W9-ARF-921

For Reference

Not to be taken from this room

ENCYCLOPEDIA
OF
AMERICAN
SOCIAL
MOVEMENTS

VOLUME ONE

ENCYCLOPEDIA
OF
AMERICAN
SOCIAL
MOVEMENTS

VOLUME ONE

EDITED BY
IMMANUEL NESS

FOREWORD BY
STEPHEN ERIC BRONNER AND FRANCES FOX PIVEN

SHARPE REFERENCE
an imprint of M.E.Sharpe, Inc.

SHARPE REFERENCE

Sharpe Reference is an imprint of M.E. Sharpe INC.

M.E. Sharpe INC.
80 Business Park Drive
Armonk, NY 10504

© 2004 by *M.E. Sharpe* INC.

Library of Congress Cataloging-in-Publication Data

Encyclopedia of American social movements / Immanuel Ness, editor.
   p. cm.
  Includes bibliographical references and indexes.
  ISBN 0-7656-8045-9 (set: alk. paper)
   1. Social movements—United States—History—Encyclopedias. 2. Social change—
United States—History—Encyclopedias. 3. Social justice—United States—History—
encyclopedias. I. Ness, Immanuel.
HN57 .E594 2004
303.48'4'097303—dc21

2002042613

Printed and bound in the United States of America

The paper used in this publication meets the minimum requirements of
American National Standard for Information Sciences—Permanence of
Paper for Printed Library Materials,
ANSI Z 39.48.1984.

BM (c) 10 9 8 7 6 5 4 3 2 1

Publisher: Myron E. Sharpe
Vice President and Editorial Director: Patricia Kolb
Vice President and Production Director: Carmen Chetti
Executive Editor and Manager of Reference: Todd Hallman
Project Manager: Wendy E. Muto
Editorial Assistant: Cathleen Prisco
Cover and Text Design: Jesse Sanchez

to comrade v.i.j.

CONTENTS

VOLUME 1

Contributors xi
Foreword xv
Acknowledgments xvii
Introduction xix

1. Antislavery Movement

Introduction 3
Antislavery Movement, 1700s–1830s 5
Antislavery Movement, 1830s–1840s 18
Antislavery Movement, 1840s–1850s 27
Antislavery Movement, 1860–1865 35
Abolition: Humanitarian and Revolutionary Ideas 47
Moderate, Radical, and Militant Abolition 62
Frederick Douglass and Antislavery 72
Free Blacks: Foundations of Polities 80
Antislavery Resistance: An Overview 89
North–South Reactions to Antislavery 96

2. Civil Rights Movement

Introduction 107
Civil Rights Movement, 1865–1910 111
Movement to Abolish Convict Labor 122
Anti-Lynching Movement 127
Civil Rights Movement, 1910–1930 136
Garvey's Universal Negro Improvement Association
    Movement 148
Brotherhood of Sleeping Car Porters 152
Civil Rights Movement, 1930–1953 158
Civil Rights Movement, 1954–1970 173
Nonviolent Direct Action 202
Congress of Racial Equality 208
Civil Rights Movement, 1970–1990 212
Racial Violence and the Civil Rights Movement 222
Black Nationalism and the Civil Rights Movement . . 227
Anti-Apartheid Movement 235
Civil Rights Movement, 1990–2000 241
Civil Rights Movement, Twenty-First Century 251

3. Women's Movement

Introduction 259
Women's Social Movement, 1800–1869 261
Moral and Dress Reform Movement, 1800–1869 . . . 268
Matilda Joslyn Gage and Woman Suffrage History . . 272
Popular Health Movement 279
Women's Cooperative Housekeeping Movement 284
Woman Suffrage Movement, 1848–1920 290
Women's Movement and Social Activism,
    1865–1920 310
African-American Women's Movement,
    1865–1920s 329
Women and the Progressive Movement 337
Women and the Anti-Imperialist Movement 341
Working Women's Movement, Early Twentieth
    Century 345

General Index I-1
Biographical Index I-53

VOLUME 2

Birth Control Movement 353
Women's Movement, 1920–1960 360
Equal Rights Amendment 373
Abortion Rights Movement 378
African-American Women's Movement,
    1930s–1940s 387
African-American Women's Movement,
    1950–Present 391
Women's Movement, 1960–1990 397
Women's Studies Movement 415
Women's Liberation Movement, 1965–1975 422
Women's Movement, 1990–Present 429
Feminist/Lesbian Separatism Movement 436
Anti-Rape Movement 445

4. Labor Movement

Introduction 455
Labor Movement, 1600–1790 458

Labor Movement, 1790–1860 464
Labor Movement, 1861–1877 473
Knights of Labor 480
Miners' Movement in the West 489
Anarchism and the Labor Movement 499
Labor Movement, 1877–1919 504
Eight-Hour Day Movement 520
Syndicalism and the Industrial Workers of the
    World 524
Railroad Workers Movement 533
Steelworkers Movement 543
Garment Workers Movement 548
Labor Movement, 1920–1934 556
Communist Movement 568
Sacco and Vanzetti 580
Unemployment Movement 584
Unemployed Councils 588
Strikes of 1934 593
Brookwood Labor College 596
Labor Movement, 1935–1947 604
Labor Law 617
Cannery Workers Movement 621
Labor Movement, 1948–1981 624
Public Workers Movement 638
Labor Movement and the Vietnam War 643
Black Lung Movement 646
Labor Movement, 1981–Present 650
PATCO and Replacement Workers 661
United Parcel Service Strike 665
Hotel and Restaurant Workers Movement 671
Wildcat Strikes 674
Organized Labor, Consumption, and Boycotts 680
Labor Culture 687

5. Native American Movement
Introduction 695
Native American Movement, Colonial Era–1800s . . . 697
Native American Movement, World War I to the
    Indian New Deal 700
Rise and Repression of the American Indian
    Movement 706
Treaty Rights and Indian Activism from Alcatraz to
    NAGPRA 725
Pan-Indianism Movement 732
Sovereignty and the Self-Determination Movement . . 735
Identity, Mascots, and Playing Indian 739
Indigenous People and Environmentalism 744
Struggle for the West: U.S. Indian Policy from Sand
    Creek to Wounded Knee 748
Identity and Literature 754

General Index I-1
Biographical Index I-53

VOLUME 3
6. Rural, Social, and Political Movements
Introduction 759
Regulator Movements and Other Rebellions,
    1760s–1790s 761
Anti-Rent Movement, 1830s–1860s 768
Southern Exodusters Movement, 1860s–1870s 773
Grange Movement 777
Farmers' Alliance Movement 783
Greenbacker Movement, 1870s–1880s 787
Populist Movement, 1890s 791
Agrarian Socialist Movement, 1890s–1920 796
Nonpartisan League, 1915–1920s 802
Women's Home Demonstration Movement,
    1920s–1930 808
Southern Tenant Farmers' Union 811
Farmer-Labor Party 818
Farm Workers Labor Movement 822
American Agriculture Movement 835

7. Moral Reform Movements
Introduction 843
Moral Reform Movements in Postwar America 845
Prostitution Reform 859
Early Anti-Vice Campaigns 862
Prohibition and Repeal 865
Anti-Drug Movement 872
Progressive Movement 881
Eugenics Movement 899
Alcoholics Anonymous 906

8. Religious, Utopian, and Health Movements
Introduction 921
Religious Movements: Overview 925
Religious Movements, 1730s–1830s 938
Religious Movements, 1830s–1870 946
Religious Movements, 1870s–Present 950
Social Gospel Movement 956
Missionary Movements 961
YMCA-YWCA 966
Rural Utopian Movements, 1820s–1850s 969
New Harmony Movement 975
Pentecostal Movement 981
Colorado Cooperative Colony Movement 983
Homeopathy Movement, 1870–Present 990
American Intentional Communities 998
Ethical Culture Movement 1007
Health Food Movement 1014

Counterculture Movement, 1960s–1970s 1020
American Buddhism 1029

9. Antiwar/Protest Movements

Introduction 1037
Antiwar Movement: Overview 1039
Anti-Preparedness Movement 1060
Antiwar Movement: World War I 1064
World War I and Civil Liberties 1073
Antiwar Movement: World War II 1077
Antiwar Movement: Vietnam War 1080
Draft Resisters in Canada During the Vietnam
    War 1097
Antiwar Movement, Twenty-first Century 1100

10. Radical and Poor People's Movements

Introduction 1115
Poor People's Movements 1117
Settlement House Movement 1141
The Unemployed Organize 1145
Tent City Movements 1152

General Index I-1
Biographical Index I-53

VOLUME 4
11. Student Movements

Introduction 1161
History of Student Movements 1163
Students for a Democratic Society Movement 1173
Free Speech Movement 1178
Vietnam Antiwar Campus Activism 1183
Weatherman Underground Organization 1196

12. Ethnic and Group Identity Movements

Introduction 1203
Nonwhite Ethnic Identity Movements 1206
Mexican Americans and the Chicano Movement . . . 1212
Asian-American Movement 1219
Mutualista Movement 1226
Gray Panthers Movement 1230
Senior Citizens Movement 1236
Disabilities Movement 1245

13. Environmental Movement

Introduction 1255
Environmental Movement, Nineteenth and Twentieth
    Centuries 1258
Conservation Movement, 1880s–1920 1285
Antinuclear Movement 1293
Environmental Justice Movement 1298
Animal Rights Movement 1309
Appropriate Technology Movement 1317

14. Lesbian, Gay, Bisexual, and Transgender Movement

Introduction 1325
Lesbian, Gay, Bisexual, and Transgender
    Movement, 1870s–1920s 1329
Lesbian, Gay, Bisexual, and Transgender
    Movement, 1920s–1969 1332
Lesbian, Gay, Bisexual, and Transgender
    Movement, 1969–Present 1344
Referenda and the Anti-Gay Rights Movement 1362
Bisexual Movement: A Brief History 1367
AIDS Coalition to Unleash Power: The ACT UP
    Movement 1373
Transgender Activism 1379

15. Conservative, Nativist, and Right-Wing Movements

Introduction 1385
Conservative Movement 1387
Women and the Conservative Movement,
    1933–Present 1411
Post–Civil War Nativism Movement 1414
Immigrant Exclusion Movement, 1870s–1920s 1422
Anti-Catholicism Activism 1428
Ku Klux Klan 1433
Militia Movement 1439

16. Global Justice Movement

Introduction 1455
Global Justice Movement: Overview 1458
Living Wage Movement 1471
Protests Against the World Trade Organization in
    Seattle 1482
Anti-Sweatshop Movement 1491
Fair Trade Coffee Campaign 1497

Bibliography 1503
General Index I-1
Biographical Index I-53

EDITOR

Immanuel Ness
Brooklyn College–City University of New York

CONTRIBUTORS

Ginette Aley
Virginia Polytechnic and State University

B.T. Arrington
National Park Service

Natalie Atkin
Wayne State University

Barbara Bair
Library of Congress

Stephanie Bateson
University of Sheffield, United Kingdom

Phil Bellfy
Michigan State University

Maria Bevacqua
Minnesota State University

Timothy G. Borden
Indiana University

Eric Boyle
University of California, Santa Barbara

Aaron Brenner
Independent Scholar

Eileen Bresnahan
Colorado College

Stephen Eric Bronner
Rutgers University

Linda Czuba Brigance
State University of New York, Fredonia

Jamie L. Bronstein
New Mexico State University

Peter Buckingham
Linfield College

John D. Buenker
University of Wisconsin, Parkside

Linnea Goodwin Burwood
State University of New York, Delhi

Malini Cadambi
New School for Social Research

David T. Canon
University of Wisconsin

Christopher Capozzola
Massachusetts Institute of Technology

Ron Capshaw
Virginia Commonwealth University

Jeffrey D. Carlisle
University of North Texas

Theresa Ann Case
University of Houston

Paula F. Casey
Women's Suffrage Historian, Memphis Tennessee

Norman Caulfield
Fort Hays Kansas State University

Kristin Celello
University of Virginia

Roger Chapman
Lincoln Trail College

Joseph Chuman
Ethical Culture Society

David S. Churchill
University of Manitoba

Ward Churchill
University of Colorado, Boulder

Christopher Clark
University of Warwick, United Kingdom

Michael Clark
University of Wyoming

Pamela Clark
University of Wyoming

Matt Clavin
American University

James H. Conrad
Texas A&M University, Commerce

Mary E. Corey
State University of New York, Brockport

Alex B. Corlu
State University of New York, Binghamton

Martha Monaghan Corpus
*Brooklyn College–City University of
New York*

Jeffrey Crane
Culver, Stockton College

David O'Donald Cullen
Collin County Community College

Prudence Cumberbatch
*Brooklyn College–City University of
New York*

George P. Cunningham
*Brooklyn College–City University of
New York*

Evan Daniel
Independent Scholar

William N. Denman
Marshall College

Jeffrey P. Dennis
Florida Atlantic University

Alesha E. Doan
*California Polytechnic State
University*

Susan Dominguez
Michigan State University

Myrna Cherkoss Donahoe
*California State University,
Dominguez Hills*

Megan J. Elias
Queensborough Community College

Michael Ezra
Sonoma State University

Kendra Field
Harvard University

Jo Freeman
Independent Scholar

Karen Garner
Florida International University

Ernest D. Green
*Brooklyn College–City University of
New York*

Richard Greenwald
*United States Merchant Marine
Academy*

Andrew Gyory
Independent Scholar

Michelle Haberland
Georgia Southern University

Donald P. Haider-Markel
University of Kansas

Jennifer Harrison
Independent Scholar

Desiree Hellegers
*Washington State University,
Vancouver*

Liz Highleyman
Independent Scholar

Tim Hodgdon
St. Thomas University

Caroline Hoefferle
Wingate University

Derek Hoff
University of Virginia

Andrew Hunt
University of Waterloo

Daniel Hurewitz
Tulane University

Loraine Hutchins
Winslow Foundation

Mandi Isaacs
Yale University

Paula Jayne
Emory University

Beth DiNatale Johnson
Ursuline College

Gregory L. Kaster
Gustavus Adolphus College

Christine Kelly
*William Paterson University of New
Jersey*

Kathleen Kennedy
Western Washington University

Jordan Kleiman
*State University of New York,
Geneseo*

Frank Koscielski
Wayne State University

Susan Applegate Krouse
Michigan State University

Barbara Kucera
Workday Minnesota

Mark Lause
University of Cincinnati

Russell M. Lawson
Bacone College

Patrick LeBeau
Michigan State University

Paul Le Blanc
La Roche College

Margaret Levi
University of Washington

James G. Lewis
Forest History Society

David M. Lewis-Colman
University of Rochester

April Linton
Princeton University

James J. Lorence
Gainesville College

John Low
Pokagon Band of Potawatomi

Norman Markowitz
Rutgers University

Donald B. Marti
Indiana University at South Bend

Joseph A. McCartin
Georgetown University

Kent McConnell
Dartmouth University

Gregory L. McDonald
*Instituto Tecnológico y Estudios
Superiores de Monterrey*

Henry M. McKiven, Jr.
University of South Alabama

Rebecca McNulty
*University of Illinois at Urbana,
Champaign*

Rebecca J. Mead
Northern Michigan University

Laurie Mercier
*Washington State University,
Vancouver*

Timothy Miller
University of Kansas

Vernon Mogensen
Kingsborough Community College

Marian B. Mollin
*Virginia Polytechnic and State
University*

Maria Mondragón-Valdéz
Independent Scholar

Peter N. Moore
Georgia State University

Michelle Moravec
Rosemont College

Angela Murphy
University of Houston

Gillian Hughes Murphy
University of Washington

R. David Myers
The College of Santa Fe

Caryn E. Neumann
Ohio State University

Mitchell Newton-Matza
University of St. Francis

Mark A. Noon
Bloomsburg University

Justin Nordstrom
Indiana University

Jean Fox O'Barr
Duke University

Tom O'Connell
Metropolitan State University

David J. Olson
University of Washington

James Paterson
University of Sydney, Australia

Ruth Percy
University of Toronto

Lisa Phillips
Edgewood College

Nicola Pizzolato
University College, London

Laura R. Prieto
Simmons College

Sarah L. Rasmusson
College of New Jersey

Jonathan Rees
Colorado State University

Marisa Richmond
Independent Scholar

Jeanette Rodda
Northern Arizona University

Paul Rubinson
University of Texas at Austin

Francis Ryan
Moravian College

Richard Schneirov
Indiana State University

Angela Schwarz
Universität Duisburg-Essen, Germany

Amy L. Scott
University of New Mexico

Cheryl Shanks
Williams College

Rebecca Sharpless
Baylor University

Benjamin Shepard
*Graduate Center, City University of
New York*

Jefferson Faye Sina
Michigan State University

Suzanne M. Spencer-Wood
Oakland University

Kimberly Springer
University of London

Candis Steenbergen
Concordia University, Canada

Erich Steinman
University of Washington

Terry Straus
University of Chicago

Gerard Sullivan
University of Sydney, Australia

Matthew A. Sutton
University of California, Santa Barbara

Paul Michel Taillon
University of Auckland, New Zealand

Beverly Tomek
University of Houston

James Swan Tuite
Brown University

William B. Turner
University of Wisconsin

Bernard Unti
American University

Kendra Van Cleave
San Francisco State University

Sue Wamsley
University of Akron

Sylvia Hood Washington
Northwestern University

Linda S. Watts
University of Washington, Bothell

Simon Wendt
Free University of Berlin, Germany

Eliot Wilczek
Tufts University

Kyle Wilkison
Collin County Community College

Joseph Wilson
Brooklyn College–City University of New York

Anne Woo-Sam
Stanford University

Cyrus Ernesto Zirakzadeh
University of Connecticut

FOREWORD

American history textbooks often convey a story of consensus, continuity, and smooth development. This encyclopedia tells the stories of social conflicts that mainstream accounts gloss over, the struggles waged by ordinary people against those who hold power over them. By filling in the blanks in this way, *Encyclopedia of American Social Movements* offers us a great gift, a richer understanding of our social legacy and the various ways people have been able to change and improve their lives.

The pages that follow turn our attention to the movements through which the poor and the exploited, the excluded and disfranchised, mobilized themselves, forged their own standards of justice, articulated new and dissident claims, and demanded responses to their grievances. Measured against the great aspirations that originally inspired the participants, some of these movements have yet to meet their goals of justice, equality, and democracy. Taken as a whole, however, they have had a remarkable impact on the fabric of American life and its institutions. And they offer valuable lessons for our own time.

This is not to say that all social movements are progressive. The frustration, anxiety, and indignation that produce social movements can take conservative, as well as progressive, political forms. Anti-vice movements helped bring about prohibition, introduced censorship laws, and fostered the oppression of women. Right-wing movements fueled our recurrent "red scares" and fought to roll back forward progress in the rights of women and all people of color. It is therefore a mistake to think of social movements as inevitably movements of the Left. With their populist impulses and sentiments, even conservative social movements have expressed resentment of the establishment.

Social movements always have challenged the normal ways of doing business. Utopian communities are obvious examples, and they have sprouted up throughout our nation's history. But the call for the new, the innovative, and the experimental, also appears—sometimes overtly and sometimes implicitly—in movements concerned with far more concrete matters. Suffragists may have concentrated on seeking the vote for women, but, in the process, they also raised questions about the legitimacy of male domination. The environmental movement has offered a critique not merely of irresponsible consumerism, but also of society's shortsightedness. In the same vein, antiwar and pacifist movements have challenged militarist policies, nationalist ideology, and, sometimes, even the state itself.

Social movements ebb and flow in response to changing historical conditions. But this encyclopedia also reveals that these movements often have deep historical roots and usually evidence at least a degree of continuity. The struggle against slavery began with protests undertaken by the Mennonites and the Quakers, was revived by the enthusiasm for radical democracy in the American revolutionary period, and was revived again by the emergence of the nineteenth-century abolitionist movement. Yet again, the struggle against racism was fostered by the birth of the National Association for the Advancement of Colored People.

Indebted to its forerunners, the subsequent Civil Rights Movement of the 1950s and 1960s had an extraordinary impact. Often forgotten are the facts that this movement broke the back of the Ku Klux Klan and that its attack on discrimination changed the face of American civil society. Its style and militancy provided an example for the Women's Movement, the Anti-War Movement, the American Indian Movement, and La Raza. The Civil Rights Movement's commitment to universal rights and its condemnation of race privilege was influenced by anti-colonial struggles elsewhere, but it also inspired others, especially the anti-apartheid movement in South Africa.

The eruption of movement activism is famously difficult to predict. Each new outbreak of protest episodes usually comes as a surprise or in reaction to an event not anticipated by most political commentators and social scientists. Prior to the outbreaks of militant protest in the 1960s, for example, social scientists were talking about the "end of ideology." When the Cold War ended, new talk arose about the "end of history," even while an international movement for global justice was taking shape with the start of the new millennium. An encyclopedia such as this reminds us that freedom is never fully actualized, that new conflicts always simmer beneath the surface of society, and that the consensus underlying the status quo is never quite as strong as establishmentarian ideologists would have us believe.

It is instructive to revisit the old debates over tactics and strategy, violence and non-violence, identity and universalism, which mark the movements in the past and influence contemporary social movements as well. In the end, however, the key questions always have to do with the conditions under which a movement can exert power and the degree to which it can force change. When all is said and done, when all the turns of tactics and strategy are reviewed, what emerges is that the power of a movement depends on its ability to mobilize mass action in defiance of existing norms and to create the threat or reality of institutional instability. The great moments of victory for these movements—whether in response to workers demanding welfare legislation or disfranchised citizens demanding civil rights—all occurred in the wake of such crises of social order.

Social movements seeking to better the conditions of the least fortunate have, again and again, attacked the idea that poverty is a natural condition. A sense of injustice inspires assaults on sweatshops, on low wages, on apartheid, on militarism, and on imperialism. It incites demands of respect for the aged and the disabled. Idealistic goals of social justice, equal human rights, and individual dignity have fueled all of the great social movements, including those with primarily materialist ideologies such as the labor movement. These same values can be found in the current anti-globalization movement with its searing critique of the effects of free market capitalism on non-western societies.

This rich encyclopedia, with its array of histories about the struggles of the exploited and disfranchised, makes clear what is perhaps the real lesson of social movements: Politics is also the mobilization of power from below.

Stephen Eric Bronner and Frances Fox Piven

ACKNOWLEDGMENTS

I am grateful to the many individuals who have made this project a success. It never could have been completed without the academic expertise that the authors of the entries have brought to this work. In particular, I thank the section editors—Beverly Tomek, Joseph Wilson, Michelle Moravec, Phil Bellfy, Kyle Wilkinson, Liz Highleyman, Benjamin Shepard, Matthew Sutton, Marian Mollin, William Turner, and James Paterson—who also brought their knowledge and scholarly insight to each of the social movement entries in this encyclopedia. In addition, I would like to thank Aaron Brenner, Ward Churchill, George Cunningham, Paul LeBlanc, and Christine Kelly for their contributions.

My greatest debt is to Frances Fox Piven for encouraging me to edit this encyclopedia. She inspired us with the potential of social movements to transform society and emphasized the importance of creating enduring structures of power. Over the years, Frances has implored that we understand social movements as potentially progressive and reactionary and that we recognize the value of defending and expanding such movements in the interest of class, racial, and women's justice.

I first met Steve Bronner several years ago in Atlanta at the American Political Science Association convention. Ever since, I have taken great interest in his work, and I applaud his unbroken commitment to social justice. I thank Steve for his friendship and his support for this encyclopedia and other projects.

Over the years, I have learned about social movements from other experts in the field. I thank Staughton Lynd for his dedicated support for workers and the oppressed in all segments of society. Staughton—teacher, activist, and friend—has helped me think about the profound questions involved in building a strong and democratic labor movement. I thank Lawrence Goodwyn for teaching me about social movements and political parties and the damage that

class inequality, elitism, and snobbery inflicts on us all. I always will be grateful to Staughton and Larry for spending hundreds of hours of their time discussing the power of solidarity.

I thank Jeanette Zelhof for putting up the good fight by tenaciously defending poor and oppressed people to preserve their homes, social services, and personal dignity. I am truly indebted for her support in very hard times. My friend Ben Goldman has been a pillar in the struggle for environmental justice and a friend through thick and thin. I thank Lori Minnite for her friendship and support through the years; I have learned so much from Lori about the meaning of loyalty, honesty, and integrity. And my brother Nero McIntosh is a true comrade in the fight for class and racial justice.

The City University of New York Affirmative Action Committee/Diversity Grants Committee provided important support for this project. The Brooklyn College Graduate Center for Worker Education of the City University of New York at 99 Hudson Street—a site of research, teaching, and scholarship—provided me with the office space and logistical support to make this work a reality. I would like to thank Doreen Grant and Maria Carosone of the Brooklyn College Department of Political Science for volunteering their help in tough times. I thank my friends Tricia Lawrence, Pam Miller, and Andrea Gordon-Smith of 99 Hudson Street for their invaluable support and encouragement.

I am particularly indebted to all those working at and with M.E. Sharpe, Inc. who have helped me through the grueling two years of work on this project. First and foremost, I thank Cathy Prisco for her invaluable efforts in systematically making this encyclopedia a reality. Cathy is simply amazing.

In editing an encyclopedia on social movements, one must make difficult choices and understand the need for clarity and balance. I thank Todd Hallman for his foresight, knowledge of reference publishing, and help in developing a comprehensive and accessible work that is balanced, even in the controversial world of social movements.

I thank Andrew Gyory, an accomplished social historian and formerly of M.E. Sharpe, for helping me transform the concept of an "Encyclopedia on Social Movements" into an actual work. Andrew is a historian in the best sense of the word—a practitioner who is breaking new ground through his published work, helping us to understand the xenophobic anti-immigrant movement against people of Chinese descent. Andrew recognized the importance of this project, and his suggestions have made it a better work.

Anne Burns is a brilliant and indefatigable free-lance photo editor, who brings to the job her broad knowledge of history, political science, sociology, and popular culture. Anne has left no stone unturned in searching for the right images for this project, and I thank her for all of her work. I was lucky to work with Anne and if I am so fortunate, I hope to work with her in the future.

I thank Wendy Muto, an untiring and dedicated project manager, as well as everyone in production and design who has assisted with this encyclopedia. I hope that I will continue to have the opportunity to work with the whole M.E. Sharpe team in the future.

Finally I thank Mike Sharpe, a man of conviction and principle, a fighter for social justice, and, most importantly, a friend.

Immanuel Ness

INTRODUCTION

If there is no struggle, there is no progress. Those who profess to favor freedom and yet deprecate agitation, are men who want crops without plowing up the ground, they want rain without thunder and lightning. They want the ocean without the awful roar of its many waters. This struggle may be a moral one, or it may be a physical one, and it may be both moral and physical, but it must be a struggle. Power concedes nothing without a demand. It never did, and it never will.

FREDERICK DOUGLASS

When Frederick Douglass uttered these words in 1857, he was a leader of the abolitionist movement, one of the greatest social movements of the nineteenth century. By "plowing up the ground" and delivering "thunder and lightning," the abolitionist movement awakened millions of Americans to the horrors of slavery and ultimately contributed to the demise of the institution in this country in 1865. Social movements—from abolition and woman suffrage to the fight for an eight-hour workday and a minimum wage; from efforts to secure civil rights and equal opportunity to campaigns for pure food, clean water, and a safer environment; from attempts to eliminate war, poverty, and sweatshop labor to the struggles for dignity, self-determination, and personal freedom—have profoundly affected every aspect of American society, shaping both the nation's history and its identity for more than two hundred years.

The *Encyclopedia of American Social Movements* is the first major reference work on the subject that seeks to examine these movements in all their complexity, power, and significance. What *is* a social movement? The term has multiple definitions, but perhaps the simplest one is the best: the coming together of large numbers of people to pursue a goal that they believe will improve society. Americans have been gathering in myriad social movements since the eighteenth century, and a comprehensive examination of these movements is long overdue.

By definition, social movements are never static: They are constantly in motion—evolving, developing, and changing, sometimes expanding, sometimes contracting. Every social movement has an aim, a goal it is heading toward. Some aims are specific, such as an end to slavery, whereas others are general, such as

moral reform. Sometimes, social movements succeed in securing their goals; other times, they fail to achieve them quickly but still have far-reaching effects on events, altering society in unanticipated ways. The abolitionist movement helped spark the Civil War in 1861; the protest movement during World War I led to the founding of the American Civil Liberties Union in 1920.

Some social movements fail outright and disappear. Others, like the prohibitionist movement, succeed but ultimately find their gains reversed and overturned. Others still, like the Populist movement, disintegrate, but then a new movement picks up parts of its cause and carries on. Many social movements have spawned other social movements—the abolitionist movement helped spawn the women's movement in the nineteenth century, much as the civil rights movement helped spawn the feminist movement in the twentieth century.

Social movements are unpredictable. They take on lives of their own and give birth to new ideas, new organizations, and new modes of thinking. Social movements frequently have complex political overtones, and this encyclopedia seeks to be as inclusive as possible in covering these nuances.

The reason that social movements have flourished in the United States for the past two centuries can be traced in part to the freedoms enshrined in the U.S. Constitution, specifically the First Amendment rights to free speech, free press, peaceful assembly, and petition. Without these four essential rights—to voice ideas, to disseminate them widely and unencumbered, to gather freely in groups, and to present grievances and demands to the government—social movements would never have spread so rapidly nor achieved such success. By utilizing these fundamental rights, Americans have made them vital and stronger, an irrevocable and unalienable part of American citizenship.

Regardless of their various goals, social movements have proved a key agent in institutionalizing and extending democracy, thus empowering individuals with a peaceful means to change their society. The Constitution provided the blueprint for these actions, but it took people—hundreds, thousands, millions of people, over many decades and generations—to seize them, actualize them, and make them real through social movements. These movements brought together diverse groups of people, the wealthy and the poor, the privileged and the oppressed, men and women, adults and children, and members of every ethnic, racial, and religious group. Through their combined actions, social movements took shape and set in motion the long, arduous process of social change.

Social movements have invented, refined, and utilized many techniques to achieve their ends. All use some form of mass communication, spreading their ideas through speeches, banners, pamphlets, newspapers, books, television, and the Internet. All incite the mass gathering of people, in meetings, marches, rallies, and demonstrations. Many create a movement culture, distinguished by its language, customs, and practices. Many also build solidarity by uniting around a motto or phrase, such as the Knights of Labor's "an injury to one is the concern of all," or a song, such as the civil rights movement's "We Shall Overcome." Some social movements even promote civil disobedience, the practice of breaking a law and going to jail, in order to bring attention to the law's perceived unjustness. Most social movements are driven by moral fervor, the deeply held belief that something in society is wrong and that mass action can highlight the problem so that society can make it right.

The causes, methods, and goals of American social movements have been as varied as its people, and no simple generalization can encompass them all. If any theme unites the diverse and myriad social movements covered in this encyclopedia, however, it is embodied in two of the words Frederick Douglass uttered in the first sentence of his speech: "struggle"—the need to fight, strive, and persevere—and "progress"—the belief that people can forge a better, safer, and more just world. These are the essential elements uniting every social movement.

As the articles in this encyclopedia show, progress does not come easily. Many Americans—from abolitionist editor Elijah P. Lovejoy in 1837 and labor leader Joe Hill in 1915 to civil rights activists James Chaney, Andrew Goodman, Michael Schwerner, Viola Liuzzo, and Martin Luther King, Jr., in the 1960s—lost their lives in the struggle for progress. And progress does not come quickly. The struggle to end slavery took more than a generation; the fight for woman suffrage took more than two generations. Indeed, the goals of many social movements remain unfulfilled.

Douglass also identified a third essential element in the phenomenon of social movements, one that is more difficult to isolate: power. "Power concedes nothing without a demand," he declared. "It never did, and it never will." Thus, this encyclopedia is also a useful tool for the study of power: who wields it, who challenges it, and who gains it. For power is never given, only taken. All social movements move against some powerful force—sometimes the government, sometimes entrenched economic interests, and sometimes tradition, custom, and popular opinion.

Whatever the opposing force, it is people with a belief, a demand, and a cause who have made social movements a mighty agent for strengthening democracy and fomenting change in the United States. By coming together, Americans have "plowed up the ground," unleashed "thunder and lightning," and produced the "awful roar" that has transformed America and made it the nation it is today.

HOW TO USE THIS ENCYCLOPEDIA

The encyclopedia is divided into 16 sections, each of which covers one of the major social movements in American history: 1) the antislavery movement; 2) civil rights movement; 3) women's movement; 4) labor movement; 5) Native American movement; 6) rural, social, and political movements; 7) moral reform movements; 8) religious, utopian, and health movements; 9) antiwar/protest movements; 10) radical and poor people's movements; 11) student movements; 12) ethnic and group identity movements; 13) environmental movement; 14) lesbian, gay, bisexual, and transgender movement; 15) conservative, nativist, and right-wing movements; and 16) global justice movement.

Each section is edited by an expert in the field and includes an introduction; articles on the critical themes, aspects, and events of the social movement or movements; biographical portraits of key leaders and figures; excerpts from primary sources and historical documents; bibliography and references; and illustrations. The articles in each section are arranged by chronology or topic, so that, together, they give a complete portrait of each movement.

It is important to keep in mind that in organizing an encyclopedia on this subject, numerous decisions had to be made regarding definition and placement. After all, many social movements overlapped, and people who participated in one movement often participated in another. Abolitionist Frederick Douglass, for example, was also a prominent supporter of women's rights. His colleague Susan B. Anthony, who became the leader of the women's movement, entered public life by joining the temperance movement. A century later, A. Philip Randolph was a prominent leader in both the labor and civil rights movements.

Many movements themselves clearly crossed boundaries. People who fought for the rights of both African Americans and women—from Sojourner Truth to Mary McLeod Bethune and Fannie Lou Hamer—belonged to the civil rights movement and to the women's movement, and many also belonged to the labor movement, student movement, poor people's movement, and other movements. These multiple movements were often interwoven, influencing and cross-pollinating each other.

Readers should bear in mind that the divisions in this reference work are not clear-cut. Movements do not arise in a vacuum, and they are far too complex to be neatly separated. Decisions had to be made about where to place articles on causes and movements that overlapped. Readers should therefore review both the table of contents and the index to find all the information they are seeking, as many causes and individuals appear in different sections, their dual or multiple roles highlighted and examined in different contexts.

This encyclopedia explores the interrelationships between the different social movements, such as the civil rights, women's, antiwar, student, and labor movements of the 1960s, and analyzes each movement's goals, tactics, membership, and outcomes. By thoroughly covering the aims, themes, and people in every American social movement and the impact they had on politics and society, the articles and material in the *Encyclopedia of American Social Movements* provide a broad and engaging overview of American history.

ANTISLAVERY MOVEMENT

Section 1 of this encyclopedia chronicles one of the first and most important social movements in American history—the struggle against slavery—from its origins in the colonial era to its demise in 1865 after the Civil War. Edited by Beverly Tomek, the articles in Section 1 demonstrate how the effort to end slavery

expanded from embryonic protests in the late seventeenth century to a broadly based social movement in the early and mid-nineteenth century. Several forms of antislavery sentiment ultimately emerged: efforts to end the importation of slaves from Africa to America; efforts to colonize blacks beyond the borders of the United States; efforts to prevent the extension of slavery to states and territories in the West; and efforts to abolish slavery throughout the nation.

From the earliest days of American slavery in the 1600s, African Americans engaged in opposition through confrontation, escape, and rebellion. Such actions reveal the intense hostility to enslavement but do not in themselves constitute a social movement. Organized opposition to slavery among European colonists began in the late seventeenth century as religious appeals by German Mennonites and Pennsylvania Quakers challenged the morality of human bondage. Questions regarding the natural rights of humanity surfaced repeatedly in the Revolutionary era, contributing to the gradual abolition of slavery in the North in the late 1700s and early 1800s.

Taking a cue from the establishment of Sierra Leone by the British, many antislavery advocates urged relocation of black Americans to Africa. In 1822, the colony of Liberia was founded in the hopes of encouraging slaveholders to free their slaves and transport them to Africa. Colonization, as it became known, dominated the antislavery movement in the early 1800s. It had many prominent supporters—James Madison and Henry Clay among them—but was scorned by most blacks, who considered America their rightful home.

The abolitionist movement was revolutionary. Ignited by David Walker, who wrote *Walker's Appeal* in 1829, William Lloyd Garrison, who founded the *Liberator* in 1831, and many others, the abolitionist movement demanded the complete and immediate end of slavery. Black and white abolitionists operated newspapers, held meetings and conventions, petitioned legislatures, and spoke out loudly against the institution at every opportunity. The mainstay of the movement was a tactic known as "moral suasion," by which abolitionists aimed to persuade slaveholders of the evils and immorality of the system and, thus, convince them to free their slaves. Garrison and his followers pioneered this tactic and emphasized its peaceful nature.

In the late 1830s and 1840s, however, a growing number of black and white abolitionists began to question the use of moral suasion alone. Proslavery mobs had begun to assault abolitionists in both the

North and the South. Many abolitionists turned to the political process, forming the Liberty Party in 1839 and the Free Soil Party in 1848. Others advocated armed self-defense, and some, such as Nat Turner and John Brown, turned to violence.

Although the abolitionist movement was never huge in terms of sheer numbers, its impact was enormous. By the 1850s, an "irrepressible conflict," as antislavery senator William Seward put it, was developing between the North and the South, as differences over slavery and its westward spread began ripping the country apart. In 1861, this conflict exploded into the Civil War.

As fighting wore on, abolitionists convinced many fellow northerners to expand the goal of the war from preserving the union to ending slavery. President Abraham Lincoln responded by issuing the Emancipation Proclamation in 1863. Two years later, the Thirteenth Amendment was added to the Constitution, abolishing slavery in the United States. By achieving its goal, the abolitionist movement was the first successful social movement in American history.

CIVIL RIGHTS MOVEMENT

The Supreme Court decision *Brown v. Board of Education* in 1954, the Montgomery Bus Boycott in 1955–56, and the battle over integrating public schools in Little Rock, Arkansas, in 1957—these are often considered the events that sparked the civil rights movement of the 1950s and 1960s. Critical as these events were, however, the fight for civil rights and racial justice had been going on for more than a century.

In the mid-1800s, many black abolitionists challenged the prevailing system of racial discrimination, which pervaded the nation, north and south. Schools, professions, and public transportation were often closed to African Americans. Many states prevented blacks from voting and serving on juries, and some communities even banned blacks from settling and living within their boundaries.

Many of these racist policies ended after the Civil War. During Reconstruction, Constitutional amendments and federal laws aimed to ensure legal equality and civil rights for African Americans. As Reconstruction collapsed in the late 1870s and 1880s, however, southern states began passing statutes designed to separate the races and keep blacks subordinate. Known as the "Jim Crow" laws, this segregationist system disfranchised blacks, denied them equal opportunity, and forced them to endure inferior treatment and accommodations. In the late nineteenth and early twentieth centuries, black activists challenged

Jim Crow, building alliances and institutions that would form the basis of the civil rights movement. Ida Wells-Barnett spearheaded the anti-lynching movement in the 1890s, and W.E.B. Du Bois led the Niagara Movement and helped found the National Association for the Advancement of Colored People in 1909. They and their colleagues mounted legal challenges to segregation and led demonstrations to rouse public opinion.

A planned march on Washington, organized by A. Philip Randolph in 1941, led President Franklin Roosevelt to ban discrimination in defense industries. By mid-century, a widespread effort to abolish segregation had emerged, and the civil rights movement took shape. Sit-ins, freedom rides, and protest marches galvanized millions of Americans in the 1960s, culminating in the Civil Rights Act of 1964 and the Voting Rights Act of 1965. These landmark statutes outlawed segregation in virtually every aspect of American public life.

After these notable achievements, the civil rights movement began to splinter. Efforts to eradicate racism and achieve economic equality have continued to prove daunting in the late twentieth and early twenty-first centuries. Section 2 of this encyclopedia, edited by Joseph Wilson, examines the complex history of the civil rights movement and its enormous impact on American society.

WOMEN'S MOVEMENT

Unlike the antislavery and civil rights movements, whose origins cannot be traced to a single event or incident, the women's movement—specifically the woman suffrage movement—effectively began in 1848 at a convention held in Seneca Falls, New York. At the time, women could not vote, married women could not own property, and any money a married woman earned belonged to her husband. Few colleges admitted women, and most professions were closed to them. Women's activism to change this system emerged in the early nineteenth century and became a full-fledged movement after the Seneca Falls Convention issued a Declaration of Principles and Sentiments demanding full emancipation and equality for women.

The "first wave" of the feminist movement in the nineteenth and early twentieth centuries embraced a wide array of issues, from dress reform and birth control to the ballot and legal equality. In 1920, the Nineteenth Amendment to the Constitution granted women the right to vote.

After this achievement, the feminist movement

declined as a unified force. Many politically active women turned to specific goals, such as an equal rights amendment to the Constitution, an end to child labor, and protections for female workers. Spurred by the civil rights movement, which aimed to eradicate racism and abolish all laws that discriminated against blacks, the "second wave" of the women's movement emerged in the 1960s, as feminists aimed to eradicate sexism and all laws that discriminated against women. The women's liberation movement, as this second wave of feminism was also called, fought for reproductive rights, a more equal division of childcare and household labor, and equal pay for equal work. Like first wave feminists, second wave feminists embraced social, economic, and political goals, which fundamentally challenged long-held beliefs and traditions.

The "third wave" of the women's movement, which developed in the late twentieth century, has not followed the same trajectory as the first two waves. The third wave is more cultural, less confrontational, and it is less likely to use the political process for change. Contemporary women's activism is still taking shape, aiming to preserve the gains of previous years while pursuing new directions.

Section 3 of this encyclopedia, edited by Michelle Moravec, covers the three waves of the women's movement from the early and mid-nineteenth century to the present.

LABOR MOVEMENT

Unlike the other three great social movements in American history—the antislavery, civil rights, and women's movements—the labor movement has been more diverse and less unified. Embracing both radical and conservative elements, often at the same time, it has pursued various aims, which have competed for allegiance and supremacy. Despite its many differences, the overriding goals of the American labor movement for the past century and a half have been better wages, safer working conditions, and greater respect and dignity in the workplace.

Workers formed the earliest labor organizations, or combinations, in the colonial period. The first trade unions appeared in the 1790s and early 1800s, organized by shoemakers, printers, and cabinetmakers. Some unions were declared illegal, as they were considered conspiracies in restraint of trade, and such rulings impeded union organizing for many years. Efforts to organize workers continued, however, spurred by the rise of industrialization and the factory system in the early 1800s. Textile workers in New En-

gland, consisting initially of young women and later of Irish immigrants, pushed for ten-hour workdays and safer working conditions. The National Trades Union, organized in 1834, was the first effort to nationalize the labor movement. The Panic of 1837 doomed this organization, the first of many times that financial crises would deal setbacks to the labor movement.

In 1866, working-class leaders formed the National Labor Union (NLU) with the overriding goal of securing the eight-hour workday. Although the NLU did not last long, the eight-hour day remained the central unifying goal of the American labor movement for the next half-century. It was in these years, between the Civil War and World War I, that the labor movement came of age, and working-class issues shaped the national agenda. These were also the bloodiest years in American labor history, with disputes between workers and employers often erupting in violence. Many of the conflicts involved soldiers and police, operating at the behest of capital, and these events mobilized workers in numerous venues.

In the 1880s, the Knights of Labor became the largest working-class organization of the century, boasting some 750,000 members at its peak. The same decade saw the birth of the American Federation of Labor (AFL), which was destined to become the most influential voice of American workers. Led by Samuel Gompers, the AFL was an organization composed of trades unions, whose members were skilled workers. These unions fought for what became known as "bread-and-butter" issues—higher wages, shorter hours, and secure jobs. Often restrictive in membership, they did not challenge the basic tenets of capitalism, American business, or society. Other workers did.

Anarchists called for the abolition of all government, while socialists advocated government ownership of all industry. Radical workers united to launch the Industrial Workers of the World (IWW) in 1905. The IWW endorsed a revolutionary program, which urged unskilled workers to unite in "one big union" dedicated to destroying the wage system and overthrowing capitalism. It attracted many supporters, particularly among the millions of European immigrants who arrived in the United States in the early part of the twentieth century.

The American labor movement secured some of its greatest victories during the Great Depression of the 1930s, when the capitalist system faced its severest challenge. With the collapse of the stock market, an unemployment rate approaching 25 percent, and an economy in tatters, the U.S. government enacted many measures long advocated by workers, including public works programs, Social Security legislation, unemployment insurance, a minimum wage, an eight-hour workday, and the right to organize. In the 1930s, workers also formed the Congress of Industrial Organizations (CIO), a militant union composed largely of miners, textile workers, steelworkers, and automobile workers. The CIO witnessed spectacular growth and merged with the AFL in 1955. As a percentage of the workforce, organized labor reached its peak in the 1950s.

During the second half of the twentieth century, the labor movement declined, as American industry itself declined, and many manufacturers closed down factories in union-friendly cities of the North and Northeast. Many companies moved to regions of the country hostile to unions and workers' rights, and others moved operations abroad, often to Third World countries where the cost of labor was far lower and protections for workers far weaker. Passage of the North American Free Trade Agreement in 1993 hastened this process, dealing setbacks to American workers. A heavy influx of immigrants, largely from Latin America and Asia, transformed the American labor movement in the late twentieth century, making it more ethnically and racially diverse than at any other time.

Section 4 of this encyclopedia covers the history of the labor movement, with articles surveying both its broad sweep and social impact, as well as the major incidents, movements, and strikes.

NATIVE AMERICAN MOVEMENT

Section 5, edited by Phil Bellfy, examines the struggle of Native Americans to defend their land and culture since the arrival of the Europeans. The European colonization of North America largely differs from that of Africa and Asia. In the Western Hemisphere, Europeans displaced indigenous peoples who had lived there for thousands of years. This process, which unfolded over several centuries, was marked by violence and massacres, the negotiation and abrogation of treaties, and the removal of native peoples to isolated reservations.

Native Americans fought these actions every step of the way, resisting both forced relocation and the stripping of their cultures. Many of these encounters proved bloody and deadly, from the Trail of Tears in the 1830s to the battles of Little Big Horn and Wounded Knee in the late 1800s.

In the twentieth century, the Native American movement focused on sovereignty, self-determination, and tribal identity, goals that continue to the present day. In the 1970s, the American Indian Movement became the voice of militant Native Americans, demanding greater rights and provoking confrontations with federal authorities. Some of these confrontations also ended in violence. Today, the Native American movement is less overtly political, focusing more on social, cultural, and economic issues.

RURAL, SOCIAL, AND POLITICAL MOVEMENTS

Until the early twentieth century, the United States was an agricultural nation with most Americans living in rural areas. Despite their isolation and scattered settlements, farmers and their rural neighbors ignited some of the most important social movements in American history, movements that often turned political.

The earliest of these began before the American Revolution, when disgruntled farmers organized against colonial legislatures, seeking better representation, lower taxes, and stronger military protection. Some protests became armed uprisings and the regulator movement, as it was called, spread through the colonies from the Carolinas to Pennsylvania. After the Revolution, a similar uprising in Massachusetts in 1786–87, known as Shays' Rebellion, revealed the weakness of the federal government and spurred drafting of the Constitution.

Rural movements, usually local in nature, arose sporadically in the nineteenth century. These included Dorr's Rebellion in Rhode Island and the anti-rent movement in New York. After the Civil War, the exoduster movement drew many adherents among former slaves who, facing hardship and oppression in the South, migrated west to Kansas in the 1870s. The West and the South also provided the backdrop for the Populist movement, perhaps the most influential rural movement in American history. Feeling strangled by railroads and dominated by an increasingly urban power structure, farmers united around a "populist" platform, which advocated government ownership of transportation and communication, cooperative storehouses that could regulate distribution and prices, and direct election of senators. The Populist movement peaked in the 1890s, electing local and national lawmakers, and many of their demands were later adopted by the Progressive movement and enacted into law.

Rural movements in the twentieth and twenty-first centuries have been less significant, as the number of people living in agricultural areas has dwindled; however, there have been exceptions. The agrarian socialist movement spread a radical economic agenda in the early 1900s and 1910s. In the 1930s, the Southern Tenant Farmers' Union drew together many impoverished blacks and whites to fight for greater job security and better working conditions. More recently, the American Agricultural Movement helped raise awareness of the plight of farmers in the late twentieth century.

Section 6 of this encyclopedia, edited by Kyle Wilkison, surveys the myriad rural social movements from the colonial era to the present. It reveals that much of the impetus for economic and political change has come from farmers and others living in agricultural regions.

MORAL REFORM MOVEMENTS

The mid-nineteenth century witnessed so many social movements that it has often been called the age of reform. The most influential of these movements—abolition and women's rights—aimed to expand human freedom. Others aimed to control human behavior by reforming people's morals and restricting their access to substances considered dangerous.

The most far-reaching of these moral reform movements was the temperance movement, which aimed to temper, or moderate, people's consumption of alcohol. The temperance movement evolved into the prohibitionist movement, which fought for a total ban on alcohol. The movement achieved its greatest success in 1919, when the Twentieth Amendment to the Constitution empowered Congress to outlaw the sale of alcohol, which it proceeded to do. Although this amendment was repealed in 1933, many counties and jurisdictions across the country still ban the sale of alcohol, an enduring legacy of the temperance movement of the nineteenth century. The temperance movement also played a role in the founding of Alcoholics Anonymous, an organization that helps individuals overcome addiction to alcohol and which became the blueprint for the self-help movement of the late twentieth century.

Other moral reform movements sought to ban prostitution, vice, and pornography. Still others sought to ban contraception, homosexuality, and drugs. Many such laws were enacted during the Progressive Era in the early twentieth century. The Progressive movement embraced multitudinous goals, from moral reform to labor legislation, from government regulation of industry to direct democracy.

Many Progressives also joined the eugenics movement, which, drawing on the new science of genetics and evolution, aimed to selectively breed children from groups deemed racially or ethnically superior.

One central theme unites these diverse moral reform movements: the drive to improve society, whether it is by changing individuals' habits and activities, by banning substances and practices deemed dangerous or wrong, or by regulating reproduction.

Section 7 of this encyclopedia, edited by Liz Highleyman and Benjamin Shepard, describes the variety and complexity of these intersecting movements, showing how some have all but vanished, while others continue to shape American society.

RELIGIOUS, UTOPIAN, AND HEALTH MOVEMENTS

Religion has played a dual role in the history of American social movements: It has been the basis and goal of various movements, and it has spurred involvement in other movements, from abolition and civil rights to utopian communities and health reform. The First Great Awakening, a widespread religious revival in the 1730s and 1740s, may rank as the first broad social movement in American history. It gave rise to the Methodist Church and spread ideas of individual responsibility and communal participation.

A century later, the Second Great Awakening of the early 1800s inspired Americans to embrace religion and the concept of perfectionism. It became the individual's duty to reform himself or herself and then to reform society. Such an ethos led many to abolition, temperance, and other movements. It also led many to join new religions, such as that of the Mormons, Seventh-Day Adventists, and Pentecostalists.

The quest to build a perfect society inspired the creation of countless utopian, or intentional, communities, which dotted the countryside in the nineteenth century. Similar ideals, coupled with a "back-to-basics" sensibility, drew many to communal societies in the 1960s.

The offshoots of religious movements are varied. The missionary movement sent proselytizers throughout the world, whereas the social gospel movement sought to bring a Christian, socialist spirit to political and social policy. Although the great majority of Americans has long been Christian, many religious movements have embraced other faiths and belief systems, including Native American religions, Santeria, Islam, Judaism, Hinduism, Buddhism, and Daoism. Also included in religious movements are *non*religious movements, such as ethical culture, which aimed to develop a system of morals and behavior based on humanistic rather than spiritual ideas.

Finally, religious movements embrace movements based on so-called alternative belief systems known as "new age." These often are an amalgam of spiritual, holistic, and traditional practices, with elements of both Eastern and Western faiths. Religion also has influenced attitudes toward the body, nutrition, and medicine, sparking various health movements such as vegetarianism, homeopathy, and a return to natural foods.

Section 8 of this encyclopedia, edited by Matthew Sutton, conveys the enormous impact of religious, utopian, and health movements, and how these movements have shaped many facets of American life.

ANTIWAR/PROTEST MOVEMENTS

Unlike most American social movements, which emerged gradually and lasted for years, antiwar movements generally sprung up quickly and were of short duration—no longer than the war being opposed. Antiwar sentiment has arisen during every war the United States has fought, though genuine antiwar movements have been rare. Whether scattered or organized, antiwar activity has had an enormous impact.

Antiwar sentiment was widespread during the American Revolution. As much as one-third of the population were loyalists. Antiwar sentiment arose during the War of 1812, mainly in New England, where some spoke of secession, and it rose again during the Mexican-American War, mostly among abolitionists and antislavery northerners. Antiwar sentiment erupted in both sections of the country during the Civil War, leading to deadly riots in the North and disunity in the South, where many regions refused to secede from the Union.

The protest movement that emerged during World War I was deemed so threatening to national security and the military effort that the federal government clamped down on it swiftly, outlawing vocal opposition to the war and jailing and deporting the movement's leaders. These government actions were among the greatest assaults on free speech in American history.

The largest and most divisive antiwar movement arose in the 1960s in opposition to the Vietnam War. Driven largely by students, the movement swelled in the course of the decade, often intersecting and overlapping with the civil rights movement, and stimulating the growth of other protest movements. The most recent antiwar movement arose in the early twenty-first century, as activists gathered to oppose U.S. intervention in Iraq. Antiwar movements have been driven by those who oppose a specific war as wrong or immoral and by pacifists who oppose all wars.

Section 9 of this encyclopedia, edited by Marian Mollin, shows how antiwar sentiment has shaped each conflict in American history and explains the far-reaching effects of antiwar movements on society at large.

RADICAL AND POOR PEOPLE'S MOVEMENTS

While poverty has been part of American history from its very beginning, poor people's movements are a product of the industrial era. The goals of poor people's movements have primarily been jobs, dignity, and financial security. Most of these movements have emerged during periods of economic depression.

One of the first was known as Coxey's Army, when unemployed workers descended on Washington, D.C., in 1894, to demand public works programs. During the same period, the settlement house movement aimed to ameliorate the social and living conditions in urban areas where many poor, uneducated immigrants had settled. During the Great Depression of the 1930s, unemployed workers organized a movement to promote public works and prevent poor people from being evicted from their homes. These movements, which often embraced more radical aims that challenged the dominance of capitalism, also motivated the enactment of many New Deal programs that provided jobs and relief to millions of Americans.

A generation later, during the widespread social upheaval of the 1960s, poor people organized with radical goals of transforming the nation's economic system. These radical and poor people's movements spurred creation of numerous antipoverty programs and often intersected with other movements, such as the civil rights movement. In fact, it was during the planning for a poor people's march for reforms in welfare, employment, and housing that Martin Luther King, Jr., was assassinated in 1968. In the late twentieth century, as homelessness became widespread, poor people organized tent city movements to secure decent housing and shelter.

For more than a century, radical and poor people's movements have spurred both public and private sector intervention in the economy with the goal of mitigating human suffering and resolving the perceived inequities of the nation's capitalist, industrial system.

STUDENT MOVEMENTS

Like poor people, students have been active in many social movements throughout American history. Not until the 1960s, however, did college students play a commanding role in reforming American society.

Discontent with what they considered widespread conformity, political and economic inequality, and corporate domination, they formed the Students for a Democratic Society (SDS) in 1960. Many students and SDS leaders joined the Free Speech Movement at the University of California in Berkeley in 1964 and played vital roles in the civil rights and antiwar movements of the decade. They created a counterculture movement, which challenged many prevailing social mores and values. More radical students joined militant organizations, such as the Weathermen, which urged overthrow of the U.S. government and the capitalist system, and used violence to pursue their aims.

In the 1980s, students galvanized opposition to apartheid in South Africa, setting up shantytowns on college campuses to raise visibility. In the 1990s and early 2000s, students provided much of the energy in the campaigns against globalization and sweatshop labor.

Students emerged as a broad social group in the second half of the twentieth century, when large numbers of Americans began attending college for the first time, and their numbers continue to grow. Although the fervor and issues have fluctuated over time, student movements remain a vibrant source for social change.

ETHNIC AND GROUP IDENTITY MOVEMENTS

The civil rights movement of the 1950s and 1960s generated many changes in American society and sparked new trends, ideas, and ways of thought. Among these was the "black is beautiful" movement that promoted pride in African-American culture and identity. Such racial and ethnic pride inspired other groups to emphasize and celebrate their past, their culture, and sense of cohesion.

Mexican Americans, other Latin Americans, and Hispanics formed the Chicano movement, while Asian Americans and other groups formed ethnic identity movements of their own. European Americans, whose ancestors came from Ireland, Italy, Poland, and other countries, also formed groups to celebrate their culture and contributions to American society.

Many of these ethnic identity movements adopted political goals that pushed for civil rights and greater economic opportunity. This, in turn, inspired formation of other groups, based not on race or ethnicity but on some specific feature. Older people formed the Gray Panthers and senior citizens' movement. Disabled people formed their own movement, which pushed for greater inclusion, acceptance, and dignity in American society. These ethnic and group identity movements have spawned an "identity politics," which has made personal association with a particular group a central element of individual identity.

ENVIRONMENTAL MOVEMENT

The origins of the environmental movement can be traced to the nineteenth century, when fishers and hunters regulated their actions to prevent depletion of fish and wildlife. Increasing settlement and encroachment on the land in the latter part of the century led to early, broad-based efforts at preservation of public space. This eventually led to the development of the National Park System, which began with the 1872 establishment of Yellowstone, the first national park.

In the early twentieth century, these efforts expanded to include preservation and conservation of natural resources such as forests, water, and soil. Publication of Rachel Carson's *Silent Spring* in 1962 generated controversy over the dangers of DDT and other widely used pesticides and helped bring about the modern environmental movement. The movement gathered strength during the 1960s, culminating in such landmark legislation as the Clean Air Act, Clean Waters Restoration Act, and Endangered Species Act, and the establishment of the Environmental Protection Agency in 1970.

As the dangers caused by pollution, toxins, and industrial waste became increasingly evident in the late twentieth century, the environmental movement became institutionalized, as powerful interest groups, manufacturers, and government agencies competed to set environmental policies. The environmental movement branched in new directions, embracing animal rights and appropriate technology, as well as efforts to close nuclear power plants.

Of all the social movements examined in this encyclopedia, the environmental movement, the subject of Section 13, is one that will most likely continue well into the twenty-first century.

Lesbian, Gay, Bisexual, and Transgender Movement

The gay rights movement emerged in the late nineteenth and early twentieth centuries, an era when sexual issues became more openly discussed in public forums. For many years, however, homosexuality was less a movement than a subculture.

In the post–World War II era, gay men and lesbians began forming organizations, such as the Mattachine Society and the Daughters of Bilitis, to build solidarity and support, as well as to fight for recognition and an end to discrimination. At the time, gay men and women faced many obstacles, from a lack of general social acceptance to specific laws banning sexual acts. Homosexuality was defined as an illness, and police often raided clubs and establishments where gay people gathered. The gay rights movement also included myriad advocates of sexual freedom, including bisexuals and transgendered people.

In June 1969, police in New York City raided the Stonewall Inn, a bar frequented by gay men and transvestites. Patrons resisted arrest and harassment, and they rioted against the police. This incident galvanized the gay rights movement. In the course of the next decade, gay men and lesbians became increasingly vocal, militant, and visible in pursuit of their aims.

The advent of AIDS in the 1980s further emboldened and solidified the gay rights movement and made homosexuality—and sexuality itself—a major public issue. Groups such as the Gay Men's Health Crisis and the AIDS Coalition to Unleash Power (or ACT-UP) drew widespread attention to the disease, treated those infected with it, and demanded greater spending, research, and social programs. By the 1990s, the gay rights movement had numerous successes, such as the passing of antidiscrimination ordinances in many states and local jurisdictions and achieving a greater degree of social acceptance.

In 2003, two judicial decisions marked a new phase in the gay rights movement: The U.S. Supreme Court struck down a Texas antisodomy law as unconstitutional, and the Supreme Judicial Court of Massachusetts ruled in favor of gay marriage. Opponents reacted swiftly with efforts to overturn or mitigate these decisions, while gay rights leaders have mobilized to preserve and extend them.

Section 14 of this encyclopedia, edited by William Turner, traces development of the lesbian, gay, bisexual, and transgendered movement over the past century and examines its impact on American society.

Conservative, Nativist, and Right-Wing Movements

Most social movements in American history have advocated greater individual rights and personal freedoms—as well as greater democracy and inclusiveness in American society—and have looked to a strong national government to help secure them. Several movements, however, do not fit neatly into this category and have sought rather to preserve the status quo or even to restore some features of an idealized past. Such movements have a variety of goals, some seeking to expand certain freedoms, some seeking to restrict them, some seeking a stronger national government, and some seeking a weaker one.

Nativist movements date back to the 1830s, when many white, Protestant Americans felt threatened by the arrival of increasing numbers of immigrants, particularly Catholic newcomers from Ireland. They engaged in violent actions and formed political parties, such as the Know Nothings in the 1850s, dedicated to restricting immigration. Anti-Irish sentiment diminished in the late 1800s, but nativism found new targets among recent immigrants, such as the Chinese, Japanese, and eastern and southern Europeans.

In 1882, the United States banned immigration from China, and, in the early 1900s, it extended this ban to most Asians and eastern and southern Europeans. These bans were repealed in the 1960s, but nativism continues to be a powerful force in the United States.

Some strands of the conservative movement focus on specific policy issues, such as opposition to gun control or support for prayer in public schools. The pro-life movement, which emerged in the 1970s, aims to outlaw abortion. By contrast, supporters of the libertarian movement focus less on specific policy issues than on their central aim of weakening the power of the national government—or any government—in personal matters. They favor maximum individual liberty without government intervention.

Many libertarians and conservatives see the national government as a threat to, rather than a guardian of, their individual rights, and they aim to reduce its size and influence. At the furthest extreme of the political right are groups that view the U.S. government as the enemy and form paramilitary bands, known as militias. An older and similarly extreme group is the Ku Klux Klan, known for its hostility toward African Americans, Catholics, Jews, and foreigners. The Klan emerged after the Civil War and committed numerous acts of terrorism against former slaves and whites sympathetic to black advancement. The group reached its greatest strength in the 1920s.

The modern conservative movement emerged after World War II in reaction to the expansion of the national government. In the decades since, it has attracted many Christian fundamentalists, whites opposed to federal support for integration, and businesspeople seeking fewer government regulations and lower taxes. A dominant force in the Republican Party, Conservatism played a key role in electing Ronald Reagan president in 1980.

Conservatives tend to favor local, rather than national, control over many social matters and often take a strict stance on issues of personal morality and individual behavior. The current conservative and right wing movement, however, embraces myriad voices, and, with strong grassroots support in many parts of the country, it continues to influence social policy and national politics.

GLOBAL JUSTICE MOVEMENT

The global justice movement is the most recent American social movement, emerging only in the last decade. As the name suggests, it is global, rather than national, in scope.

Following World War II, wealthier nations created several global organizations, such as the International Monetary Fund and World Bank, to promote economic development and world trade. These organizations wielded influence over international commerce and investments in Third World countries. In the 1990s, Mexico, Canada, and the United States ratified the North American Free Trade Agreement to lower trade barriers between these nations. Critics have charged that such transnational organizations have weakened environmental protections, exploited Third World workers, and reduced American jobs.

The global justice movement has challenged these organizations and demanded greater participation of the poor in setting economic policy and improving working conditions worldwide. They have fought for a "living wage" that would lift incomes of poorer workers, fair trade laws, and elimination of sweatshop labor. The global justice movement burst into national consciousness in 1999, when protesters violently disrupted a meeting of the World Trade Organization in Seattle. Similar protests have occurred in Canada, Switzerland, Italy, and Mexico.

Section 16 of this encyclopedia, edited by Liz Highleyman, traces the origins of this still-emerging movement and its effort to build support, both nationally and globally.

THE DYNAMICS OF SOCIAL MOVEMENTS

The *Encyclopedia of American Social Movements* aims to be comprehensive, authoritative, and balanced. Its goal is neither to champion nor glorify the people in these movements but rather to examine their ideas and motives and understand how their united actions shaped American life. As democracy in motion, social movements are the epic story of the nation's past, providing Americans with a forum—a mechanism—to come together, voice grievances, and change society. Indeed, social movements define, in part, what it means to be American.

Every social movement has begun the same way: with the belief that the world can be a better place and that people can make this happen. By uniting in a movement, people's voices become magnified, precipitating the actions that move the nation in a new direction.

Many of the nation's greatest goals and accomplishments have been the result of social movements through which people have challenged the established order in the struggle for progress. "Our lives begin to end," Martin Luther King, Jr., said, "the day we become silent about things that matter." As this encyclopedia shows, Americans break their silence every time they create and join a social movement and become part of the "awful roar" that transforms the world.

1

ANTISLAVERY MOVEMENT

Introduction

Shortly after the Civil War, long-time abolitionist and Union colonel Thomas Wentworth Higginson looked back with pride and optimism at the fight he and his troops had just helped win. For Higginson and other abolitionists, the war's significance lay primarily not in the preservation of the Union but rather in the achievement of black freedom. By the time the war broke out, abolitionists—black and white, male and female—had been struggling for generations to end slavery.

The fight against human bondage in the United States had a long history. European colonists in North America began relying upon enslaved African laborers within the first generation of settling in the New World. Protest against the system erupted almost immediately. German Mennonites and Quakers in Pennsylvania led the way, petitioning against slavery as early as the 1680s. They argued that slavery broke the Golden Rule of Christianity and defeated their purpose for settling in the New World. For these settlers, the colonies offered a chance to create model societies that emphasized freedom of conscience and an opportunity to live in "Godly" simplicity. Slavery defeated both goals. Unfortunately, most of their neighbors did not share their concerns, and slavery became deeply entrenched in the legal and social fabric of the colonies.

More colonists began to question slavery in the decades before the American Revolution. Concerned more with self-preservation than the welfare of the enslaved, this generation of antislavery leaders struggled to halt the importation of new slaves. A 1712 conspiracy in which a group of slaves plotted to burn the town of New York convinced a growing number of whites to oppose human bondage by emphasizing the dangers of retribution. Following the conspiracy, a number of state assemblies tried to impose substantial taxes on slave importation to keep the black population, and thus the threat of retaliation, from growing. The colonies, however, still belonged to En-gland, and the home government overrode such efforts. Slavery was a profitable system that brought great wealth to the empire.

During the Revolutionary Era, this fear of the enslaved combined with a new emphasis on natural rights to lead a growing number of whites to question human bondage. In the original draft of the Declaration of Independence, Thomas Jefferson criticized the English government for introducing slavery into the colonies. For Jefferson and other aristocratic Virginia planters, the system served as a daily reminder of the contradiction between the freedom they celebrated and the reality of their own greed. They also worried that their bondspersons would eventually strike for their own liberty. Jefferson compared the situation to having a "wolf by the ears," and the Haitian Revolution in August 1791, now known as the only successful slave revolt in history, compounded his fears. Most Northern states, less dependent on slave labor than the Southern states, took steps during and immediately after the Revolution to end slavery, with most providing for gradual emancipation.

Many antislavery leaders of the Revolutionary generation dreamed of solving the problem by returning the slaves to Africa. They saw repatriation as a way to make up to Africa for past wrongs, to "civilize" the inhabitants, and to teach them legitimate trades while also ridding themselves of the dangers of slaveholding. This idea was not new. Britain had created the African colony of Sierra Leone in the 1790s as a "haven" for poor blacks from London, Loyalists from the American Revolution, and "recaptives" saved from the illicit slave trade. Hoping to create a similar colony, a number of influential Americans came together in December of 1816 to form the American Society for Colonizing the Free People of Colour of the United States, more commonly known as the American Colonization Society. This group initially enjoyed success in both sections of the country, winning support from Virginia slaveholders as well as re-

3

ligious and missionary groups from Pennsylvania and other Northern states. Taking their cue from British efforts at Sierra Leone, they founded the African colony of Liberia in 1822. They hoped the formation of such a colony would encourage American slaveholders to free their laborers by providing an outlet for their removal. They also hoped that their colony, like Sierra Leone, would serve as a home for recaptives. At first, a few key black leaders such as Paul Cuffee and James Forten also considered the merits of the plan.

Most African Americans, however, saw colonization as a scheme to strengthen slavery by removing free blacks from the country. They argued that if able free black leaders went to Liberia, American slaves would be deprived of valuable leadership in the freedom struggle at home. By the 1830s, a growing number of whites, led by William Lloyd Garrison, had begun to listen to black protests and joined with them in calling for immediate and uncompensated emancipation. Influenced largely by the evangelical nature of the Second Great Awakening, white leaders like Garrison, Gerrit Smith, Arthur and Lewis Tappan, and Theodore Dwight Weld joined the efforts of black leaders and together created the biracial abolitionist movement. Abolition and antislavery became two distinct movements in the 1830s.

The abolition movement was revolutionary. Abolitionists not only called for immediate freedom for the enslaved, but they also, at least in theory, insisted upon racial equality. While white abolitionists continued to hold their own racial biases, they went beyond the antislavery advocates of previous generations by working directly with African Americans. Black and white abolitionists operated newspapers, held meetings and conventions, petitioned legislatures, and spoke out loudly against the institution at every opportunity. The mainstay of the movement was a belief in a tactic known as *moral suasion*. According to this theory, abolitionists could convince slaveholders of the evils of the system and, thus, encourage them to release the slaves. Garrison and his followers pioneered this tactic and emphasized its peaceful nature.

By the 1840s, however, a growing number of black and white abolitionists began to question the use of moral suasion alone. Pro-slavery mobs had begun to assault abolitionists in both the North and the South. In 1837, abolitionist editor Elijah P. Lovejoy, having been previously attacked by mobs, decided to abandon his antiviolence stance in favor of armed self-defense. Despite his decision to fight back, he was killed while trying to defend his press. This incident,

as well as attacks upon other leaders, including Garrison himself, led a number of abolitionists to question nonviolence. At the same time, the passage of a strong fugitive slave law and an outbreak of proslavery violence in Kansas convinced others to embrace a more militant stance. It was at this point that those of Higginson's generation joined the struggle.

By the end of the 1850s, agitation on both sides had reached the boiling point, and Northern abolitionists and Southern slaveholders were both calling for disunion. When the Civil War broke out, President Abraham Lincoln professed a commitment to save the Union at all costs, but many abolitionists saw a greater purpose to the fight. Both blacks and whites pushed the president to make abolition a war goal. Blacks were excluded from joining the army during the first years of the war, but slaves began escaping immediately. They served the Union troops as spies, cooks, manual laborers, and nurses. A number of free black leaders approached Lincoln personally, asking him to let them participate in what they saw as the logical culmination of their decades of struggle. As soon as the president issued the Emancipation Proclamation and the Union Army began accepting black recruits, African Americans began enlisting. They exhibited valor in battles such as Milliken's Bend, Port Hudson, and, most notably, Fort Wagner.

Black abolitionists saw the Civil War as an opportunity to prove racial equality by earning freedom rather than having it handed to them. A number of civil rights victories during the war reinforced their optimism that their efforts in battle would bring lasting changes. To begin with, by allowing black men to take up arms for the country, the U.S. government acknowledged black citizenship. The government also passed a number of antidiscrimination measures, repealing an 1825 law barring blacks from carrying the mail, admitting blacks to the visitors' galleries in Congress, and initiating a process that would lead to the end of legal segregation in the North within three decades. Most importantly, the Union victory led to the Fourteenth and Fifteenth amendments to the Constitution, freeing the slaves and declaring them citizens, respectively. For white and black abolitionists alike, these changes served as evidence that they had won much more than the Civil War. They had reached their decades-long goal of removing the stain of slavery from the nation and had secured freedom for those in bondage.

Beverly Tomek

ANTISLAVERY MOVEMENT
1700s–1830s

Bound labor played an indispensable role in the development of the Americas. Hoping to extract profit from this vast territory, European leaders and their colonial agents began immediately to force indigenous populations to provide labor in the colonies. When that arrangement failed, the Europeans turned to Africa. These enslaved workers produced wealth for European nations by mining for precious metals in Spain's Central and South American colonies and planting, cultivating, and harvesting cash crops such as sugar, tobacco, and cotton in the English and French colonies of the Caribbean and North America. By using slave labor, European leaders created profitable empires.

By the time of the American Revolution, however, a growing number of people in Europe, as well as in the colonies, began to speak out against slavery. Although the abolition crusade did not emerge as an organized, coherent movement until the 1830s, antislavery sentiment has a much longer history. Examination of the long legacy of antislavery thought in the North American colonies, the effect of the American Revolution on slavery, and the early efforts of organized antislavery reveal that the abolitionists of the Antebellum years were adding to, and improving upon, an existing foundation.

ANTISLAVERY IN COLONIAL AMERICA

Antislavery efforts in North America began almost immediately. German Mennonites and Quakers in Pennsylvania began protesting human bondage as early as the 1680s. In 1688, a group of Dutch-speaking Quakers from the Germantown settlement presented an antislavery petition that made its way to the Philadelphia Quarterly Meeting. They pointed out that slavery broke the Golden Rule of Christianity, made a mockery of the colony's claim to be a Holy Experiment and a haven for freedom, and created a situation fraught with danger.

The petition employed each of these arguments to persuade fellow Quakers to oppose slavery. It began by invoking God's commandment to "doe to all men like as we will be done to ourselves" and reminding Quakers of the colonial promise of "liberty of conscience." The petitioners then pointed out that slavery hampered their religious mission in America, comparing racial oppression in the colonies to their own spiritual repression in Europe, warning that "this makes an ill report in all those countries of Europe where they [hear that] Quakers . . . here handel men as they handel there . . . cattle." Finally, although many historians have failed to emphasize this point, the petitioners cried out against slavery in a quest for self-preservation. They warned that the slaves, described by their owners as "wicked and stubborn men," could join together, "fight for their freedom," and "handel their masters and mistresses" as they had been "handled" themselves. The petitioners argued that the "poor slaves" had the right to such retaliation, and they feared the consequences for all white colonists, slave owners or not. Their petition was tabled by the Yearly Meeting, and many Quakers continued to own slaves, but it serves as an important record of early protest against slavery. It combined compassion for the slaves with concern for white settlers by arguing that the system robbed blacks of their freedom and put white settlers in danger by encouraging a future race war.

The Germantown effort was followed by attempts to at least halt the importation of more slaves. In 1712, a conspiracy among slaves to burn the town of New York confirmed the petitioners' fears of retaliation and led Pennsylvania's Quaker-dominated assembly to impose a substantial tax of 20 pounds per head on any slave imported into the colony. The New York insurrection involved only twenty slaves, but it resulted in the death of nine whites. Even these small numbers spread terror throughout the North Ameri-

5

can colonies because any challenge to complete black subjugation posed a threat to the entire system of bound labor and put white lives in jeopardy. The Pennsylvania tax effort failed, however, because the Crown overrode the duty, and the slave trade in this and other colonies continued despite the protest of some Quakers, most notably Ralph Sandiford and Anthony Benezet. Even after the 1739 Stono Rebellion in South Carolina led to the death of approximately twenty whites at the hands of fifty slave rebels, importation of Africans into North America continued.

Northern opposition to slavery began to grow in the decades leading up to the American Revolution. To begin with, the plantation economy, which made cash crops crucial in the Southern states, did not develop in the colonies above Virginia. The mixed economy of the Middle States made small-scale slavery profitable as bound laborers learned a variety of farming and artisanal skills, but large-scale commercial farms dependent upon gang labor remained largely a Southern phenomenon. In addition, most New Englanders came to America in search of self-sufficiency rather than large profits, and slavery did not fit in well with their religious ideals. These settlers, known as Puritans, came to the colonies in hopes of creating what they called a "city upon a hill." This society, they hoped, would serve as an example of perfection to the rest of the world and encourage observers to follow a "Godly" lifestyle of simplicity and morality. Although slavery existed in New England, growing numbers of whites began to regret their complicity. They began to fear that the taint of human oppression would put all colonists in danger of Divine retribution. Many Quakers agreed with the Puritans, and a large number saw the Seven Years' War as God's punishment for extravagant lifestyles and abuse of fellow humans. This crisis in conscience, combined with the fact that slavery remained much more important economically in the South than in the North, encouraged the growth of opposition to the system.

GROWTH IN ANTISLAVERY SENTIMENT

Scholars have long debated the reasons for the growth of antislavery sentiment in the eighteenth century. In his monumental 1944 study, *Capitalism & Slavery*, Eric Williams attributed the growth in antislavery arguments throughout the British Empire to the declining profitability of the system. He argued that the crusade to end the slave trade emerged only after it had "become less profitable and less vital" to the home government. According to Williams, before the American

Notices advertising slave sales and slave auctions appeared regularly in American newspapers throughout the eighteenth century. *(Library of Congress)*

Revolution, "all classes in English society . . . supported the slave trade" and even fought against colonial assemblies' efforts to curtail the growth of the slave population by placing restrictions on importation. He added that English Quakers, unlike those of the northern American colonies, approved of the slave trade as essential to the growth and success of the empire. He used this idea to support his larger argument that profits from the slave trade "provided one of the main streams of that accumulation of capital . . . which financed the Industrial Revolution."

Thus, according to Williams, slavery and the slave trade enjoyed widespread support while they contributed to the economic growth of the empire. The system planted the seeds of its own destruction, however, by fueling the industrial revolution. Once industry began to dominate, fewer were willing to support the plantations because they had outlived their usefulness to the empire. They had fueled the shipping and shipbuilding industries, provided markets for English goods, spurred the growth of English seaport towns, and provided raw materials used by British industry.

With American independence, Britain became primarily concerned with processing raw materials and manufacturing finished goods. The most important of these raw materials—cotton—came from the United States. Thus, slavery became largely an American problem. By the time British abolitionists began to attack the system in the British West Indian colonies, according to Williams' argument, it was no longer essential to the empire. Since Williams's time, scholars such as Seymour Drescher and David Brion Davis have challenged these assumptions, yet Williams's explanation remains thought-provoking.

While Williams focused on economic reasons for the growth of antislavery, others have argued that ideology played a larger role. Davis, in his Pulitzer Prize-winning book, *The Problem of Slavery in Western Culture* (1966), emphasized the role of religion and Enlightenment thought in fostering the attack on slavery. He agreed with Williams that slavery "played a major role in the early development of the New World and in the growth of commercial capitalism," but he insisted that "slavery had always been more than an economic institution." He argued that bound labor was "a genuine moral problem" and antislavery crusaders saw emancipation as "proof of moral progress in history."

According to Davis, the rise of dissenting sects like the Quakers led to changes in religious ideas, which ultimately affected attitudes toward slavery. Traditional Christianity supported slavery because of the belief in the doctrine of original sin. In this case, the original sin was committed when Noah's son Ham stared at his father's nude body, causing all of his descendants to bear his curse as punishment. As Europeans began to explore Africa and study its people, they began to believe that this "Curse of Ham" had caused the difference in skin color. According to this theory, Africans descended from Ham, and their black skin served as physical evidence of the curse. They extended this idea of original sin and punishment to justify enslaving blacks by arguing that Africans were relegated to the status of servants by God as a result of Ham's sin.

According to Davis, however, some new Christian sects that emerged after the Protestant Reformation began to question traditional doctrines, including that of original sin. In the process, they "undermined the ideology which rationalized the existing social order." Davis added that by mid-century Quaker belief especially began to provide "a cultural setting in which hostility to slavery could become something more than individual dissent," especially in Pennsylvania

where Friends played a large role in the colonial government. He described a similar transformation of opinion on slavery in other Protestant denominations, concluding that "it is hardly conceivable that antislavery could have become a powerful international force had it not been preceded by a revolutionary shift in attitudes toward sin, human nature, and progress."

According to Davis, the Enlightenment also contributed to the growth of antislavery by challenging traditional secular authority. Although the Protestants "searched for authentic standards in the revealed word of God," Enlightenment thinkers looked to human nature for answers. Men like John Locke and Jean Jacques Rousseau argued that human nature in an uncorrupted state was good, or at least malleable, rather than evil. Such reasoning led to a "heightened concern for individual happiness" and led growing numbers of thinkers to question human bondage. Thus, by the eve of the American Revolution, the ideas of the French Enlightenment had laid the groundwork for both white and black freedom movements.

Abolition societies began to form in the colonies before the Revolution. Pennsylvania's Society for Promoting the Abolition of Slavery was founded in 1775 by Benjamin Franklin, but the turmoil of the war led to its demise. It was reorganized in 1784 as the Pennsylvania Society for Promoting the Abolition of Slavery and for the Relief of Free Negroes Unlawfully held in Bondage, and for Improving the Condition of the African Race. As president of this society, Franklin pledged to "instruct; to advise; to qualify those who have been restored to freedom . . . To promote in them habits of industry; to furnish them with employments suited to their age, sex, talents, and other circumstances; and to procure their children an education calculated for their future situation in life." For early abolitionists like Franklin, the end of slavery had to be gradual and required training for the freed so that they could become useful members of society.

Most Northern states took steps to end slavery during and immediately after the war. Vermont adopted an antislavery clause in its 1777 state constitution, but it was not one of the original thirteen colonies and was not admitted into the new nation until 1791. Pennsylvania was the first state to adopt legislation against slavery, providing for gradual emancipation with a 1780 abolition act. Most New England states followed suit around the same time, also providing for gradual emancipation. Some states, including Rhode Island and Connecticut, passed statutes promising freedom to future generations. Under most of these gradual abolition acts, the children of current slaves would become free upon their maturity, usually in their late twenties. States such as Massachusetts and New Hampshire relied upon judicial decisions to provide the same effect.

Most of these measures were products of a combination of economic, religious, and ideological motivations. Williams and Davis each presented valid points as to the importance of economics and ideology in the emergence of the transatlantic antislavery movement. A comprehensive look at the growth of antislavery sentiment, specifically in North America, however, reveals a unique, and sometimes overlooked, factor: fear. Unlike British abolitionists, who lived thousands of miles away from the slaves they hoped to free, Americans were motivated by distrust for the growing number of bound laborers in their midst. The Germantown petition, though arguing that the enslaved had a right to retaliate, hoped to convince fellow Quakers to stop importing slaves in the interest of self-preservation. Although large-scale, well-organized slave rebellions were rare in the North American colonies, white settlers heard reports of frequent rebellion in the English West Indies. Most realized that the key difference was population balance. In the Caribbean, a high rate of absenteeism and the large-scale nature of the plantation workforce left whites greatly outnumbered by blacks. In North America, the only colony with a black majority was South Carolina. As long as whites outnumbered blacks in most colonies, they could hope to be safe from rebellion. However, if more colonies followed South Carolina's lead in importing large numbers of slaves from Africa and the Caribbean, whites throughout North America would face the danger of retaliation. Another fear shared by North Americans from the beginning of colonial settlement was the fear of racial intermixture. In 1691, the Virginia legislature passed a statute that made interracial sexual acts illegal and effectively outlawed interracial marriage, and most other colonial legislatures at least considered similar acts.

Because of such fear, the earliest antislavery initiatives, like the attempt by the Pennsylvania assembly to tax slave imports, were actually aimed at limiting the growth of the black population rather than freeing those currently held in bondage. Founding Father and early abolitionist Franklin best summed up this desire in his 1755 pamphlet, *Observations Concerning the Increase of Mankind*. In this essay, Franklin argued against increasing "the Sons of Africa, by Planting them in America, where we have so

Slave importers crowded Africans as closely as possible on ships crossing the Atlantic Ocean. Because of the wretched conditions on board, an estimated 10 to 25 percent died on the grueling "Middle Passage" from Africa to America. *(Library of Congress)*

fair an Opportunity, by excluding all blacks and Tawneys, of increasing the lovely White and Red [races]." Other early abolitionists agreed. Quaker Anthony Benezet argued in his 1767 *Caution and Warning to Great Britain and Her Colonies* that slavery posed a danger to white morals while also exciting "continual apprehension of dangers and frequent alarms, to which the whites are necessarily exposed from so great an increase of a people that, by their bondage and oppression, become natural enemies." In this climate of fear, antislavery advocates hoped, above all, to purge society of the evil system and the menacing presence of an unwanted population. Justice for the men and women in bondage was of secondary concern at best. Even for men of conscience like Benezet, sympathy for the enslaved and fear of the black population could easily go hand in hand.

SLAVERY AND THE AMERICAN REVOLUTION

These early antislavery rumblings gained volume during the American Revolution. As American lead-

A PETITION FOR FREEDOM
BY AFRICAN AMERICANS OF
MASSACHUSETTS, 1777

The fight against British colonialism in the Americas calling for liberty, freedom, and equality raised the crucial question of the dehumanized status of enslaved African Americans who were oppressed by the same colonial white population that demanded liberty. The following is a demand made on the Massachusetts General Court in 1777 by African Americans seeking freedom from slavery. The language is in the original.

To the Honorable Counsel and House of Representatives for the State of Massachusetts Bay in General Court assembled, January 13, 1777

The petition of A Great Number of Blackes detained in a State of slavery in the Bowels of a free & Christian Country Humbly shuwith [showeth] that your Petitioners apprehend that thay [they] have in Common with all other men a Natural and Unaliable [inalienable] Right to that freedom which the Grat Parent of the Unavers hath Bestowed equalley on all menkind and which they have Never forfuted by any Compact or agreement whatever—but thay wher Unjustly Dragged by the hand of cruel Power from their Derest friends and sum of them Even torn from the Embraces of their tender Parents—from A popolous Pleasant and plentiful contry and in violation of Laws of Nature and off Nations and in defiance of all the tender feelings of humanity Brough[t] hear Either to Be sold Like Beast of Burthen & Like them Condemnd to Slavery for Life—Among A People Profesing the mild Religion of Jesus A people Not Insensible of the Secrets of Rational Being Nor without spirit to Resent the unjust endeavours of others to Reduce them to a state of Bondage and

Subjection your honouer Need not to be informed that A Life of Slavery Like that of your petioners Deprived of Every social privilege of Every thing Requisit to Render Life Tolable [Tolerable] is far worse then Nonexistence.

. . . .

[T]he Good People of these States your petitiononers have Long and 'Patiently waited the Evnt of petition after petition By them presented to the Legislative Body of this state and cannot but with Grief Reflect that their Success hath ben but too similar they Cannot but express their Astonishment that It has Never Bin Considred that Every Principle form which Amarica has Acted in the Cours of their unhappy Dificultes with Great Briton Pleads Stronger than A thousand arguments in favowrs of your petioners they therfor humble Beseech your honours to give this petion [petition] its due weight & consideration & cause an act of the Legislatur to be past Wherby they may be Restored to the Enjoyments of that which is the Naturel Right of all men—and their Children who wher Born in this Land of Liberty may not be heald as Slaves after they arrive at the age of twenty one years so may the Inhabitance of this Stats No longer chargeable with the inconsistancey of acting themselves the part which they condem and oppose in others Be prospered in their present Glorious struggle for Liberty and have those Blessing to them, &c.

Lancaster Hill	Jack Purpont
Peter Bess	Nero Suneto
Brister Slenten	Newport Symner
Prince Hall	Job Lock

Source: Collections of the Massachusetts Historical Society. 5th Series, III (Boston, 1877), pp. 436–437.

---

ers began to employ the rhetoric of freedom and equality, they were forced to grapple with the paradox of slavery in their "free" society. Unlike slaveholders of the Antebellum era, those of the colonial and revolutionary periods generally accepted the idea that slavery was harmful to whites and blacks alike, and most Americans, North and South, expressed reservations about human bondage.

Historian Gary Nash cited five reasons that the period of the 1770s and 1780s offered an "opportune time for abolishing slavery." He emphasized the widespread antislavery sentiment, adding that al-

though the lower South still depended largely upon and thus strongly supported slavery, that section was too weak to resist a sustained antislavery effort from the rest of the nation at that time. He added that most thinkers of the time believed in environmentalism, a theory that offered a possible tool in the struggle against racism. Environmentalists argued that the "degradation" of blacks was due to the condition of enslavement rather than racial inferiority. Thus, blacks and whites were naturally equal and held the same capacity for education and improvement. Finally, he maintained that the unsettled western territories offered hope for the antislavery movement in two ways. The land could be used to provide compensation to owners for releasing their human property, and it could also provide a place for resettling the freed. According to Nash, however, greed prevented the founders from seizing the moment. He argued that the North and Upper South, though opposed to slavery in theory, enjoyed too much residual economic benefit from slavery's contribution to a strong national economy.

Nash's argument is certainly valid, but it addresses only one aspect of a double-sided issue. The economic greed he describes was coupled by fear. Thomas Jefferson, as the author of the Declaration of Independence and the famous assertion that "all men are created equal," provides the most famous case study. Like others of his time, he profited from slavery. He also feared both the continuation of the system and the immediate emancipation of the bondspeople, worrying that blacks, free or slave, would destroy the white race either by armed, physical retribution or through genetic mixing.

FEAR OF REVOLTS

Jefferson's fear of the biracial climate in America surfaced early in his career, most notably in his rough draft of the Declaration of Independence. In his original draft, he not only blamed the British slave trade for imposing a volatile black population among the colonists, but he also publicly articulated his fear of slave insurrection. He insisted that King George not only "waged cruel war against human nature itself" by bringing slaves to the colonies, but that he had also blocked colonial measures to prevent further importation of slaves. Referring to a proclamation in which Virginia's royal governor, Lord Dunmore, promised freedom to slaves who would join the British forces in putting down the colonists' rebellion, he blamed the British government for "exciting those very people to rise in arms among us, and to purchase that liberty of which [the King] has deprived them, by murdering the people on whom he also obtruded them." Jefferson's fear of the slaves' reaction to Dunmore's proclamation was genuine, and other Virginians had expressed similar worries. Some had begun calling for more troops, and one Virginia leader even wrote to his state's delegates in Congress to request that the federal government hire regular officers to protect residents of the state against their slaves.

Fears of slave revolt did not end after the Revolutionary War. Instead, they increased markedly between 1790 and 1801 in light of foreign and domestic slave rebellion. The fervor of revolution in America spread to Europe, fueling a similar revolt in France, which led to the overthrow of the king. Blacks in the French West Indian colonies took advantage of the chaos of the French Revolution to strike for their own freedom in the early 1790s, and many Americans feared that blacks in the United States would follow their lead. The best known of these rebellions occurred on the island of St. Domingo, in the country now known as Haiti. This revolution ended with Haiti becoming the first independent Caribbean nation and the only republic led by blacks. American blacks were aware of this victory and argued that the Haitian example proved that blacks were capable of governing themselves.

Jefferson, who had expressed concern about the growing black population in the United States, received dispatches of the Haitian revolt and a copy of the 1790 American census report at the same time. The Census of 1790 was alarming to a man who had shown continual concern for the growing number of blacks in America. As early as 1785, he expressed irritation that, despite his inducements for the government to end the slave trade, three states were still importing African laborers. He learned that South Carolina had imported more than 4,000 blacks from Africa that year and that over 1,000 black loyalists who had supported the British during the Revolutionary War had been returned to their masters. Two years later, North and South Carolina and Georgia were continuing to import slaves, and Jefferson voiced his irritation that there were 650,000 blacks in the five Southern states alone and that the prospects of the complete cessation of the slave trade did not look promising. By the time of the 1790 Census, the Virginia black population, both slave and free, was more than half the size of the white population, and states such as North Carolina and Georgia were seeing similar increases. In this atmosphere, the dispatches Jefferson received from Haiti could only have served to heighten his existing fears. In his 1781 *Notes on the State of Virginia*, Jefferson had warned that blacks posed a constant danger to the new republic, arguing that "ten thousand recollections . . . of the injuries they have sustained . . . will divide us into parties, and produce convulsions which will probably never end but in the extermination of the one or the other race." The Haitian events served as a chilling reminder of his own insights.

The U.S. consul to Haiti, Nathaniel Cutting, sent reports that reinforced Jefferson's own fears. Declaring that "their whole plan is marked with bitter resentment for former injuries," he concluded that "here we have a lively instance of the baneful effects of Slavery, and I wish that America might add another laurel to her wreath of Fame, by leading the way to a general emancipation." To strengthen his point, Cutting included vivid accounts of atrocities committed by the insurrectionists. In his letters, he recounted horrifying instances of black violence against whites, telling of cases in which the "remorseless savages" entered hospitals and "inhumanely murder'd" the "unfortunate Invalids," "stripped naked and mangled in a most horrid manner" French soldiers, and "in the most cruel manner murder'd in cool blood great numbers of those whom they had thus render'd defenceless." He added that "their savage barbarity has spared neither age nor sex," and he attributed this level of violence to "the ebullitions of uncultivated spirits which have made a sudden transition from the extreme of ignorance and despotic restraint, to certain mistaken ideas of the Rights of Man." This thought haunted Jefferson throughout the conflict, and he wrote to James Monroe two years later saying, "I become daily more and more convinced that all the West India islands will remain in the hands of the people of color, and a total expulsion of the whites sooner or later take place. It is high time we should foresee the bloody scenes which our children certainly, and possibly ourselves . . . have to wade through, and try to avert them."

In addition to stirring Jefferson's fears of armed black retaliation, Cutting's dispatches also touched upon Jefferson's paranoia of factionalism among the white community. Like other leaders of the Revolutionary era, Jefferson worried that factionalism could destroy the republican experiment, but his fears were compounded by his concern that slavery would eventually prove to be the "knell of the Union." Jefferson had begun to grow concerned about the fate of the Union at least as early as 1791 when he sent George Washington a packet of information recounting tensions between Pennsylvania and Virginia over the question of slavery. Seeing such factional bickering as dangerous to the greater society, Jefferson must have been alarmed by Cutting's assertions that French colonists in Haiti were hurting their own cause because they "had not learn'd to sacrifice private opinion to public utility" and were unable to put up a united front against the rebels. This fear grew for Jefferson and other white Americans as political bickering between the Republicans and Federalists in 1800 encouraged Gabriel, a slave of Virginian Thomas Prosser, to develop his own scheme of liberation.

While this conspiracy was betrayed by a nervous member and put down before any whites were harmed, it ended in the execution of twenty-seven slaves.

EARLY ORGANIZED ANTISLAVERY EFFORTS

These events had a profound impact on the American antislavery movement. Jefferson, like others of his time, wanted to end slavery and yet he did not want America to contain a large population of free blacks. The Founders at the 1787 Constitutional Convention shared his concern and feared splitting the young nation by overemphasizing the issue of slavery. They did manage to include a provision in the Constitution that would provide an opportunity to end the foreign slave trade in 1808. But this allowed for twenty more years of importation. This conundrum led almost all early antislavery advocates to support the colonization of blacks to other parts of the world. Some called for the creation of black settlements in the American West, but most hoped to send freed slaves either to the new republic of Haiti or "back" to Africa.

The idea of "returning" blacks to Africa was not new. The British slave trade became an organized commercial enterprise in 1563, but by 1596 Queen Elizabeth, like American leaders two centuries later, began calling for the removal of blacks from the country. Ignoring the fact that her own encouragement of the slave trade caused the growth of the black population, Elizabeth continued to support the trade while making appeals to remove blacks, both free and bound, from England. In 1601, she issued a Royal Proclamation ordering the expulsion of blacks from Britain, insisting that indigent free blacks were consuming relief that should be available to the white poor. This proclamation met little success, but almost two centuries later the government officially concluded that there was "no place so fit and proper [for Africans] as the grain coast of Africa." Accordingly, they helped finance and recruit settlers for an African settlement, which became known as Sierra Leone.

Although the government's motives for supporting repatriation were based on self-interest, a number of British philanthropists supported the scheme for humanitarian reasons. Many saw colonization as a humane means of restoring the freedom and dignity of Africans while also providing an opportunity to civilize and Christianize the entire continent. According to this line of thought, which gained momentum throughout the nineteenth century, blacks who had been trained and educated by Europeans would return to Africa and teach natives the values of Western civilization and Christianity. British leaders such as Granville Sharp, John Wesley, James Ramsay, Thomas Clarkson, and William Wilberforce laid the foundation for the expansion of this humanitarian sentiment as they argued for the rights of blacks. Specifically, they sought to convince the public that, although slavery may have conditioned the bondsmen to adopt the traits that had become stereotypically assigned as racial characteristics, the slaves were indeed human beings. The logical conclusion to this reasoning was that slavery was morally wrong, and as enlightened members of the British middle class began to embrace these ideas, they created a strong abolition movement. To make up for past transgressions against blacks, many of these philanthropists sought a means not only to free the slaves but to positively affect the continent they had been ruthlessly exploiting for centuries. For many, the logical solution was to send a select number of the most educated and skilled blacks to Africa where they could serve as colonial leaders, creating societies that would in turn influence the remaining indigenous population.

Taking their cue from British efforts in Sierra Leone, a number of influential Americans came together in December of 1816 to form the American Society for Colonizing the Free People of Colour of the United States, also referred to as the American Colonization Society (ACS). Although Jefferson himself never joined the ACS, the founders of the Society built upon many of the ideas he had presented throughout his lifetime, particularly in his *Notes on Virginia*. He had described his fears of retribution, racial mixing, and political infighting as he explained the challenges slavery posed to the American experiment in Democracy. Other Virginians had agreed, and Ferdinando Fairfax had even proposed that Congress follow the British lead and acquire a colony in Africa where free blacks could be sent. Many believed that the existence of such a colony would encourage slaveholders to free their slaves by offering an alternative to the dangers of coexistence. Leaders in other states such as Pennsylvania began to embrace the idea of gradual emancipation combined with colonization, and a number of different colonization plans had developed by the time the ACS emerged in 1816.

When the ACS founders met, they brought with them a number of ideas and hopes. Some leaders cited the example of a group of New Englanders, led by Samuel Hopkins and Ezra Stiles, who had proposed a missionary colony in Africa as early as 1773. The New England plan had called for sending a few dozen "well instructed Negroes" to Africa to spread Christianity. Proponents had hoped that this would stop the slave trade at the source and make up for past exploitation of Africa and its people. William Thornton, an English Quaker who came to America after the Revolution, expanded upon this plan by adding a commercial element. He shared some of the philanthropic motivation, but he also saw a possibility for economic gain. He argued that free blacks sent to the colony could achieve wealth as well as independence by trading in legitimate tropical products such as spices, ivory, gold, and dyes.

Important leaders from both sections of the country attended the founding meeting of the ACS in 1816. These men included religious leaders such as the Reverend Robert Finley of New Jersey, traveling missionary Samuel Mills, American Bible Society founder Elias Boudinot, and John E. Caldwell of New York. Important political leaders at the meeting included Supreme Court clerk Elias Boudinot Caldwell, well-known Washington, D.C., lawyer Francis Scott Key, Supreme Court Justice Bushrod Washington, House of Representatives Speaker Henry Clay, Virginia politicians Charles Fenton Mercer and John Randolph Fairfax, and Congressman Daniel Webster also participated. These men shared a fear of a biracial America and hoped to solve the problem by removing blacks. Although Clay, a leading Southern politician, warned the others that too much emphasis upon emancipation would alienate possible Southern support, most of the men at the meeting shared a desire not only to remove free blacks, but also to encourage emancipation by offering a distant outlet for freed slaves. Finley, who many historians agree played a crucial role in creating the society, insisted throughout his life that the group's primary goal, despite the caution of Southerners like Clay, was emancipation.

Finley and other philanthropists insisted that the American racial climate would leave blacks permanently relegated to an inferior status. Many argued that white racism, not black inferiority, would prevent blacks from achieving equality in the United States. They also shared an optimism that slaveholders could be convinced to free their laborers if only they could be assured that they would not have to live in a biracial society. Like British philanthropists, many Americans also believed in the missionary potential of their proposed colony.

COLONIZATION IN AFRICA?

The first annual ACS report illustrated the founders' optimism that colonization offered a valid solution to America's twin problems of slavery and racism. The author began by celebrating apparent support for the Society among Virginia slaveholders, looking forward to future funds, and expressing "a confident hope that our labors will be rewarded by the willing contributions of a generous and enlightened people." Summarizing the group's goals, he argued that colonization would "be alike propitious to every interest of our domestic society" by encouraging the "slow but gradual abolition of slavery" while also removing from America's political institutions "the only blot which stains them." Finally, the report described the ACS's hope that the U.S. government would eventually endorse, and some day even take over, the colonization effort. Although the government did eventually offer limited support, this final goal was never realized.

Initially, the ACS enjoyed growing support from whites in both sections of the United States and some African Americans as well. Paul Cuffee, a wealthy American sailor of African and Native American ancestry, had already supported the British Sierra Leone venture. He had transported a group of North American settlers to the colony and made plans for future voyages. He became active in the British abolition and repatriation society known as the African Institution, and he corresponded with white British philanthropists such as Thomas Clarkson. He enlisted his friend James Forten, a wealthy African-American sail manufacturer from Philadelphia, in his recruiting efforts in the United States, and both men became agents of the African Institution. They sought to recruit suitable colonists with useful skills. The War of 1812, however, hampered their efforts when wartime restrictions on trade with Britain prohibited voyages from America to Sierra Leone. Even so, Cuffee and Forten remained active in the Institution, and white American philanthropists even began to consult them with their plans for a similar settlement. Samuel J. Mills, a key ACS figure, was among those who sought the black colonizationists' advice.

Cuffee shared white fears of a possible future race war. He warned Mills that only manumission would allow slaveholders to free themselves from fears of servile retribution. He agreed with many whites, however, that most owners would rather take chances by continuing to keep slaves than risk living with large numbers of free blacks. The solution, he argued, was for white American philanthropists to emulate their British counterparts and help found and support a settlement in Africa. Finley, another key ACS founder, sought to capitalize on Cuffee's support and contacted

him as he made plans for the founding meeting of the organization.

Society leaders realized that the success of Sierra Leone was due largely to the aid of the British government, so they appealed to the American government for similar assistance. They sent agents to explore Africa, find a location for a settlement, and report back on the feasibility of such a colony. The plan was to use such reports to convince the government, especially President James Monroe, to provide funding for the resettlement efforts. ACS managers decided to emphasize the value of such a colony in suppressing the slave trade. The government had outlawed the traffic a decade before, but smugglers continued to evade the law and illegally import African captives.

Just as British abolitionists had used gory propaganda to advertise their colony as an attack on the trade, ACS managers hoped to use similar tactics to gain federal assistance. Charles F. Mercer used his role in Congress to introduce a bill that made the plight of rescued Africans a federal concern. The bill also gave the president the authority to send a naval squadron to patrol African waters and to establish an agency on the coast of Africa for resettling victims of this illicit slave trade. This bill passed and became known as the Slave Trade Act of 1819. A committee of ACS managers then met with President James Monroe to urge him to interpret the act loosely in order to help them create a colony modeled after Sierra Leone. Opposition from Secretary of State John Quincy Adams prevented Monroe from using the act to purchase territory in the name of the United States government, but the president did agree to help with the transportation of colonists. He also appointed federal agents to go to Africa and prepare a station from which the government would operate in policing against the slave trade.

Black settlers to Liberia included "recaptives," or those rescued from the slave trade, free blacks from the United States, and former American slaves. Most settlers who left America for Liberia before 1827 were free blacks who applied to the Society for passage to the colony. After that time, however, most settlers were recently manumitted slaves. Many of these former slaves were freed on the provision that they would emigrate to the colony. According to recent research, approximately 6,000 slaves were emancipated under the ACS agenda between the colony's founding and the Civil War.

BLACK RESISTANCE

Because of later abolitionist accounts, many historians have portrayed black resistance to colonization as immediate. In reality, however, black reaction was more complicated. Forten himself allowed his earliest biographers to ignore this initial support for African colonization and credit him with leading a resistance movement beginning in 1817. His most recent biography, however, has revealed in great detail his work with the African Institute and his role as a follower, rather than a leader, of the resistance movement. In reality, free blacks in three cities—the District of Columbia, Philadelphia, and Richmond—protested the ACS founding, expressing fears that colonization would lead to forced deportation. These protests occurred in 1817, and the Philadelphia meeting helped change Forten's mind. However, they did not lead to a sustained anticolonization movement.

Black resistance to colonization became strong in the late 1820s and early 1830s. Records reveal that throughout the early to mid-1820s most emigrants were free blacks. They applied for passage to Liberia hoping to find opportunities they had been denied in the United Sates. According to historian Marie Tyler McGraw, these early colonists saw emigration as a chance for political, religious, and commercial liberty, and they believed that they would be allowed important roles in governing the new colony. As McGraw points out, they hoped Liberia would provide "true citizenship based on virtue or merit." This elusive goal had been "the one thing not possible in the United States for free blacks whose 'energy and self-educating force' would have gained them every civic honor had they been white."

Two men who went to Liberia with such aspirations were Lott Cary and Colin Teague. Both men were influential members of Richmond, Virginia's free black community. Both served as elders in the First Baptist Church, and both volunteered to go to Africa to serve as missionaries. Other free blacks in Richmond waited for these leaders to send word of conditions and prospects in the colony before deciding whether or not they would join them. By the late 1820s, however, Cary was dead and white colonizationists had taken over recruiting efforts in Richmond. At the same time, some of the initial colonists returned to the United States with negative descriptions of conditions in Liberia. After Nat Turner's slave revolt in 1831, whites became increasingly active in the colonization society, and the emphasis shifted from one of a missionary society to one of an emigration

agency. In this atmosphere, fewer free blacks were willing to volunteer to participate in the African venture.

Thus, by the late 1820s the initial anticolonization rumblings of 1817 had reached a crescendo. More and more African Americans were beginning to see the ACS as a thinly veiled scheme to remove free blacks in an effort to strengthen slavery. According to this logic, if able free black leaders went to Liberia, American slaves would be deprived of valuable leadership in the freedom struggle at home.

In response to their fears of forced deportation, African Americans strengthened their own antislavery efforts. Since colonial times, blacks had petitioned for freedom. During the Revolutionary era they expanded their efforts and employed the rhetoric of freedom and equality. A number of successful blacks had achieved economic wealth and earned respectable roles in their own churches. They lived exemplary lives in hope of proving black equality, and they felt uniquely qualified to lead the crusade against slavery. The colonization movement threatened their efforts.

Within a decade of the ACS's founding, black leaders began to embark on a crusade of their own. A growing number decided to fight for freedom and equality at home and prove to whites that blacks could contribute to the future success of the young nation. In 1827, John Russwurm and Samuel Cornish launched Freedom's Journal, the first newspaper operated by African Americans.

Appearing four years before William Lloyd Garrison's Liberator, this abolitionist paper began by declaring black independence in the antislavery movement. Russwurm was a colonizationist, but he, like many other black supporters, hoped that the endeavor would allow blacks an opportunity at self-determination. His partner disagreed. Like a growing number of black leaders in the 1820s, Cornish aided in the attack on the ACS, calling for black independence, not in an African colony, but in the United States. Both agreed that African Americans need to speak up for themselves. Citing the "many schemes . . . in action concerning our people" the editors vowed "to plead our own cause" and to lead the way in efforts to uplift the black community. Tired of being portrayed negatively in the white press and characterized as dangerous and degraded, the editors insisted in the opening editorial that "the virtuous part of our people feel themselves sorely aggrieved under the existing state of things" because "our vices and our degradation are ever arrayed against us, but our virtues are passed by unnoticed."

BISHOP RICHARD ALLEN IN
FREEDOM'S JOURNAL November 2, 1827

*Bishop Richard Allen, born into slavery, was founder of the
African Methodist Episcopal Church. Writing in* Freedom's
Journal, *the first African-American newspaper, Allen argues
that the scheme of sending blacks to Liberia is a means to
deny them their rightful place in American society.*

I have for several years been striving to reconcile my
mind to the colonization of Africans in Liberia, but
there have always been, and there still remain great
and insurmountable objections against the scheme. We
are an unlettered people, brought up in ignorance, not
one in a hundred can read or write; not one in a thousand has a liberal education. Is there any fitness for
such to be sent into a far country, among Heathens, to
convert or civilize them; when they themselves are neither civilized nor christianized? See the great bulk of
the poor ignorant Africans in this country; exposed to
every temptation before them; all for the want of their
morals being refined by education, and proper attendance paid unto them by their owners, or those who
had the charge of them. It is said by the southern slaveholders, that the more ignorant they can bring up the
Africans, the better slaves they make. It is enough for
them to know the words, "go and come." Is there any
fitness for such people to be colonized in a far country,
to be their own rulers? Can we not discern the project
of sending the free people of color away from this
country? Is it not for the interest of the slave holder, to
select the free people of color out of the different states,
and send them to Liberia? Will it not make their slaves
uneasy to see free men of color enjoying liberty? It is

against the law in some of the southern states, that a
person of color should receive an education under a severe penalty. Colonizationists speak of America being
first colonized, but is there any comparison between
the two? America was colonized by as wise, judicious,
and educated men as the world afforded. William Penn
did not want for learning, wisdom, or intelligence. If
all the people in Europe and America were as ignorant,
and in the same situation as our brethren, what would
become of the world; where would be the principle or
piety that would govern the people? We were stolen
from our mother country and brought here. We have
tilled the ground and made fortunes for thousands,
and still they are not weary of our services. But they
who stay to till the ground must be slaves. Is there not
land enough in America, or "corn enough in Egypt?"
Why would they send us into a far country to die? See
the thousands of foreigners emigrating to America
every year: and if there be ground sufficient for them
to cultivate, and bread for them to eat; why would
they wish to send the first tillers of the land away? Africans have made fortunes for thousands, who are yet
unwilling to part with their services, but the free must
be sent away, and those who remain must be slaves? I
have no doubt that there are many good men who do
not see as I do and who are for sending us to Liberia,
but they have not duly considered the subject—they
are not men of color. This land which we have watered
with our tears and our blood, is now our mother country and we are well satisfied to stay where wisdom
abounds and the gospel is free.

Source: Freedom's Journal, [New York], November 2,
1827.

The editors disagreed over the colonization issue,
but the paper's Boston agent harbored definite opinions. David Walker began working with *Freedom's
Journal* shortly after its founding and played an important role in encouraging readers to reject colonization and support the quest for immediate abolition.
He is most famous for his 1829 *Appeal to the Colored
Citizens of the World*, a pamphlet that portrayed colonization as pro-, rather than antislavery. Other American blacks had already made that claim, but Walker
added a new militancy by insisting that African
Americans had a right to U.S. citizenship. He also
wrote that blacks, slave or free, had a right to defend
themselves from white violence.

Before this time, white antislavery advocates had

focused on preventing violence by removing blacks,
conveniently ignoring the reality that whites in both
sections, especially the South, abused blacks by beating them. Most racial mixing, as Jefferson himself was
aware, occurred when white men raped and abused
black women. Walker, though born free, had seen
much of this abuse firsthand, and he had grown tired
of hearing about dangerous blacks from a society that
chose to ignore dangerous whites. He called upon
black men to defend their families and assert their
rights as Americans. Appealing to both slaves and
free blacks, he frightened whites by showing that abolitionists and slaves could work together to overthrow the system. He also scared whites by describing
the incidents in Haiti and predicting that, unless the

DAVID WALKER (1785–1830)

Born in Wilmington, North Carolina, Walker was the son of a free black woman and slave father. According to the laws of his home state, he assumed the free status of his mother. He traveled the South widely and became greatly concerned over the conditions of his fellow blacks, including the mistreatment of his mother and restrictions placed upon his father. He then determined to leave the South and moved to Philadelphia, where he became a devout follower of Richard Allen, the black bishop of the AME church, and then to Boston in 1827. There he taught himself to read and write and opened a second-hand clothing business.

Walker quickly involved himself in local black antislavery activities, most notably the anticolonizationist General Colored Association of Massachusetts. In 1828, in a speech to that organization, he urged free blacks to act collectively to undermine both the institution of slavery in the South and the recovery of fugitive slaves in the North. The following year he issued the first of three editions of his pamphlet, *David Walker's Appeal, in four Articles; Together with a Preamble to the Coloured Citizens of the World, But in Particular, and Very Expressly, to Those of the United States* (often referred to as Walker's *Appeal*)

Some historians date the beginning of the modern abolitionist movement to this publication, which antedated William Lloyd Garrison's abolitionist newspaper by two years. Walker's antislavery pamphlet made its arguments in eloquent, soundly reasoned terms. It urged slaves to rise up against their oppressors, violently if necessary, but urged forgiveness if slaveholders voluntarily repented and let them go. In other words, it called for immediate abolition, an unusual proposition at the time. The pamphlet also contained the major principles of black nationalism: the belief that blacks must eventually reside in their own nation; the assertion that blacks must provide their own leadership and defense; and the conviction that blacks must play a messianic role.

Distributed in the South by sailors sympathetic to abolition, the *Appeal* frightened slaveholders. Some state legislatures not only banned it but made it a crime punishable by death to introduce similar literature. Throughout the South, a price was set on Walker's head. After issuing an even more militant appeal to end slavery, he was found dead near his shop in June 1830. It was rumored and widely believed, though never proven, that he was poisoned. Later scholarship suggests he died of tuberculosis, the same disease that killed his daughter.

James G. Lewis

racial climate changed in America, Providence would assure a similar fate. He promised his readers that God would send "a Hannibal" to "deliver you through him from your deplorable and wretched condition." When this leader arrived, he insisted, it was the duty of all blacks to "give him your support and let him go his length" and "lay no obstacle in [redemption's] way." To Walker, such events were inevitable, but he added that he would like to see whites "repent" before it was too late so that "God may have mercy on them."

By 1830, black leaders like Walker had begun to attract the attention of white antislavery advocates. They succeeded in convincing a number of white colonizationists, most notably Garrison, that blacks and whites could live together in a biracial society. As blacks fought against colonization and leaders such as Garrison joined their crusade, they formed an important partnership. Together these black and white anticolonizationists initiated the abolitionist movement, calling for immediate freedom for the enslaved without compensation for the masters or repatriation of the freed.

CONCLUSION

Although many, if not most, colonizationists truly opposed human bondage, their movement suffered from a number of crucial errors that the abolitionists managed to overcome. To begin with, they failed to make slavery truly a moral issue. Focusing on the practical need to end slavery without alienating whites in either section, they refused to criticize slave owners. Many have argued that their moderation was laudable. A number of early historians of the movement have pointed out that colonizationists hoped to avert race war and sectional discord. Unfortunately, however, their patience led them to sacrifice the immediate rights of the enslaved. Even those who saw blacks and whites as naturally equal shared a defeatist attitude toward American race relations. They did not challenge the racism around them because they saw it as insurmountable. This led to their most tragic error. They refused to treat blacks as equals in the crusade against slavery. Some blacks initially agreed that American racism would prevent them from achieving equality, and they joined the colonization movement. They became alienated, however, when their hopes for self-determination were crushed in the late 1820s. Even Forten realized that colonization through the American Colonization Society was and would remain a white-initiated effort. This tendency only increased as events like the Nat Turner insurrection and growing sectional strife increased white fears. Just like Jefferson, the colonizationists of the ACS feared that a biracial America would naturally result in race war, racial mixing, or sectional division. Unlike the abolitionists, they harbored no optimism for racial co-existence. They also held out little hope for interracial cooperation and friendship in the anti-slavery crusade.

Beverly Tomek

BIBLIOGRAPHY

Ackerson, Kenneth Wayne. "The African Institution of London and the Antislavery Movement in Great Britain." Ph.D diss., Temple University, 1999.

Birnbaum, Jonathan, and Clarence Taylor. *Civil Rights Since 1787: A Reader on the Black Struggle*. New York: New York University Press, 2000.

Blackburn, Robin. *The Overthrow of Colonial Slavery, 1776–1848*. New York: Verso, 1996.

Brown, Kathleen M. *Good Wives, Nasty Wenches & Anxious Patriarchs: Gender, Race, and Power in Colonial Virginia*. Chapel Hill: University of North Carolina Press, 1996.

Burin, Eric A. "The Peculiar Solution: The American Colonization Society and Antislavery Sentiment in the South, 1820–1860." Ph.D. diss., University of Illinois, 1998.

Davis, David Brion. *The Problem of Slavery in Western Culture*. Ithaca, NY: Cornell University Press, 1966.

———. *The Problem of Slavery in the Age of Revolution, 1770–1823*. Ithaca, NY: Cornell University Press, 1975.

Drake, Thomas E. *Quakers and Slavery in America*. Gloucester, MA: Yale University Press, 1965.

Drescher, Seymour. *Econocide: British Slavery in the Era of Abolition*. Pittsburgh, PA: University of Pittsburgh Press, 1977.

Eggerton, Douglas R. "Averting a Crisis: The Proslavery Critique of the American Colonization Society." *Civil War History* 43:2 (June 1997): 142–157.

Finkelman, Paul. *Slavery and the Founders: Race and Liberty in the Age of Jefferson*. Armonk, NY: M.E. Sharpe, 1996.

Fox, Early Lee. *The American Colonization Society, 1817–1840*. Baltimore, MD: Johns Hopkins University Press, 1919.

Fredrickson, George M. *The Black Image in the White Mind: The Debate on Afro-American Character and Destiny, 1817–1914*. New York: Harper & Row, 1971.

Harding, Vincent. *There Is a River: The Black Struggle for Freedom in America*. New York: Harcourt Brace Jovanovich, 1981.

Harrold, Stanley. *American Abolitionists*. New York: Longman, 2001.

Jordan, Winthrop. *White over Black: American Attitudes Toward the Negro, 1550–1812*. Chapel Hill: University of North Carolina Press, 1968.

McColley, Robert. *Slavery and Jeffersonian Virginia*. Urbana: University of Illinois Press, 1964.

McGraw, Marie Tyler. "Richmond Free Blacks and African Colonization, 1816–1832." *Journal of American Studies* 21:2 (August 1987): 207–224.

Melish, Joanne Pope. *Disowning Slavery: Gradual Emancipation and "Race" in New England, 1780–1860*. Ithaca, NY: Cornell University Press, 1998.

Miller, John Chester. *The Wolf by the Ears: Thomas Jefferson and Slavery*. New York: Meridian, 1977.

Nash, Gary B. *Forging Freedom: The Formation of Philadelphia's Black Community, 1720–1840*. Cambridge, MA: Harvard University Press, 1988.

———. *Race and Revolution*. New York: Madison House, 1990.

Quarles, Benjamin. *Black Abolitionists*. New York: Oxford University Press, 1969.

Soderlund, Jean R. *Quakers and Slavery: A Divided Spirit*. Princeton, NJ: Princeton University Press, 1985.

Staudenraus, P.J. *The African Colonization Movement, 1816–1865*. New York: Columbia University Press, 1961.

Williams, Eric. *Capitalism & Slavery*. Chapel Hill: University of North Carolina Press, 1944.

Winch, Julie. *A Gentleman of Color: The Life of James Forten*. New York: Oxford University Press, 2002.

ANTISLAVERY MOVEMENT

1830s–1840s

By the 1830s, the antislavery movement had evolved into the abolitionist crusade. Although some African Americans began to consider the idea of emigration to places like Canada or Haiti independent of the American Colonization Society (ACS), most black leaders opted to stay in the United States and fight against slavery. These leaders had convinced many white colonizationists to join in their effort to resist colonization. They insisted that, despite the stated motives of many ACS members, the true goal was the eventual forced removal of all free blacks to Africa in an effort to strengthen slavery in the United States. This prodding by black leaders occurred at an opportune moment. American society was becoming more modern during this time period, undergoing what historians call a "market revolution." At the same time, the Second Great Awakening was creating a new wave of evangelicalism, which encouraged many Americans to seek benevolent reform in a number of areas. Both of these factors supported the growth of what is known as immediate abolition.

THE MARKET REVOLUTION AND MODERNIZATION OF AMERICAN SOCIETY

Important aspects of the market revolution included advances in transportation, communication, and agriculture as well as changing ideas about the family. Before the 1800s, localism prevailed in the United States. The economy had been based largely on self-sufficient farms, local markets, and individually handcrafted products made by independent artisans. By the Civil War, however, this would all change drastically.

A number of key developments aided in the transformation of the country. To begin with, the population grew drastically between 1800 and 1860 from 5.3 to 31 million. Both the natural population growth and high levels of immigration contributed to this demographic expansion. The population began expanding westward beyond the Appalachian Mountains, and the North grew faster than the South. This situation invited conflict over slavery by raising questions over its expansion into the new territories, at the same time that significant numbers of Americans were becoming dependent upon wage labor in the industrializing cities of the North.

Farming remained important, however, especially in the newer territories of the West and Deep South. In the West, improved axes and John Deere's stronger plow allowed for more cultivated acreage. Farmers began to plant wheat in these new areas, especially the Midwestern states like Illinois, and other advancements like Cyrus McCormick's reaper made farming profitable in this area. In the newly settled Deep South states like Texas, Louisiana, Mississippi, and Alabama, Eli Whitney's cotton gin was making slavery more profitable than ever. This invention took the seeds out of the mature cotton and helped make it easier to prepare for market, but it also led to an increased demand for the product. Thus, the need for slaves increased as plantations began to grow along the coast of the Gulf of Mexico.

Transportation and communication advances made it easier to market these products and led to a growing dependency between the different sections of the nation. Improved roads with gravel surfaces, longer and more sophisticated canals such as New York's Erie Canal, the development of steamboats, and the expansion of the railroad played important roles in the market revolution. These innovations helped replace local markets with a national trade network. Samuel Morse's telegraph and the rotary printer, with its resulting "penny press," also brought Americans together by allowing for more efficient communication across greater distances.

Other characteristics of the market revolution included the emergence of a more industrial system of manufacturing finished products and a more modern system of banking and finance. The general trend in manufacturing included a decline in handmade and homemade goods. Whereas many goods had been produced in the home individually in the eighteenth century, beginning in the early 1800s more people began to work in factories, allowing for mass production. One of the most important examples was the textile industry. Textile factories became an important part of the New England landscape, using cotton from the South to produce cloth. Another industry that saw substantial growth was the iron industry, which produced materials for the railroads and agricultural implements. Finally, banking and finance moved from small-scale business and bartering to larger enterprises that relied upon cash and credit.

Along with all these changes came a new outlook on labor. During the colonial period, workers enjoyed limited options. They served apprenticeships and learned a trade from a master craftsman. They then worked and lived with that craftsman, serving as journeymen, as they waited until they could open their own shops. They generally remained in one trade throughout their lifetime, despite their level of satisfaction with that trade. With the rise of the capitalistic system, however, workers no longer served as apprentices. Assembly lines replaced skilled craft work, so workers simply sought jobs in whichever industry was hiring. They worked for a wage and could quit and seek different opportunities, limited only by the competition of other workers for the available jobs. This focus on competition and a more "independent" workforce led more people to criticize slavery. They argued that free labor was based on incentive because workers increased their output in hopes of better pay and job security. Accordingly, they insisted, the new system was more efficient and, thus, more profitable. Therefore, slavery was not only immoral, it was economically unsound in the modernizing economy.

Traditional views of the family also changed. As more people began to work out of their homes for wages, a new "cult of domesticity" emerged. Based on an ideology known as "separate spheres," this line of thought justified the changes by arguing that men fulfilled their "natural" roles by entering the competitive job market. According to this reasoning, men were inherently competitive, endowed with business sense because of their rationality, and strong enough to handle the cold, competitive outside world. Women, on the other hand, were inherently sensitive,

talented at nurturing both their husbands and their children, naturally moral, and inclined to Christian virtues. Thus, they were uniquely qualified to take care of the home and create a haven in which their husbands could seek comfort and security in an increasingly cold and hostile world.

This new attitude toward the family greatly affected the abolition crusade. Most white middle-class abolitionists emphasized the harmful effects of slavery on the family. They argued that enslaved women were prevented from upholding the feminine virtues of piety and purity when their male owners raped them or encouraged them to provide sexual favors for better treatment of themselves or their families. They insisted, moreover, that enslaved men were denied the opportunity to provide for their families because providing for all slaves remained the domain of the master. Under such conditions, they insisted, gender roles became corrupted and the family was destroyed.

Both black and white abolitionists employed these themes in their speeches and writings, but the new gender ideals posed special problems for black leaders. Victorian middle-class gender ideology emphasized the importance of a nuclear family with a patriarchal leader. The man, as the leader of this unit, labored out of the home to provide sustenance for his dependents, so that the woman could remain inside the domestic realm, providing a haven for him and cultivating the morals of their children. Family and personal honor centered on the man's ability to exert control over himself, his dependents, and his property while protecting his wife and children and overseeing their moral development. According to historian Charles Rosenberg, nineteenth-century men had two basic role models to follow: the Masculine Achiever, which focused on rugged individualism and commercial success, and the Christian Gentleman, which stressed gentleness, moral and communal values, self-sacrifice, and self-restraint. Black men were excluded from most lucrative commercial endeavors, and they had to refute stereotypes that they were inherently violent and brutal. Therefore, many chose to emphasize their roles as Christian Gentlemen. This tactic, however, threatened their masculinity by forcing them to focus on characteristics that were most often used to describe women.

EVANGELICALISM AND THE GROWTH OF AMERICAN REFORM

By changing most Americans' outlook on such issues as labor and the family, the modernization of America encouraged the development of a reform impulse with a broad agenda. Abolition was only one of many efforts to improve society. Most reform advocates were middle-class men and women who felt that all Americans shared in the guilt of slavery. They also shared what historian Ronald Walters has described as "confidence in progress and human will." According to Walters, the growing cities were "especially ripe for moral crusades" and "provided reformers with problems in need of solutions." He added that the political climate of the "Jacksonian Era" also alarmed middle-class moralists by revealing what they perceived to be a decline in honesty and "virtue." Advances in transportation and improvements in communication, especially the proliferation of cheap newspapers, aided the reformers by allowing them a forum for disseminating their solutions. Finally, evangelical Protestantism provided an intellectual framework for the quest to create a perfect society.

Evangelicalism played a large role in antebellum reform. The Second Great Awakening spread evangelical ideas through a series of revivals, reaching out to all who would join the crusade and emphasizing the personal responsibility of all people to help eliminate sin. Most importantly, it emphasized the notion that both the individual and society could reach a state of perfection. According to this logic, each person, no matter how lowly, should seek to live a perfect life so that society in general could follow. Reformers believed that the individual had to want to be part of this general improvement, so they sought to enlighten people rather than force them to behave in a prescribed manner.

These beliefs had a number of implications for the abolition movement. First, evangelicalism empowered all believers by insisting that everyone could seek perfection. A number of studies, most notably Nell Painter's work on former slave Sojourner Truth, have traced the effects of this ideology on black abolitionists. Even though many had been denied education and had endured their masters' efforts at making them feel inferior, evangelical Protestantism gave them the confidence to join public antislavery efforts. Just as importantly, evangelicalism's emphasis on improving the individual through enlightenment led most abolitionists to subscribe to a concept known as "moral suasion."

This tactic became the keystone of the movement as abolitionists struggled to convince slaveholders and proponents of human bondage of their evil ways.

THE GROWTH OF IMMEDIATISM

William Lloyd Garrison subscribed to the beliefs of evangelical Protestantism, and by 1830 he had begun to listen to African Americans' assessment of the eighteenth-century antislavery movement. He had considered the merits of colonization and even supported the endeavor earlier in his career, but in the 1830s he embarked upon a personal crusade to destroy the society after black acquaintances convinced him that the organization was indeed pro-slavery. A number of other important white colonizationists, including Simeon S. Jocelyn, James G. Birney, and Gerrit Smith, followed suit and joined the new cause. These abolitionists used a number of tactics in their campaign for immediate emancipation. They embarked on lecture tours and relied heavily on the press to convince Americans that the enslaved should be freed immediately without compensation for their masters. They even took their cause to England and formed abolitionist societies to coordinate their activities. Although white leaders never truly overcame their own racial biases, they reached out to free blacks, joining efforts in the struggle against institutionalized racial oppression and human bondage. Blacks continued to play crucial roles in this movement, and women joined the cause as well.

Like other reformers of their time, abolitionists took advantage of improvements in transportation and communication, relying heavily on the lecture circuit and the printing press. Colonizationists employed similar means, and immediatists set out to beat them at their own game. Garrison set the stage for the debate by announcing on New Year's Day 1831 that, unlike the colonizationists, the abolitionists would not seek the support of slaveholders at the expense of black freedom. He emphasized this point by referring to them as "oppressors," "mansteelers," and "tyrants." He directed his crusade against both groups and in his 1832 *Thoughts on African Colonization*, he proclaimed all-out "warfare . . . against the American Colonization Society."

Garrison's pamphlet synthesized the arguments that black abolitionists had put forth against the colonization society. In this pamphlet, Garrison used the ACS's monthly journal, *The African Repository*, to illustrate the point that colonization was "a conspiracy to send the free people of color to Africa under a benevolent pretence, but really that the slaves may be held more securely in bondage." He had arrived at this assessment after listening to, and reading articles by, the black leaders he had met during his own early

WILLIAM LLOYD GARRISON

(1805–1879)

William Lloyd Garrison was born in Newburyport, Massachusetts, to a poor but pious family. He supplemented his limited schooling with newspaper work and in 1829 went to Baltimore, Maryland, to work for Benjamin Lundy's antislavery *Genius of Universal Emancipation*. He left there in 1830 and returned to New England pledged to abolitionism. On January 1, 1831, he published the first issue of *The Liberator*, a paper that he continued for thirty-five years (the last number was dated December 29, 1865), until after the Thirteenth Amendment had been adopted. In *The Liberator*, Garrison took an uncompromising stand for the immediate and complete abolition of slavery. Although its circulation was never over 3,000, the paper became famous (notorious, to Southerners) for the frank and quotable language Garrison used to denounce slavery and advocate moral uplift and social change. Garrison advocated neither force nor the ballot to reach this goal and instead relied wholly upon moral persuasion.

That same year he founded the New England Anti-Slavery Society and served as a paid agent for it. In his *Thoughts on African Colonization* (1832), Garrison announced his opposition to the work of the American Colonization Society, which wanted to colonize slaves abroad rather than liberate them and guarantee their rights as free men and women. In 1833, he formed the American Anti-Slavery Society (AAS), of which he was president from 1843 to 1865. The AAS became another vehicle through which he called on Americans to immediately cease their support of slavery and all slaveholders, a position he laid out in its *Declaration of Sentiments*. The organization also demanded that churches, political parties, and even the federal government cut all ties with slavery.

In 1835, Garrison was physically attacked in Boston by a mob composed of seemingly respectable people. The attack won a valuable convert to his cause in Wendell Phillips, who became an abolitionist even more radical than Garrison. Garrison and his followers proclaimed that slavery contradicted the nation's religious and republican values. His statements helped split religious denominations and undermine national political coalitions. Garrison's attacks included clergy who were apathetic to his cause or who were apologists for slavery. Believing there was no higher government than the government of God, he attacked the federal government, called both major parties proslavery, and described the United States Constitution as a "covenant with death and an agreement with hell." He pushed resolutions through the Massachusetts Anti-Slavery Society and the AAS that made statements to that effect. This type of agitation contributed to the transformation of Northern attitudes in the 1850s from one of mild objection to slavery to widespread anti-Southernism. He burned the Constitution publicly at an abolitionist meeting in Framingham, Massachusetts, on July 4, 1854, and opposed the Civil War until President Abraham Lincoln issued the Emancipation Proclamation. With the end of the war and passage of the Thirteenth Amendment, Garrison declared his crusade a triumphant one and resigned from the AAS. He then turned to other reform issues, but none of them ever held his attention and passion as had abolitionism.

Garrison's positions were not always popular within the antislavery movement. His crusades for other reforms that he united with abolitionism, notably woman suffrage and prohibition, split the AAS in 1840 into two factions, one wanting to move beyond antislavery and the other wanting to focus only on that subject. Garrison, supportive of the work and efforts of Sarah and Angelina Grimké, insisted on equal participation for women in the antislavery movement. His opponents left and formed the American and Foreign Anti-Slavery Society in 1840 as well as the Liberty Party.

The weight of historical evidence seems to indicate strongly that, although Garrison attracted national attention, his extremism carried little political influence. Instead, he served more as a symbol and prophet of things to come, including passage of the Thirteenth Amendment, which abolished slavery, and eventual support of full civil rights for blacks. Furthermore, the effective fight against slavery was carried on by less well-known men who tackled the problem in a realistic manner. Garrison, who antagonized and outraged other abolitionists, was not a good organizer. Even so, his contribution to the cause, though it was not as great as many consider it, was important.

James G. Lewis

antislavery work. Although he never completely overcame his own paternalistic racial ideas, he and other whites who left the ACS to work with black abolitionists for freedom in the United States contributed significantly to the fight against slavery by showing that blacks and whites could work together.

Garrison was not the only important abolitionist speaker and writer. The evangelical emphasis on inherent human equality created a climate in which African Americans and women of both races felt empowered enough to speak out. One of the most famous examples is that of Sarah and Angelina Grimké. These sisters were born in the South to a slaveholding family but through their own "moral suasion" had come to the conclusion that human bondage was wrong. They entered the lecture circuit to speak out against slavery, becoming the first widely known female antislavery agents.

When the Grimkés embarked on an unprecedented nine-month speaking tour in 1837, they faced a number of challenges. Most importantly, women were not expected to speak publicly in front of mixed or, in the words of the time, "promiscuous," audiences. According to their biographer, Gerda Lerner, however, their "piety and respectability" served as a "shield against all attacks" from those who opposed their right to play an active role in the movement. Their origins as part of the "refined" class of the South also helped, offering them legitimacy by allowing them to speak with the voice of experience. Their talks were punctuated with a sense of wisdom as they described the ways in which slavery harmed all of American society, not just the forced laborers.

By the end of their tour, in February of 1838, they managed to break another precedent by speaking to the Massachusetts state legislature. Angelina began by explaining that they were there "on behalf of the 20,000 women of Massachusetts whose names are enrolled on [antislavery] petitions which have been submitted to the Legislature." In response to previous criticism that women, excluded from politics, "had nothing to do with" slavery, she justified her mission by arguing that "American women have to do with this subject, not only because it is moral and religious, but because it is *political*, inasmuch as we are citizens of this republic." As a "southerner, exiled from the land of my birth by the sound of the last and the piteous cry of the slave," she appealed to her audience to help "overturn a system of complicated crimes, built upon the broken hearts and prostrate bodies of my countrymen in chains and cemented by the blood, sweat and tears of my sisters in bonds."

Black abolitionists also spoke out vociferously on behalf of their "brothers and sisters in bonds." Their racial ties led them to emphasize a self-help concept that held that free blacks had a duty to live exemplary lives and remove much of the white justification for slavery by proving racial equality. This idea was crucial to their efforts against colonization. Black leaders Abraham D. Shadd, Peter Spencer, and William S. Thomas explained to a Wilmington, Delaware, audience in 1831 that the "degraded" condition of blacks described by colonizationists "cannot be bettered by removing the most exemplary individuals of color from amongst us." They insisted that, under the ACS plans, "the industrious part [of the black community] would emigrate" while "in the same proportion those who would remain would become more degraded, wretched and miserable, and consequently less capable of appreciating the many opportunities which are now offering for the moral and intellectual improvement of our brethren."

Abolitionists—black and white, male and female—sought to reach even broader audiences by presenting their antislavery arguments in the printed form. Pamphlets like Garrison's were a popular tool. Even more important, however, a number of antislavery advocates operated their own newspapers. Benjamin Lundy, a white Quaker who served as Garrison's mentor, edited one of the earliest antislavery papers, the weekly *Genius of Universal Emancipation* in Baltimore in the 1820s. Garrison became co-editor of the paper in 1829, but he began publishing his own weekly, *The Liberator*, in Boston two years later. James Forten, a wealthy black businessman from Philadelphia, provided financial backing, and 60 percent of *The Liberator's* subscribers were African Americans.

Beginning in 1827, black abolitionists offered their own newspapers. John B. Russwurm and Samuel Cornish began their paper, *Freedom's Journal*, that year, and Cornish became editor of another periodical, the *Colored American*, in 1837. In this paper, Cornish insisted on the need for strong black leadership, challenging the idea that Garrison was the leader of the abolition movement. He appreciated white assistance, but he appealed to blacks to lead the way and to "speak out in THUNDER TONES" for freedom for the slaves and equality for all. According to historian C. Peter Ripley, this newspaper "helped to establish the value of a black press" and forced abolitionists to consider more deeply the need for racial equality.

Throughout the 1830s, black and white abolitionists reached out to reading and listening audiences throughout the world as they sought converts to their

APPEAL TO THE CHRISTIAN WOMEN OF THE SOUTH
ANGELINA E. GRIMKÉ 1836

In the pamphlet "Appeal to the Christian Women of the South," Angelina E. Grimké, the daughter of a slaveholding judge in the South, calls on women to help end the system of slavery on the basis of morality and Christian values.

It is because I feel a deep and tender interest in your present and eternal welfare that I am willing thus publicly to address you. Some of you have loved me as a relative, and some have felt bound to me in Christian sympathy, and Gospel fellowship; and even when compelled by a strong sense of duty, to break those outward bonds of union which bound us together as members of the same community, and members of the same religious denomination. . . .

But perhaps you will be ready to query, why appeal to women on this subject? We do not make the laws which perpetuate slavery. No legislative power is vested in us; we can do nothing to overthrow the system, even if we wished to do so. To this I reply, I know you do not make the laws, but I also know that you are the wives and mothers, the sisters and daughters of those who do; and if you really suppose you can do nothing to overthrow slavery, you are greatly mistaken. You can do much in every way: four things I will name. . . .

1. Read then on the subject of slavery. Search the Scriptures daily, whether the things I told you are true. . . . I want you to read in the spirit of inquiry, and the spirit of prayer. Even the enemies of Abolitionists, acknowledge that their doctrines are drawn from it. In the great mob in Boston, last autumn, when the books and papers of the Anti-Slavery Society, were thrown out of the windows of their office, one individual laid hold of the Bible and was about tossing it on the ground, when another reminded him that it was the Bible he had in his hand. " 'tis all one,' " he replied, and out went the sacred volume, along with the rest.

2. Pray over this subject. When you have entered into your closets, and shut to the doors, then pray to your father, who seeth in secret, that he would open your eyes to see whether slavery is sinful, and if it is, that he would enable you to bear a faithful, open and unshrinking testimony against it, and to do whatsoever your hands find to do, leaving the consequences entirely to him, who still says to us whenever we try to reason duty away from the fear of consequences, "What is that to thee, follow thou me."

3. Speak on this subject. It is through the tongue, the pen, and the press, that truth is principally propagated. Speak then to your relatives, your friends, your acquaintances on the subject of slavery; be not afraid if you are conscientiously convinced it is sinful, to say so openly, but calmly, and to let your sentiments be known. If you are served by the slaves of others, try to ameliorate their condition as much as possible; never aggravate their faults, and thus add fuel to the fire of anger already kindled, in a master and mistress's bosom; remember their extreme ignorance, and consider them as your Heavenly Father does the less culpable on this account, even when they do wrong things. Discountenance all cruelty to them, all starvation, all corporal chastisement; these may brutalize and break their spirits, but will never bend them to willing, cheerful obedience. If possible, see that they are comfortably and seasonably fed, whether in the house or the field; it is unreasonable and cruel to expect slaves to wait for their breakfast until eleven o'clock, when they rise at five or six. Do all you can, to induce their owners to clothe them well, and to allow them many little indulgences which would contribute to their comfort. Above all, try to persuade your husband, father, brothers, and sons, that slavery is a crime against God and man, and that it is a great sin to keep human beings in such abject ignorance; to deny them the privilege of learning to read and write. . . .

4. Act on this subject. Some of you own slaves yourselves. If you believe slavery is sinful, set them at liberty, "undo the heavy burdens and let the oppressed go free." If they wish to remain with you, pay them wages, if not let them leave you. Should they remain, teach them, and have them taught the common branches of an English education; they have minds and those minds, ought to be improved. . . .

. . . And why not try it in the Southern States, if it never has occasioned rebellion; if not a drop of blood has ever been shed in consequence of it, though it has been so often tried, why should we suppose it would produce such disastrous consequences now? . . .
There is nothing to fear from immediate Emancipation, but every thing from the consequences of slavery.

Your sympathizing Friend,

Angelina E. Grimké

Source: The Anti-Slavery Examiner. 1:2 (September 1836). New York Anti-Slavery Society. Available at memory. loc.gov/ammem/aapchtml/aapcpres07.html.

GRIMKÉ SISTERS
SARAH MOORE GRIMKÉ (1792–1873) and
ANGELINA EMILY GRIMKÉ (1805–1879)

The Grimké sisters were born the sixth and fourteenth of fourteen children to John Faucheraud Grimké, a Cambridge University-educated French Huguenot and prominent member of the South Carolina judiciary, and Mary (Smith) Grimké, who came from one of South Carolina's leading families. Sarah was born on November 26, 1792, and Angelina on February 20, 1805. Raised in Charleston in a major slaveholding family, they witnessed brutal mistreatment of slaves carried out by their family and others with whom they socialized. Sarah first encountered antislavery sentiments and found them agreeable to her own views when she accompanied her father on a trip to Philadelphia in 1819. In 1821, she left her Southern home permanently for Philadelphia and became a member of the Society of Friends (Quakers). Angelina followed her in 1829 and also became a Quaker.

Angelina, the more outgoing of the two sisters, joined the Philadelphia Female Anti-Slavery Society in 1835 and decided to speak out publicly. A letter published that year in *The Liberator* helped launch her abolitionist career. She wrote *An Appeal to the Christian Women of the South* in 1836 in which she urged those addressed to use their moral force against slavery. The pamphlet called upon its readers to "*overthrow* [her emphasis] this horrible system of oppression and cruelty, licentiousness and wrong." It created such outrage in the South that Southern postmasters destroyed copies of it and Angelina was warned never to return to Charleston. That same year she and her sister began speaking to small groups of women around New York

City. Sarah refuted the biblical basis for slavery in her own pamphlet, *Epistle to the Clergy of the Southern States*, in 1836.

The sisters spent the following two years touring New England and speaking out against slavery and earned the condemnation of the General Association of Congregational Ministers of Massachusetts in July 1837. The sisters' willingness to discuss "things which ought not to be named," such as the abuse of women slaves, elicited their denunciation of women preachers and reformers. This led the sisters to crusade equally for women's rights. There followed Angelina's *Appeal to the Women of the Nominally Free States* (1837) and Sarah's *Letters on the Equality of the Sexes and the Condition of Woman* (1838). Their lectures at Odeon Hall, Boston, in the spring of 1838 attracted thousands.

Angelina's three appearances before the Massachusetts legislative committee on antislavery petitions early in 1838 constituted a triumph. That same year she married Theodore Dwight Weld, also an active abolitionist. Ill health after her marriage led her to retire from public life, but she continued to aid Weld in his abolitionist work. Sarah lived with the couple thereafter and helped to raise the couple's children. After collaborating with Angelina's husband on *Slavery As It Is: Testimony of a Thousand Witnesses* (1839), the sisters retired from public activity. They assisted in Weld's progressive schools in Belleville and later Perth Amboy, New Jersey, from 1848 to 1862. In 1863, the three moved to Massachusetts, where they remained the rest of their lives. There the sisters died, Sarah on December 23, 1873, and Angelina on October 26, 1879.

James G. Lewis

cause. Beginning in 1830, they took their message to England. According to Richard Blackett, historian of the transatlantic abolition movement, the fight against colonization led every major black abolitionist, as well as Garrison, to appeal to the British public for moral and financial support of immediate, uncompensated abolition. Throughout the decade, colonizationists and abolitionists competed for British support. The colonizationists cited British efforts in a similar African colony, Sierra Leone, as precedent for their own work in Liberia, hoping to enlist the aid of British colonizationists. By the 1830s, however, public sentiment had largely shifted in favor of immediate release of those in bondage. Like Garrison, most British ab-

olitionists had been greatly influenced by African-American resistance to repatriation.

AMERICAN ANTI-SLAVERY SOCIETY

A number of important organizations grew out of this new phase of antislavery. The New England Anti-Slavery Society was the first and was formed in 1832. The most famous, however, the American Anti-Slavery Society (AASS), was established in Philadelphia in 1833. Garrison helped found this group, but it was controlled primarily by New York abolitionists, especially Lewis Tappan. This group undertook a famous postal campaign in 1835, flooding the post throughout the nation, but especially the South, with antislavery literature. It also led numerous petition drives. By 1838, through the efforts of diligent abolitionists, especially women like the Grimkés, the group had sent more than 400,000 signatures to Congress.

Under Tappan's leadership, the AASS also began to recruit agents to spread their antislavery message across the country. Many of these agents, the most famous of which was Theodore Dwight Weld, were former ministers, and their speaking ability convinced their listeners to form many antislavery auxiliaries at the town, county, and state levels. This network of abolitionist groups included 1,300 branches with a total of over a quarter of a million members by the end of the decade.

Abolitionists fought a successful battle against colonizationists, but, unfortunately, they began to argue with each other in the latter half of the decade, causing the movement to split. Garrison's increasing radicalism played a large role in the conflict. He began to question many aspects of the evangelical faith, which had served as the cornerstone of the movement. He accused Protestants of encouraging "sectarianism," citing the various denominations that were developing. He also argued that all days, not just Sunday, should be treated as holy, and he embraced Christian anarchism and its belief in "nonresistance," denouncing all forms of force and violence. He also drew criticism from some other abolitionists for embracing the women's rights movement. Finally, he resisted political involvement even when a number of his colleagues were embracing such action.

Although the final split in the AASS occurred when Abby Kelley was elected to a formerly all-male committee, each of these issues played an important role in causing the schism. Abolitionists had begun arguing over religious ideas and the role of women in the movement in 1837 when clerical abolitionists such as Henry B. Stanton, Elizur Wright Jr., and Charles Torrey left the Massachusetts Anti-Slavery Society after unsuccessfully challenging Garrison on these issues. They then formed their own state society and attended the national AASS annual meeting in 1839. At this meeting Garrison and his supporters earned for women the right to vote in the organization but, as historian Stanley Harrold pointed out, "neither side won a clear victory on the issue of political tactics." A year later, at the 1840 gathering, Kelley's election signaled a victory for the Garrisonians, and Tappan and the other evangelicals left the organization.

Most historians have emphasized the debate over the role of women as the catalyst for the split, but Ronald Walters, a specialist in American reform, stressed a growing political tension as equally crucial. He cited the efforts of a group of New York and Ohio abolitionists such as James G. Birney, Myron Holley, and Stanton to enter the political arena in the late 1830s. Garrison and his followers believed that the politicians, who bent to the public will rather than leading Americans in a quest for a higher morality, were corrupt. Furthermore, as a Christian anarchist, he saw human government as inherently corrupt and sinful, and he had also come to the conclusion that the United States Constitution was proslavery and, thus, the American system was particularly evil. Political abolitionists, however, had concluded that both major parties were tainted and "chained to southern votes," but they were not ready to give up on the system in general. They decided that the best solution was to form their own antislavery party and run their own candidates. In 1840, as the evangelicals left the AASS over the women's rights issue, Birney ran for president under the newly formed Liberty Party.

As the new decade began, the abolitionist movement could look back on a number of important achievements despite their current difficulties. Blacks and whites had begun to work together for the common goal of ending slavery, and increasing numbers were coming to see the need for civil rights and equality for free blacks. Black leaders had met success in their efforts to convince many important white antislavery leaders of the limitations of compensated, gradual emancipation and colonization. Men and women were working together to help society reach the perfection emphasized by evangelical reformers in general. Although the Garrisonians grew increasingly radical, they remained the minority among abolitionists. In the tumultuous decades ahead, most would continue to work together to spread their antislavery message to a growing number of listeners and readers.

Beverly Tomek

BIBLIOGRAPHY

Blackett, R.J.M. *Building an Antislavery Wall: Black Americans in the Atlantic Abolitionist Movement, 1830–1860.* Ithaca, NY: Cornell University Press, 1983.

Goodman, Paul. *Of One Blood: Abolitionism and the Origins of Racial Equality.* Los Angeles: University of California Press, 1998.

Harrold, Stanley. *American Abolitionists*. New York: Longman Press, 2001.

Horton, James Oliver. *Free People of Color: Inside the African American Community*. Washington, DC: Smithsonian Institution Press, 1993.

Lerner, Gerda. *The Grimké Sisters from South Carolina: Pioneers for Women's Rights and Abolition*. New York: Houghton Mifflin Company, 1967. Reprint, 1998. New York: Oxford University Press.

Painter, Nell. *Sojourner Truth: A Life, A Symbol*. New York: W.W. Norton, 1996.

Quarles, Benjamin. *Black Abolitionists*. New York: Oxford University Press, 1969.

Ripley, C. Peter, ed. *The Black Abolitionist Papers*. Chapel Hill: University of North Carolina Press, 1991.

Rosenberg, Charles. "Sexuality, Class and Role in Nineteenth Century America." In Elizabeth Pleck and Joseph E. Pleck, eds., *The American Man*, 219–257. Englewood Cliffs, NJ: Prentice-Hall, 1980.

Walters, Ronald G. *American Reformers, 1815–1860*. New York: Hill and Wang, 1997.

ANTISLAVERY MOVEMENT
1840s–1850s

Abolitionists spent the 1830s building a movement, but by 1840 its structure was beginning to fall apart. From the beginning, most Americans resented their efforts, accusing them of putting the nation in jeopardy by stirring up both the slaveholders and the slaves. Throughout the 1830s and 1840s, abolitionists faced increasingly violent mobs, and they made fewer converts to the cause than most people today realize. In general, Americans in the antebellum years remained unwilling to challenge slaveholders as long as the system of human bondage did not affect them directly.

By the 1850s, this situation was beginning to change a little, but many who came to oppose slavery during this time did so in the tradition of "antislavery" rather than "abolition." The Compromise of 1850, the Kansas-Nebraska Act of 1854, and the *Dred Scott* U.S. Supreme Court decision in 1857 all made more and more Northerners feel threatened. Throughout the free states, people began embracing a theory that the Southern "oligarchy" or "slaveocracy" had been ruling the entire nation from the beginning. This "slave power" thesis became very popular as both politicians and abolitionists began to argue that slaveholders must be stopped before they found a way to force their system back into the North as well as the newly settled territories of the West. Thus, slavery became a major political issue during these years.

As antislavery entered the political arena with greater force, the social aspect of the abolitionist movement began to suffer. One group followed Myron Holley, Charles Torrey, Joshua Leavitt, Gerrit Smith, and James G. Birney into the political arena, forming their own third party, the Liberty Party, in 1840. Another group continued to follow William Lloyd Garrison even as he grew increasingly radical by adding women's rights to his overall agenda and calling for larger cultural and political changes. Others followed Lewis Tappan in his efforts to work through the churches to gain support for abolition. Finally, as the American Anti-Slavery Society (AASS) fell apart under such stress, many black abolitionist leaders began to reassert their independence in the movement, continuing to adhere to their own theories of self-help and racial uplift.

ANTISLAVERY IN THE POLITICAL ARENA

When the AASS split in 1840, one group of abolitionists chose to pursue their goals through the political arena. They argued that the United States Constitution was an antislavery document, and, therefore, the federal government could legally take steps to end slavery in the South. Since they believed that slavery was not sanctioned by the government, some members of this group could justify actively helping slaves escape while they waited for the day in which they could destroy the system through political means. Although their belief in the American political system made them philosophically less radical than the Garrisonians, their use of physical force to aid in self-liberation made their tactics more radical.

The more radical political abolitionists, led by Gerrit Smith of New York, took the most aggressive stance toward the South. According to historian Stanley Harrold, their militance was inspired by the increasing efforts, during the early 1840s, of the enslaved to liberate themselves through escapes and shipboard revolts. Smith demonstrated this new effort to appeal to the slave rather than the master in his 1842 *Address to the Slaves in the United States of America*. In the tradition of black abolitionist David Walker, he called upon the enslaved to avail themselves "of any feasible, peaceable mode" of securing their own freedom. Discouraging them from "recourse to violence and blood-shed for the termination of slavery," he nevertheless encouraged "every slave, who has the reasonable prospect of being able to run away from slavery, to make the experiment." He boasted that, through abolitionist influence, the rate of successful escapes had reached "a thousand a year," and he assured those hoping to follow this course of action that "under the influence of anti-slavery lessons, nineteen-twentieths" of whites in the border free states had decided to help, rather than return, fugitives.

This emphasis on helping the slaves with direct assistance appealed to many black abolitionists, and Henry Highland Garnet offered a similar appeal to the slaves a year later. Taking his appeal a step further than Smith, he suggested that violence could be necessary and justified in some cases. Garnet's father had led his family to freedom, and the memory of his father's bravery, as well as the influence of Walker's earlier appeal, led him to call upon those still in bondage to "USE EVERY MEANS, BOTH MORAL, INTELLECTUAL, AND PHYSICAL, THAT PROMISES SUCCESS." Like Smith, however, Garnet stopped short of calling for armed revolt; instead he encouraged the enslaved to appeal to their masters' "sense of justice" and to "promise them renewed diligence in the cultivation of the soil, if they will render to you an equivalent for your services."

Radical political abolitionists did more than talk. They actively helped slaves in many ways. They purchased the freedom of a number of slaves, including Frederick Douglass. This tactic drew criticism from the Garrisonians, who insisted that purchasing people for any reason legitimized slavery by acknowledging slaveholders' property rights.

Theoretical issues aside, this tactic remained popular, and abolitionists raised funds in both the United States and England for this purpose. In addition to raising money and helping slaves purchase themselves or their families, this group of abolitionists also helped many sue for their freedom. Perhaps most important, they helped slaves escape and even intervened and tried to rescue some, such as Anthony Burns, a fugitive slave known as Shadrack, and another known as Jerry, from slave catchers. According to Harrold, these tactics made the abolition efforts more public and helped gain sympathy for the cause, spreading "an antislavery morality" throughout many Northern communities.

The rescue of fugitives strengthened the overall movement by encouraging biracial cooperation and making abolitionists appear to Southerners as a unified, formidable opponent. According to Harrold, "the notoriety of a half-dozen dramatic rescues encouraged white Southerners to believe that the North was full of militant abolitionists who favored African-American freedom over the vested interests of slaveholders." It

also greatly influenced the future generation of white abolitionists such as Thomas Wentworth Higginson while further alienating nonresistants such as Garrison.

These biracial efforts at direct, physical resistance increased throughout the 1840s and 1850s, and a number of contemporary newspapers began referring to an "Underground Railroad" at the beginning of this time period. This term has gained popularity ever since, but modern students of abolition have shown that the idea of a centralized, unified operation is often exaggerated. In reality, black abolitionists had been helping slaves escape throughout U.S. history. By the 1790s, they had managed to gain the support of some sympathetic whites in the Upper South. During the early 1840s, such efforts intensified, and more abolitionists began to actually go South and lead slaves to freedom. This became an important component of the abolitionist movement, especially as the growth in the domestic slave trade led more masters to sell slaves to the Deep South, thus splitting families.

Black and white radical political abolitionists played key roles in this movement, and they did form a loose network, so the idea of an "underground railroad" has validity. Former slaves such as Harriet Tubman, "The Moses of Her People," Josiah Henson, and John P. Parker all went South to lead slaves northward to freedom. Free blacks, including Philadelphia vigilant association leader William Still, also assisted runaways along their journey. Finally, a number of white abolitionists such as Jacob Bigelow, Smith, and Tappan also aided in escape and rescue efforts.

Although a number of political abolitionists adhered to Smith's belief in radical tactics and participated in such militant efforts, others shared his political goals but took a less antagonistic stance toward the South. This group, led by Salmon P. Chase and Gamaliel Bailey, continued to reach out to the masters rather than the slaves. They remained confident that slaveholders could be made to see the errors of their ways and free their bondspersons out of love for the country and concern for the good of society. In his periodical, the *National Era*, Bailey tried to appeal to Southerners by explaining that the Liberty Party was "not sectional in its creed or spirit."

Unlike the radical political abolitionists, who insisted that the federal government had the legal authority to intervene and abolish slavery in the South, Bailey and Chase held to the states' rights arguments stressed by the earlier antislavery generation. Like the colonizationists of the 1820s and 1830s, they insisted that their party hoped to appeal to each state to change rather than to force change upon them. To emphasize this point, Bailey promised that "so far as slavery may exist by act of Congress, affect Federal legislation or general politics" the Liberty party "will act against it by federative powers." He added, however, that "where it exists by the law and within the jurisdiction of the State, it leaves its members in that State to resort to State legislative or judicial action for its removal, seconding their efforts by the moral influence of the rest of the organization."

This disagreement over whether to focus on slaveholder or slave led the Liberty Party to split in the late 1840s. By this time, the intellectual climate in the North was becoming increasingly antislavery, though not abolitionist. Put simply, more and more Northerners were growing concerned over the spread of slavery throughout the free territories. In 1848, a number of northern Whigs, some Democrats, and some abolitionists came together to form another third party, the Free Soil Party.

Although the party enjoyed the support of a small number of abolitionists, it was actually "antislavery" in the tradition of the colonizationists. Most supporters of Free Soil were not concerned with the fate of the enslaved. Instead, they hoped to keep African Americans, slave or free, out of the newly settled territories. They acknowledged the right of slaveholders in the South to keep their human property, but they also argued that slaveholders had been corrupted by the system that gave them such complete power over others. They insisted that this "slaveocracy" was seeking to extend its power by forcing its system, and its slaves, upon the rest of the nation. This idea, known as the "slave power" thesis, was not new, but it became more theoretically sophisticated and widespread during the 1850s. It became the primary tool of the Free Soilers during the 1840s and helped the Republicans gain power in the 1850s.

Although abolitionists often used slave power rhetoric in their quest for social reformation of the country, most who employed the thesis in the political arena disliked both the slave and the slaveholder. Thus, both abolitionists and antiblack antislavery leaders could unite in their denunciation of the "slave oligarchy." With the rise of the Free Soil and Republican parties, slavery became an openly sectional political issue as leaders attacked slaveholders for trying to corrupt the entire nation. According to historian Leonard Richards, leaders of these two parties "had a decisive advantage" because their power base was en-

tirely from the North and they "had no need, much less desire, to placate the South." At first glance this development could seem advantageous for abolitionists, but it actually hurt the movement by leading some to settle for an attack on slavery that included a racist, exclusionary element rather than pushing for abolition based on the rights of blacks as human beings. Unfortunately, such emphasis on the need to protect white Northerners from power-hungry slaveholders and their potentially dangerous chattel proved a crucial tool in turning most Northerners against slavery.

The Compromise of 1850, the Kansas-Nebraska Act of 1854, and the *Dred Scott* decision in 1857 would all play crucial roles by providing most Northerners, abolitionist or not, with evidence that slaveholders were indeed trying to extend their power and their system throughout the entire nation. The Compromise of 1850 included a Fugitive Slave Law that removed the burden of proof from the master and placed it on the slave. It offended many Northern whites, making them feel that the federal government was attempting to use them to enforce its dirty business by requiring citizens in general to assist in apprehending accused escapees. This law enhanced their fears of "slave power" by denying them their freedom of conscience, since it made it illegal not to give assistance to the slave catchers. The Kansas-Nebraska Act added to the growing fear by opening the door for the possibility of slavery in territories that had been previously declared free. Under this act, settlers in these territories would vote on whether or not to allow slavery, despite the fact that previous legislation had prohibited slavery in these territories. Finally, the *Dred Scott* decision protected the rights of slave owners to take their slaves anywhere in the country and denied citizenship even to free blacks in the United States.

ABOLITION IN THE SOCIAL ARENA

At the same time that Smith, Bailey, and their followers were struggling for a place in the political arena, other abolitionists such as Garrison and Tappan kept the social movement alive. Garrrison refused to work through the government or mainstream religious channels, arguing that both had become corrupt beyond repair. As a result, he embraced an ideology sometimes described by scholars as "Christian anarchism." Tappan, on the other hand, argued that the best hope for the movement was to work through the churches. He continued to build upon the evangelical framework of the abolition movement event after the

Fugitive Slave Law led him to join the political radicals in the early 1850s.

Although Garrison and his followers maintained control of the AASS after the split in 1840, their radical ideas left them in the minority within the overall abolition movement. To begin with, Garrison alienated many potential followers by attacking the churches. He criticized them for refusing to speak out and unequivocally label slavery as sinful. He embraced "anti-sabbatarianism," which held that Sunday was no holier than the other days of the week, and he adopted the doctrine of "Christian Perfectionism." This ideology insisted that each person should strive for total abstinence from sin, on an individual level, relying upon his or her own inner strength rather than the guidance of organized religion.

Garrison and his followers also attacked the American social order, most notably by pushing for civil rights for African Americans and women. Scholars continue to debate the extent to which any white abolitionist truly embraced racial equality, but historian Paul Goodman argued that radical social abolitionists like Garrison challenged the larger American social structure not just by calling for an end to slavery but also by pushing for "full human equality." According to Goodman, white abolitionists developed sympathy for their black coworkers after listening to their assessment of the social structure and learning to deal with them as equals.

Goodman's thesis provides a heroic view of white abolitionists; however, contemporary accounts by black leaders like Douglass and Martin R. Delany describe a great deal of paternalism. Historian C. Peter Ripley has shown that Garrison and others, while working closely with black leaders, failed to share important offices with them. According to Ripley, blacks worked diligently in the AASS and its auxiliaries and contributed a great deal financially, yet the group's leadership "remained almost exclusively white." He cited as evidence the cases of William Still and William Cooper Nell, two black men who devoted decades to the AASS but never rose above the position of clerk.

Such exclusion is lamentable, but Garrison and his followers should be credited for rising above the prejudices of their time and at least addressing social inequality. By responding to African Americans' quest for freedom and equality, the Garrisonians initiated a course followed by later generations of white abolitionists. They challenged the social order by working with black leaders and arguing not only that the en-

M. R. DeLANEY.

Editor, author, black nationalist, and colonizationist, Martin Delany emerged as one of the most militant abolitionists in the 1840s and 1850s. During the Civil War, he was commissioned as a major in the Union Army, thereby becoming the nation's highest-ranking black field officer. *(Ohio Historical Society)*

slaved must be freed but also that, once free, they must be allowed to remain in the United States.

In addition to calling for black civil rights, Garrison embraced the crusade for women's rights. He helped secure the election of a woman, Abigail Kelley, to the business committee at the 1840 AASS convention. Unlike many other abolitionists, Garrison believed that women's rights and antislavery were compatible and were, indeed, both necessary to the overall agenda for improving American society. This stance led many women abolitionists into his camp, and Frederick Douglass, one of the most famous black Garrisonians of the 1840s, attended the first women's rights convention at Seneca Falls, New York, in 1848.

Garrisonians ignited controversy by attacking organized religion and calling for women's rights, and their political views only increased their alienation

MARTIN ROBISON DELANY (1812–1885)

Delany was born in Charles Town, Virginia (now West Virginia), on May 6, 1812, of a freed black woman and a slave father. His mother moved Delany and his siblings to Chambersburg, Pennsylvania, after it was discovered they could read and write and were teaching other slaves to do so. In 1831, Delany moved to Pittsburgh and studied the classics, Latin, and Greek at Jefferson College. Two years later, he became a physician's assistant as a cupper and leecher. During his time in Pittsburgh, he became involved in the abolition and temperance movements and began to form his idea of a separate black nation in Africa.

Delany founded a black weekly magazine, *Mystery* (1843–1847), which publicized the grievances of blacks in the United States and also championed women's rights, and he helped Frederick Douglass publish his abolitionist newspaper, the *North Star* (1847–1849). While on a speaking tour of Ohio, he was threatened by mobs on several occasions. He was admitted to Harvard Medical School in 1851 but had to leave because of classmates' protests. The following year he published *The Condition, Elevation, Emigration, and Destiny of the Colored People of the United States, Politically Considered*. This landmark book alienated virtually all abolitionist leaders by advocating the need for blacks to leave America and start anew with a new nation elsewhere. His book also attacked white abolitionists for discrimination, in not hiring able blacks for their businesses, and for disallowing leadership positions to blacks in their organizations. He followed that book up with his "reply" to Harriet Beecher Stowe's *Uncle Tom's Cabin* (1852) called *Blake, or The Huts of America*, about the secret travels through slave communities by an insurrectionist (a portion of which originally appeared

serially in the *Anglo-African Magazine* from January to July 1859). Modern scholars consider his portrayal of antebellum black culture as being among the most accurate. Delany moved to Chatham, Canada, in 1856.

Delany traveled to Liberia in Africa in 1859 seeking lands in the Niger Delta region for resettlement. Delany and Robert Campbell signed a treaty with eight chiefs, but it was later dissolved owing to warfare in the region, subversive opposition by white missionaries, and the outbreak of the Civil War in America. During the Civil War, Delany recruited black men for Massachusetts' Fifty-fourth Regiment, as well as in Rhode Island and Connecticut, and in Cleveland and Chicago. After meeting with President Abraham Lincoln, he was commissioned as a major in the U.S. Army, the first black to receive a regular army commission. He crafted a scheme for recruiting a black guerrilla army to arm slaves, but the war ended before he could implement his plan.

After the war, Delany lived in South Carolina while working for the Freedmen's Bureau for three years and was active in politics. He was nominated for lieutenant governor of South Carolina on the Independent Republican ticket in 1874 but lost. From the summer of 1877 until 1880, Delany served as chairman of the finance committee of the Liberia Exodus Joint Stock Steamship Company, which was organized to settle blacks in Africa. He moved to Xenia, Ohio, several years after Reconstruction ended to provide for his family, and he died there on January 24, 1885. Although never as well known as other African-American leaders, Delany's work has been recognized as a precursor to more militant Black Nationalist movements.

James G. Lewis

from the mainstream. Unlike the radical political abolitionists, Garrison argued that the United States Constitution was a pro-slavery document. Accordingly, political action was futile. Garrisonians also continued to adhere to the tactic of "nonresistance," which led them to criticize any form of physical self-defense. Their refusal to move beyond strict adherence to moral suasion and enter the political fight lost them a great deal of black support, most notably that of Frederick Douglass in 1851.

After the AASS split, a third faction, led by Tappan, appealed to a larger number of abolitionists, both white and black. Tappan's group remained flexible, maintaining contacts in the social as well as the polit-

ical scene. Unlike Garrison, Tappan was willing to consider the arguments of political abolitionists. More important, however, he gained the support of black and white religious leaders by working through, rather than criticizing, organized religion. His group, the American and Foreign Anti-Slavery Society (AFASS), worked to convince church leaders to embrace abolition. At the same time, the AFASS supported abolitionists who chose to leave churches they considered pro-slavery. According to Harrold, this tactic profoundly increased the sectional nature of the abolitionist struggle by encouraging a number of denominations to split over the issue of slavery. For example, when the Methodist Episcopal Church failed to denounce slavery, the Wesleyan Methodists left to form their own organization in 1842. Other examples include the formation of the American Baptist Foreign Mission Society in 1845 and the Free Presbyterians in 1846. According to Harrold, these groups provided crucial grassroots support for the cause during the 1840s, 1850s, and 1860s. Tappan himself also helped create the American Missionary Association in 1846, and Harrold describes that group as "the largest antebellum abolitionist organization and the most active supporter of evangelical opponents of slavery in the South." Thus, Tappan's efforts to work through the churches helped create and sustain much of the movement's growth in the Antebellum years.

BLACK ABOLITIONISTS AND THE SPLITTING OF THE MOVEMENT

The changes of the 1840s and 1850s greatly affected the black abolitionist movement. During the 1830s, blacks gained white support in their opposition to the colonization movement and their quest for immediate freedom. Initially, they harbored a great deal of hope for a biracial assault on the institution of slavery. By the 1840s, however, many had become disenchanted with infighting among white leaders and lack of substantial opportunity for black leadership within the movement.

Many black leaders felt that whites were becoming distracted just when the cause was gaining urgency. While the Compromise of 1850, the Kansas-Nebraska Act, and *Dred Scott* made Northern whites feel threatened, they posed a substantial threat to black freedom. Most black leaders continued to push for self-help and racial uplift, but some began to propose a new type of colonization—a black-initiated, black-led emigration.

After the AASS split, most black leaders chose to focus on political action. Some, such as Henry Bibb and Samuel Ringgold Ward, joined the Liberty Party. Black clergymen, including Samuel Cornish, Theodore S. Wright, and Henry Highland Garnet, were attracted to Tappan's AFASS. By and large, however, most black leaders began to call for independence from white leaders and their squabbles. According to Ripley, white and black abolitionists had distinct movements by the 1840s, with whites focusing on the abstract and ideological aspects of antislavery and blacks defining both slavery and freedom "in more concrete, experiential terms." According to Ripley, "white abolitionists insisted that antislavery strategies and tactics conform to abstract moral principles,"

while black leaders "sought practical change, usually more concerned with results than tactics."

Free blacks and slaves shared a common struggle against slavery and oppression, and events of the 1850s highlighted this connection. The Fugitive Slave Law of 1850, for example, had a huge impact on the free black community. Replacing the Fugitive Slave Law of 1793, this new act threatened the security of all Northern free blacks by denying them the right to trial by jury and placing the burden on them to prove their innocence. It even created a bounty system that awarded commissioners ten dollars for each case in which a slave was returned to the master, but only five dollars for each case in which the accused escapee was released. Realizing the danger to the union if the law was not respected, most Northerners reluctantly accepted the new law and their role in its execution, making a clear distinction between their right to oppose the spread of slavery and their duty to enforce the law.

Black abolitionist leaders knew what was at stake. Delany warned in his 1852 book, *The Condition, Elevation, Emigration, and Destiny of the Colored People of the United States*, that whites would not consider disobeying the law because of the growing fear for the union. He warned his readers that "the existence of the Fugitive Slave Law [is] *necessary* to the continuance of the national compact." Other free blacks also immediately recognized the danger to their liberty. Tying them directly to slaves by emphasizing their ethnic connection, the law required nothing more than a sworn affidavit from a slave owner who wished to claim a black as renegade property.

This law brought about one of the most militant periods in the abolition struggle, as many fugitives, including Anthony Burns, were returned to slavery despite public outcries. As a result, many black leaders began to encourage civil disobedience more than ever before. Delany emphasized that fugitive slaves were not the only ones who should fear for their freedom. He claimed that the law was especially dangerous for Northern free blacks because, unlike Southern free blacks, they usually did not possess documentation of their status.

In this climate, the black movement split as well, as some leaders began to consider emigration. Blacks who turned to emigration sought refuge in a number of places. A few advocated going to Mexico, while others chose to join the transatlantic abolitionist crusade and set sail for Great Britain. Canada, however, was the most popular destination. Despite the various choices for settlement, most of these Antebellum emi-

Death of Capt. Ferrer, the Captain of the Amistad, July, 1839.

Don Jose Ruiz and Don Pedro Montez, of the Island of Cuba, having purchased fifty-three slaves at Havana, recently imported from Africa, put them on board the Amistad, Capt. Ferrer, in order to transport them to Principe, another port on the Island of Cuba. After being out from Havana about four days, the African captives on board, in order to obtain their freedom, and return to Africa, armed themselves with cane knives, and rose upon the Captain and crew of the vessel. Capt. Ferrer and the cook of the vessel were killed; two of the crew escaped; Ruiz and Montez were made prisoners.

After being illegally abducted as slaves from Sierra Leone in 1839, Joseph Cinque and fifty-two fellow captives escape from their chains and rise up in rebellion on the *Amistad*, killing the ship's captain and a crew member. Cinque and the rebels were later arrested and tried for murder, but the court found them not guilty because they had been seized illegally. Cinque and most of the rebels returned to Africa in 1842. *(Library of Congress)*

grationists shared a desire to eventually return to the United States once conditions improved. In most cases, they hoped their settlements would help facilitate progress in American race relations by providing evidence of black self-reliance and achievement. These settlers, much like the Puritans who founded New England, strove to create a "city on a hill" that would showcase black achievement and prove that African Americans were capable of contributing to American society.

Such emigration schemes gained popularity in waves, first after the Kansas-Nebraska Act threatened to allow the extension of slavery into the territories and then after the *Dred Scott* decision denied black citizenship. After the first of these setbacks, Delany decided that the time was right to call a convention to discuss black prospects in America and other countries. Two years later, he left for Canada. When the U.S. Supreme Court ruled the following year that blacks were not American citizens, a renewed interest in Canadian emigration led a number of blacks to follow his lead. William Wells Brown, another black abolitionist and one of the earliest black historians, argued in his book, *The Rising Son* (1873), that by the end of the decade, "the subdued tone of the liberal

portion of the press, the humiliating offers of Northern political leaders of compromises, and the numerous cases of fugitive slaves being returned to their masters, sent a thrill of fear to all colored men in the land for their safety, and nearly every train going North found more or less negroes freeing to Canada." But still, most did not give up. Brown added that while *Dred Scott* was a setback, it did not prove that blacks would never be accepted in America. He chose to believe that, though the Supreme Court bowed to the South in this case, the "good men at the North felt ashamed of the Government under which they lived." During this time, black leaders produced their most militant rhetoric as their disenchantment with American racism grew, yet, like Brown, most maintained a degree of optimism that they could change things by proving their own equality, and they never gave up on their quest for American acceptance.

The emigration schemes some embraced, ironically, embodied this hope. Delany's scheme is perhaps the most well known. It is important to note that he did not seek mass emigration of American blacks to any other part of the world at this time. Instead, he infused the Puritan concept of the "city on a hill" with the capitalistic values of his own time, seeking to create a black-led colony that would enjoy moral and economic success, proving that the black community had capable leaders and industrious citizens. An extension of his self-help, moral suasion agenda, this colony would prove black equality, generate self-confidence among the larger black community, and beat whites at their own economic game while also spreading Western culture to other parts of the world. This scheme illustrates both the "racial uplift" agenda of the black abolitionist crusade and the missionary atmosphere of the time. Alexander Crummell, another black abolitionist who turned to emigration, focused particularly on the missionary aspect, insisting that colonies in Africa would prove black equality while also propagating Christianity to the "benighted" parts of the world.

CONCLUSION

The American Civil War opened the door for both black and white abolitionists to pursue their goals with greater fervor. Even the Garrisonians could contribute to the Union effort in hopes of creating a new nation that, unlike the one created by the Constitution, did not sanction human bondage. The spirit of hope embodied in the war led many to forget old wounds, and abolitionists of all factions sought to pressure the government to turn the struggle into a war for black freedom. Garrison had called for the North to dissolve the Union rather than compromise with the South during the past decade. Once the

South made the decision to leave, he hoped to influence the results of their endeavor. Even the emigrationists came home to help in the struggle, seeing the war as their chance to earn a place in an improved postwar America. Most had cited black service in past wars as a claim to citizenship and equality, and they extended their self-help philosophy to the battlefield.

Beverly Tomek

BIBLIOGRAPHY

Delany, Martin R. *The Condition, Elevation, Emigration and Destiny of the Colored People of the United States*. 1852. Reprint, Baltimore, MD: Black Classics, 1993.

Goodman, Paul. *Of One Blood: Abolitionism and the Origins of Racial Equality*. Los Angeles: University of California Press, 1998.

Harding, Vincent. *There Is a River: The Black Struggle for Freedom in America*. New York: Harcourt Brace Jovanovich, 1981.

Harrold, Stanley. *American Abolitionists*. New York: Longman, 2001.

Mayer, Henry. *All on Fire: William Lloyd Garrison and the Abolition of Slavery*. New York: St. Martin's Press, 1998.

Richards, Leonard L. *The Slave Power: The Free North and Southern Domination, 1780–1860*. Baton Rouge: Louisiana State University Press, 2000.

Ripley, C. Peter. *The Black Abolitionist Papers*. 5 vols. Chapel Hill: University of North Carolina Press, 1991.

Wyatt-Brown, Bertram. *Lewis Tappan and the Evangelical War Against Slavery*. 1969. Reprint, Baton Rouge: Louisiana State University Press, 1997.

ANTISLAVERY MOVEMENT   1860–1865

If most Americans remember anything about Civil War history, it is that Abraham Lincoln freed the slaves with the Emancipation Proclamation. Traditional Civil War historians agree. Lincoln freed the slaves, first and foremost by labeling slavery a moral evil and calling for an end to bound labor. This position also argues that Lincoln's election in 1860 provoked the South to secede and that his refusal to compromise on the expansion of slavery and on Fort Sumter were also crucial. It also cites Lincoln's creation of a Unionist coalition in the first year of war, his later commitment to emancipation, and his insistence upon unconditional victory. For traditionalists, Abraham Lincoln clearly played the lead role in the drama of the war, and the soldiers of the Union Army served as the supporting actors. As for most slaves, they were simply the lucky beneficiaries of policies passed by the "Great Emancipator" and enforced by his warriors.

Beginning in the 1960s, however, a new group of historians started looking at the role of everyday people in American history. Known as "social historians," many of this generation began to discover that enslaved African Americans played central roles in the Civil War and emancipation. Led by the team of Ira Berlin, Barbara Fields, Steven Miller, Joseph Reidy, and Leslie Rowland, these writers argued that the slaves earned their own freedom. Through their multivolume project, *Free at Last: A Documentary History of Slavery, Freedom, and the Civil War* (1992), these historians traced the efforts of African Americans to claim their own freedom by escaping from their masters during the war, working in Union camps, and, eventually, fighting in the Union Army. Their work supports the idea that Lincoln was a hesitant leader who issued the Emancipation Proclamation only after escaping slaves forced him to deal with the issue of slavery head-on. Thus, the slaves freed themselves by leaving the plantations and forcing the government to create policies that dealt with them as people. According to Berlin, "Whatever he believed about slavery, in 1861 Lincoln did not see the war as an instrument of emancipation. The slaves did. Lincoln's commitment to emancipation changed with time because it had to."

WHO FREED THE SLAVES?

Although proponents of both schools of thought present important arguments, neither has provided a comprehensive answer to the question of who actually freed the slaves. The truth is that both the enslaved population and President Lincoln played key roles. Just as important, however, were the efforts put forth by the free black population of the North in securing the end of slavery. The most important contribution of social history to the story of the Civil War lies in a clearer understanding of the importance of the broader African-American community in what became a quest not only for emancipation but also for civil rights. This quest began with the efforts of black abolitionists, many of whom were escaped slaves themselves. Building on this legacy, free and enslaved African Americans worked together once the war broke out to force a change in war goals from preservation of the union to emancipation of the enslaved. After they convinced Lincoln to issue his Proclamation, both groups continued to contribute to the war effort.

By the time of the Civil War, black Americans had been emancipating themselves for generations. Many of the escapees, most notably Frederick Douglass, became activists by fighting publicly for the abolition of slavery. Until the 1850s, most of them relied on a tactic they called "moral suasion." They tried to convince the public that slavery was an evil institution that hurt black and white Americans. By the 1850s, however, many had begun to worry that America could not be reformed through moral suasion alone. They saw the

Fugitive Slave Law of 1850 and the Dred Scott decision of 1857 as assaults not only on themselves but on American liberty in general, and some abolitionists—both black and white—even began to call for the Northern states to secede from the Union.

The Fugitive Slave Law linked Southern slaves with Northern free blacks by declaring that all African Americans were slaves until proven otherwise. Although the previous fugitive slave law had placed the burden of proof on masters and required them to apprehend their own slaves, the new law placed the burden of proof on the slave and provided masters with federal assistance in recapturing escaped slaves. It also denied the accused the right to trial by jury and required law enforcement officers and citizens in general to assist in apprehending accused escapees. It even created a bounty system in which commissioners were awarded ten dollars for each case in which a slave was returned to the master but only five dollars for each case in which the accused escapee was released. Realizing the danger to the Union if the law was not respected, most Northerners reluctantly accepted the new law and their role in its execution.

CIVIL DISOBEDIENCE

As if being assumed a slave was not bad enough, the *Dred Scott* decision compounded the humiliation. In this decision, the U.S. Supreme Court ruled that no black, whether free or enslaved, was an American citizen. In the wake of these two measures, abolitionists began to encourage civil disobedience more than ever before. Martin R. Delany, an important free black leader in the North, emphasized that fugitive slaves were not the only ones who should fear for their freedom. In an 1854 speech to the Cleveland Emigration Convention, he claimed that Northern free blacks faced the greater danger because, unlike Southern free blacks, they did not usually possess documentation of their status. Black abolitionist William Wells Brown argued in his 1867 book, *The Negro in the American Rebellion*, that after the *Dred Scott* decision, "the Constitution . . . became the emblem of the tyrants and the winding sheet of liberty and gave a boldness to the people of the South." Immediately following these oppressive developments, many African Americans considered emigration to various parts of the world, and a large number moved to Canada. However, most realized that even Northern whites were growing tired of Southern aggression as rising numbers began to cry out against what they called the "slave power."

CIVIL WAR

When the war first broke out, most Northerners claimed that it would be a war for the Union rather than a war to end slavery, but enslaved and free African Americans saw greater potential. Even those who had begun to call for emigration had only done so because the Fugitive Slave Law had cast into legal code dangerous distinctions based solely on race. Delany, one of the most famous emigrationists of the period, had insisted in his 1852 book, *The Condition, Elevation, Emigration and Destiny of the Colored People of the United States*, that the situation could "never be changed except by legislation," and that it was "the height of folly to expect such express legislation, except by the inevitable force of some irresistible internal political pressure." The Civil War provided just such pressure.

African-American intellectuals had cited black service in past wars as a claim to citizenship and equality, and they immediately saw the opportunity to earn respect by fighting for the Union. Seeing that pressure from blacks could influence the goals and outcome of the war, many began to hope that African Americans could prove their worth by actively fighting to enjoy the privileges of American citizenship. Only blacks could make it a successful war for freedom, Delany argued, because "the rights of no oppressed people [had] ever . . . been obtained by a voluntary act of justice on the part of the oppressors." He added that the war offered blacks a chance to use "muscles, hands, limbs, might and strength" to overthrow the powerful slave owners and force America along in its journey toward enlightenment and progress.

Although the war did not become a war for black freedom until Lincoln issued the Emancipation Proclamation on January 1, 1863, most blacks realized immediately that agitation over slavery caused secession. Many logically concluded that drastic changes were imminent, and they decided that a Northern victory would mean freedom for all, whereas a Southern victory would cause the death of black liberty throughout the country. Most African-American leaders determined that blacks had a unique opportunity, as well as an obligation, to turn the war for the Union into a war against slavery. Abolitionists had been pushing for a separation of the North and South for nearly twenty years, and now was their chance to seize the reigns from the slave owners. Leaders such as David Walker and Henry Highland Garnet had chided Southern blacks to stand up and fight in ear-

This series of images drawn by illustrator Thomas Nast in 1865 juxtaposes the horrors of slavery with the benefits—and triumph—of emancipation. *(Library of Congress)*

lier, less propitious times, and by the time the Civil War broke out, most black leaders had decided that violence and armed insurrection were the only solution. Now that the time was right, black participation would be crucial in securing freedom for the bondsmen and civil rights for all.

Though initial enthusiasm was dampened by exclusionary policies aimed at keeping them out of the struggle, blacks remained determined to take part. As the events of the war unfolded, most blacks began to put aside the persecution of the past decade, becoming determined to contribute to the war effort in a number of ways. To begin with, they built upon black service in previous wars to push for the government to adopt emancipation as a war goal and extend the right of blacks to participate on the battlefield. Some also offered their skills as laborers, scouts, and spies. Finally, after the war was opened to black participa-

tion, they fought for the Union and assisted in efforts to educate the freedmen and prepare them for the future.

Whether or not Abraham Lincoln was the "Great Emancipator" mythologized in history, a number of policies under his administration gave black Americans hope for acceptance in the United States even before emancipation. Delany told his earliest biographer that he immediately saw the potential in the Lincoln administration. He claimed that he saw Lincoln as a clever politician early on, realizing that the war would ultimately resolve the issue of black freedom. For many, the Civil War was nothing less than the culmination of the work begun by Gabriel Prosser, Denmark Vesey, and Nat Turner, and they recognized that blacks could play a unique role in securing their own freedom. In his 1874 book, *The Rising Son*, Brown looked back upon the early war years and described what he called a "change . . . over the dreams of the people." He cited stricter enforcement of the ban on the African slave trade, the abolition of slavery in the District of Columbia, and diplomatic recognition of the black republics of Haiti and Liberia as causes for the optimism of 1862. Delany agreed and emphasized the important role of blacks in these developments. He wrote to Douglass proclaiming that "the recent recognition of Haiti and Liberia, was due more to the presence of intelligent black representatives from Liberia at Washington than a thousand whites." In a statement that also reflected his attitude about the war, he concluded: "If I have one great political desire more than another it is that the black race manage their own affairs instead of entrusting them to others."

BLACK ACTIVISM

Even before Delany expressed his desire, some had indeed taken the initiative to manage their own affairs, seeking to pressure the government to make emancipation a goal of the war and to allow blacks to serve as soldiers. Alfred M. Green, a black abolitionist from Philadelphia and one of the earliest advocates of black participation in the war, insisted that the conflict was the vehicle by which to complete the Revolution of 1776. In an October 1861 letter to The Weekly Anglo-African, he maintained that "the world is rushing like a wild tornado in the direction of universal emancipation." He insisted that blacks must "grasp the sword—grasp this most favorable opportunity of becoming inured to the service that must burst the fetters of the enslaved and enfranchise the nominally free of the North." In light of white resistance to black participation, he added, "let us say to the demagogues of the North, who would prevent us now from proving [our] manhood and foresight in the midst of all these complicated difficulties, that we will be armed . . . and if our fathers were cheated and disfranchised after nobly defending the country, we, their sons, have the manhood to defend the right and the sagacity to detect the wrong."

Through this argument, Green expanded upon a common tradition among black abolitionists to use service in past wars as a justification for freedom as well as citizenship and equality. Aware that a number of slaves had earned their own freedom through service in the Revolution and the War of 1812, black leaders, particularly early historians such as William Cooper Nell and Delany, had tried for the past decade to prove that such service had earned for blacks the same freedoms as whites. Both writing in the early

1850s, Nell and Delany recounted black heroism in these wars, particularly the War of 1812. They both claimed that slaves had given Andrew Jackson the famous idea of hiding behind cotton bales as the enemy approached during the Battle of New Orleans, and they made good use of Jackson's famous speech in which he referred to his black soldiers as "citizens."

In both his Services of Colored Americans (1851) and The Colored Patriots of the American Revolution (1855), Nell provided not only accounts of black valor but also descriptions of the effects of such heroism on a number of important white statesmen. His goal was not only to prove that blacks had helped earn American freedom but also to raise consciousness of the fact that blacks were being denied their rightful heritage by an ungrateful country. His works end on optimistic notes, however, calling for a "second revolution" in which blacks would "prove valid their claim" to the title of patriots and demonstrate to the world their equality.

Delany's Condition, Elevation, Emigration was similar to Nell's work in many respects. He also struggled desperately to prove that blacks deserved citizenship because of their efforts in past wars. He insisted that "amor patria, or love of country, is the first requisition and highest attribute of every citizen," and that "he who voluntarily ventures his own safety for that of his country, is a patriot of the purest character." He even paraphrased Jefferson, attributing to him the argument that "the descendants of all who have borne arms in their country's struggle for liberty, should be always entitled to all the rights and privileges [of citizenship]." He concluded, almost prophetically, that in times of danger the country turned to "him who braves the consequences, and fights his country's battles . . . who shoulders his musket, girds on his sword, and faces the enemy on to the charge."

A number of leaders expressed the view that only force would end slavery and that blacks themselves must deliver that force. In his letter to The Weekly Anglo-African, Green maintained that service in the war would allow blacks to "enforce the doctrine we have ever taught of self-reliance." He further maintained that God was "opening the way for us to free ourselves" and that "the prejudiced never will respect us until they are forced to do it by deed of our own."

Many slaves had already arrived at similar conclusions and had been participating in the war effort since 1861. Their work began a few weeks after the war broke out, when a group of Virginia slaves seeking asylum behind enemy lines stole a canoe and snuck across Chesapeake Bay. Presenting themselves to General Benjamin Butler, the Union commander at Virginia, they forced the government to develop a policy for dealing with black refugees. Instead of returning them to their masters, Butler declared them "contraband," or captured enemy property, and put them to work in the camp. Seeing opportunity for freedom, others began to approach Butler's camp, and within two months he had 900 "contraband" workers serving as teamsters, blacksmiths, cooks, and laundresses.

Butler's "contraband" set the precedent for allowing black participation in the war by assisting as laborers in his camp in 1861. At least 150,000 black laborers had assisted in the quartermaster and engineering departments in such capacity by the end of the war, and by 1865, approximately 500,000 slaves joined the effort as either laborers or soldiers. The government was well aware of the value of such assistance. Union soldiers, many of whom entered the war with racist sentiments, began to see the value and skills of the escaped slaves with whom they came into contact. In addition to protecting them from recapture, some even began to argue that black men should be allowed to participate in combat. A Quartermaster General's "Report on Negro Labor" concluded that "if black men could wield a shovel they could shoulder a musket."

This sentiment strengthened as Northern troops entered the deeper areas of the Confederacy and began to rely more upon contraband assistance. By the summer of 1862, much of the Northern public even began to see how essential arming ex-slaves would be to victory, and many, regardless of their views on racial equality or emancipation, began to advocate enlisting black soldiers as an expedient measure.

Evidence shows that the contrabands' efforts at self-help earned them respect from many soldiers. In fact, despite official policy to return escapees, a congressional committee on the conduct of war found that not only did some troops refuse to return slaves, but some even avenged their maltreatment. Testimony of General Daniel E. Sickles revealed a couple of instances in which owners who had regained possession of slaves proceeded to flog them in sight of the officers only to find themselves on the other end of the whip at the mercy of the troops. The situation was particularly distressing to Washington officials because, in many cases, the officers were encouraging the men to defend the slaves. William T. Sherman set an example by refusing to help a West Point classmate retrieve slaves from Union-occupied Memphis, and General John Phelps not only welcomed runaways to

his camp, but he even ordered occasional retributive raids on particularly cruel masters. Furthermore, the congressional investigation concluded that lesser officers sometimes allowed soldiers to beat slave owners who entered their camps to claim contraband. This spirit of defiance was contagious and served to reinforce black resistance and independence.

BLACKS IN THE CIVIL WAR

Not only did Union officers encourage blacks to escape and work in the camps, but they also began to arm and train blacks for military service before Lincoln's proclamation allowed them to do so. General David Hunter played a key role in this effort. Commander in the South Carolina Sea Islands, he sought Lincoln's permission to enlist escaped slaves for combat duty in April of 1862. When Lincoln failed to respond, Hunter began recruiting on his own authority until he learned that the War Department would not pay the black soldiers or provide them necessary supplies. Because of the lack of support, he disbanded his regiment until the War Department finally authorized his efforts in August. During that same month, Butler incorporated several units of free black soldiers into the Union forces under his command. In addition to these "Native Guard" units, he later began recruiting both free blacks and escaped slaves.

The eagerness of both free blacks and escaped slaves to fight and the Union's need for as many hands as possible converged, and blacks won their first Civil War goal on January 1, 1863, when President Lincoln issued the Emancipation Proclamation. This famous document not only declared free all slaves in the Confederate states but also made freedom a war goal and announced the Union's new policy of enlisting African Americans as soldiers and sailors.

Soon after Lincoln opened the door for black participation, Henry McNeal Turner, a long-time black abolitionist who became a recruiter for the Union, challenged black men to enlist. In a February 1863 letter to the *Christian Recorder,* he appealed to black men to prove their equality by joining the war effort. He maintained that "the cry has long been, Give us the opportunity; show us a chance to climb to distinction, and we will show the world by our bravery what the negro can do." He argued that, "as soon as we are invited to stand on such a basis as will develop these interior qualities, for us to deride the idea and scornfully turn away, would be to argue a self-consciousness of incapacity." James Henry Gooding, a New Hampshire native who became a corporal in the famous Massachusetts Fifty-fourth Regiment, took Turner's challenge a step farther by warning of dire consequences if blacks failed to seize the opportunity at hand. He sent a series of letters to the New Bedford *Mercury* in an effort to gain recruits for his regiment. He pointed out that if slavery was defeated by whites alone, "language cannot depict the indignity, the scorn, and perhaps the violence, that will be heaped upon us; unthought of laws will be enacted, and put in force, to banish us from the land of our birth." In light of that possibility, he insisted, "now is the time to *act*."

In May of 1863, the government further sanctioned black participation in battle by creating a Bureau of Colored Troops within the War Department, and black soldiers immediately began to distinguish themselves in battle. They began to earn acclaim just five days after the bureau was established by participating in an assault on Port Hudson, Louisiana. Two regiments of free blacks and ex-slaves from New Orleans participated in this Union assault on the Confederate stronghold on the Mississippi River. Although the Union failed in this effort, the press began to take notice of black heroism. Ira Berlin, Barbara Fields, and their team of researchers have reprinted a number of glowing reports of black efforts in these and other battles in their multivolume *Free at Last: A Documentary History of Slavery, Freedom, and the Civil War*. Among these reports is one by an officer who admitted to entertaining "some fears as to their pluck." After seeing black troops in battle, however, he reported that the "heroic descendants of Africa [moved] forward . . . under a murderous fire" from enemy guns. His report concluded that "their gallantry entitles them to a special praise." Evidently, other witnesses shared his assessment of black bravery, as he reported to a Louisiana recruiter of black troops that "the sneers of others are being tempered into eulogy." A month later at Millikens Bend, another battle in Louisiana, both ex-slaves and free Southern blacks again demonstrated bravery that shocked many whites. Even a Confederate officer was impressed. In another report reprinted by Berlin's group, he admitted that the black troops had resisted "with considerable obstinacy, while the white or true Yankee portion ran like whipped curs."

Observers reported black bravery in many battles, but none has captured as much attention as the famous assault on South Carolina's Fort Wager in July of 1863. Led by the first black Northern regiment, the now-famous Massachusetts Fifty-fourth, the attack ended in failure and massive loss of life, but the black soldiers proceeded bravely under unrelenting Confederate fire. William H. Carney earned a Congressional Medal of Honor for his bravery in bearing the regimental colors. According to the battle report of Colonel M.S. Littlefield, a witness, Carney "refused to give up his sacred trust until he found an officer of his regiment" to pass the colors to, despite severe wounds in his leg and head.

Less celebrated but just as important to the Union cause were the naval contributions of African Americans during the war. Frederick Douglass reported in *Douglass' Monthly* in 1861, well before the Emancipation Proclamation, that a black sailor gave the Union its first naval victory. According to Douglass, a Confederate privateer had captured a schooner, the *S.J. Waring*, off the coast of New York and captured black crew members to be sold into slavery in Charleston. William Tillman, the steward, decided that he would not allow himself to be sold, and he convinced a fellow prisoner to help recapture the ship. Though neither Tillman nor his companions had experience in navigation, they managed to take the ship when it was within fifty miles of Charleston, turn it around, and reach New York. This feat earned praise from the New York *Tribune*, which thanked Tillman for the "first vindication of [the nation's] honor at sea."

A number of black sailors, free and enslaved, achieved similar victories. Robert Smalls, the most famous slave to contribute to the war, managed to commandeer a Confederate gunboat, the *Planter*, and surrender it to Union forces. The twenty-three-year-old pilot recounted to an 1864 audience in Philadelphia that he and his crew of fellow slaves waited for the captain to leave the ship on the night of May 13, 1862, picked up their families and friends, and "proceeded down Charleston River slowly." Smalls told his listeners that, upon reaching Fort Sumter, he "gave the signal which was answered from the fort, thereby giving permission to pass," and then "made speed for the blockading fleet." Once beyond the range of Sumter's guns, he hoisted a white flag and turned the vessel over to a Union captain. Both black and white newspapers celebrated Smalls's feat and reported his promotion as captain of the vessel in 1866.

Seeing that black valor on land and sea forced a number of white soldiers, commanders, and members of the general public to rethink their attitudes, many blacks became confident that, despite the failures of past wars, they could help end prejudice by proving themselves on the battlefields. By the war's end, 70 percent of all Northern black males of military age joined this crusade by enlisting in the Union Army.

Proportionate to the population, black enlistment in the North was three times that of white enlistment. Black men provided nearly 10 percent of Union fighters, and Northern and Southern blacks participated in 449 engagements, 39 of which were major battles. Approximately 37,300 blacks died while serving, and 21 earned Congressional Medals of Honor. These men had earned citizenship for all African Americans by forcing the government to disregard and even denounce the *Dred Scott* decision.

REPEAL OF RACIST LAWS

In addition to acknowledging black citizenship, the government passed a number of antidiscrimination measures during the war. In 1862, the Senate repealed an 1825 law barring blacks from carrying the mail, and Congress ruled that blacks could no longer be excluded as witnesses in the courts of the District of Columbia. Following this lead, some states also began to allow blacks to testify in court. Also during the war, Congress admitted blacks to its visitors galleries for the first time, the Smithsonian finally began to welcome blacks to public lectures, organizers of the president's public reception on New Year's Day allowed blacks to attend, and black troops were included in the Inauguration Day parade. Finally, black contributions to the war effort caused many whites to develop more positive attitudes that led to lasting changes in education and public transportation, and legal segregation ended in most parts of the North within three decades of the war's end.

The connection between these advances and black heroism in the war was obvious. Writing during Reconstruction, Brown, a pioneer in black history and a leader in the freedom struggle, looked back at the war years with optimism and pride in the fact that black heroism had "raised the colored men in the estimation of the nation." Insisting that because slavery had caused "all the prejudice against the negro," he had maintained in *Rising Son* that racism would end since slavery had been abolished. He also cited black bravery as crucial not only to ending slavery but also to dispelling racist sentiment.

DISCRIMINATION

The idea that the end of slavery could mean the end of racism had been common throughout the black abolition struggle, and it served as one of the strongest inducements for Northern blacks to participate in the war effort. In fact, while slaves escaped and fought for their own liberty early on, most Northern blacks did not officially join the effort until after the Emancipation Proclamation had been issued. Whereas most Southern blacks, as former slaves, fought with the motivation of freedom, Northern blacks joined the struggle to prove their equality and earn the rights of American citizenship. H. Ford Douglas, one of the youngest black abolitionist leaders before the war, seized the opportunity to supplement rhetoric with action. In a February 1863 letter to *Douglass' Monthly*, he expressed hopes that America would "pay back to the negro in spiritual culture [and] in opportunities for self-improvement, what they have take[n] from him." According to a contemporary observer, the crusade was successful, since even the pro-slavery press had begun to praise the black soldiers.

Although contemporary observers and Reconstruction-era black historians focused on positive changes in public attitude, the soldiers themselves faced a great deal of discrimination and injustice. To begin with, the sight of a black in the Union uniform offended extremist racists, and in some instances mobs attacked black soldiers. In addition, Confederates treated black prisoners as insurrectionists rather than prisoners of war, brutally murdering them or selling them back into slavery. Although Southern maltreatment was expected, black soldiers were often shocked to find discrimination within the Union Army as they were sent to the front lines of battle, given inadequate pay, and prevented from rising to the rank of commissioned officers.

A number of instances of racism and discrimination, however, were followed by renewed hope, and most blacks chose to stress the good and forgive the bad. For most cases of harassment of black soldiers, optimists could emphasize the dismayed reaction and intervention of white onlookers. Prejudiced actions of officers also were often met with criticism by their superiors or government officials. Confederate threats of murder and enslavement were answered with similar promises of retaliation by the United States government and Union officers. Finally, many blacks were encouraged by the support of their commanders, particularly in the struggle for equal pay.

Although the pay issue was eventually rectified, the quest for black officers was left largely unanswered. At issue was the fact that black soldiers wanted leaders of their own color to further their self-help agenda, but most whites resented the idea of having to salute or take orders from blacks. Although they could not become line officers, blacks could earn commissions as chaplains and surgeons, but such positions did not involve battlefield command.

RESISTANCE TO DISCRIMINATION

Those who entertained aspirations for these few leadership roles realized that the shortest avenue was through recruiting efforts. Not only had many white men earned high rank after starting out as recruiters, but many chaplains had received commissions because they had served successfully in that capacity. Frederick Douglass, John Mercer Langston, Charles Lenox Remond, Henry Highland Garnet, Rock, Brown, and Delany were among the abolitionists who recruited for the Union cause. While recruiting in the South, Rock spoke to the soldiers of the Fifth United States Colored Heavy Artillery Regiment. He stressed the connection between blacks of both regions, employing the rhetoric of self-help. He told his audience that "God gives men their liberty who can and dare defend them," and that God was on their side. He spoke down to the recruits, however, informing them that after the war they would "enjoy the rights and privileges of freemen," but that their Northern "families . . . shall expect you to educate and prepare yourselves and your families to become useful and respected members of society." Despite his elitist outlook, he was about to help recruit 147,000 soldiers.

Although a cultural chasm existed between Northern recruiters and Southern blacks, most recruiters did feel a genuine concern for their enlistees. Brown and Rock both resigned their position as recruiters over the equal pay issue. Though disgusted over the inequality, Rock refused to give up. He addressed the National Convention of Colored Men in Syracuse, New York, asking them to stand by the black soldiers and their families and cheer them on for the good of the United States' future. He was rewarded for his optimism in February of 1865 as he was sworn in to practice law before the Supreme Court.

Rock was not the only recruiter eventually rewarded for his efforts. Delany was eventually commissioned as the first black field officer in the U.S. Army on February 27, 1865. This position came after years of recruiting and a failed attempt to join the army as a surgeon. The first black to be awarded a recruiting contract by any state, Delany had been one of the most successful black recruiters, and his handbills and posters reflected his philosophy of racial uplift and self-help. He emphasized his racial affinity with his recruits and emphasized that it was "the duty of every colored man to vindicate his manhood by becoming a soldier, and with his own stout arm to battle for the emancipation of his race." With his commission, the acceptance of John Rock as a Supreme Court lawyer, and the opportunity for Henry Highland Garnet to preach at the capitol, Delany felt that the government had finally recognized the talents of black men of his class. In a report on a March 1865 speech delivered at New York's Shiloh Church, *The Weekly Anglo-African* quoted Delany's argument that although past governments had "progressed toward barbarism, and . . . were monuments of the barbarity of the times," President Lincoln and Secretary of War Edwin Stanton were leading a government that was progressing "toward truth, justice, liberty, Union and greatness." In Delany's assessment, "much progress had been made toward each." He believed that his hopes of black participation in the government were well within reach, since the country had "reached the innovation of elevating colored men to the grade of officers of the United States army."

Delany had earned his commission after approaching Lincoln with a plan to encourage self-liberation of slaves under black leadership. According to his plan, Delany would travel throughout the South, liberating slaves and organizing them in a large-scale uprising. This uprising, however, would be against the Confederate States instead of the United States. Concerned that the rebels would force the slaves to take up arms in defense of their own bondage, Delany proposed a plan in which he would follow the Underground Railroad south, spreading news of emancipation and gathering the newly freed to fight for their liberty rather than against it.

Delany's plan was the embodiment of black self-liberation. In presenting his plans to President Lincoln and Secretary Stanton, he emphasized his ethnicity as well as the fact that he was offering his assistance rather than asking a favor. Francis Rollins's 1883 biography, the *Life and Public Services of Martin R. Delany*, recounts Delany's claim that he had determined that "to wait upon the president at such a time to obtain anything from him could only be realized by having something, [a] plan, to offer the government." According to Delany, he had decided that to ask "Mr. President, what have you to give me?" would elicit the response "Sir, what have you to offer me?" and he was equipped with the answer. Pragmatically, he told Lincoln that he was aware of the barriers to appointing black officers. His solution was "an army of blacks, commanded entirely by black officers . . . to penetrate through the heart of the South, and make conquests, with the banner of Emancipation unfurled, proclaiming freedom as they go, sustaining and protecting it by arming the emancipated [and] taking them as fresh troops." He told Lincoln that his black-led liberation army would "give confidence to the slaves, and retain them to the Union, stop foreign intervention, and speedily bring the war to a close." Although he emphasized what his plan would do for the country when presenting it to Lincoln, he was most concerned with what it would do for African Americans. He believed that blacks needed black leadership, and he felt that he was uniquely qualified to provide it.

Although the war ended before Delany could implement his plan, others had used similar means to contribute to Union efforts. Northern abolitionists such as Harriet Tubman, as well as more recently liberated slaves, served as scouts, spies, and liberators by heading back south. Tubman, who for years had led slaves northward along the Underground Railroad, reversed directions and traveled southward to spread the news of emancipation. Her raids not only freed slaves and weakened rebel forces by taking away valuable laborers, but also aided the Union cause because many of the able-bodied among her contraband were willing to fight on the battlefield. Sent south at the beginning of the war by the governor of Massachusetts, she delivered slaves to freedom and recruited the men as soldiers; she also worked as a spy and a nurse. She was quite valuable in each of these roles because her life as a slave and her work in the Underground Railroad had made her familiar with the Southern landscape, and she was accustomed to tending to the needs of others.

THE BLACKS' ROLE IN THE SOUTH

Most other blacks who served the Union as scouts and spies had recently escaped, and they used intimate knowledge of their home terrain to help the cause. Confederates blamed the escapees for successful Union raids. Union Major-General O. M. Mitchell agreed. He admitted to Secretary of War Edwin Stanton in a May 4, 1862, report that much of "the most valuable and reliable information of the enemy's movements . . . that we have been able to get we have derived from Negroes who have come into our lines." Some of the most valuable spies and scouts had once served Confederate leaders. Garland H. White, former slave of Senator Robert Toombs, offered his services as a guide for Sherman's army in Georgia. He offered his assistance in a July 29, 1864, letter to Secretary of State William H. Seward. Calling for a campaign through his area of the state, he described his intimate knowledge of the plantations, railroads, rivers, and general terrain. He even cited his acquaintance with

an area that contained a prison that held "several thousands of our Union soldiers."

White was one of two chaplains known to have been born a slave, but as the slave of a former U.S. senator, he had extensive contact with Northern culture. He had even met a variety of government officials, including Seward, before running away from Toombs in 1859 or 1860. After escaping, he went to Canada and became an African Methodist-Episcopal pastor. As soon as the war broke out, he offered his services and began recruiting, and in October 1864 he was awarded with a commission as chaplain. Through this route he, like other chaplains, also became an educator of the freedmen. Believing that education would be crucial in preparing freedmen for full citizenship, most chaplains encouraged their listeners to seek literacy to earn white respect. They held strong beliefs that education would serve as the means of racial elevation.

Chaplains were not the only proponents of education. James Monroe Trotter, a black who gained the lieutenancy by the end of the war, argued that many noncommissioned officers and private soldiers also helped educate their fellow soldiers as well as Southern black civilians. Many of these officers and soldiers were from the North and had encountered Southern blacks for the first time in their army camps. Despite regional cultural differences, however, blacks from both areas agreed on one point: education was a must.

EDUCATION AND ECONOMIC ADVANCE

Most Northerners believed that racial uplift hinged on the ability of all blacks to prove their equality through education and economic achievement. Accordingly, they decided that it was their duty to assist in the betterment of the entire race by helping educate the newly liberated in an effort to fight racial prejudice. Though bound by race, many Northern black soldiers were as culturally distant from the freedmen as were Northern whites. Gooding's account of his army life shows the same condescending attitude and belief in stereotypes as abolitionist Thomas Wentworth Higginson's despite the fact that he was black and Higginson was white. Echoing Delany's arguments in the *North Star* that liberal education without practical training would be useless, one black sergeant-major explained in a July 1865 letter to *The Weekly Anglo-African* that while he was "happy" to know of strides taken for elevation in more academic fields, he was worried that "these qualifications alone will not enable us to perform all the duties of independent and good citizens." A barber from Pittsburgh, this soldier insisted that "our education needs to be practical, such as will profit us and our families. . . . Let no one harbor a thought that, because he is not permitted to occupy the most prominent position in society, there is nothing left worthy of his attention." Explaining that farmers and mechanics were just as important as statesmen, lawyers, and doctors, he went on to celebrate the self-made man and encourage frugality and hard work. He concluded that economic equality would be even more important to racial uplift than civil rights: "While we have to look to others for equality before the law, we must depend entirely on our own hands and heads for equality in financial resources."

The desire of the ex-slaves for education, however, extended beyond the practical avenues outlined by some elitist Northerners. Like Northerners, many Southern blacks subscribed to the idea that ignorance was the cause of their oppression and that education was the solution. Their educational goals, however, were more wide-ranging than a simple need to learn work skills. After all, they had learned practical skills through their manual labor as slaves. Now they wanted to read and write and learn skills that would prepare them for leadership. Many attributed the government's refusal to commission black officers to the inferior education blacks had received.

Joseph T. Wilson, a veteran of both the Second Louisiana Native Guards and the Massachusetts Fifty-fourth, produced the most comprehensive history of black participation in the war, and he described in detail the quest of most blacks for education. He argued in his 1887 book, *The Black Phalanx: African-American Soldiers in the War of Independence, The War of 1812, and the Civil War,* that "each soldier felt that but for his illiteracy he might be a sergeant, company clerk, or quartermaster, and not a few, that if educated, they might be lieutenants and captains." He further maintained that "this was not an unnatural conclusion for a brave soldier to arrive at, when men no braver than himself were being promoted for bravery." He also suggested that black soldiers saw most white Union soldiers as superior to white Confederate soldiers because they were more educated, and they sought to emulate them as a result.

Whether or not they equated education with promotion in the service, black soldiers were eager to learn as much as possible. Wilson reported that, sensing that education "somehow made them better men," the soldiers paid teachers' salaries out of their own earnings and contributed money to help build

schools. They crowded school rooms and used their free time to study and drill each other, and they eagerly called for education for themselves and their families to continue after the war.

Not all Northern blacks who contributed to the education of the freedmen were affiliated with the military. For many antebellum black abolitionist leaders, the war provided a great opportunity to further their self-help agenda and expand their missionary work to Southern blacks. Crusaders like Robert Hamilton saw the Emancipation Proclamation as a call to action. According to his editorial in the January 17, 1863, edition of *The Weekly Anglo-African,* "the process of transforming three million of slaves into citizens requires the aid of intelligent colored men and women." Though he recognized a cultural difference, he insisted "we are, and can be, nearer to them than any other class of persons; we can enter into their feelings and attract their sympathies better than any others can. We can more patiently help and teach, and more jealously defend them, than any others can." Seeing the hand of fate in the situation, he further argued that "we are manifestly destined for this work of mercy. It is for this trial God has given us the partial freedom, and such education, and the irrepressible desire for equality which consumes our souls."

Women from both regions played an important role in these efforts. Susie King Taylor, who had been educated while she was a slave, escaped and joined a regiment of ex-slaves in the Sea Islands as a cook, nurse, and teacher. Satirra Douglas, wife of H. Ford Douglas, traveled to Kansas under the auspices of the Women's Loyal League of Chicago to work in a freedmen's school, and Charlotte Forten built upon her work in the abolition struggle by also teaching blacks in the Sea Islands. In a dispatch to the *Atlantic Monthly* in 1864, she described children who were eager to learn and parents who were making sacrifices so that their children could attend school. Among her pupils were a grandmother and a mother who came and brought her baby. Happy to participate in the uplift of her "long-abused race," she saw herself as working toward the long-term goal of "promoting a higher, holier, and happier life on the Sea Islands." Though enthusiastic about her work, like other Northerners she described her students with an amused detachment. Stating the obvious, she explained that "there is [not] a man, woman, or even a child that is old enough to be sensible, that would submit to being made a slave again," and she expressed amusement at their manners and speech patterns. She did, however, praise their musical talent.

Although the doctrine of racial uplift shared by Northern black abolitionists prevented a true appreciation of Southern culture on its own merits, wartime missionaries and educators did leave an important legacy. In his early history of black contributions to the war, Wilson explained that many of these pupils pursued their education in the postwar years. According to Wilson, "since the war I have now heard of more than one who have taken up the profession of preaching and law making, whose first letter was learned in camp; and not a few who have entered college." Although much of the reform from the war years and Reconstruction was later abandoned or forced backwards, "the seeds of educational advance planted during the war years were never completely uprooted."

As the war came to a close, things were looking up. The leaders of what had been a crusade for the abolition of slavery a decade before could concentrate all their energies on civil rights. Even better, they were leading a movement that appeared to have a promising future. The accomplishments of Garnet, Rock, and Delany served as encouragement that blacks would be accepted as equals in the church, the government, and the military. Strides had been made in Northern and Southern education, desegregation had begun in the public facilities in some Northern cities, and blacks were being chosen as jurors and even elected to office. Furthermore, government and military leaders were aware of the important role blacks had played in the war. With military and government leaders praising black efforts for the Union, blacks from both regions shared the optimism that America had awakened. As Brown explained in *Rising Son*, "one by one, distinguishing lines have been erased, and now the black man is deemed worthy to participate in all the privileges of an American citizen."

The gains of the Civil War resulted from a joint effort of abolitionists, military leaders, President Lincoln, and the enslaved. Black abolitionists and slaves fought because they believed that the fate of their entire race was at stake. Lincoln's willingness to shift the goals of the war was crucial, but it did not arise solely out of an intrinsic need to do what was right. A number of black abolitionists, including Douglass and Delany, had approached him to discuss the need for emancipation. More important, the enslaved of the South decided that the time for freedom had ar-

rived. Ultimately, their mass exodus from the plantations and arrival in Union camps forced military leaders and the president to develop fair policies. White conscience changed only after black efforts left no alternative.

Beverly Tomek

BIBLIOGRAPHY

Adams, Virginia, ed. *On the Altar of Freedom: A Black Soldier's Civil War Letters from the Front*. Amherst: University of Massachusetts Press, 1991.

Aptheker, Herbert, ed. *A Documentary History of the Negro People in the United States*. New York: Citadel, 1951.

Berlin, Ira, Barbara J. Fields, Steven Miller, Joseph Reidy, and Leslie Rowland, eds. *Free at Last: A Documentary History of Slavery, Freedom, and the Civil War*. New York: Free Press, 1992.

Blassingame, John. "The Union Army as an Education Institution for Negroes, 1862–1865." *Journal of Negro Education* 34 (1965): 152–159.

Bradford, Sarah. *Harriet Tubman, the Moses of Her People*. Bedford, MA: Applewood Books, 1886.

Brown, William Wells. *The Negro in the American Rebellion: His Heroism and His Fidelity*. Boston: A.G. Brown, 1880.

———. *The Rising Son; or, the Antecedents and Advancement of the Colored Race*. Boston: A.G. Brown, 1874.

Burchard, Peter. *One Gallant Rush: Robert Gould Shaw and His Brave Black Regiment*. New York: St. Martin's Press, 1965.

Cornish, Dudley Taylor. *The Sable Arm: Black Troops in the Union Army, 1861–1865*. Lawrence: University Press of Kansas, 1987.

Delany, Martin R. *The Condition, Elevation, Emigration and Destiny of the Colored People of the United States*. 1852. Reprint, Baltimore: Black Classics, 1993.

Durden, Robert F. *The Gray and the Black: The Confederate Debate on Emancipation*. Baton Rouge: Louisiana State University Press, 1972.

Glatthaar, Joseph. *Forged in Battle: The Civil War Alliance of Black Soldiers and White Officers*. New York: Free Press, 1990.

Harding, Vincent. *There Is a River: The Black Struggle for Freedom in America*. New York: Harcourt Brace Jovanovich, 1981.

Higginson, Thomas Wentworth. *Army Life in a Black Regiment*. 1870. Reprint, New York: Penguin Books, 1997.

Katz, William Loren, ed. *Eyewitness: A Living Documentary of the African American Contribution to American History*. New York: Simon & Schuster, 1967.

Litwack, Leon, and August Meier, eds. *Black Leaders of the Nineteenth Century*. Chicago: University of Illinois Press, 1991.

MacGregor, Morris J., and Bernard C. Nalty, eds. *Blacks in the United States Armed Forces, Basic Documents*. 3 vols. Wilmington, DE: Scholarly Resources, 1977.

McPherson, James. "Who Freed the Slaves?" *Reconstruction* 2:3 (1994): 35–40.

———, ed. *The Negro's Civil War: How American Negroes Felt and Acted During the War for the Union.* New York: Pantheon Books, 1965.

Messner, William. "Black Education in Louisiana, 1863–1865." *Civil War History* 22 (1976): 41–59.

Miller, Edward A. *The Black Civil War Soldiers of Illinois: The Story of the Twenty-Ninth U.S. Colored Infantry.* Columbia: University of South Carolina Press, 1998.

Nell, William C. *The Colored Patriots of the American Revolution, with Sketches of Several Distinguished Colored Persons: To Which Is Added a Brief Survey of The Condition and Prospects of Colored Americans.* Boston: Robert F. Wallcut, 1855.

———. *Services of Colored Americans in the Wars of 1776 and 1812.* Boston: Prentiss & Sawyer, 1851.

Quarles, Benjamin. *The Negro in the Civil War.* New York: Da Capo, 1989.

Redkey, Edwin S. "Black Chaplains in the Union Army." *Civil War History* 33 (1987): 331–350.

———, ed. *A Grand Army of Black Men: Letters from African-American Soldiers in the Union Army, 1861–1865.* New York: Cambridge University Press, 1992.

Ripley, C. Peter, ed. *The Black Abolitionist Papers.* 5 vols. Chapel Hill: University of North Carolina Press, 1986–1992.

Rollins, Francis. *Life and Public Services of Martin R. Delany,* 1883. Reprint, New York: Arno, 1969.

Sterling, Dorothy, ed. *Speak Out in Thunder Tones: Letters and Other Writings by Black Northerners, 1787–1856.* New York: Da Capo, 1973.

Taylor, Susie King. *Reminiscences of My Life in Camp.* Boston: Susie King Taylor, 1902.

Ullman, Victor. *Martin R. Delany: The Beginnings of Black Nationalism.* Boston: Beacon, 1971.

Weaver, C.P. *Thank God My Regiment an African One: The Civil War Diary of Colonel Nathan W. Daniels.* Baton Rouge: Louisiana State University Press, 1998.

Williams, George W. *A History of the Negro Troops in the War of the Rebellion, 1861–1865.* New York: Harper & Brothers, 1888.

Wilson, Joseph T. *The Black Phalanx: African-American Soldiers in the War of Independence, The War of 1812, and the Civil War.* 1887. Reprint, Da Capo, New York, 1994.

Yacovone, Donald, ed. *A Voice of Thunder: A Black Soldier's Civil War.* Chicago: University of Illinois Press, 1998.

ABOLITION: HUMANITARIAN AND REVOLUTIONARY IDEAS

The principle of abolitionism promotes the immediate, unconditional, and universal abolition of the institution of slavery. The crusade to end slavery and secure racial justice in American society was part of a broader movement within the Americas that sought to rid the British, Dutch, French, Portuguese, and Spanish empires of their unfree labor systems. This cultural transformation in North America took place from approximately 1750 to 1890. In the United States, the abolitionist movement included individuals of varying ethnicities, genders, and socioeconomic positions. Abolitionism became one of the great reform movements in the nation's history whose popular growth may be traced in part to the philosophical principles governing the American Revolution.

The precise origins of this extraordinary movement are difficult to locate. According to some of the earliest studies of abolitionism, those who espoused an immediatist position on the institution of slavery were an autonomous and aberrant group of pious radicals who imposed their religious convictions and ideological principles on the broader society. While not denying the independent spirit and convictions governing abolitionists, scholars since then have sought to evaluate these Northern reformers within the wider cultural changes that took place in the antebellum period. That is, later scholars asked not only what forces of intellectual and social change gave rise to abolitionism, but also what changes took place that allowed their slow and perhaps begrudging acceptance among great numbers of Americans. Scholars have postulated several theories to answer these questions.

Some have suggested that by the turn of the nineteenth century a new form of humanitarianism had found expression in America. Both Enlightenment rationalism and the religious piety spawned by the Great Awakenings profoundly shaped this perspective. Describing the cultural forces at play by the turn of the century, historian Henry May's *The Enlightenment in America* (1976) notes:

> In the first years of the century important and obvious innovation was taking place mostly in two spheres, politics and religion, and in these what was new was method and organization rather than theory. Beyond these all-important realms, and also in the center of both, the real movement was taking place in the elusive realm of feeling. What was expressed in crude assertions Europeans found so hard to take was an ardent and emotional insistence on social equality. Egalitarian feelings, in America, often ran far ahead of fact, but yet in the long run affected many kinds of reality.

The resulting adjustment in individual perceptions brought the institution of slavery under considerable scrutiny. To varying degrees, in both North and South, slavery was seen as an antiquated and often morally repugnant practice of the Old World.

Another theory posits that the formation of economic free markets in the emerging capitalism and the industrial order of the West created a sphere of casual perception within the everyday affairs among the bourgeoisie class. This thesis suggests capitalist and market expansion broadened social perception among Americans and Europeans concerning the productivity of market goods and, in turn, promoted a sense of moral responsibility. The newly born relationship, albeit subtle and casually perceived by Westerners, goaded many to a point where passive sympathy for antislavery arguments no longer seemed to be an adequate response to the dehumanizing effects of slavery. The application of the Golden Rule to new arenas became part of an ethical dialogue concerning various social practices, including the long-standing practice of slavery in the Western Hemisphere. The result was the emergence of antislavery reform, which was but one manifestation of a new humanitarian sentiment that shaped the nineteenth century. Still, some scholars dismiss the idea that free markets had an overwhelming effect on changing public morality. Instead, they argue that the emergence of a new humanitarian sensibility was only minimally nourished by capitalists, who only sparingly advocated immediate abolition in both the North and South.

Although questions remain concerning the degree of influence the free market had on the development of a new humanitarian perspective, there is general agreement that the emergence of a new industrial order, coupled with the egalitarian principles engendered by the American Revolution, and the development of evangelical sensibilities provided Americans with an alternative lens through which they could discern previously accepted social norms. For many colonists, the assertion that their independence from England was justified on the grounds of humanity's inalienable right to the pursuit of liberty now more than ever conflicted with the fledgling nation's willingness to enslave approximately 500,000 African Americans, or nearly one-sixth of the total population of the colonies.

SECTARIAN CONVICTIONS AND ORGANIZING ANTISLAVERY REFORM

The earliest distinct sector of American society that consistently questioned the legitimacy of slavery and demanded its abolition was the Society of Friends, particularly those living in the port city of Philadelphia. As descendants of the Protestant Reformation, these Pennsylvania Quakers proclaimed the universality of God's love and the equality of all humanity as recipients of divine love. The Friends also believed that physical coercion was an evil; it was this belief that led them to become outspoken critics of the institution of slavery. Such criticism largely fell upon deaf ears until the mid- to late eighteenth century when evangelical revivals, with their emphasis on personal accountability regarding sin, coupled with the ideological conviction of inalienable rights, helped find receptive audiences for the Quakers' abolitionist message. Hoping to channel these concerns into social action, the Philadelphia Quakers created the first antislavery society in the world in 1775. Despite these encouraging developments in the North, the antislavery message found only sporadic support in the South as the nation's slave population nearly doubled by the close of the eighteenth century. Over the next thirty

years the nation's slave population would again double, securing its position in American society.

Running parallel to this sectarian cause were other national efforts of reform. One idea that sought to end slavery through voluntary manumission and the subsequent expulsion of slaves to Africa was colonization. The initial popularity of the American Colonization Society, founded in 1817 by Robert Finley, a Presbyterian minister from New Jersey, was largely due to its loose organizational structure, which enabled its promoters to appeal to local constituencies while circumventing the problem of a national coherent agenda concerning race. Colonization won support among Northerners and Southerners alike and received the backing of several would-be abolitionists. The development of new humanitarian sensibilities amidst the national democratic experiment led some proponents to naively believe that slaveholders would no longer participate in overt acts of physical barbarity toward the slaves and that in due time the institution of slavery would end following its proscribed course evident in the North. Advances in antislavery reform served to solidify these beliefs, including Congress's prohibition of the slave trade in 1808, the debates of the Virginia legislature concerning colonization in 1816, state bans on the importation of slaves, and a spike in the number of private manumissions in the upper South. So promising were the plans for colonizing that Henry Clay, the leader of the National Republican Party, incorporated the concept of colonization into his party's platform. These halcyon days of colonization, however, were short lived with the growth of "King Cotton" and the continued expansion of slavery in the West.

The Missouri debates mark a significant, yet subtle, change in the colonization movement. For the first time in colonization's brief history, distinct regional concerns began to surface that deeply influenced the spoken objectives of colonization along regional lines. By the first half of the 1830s, colonization's musings about "justice" and "self-preservation" shifted from a national to a distinctly Southern orientation. Soon internal and external forces would significantly cripple the power of the movement.

Shortly following the Virginia legislature's debates over slavery in 1832, William Lloyd Garrison published his *Thoughts on African Colonization,* leveling a scathing critique at the presuppositions governing arguments for colonization. Garrison's pamphlet suggested that the principle of melioration through the removal of blacks was "a libel upon humanity and justice—a libel upon republicanism—a libel upon the

Declaration of Independence—a libel upon Christianity." Garrison's words were without compromise. No longer, he exclaimed, could the institution of slavery be dismissed as the remnant of a foreign oppressor (the claim of James Monroe); the imposition of international trade (the assertion of William Thorton); or an "insurmountable barrier" of humanity—(the reflection of Thomas Jefferson). Garrison's critique gave shape to the argument of those advocating immediate abolition by its resolute belief that contemporary Americans were responsible for the continuation of slavery. More important, Garrison made the novel assertion that the semireligious principles of the Declaration of Independence guaranteed instant, uncompensated emancipation without repatriation. The following year the American Anti-Slavery Society was founded by former colonization advocates Arthur and Lewis Tappan, Garrison, and Gerrit Smith. Now for a new generation of reformers, immediate abolition and black equality were the only logical measure that would truly redeem the nation, a position that dramatically shaped the careers of these men.

The Tappans were wealthy merchants and social reformers from a strong Calvinist family, Lewis perhaps best remembered for his role in organizing the defense of Joseph Cinque in the Amistad trial. The brothers helped to fund numerous antislavery journals and publications but eventually parted ways with the American Anti-Slavery Society over their disapproval of the women serving as officers for the organization. Smith, on the other hand, chose a more radical approach to reform. A philanthropist and social reformer from Utica, New York, Smith was converted to abolitionism in 1835 after hearing a speech by Garrison. He served in Congress and notably ran as a presidential candidate in 1848. Failed attempts to secure immediate abolition eventually led Smith to financially back John Brown's raid at Harpers Ferry, becoming one of the famed "Secret Six." The society and its largely Quaker constituency renounced the use of "all carnal weapons" to accomplish these directives instead of encouraging the abolition of slavery through "the potency of truth" and the "power of love."

NASCENT ABOLITIONISM, GARRISONIANS, AND PUBLIC RESISTANCE

Abolition's greatest articulator and celebrity in the United States emerged during the 1830s in the person of William Lloyd Garrison. In many ways the North was primed to receive Garrison's message. A gener-

ation of young Northerners had grown up with limited or no personal experience of slavery. For a new generation of Americans, the physical discipline and cruelty of slavery came as a cultural shock, and many welcomed the abolitionist message.

In 1828, Garrison was converted to abolitionism by Benjamin Lundy, a Quaker. Shortly after taking up the antislavery cause, Garrison, a Baptist of deep conviction, was sued for libel by the owner of a ship that transported slaves. The converted abolitionist declared the ship owner a highway robber and murderer, for which Garrison received a six-month sentence in prison. Upon his release from prison, Garrison undertook a speaking tour in the Northeast linking immediatism with the call for black equality. Upon the completion of his tour, Garrison pursued other venues for spreading his message. Receiving financial support from James Forten, a wealthy African-American abolitionist from Philadelphia, Garrison, a trained printer from Newburyport, Massachusetts, began to publish a weekly antislavery newspaper in Boston on January 1, 1831. Over the next thirty-four years, The Liberator served as a repository for Garrison's ideas, attracting an audience among African Americans and social reformers in the North. Its earliest publications reflected the influence of Finneyite perfectionism, an evangelical revival current that allowed writers to ground their antislavery argument in moral absolutes. Such ideas would saturate the pages of The Liberator and were widely evident in contributions by men such as Henry Wright and James Boyle. Yet it was Garrison's cantankerous personality and inflammatory rhetoric that captured public attention and quickly gained him a national reputation. The weekly soon became an essential medium for the movement, enabling abolitionist ideology to spread like wildfire throughout the nation. While the abolitionist message spread quickly, the public attention the movement was drawing outstripped the movement's actual numbers.

But the reform movement's appeal to a kind of evangelical perfectionism enabled it to find a receptive audience among certain sectors within the nation's religious life. A little more than a year following the founding of Garrison's weekly, the New England Anti-Slavery Society was organized at the African Baptist Church in Boston. Organized by Garrison, the group pledged itself to nonviolent means to procure the freedom of African Americans. Other groups followed shortly thereafter. In the fall of 1833, Lewis Tappan organized the New York Anti-Slavery Society, which grounded its working principle in the theological conviction that Christianity "forbid[s] the doing of evil that good may come." Despite evidence of growing support for abolitionism within New England religious circles, particularly among Congregationalists, the majority of co-religionists continued to express hope in colonization schemes. With increasing virulence Garrison attacked supporters of colonization, further alienating evangelicals by asserting that supporters of colonization were racists and equivocal on the Gospel message.

It was in this volatile atmosphere that the United States government sought to quell the potentially explosive message of abolitionism. Fearful of disrupting the delicate party alliance between the North and South, President Andrew Jackson in 1835 endorsed the suppression of abolitionist literature being sent to the South. In addition to this attempt to deflect abolitionist criticism of the South, Southern members of the House of Representatives supported by significant numbers of Northern representatives successfully passed a "gag rule" that automatically tabled several antislavery petitions that appeared from 1836 to 1844.

Outside New England, however, Garrison's message of immediatism and nonviolence was finding a receptive audience in places such as upstate New York, Pennsylvania, and the Old Northwest. The success and spread of immediatism outside New England was due in large part to the American Anti-Slavery Society. Founded in 1833, the society's executive office was located in New York City, which became a hub of antislavery activity. The New York office employed traveling speakers, distributed literature, coordinated petition drives, and published the widely read weekly *Emancipator*. By 1837, 145 local societies had formed in Massachusetts, while neighboring New York saw nearly double that number of local organizations. Ohioans also saw strong support for abolitionism within their borders, with more than 200 active societies. The following year, the American Anti-Slavery Society consisted of 1,350 local affiliates with approximately a quarter of a million members.

As antislavery groups spread across the North, their resolute message and moral absolutism made them the targets of verbal threats and personal assaults. Particularly alarming to many Northerners and Southerners was the praise many abolitionists bestowed upon a pantheon of African-American liberators, including Denmark Vesey, Nat Turner, and Joseph Cinque. The bestowal of such praise, however, was not without consequences. Crowds of pro-slavery men were easily incited to violent action against abolitionists to protect "their freedoms" against a group

of zealous reformers whose principal objective seemed to be the destruction of a lawful and ordered society. Further fanning the flames was the widespread assertion that abolitionists were encouraging interracial marriage and other practices that cut across society's color caste. Political cartoonist Edward W. Clay's work "Practical Amalgamation" reflected these fears by depicting Garrisonian abolitionists as self-gratifying opportunists whose reforms of civil equality would ultimately lead to miscegenation.

It was not long before the leaders of the movement became the targets of angry reprisals. A New York mob ransacked Tappan's house in 1834. The severity of these attacks steadily increased. The following year in Boston, Garrison barely escaped lynching by an angry crowd. Elijah P. Lovejoy, an editor and Presbyterian minister, was not so fortunate. In November 1837, an angry crowd gathered outside the Godfrey & Gilman warehouse in Alton, Illinois, vowing to destroy his antislavery newspaper operations. When Lovejoy climbed to the roof to try and put out the fire set by the mob, he was fatally shot.

Public reaction to Lovejoy's death was swift and emphatic. On December 8, 1837, nearly 5,000 Bostonians packed Faneuil Hall to demonstrate against Lovejoy's murder. U.S. Attorney General James T. Austin surprised the crowd gathered by denouncing Lovejoy for frightening slaveholders with his abolitionist message and suggesting that those who had murdered him had done so as a form of self-protection. The eloquent abolitionist and attorney Wendell Phillips responded to Austin on behalf of abolitionists, drawing an analogy between Lovejoy and those who died in the Boston Massacre. These were the men, Phillips decreed, who were the true patriots and martyrs of liberty. Phillips's words carried the day and helped to galvanize Northern sentiment in the months that followed.

Lovejoy's murder shocked the conscience of many moderate Americans who had previously been unmoved by the sporadic violence witnessed in 1834 and 1835. It also bespoke the violence that lay just beneath the surface of the movement as it developed. Countless numbers of the nation's citizens, alarmed by the death of a Protestant cleric at the hands of pro-slavery advocates, went on the defensive against the South. But within the abolitionist movement Lovejoy's death signaled a change in temperament. Now more than ever before, proponents of abolitionism saw the need to abandon Garrisonian principles of nonviolence in order to adopt methods and approaches that would directly confront the powers that be in the South. The following year, Quaker and long-time Garrison supporter John Greenleaf Whittier's publication *Ballads and Anti-Slavery Poems* reflected the evolving character of the movement with poems such as "Stanzas for the Times" and "The Moral Warfare." With new agitators for abolition airing their claims in the aftermath of Lovejoy's death, the 1840s witnessed a shift in focus of the abolitionist debate.

"RIGHTEOUS VIOLENCE" AND THE SPLINTERING OF ANTISLAVERY REFORM

By 1840, abolitionism had become a formidable social force in the North, but abolitionists were not of one mind concerning the trajectory of reform. Massachusetts had emerged as the most radical antislavery state in the Union and was the home of many prominent non-Garrisonian abolitionists, including Henry Wilson and Charles Sumner, two of the strongest antislavery senators in Congress. Partly fueled by the popularity of evangelical revivalism, which closely tied human sin to acts of individual and social reform, the cause of abolitionism also found receptive audiences in areas of Ohio and upstate New York. Geographical expanse led to a greater diversity of abolitionist sentiment, which, in turn, raised questions concerning the timing and method of securing antislavery reform.

Lovejoy's murder brought to the surface divisions that had been brewing between Garrisonians, abolitionists, and evangelical reformers for several years. Deep divisions between evangelicals and Garrisonians had occurred the previous year following a literary polemic carried out between Garrison and the prominent divine Lyman Beecher. That year Beecher had persuaded associations of Congregational clerics in Connecticut and Massachusetts to exclude from their pulpits speakers with "erroneous and questionable views" concerning scriptural interpretation. Then in 1836 he addressed the Presbyterian General Assembly, dissuading members from holding any discussion concerning slavery. Garrison interpreted these efforts as a sign of the spiritual lifelessness of all Northern churches. By midsummer, he responded to these tactics by publishing three separate articles in *The Liberator* attacking Beecher. Garrison suggested that Beecher was all too ready to denounce Sabbath-breaking while overlooking Southern slaveholders' disregard for not only the Fourth Commandment, but the entirety of Mosaic Law. The following year, well-respected clerical abolitionists within the Massachusetts Anti-Slavery Society, including Henry B. Stanton,

Elizur Wright Jr., and Charles T. Torrey, challenged Garrison on his assertions of religious orthodoxy.

Throughout the decade, Garrison and his followers grew increasingly radical in their calls for reform. Unlike other abolitionist constituencies, Garrisonians admitted both women and African Americans into their membership while becoming increasingly antagonistic toward most denominations, which they believed had sullied the Gospel message in order to preserve their social status and organizational structures. True to this spirit, Garrison condemned all human governments as resting on immoral forces, and in 1843, he denounced the U.S. Constitution as a proslavery document. He went so far as to call upon Northerners to dissolve the Union to terminate its sinful support of the slave South. These antislavery reformers also adhered to their namesake's principle of nonviolence, arguing that it was the only means to bring about social change.

Although many of these positions were unpopular, support for Garrison remained strong and was evident when he and several hundred supporters gathered at Marlboro Chapel on September 20, 1838, to lend their support to the formation of the New England Non-Resistant Society. Garrison heralded the day's events as the opening of a new epoch in human history in which the existing civil order would one day be overthrown by spiritually regenerate subjects peacefully working for the social good. Like the rhetoric he so frequently championed, Garrison's reform efforts challenged prevailing standards of public morality by offering an alternative vision to accepted social norms. These views found pockets of staunch support in areas such as New York City, Massachusetts, Pennsylvania, and Ohio but overall alienated both evangelical reformers working for the cause of immediate abolition and those who advocated political, even violent, overthrow of the South's "slaveocracy." Ever-increasing numbers of reformers were not persuaded by Garrison's willingness to sacrifice social and political expediency for what many considered his obtuse moral absolutism.

These philosophical differences were compounded by frequent episodes of violence against abolitionists, limited opposition by Northerners to slavery, and the immediate failures of the 1835 postal campaign; an effort headed by Garrisonian abolitionists who flooded the nation's mails with vociferous tracts calling for the immediate end of slavery. In the hopes of avoiding a national debate, external pressures helped to splinter the antislavery movement into several factions, raising doubts about the abilities and leadership of the founding generation of antislavery agitators. Greater numbers of abolitionists began to question the expediency of rejecting political engagement as was advocated by an earlier generation of abolitionists. With the election of Abigail Kelley Foster, a nonresistant feminist, to the executive business committee of the American Anti-Slavery Society, Lewis Tappan led evangelicals out of the organization to the rival American and Foreign Anti-Slavery Society in 1840, leaving the original organization greatly diminished in both its constituency and powers of persuasion among religious groups.

In its most extreme expression, evangelicalism prodded individuals into sanctifying every aspect of daily life, making them sensitive not only to their own sins and those of society, but also, acutely so, to the hypocrisy found among many churches when it had come to African Americans. For many, slavery was incompatible with the will of God and the national calling; more than this, they believed that if this practice continued, God would exact retribution upon the nation. Such a consistent and thorough articulation of antislavery reform and Christian belief was best exemplified in individuals like Arthur and Lewis Tappan, Theodore Dwight Weld, and James G. Birney. With the breakup of the American Anti-Slavery Society, Lewis Tappan, a wealthy New York City businessman and evangelical reformer, led the American and Foreign Anti-Slavery Society. From 1840 to 1855, this organization focused its efforts on reforming churches to take up the cause of abolition. These efforts proved to be successful as Wesleyan Methodists formally severed ties with the Methodist Episcopal Church in 1842, Free Presbyterians formed in 1846, and the American Baptist Free Mission Society was founded a year earlier. These organizations provided thousands of churchgoing activists a forum for exercising their religious convictions while alienating other abolitionists by their belief that ultimate success lay "mainly on the blessings of the Almighty."

Although abolitionists found some of their most vocal supporters among various Protestant denominations in the North, they also found some of their greatest detractors in these same circles. Many in the pew and behind the pulpit felt threatened by these antislavery reformers who demanded allegiance to abstract principles like the social equality of blacks and whites while vehemently denouncing the literal authority of the Bible that appeared to affirm the practice of slavery. For many churchgoers, eradicating the unpleasant practices associated with the institution of slavery, not the institution in and of itself, was the

target of their reform concerns. A paternalism couched in racist assumptions allowed many of the nation's faithful to worry about efforts to Christianize slaves rather than systemic reforms that would secure their freedom. So common was this tack that in 1849 Frederick Douglass felt compelled to counsel his sympathetic largely white audience, "There are many Madison Washingtons and Nathaniel Turners in the South who would assert their rights to liberty, if you would take your feet from their necks, and your sympathy and aid from their oppressors."

Equally alarming for some was the debate among immediatists during the decade concerning acceptable forms of violence to secure immediatism. With greater frequency abolitionists agitated for reform at any cost, even to the point of disunion. In 1843, at the National Negro convention in Buffalo, New York, Presbyterian minister Henry Highland Garnet addressed the crowd, admonishing slaves in the South to "resist" and "torment the God-cursed slaveholders." That same year church leaders condemned Garrison, who burned a copy of the Constitution charging it as a proslavery tract that had led the nation into "a covenant with death, and an agreement with Hell." Even Joshua Leavitt, one-time editor of the *New York Evangelist* and leader of the fledgling Liberty Party, maintained that slaves had a "God-given" manhood to lead revolts against their oppressors. Other radical political abolitionists, Gerrit Smith and Garnet, would evoke a similar refrain.

As the nation's politics became more embroiled in debates over the issue of slavery, many denominational leaders in the North became increasingly weary of such rhetorical jousts and guarded about the forums in which abolitionists could air their message. Editors of the nation's religious weeklies were hostile to the message of immediatism, leading to the development of abolitionist weeklies. Periodicals such as the *Antislavery Bugle* served as an essential organizational tool for antislavery groups, particularly in rural areas of the Western Reserve of Ohio. Garrisonians soon realized that abolitionist literature, such as *The Liberator,* could not puncture the mass of indifference encompassing the nation's churches. As an alternative to the medium of the religious weeklies, abolitionists carried their message to the masses by developing a system of traveling agents to address audiences directly.

By the end of the decade, abolitionism had undergone several major developments. With the creation of new and ideologically diverse societies within the movement, abolitionism was able to attract a more diverse constituency. Those who later championed their own reform efforts, such as Elizabeth Cady Stanton and women's rights, or Frederick Douglass with the calls for civil rights, found a home in the abolitionist movement of the 1840s. The movement had also grown to accommodate those with differing religious convictions concerning issues of government and strong-arm reform. But perhaps most important was the movement's increasing participation in the political process, which forever changed the landscape of American politics in the nineteenth century.

THE LIBERTY PARTY: PARTY POLITICS OF THE 1840S AND 1850S

Outraged over the censure of abolitionist petitions before Congress, dissident Whigs and Democrats from the North began to agitate the body politic to entertain questions concerning abolitionism. These calls for direct political engagement grew louder as slave unrest in the South increased in the 1830s. The political response took shape in the formation of two groups, the Liberty Party and the Free Soil Party. This development also illustrated the concessions made by an earlier generation of abolitionists like Garrison who, while refusing to cast a vote himself for political parties or candidates, urged younger abolitionists and Americans in general to endorse antislavery ballots. Leading the way for political activity were abolitionists such as Alvan Stewart and Myron Holley of western New York. By 1840, these men had grown disillusioned with abolitionist arguments concerning moral persuasion, which inspired them to officially organize a political party among abolitionists. In April of that year, the newly formed Liberty Party nominated James G. Birney, a former slaveholder, for president. The party platform included a call to end the domestic slave trade, a restriction of slavery in the territories, and the abolition of slavery in the District of Columbia and all territories where the federal government had jurisdiction. Additional support for Birney came from Massachusetts politicians Joshua Leavitt and Henry B. Chase.

Birney garnered only 7,056 votes out of a total 2,411,187 popular votes. Following the presidential election of 1840, the party gained the support of Ohio abolitionist Salmon P. Chase. Soon, the leadership of the party changed hands as Smith, William Goodell, and Douglass became the party's leading spokesmen. The party's central mouthpiece, *Principia,* was edited in New York City and helped to shape the party's constituency in Massachusetts, New York, and Ohio.

During the presidential election of 1844, the Liberty Party once again nominated Birney as its candidate to run against the Democratic candidate James K. Polk and the Whig nominee Henry Clay. This time Birney received 65,608 votes out of a total 2,871,906 popular votes. While the party's efforts captured only 16,000 votes in the state of New York, Birney's candidacy captured enough of the popular vote in the state to thwart the Whig Party's efforts, ultimately allowing the Democrats to carry New York and win the election. Polk's pro-slavery policies, which included the annexation of Texas, resulting in the Mexican War, seemed to confirm earlier claims by the leaders of the Liberty Party that a Slave Power Conspiracy had usurped republican principles.

With these developments it appeared that Northern institutions were ultimately threatened by the South's "peculiar institution." Liberty Party abolitionists from New York and Massachusetts rejected Garrisonian nonresistance and the assertion that the Constitution was a pro-slavery document. Furthermore, under the leadership of Garnet and Douglass, the party supported direct intervention against slavery in the border South and suggested that the Constitution made slavery illegal throughout the United States.

Ohio constituents of the party were more moderate in their calls for political change. Unlike their Eastern counterparts, Western leaders distinguished between abolitionism as a moral position and the Liberty Party as a conventional political party. This element of the party differed from Easterners by maintaining that the proper objective of the party was to denationalize slavery by abolishing it in those areas of Congress's jurisdiction. By 1846, the Liberty Party was adrift. With the Wilmot Proviso's call to contain, not abolish, slavery, party members split over taking a harder abolitionist position or appealing to a broader coalition. The party became leaderless, bringing about its demise shortly thereafter.

In its place emerged the Free Soil Party, which was formed under the direction of "Barnburner" Democrats from New York (a radical faction of the party that developed the free labor arguments under the direction of John Van Buren, son of Martin Van Buren, whose commitment to social and monetary reforms was likened to a farmer's burning his barn to rid it of rats), radical antislavery Whigs, and Liberty Party supporters. Though having no former ties to its political predecessor, this group included old Liberty Party stalwarts who eventually followed Stanton, Leavitt, and Wright into the Free Soil Party in 1848.

The two factions of Free Soilers met with Liberty Party representatives in Buffalo in 1848 and forwarded Martin Van Buren as their presidential candidate. In the February 2, 1849, edition of *The Liberator*, Phillips reportedly made the following comment on the leadership of the abolitionist movement: "look upon the Free Soil movement as the unavoidable result of our principles and agitation." Others were not so pleased with recent political developments. At the close of the decade, George Whipple wrote to Smith, suggesting that to vote Free Soil was "to sin against God and incur his displeasure."

Shifting political alliances had led many Western abolitionists to submerge their abolitionist identity into weaker antislavery principles. Many abolitionists would become key members of the Republican Party in later years. The formation of the Liberty Party and its envelopment by Free Soilers forever changed the landscape of the antislavery movement in America. For the first time an antislavery candidate and platform had attracted the support of thousands of Northerners, helping to sunder the wings of the North's major parties. But this development alienated many abolitionists who were dismayed by the Free Soil Party's refusal to include equal social and political rights for African Americans in their platform. By the close of the decade, Lewis Tappan and many of his followers rebuffed these developments, arguing that concerns for party politics had detracted from the moral and religious aspects of the cause.

ABOLITIONISM AND GENDER IN THE 1840s AND 1850s

No less important to the development and character of abolitionism in American society in the 1840s and 1850s was the issue of gender in the movement. Like those issues concerning nonviolence, abolitionism and denominationalism, and the appropriation of party politics in order to secure reforms, conceptions of gender were ever present in the dialogue of nineteenth-century abolitionists. Among certain sectors of abolitionism, women in the movement played a prominent role in shaping the direction of reform. In structural and theoretical terms, it has been suggested that immediate abolitionism during the 1830s and early 1840s served as a precursor to and testing for the women's rights movement, which was formalized at Seneca Falls, New York, in 1848. Among sectors of Garrisonians in the late 1830s, many women enjoyed full participation in the movement, including political action, acts of moral suasion, and the liberation of slaves. So compelling was the working relationship of female abolitionists to their male counterparts that some, with varying levels of consistency, began to conceptualize and embrace new feminized constructions of masculinity. Although the practices of abolitionists often dramatically failed to mirror the rhetoric of abolitionists, the movement's grappling with these issues on various fronts gave women a platform on which to frame issues and develop their abilities as social reformers.

Prior to the 1840s and 1850s, male and female abolitionists largely maintained separate spheres in carrying out their reform efforts. Indicative of gender constructions of the day that firmly distinguished between the working spheres of men and women, female abolitionists carried out efforts for immediatism through their own emancipation networks. As the paragons of Christian piety, women were actively involved in social reform efforts that sought to secure Protestant America's "Benevolent Empire." Immediate abolition, however, was one activity that fell outside the permissible boundaries of social reform because it threatened to overturn both racial and gender assumptions structuring the social order. Women who engaged in such activities were viewed as particularly threatening and were often ridiculed by both pro-slavery forces and those weary of loosening patriarchal controls. Despite these formidable obstacles and the increasing threat of violence being perpetrated against those espousing abolitionism, some individuals—such as Elizabeth Chandler, a Quaker from Delaware, Maria W. Stewart, an African American from Boston, and Lucretia Mott, a Quaker preacher from Philadelphia—rose to the cause.

Elizabeth Chandler's earliest and primary contribution to the abolitionist movement was as a contributing columnist to Benjamin Lundy's *Genius of Universal Emancipation*. As her reputation grew, Chandler organized female antislavery groups in both Philadelphia and Michigan, appealing to prevailing assumptions about a woman's superior moral disposition and potential abilities for moral suasion. Stewart, a contemporary of Chandler, had a brief but notable career as an advocate for her race. In 1833 and at the young age of twenty-six, Stewart stood before a Masonic lodge of African Americans urging them to actively engage in the antislavery cause. The young African American's comments boldly addressed the moral indifference some Northern blacks had demonstrated toward Southern blacks and the institution of slavery. But more poignantly the speech, delivered

SOJOURNER TRUTH (c. 1797–1883)

Sojourner Truth was born in Ulster County, New York, the daughter of slaves of a wealthy Dutch owner, and was originally called Isabella. Her first language was Dutch. She was sold several times and was forced into a marriage with a fellow slave. Between 1810 and 1827, she bore at least five children to him, at least three of whom were sold to other slaveholders. Just before New York State abolished slavery in 1827, she ran away and found refuge with Isaac Van Wagener, a Quaker, who took her in and whose name she took. With the help of Quaker friends, she waged a court battle in which she recovered her small son, who had been sold illegally into slavery in the South. In about 1829, she went to New York City with her two youngest children, supporting herself through domestic employment for the next several years.

In 1843, she left New York City and was introduced to abolitionism at a utopian community in Northampton, Massachusetts, and thereafter spoke in behalf of the movement throughout the state. She also took the name Sojourner Truth, which she used from then on. Obeying a supernatural call to "travel up and down the land," she embraced evangelical religion and began her career of street-corner preaching, insisting her listeners accept the biblical message of God's goodness and turn away from sins, including slavery. Though illiterate, she demonstrated a wide knowledge of the Bible. Six feet tall and wearing a white turban and gray dress that accentuated her skin color, she made a striking figure at antislavery and women's rights meetings. Her witty, direct sayings delivered in a Dutch accent only increased interest in her, bringing her greater popularity.

In 1850, Truth traveled throughout the Midwest. The following year, at a women's rights convention in Akron, Ohio, she gave her famous speech, "Ain't I a Woman," challenging the notion that men were superior to women. Encouraged by other women leaders, notably Lucretia Mott, she continued to appear before suffrage gatherings for the rest of her life.

In the 1850s, Truth settled in Battle Creek, Michigan. At the beginning of the American Civil War, she gathered supplies for black volunteer regiments in Michigan, and in 1864 she went to Washington, D.C., where she helped integrate streetcars and was received at the White House by President Abraham Lincoln. That same year, she accepted an appointment with the National Freedmen's Relief Association counseling former slaves, particularly in matters of resettlement. After the war, she supported herself by selling copies of her book, *Narrative of Sojourner Truth* (1850), which she had dictated to Olive Gilbert. She continued working for women's suffrage and initiated a petition drive to obtain land for former slaves. As late as the 1870s she encouraged the migration of freedmen to Kansas and Missouri. In 1875, she retired to her home in Battle Creek, where she died on November 26, 1883.

James G. Lewis

by a woman, confronted the prevailing gender assumptions concerning public leadership in Northern society. Alarmed by such rhetoric, the black community in Boston drove Stewart out of town, thereby ending her brief career as a public speaker for antislavery.

One of the more formidable figures to emerge within female abolitionist circles during these early years was Lucretia Mott. Known as the "Black Man's Goddess," Mott entered the antislavery movement by way of her Quakerism, which initially led her to boycott all slave-made products and goods. Meeting William Lloyd Garrison in 1830, Mott took up Garrison's call for nonviolent reform and immediatism. She was one of four women present at the inaugural meeting of the American Anti-Slavery Society the following year. Nearly a decade later, in May 1841, Garrison appointed Mott to serve on the executive committee of the society. In addition to these duties, Mott continued to campaign for antislavery reform before the public, basing her argument on the theological conviction that humans were fashioned in the image of God and should be accorded such value regardless of the color of their skin. She preached this message for over three decades in the District of Columbia and areas of Maryland and Virginia. Her continuous work for antislavery reform gained Mott much notoriety, particularly among black abolitionists who admired her zeal for the cause. Despite these alliances, Mott remained true to her nonviolent principles, and she parted with other abolitionists like Frederick Douglass who openly supported John Brown's raid on Harpers Ferry in 1859.

Female abolitionists figured prominently in the movement by the 1840s. Critical to the rise of the feminist voice within the movement was Garrison's and other abolitionists' espousal of nonresistance and its implicit indictment of physical force, which leading female voices in the movement directly associated with women's "domestic slavery" and society's patriarchy. Two of the movement's earliest feminist voices were those of Angelina and Sarah Grimké, who in 1837 went on a speaking tour sponsored by Garrison. Central to the Grimkés' message was their renouncement of their slaveholding origins in South Carolina and their conversion to Quaker principles in Philadelphia.

Some women such as the Grimkés assumed leadership roles within the movement, but their criticism of patriarchy often fell upon deaf ears. Moreover, factions within the abolitionist movement resisted women's overtures to promote the cause of women under the larger canopy of abolitionism. Such sentiment was evident at the 1840 World Anti-Slavery Convention in London when Lucretia Mott and Elizabeth Cady Stanton were banished to the women's balcony during the meetings. As a sign of protest, Garrison joined the two stalwarts of the feminist cause in the balcony rather than the male delegates on the floor of the hall.

In neighboring Philadelphia, antislavery reform was structured along gender lines. Organized in the same year as the American Anti-Slavery Society, the Philadelphia Female Anti-Slavery Society was headed by Mott, Mary Grew, and Sarah Pugh. Still another state organization growing out of the Garrison movement was the Pennsylvania Anti-Slavery Society headed by James and Lucretia Mott and J. Miller McKim. In neighboring New York State, several fledgling Garrisonian groups emerged. These groups of abolitionists often differed on points of procedure or emphasis but were united in their efforts on the main objectives of the abolitionist crusade.

As women assumed greater prominence in the abolitionist movement, their roles in the reform movement diversified. One area of work open to them was the Underground Railroad, first established in 1838 by white students attending Mission Institute in Quincy, Illinois. Shortly thereafter, two other networks were quickly up and running, bringing escaped slaves from the West to Canada. Though not well known in her day, Harriet Tubman is perhaps the best remembered agent of the network. After escaping slavery in 1849, she became an active agent in the Underground Railroad in the 1850s, helping to liberate more than 300 slaves from Maryland. Tubman's commitment to the cause of liberation was beyond question: she returned to the land of her bondage as many as nineteen times. Tubman followed in the steps of others such as Thomas Smallwood who participated in the liberation

In this painting by Michigan artist R.D. Bayley, President Abraham Lincoln shows abolitionist Sojourner Truth the Bible given him by the African-American community of Baltimore in 1864. *(Library of Congress)*

of Southern slaves in 1842–1843. Torrey was eventually arrested for these efforts and was given a six-year prison term in the Maryland Penitentiary, where he died in 1846.

Tubman's fame as an African-American abolitionist was surpassed only by that of Sojourner Truth. A former illiterate slave, Truth began her career auspiciously as a member of a religious sect, the Kingdom of Matthias, which was led by the self-styled prophet Robert Matthews. On the day of Pentecost in 1843, Truth felt called by the Holy Spirit to preach, exhorting others to embrace the Gospel message. Taking the name "Sojourner Truth," she made her way from New York City to Northampton, Massachusetts, where she met social reformers, including antislavery activists such as Frederick Douglass. Quickly embraced within these circles, Truth made a career

SPEECH BY SOJOURNER TRUTH
WOMEN'S RIGHTS CONVENTION, 1851

The following is a speech by Sojourner Truth presented at the Women's Rights Convention, 1851, in Akron, Ohio, as recalled by Frances Gage. Born Isabella Baumfree to slave parents in a Dutch-speaking settlement in Ulster, New York, Truth became a leading African-American advocate for abolition and women's rights.

"Wall, chilern, whar dar is so much racket dar must be somethin' out o' kilter. I tink dat 'twixt de niggers of de Souf and de womin at de Nork, all talkin' 'bout rights, de white men will be in a fix pretty soon. But what's all dis here talkin' 'bout?

"Dat man ober dar say dat womin needs to be helped into carriages, and lifted ober ditches, and to hab de best place everywhar. Nobody eber helps me into carriages, or ober mud-puddles, or gibs me any best place!" And raising herself to her full height, and her voice to a pitch like rolling thunders, she asked "And a'n't I a woman? Look at me! Look at me! Look at my arm! (and she bared her right arm to the shoulder, showing her tremendous muscular power). I have ploughed, and planted, and gathered into barns, and no man could head me! And a'n't I a woman? I could work as much and eat as much as a man—when I could get it—and bear de lash a well! And a'n't I a woman? I have borne thirteen chilern, and seen 'em mos' all sold off to slavery, and when I cried out with my mother's grief, none but Jesus heard me! And a'n't I a woman?

"Den dey talks 'bout dis ting in de head; what dis dey call it?" ("Intellect," whispered some one near.) "Dat's it, honey. What's dat got to do wid womin's rights or nigger's rights? If my cup won't hold but a pint, and yourn holds a quart, wouldn't ye be mean not to let me have my little half-measure full?" And she pointed her significant finger, and sent a keen glance at the minister who had made the argument. The cheering was long and loud.

"Den dat little man in black dar, he say women can't have as much rights as men, 'cause Christ wan't a woman! Whar did your Christ come from?" Rolling thunder couldn't have stilled that crowd, as did those deep, wonderful tones, as she stood there with out-stretched arms and eyes of fire. Raising her voice still louder, she repeated, "Whar did your Christ come from? From God and a woman! Man had nothin' to do wid Him." Oh, what a rebuke that was to that little man.

Turning again to another objector, she took up the defense of Mother Eve. I can not follow her through it all. It was pointed, and witty, and solemn; eliciting at almost every sentence deafening applause; and she ended by asserting: "If de fust woman God ever made was strong enough to turn de world upside down all alone, dese women togedder (and she glanced her eye over the platform) ought to be able to turn it back, and get it right side up again! And now dey is asking to do it, de men better let 'em." Long-continued cheering greeted this. "Bleeged to ye for hearin' on me, and now old Sojourner han't got nothin' more to say."

Amid roars of applause, she returned to her corner, leaving more than one of us with streaming eyes, and hearts beating with gratitude. She had taken us up in her strong arms and carried us safely over the slough of difficulty turning the whole tide in our favor. I have never in my life seen anything like the magical influence that subdued the mobbish spirit of the day, and turned the sneers and jeers of an excited crowd into notes of respect and admiration. Hundreds rushed up to shake hands with her, and congratulate the glorious old mother, and bid her God-speed on her mission of "testifyin' agin concerning the wickedness of this 'ere people."

Source: Elizabeth Cady Stanton, Matilda Joslyn Gage, and Susan B. Anthony, *History of Woman Suffrage,* vol. 1 (New York: Fowler and Wells, 1881).

preaching and addressing large audiences concerning her enslavement. Her popularity increased with the publication of her autobiography, *Narrative of Sojourner Truth,* in 1850. At the women's rights convention in Akron, Ohio, in 1851, Truth's public image as an abolitionist and advocate of women's rights was secured in a legendary speech. During the Civil War, she aided in the enlistment of African-American troops, administered to the wounded, and continued to advocate for equal rights at the highest levels of the United States government.

The tireless work of women such as Mott, Truth, and Tubman challenged both the prevailing gender assumptions of the day and paternalism governing race relations. Although some members of the Garrisonian camp were skeptical about these efforts and their limited effects, other abolitionists were inspired by the heroic efforts taking place in the Border States.

Like no other effort by abolitionist women, the Underground Railroad exacerbated deeply held fears among Southern whites concerning the ties between Northern abolitionists and slaves.

SECTIONALISM, VIOLENCE, AND POLITICAL OPPOSITION IN THE 1850s

Other significant developments in the 1840s would shape abolitionism in the decade that followed. One of these developments was the growing division between black and white abolitionists over the measures necessary to end slavery. At the Buffalo Convention of Free People of Color in 1843, Henry Highland Garnet contradicted the Garrisonian doctrine of passive resistance by calling for slave revolts. Such open advocation of violence alienated many white evangelicals who sought antislavery reform. Two years later, Frederick Douglass galvanized abolitionist sentiment among African Americans, helping to nurture leaders within the black community with the publication of his autobiography, *Narrative of the Life of Frederick Douglass,* which detailed his life as a slave in Maryland. Douglass's compelling autobiography was such a success that it propelled him into the limelight, giving the former slave unprecedented public appeal for an African American. By 1847, Douglass had broken his ties with white abolitionists and had launched his paper *The North Star,* in Rochester, New York. Stung by these developments, Garrison vilified Douglass before both abolitionists and the press. Increasingly, black abolitionists were developing independent leadership through participation in the Northern lecture circuit and the publication of slave narratives like Douglass's. This internal divisiveness, however, was but one reflection of the volatile atmosphere immersing abolitionists during the 1850s.

Violence, or the support of violence as a means to bring about slavery's end, shaped the 1850s. In May 1854, the Kansas-Nebraska Act repealed the Missouri Compromise of 1820, opening up the Nebraska country to settlement on the basis of popular sovereignty and undoing the sectional truce of 1850. Political realignments of territories concerning popular sovereignty helped to usher in the fight for "Bleeding Kansas," an era of American politics in which questions over territorial expansion were irreducible from the national debate over slavery. In April 1854, the New England Emigrant Aid Society was formed to colonize Free Soilers in Kansas, arousing pro-slavery opposition. In 1856, pro-slavery border ruffians from Missouri attacked the town of Lawrence, Kansas. On

JOHN BROWN EXHIBITING HIS HANGMAN!

In this imaginary scene, the martyred John Brown returns from the grave to hang Confederate president Jefferson Davis. In reality, Davis was imprisoned for two years after the Civil War, indicted—but never tried—for treason, and released in 1867. *(Library of Congress)*

May 24, 1856, John Brown staged a massacre at Pottawatomie Creek. In 1857, tensions erupted over the *Dred Scott* decision offered by the U.S. Supreme Court, which declared the Missouri Compromise unconstitutional on the grounds that Congress had no right to enact a law depriving persons of property in the territories of the United States. In this climate of rising violence, some abolitionists became more militant in their message and means of carrying out their reforms.

Abolitionists openly defied the Fugitive Slave Law of 1850 on several occasions. In February 1851, only one month after the law had gone into effect, a black mob stormed a Boston courtroom to rescue a fugitive slave known as Shadrack. White and black abolitionists in the area applauded these efforts, and later that same year two similar attempts were made

THOMAS HAMILTON ON THE JOHN BROWN TRIAL AND THE NAT TURNER REBELLION, 1859

Thomas Hamilton, the publisher of The Weekly Anglo-African, *an influential black newspaper in New York, writes on the relationship between the John Brown trial and execution and the Nat Turner rebellion.*

There are two reasons why we present our readers with the "Confessions of Nat Turner." First, to place upon record this most remarkable episode in the history of human slavery, which proves to the philosophic observer that in the midst of this most perfectly contrived and apparently secure system of slavery, humanity will out, and engender from its bosom, forces that will contend against oppression, however unsuccessfully; and secondly, that the two methods of Nat Turner and of John Brown may be compared. The one is the mode in which the slave seeks freedom for his fellow, and the other mode in which the white man seeks to free the slave. There are many points of similarity between these two men: they were both idealists; both governed by their views of the teachings of the Bible; both had harbored for years the purpose to which they gave up their lives; both felt themselves *obeyed* as by some divine, or at least, spiritual impulse; the one seeking in the air, the earth, and the heavens for signs which came at last; and the other, obeying impulses which he believes to have been fore-ordained from the eternal past; both cool, calm, and heroic in prison and in the prospect of inevitable death; both confess with child-like frankness and simplicity the object they had in view—the pure and simple emancipations of their fellow men, both win from the judges who sentenced them, expressions of deep sympathy—and here the parallel ceases. Nat Turner's terrible logic could only see the enfranchisement of one race, compassed by the extirpation of the other; and he followed his glory syllogism with rude exactitude. John Brown, believing that the freedom of the enthralled could only be effecting by placing them on an equality with the enslavers, and unable in the very effort at emancipation to tyrannize himself, is moved with compassion for tyrants, as well as slave, and seeks to extirpate this formidable cancer, without spilling one drop of Christian blood.

These two narratives present a fearful choice to the slaveholders, nay, to this great nation—which of the two modes of emancipation shall take place? The method of Nat Turner, or the method of John Brown?

Emancipation must take place, and soon. There can be no long delay in the choice of methods. If Joe Brown's be not soon adopted by the free North, then Nat Turner's will be by the enslaved South.

Had the order of events been reversed—had Nat Turner been in John Brown's place at the head of these twenty-one men, governed by his inexorable logic and cool daring, the soil of Virginia and Maryland and the far South would by this time be drenched in blood and the wild and sanguinary course of these men, no earthly power could stay.

The course which the South is now frantically pursuing will engender in its bosom and nurse into maturity a hundred Nat Turners, whom Virginia is infinitely less able to resist in 1860, than she was in 1831.

So, people of the South, people of the North! Men and brethren, Men and brethren, choose ye which method of emancipation you prefer—Nat Turner's, or John Brown's?

Source: The Weekly Anglo-African, [New York], December 31, 1859.

---

in Christiana, Pennsylvania, and Syracuse, New York. Both efforts to free fugitive slaves were met with stiff resistance, and in Pennsylvania, three African Americans and one slaveholder were dead in the aftermath of these efforts. Similar episodes took place later in the decade once again in Boston and also in Oberlin, Ohio.

Abolitionists employed yet other means to loosen the grip of slavery on the South. In Kentucky and Virginia efforts to establish free-labor colonies were made in 1854. Delia Webster, a former member of the Underground Railroad and a native of Vermont, traveled to northern Kentucky to establish one such colony. Webster encountered stiff resistance by locals, which limited her progress. After four years, she enlisted the help of Lewis Tappan. In 1855, John G. Fee, an evangelical and abolitionist from Kentucky, started a similar colony in nearby Berea. With the support of the American Missionary Association, founded by Tappan, George Whipple, and Simon Jocelyn in 1846, Fee's efforts met with some success. An ostensibly nonsectarian group, the association helped to organize antislavery churches in the western United States and founded Berea College that same year. Eli Thayer and John C. Underwood undertook similar efforts in Virginia. In the late 1850s, these men organized a free-labor colony at Ceredo, in the northwestern portion of the state.

Although these efforts evoked the disdain of many Southerners, no event captured the attention of the nation more or raised greater fear in the hearts of Southerners than John Brown's raid at Harpers Ferry, Virginia, on October 16, 1859. Three years earlier Brown and his five sons had moved to Kansas, eventually joining the Pottawatomie Rifles in the Free Soil defense of Kansas. On May 24 and 25, 1856, the "Pottawatomie massacre" took place in which five pro-slavery men were killed with broadswords by Brown's men. In just two weeks following the event, the play *Osawatomie Brown* appeared on Broadway. This event helped to trigger guerrilla warfare throughout Kansas, which lasted throughout the fall. In the months that followed, Brown and his sons established the Kansas Regulars, taking up a career fighting in both Kansas and Missouri.

With his popularity on the rise, Brown returned East in October 1856, to secure funds for his military exploits out West. He briefly returned to Kansas two years later, where he launched an invasion into Missouri, killing a slave owner and freeing eleven slaves. Despite having a $200 bounty placed on his head, Brown returned East to continue his speaking tour. He delivered speeches in Ohio, New York, Massachusetts, and Connecticut while meeting with politicians such as Representative Joshua Giddings of Ohio and Senator Henry Wilson of Massachusetts. During this time Brown met with the "Secret Six," who helped to subsidize Brown's campaign into Virginia, Gerrit Smith being one of the leading financiers.

That summer Brown visited his home in North Elba, New York, for the last time. After saying good-bye to his wife and family, Brown and his two sons, Oliver and Owen, reached Harpers Ferry in July 1859. They rented a farm in Maryland expecting large numbers of abolitionists to join their army. By mid-September, only eighteen recruits had arrived. Disappointed but not deterred, Brown and his men took up their self-declared abolitionist cause on Sunday, October 16. Two days later, the siege in Virginia was over. For his crime, Brown was hanged on December 2, 1859. In the month between his sentencing and execution, Brown engaged in a correspondence campaign, creating his martyrdom in the minds of some and securing the threat of violent abolitionism among others.

CONCLUSION

Scholars have suggested that it was in the years following the election of Abraham Lincoln that abolitionism reached its zenith of power. This understanding is based on several significant developments that took place during the Secession Crisis and the Civil War. First, as Americans took to arms, Northern perceptions of abolitionism were transformed nearly overnight. Antislavery spokespersons were no longer perceived as fanatical leaders of a fringe and much despised movement, but were now viewed as respected critics of contemporary society. Next, those with abolitionist sentiment were able to merge with Free Soil Republicans who, prior to 1861, were committed to the geographical limitation and not the immediate extermination of slavery. Finally, Garrison's longstanding antislavery weekly, *The Liberator,* ceased publication in 1865 once the Northern forces had achieved victory and the Southern slaves had been emancipated.

Some scholars, however, have criticized this analysis on two crucial fronts. First, it does not take into account the rapid demise of the abolitionist cause for the equal rights of African Americans following the Civil War. Second, it places too great a weight on the United States government's conversion to abolitionism as truly a long-term commitment to African-American equality rather than a calculated move of military and political expediency. Despite these different perspectives, scholars acknowledge the achievements of the abolitionists themselves, particularly the social reforms abolitionists achieved in the 1840s and 1850s, which included the repeal of several Northern laws discriminating against blacks. In addition, the abolitionist movement of the 1840s and 1850s incorporated a wide spectrum of American society utilizing traditionally discriminated people—women and African Americans—as principal actors in their reform efforts. In this sense, abolitionism was an extremely radical social movement that profoundly shaped not only antebellum America, but also generations of Americans beyond.

Kent McConnell

BIBLIOGRAPHY

Bell, Howard H. "National Negro Conventions of the Middle 1840s: Moral Suasion vs. Political Action." *Journal of Negro History* 42: 4 (October 1957): 247–260.

Bender, Thomas, ed. *The Antislavery Debate: Capitalism and Abolitionism As a Problem of Historical Interpretation.* Berkeley: University of California Press, 1992.

Bretz, Julian P. "The Economic Background of the Liberty Party." *The America Historical Review* 34:2 (January 1929): 250–264.

Davis, David Brion. *The Problem of Slavery in Western Culture.* Ithaca, NY: Cornell University Press, 1966.

Foner, Eric. "Politics and Prejudice: The Free Soil Party and the Negro, 1849–1852." *Journal of Negro History* 50:4 (October 1965): 239–256.

Friedman, Lawrence J. "Confidence and Pertinacity in Evangelical Abolitionism: Lewis Tappan's Circle." *American Quarterly* 31:1 (Spring 1979): 81–106.

———. *Self and Community in American Abolitionism, 1830–1870.* Cambridge, MA: Cambridge University Press, 1982.

Goodheart, Lawrence B., and Hugh Hawkins, eds. *The Abolitionists: Means, Ends, and Motivations.* 3d ed. Lexington, MA: D.C. Heath, 1995.

Hammond, John L. "Revival Religion and Antislavery Politics." *American Sociological Review* 39:2 (April 1974): 175–186.

Harrold, Stanley. *American Abolitionists.* Essex, England: Pearson Education Limited, 2001.

Huston, James L. "The Experiential Basis of Northern Antislavery Impulse." *The Journal of Southern History* 56:4 (November 1990): 609–640.

May, Henry F. *The Enlightenment in America.* New York: Oxford University Press, 1976.

Mayer, Henry. *All on Fire: William Lloyd Garrison and the Abolition of Slavery.* New York: St. Martin's, 1998.

McKivigan, John R. *The War against Proslavery Religion: Abolitionism and the Northern Churches, 1830–1865.* Ithaca, NY: Cornell University Press, 1984.

Quarles, Benjamin. *Black Abolitionists.* New York: Oxford University Press, 1969.

Ripley, C. Peter, ed. *The Black Abolitionist Papers.* Vol. IV, *The United States, 1847–1858.* Chapel Hill: University of North Carolina Press, 1991.

Staudenraus, P.J. *The African Colonization Movement, 1816–1865.* New York: Columbia University Press, 1961.

Strong, Douglas M. *Perfectionist Politics: Abolitionism and the Religious Tensions of American Democracy.* Syracuse, NY: Syracuse University Press, 1999.

Walters, Ronald G. *American Reformers, 1815–1860.* New York: Hill and Wang, 1978.

———. *The Antislavery Appeal: American Abolitionism After 1830.* Baltimore, MD: Johns Hopkins University Press, 1976.

Wyatt-Brown, Bertram. *Lewis Tappan and the Evangelical War Against Slavery.* Cleveland, OH: Press of Case Western Reserve University, 1969.

Wyly-Jones, Susan. "The 1835 Anti-Abolition Meetings in the South: A New Look at the Controversy over the Abolition Postal Campaign." *Civil War History* 47 (December 2001): 289–309.

Moderate, Radical, and Militant Abolition

Although the terms *antislavery* and *abolition* are often used interchangeably, in reality they represent two vastly different movements. Antislavery efforts began during the colonial era, especially in the Quaker stronghold of Pennsylvania. The abolition movement developed much later, in the 1830s, only after black and white reformers came together in a full-scale attack upon human bondage.

Although various groups had argued for emancipation of the enslaved since before the American Revolution, earlier programs differed greatly from the program proposed by nineteenth-century abolitionists. To begin with, emancipationist proposals had called for gradual freedom that, supporters argued, would allow for time in which blacks could be "prepared" for independence. Abolitionists, in contrast, argued that slaves should be freed immediately. Also, emancipationists argued that the government should compensate slave owners for releasing their bondspeople. Immediatists, however, insisted that such proposals condoned slavery and tainted the government with the guilt of slave ownership. Finally, many emancipationists subscribed to the theory that, once freed, blacks must be relocated and settled in their own colonies, either in South or Central America, the unsettled territories in the American West, or Africa.

Garrison and the Black Community

Abolitionists disagreed. Though a few early African-American leaders such as Paul Cuffee and James Forten briefly flirted with the idea of repatriation, they quickly learned that the black masses were not interested in "returning" to a distant, unfamiliar continent. After learning this lesson, black leaders began to take the message to whites like William Lloyd Garrison, and together they turned the movement for gradual, conditional emancipation into one of immediate, unconditional freedom. A biracial crusade from the beginning, this new abolition movement drew upon the broader reform impulse of the antebellum years. It relied on evangelical Christianity, the idea of history as progress, and self-help in the black community to prove racial equality and earn freedom and citizenship for African Americans.

Garrison played a crucial role in transforming the antislavery movement into a crusade for immediate abolition. His working relationship with the free black community provided a major catalyst for this transformation. Like most white abolitionists, he began his antislavery career as a supporter of the American Colonization Society. By 1831, however, he was ready to accuse that group of "Persecution," "Falsehood," "Cowardice," and "Infidelity." Citing the American Colonization Society (ACS) periodical, *The African Repository*, speeches by slaveholding ACS supporters, and editorials from African-American newspapers, Garrison set out to prove that the society's work actually strengthened slavery by removing free blacks and that African Americans opposed colonization. In his 1832 book, *Thoughts on African Colonization*, he declared war on the society. Admitting that he had once supported colonization, he explained that his examination of the society's reports and journal had revealed "a conspiracy to send the free people of color to Africa under a benevolent pretence, but really that the slaves may be held more securely in bondage." He then expressed confidence that "the great mass of [ACS] supporters at the north did not realise its dangerous tendency," and that careful reasoning would convince the benevolent to abandon the colonization movement and join his crusade.

Throughout the 1830s, a number of white reform leaders did just that. After joining Garrison's crusade, white leaders began to reach out to the masses in an effort to broaden the movement. They met with success in the North. By the end of the decade, approximately 140,000 Northerners had joined nearly 1,350 different immediatist groups.

AFRICAN-AMERICAN STUDENTS IN OHIO, 1834

The following are written statements of unnamed young students in Ohio opposing the institution of slavery.

We are going next summer to buy a farm and to work part of the day and to study the other part if we live to see it. . . . [We hope to] come home part of the day to see our mothers and sisters and cousins . . . and see our kind folks and to be good boys and when we get [to be men] to get the poor slaves from bondage.

_____, aged seven years

I now inform you in these few lines, that what we are studying for is to try to get the yoke of slavery broke and the chains parted asunder and slave holding [to] cease for ever. O that God would change the hearts of our fellow men.

_____, aged twelve years

This is to inform you that I have two cousins in slavery who are entitled to their freedom. They have done everything that the will requires and now they won't let them go. They talk of selling them down the river. If this was your case what would you do? Please give me your advice.

_____, aged ten years

Students with friends and family members in slavery in the South.

Source: "Report of the Condition of the Free Colored People of Ohio." Proceedings of the Ohio Anti-Slavery Convention Held at Putnam on the Twenty-Second, Twenty-Third, and Twenty-Fourth of April 1835.

Although they all fought for the same general goal, abolitionists disagreed on a number of issues. At first, most immediatists joined the American Anti-Slavery Society (AASS), which was founded in 1833. The overall goals of the society were simple: immediate and uncompensated emancipation of all slaves and the rights of citizenship for all African Americans. They relied upon a concept known as moral suasion. According to this nonviolent method, abolitionists would appeal to Americans' sense of justice and humanity through the principles of Christianity and the natural rights arguments of the American Revolution.

They used petition campaigns and public speaking tours to convince whites of the evils of bondage.

Failure to gain support in the South, the tepid nature of Northern support, and violence against abolitionists throughout the country, however, caused antislavery leaders to split into a number of factions between 1837 and 1840. At base was a disagreement over tactics and short-term goals. This tension centered around the movement's relationship with the national government and established churches, the need for an independent political party, and the role of women and women's rights. Because the long-term goal—immediate freedom for the enslaved—was a radical demand, many historians and contemporaries labeled the entire movement as radical. In reality, however, abolitionists and the theories they developed fit into a broad spectrum ranging from moderate to radical to militant.

Moderate abolitionists included orthodox Christian and political groups that sought to work within existing institutions to further their agenda. Louis Tappan led a group of orthodox evangelical Christians that hoped to use the political arena to further their cause. Based primarily in New York, these abolitionists created the American and Foreign Anti-Slavery Society (AFASS). They believed in the importance of the American government and hoped to use their religious venue to remove the corruption of slavery. They tried to work through the major Christian denominations, but they were willing to leave churches that refused to adopt an antislavery stance. Members of this group created such churches as the Wesleyan Methodists, the American Baptist Free Mission Society, and the Free Presbyterians in the 1840s. Tappan also helped create the American Missionary Association in 1846. This group supported antislavery evangelical activity in the South. Although they acknowledged the important role women played in moral suasion, they maintained traditional gender attitudes.

Other leaders, such as Joshua Leavitt of Boston and Gamaliel Bailey and Salmon P. Chase of Ohio, hoped to work primarily within the American political structure. They recognized that Southern states had the right to maintain slavery within their borders, but they hoped to use moral suasion to convince Southerners to abandon the institution. Meanwhile, they hoped to convince the federal government to end slavery in the national domain. This focus on the containment of slavery led them to join the Free Soil Party in 1848.

RADICAL ABOLITIONISTS

Radical abolitionists went a step further. By the early 1840s, they became disenchanted with milder forms of political protests, and they grew increasingly disgusted by the domestic slave trade's tendency to separate African-American families. Also, they admired the direct action of slaves who took the initiative of "stealing themselves," and they began to see it as their duty to assist.

Political radicals such as Beriah Green and Gerrit Smith of New York argued that such direct action was not in violation of the law because slavery itself was an illegal institution. They maintained that the Constitution was being misinterpreted as pro-slavery when it was actually an antislavery document. Despite their admiration for escaped slaves, however, most refused to condone full-scale violence. They also labored under a patriarchal assumption that blacks needed their leadership, an attitude that kept them from treating black abolitionists as equal partners in the antislavery crusade.

Gerrit Smith's 1842 *Address to the Slaves in the United States of America* demonstrates political abolitionist sentiment. In this address, Smith argued that abolitionists had a right to "go into the south, and use . . . intelligence to promote the escape of ignorant and imbruted slaves from their prison-house." He also discouraged full-scale violence, instead prompting the enslaved to endure their condition for the time being because "recourse to violence and blood-shed for the termination of slavery, is very likely . . . to result in the confirmation and protraction of the evil." His aversion to violence was based on expediency rather than "on the high ground of absolute morality." Encouraging slaves to escape whenever a feasible, peaceful opportunity presented itself, he celebrated the growing rate of self-manumission, claiming that "there are now a thousand a year; a rate more than five times as great as that before the anti-slavery effort." He also pledged Northern support for escapees, explaining that "under the influence of anti-slavery lessons, nineteen-twentieths" of white Northerners had been convinced not to return fugitives.

Radical political abolitionists like Smith also rallied for the creation of an antislavery third party. They insisted that the Constitution, as an antislavery document, made slavery illegal throughout the country and gave either Congress or the Supreme Court the power to abolish slavery in the South. During the late 1830s, they began to abandon existing political parties in favor of their own Liberty Party, and they nomi-

nated James G. Birney for president in 1840 and 1844. Their tactic of fighting slavery within a political context appealed to some black abolitionists, most notably Henry Highland Garnet and Frederick Douglass. Interparty strife led most Liberty Party members to defect and join moderate political abolitionist Whigs and Democrats in forming the Free Soil Party in 1848.

The most famous radical abolitionists, however, eschewed all involvement with churches or political parties, new or old. Led by Garrison, this group believed that the American system had become so corrupt that full-scale cultural and political restructuring was necessary. They followed the perfectionist doctrine of utopian socialist John Humphrey Noyes in rejecting all violence, refusing to employ physical means even in self-defense. Also known as Christian anarchism, or nonresistance, Noyes's system rejected all forms of physical coercion and insisted that human governments, by nature, rested upon force. Abolitionists who joined Garrison in following perfectionist doctrine insisted, moreover, that the United States Constitution was a pro-slavery document. Thus, they called upon the North to dissolve the Union and remove itself from the corruption of the South. They also chided the churches for refusing to condemn slavery as sinful. Finally, they insisted on equal rights for women and allowed them to vote and serve as delegates. Their election of Abigail Kelley to the AASS business committee precipitated the final split between antislavery factions in 1840. Despite such opposition, women were able to work through Garrisonian organizations to play important roles in the overall movement. Though the minority, Garrisonians maintained control of the AASS after 1840, and although they remained theoretically radical, they were less likely than the political group to assist in slave escapes and Underground Railroad activities.

Even the most radical immediatists initially called for nonviolence in the antislavery crusade. For Garrison and his group it was a matter of moral choice, but for most others the issue was one of expediency. Violent rhetoric, they argued, would cause a backlash in the South, especially since most Southerners already lived in fear of slave revolts. The Garrisonians also pointed out that violent tactics ran counter to the law, and they saw no benefit in associating the movement with lawlessness.

ABOLITION AND VIOLENCE

Between the 1830s and the beginning of the Civil War, a number of circumstances led to the growth of a more militant strain of abolition. To begin with, the

On the night of November 7, 1837, a mob attacks the office of abolitionist printer Elijah P. Lovejoy in Alton, Illinois. In one of many instances of anti-abolitionist violence in the mid-nineteenth century, the mob murdered Lovejoy and destroyed his printing press. No one was ever punished for the crime, but the murder electrified abolitionists throughout the nation. *(Brown Brothers)*

political radicals had admired direct action on the part of the enslaved from early on, and growing numbers of white abolitionists began to understand that the nonviolent ideal was often impractical. Revolts such as Nat Turner's and that of the *Amistad* captives taught them that blacks were willing and able to fight back when the opportunity presented itself. They also came increasingly to see slavery as a race war in itself, and many began to understand that, just as their own ancestors had fought for independence from British "tyranny," the slaves struggled to secure their own liberty. In addition, a number of white abolitionists learned firsthand the need for active self-defense.

The most tragic example of their self-defense efforts is that of Elijah P. Lovejoy, a white abolitionist newspaper editor from Illinois. He had been attacked by anti-abolitionist mobs before, but when he and his press came under attack in 1837, he fought back by opening fire on the mob. After having two presses

destroyed previously and having been chased from his mother-in-law's home, he vowed to defend his family. A month before the final attack, he wrote that his wife suffered from constant fear and exhaustion. Contrary to his own nonviolent inclinations, he had resorted to keeping loaded arms available should another attack occur. He admitted to having four loaded muskets in addition to pistols and ammunition ready. He felt "inexpressible reluctance to resort to this method of defence," but "dear-bought experience" had taught him not to rely on the law or public sentiment for protection. Even in the face of mortal danger, Lovejoy had resisted armed defense until he felt he had no other recourse. A month after he wrote to justify his conversion to self-defense, his stalkers got the final word, destroying his press and taking his life.

The passage of a stronger fugitive slave law and pro-slavery violence in Kansas converted others to the militant cause. The Fugitive Slave Law of 1850 threatened the freedom of all African Americans, especially in the North where generations had been born into freedom and no longer carried free papers. Sympathy for the plight of their fellow crusaders led white abolitionists to join in active resistance to this law, and the joint efforts of black and white abolitionists in rescuing those arrested provide the best examples of interracial cooperation in the freedom struggle. A young generation of white abolitionists, including Thomas Wentworth Higginson, who would become the leader of a black regiment during the Civil War, entered the movement during the struggle over the Fugitive Slave Law and became particularly willing to employ violence when necessary.

Others embraced defensive violence after experiencing or reading about the bloody conflict in Kansas between the pro-slavery and antislavery settlers. Northern free-soil supporters made up the majority in this new territory, but pro-slavery "border ruffians" from Missouri and territorial officials fought to add Kansas to the list of slave states. Abolitionists such as Charles B. Stearns, John Henry Kagi, and John Brown traveled to Kansas to witness the struggle firsthand, and Kagi and Brown both joined the battle by killing pro-slavery men. Stearns left for Kansas a Garrisonian nonresistant, but his experiences led him to conclude that "pro-slavery Missourians are demons from the bottomless pit and may be shot with impunity." By the late 1850s, even the most nonviolent abolitionists had concluded that the Compromise of 1850 and the deadly agitation in Kansas served as evidence of a "Slave Power" conspiracy. This theory held that Southerners were aggressively seeking to extend their economic system throughout all new territories in a quest to maintain political control of the nation and guarantee the protection of slavery. As a result, many abolitionists began to call for slave revolt, and John Brown pledged his life to the cause of direct action.

Many historians emphasize the biracial nature of this violent phase of the abolition struggle, supporting the idea that black abolitionists were more militant from the beginning. More recent studies have shown a much closer parallel between black and white efforts throughout all phases of the movement. Although many blacks gained freedom through the militant tactic of self-emancipation, the Northern free black abolitionist community, which developed and matured during the first half of the nineteenth century, embraced the typical American reform values shared by its white contemporaries. The assumption of black militance stems largely from the appeals of David Walker and Henry Highland Garnet. Both writers called upon the enslaved to rise up; Walker's *Appeal to the Colored Citizens of the World* (1829) scared Southerners so badly that they struggled to keep it out of the hands of the slaves.

Although Walker is often cited as an early example of black militance, his *Appeal* served also as an appeal to whites to acknowledge black humanity. Like other black reformers of his day, Walker embraced the dominant American culture, especially the Victorian family and gender roles. What he wanted most was for blacks to prove to whites that they were equal and thus deserved equal opportunities in the United States. Prophetically, he began by arguing that God, not the enslaved, would seek revenge on the oppressors by dividing their ranks and setting them against each other. He added, however, that it was the duty of the enslaved to help "fight under our Lord and Master Jesus Christ, in the glorious and heavenly cause of freedom." He then employed the same rhetoric of Victorian morality that white abolitionists used to graphically describe the tragic nature of family life under slavery.

Although Walker expressed admiration for the Haitian Revolution, he was aware of the pro-slavery horror stories of blacks slaughtering babies, raping women, and murdering men. Thus, he called upon his black readers not to rise up and kill whites but to prove equality by fighting against their own ignorance as a means of actively refuting racist arguments. He argued that force in defense of self or family was justified, but he insisted that whites were naturally more violent than blacks. Finally, he prevailed upon educated and enlightened black men to lead the rest of the race out of degradation through the dissemination of education and religion and "prove to the Americans and the rest of the world, that we are MEN, and not *brutes.*"

Near the end of his address, Walker introduced the argument that, regardless of how black men felt about violence toward whites, whites feared retribution. He argued that if black men would shed their "servile spirit" and "death-like apathy," they could stand up for themselves and prove their equality. He did not encourage violence, instead arguing that vengeance belonged "to the Lord" and even offering hope that God would forgive the oppressors if they would repent and aid in black enlightenment. "Treat us like men," he concluded, "and there is no danger but we will all live in peace and happiness together."

Henry Highland Garnet presented similar arguments a decade later in his 1843 "Address to the Slaves." An ally of Gerrit Smith and the son of an escaped slave, Garnet called upon the enslaved to act for their freedom, insisting that "if hereditary bondsmen would be free, they must themselves strike the blow." After arguing that voluntary submission was sinful and disgraceful, he told slaves not to rise up and kill their masters but to "appeal to their sense of justice, and . . . Promise them renewed diligence in the cultivation of the soil, if they will render to you an equivalent for your services." He then advised slaves to "torment the God-cursed slaveholders, [so] that they will be glad to let you go free," but he warned them that "we do not advise you to attempt a revolution with the sword, because it would be INEXPEDIENT." Like his white allies, he had become convinced that self-defense was justified, but, like Smith, he realized that violence would lead to retribution and hurt the antislavery cause in the long run.

Despite the occasional militant rhetoric of leaders like Walker and Garnet, almost all black leaders preferred the nonviolent tactic of moral suasion. To this doctrine they added the concepts of self-help and racial uplift, as they developed their own peaceful crusade. Most, including Walker, shared white abolitionists' belief in evangelical religion and contemporary gender prescriptions. Black leaders embraced the masculine reform ideal of the "Christian Gentleman," arguing for restraint. They handled militant ideas with caution because of two stereotypes they were forced to struggle against. They needed to show that black men were capable of standing up for themselves and their loved ones to counter the Sambo image of docility and childlike innocence. At the same time, they had to stress reluctance to violence and willingness to forgive as they refuted the pro-slavery argument that most black men were violent brutes like Nat Turner.

ABOLITION, MORALITY, AND SELF-ELEVATION

Even as they fought against these images, black leaders themselves were unsure of the extent to which fellow blacks, particularly the enslaved, would employ violence even when needed. Like the white abolitionists they worked with, they adhered to a doctrine of racial difference that countered the pro-slavery rhetoric of black brutality and savagery by attributing the feminine qualities of submission, generosity, and peacefulness to black men. The result was an idea that black men were naturally inclined toward the Christian action of forgiving oppressors rather than seeking vengeance. This idea was an im-

portant tool in the abolitionist crusade to prove that, if freed, blacks would not revert to savagery. Many, like Walker, argued that whites were more likely to resort to violence than were blacks, but most remained concerned that violence would some day be necessary, and they hoped that blacks would be able to fight for their own freedom if they had to. They drew upon a legacy of black participation in the American Revolution and the War of 1812 to argue that violence in defense of home and country was justified, regardless of race.

Although active defense of home and family became a reality for many free blacks throughout the 1850s, most never really abandoned moral suasion and self-elevation as chief tactics. The concept of self-elevation had three main components: moral uplift, educational attainment, and economic self-sufficiency. White reform leaders of the day encouraged the white masses to strive for success in each of these areas, just as black leaders preached the tenets to the black masses. The crucial difference was that more was at stake for the black community. Self-elevation, black leaders hoped, not only would force whites to accept racial equality, but would also eventually lead to the abolition of slavery by defeating pro-slavery arguments that the system itself was a civilizing force.

Self-elevation was deeply ingrained in the philosophies of black leaders, and self-help arguments strongly punctuate their writings. Lewis Woodson, a respected black leader in Pittsburgh during the 1830s, told fellow black reformers that "CONDITION and not *color,* is the chief cause of the prejudice, under which we suffer," and he spent his life convincing others that uplift was crucial to the black community. He insisted that blacks must achieve elevation without the help of whites.

One of Woodson's most famous admirers, Martin R. Delany, took his message to a younger generation of black abolitionists. He called for self-elevation throughout his novel *Blake; or the Huts of America* (1859). His political and historical work, *The Condition, Elevation, Emigration, and Destiny of the Colored People of the United States* (1852), and many of his writings in the *North Star,* a newspaper he edited with Frederick Douglass, stressed the importance of self-help and black leadership by celebrating "uplifted" blacks. Like most other leaders of his time, including Garrison, Delany firmly believed that blacks had to be prepared morally, intellectually, and economically to be productive members of society.

Moral uplift required a number of reform measures. Leaders especially emphasized frugality and temperance. Maria W. Stewart, a pioneer in the women's rights movement as well as an influential Northern free black abolitionist lecturer of the 1830s, implored young black men to "flee from the gambling board and the dance hall." She further advised them to save their hard-earned money for more useful purposes such as "mental and moral improvement." Samuel Cornish, a black pioneer in the field of American journalism, agreed. He insisted that if blacks could establish a "character" and "become more religious and moral, more industrious and prudent, than other classes of the community, it will be impossible to keep us down." On the other hand, he warned that "should we prove unworthy [of] our few privileges, we shall furnish our enemies the strongest arguments, with which to oppose the emancipation of the slave, and to hinder the elevation of the free." He held free blacks responsible for the enslaved, concluding that the salvation of the slave depended upon the conduct of free blacks, and he urged all to live by the moral reform principles of "temperance, hard work, education, and piety."

As products of the American reform movement, many black leaders emphasized several of its principles, particularly temperance. Delany was proud of his own restraint, and he urged others to "let your habits be strictly temperate, and for human nature's sake, abstain from the erroneous idea that some sort of malt or spirituous drink is necessary." He emphasized his disapproval of "ardent liquid" in *Blake,* characterizing one of the white slave traders as drunk and reckless, while his main character, a black man, was sober and levelheaded at all times.

William Whipper, another Northern free black leader, also strongly supported the temperance movement, claiming that intemperance was as evil as slavery. He insisted that "the slave may escape from the rule and presence of his master, by flying to a land of freedom; but the subject of intemperance finds that *his* master is almost omnipresent." He went on to argue that one of the "earliest achievements" of intemperance was "to secure the 'slave trade' by inducing the native Africans to sell their brethren while under its influence." He concluded that temperate blacks could redeem past wrongs by working to uplift Africans as well as fellow African Americans. Jacob C. White, a member of Philadelphia's black elite, also argued that temperance was important in the redemption of the black community. He urged young men to spend their money "for the purpose of elevating our people and promoting the cause of education among them" rather than on rum. He insisted that once youth were

"trained in such a manner that they will be fitted for usefulness" they would be prepared to fight for black rights, and their work would lead to a "marked difference in the Colored People of this country, in a political and social point of view." Finally, William C. Nell, an early black historian who chronicled the lives of important African-American leaders, stressed throughout his work that the heroes he described were all temperate.

RELIGIOUS STRAINS OF ABOLITIONISM

Many leaders of the Northern free black community had embraced self-elevation and moral uplift early in their careers, and a number of them even gained their leadership experience through self-improvement societies. Delany was a member of the Young Men's Bible Society, the Young Men's Anti-Slavery and Literary Society, and a founder of the Theban Literary Society. He was also manager of the Moral Reform Society and founder of the first total abstinence society for blacks. Garnet was an officer of the Garrison Literary and Benevolent Association, and Crummell was a charter member of the Phoenixonian Literary Society, both in New York. Many of these societies opened libraries, founded evening schools, and encouraged intellectual enlightenment through group discussions. They also organized lyceum-style lectures in which experts spoke about scientific, political, historical, and moral topics.

Membership in these groups gave future leaders the confidence and optimism necessary to spread their self-help crusade through missionary work. Garnet believed that encouraging self-elevation would "show [our] love to the slave at the South, by doing good to the free black man at the North." He wrote to Simeon S. Jocelyn, a white reformer who worked with the American Missionary Association (AMA), to encourage the organization to reach out to the poor of both races in New York City, "sympathise with them, and teach them in divine things." He also urged the AMA to "encourage them in everything that belongs to well ordered living." In the same spirit, using words that indicate a distance between herself and her subjects, Northern free black leader Frances Ellen Watkins Harper outlined a plan to take her missionary crusade to the West, "lecturing among the colored people." She maintained that the most useful contribution she could make to the abolitionist cause would be to "labor earnestly and faithfully among those with whom I am identified by complexion, race and blood." She concluded that "so long as they are down, I belong to a downtrodden race." While both of these leaders were referring to the need for black uplift in the United States, other African-American leaders began to see a need to spread similar missionary efforts to Africa in a broader effort to prove that people of color throughout the world could achieve the same levels of success as white Americans, if given the chance.

BLACK EQUALITY THROUGH EDUCATION

Advocates of self-elevation agreed that moral uplift was only the beginning. Education was equally crucial in the crusade for equality. Black leader H. Ford Douglas argued that both blacks and whites needed to be educated for the betterment of the entire American society, insisting that "if anything is to be done for freedom, we must make this question of slavery, not a colored question, but a white question as well." Speaking in Ohio in 1860, he informed whites that "while the colored people are bowed down by slavery, they can accomplish nothing great or noble; nor can you, while you oppress them." Douglas, a self-taught fugitive slave, valued education in general, but, like most former bondsmen, he especially emphasized the need for black education. Another former slave, James R. Bradley, insisted that slaves wanted not only liberty but education as well. He enrolled in Lane Seminary immediately upon buying his own freedom and later produced a written account of his life. Emphasizing his desire for an education and his efforts to teach himself to read and write, he explained that he had been "praying to God for years that my poor dark mind might see the light of knowledge." Frederick Douglass, Henry Bibb, and William Wells Brown, all of whom were escaped slaves, also drew upon their experiences in slavery to argue the need for black education in the struggle for freedom.

Former bondsmen were not the only ones to recognize the value of education. Some leaders encouraged youth to participate in integrated schools whenever possible. A strong proponent of racial cooperation, Nell insisted that "the colored youth should be stimulated to establish such a character in these seats of learning, by his energy in study and gentlemanly deportment towards teachers and pupils, as to disarm opposition, show himself an equal, and, in spite of cold looks and repulsive treatment, hew a path to eminence and respect." He concluded that, "like the gem which shines brighter by attrition," the black youth must "become himself, among good scholars, the very best."

Denied equal privileges in the public school system, however, most Northern black communities boasted their own schools. The New York African Free School was a great source of pride for the black community, training important leaders such as Garnet, Alexander Crummell, John B. Russwurm, and James McCune Smith. Students' accomplishments were celebrated each year with exhibitions displaying their work. Even girls were allowed to attend such schools, but, like white girls, they were taught gender-specific skills such as knitting and sewing.

By the mid-1830s, higher education was available to Northern free blacks at schools such as Noyes Academy, the Oneida Institute, Wesleyan University, Oberlin College, and Dartmouth. However, many avenues of opportunity remained closed to blacks. Delany and James McCune Smith were both denied access to medical training at the major medical schools. Delany managed to get into Harvard but was asked to leave after a semester because of the protests of white students, and Smith was forced to turn to Scotland's Glasgow University for his degree. Many divinity schools also refused to admit black students. Crummell, like Smith, eventually turned to Great Britain for an opportunity to earn advanced training, and J.W.C. Pennington, after hiding behind doors at Yale to learn as much as possible for intrinsic benefit, eventually earned his Doctor of Divinity degree at the University of Heidelberg.

Many abolitionists emphasized the practical role of industrial education over traditional academic training. Samuel Cornish called for a manual labor college in 1829, and Abraham Shadd, William Hamilton, and William Whipper reported on the need for such a school to the 1832 national convention of black leaders. These men argued that their proposed colleges would impart both classical knowledge and practical skills to their students.

By the 1850s, the call for manual education had become even stronger, as both black and white leaders began to see its value as a vehicle for autonomy and self-elevation. Charles Reason, former pupil and professor at the African Free School, maintained that abolitionists were responsible for "not only chattel slavery, but that other kind of slavery, which, for generation after generation, dooms an oppressed people to a condition of dependence and pauperism." The best way to ameliorate the condition, he insisted, was through industrial education.

Like moral uplift, education was only a step in the process of proving black equality. Once blacks gained education, the next important step was to earn economic self-sufficiency. In an effort to encourage black entrepreneurs, Delany and Nell both wrote books that catalogued successful black businessmen. John N. Still, a successful black merchant, also believed in the power of black ownership of the means of capital. He voiced irritation that blacks were so willing to spend their money to support churches when they should be investing capital in black businesses. Peter Lester, another black Northern merchant, found what he considered concrete evidence that economic self-sufficiency by blacks would help end racial prejudice. Encouraged by the freedom and degree of equality he found after emigrating to Canada in 1859, he concluded that "the day that we are engaged in business matters, so as to bring about a commercial intercourse between the whites and ourselves, that very day our chains will commence to fall."

Given the American tradition of Jeffersonian thought and the opening of the West to farming ventures, many black leaders concluded that the best way to economic self-sufficiency was through agriculture. Woodson had argued as early as the 1830s that agriculture was an honorable trade that would lead to black autonomy, and a number of black abolitionists developed schemes for agricultural settlements both before and after the Civil War. Some maintained that the American West was the ideal location for such communities, while others wanted to create agrarian communities in Canada, Haiti, or Africa.

After the passage of the Fugitive Slave Law of 1850, a handful of black abolitionist leaders began to consider emigration to such distant places, and some saw agriculture as the key to successful communities. Relying heavily on the idea of "free produce," Delany developed a plan for a settlement in the Niger Valley. He believed that Africa provided the ideal climate for growing crops that were currently being cultivated by slave labor in the United States. He also maintained that Africans were talented farmers already accustomed to agricultural tasks, and he cited the cultivation he saw in Africa and the sophisticated agricultural division of labor as proof that Africans were qualified to become the producers of the world's wealth and thus prove racial equality. Ironically, emigrationist leaders like Delany are sometimes considered the most radical leaders of the antebellum black community, but they were also some of the strongest adherents to the moral suasionist, self-help philosophy.

CONCLUSION

Although black abolitionist emphasis on self-help and the movement's overall reliance on moral suasion show a conservative tendency, it is important to realize that the abolition movement was indeed radical. Even the moderate abolitionists hoped to drastically alter American society by forcing Southerners to give up valuable private property. Historians have pointed out that even the most radical white abolitionists, including Garrison, held their own paternalistic assumptions that blacks needed white guidance to help them prepare for freedom. Black abolitionists saw this tendency and struggled to prove otherwise through their self-help agenda. It is important to note, however, that Garrison, Smith and other white abolitionists were willing to put their safety on the line to argue for black freedom, and black abolitionists realized that, despite their own biases, white abolitionists had good intentions.

The struggle to end slavery began when Africans and African Americans fought for their own freedom. It became a viable movement when white abolitionists listened to black objections to colonization and joined in the fight to end slavery and push for a racially inclusive society in America. Both groups played crucial roles in the overall crusade.

Beverly Tomek

BIBLIOGRAPHY

Aptheker, Herbert. *Abolitionism: A Revolutionary Movement*. Boston: Twayne, 1989.

Bennett, Lerone. *Before the Mayflower: A History of the Negro in America, 1619–1964*. New York: Penguin Books, 1961.

Blackett, R.J.M. *Building an Anti-Slavery Wall: Black Americans in the Atlantic Abolitionist Movement, 1830–1860*. Ithaca, NY: Cornell University Press, 1983.

Delany, Martin R. *Blake, or the Huts of America*. 1859–1862. Reprint, Boston: Beacon, 1970.

———. *The Condition, Elevation, Emigration and Destiny of the Colored People of the United States*. 1852. Reprint, Baltimore: Black Classics, 1993.

———. "Official Report of the Niger Valley Exploring Party." In *Search for a Place: Black Separatism and Africa, 1860*, ed. Howard Bell, 23–148. Ann Arbor: University of Michigan Press, 1969.

Dumond, Dwight Lowell. *Antislavery Origins of the Civil War in the United States*. Ann Arbor: University of Michigan Press, 1939.

Filler, Louis. *The Crusade Against Slavery, 1830–1860*. New York: Harper & Brothers, 1960.

Goodman, Paul. *Of One Blood: Abolitionism and the Origins of Racial Equality*. Los Angeles: University of California Press, 1998.

Harding, Vincent. *There Is a River: The Black Struggle for Freedom in America*. New York: Harcourt Brace Jovanovich, 1981.

Harrold, Stanley. *American Abolitionists*. Essex: Pearson Education Limited, 2001.

———. *The Abolitionists and the South, 1831–1860*. Lexington: University Press of Kentucky, 1995.

Litwack, Leon, and August Meier, eds. *Black Leaders of the Nineteenth Century*. Chicago: University of Illinois Press, 1991.

Mayer, Henry. *All on Fire: William Lloyd Garrison and the Abolition of Slavery*. New York: St. Martin's, 1998.

McKivigan, John R., and Stanley Harrold. *Antislavery Violence: Sectional, Racial, and Cultural Conflict in Antebellum America*. Knoxville: University of Tennessee Press, 1999.

Nell, William Cooper. *The Colored Patriots of the American Revolution with Sketches of Several Distinguished Colored Persons: To Which Is Added a Brief Survey of the Condition and Prospects of Colored Americans*. Boston: Robert F. Wallcut, 1855.

Quarles, Benjamin. *Black Abolitionists*. New York: Oxford University Press, 1969.

Ripley, C. Peter. *The Black Abolitionist Papers*. 5 vols. Chapel Hill: University of North Carolina Press, 1986–1992.

Sterling, Dorothy. *Speak Out in Thunder Tones: Letters and Other Writings by Black Northerners, 1787–1856*. New York: Da Capo, 1973.

Ullman, Victor. *Martin R. Delany: The Beginnings of Black Nationalism*. Boston: Beacon, 1971.

Wyatt-Brown, Bertram. *Lewis Tappan and the Evangelical War Against Slavery*. Baton Rouge: Louisiana State University Press, 1969.

Yee, Shirley J. *Black Women Abolitionists: A Study in American Activism, 1828–1860*. Knoxville: University of Tennessee Press, 1992.

FREDERICK DOUGLASS AND ANTISLAVERY

For most of the English-speaking world, Frederick Douglass is the black voice of antislavery. Born a slave, he entered public life within three years of his escape. A modern man, his mastery of the spoken and written word has sustained him as a preeminent figure of nineteenth-century American political life. One of the paradoxes of slavery in the United States is that it produced such men and women. The history of American slavery and the struggle against that "peculiar institution" is filled with the unique vantage points of articulate slaves, fugitives, and free black men and women. Among them, Douglass left the most extensive record, inscribed himself into his own time and history, and made his struggles as a slave to free himself and as a freeman to bring slavery to an end a central part of the drama of the nineteenth century.

THE "SCHOOL" OF SLAVERY

Douglass was born Frederick Augustus Washington Bailey in February of 1818 on the Eastern Shore of Maryland. He was the son of Harriet Bailey and a white man most often identified as Aaron Anthony, his owner. On his mother's side he descended from blacks who had lived in Talbot County as a stable extended family for more than a century. Harriet Bailey's father, Isaac, was free and earned his living as a sawyer. Her mother, Betsy, was a slave but lived independently in the family's modest cabin where she earned money and considerable respect as a net maker. Her children, however, were slaves, and her only obligation to her master seemed to have been the care of her grandchildren, a task for which she was sometimes paid. Douglass was one of her charges, and he was raised in the relative freedom and familial stability of his grandparent's cabin until he was six years old.

Douglass recorded in his autobiographies the shock he experienced when his grandmother abruptly left him with Aaron Anthony and he became a part of his owner's household. A newcomer to slaveholding, Anthony inherited Harriet Bailey and her children through marriage to the daughter of one of the most distinguished families in the region. A widower in his late fifties when Douglass came to live with them, he arose from relative poverty to own several small farms and more than two dozen slaves, most of them the children and grandchildren of Betsy Bailey. Not a planter himself, he rented out his farms and slaves while he served as principal overseer of Edward Lloyd's plantations. The home to which Douglass was taken was on Lloyd's Wye River plantation.

The Lloyd family was one of the oldest in the region, with traditions of economic self-sufficiency, grandeur, and hospitality dating back to the colonial period. The Wye River plantation's present owner, a former governor and senator and one of the largest slaveholders in the region, was by blood and tradition an aristocrat of slaveholding society. The splendor of the Wye River was unequaled in the state, but that splendor was supported by 500 slaves spread out over a series of outlying plantations run by overseers under the supervision of Lloyd and Anthony. The home plantation was populated by house servants and artisans with the skills to underwrite the estate's independence and opulent life.

In Anthony's house on the Wye River plantation, Douglass began to experience slavery's extremes. Despite the wealth of the Lloyds, slavery as an institution was declining in Maryland, and the more meager fortunes of Anthony's family as well as the stability of the Bailey clan suffered. Throughout his youth, Douglass experienced the dissolution and dispersal of the century-old black community into which he was born, with more than a dozen members of his own family being sold out of state. His mother worked on a distant plantation, and he rarely saw her. Placed under the supervision of Anthony's slave cook, he rarely had enough to eat, and he witnessed and heard about the harsh beating of the Lloyd slaves. Lloyd's slaves were considered poorly fed and harshly treated, even by the standards of the time.

Yet Douglass was relatively favored, and though they were small favors, he had the natural instincts to make the best of them. He soaked in experiences and constantly remade himself to the extent of the boundaries that confined him. Douglass spared no energies in his later career in cataloging the horrors of slavery on the Eastern Shore, but the considerable talents he brought to that denunciation were ironically nurtured in the unevenness and paradoxes of that very institution. Lloyd selected him to be the companion to his son. Anthony's daughter, Lucretia, also singled him out for special protection and favors. Perhaps the greatest favor that was done him was in 1826, as Anthony retired from Lloyd's service and a younger man replaced him at Wye River. Douglass was sent to Baltimore to live with Hugh Auld, the brother of Lucretia's husband, to be his son's companion.

Free blacks in Baltimore outnumbered slaves four to one. Douglass lived for seven years amid the porous boundaries between the life of urban and mostly domestic slaves and the social and political structures of free black domestics, day laborers, artisans, and seamen. In Auld's household, his mistress, Sophia Auld, treated him with unexpected kindness and even began to teach him to read until her husband forbade her to do so. As an errand boy in Auld's shipbuilding firm, he taught himself the alphabet by copying letters used to identify ship parts and learned to write by transcribing the work in "Little Tommy" Auld's cast of copy books. Among free blacks he became an active member of the all-black Bethel African Methodist Church, where he was converted and heard the important black and white evangelical preachers of his day. Together with one member of the church, Uncle Lawson, Douglass read and pondered the Bible.

A disagreement between Hugh and Thomas Auld forced his return to the Eastern Shore, and after seven years' absence much had changed. Anthony and his daughter Lucretia had died, leaving him the property of her husband Thomas Auld. At fifteen, Douglass, too, had changed. He was old enough to be put to work, but it became clear to slaves and masters alike that he was interested in his freedom and the freedom of other slaves. He opened a Sabbath school and began to teach a group of his fellow slaves how to read and write. When his activities were discovered, Auld hired him out to Edward Covey who had a reputation for breaking the spirit of rebellious slaves. A slave

Abolitionist, orator, editor, and author Frederick Douglass was the preeminent African American of his generation. After escaping from slavery in 1838, he devoted his life to the causes of emancipation, universal suffrage, and equal rights. *(Brown Brothers)*

beater of some enthusiasm, Covey beat him until Douglass resolved to resist. In the ensuing fight, Douglass was the victor, and he cites this battle as having ushered him into symbolic manhood. Auld then hired him out to another slaveholder who had the reputation for treating his slaves more humanely. Soon Douglass was found organizing a group of slaves to run away. Ultimately, Auld returned Douglass to Baltimore, promising him that he would free him at the age of twenty-four.

Douglass returned to Baltimore a self-confident young man determined to attain that freedom. Thomas Auld apprenticed Douglass to learn the caulking trade at a shipyard. Where blacks and whites had worked side by side in the past, the influx of free blacks and Irish immigrants made competition between them inevitable. While Douglass was employed, the white workers struck in order to have all the free black workers fired. That animosity also applied to the slave apprentices, and he frequently found himself the source of derision and was provoked into fighting.

At the same time, Douglass became a full participant in churches, benevolent societies, and Sabbath schools. His independence was facilitated by making an agreement with Auld in which he would hire himself out and pay all of his own expenses. He and several friends formed the East Baltimore Mental Improvement Society, a debating society where they read and argued religion, morality, and abolition. They became increasingly politically conscious and withdrew from Bethel when church leaders took a stand against radical abolition. During this time, Douglass met and became engaged to Anna Murray, a free black woman, who also came from the Eastern Shore.

After a series of almost violent confrontations with Auld, Douglass decided to run away, fearing that he would be sold South. He borrowed a black seaman's protection papers and traveled by train from Baltimore to Wilmington, Delaware, where he boarded a ship to Philadelphia, and then took another train to New York. He left slavery with considerable personal resources. He was literate and urbane, and he was also something of a preacher. He had the confidence of a young man who was considered by all to have promise, and he had the experience of leadership among the free blacks of Baltimore and the slaves of the Eastern Shore. He would later speak with characteristic irony of having been educated in the "school" of slavery, yet there is more truth to that claim than his rhetoric suggested.

RADICAL ABOLITION

Like so many fugitive slaves before him, Douglass, going by the name Johnson, found his safety first in the familiar world of the free black community of New York. He stayed at the home of David Ruggles, the secretary of the New York Vigilance Committee, where Murray joined him and where they married. Although his later colleagues saw their marriage as a mismatch, Murray was typical of the women, white and black, whom Douglass knew and admired all of his life. She never learned to read and write, but like Betsy Bailey she was personally and financially independent, having saved enough money to help Douglass pay his fare to New York. Murray was never comfortable in the interracial social circle that Douglass came to live in, but her frugality, domestic management, and personal industry underwrote Douglass's public life, leaving him free to travel extensively, secure that in his absence she could manage

his household and raise the five children they had together.

From New York, Douglass and his new wife moved to New Bedford, Massachusetts, where he changed his name from Johnson to Douglass, and began his new life as a free man. Although smaller than Baltimore, the New Bedford black community was similarly organized by its churches and other institutions. Like Baltimore, there was tension between white and black workers. Douglass was an experienced caulker, but whites already in that profession opposed his employment, confining him to unskilled and occasional labor. Nevertheless, the free black community of New Bedford afforded Douglass some considerable opportunity for his talents. He joined the New Bedford Zion Methodist Church and was later licensed to preach by the African Methodist Episcopal Zion denomination. Through his appearances in various New Bedford pulpits he continued his apprenticeship as a public speaker.

New Bedford's blacks were openly abolitionist, in a way that Southern free blacks could not be, and their institutions were at one with national abolitionist and moral reform movements. Douglass became a subscriber to *The Liberator* and heard its editor, William Lloyd Garrison, and other black and white abolitionists as they spoke in his town. In August of 1841, Douglass attended the state convention of the Massachusetts Anti-Slavery Society. His reputation led to an invitation to speak, and that speech, which would become the crowning moment in his *Narrative of the Life of Frederick Douglass* (1845), launched his public career as an abolitionist. Garrison recounts the inspiration Douglass's listeners felt in his "Preface" to the *Narrative*. He was an immediate success, and John A. Collins offered him a position as general agent for the Massachusetts Anti-Slavery Society.

Douglass surpassed in fame other black abolitionist lecturers. A compelling speaker in an age when public oratory was the preeminent art of political life, he lectured throughout New England with Garrison, Wendell Phillips, and the other principal white abolitionists seeking converts, raising money, and selling subscriptions to *The Liberator* and the *Anti-Slavery Standard*. He became a "regular speaker" at the American Anti-Slavery Society's annual convention. The precarious life of the abolitionist circuit was not without its hardships. Speakers frequently met with violent opposition from their audience and on the streets, and black and interracial speaking teams were more likely to suffer attacks. In addition, for blacks, formal and informal discrimination in transportation and lodging presented constant outrages and challenges.

Douglass shared Garrison's commitment to moral suasion, immediate emancipation, civil equality for free blacks, and opposition to colonization—positions that separated radical abolition from the more conservative and Southern-based antislavery and brought Garrison many black supporters to *The Liberator* and the Massachusetts and American Anti-Slavery Societies. Although theory often outstripped practice, Garrison's views made an interracial abolitionist movement possible. Few shared Garrison's belief that the United States Constitution was tainted by articles that recognized and protected slavery, and most did not follow his call to avoid voting and the political process, or his more extreme advocacy of disunion with slaveholding states. Nonetheless, Douglass followed the tenets of Garrisonian abolition that were contested and split radicals into factions in the 1840s.

Douglass's abolitionism was also of a piece with his commitment to the broad national moral reform that embraced temperance, women's rights, and self-improvement. He was the only one of the thirty-two men who attended the 1848 Women's Rights Convention at Seneca Falls, New York, to speak, urging the convention to resolve itself in favor of women's suffrage. Within the black community, he became active in the variety of organizations that sustained community life. Some of these organizations, like the League of Colored Laborers, were short-lived, but most urged temperance, economic and cultural self-improvement, and an end to discriminatory laws and social practices. He regularly attended the National Conventions of Colored Citizens. At the 1843 convention, he unsuccessfully opposed a resolution in support of the emerging antislavery Liberty Party. He also opposed, successfully, Henry Highland Garnet's resolution urging an uprising among slaves. He was also a strong supporter of the Convention's attempts to establish an industrial arts school for blacks in Connecticut.

Douglass's rapid emergence into leadership of both the interracial abolitionist movement and the all-black convention movement led many to question his credentials as a fugitive slave. In response to those doubts as well as to raise money, in 1845 he published the first of his three autobiographies, *Narrative of the Life of Frederick Douglass, an American Slave, Written by Himself.* Written under his adopted name, the work revealed the details of his experience in slavery and the development of his resolve to gain his freedom. Although the written and dictated narratives of ex-slaves was a staple of abolitionist literature, his *Narrative* was better crafted than most and, as a result, was exceedingly popular both in the United States and Great Britain. His quest for literacy, independence, family, and social status were ambitions with which most of his readers could identify. Through the *Narrative*, Douglass convincingly converted himself and his life into a symbol of the struggle against slavery.

The success of the *Narrative* and the specificity of Douglass's revelations about his early life made him a prime target for recapture. He decided to leave the country, and between the fall of 1845 and the spring of 1847 he toured England, Ireland, Scotland, and Wales giving antislavery lectures and championing moral reform causes. The abolitionists and moral reformers of Great Britain embraced and supported him with enthusiasm. His sympathetic British followers not only contributed money to his cause, but also sought to further Douglass's individual voice and position. Most importantly, several friends raised funds and arranged for his manumission. Although the purchasing of freedom was against the strict tenets of many of his antislavery colleagues, Douglass welcomed this opportunity and, with Garrison's support, was able to deflect some of the criticism.

Douglass returned from England in the spring of 1847 free from the claims of any master and poised financially, politically, and intellectually to pursue his own course. Gradually, he began freeing himself from the claims of his most important mentor, William Lloyd Garrison. The relative social ease he experienced in Britain made him chafe at the awkwardness and anxiety with which white abolitionists treated him in the United States. Twelve years his senior, Garrison had become something of a father figure to Douglass, shepherding his way into the top ranks of the abolitionist movement, but the publication of Douglass's *Narrative* and the success of his foreign tour gave Douglass a sense of his unique importance to the antislavery cause. Almost thirty, he was offended by the paternal relations. He had become an important force in the antislavery movement in the English-speaking world and was supported and courted by the leaders of its various divisions. Throughout the rest of his career, he would negotiate the various factions of the antislavery and reform movements in order to chart a course that was uniquely his own.

Over Garrison's objections, Douglass used the money raised on his British tour to establish his own newspaper, the *North Star*, which published its first

THE MEANING OF JULY FOURTH FOR THE NEGRO, 1852

Perhaps one of Frederick Douglass's most passionate addresses was delivered on July 5, 1852, at an affair celebrating the signing of the Declaration of Independence at Rochester's Corinthian Hall. In a scathing speech, Douglass submits that Independence and the "Fourth of July is yours, not *mine. You may rejoice, I must mourn."*

Fellow Citizens—Pardon me, and allow me to ask, why am I called upon to speak here, today? What have I, or those I represent, to do with your national independence? Are the great principles of political freedom and of natural justice, embodied in that Declaration of Independence, extended to us? . . .

Such is not the state of the case. I say it with a sad sense of the disparity between us. I am not included within the pale of this glorious anniversary! Your high independence only reveals the immeasurable distance between us. The blessings in which you this day rejoice, are not enjoyed in common. The rich inheritance of justice, liberty, prosperity, and independence, bequeathed by your fathers, is shared by you, not by me. The sunlight that brought life and healing to you, has brought stripes and death to me. This Fourth of July is *yours*, not *mine*. You may rejoice, I must mourn. . . .

Fellow-citizens, above your national, tumultuous joy, I hear the mournful wail of millions, whose chains, heavy and grievous yesterday, are to-day rendered more intolerable by the jubilant shouts that reach them. If I do forget, if I do not faithfully remember those bleeding children of sorrow this day, "may . . . my tongue cleave to the roof of my mouth!" . . . My Subject, then, fellow-citizens, is AMERICAN SLAVERY. I shall see this day and its popular characteristics from the slave's point of view. Standing there, identified with the American bondman, making his wrongs mine, I do not hesitate to declare, with all my soul, that the character and conduct of this nation never looked blacker to me than on this Fourth of July. Whether we turn to the declarations of the past, or to the professions of the present, the conduct of the nation seems equally hideous and revolting. America is false to the past, false to the present, and solemnly binds herself to be false to the future. Standing with God and the crushed and bleeding slave on this occasion, I will . . . denounce, with all the emphasis I can command, everything that serves to perpetuate slavery—the great sin and shame of America! . . .

For the present, it is enough to affirm the equal manhood of the Negro race. Is it not astonishing that, while we are plowing, planting, and reaping, using all kinds of mechanical tools, erecting houses, constructing bridges, building ships, working in metals of brass, iron, copper, silvery, and gold; that, while we are reading, writing and ciphering, acting as clerks, merchants, and secretaries, having among us lawyers, doctors, ministers, poets, authors, editors, orators, and teachers; that, while we are engaged in all manner of enterprises common to other men—digging gold in California, capturing the whale in the Pacific, feeding sheep and cattle on the hillside, living, moving, acting, thinking, planning, living in families as husbands, wives, and children, and above all, confessing and worshiping the Christian's God, and looking hopefully for life and immortality beyond the grave,—we are called upon to prove that we are men!

What! am I to argue that it is wrong to make men brutes, to rob them of their liberty, to work them without wages, to keep them ignorant of their relations to their fellow-men, to beat them with sticks, to flay their flesh with the lash, to load their limbs with irons, to hunt them with dogs, to sell them at auction, to sunder their families, to knock out their teeth, to burn their flesh, to starve them into obedience and submission to their masters? Must I argue that a system, thus marked with blood and stained with pollution, is wrong? No; I will not. I have better employment of my time. . . .

What to the American slave is your Fourth of July? I answer, a day that reveals to him, more than all other days in the year, the gross injustice and cruelty to which he is the constant victim. To him, your celebration is a sham; . . . your sounds of rejoicing are empty and heartless; . . . your shouts of liberty and equality [are] hollow mockery; your prayers and hymns . . . are to him mere fraud . . . and hypocrisy—a thin veil to cover up crimes which would disgrace a nation of savages. There is not a nation on the earthy guilty of practices more shocking and bloody, than are the people of the United States, at this very hour.

Source: Philip S. Foner, *The Life and Writings of Frederick Douglass*, Vol. II, *Pre-Civil War Decade 1850–1860* (New York: International, 1950).

issue on December 3, 1847. The *North Star* was published from Rochester, New York, where Douglass and his family took up residence. In New York, Douglass developed and had the financial support of Gerrit Smith, a philanthropist, reformer, and one of the founders of the abolitionist Liberty Party. Perhaps his most important ally was Julia Griffiths, whom he had met in England. She came to the United States and assisted Douglass as business manager and assistant editor of the *North Star*. She was particularly adept at helping Douglass secure funds for the always poorly financed paper. Her presence allowed him to travel and lecture while she took care of the business of publishing the newspaper.

During the 1850s, Douglass remade his abolitionist vision and sought new allies. Black and white abolitionists experienced this decade as a series of political defeats further entrenching what they came to call "Slave Power" in the American polity. The Compromise of 1850 with its newly strengthened Fugitive Slave Law, the Kansas-Nebraska Act of 1854 with the attending warfare in Kansas between pro and antislavery forces, and the U.S. Supreme Court's *Dred Scott* (1857) decision challenged Douglass to rethink his political views. These events left little cause for optimism that the tactics of moral suasion would lead the nations to political regeneration. Douglass abandoned the Garrisonian view of the Constitution, announcing his changed position at the annual convention of the American Anti-Slavery Society in 1851 and in *The Liberator*. The Convention withdrew its support of the *North Star*, but Douglass had already secured another means of support. Casting his lot firmly with political abolitionists, the *North Star* merged with the less successful Liberty Party Paper reemerging under Douglass's editorship as *Frederick Douglass's Paper*. Douglass's newfound positions and alliances were bitterly resented by the Garrisonians, and in a manner that was typical of that age, Douglass found himself increasingly the subject of hostile comments in the Garrisonian papers. These comments culminated when Garrison quietly questioned in print the role of Julia Griffiths in Douglass's household. Anna Murray Douglass issued a statement denying any irregularities. Thereafter, the breach between Douglass and Garrison was complete, and Douglass no longer attended the meetings of the American Anti-Slavery Society.

Throughout the rest of the 1850s, Douglass and his paper were deeply involved in the political process. He spoke at political conventions and endorsed candidates for national and local office. Although his first allegiance was to Gerrit Smith's single-issue Liberty and Radical Abolitionist parties, he flirted even while he criticized with the emerging Free Soil and Republican parties. He also turned with more conviction to elevating the condition of free blacks, advocating a dual strategy of eradicating barriers to their equal participation in civil society, such as his campaign to eliminate the property qualification that was only imposed on blacks in New York, while supporting attempts to establish an industrial education school for blacks in the North. In 1855, he published another autobiography, *My Bondage and My Freedom*, in which he sought to explain his changes of political views and in which he criticized his old friends for their racial practices.

Still Douglass could not imagine abandoning the interracial coalition the abolitionists had created. He merely shifted his sense of who would be the best allies to the political abolitionists. He rejected the increasingly strong minority voice in the black national conventions advocating immigration to Africa, the Caribbean, and Latin America. He also rejected John Brown's plans to capture the Arsenal at Harpers Ferry. Just before the raid was executed, Douglass met Brown in Chambersburg, Pennsylvania, in hopes of dissuading him from a plan he felt was destined to fail. After Brown was defeated and captured, correspondence was found among his possessions that seemed to implicate Douglass and other prominent abolitionists in his raid. Douglass found it expedient to follow through on his plans to lecture in England and Scotland in order to avoid arrest and possible extradition to Virginia.

CIVIL WAR AND RECONSTRUCTION

When Douglass returned from England, the United States was in the midst of the election of 1860. He warmed only slowly to Abraham Lincoln, instead supporting Smith's campaign as the presidential candidate of the Radical Abolitionist Party. Whatever initial reservation Lincoln had about directly addressing the issue of slavery, the Civil War and Reconstruction put the abolitionist goal within reach. After twenty years of swimming against the national tide, Douglass found himself with the much more complex task of trying to influence a rush and flow of events that seemed to be going his way. The Emancipation Proclamation, the enlistment of black troops, the emergence of Radical Republicans, the creation of the Freedman's Bureau, the Reconstruction amendments to the Constitution—all policies that he advocated before they came into effect—gave reality to Douglass's most cherished goals. Undaunted by having to end publication of his newspaper in 1860 and his magazine, *Frederick Douglass' Monthly*, in 1863, Douglass became a propagandist for the war as he wished it to be, and more slowly he also became a Republican Party operative.

The most prominent among blacks in the abolitionist movement, Douglass became the national black politician whom the nation needed, someone who could represent a group of men and women whose actions and opinions were important to the successful pursuit of the war effort, and after the passage of the Fifteenth Amendment a group that played a significant role in Republican Party politics. On August 10, 1863, Douglass led a group of blacks who met Abraham Lincoln in the White House. Although they discussed significant differences between their respective positions on the war aims, the symbolic importance of the meeting was unmistakable. Thereafter he met with most Republican presidents, as well as senators, congressmen, and cabinet members. Even Andrew Johnson, who had no sympathy for Douglass's vision of America, met with him.

In 1872 Douglass's house in Rochester burned down, and he moved his family to the District of Columbia, where he took over ownership and active editorship of the *New National Era*. In that same year he urged the National Convention of Colored People to endorse the presidential candidacy of Ulysses S. Grant. He served as one of Grant's electors in New York State, and he lectured in New England and Middle Atlantic States for Grant's elections. His only major misstep of the period was in 1874 when he accepted the presidency of the Freedman's Savings and Trust Company without being fully aware that this bank, with branches throughout the South and with millions of dollars in deposits, had been mismanaged and was insolvent. When Douglass was unable to restore confidence in the institution, the bank closed and thousands lost their deposits.

THE SAGE OF ANACOSTIA

The year that Rutherford B. Hayes was nominated, Douglass attended his first Republican National Convention, and he missed only one thereafter. The Compromise of 1877 brought Hayes the presidency in exchange for his withdrawal of federal troops from the South, effectively ending Reconstruction. If the black vote could no longer elect candidates in the post-Reconstruction South, it remained important in nominating Republican candidates to national office, and blacks like Douglass had limited access to the

party's patronage machine. Hayes appointed Douglass U.S. marshall of the District of Columbia, his first political patronage position, and accepted his advocacy for others. The series of positions Douglass received from Republican presidents gave him a regular income and relieved him of the necessity of constant speech making and article writing, while allowing him the time to speak and write as he pleased. He bought a large house for himself and his family along the Anacostia River, called "Cedar Hill," and there he wrote his third autobiography, *The Life and Times of Frederick Douglass*. Published in 1881, it was less successful than his previous volumes, but it recorded his view of the volatile Civil War and Reconstruction periods.

The last decade of Douglass's life was marked by two controversies, one in his private life and one in his public career. In 1884, after Anna died, Douglass remarried. His wife, Helen Pitt, a clerk in the Office of the Recorder of Deeds, was the daughter of an abolitionist and descendant of the *Mayflower*. It was an interracial marriage criticized for different reasons by both blacks and whites, and to which his children were cool. In 1889, Douglass accepted appointment as America's resident minister and consul general to Haiti. In addition to the many small tasks he had to perform for American citizens, he was also expected to further American economic and military interests. The United States was particularly interested in establishing a naval base at Môle St. Nicolas. The American press blamed Douglass's support for Haitian interests for the failure of the negotiations, and after returning to the United States Douglass resigned the consulship. For their part, Haitians still honored him and in 1893 appointed him their commissioner to the World's Columbian Exposition in Chicago.

Douglass revised and updated his last autobiography in 1892, and in his last days he took up new causes and renewed his commitment to old ones. He became an enthusiastic supporter of Ida B. Wells's crusade against lynching. On February 20, 1895, Douglass spoke at a meeting of the National Council of Women, where he was with his old friend and sometime adversary, Susan B. Anthony. Shortly after returning to Cedar Hills, he died of heart failure.

The degree to which Douglass had come to embody the central American political struggle of his century became almost immediately apparent. His memorial service in Washington, D.C., was followed by others throughout the nation. The new group of leaders, wary of his views when he was alive, quickly reached out to embrace his legacy. No two leaders fought more for Douglass's legacy and mantel than Booker T. Washington and W.E.B. Du Bois, each claiming to be continuing his tradition.

George P. Cunningham

BIBLIOGRAPHY

Blassingame, John W., et al. *The Frederick Douglass Papers: Series One: The Speeches, Debates, and Interviews*, Vols. I–V. New Haven, CT: Yale University Press, 1979–1992.

————. *The Frederick Douglass Papers: Series Two: Autobiographical Writings*, Vol. I. New Haven, CT: Yale University Press, 1999.

Blight, David W. *Frederick Douglass' Civil War: Keeping Faith in Jubilee.* Baton Rouge: Louisiana State University Press, 1989.

————. *Frederick Douglass and Abraham Lincoln: A Relationship in Language, Politics, and Memory.* Milwaukee, WI: Marquette University Press, 2001

Dickinson, Preston J. *Frederick Douglass: The Maryland Years.* Baltimore, MD: Johns Hopkins University Press, 1980.

Diedrich, Maria. *Love Across Color Lines: Ottilie Assing and Frederick Douglass.* New York: Hill & Wang, 2000.

Foner, Philip S., ed. *Frederick Douglass on Women's Rights.* New York: Da Capo, 1994.

Gates, Henry Louis, Jr., ed. *Frederick Douglass: Autobiographies.* New York: Library of America, 1994.

Huggins, Nathan I. *Slave and Citizen: The Life of Frederick Douglass.* Boston: Little, Brown, 1980

McFeely, William S. *Frederick Douglass.* New York: Simon and Schuster, 1991.

Martin, Waldo E., Jr. *The Mind of Frederick Douglass.* Chapel Hill: University of North Carolina Press, 1984.

Quarles, Benjamin. *Frederick Douglass.* Washington, DC: Associated, 1948.

Sundquist, Eric J., ed. *Frederick Douglass: New Literary and Historical Essays.* New York: Cambridge University Press, 1990.

FREE BLACKS: FOUNDATIONS OF POLITIES

Shortly after South Carolina troops fired on Fort Sumter, blacks in Boston assembled at their Twelfth Baptist Church to rally themselves to the Union cause and to volunteer as soldiers. Similar events took place in Providence, New York, Washington, Cleveland, and Philadelphia. These men and women, the free blacks of the North, were the fruits of the Northern emancipation, and they could justly feel that if their own history could be replicated in the South, they had reason to be optimistic about their future and the future of their brothers and sisters in bondage. In the eighty years between the Revolutionary and the Civil wars, they had created a community that spoke in words and by the example of their lives for universal liberty and unrestricted citizenship. They had lived in a margin of freedom that was far smaller than that of their white contemporaries, but within that margin they had also made the transition from slavery to freedom, absorbed a large number of fugitive slaves and free black migrants from the South, and built a network of local and national institutions. Despite, and in part because of, civil, social, and economic proscriptions, the free blacks of the North welded themselves into a community, with an institutional infrastructure, a purposeful official culture, and the means of sustaining their voices in the public debates about race and slavery. The clarity with which they saw their role in the Civil War was the product of eighty years of building a culture that stressed the intertwined nature of their status and that of the slave, and imposed on them the obligation to be a vanguard in the movement toward total emancipation.

SHAPING A FREE COMMUNITY

The impulse toward institution building was shared by free blacks in both the North and the South. The first black church was organized in Silver Bluff, Georgia, in 1773. It was followed by the Harrison Street Baptist Church, organized in Petersburg, Virginia, in 1776; the First African Baptist Church, organized in Richmond, Virginia, in 1785; and the Colored Baptist Church, organized in Williamsburg, Virginia, in 1785. Throughout the antebellum period, black churches, often with mixed congregations of slave and free, and pastored by blacks, existed in the South. In like manner, mutual aid societies and schools existed intermittently in numerous Southern cities. The history of the Southern black church and other social institutions, however, was one of valiant efforts to maintain some autonomy against increasing hostility toward them from the white population. Often the churches had to give up their ambitions of having a black minister, or they had to accept nominal or very stringent white control. These churches and other institutions remain as testimony to the impulses of their creators, but stable institutions could be built by blacks only in the cities and towns of the North, and it is in that region that the uninterrupted history of all-black organization and institutions allowed them to reach their intended potential.

The abolition of slavery in the Northern states during the era of the American Revolution established the basis for freedom, but emancipated slaves took it upon themselves to define what it was to be free men and women. The most important component of freedom for them was to move from being dependents and subordinates in white households to becoming economically and culturally independent householders. In his study of blacks in Providence, Rhode Island, *The Afro-Yankees: Providence's Black Community in the Antebellum Era* (1982), historian Robert Cottrol concludes that householders "had to make decisions for their families on such matters as the education of their children, the religious environment of their families, and how to protect their families in an increasingly hostile society." The formation of households in an environment that was hostile to the economic, cultural, and political ambitions of blacks called for a variety of institutions to sustain and support the ideal as well as the reality.

The founding of the independent black religious denominations was pivotal in the development of the free black community. The early history of the independent black church begins in Philadelphia. The principals in the first act of that history were two men of similar background and vision—Richard Allen and Absalom Jones. Both men purchased their freedom before the general emancipation in Pennsylvania, educated themselves, and became property holders. Allen, after converting to Methodism, traveled with white preachers in Maryland, New Jersey, Delaware, and Pennsylvania as an exhorter.

Like most Northern free blacks, Allen and Jones worshiped at a white church, St. George's Methodist Episcopal. In 1787, their church instituted the Southern policy on rear balcony seating for blacks. In part, the segregation policy was a reaction to an increase in the black membership through Jones and Allen's evangelical activities in the black community. Jones, Allen, and other black parishioners were forcibly evicted from their seats and forced to sit in the balcony. They withdrew from the church and formed the African Free Society.

The African Free Society was a mutual aid society that collected dues and dispensed benefits for its sick members, widows, and dependent children. Blacks throughout the North created similar societies to establish and protect their economic standing. Predating the Philadelphia group was the Free African Union Society of Newport, Rhode Island, which was founded in 1780. The African Benevolent Society was founded in that same city in 1807, and a satellite unit of the Free African Union Society was founded in Providence in 1789. In 1796, the Free African Society of Boston was founded. Although by nature ephemeral and short-lived, mutual aid societies became a constant part of the life of free blacks in the North.

At the core of the Free African Society and the various other mutual aid societies was a vision of the necessary characteristics that Afro-Americans needed to cultivate in order to prosper socially, economically, and politically. The men and women who developed the society tried to preserve, support, and ultimately reproduce themselves and their accomplishments. They were classically self-made men and women, and their institutions embodied the goal of "racial elevation," which they saw in their lives. The preamble of the Free African Society's constitution is more than anything else a statement of an achieved identity. It declared: "Whereas, Absalom Jones and Richard Allen, two men of the African race, who, for their religious life and conversations, have obtained a good report among men, these persons for a love of the people of their own complexion whom they beheld with sorrow, because of their irreligious and uncivilized state, often communed together upon this painful and important subject in order to form some kind of religious body; . . . till it was proposed after a serious communication of sentiments that a society should be formed without regard to religious tenants [sic], provided the persons live an orderly and sober life, in order to support one another in sickness, and for the benefits of their widows and fatherless children." The society sought to promote education, thrift, industry, marital fidelity, and temperance. These values were written into their constitution, and loss of benefits and membership was the punishment for straying outside the strictures of behavior. In addition, as the society grew, a committee was appointed to "visit the members and give such advice as may appear necessary." As the antebellum period progressed, the personal qualities called for by the society would become the official standards of the free black community. In the society's structure were the seeds of the independent black church, literacy societies, temperance societies, and other organizations that would promote and sustain official standards.

The Free African Society of Philadelphia began holding Sunday services and organized the African Church in 1791. In 1794, the society raised the funds for and built St. Thomas African Episcopal Church. The church, under the leadership of Jones, was accepted by the Episcopalian denomination in that same year. Jones became the first black Episcopalian priest in 1804. Allen, however, remained faithful to the Methodist doctrine and established Bethel African Methodist Episcopal Church in 1794. He became a deacon and was ordained in 1799. African Methodist Episcopal (AME) churches were established in other Northern cities, and in 1816, the various independent churches met and established a denomination with Allen as its first bishop. Despite the different denominational affiliations, Jones and Allen remained friends and worked together in many common endeavors. They shared the same broad goals and methods; under their guidance, the activities of St. Thomas and Bethel AME were mirror images of each other. At St. Thomas, Jones founded the Female Benevolent Society, the African Friendly Society, and a school. In 1795, Allen opened a school, and in 1804, he organized the Society of Free People of Color for Promoting the Instruction and School Education of Children of African Descent. Together Jones and Allen petitioned both the Pennsylvania and the United

States Congress for the abolition of slavery, provided leadership for the Philadelphia lodge of black Masons, and founded the Society for the Suppression of Vice and Immorality.

In similar ways, other all-black denominations were founded. In 1796, James Varick led a group of New York blacks in the establishment of Zion Church, which became one of the founders of the African Methodist Episcopal Zion denomination in 1822 with Varick as its first bishop. Baptist churches also began to make an appearance in the North. In 1805, the Jay Street Baptist Church was founded in Boston; in 1808, the Abyssinian Baptist Church was founded in New York; and in 1810, the First African Baptist Church was founded in Philadelphia. By 1840, there were 300 independent black congregations in the North. These churches existed in almost every major Northern city, and equally important, denominations had been established that tied the black churches together into regional units. Local leadership had developed, as had national leaders with strong local bases. The black community under these leaders began to establish a degree of political, social, economic, and cultural autonomy.

Although the church was the most successful and most permanent of the institutions built by free blacks, second in importance was the establishment of schools. The establishment of schools did not proceed with the directness of the establishment of independent black churches. Each political jurisdiction had differing ideas about the education of blacks. Some made no provisions for black education, others had an integrated school system, while still others provided for a segregated school system. Where education was lacking or deficient, blacks tried through various institutions to create independent black schools. At the simplest level, churches established Sunday schools and Bible classes. By the 1830s, blacks in all of the major cities supported schools, and Philadelphia had ten such institutions. In 1844, the African Methodist Episcopal Church Ohio Conference took the first step toward founding a theological seminary. Union Seminary was opened in 1847 and paralleled the activities of white Methodists of that state to found a college for blacks. The institution they founded was named after the British abolitionist William Wilberforce and opened in 1856. During the Civil War, the Methodist Episcopal church purchased Wilberforce and merged it with their Union Seminary, thereby creating the oldest of the historically black colleges.

In the 1830s, two new types of organizations arose: literary societies and temperance societies. Early in the 1830s, blacks made a concerted effort to establish literary societies. Blacks found themselves denied access to white forums for the discussion of ideas and to white reading rooms; the literary societies tried to ensure that free blacks would not be denied these avenues to self-culture. In her survey of antebellum black literary societies, *Early Negro Writing, 1760–1837* (1971), Dorothy Porter lists eleven in Pennsylvania; sixteen in New York State; six in Massachusetts; three in the District of Columbia; two each in Rhode Island, Ohio, and Maryland; and one each in Connecticut, Michigan, and New Jersey. Most met at regular intervals to discuss books, to read, and to discuss original works by their members. They also sponsored libraries. In a similar fashion, temperance and total abstinence societies grew throughout the 1830s and 1840s. Aimed at both the old and the young, these societies elicited pledges of total abstinence, lectured on the evils of drink, and encouraged blacks to spend their money in more profitable areas.

By the 1830s, the main lines through which blacks wished to develop their communities were established. The free blacks of the North found, in the prevailing ethos of the nation, forms and frames of reference that were meaningful to them. They adopted these frames of reference to their own condition, and through a variety of organizations made them suitable vehicles for their own elevation. The church, mutual aid societies, educational institutions, temperance societies, and literary societies formed an interrelated network of organizations that aimed at racial elevation. Many of these institutions worked together and shared membership. In particular, the church encouraged and housed a number of other organizations.

Much of the effort of free blacks was spent looking inward, establishing a distance between themselves and the condition of blacks in slavery, and defining the nature of being for free men and women. Free blacks borrowed liberally and, indeed, self-consciously from Anglo-American culture. At the core of their personal identities and the culture they were forming for themselves was the prevailing nineteenth-century notion of character. If in the formative period of the free black community, there was an emphasis on self-mastery, the other side of the notion of character—the presentation of the self to society and the interrelationship between the social and the moral—was ever present. Indeed, the presentation of their achieved identity as free men and women was central to their political stances.

SHAPING A POLITICAL VISION

Free blacks of the North sought to achieve a personal and public identity that could not be realized while slavery existed in the South or racial discrimination existed in the North. Their quest to define themselves as free men and women had to entail a struggle against slavery. Beginning with tentative pleas to the consciences of men and women of goodwill and ending with strident outcries in voices that presumed a moral authority, free blacks protested the slave trade, slavery, and racial discrimination in free states. Drawing heavily on the ideal of a universal brotherhood of man under God, and the mixed secular-sacred language of the Declaration of Independence, they launched an ever-increasing attack on racial discrimination in the North and slavery in the South. Racial elevation, as they developed the notion, was a dual project that called for the development of character within the race and the recognition of civil liberty by American society. So completely interwoven were these twin aspects of the same project that each was conceived and described in terms of the other. Almost always including a statement of their achieved identity in their numerous petitions, memorials, articles, and speeches, they argued their accomplishments in liberty as living proof of the unreasonableness and immorality of racial distinctions in civil and economic matters. In doing so, free blacks gradually established themselves as the national spokesmen for the interests of slaves and became significant theorists, actors, and voices in the abolitionist movement.

In 1792, Benjamin Banneker, a free black who had achieved international distinction as a mathematician and astronomer, wrote Secretary of State Thomas Jefferson. Within his letter are the main lines of the argument that the free blacks used against slavery. He said: "I freely and cheerfully acknowledge that I am of the African race, and in that color which is natural to them of the deepest dye; and it is under a sense of the most profound gratitude to the supreme Ruler of the Universe that I now confess to you that I am not under that state of tyrannical thralldom and inhuman captivity to which too many of my brethren are doomed, but that I have abundantly tasted of the fruition of those blessings, which proceed from that free and unequalled liberty with which you will willingly allow you have mercifully received from the immediate hand of that Being from whom proceedeth every good and perfect Gift." As proof of these blessings that liberty conferred on men, Banneker offered his own almanac, the first of six derived from his astro-

nomical calculations. Reminding Jefferson of America's won struggle for liberty, he suggested that "it is the indispensable duty of those who maintain for themselves the rights of nature, and who profess the obligations of Christianity, to extend their power and influence to the relief of every part of the human race," according to historian Sidney Kaplan in his *Black Presence in the Era of the American Revolution* (1989).

In 1817, the establishment of the American Society for the Colonizing the Free People of Color of the United States, popularly known as the American Colonization Society, presented the free black population with a strong challenge to their goals for themselves and for the country. Through the American Colonization Society, distinguished white Northerners and Southerners united around deportation to Africa as the solution to the problems of free blacks and part of the ultimate solution to the problem of slavery. The Colonization Society quickly brought together the antislavery elements of American society with slaveholders and established a national consensus around deportation. Under the society, antislavery became almost synonymous with colonization. The prestige of its membership and the resources at its command threatened to drown out the emerging voice of free blacks as spokesmen for their own interests.

Emigration to Africa was neither a new idea to blacks nor one that they were opposed to under all circumstances. In 1783, the mutual aid societies of Boston, Newport, Providence, and Philadelphia corresponded with one another to discuss the idea of emigrating to Africa. In 1815, Paul Cuffe, a wealthy black sea captain in Westport, Massachusetts, used his own resources to take thirty-eight black settlers to the British colony of Sierra Leone. Free blacks, however, envisioned emigration in quite a different way from the members of the Colonization Society. For free blacks, emigration was to be selective and missionary in nature. Just as they sought to replicate themselves in America, they felt it was their duty and obligation to play a role in the elevation of Africa by evangelizing, promoting education, encouraging modern approaches to cultivation, and spurring commerce. The formation of the American Colonization Society virtually ended discussion on emigration in the black community for two decades. The colonization idea challenged the basic tenets of the identity that free blacks were building for themselves, the universality of humankind under God and the American Constitution. This appellation "African" ceased to be used in the titles of new black organizations. Henceforth, free blacks would look at themselves and describe themselves as Americans. Equally important, they would bend their resources toward establishing themselves as the legitimate voice for their race in America and sometimes in Africa.

Although the Colonization Society had some black supporters, the majority of free blacks were swift and clear about their rejection of colonization. Almost immediately following the formation of the society, a rally at Bethel AME Church in Pennsylvania, attended by over 3,000, declared the collective opposition of free blacks to colonization. At a second rally, James Forten, a wealthy sailmaker and influential leader of Philadelphia's black community, declared: "Relieved from the miseries of slavery, many of us by your aid possessing the benefits which industry and integrity in this prosperous country assures to all its inhabitants, enjoying the rich blessings of religion, by opportunities of worshipping the only true God, under the light of Christianity, each of us according to his understanding; and having afforded to us and our children the means of education and improvement; we have no wish to separate from our present home." Forten made clear the opposition of free blacks to colonization. He also denied that the expatriation of slaves would be of benefit either to the slave or to Africa. As noted by Porter, he felt that a community of freed slaves "without arts, without habits of industry, and unaccustomed to provide by their won exertions and foresight for their wants, the colony will soon become the abode of every vice, and the home of every misery." Forten further argued that the deportation of free blacks would strengthen slavery, not weaken it.

One of the most effective responses to the Colonization Society was the development of the black press. Although by the 1820s blacks were well organized on the local level, they had not created a means of systematic national communication. In 1827, John B. Russwurm and Samuel E. Cornish founded the first black periodical, *Freedom's Journal,* which Russwurm renamed and edited alone under the title *The Rights of All* until its demise in 1830. The *Journal* was above all anticolonization, but it also drew portraits of famous blacks in history, defended the character and the intellectual and cultural capabilities of blacks, and championed immediate and unconditional abolition of slavery. James Forten, Richard Allen, and abolitionist David Walker were among its contributors.

Other periodicals followed the demise of *The Rights of All.* Cornish himself founded the second national periodical, *The Weekly Advocate* (1837–1842),

which was renamed *Colored American.* The AME church established three periodicals in this period: the *African Methodist Episcopal Church Magazine* (1841–1848), which was largely devoted to denominational news; the *Christian Herald* (1857–), which is still published in the twenty-first century as the *Christian Recorder;* and the *Repository of Religion and Literature and of Science and Art* (1858–1864), a general interest magazine. Perhaps the best known and the longest lived of the antebellum black journals was *The North Star,* edited by Frederick Douglass. First published in 1847 and rechristened *Frederick Douglass's Paper* in 1851, it remained in publication until 1860. Also of particular note was the *Anglo-African Magazine* (1859), which distinguished itself by the fame and caliber of its contributors. The goal of a consistent national black press was never reached, but after 1838 a periodical edited by a black was almost always available.

Along with the desire to create a national press, free blacks wanted to create a secular national organization. Samuel Cornish in *Freedom's Journal* called for a national convention of free blacks. The first national convention of free blacks met in 1830. Although it was the first secular institution to attempt to achieve national status, its origins were rooted in the black churches and in Philadelphia. The first convention was held at Bethel AME Church in Philadelphia and was presided over by Bishop Allen. For the next five years conventions were held annually, all but one of them hosted by Philadelphia's blacks. The activities of the conventions of the 1830s were decidedly inward looking and focused on the elevation of free blacks. Many of the delegates to these first conventions had come of age in the period of the Revolutionary War and were shaped by their earlier organizational activities; they were in may ways trying to reconstruct on a national scale the early free African societies.

One of the primary aims of the convention was to discredit the idea of colonization among white antislavery advocates, but in the initial three years the delegates also voted to support the efforts of Cincinnati blacks to emigrate to Canada. Second, there was a plan for the establishment of a black college of manual labor in New Haven, Connecticut. The delegates made ambitious plans for an "American Society of Free Persons of Colour, for Improving their Condition in the United States; for Purchasing Lands; and for the Establishing of a Settlement in Upper Canada." They stressed the official virtues of temperance, education, and economic development. In the 1831 convention, the Committee on the Convention of the Free People of Colour said: "Education, Temperance, and

THE BLACK FREE PRESS 1837

In the early nineteenth century, African Americans contended that the right to a free press should not be limited to white Americans but should extend to blacks as well. In 1837, Samuel Cornish founded The Weekly Advocate *as a means to advance this cause. The following is an editorial to the readers, justifying the newspaper's founding.*

The addition of another Paper to the list of those already before the Public, may be, and is probably considered by some persons of common observations and superficial reflection, as unnecessary and uncalled for; but numerous, however, as we freely allow them to be, it is believed by many of our people, that there is still a vacancy to be supplied, a chain to be filled up; and that there is NOW a clear opening for one of a different character, which shall be devoted to the moral improvement and amelioration of our race. After the most mature deliberation we have commenced the noble enterprise. Our paper, thought somewhat small in size, will be found valuable in contents. The advantages of the present undertaking are not to be estimated by words, they are incalculable. If the Press, a "FREE PRESS," be a foe to the tyrant—if its blessings be so great and innumerable; the Question naturally presents itself, why do we not have one of our own? We now have a Press and Paper under our own entire control and we call upon our friends, one and all, to come forward and assist us in this work and labor of love, and share in the consequent blessings thereof. Are there not hundreds among you, who will welcome the Advocate as a Friendly Visitor?—Philanthropists! Shall we have LIGHT, clear and irresistible Light on all the important topics of the day, or shall we live and expire in the gloom of ignorance, with the lights of science shining around us.

The *Advocate* will be like a chain, binding you together as ONE. Its columns will always be the organ of your wishes and feelings, and the proper medium for laying your claims before the Public. What then, in the name of common sense, is wanted to enable us to GO FORWARD, in the successful prosecution of this new enterprise?—Judging from numbers, we are abundantly able. O how often have we been insulted and degraded, and how frequently do we feel the want of an ADVOCATE among us! Those of us who shall be instrumental in establishing such a paper, will reap a rich reward in their own bosoms—not in silver and gold—but in the intelligence and improvement of our race in intellectual knowledge and refinement. And when time has consigned us to our honored graves, the good we have done will live after us. Future generations will partake largely and freely of the fruits of the tree planted by our bounty, rise up and call us blessed.....

We need scarcely say, we are opposed to *Colonization*. It matters not to us what features it may assume whether It presents in the garb of philanthropy, or assumes the mild and benign countenance of Christianity, or comes with the selfish aspect of Politics; we will believe, assert and maintain (So help us God!) that we are opposed to the exclusive emigration and colonization of the People of Color of these United States. We hold ourselves ready, at all times to combat with opposite views, and defend these our principles to the last! In regard to TEMPERANCE, we go the whole in this good cause. But our motto is *Temperance in all things*. We shall advocate Universal Suffrages and Universal Education, and we shall oppose all Monopolies, which oppress the poor and laboring classes of society....

We need not say that our entire dependence for support is upon the colored portion of this great community, when we tell them that the ADVOCATE is their paper, in every sense of the word—that it will advocate their just claims and rights—sustain them in every proper appeal to manly generosity and justice. And as the cause of IMMEDIATE EMANCIPATION is based on incontrovertible right, we shall at all times, take it up with resolution, and defend it with firmness. We trust we possess sufficient moral courage to assert THE TRUTH and maintain it at all hazards. We shall neither be frightened nor coaxed from our duty. The empty threats of the oppressor we despise. We shall, however, always point out that course to the friendless and unprotected, which will bring *happiness* to the mind, and will give such advice as will prove useful to all in the wearisome journey of human life.

The people of color have often said among themselves. We want an Advocate of our own—devoted particularly to our own interests—conducted by ourselves, devoted to our moral, mental and political improvement, containing the news of the day, and a variety of scientific and literary matter; and ONE in which we can make known our various and respective occupations in life, through the medium of advertising. To such we say, Look here! Today you have spread before your eyes the desideratum you have so long, and ardently prayed for.

Source: The Weekly Advocate, *New York, January 7, 1837.*

Economy, are best calculated to promote the elevation of mankind to a proper rank and standing among men, as they enable him to discharge all those duties enjoined on him by his Creator. We would therefore respectfully request an early attention to those virtues among our brethren, who have a desire to be useful."

Until the 1830s, the trend among blacks was to create independent organizations. Perhaps the original impetus to separation was discrimination in, and exclusion from, white institutions, but the institutions of free blacks clearly gave them an independence that they came to regard as inherently valuable. The emergence of the militant abolitionist movement among whites created an important point of convergence between independent black institutions and white organizations. William Lloyd Garrison was one of the benefactors of the infrastructure of the black community. It provided him with his crucial early support and encouragement. For the first four years of the publication of *The Liberator,* blacks were three quarters of the subscribers, and Garrison's pivotal journey to England to gather the support of the British antislavery movement was largely underwritten by blacks. The New England Anti-Slavery Society was founded in the schoolroom of the African Baptist Church in Boston, and much of the planning for the American Anti-Slavery Society took place at the home of James Forten in Philadelphia.

The early support given by free blacks was essential for Garrison's development from a lonely voice into the voice of American antislavery. They supported him with such enthusiasm because he was the first prominent white to espouse the black view on slavery. Garrison championed immediate abolition, uncompensated emancipation, and equality for free blacks. His full entry into the fold came in 1832 with the publication of his *Thoughts on African Colonization* in which he cited black opposition to the Colonization Society as a primary reason against it. In later years, blacks would claim a prominent role in converting Garrison away from the colonization solution.

Where the Colonization Society competed with the blacks for authority, the post-1830s abolitionist crusade sought part of its authority from blacks. They became central in the new abolitionist crusade. Free blacks gave eloquent testimony to the genius of liberty, and the former slaves bore shocking witness to the brutality of slavery. Charles Lenox Remond, a free man, was one of the first blacks appointed as a lecturer on the abolitionist circuit. Remond was joined

by others, most notably the fugitive slave William Wells Brown and Frederick Douglass. The fugitives from the plantation added another dimension to the crusade through their published autobiographies. Many were written by the fugitives themselves, which doubly struck at the arguments of black inferiority used to justify slavery.

The rise of militant abolitionism supplemented, but did not supplant, black-led institutions; in fact, it perhaps encouraged the growth of these organizations. The National Negro Conventions expanded their reach by establishing state-affiliated organizations. The conventions that met in the 1840s and 1850s did so in a different atmosphere and under new leadership. Many of the older leaders died or were in declining health: Allen died in 1831; Forten's health declined in the late 1830s, and he died in 1842. Escaped slaves like Frederick Douglass and William Wells Brown, whose base of influence was the abolitionist movement, not traditional black institutions, came to national prominence on the lecture circuit. They joined with traditional black leaders, who were becoming increasingly militant, in focusing the efforts of free blacks outward. A decade of militant abolitionism had placed the issues of slavery and the role of free blacks at the center of national attention. The conventions of the 1840s, therefore, were decidedly more political.

As time progressed, the abolitionist movement was failing to live up to the hopes that blacks had for it. Blacks found that their white co-workers in the struggle to end slavery were not untainted by the habits of racism and paternalism. In the 1840s, the movement itself split between the moral suasionist led by William Lloyd Garrison and the political pragmatist led by Garrett Smith. Debate on central goals and tactics spread to the conventions, where blacks debated encouraging slaves in the South to revolt. After the black community had successfully shifted the abolitionist movement away from the path of colonization, it reopened the debate on emigration.

Where consensus and the development of culture were essential to the first convention, the conventions of the 1840s took their existence within their community for granted. Despite the significant issues that divided black leadership in the 1840s and 1850s, the cultural ideals that were established prior to the 1830s held sway. Education, for example, was a consistent focus for all conventions. In the 1830s, the conventions made plans to create a manual arts college in New Haven, Connecticut. The conventions of 1847 and

1853 would also support similar plans. Among those who proposed emigration, the vision of civilizing Africa, or making Africans like themselves, still held sway and was the key to the reestablishment of African greatness. Garnett's address to the slaves encouraging violent resistance was so steeped in the ideas of the universal need of man to be free that at times it seemed to condemn slaves for their submission to bondage.

The decade of the 1850s was indeed a difficult one for free blacks. The abolitionist movement was disappointing, and the fruits of militant abolitionism were few, scattered, and sometimes bitter. As the issue of slavery became part of a national debate, the instinct of most Americans was to compromise. The decade was inaugurated with the Compromise of 1850, which once again tried to find a *modus vivendi* between the diverging interests of the North and South. That compromise, however, contained a Fugitive Slave Act, which endangered not only runaway slaves but many prominent abolitionists and free blacks as well. The U.S. Supreme Court's *Dred Scott* decision of 1857 undercut constitutional efforts to give blacks citizenship. Some blacks reacted with increasing militancy, and a handful joined John Brown's assault on Harpers Ferry. Others tried violence in the North to block the return of fugitive slaves, and still others looked toward Africa or the Caribbean as a home.

From the vantage point of the late 1850s, free blacks had reason to despair. Viewed by objective standards, many of the organizations they founded were feeble and others were short-lived. Only the black church maintained a stable and consistent presence. Yet, at the same time, many of the larger goals of the institutions were reached. Free blacks had developed a broad consensus around thrift, industry, temperance, and Christian piety as internal measures of character. If not all possessed or even aspired to these "virtues," these characteristics were the official goals of the leaders of the free black community. Free blacks had also established a history of their own transformation in adversity from slaves to free men and women. That history served up its own institutions and representative men and women as examples and models for themselves and their progeny. Equally important, free blacks had achieved an independent voice in American politics. Despite the divisions of basic political goals on the eve of the Civil War, free blacks had become a culturally unified community with internally determined values, visions, and goals, and with models for achieving those goals.

CONCLUSION

The Civil War, emancipation, and the enlistment of black soldiers healed many of the divisions of the 1850s and reaffirmed the main lines of the dual project of freedom developed by free blacks. In the Civil War, blacks prepared as soldiers against slavery, as missionaries to the emancipated slaves, and as spokesmen for the next phase of their struggle, the replication of their history in the South.

On October 4, 1864, the last of the National Conventions of Colored Men convened in Syracuse, New York. In addition to delegates from Northern states, delegates attended from Virginia, North Carolina, Florida, Louisiana, Tennessee, Missouri, and Mississippi. In accepting election to the presidency of the Convention, Frederick Douglass declared ". . . nowhere, in the wide, wide world, can men be found coupled with a cause of greater dignity and importance than that which brings us here. We are here to promote the freedom, progress, elevation, and perfect enfranchisement, of the entire colored people of the United States; to show that, though slaves, we are not contented slaves, but that like all other progressive races of men, we are resolved to advance in the scale of knowledge, worth, and civilization, and claim our rights as men among men." The convention's business took place in front of the battle flag of the First Louisiana Colored Troops. Each evening session was reserved for oration. Perhaps P.B. Randolph of New York echoed the majority sentiment in declaring:

> we are here to prove our right to manhood and justice, to maintain these rights not by force of more appeal, not by loud threats, not by battle-axe and sabre, but by the divine rights of brains, of will, of true patriotism, of manhood, of womanhood, of all that is great and noble and worth striving for in human character. We are here to ring the bells at the door of the world: proclaiming to the nations, to the white man in his palace, the slave in his hut, kings on their throne, and to the whole broad universe, that WE ARE COMING UP.

The convention looked to the future: it founded the National Equal Rights League whose purpose was "to encourage sound morality education, temperance, frugality, industry and promote every thing that pertains to a well-ordered and dignified life; to obtain by appeals to the minds and conscience of the American people, or by legal process when possible, a recognition of the rights of the colored people of the nation as American citizens."

George P. Cunningham

BIBLIOGRAPHY

Andrews, William L. *To Tell a Free Story: The First Century of Afro-American Autobiography, 1760–1865.* Urbana: University of Illinois Press, 1986.

Bartlett, Irving H. *From Slave to Citizen: The Story of the Negro in Rhode Island.* Providence, RI: Urban League of Greater Providence, 1954.

Bell, Howard H., ed. *Minutes of the Proceedings of the National Negro Conventions, 1830–1864.* New York: Ayers, 1969.

Berlin, Ira. *Slaves Without Masters: The Free Negro in the Antebellum South.* New York: Pantheon Books, 1974.

Bethel, Elizabeth R. *The Roots of African-American Identity: Memory and History in Free Antebellum Communities.* New York: St. Martin's, 1997.

Cottrol, Robert J. *The Afro-Yankees: Providence's Black Community in the Antebellum Era.* Westport, CT: Greenwood Press, 1982.

Curry, Leonard P. *Free Blacks in Urban America, 1800–1850: The Shadow of a Dream.* Chicago: University of Chicago Press, 1981.

Horton, James O. *Free People of Color: Inside the African American Community.* Washington, DC: Smithsonian Institute, 1993.

Horton, James O., and Lois E. Horton. *Black Bostonians: Family Life and Community Struggle in the Antebellum North.* New York: Holmes and Meier, 1979.

———. *In Hope of Liberty: Culture, Community, and Protest among Northern Free Blacks, 1700–1860.* New York: Oxford University Press, 1998.

Kaplan, Sidney. *The Black Presence in the Era of the American Revolution.* Rev. ed. Amherst: University of Massachusetts Press, 1989.

Litwack, Leon. *North of Slavery: The Negro in the Free States, 1790–1860.* Chicago: University of Chicago Press, 1961.

Miller, Floyd J. *The Search for a Black Nationality: Black Colonization and Emigration, 1787–1863.* Urbana: University of Illinois Press, 1975.

Nash, Gary B. *Forging Freedom: The Formation of Philadelphia's Black Community, 1720–1840.* Boston: Harvard University Press, 1991.

Porter, Dorothy, ed. *Early Negro Writing, 1760–1837.* Boston: Beacon, 1971.

Quarles, Benjamin. *Black Abolitionists.* New York: Oxford University Press, 1969.

Raboteau, Albert J. *Slave Religion: The "Invisible Institution" in the Antebellum South.* New York: Oxford University Press, 1978.

Reed, Harry A. *Platform for Change: The Foundations of the Northern Free Black Community, 1775–1865.* East Lansing: Michigan State University Press, 1994.

Thorborough, Emma. *The Negro in Indiana: A Study of a Minority.* Indianapolis: Indiana University Press, 1957.

Winch, Julie. *Black Elite: Activism, Accommodation, and the Struggle for Autonomy, 1787–1848.* Philadelphia: Temple University Press, 1993.

Wright, Richard R., Jr. *The Negro in Pennsylvania: A Study in Economic History.* Philadelphia: A.M.E. Book Concern, 1910.

ANTISLAVERY RESISTANCE: AN OVERVIEW

Slavery was America's paradox, for while white citizens increasingly enjoyed an unprecedented level of individual liberty and social equality African Americans were treated as chattel. The enslavement of one group of people made little sense in a nation that proclaimed, "all men are created equal," and when the rhetoric of the Enlightenment ideals of the inherent rights of men and individual liberty crossed the Atlantic Ocean in the second half of the eighteenth century, the walls supporting the institution of slavery began to come down.

In the two decades after the American Revolution, every Northern state legislature took steps to abolish slavery; but in the South, with the invention of the cotton gin and the rise of "King Cotton," the value of slave labor to the region's economy and culture increased. Here, as in other slave societies throughout the Western Hemisphere, emancipation would come neither quickly nor easily. Consequently, a movement developed among both free and enslaved Americans in the first half of the nineteenth century to destroy the South's "peculiar" institution. Like other reform movements inspired by the evangelical Protestant revivals of the 1820s, the crusade to abolish slavery aimed to remake America into a more perfect and Christian nation; but unlike the others, this one reached its stated objective.

THE MOVEMENT TO ABOLISH SLAVERY

A number of important historical events served as catalysts to the organized movement to abolish slavery in the United States. First, in 1829 a free black clothier in Boston published the most incendiary piece of antislavery literature ever written by an American. Known as the *Appeal to the Colored Citizens of the World*, David Walker's written attack on slavery and the failure of the American dream shocked readers, for Walker not only charged Northerners with complicity in perpetuating the inhumane institution, but criticized Southern slaves for refusing to rise up and slaughter their masters.

Second, on January 1, 1831, also in Boston, William Lloyd Garrison, a young, controversial, and intensely religious newspaper editor, began publishing an antislavery newspaper called the *Liberator*. Writers and editors had written in opposition to slavery in American newspapers before, but the *Liberator* was different, for according to its creator its goal was to bring about the abolition of slavery *immediately*. In language reminiscent of Walker's *Appeal*, Garrison insisted that the time to solve the problem of slavery had arrived, and Northerners would play an important role.

Third and lastly, just months after the *Liberator* first appeared, the bloodiest slave insurrection in American history took place in Southampton, Virginia, on August 21, 1831, when Nat Turner, a spiritually and intellectually transcendent field slave, led more than sixty slaves across the plantations of Southampton County, Virginia, killing fifty-seven whites. Turner's revolt horrified white Southerners, convincing many of an imminent racial apocalypse, but it had a much different impact on white Northerners, who interpreted it as a divine sign that an oppressed people were seeking and in need of deliverance. For this, some were ready to answer the call.

THE AMERICAN ANTI-SLAVERY SOCIETY

In December 1833, Garrison founded the American Anti-Slavery Society, and within five years, more than 1,000 local societies with 250,000 members had organized under the national group. For the next three decades, these societies would serve as the organizational framework on which the movement to abolish slavery rested. Through formal and informal networks of communication, they provided a vehicle for individual Americans to change society collectively, and their diversity testifies to their widespread ap-

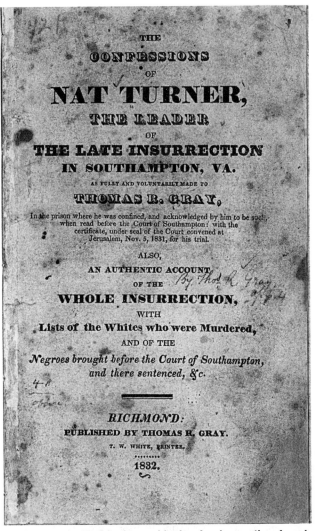

Nat Turner was a Virginia slave and leader of an insurrection of nearly eighty slaves that left approximately sixty whites dead in August 1831 in Southampton County, Virginia. *The Confessions of Nat Turner* is an account of the uprising, countered by the killing of about 100 blacks by white vigilantes. *(Library of Congress)*

peal: some societies were all-male; others were all-female; some were racially integrated; others were racially segregated; some were short-lived; others lasted for decades. Despite this diversity, these disparate and at times distant groups shared much in common. Members were committed social reformers who demonstrated great courage when they paid a membership fee of anywhere from twenty-five cents to one dollar and took part in initiation rites, for by joining an antislavery society they sided with an unpopular cause.

It is estimated that no more than 1 percent of Americans were abolitionists at one time; thus, the members of antislavery societies took great risks when they took a stand on slavery. They faced personal and social ostracism and became vulnerable to verbal and physical attacks. There were also financial risks, for few had time or money to spare. Although some organization members earned a living working for these societies as writers, lecturers, and administrators, typical members volunteered their time. Members were businessmen, manufacturers, and lawyers. They were also wives, schoolteachers, and artisans.

The American Anti-Slavery Society took the lead in recruiting members, hiring and training traveling lecturers, funding the publication and distribution of antislavery literature, and hosting annual conventions. In short, they organized the work of the local societies, which formed after a group of people established an organizing committee, drafted a Constitution, elected officers, and then contacted peer agencies for guidance and assistance. The men and women of antislavery societies considered slavery a sin, and they set out to convince others. To do this they needed money, so fundraising became a central concern. Wealthy businessmen like Arthur and Lewis Tappan donated large sums of money; nonetheless, abolitionism remained largely a grassroots movement. Under the leadership of Elizabeth Cady Stanton, Lucretia Mott, and Susan B. Anthony, women especially played an essential fundraising role. They formed sewing circles and "cent-a-week" societies, and hosted antislavery fairs and bazaars to raise funds that went not only to supporting society functions, but were forwarded directly to fugitive slaves and free black communities in the North and Canada, to provide food, clothing, education, and shelter.

RISING OPPOSITION TO SLAVERY

Antislavery lectures formed the nucleus of society life and were held wherever an audience could gather: outdoors, in schools, halls, clubs, and private homes. The emotion speakers exhibited and evoked from audience members at these events reminded observers of the religious revivals that had swept parts of the Northeastern and Midwestern United States as part of the Second Great Awakening. But antislavery lectures were also part of the nineteenth-century lyceum movement in which rhetorical addresses became public spectacles of erudition, discourse, and debate, making political and cultural icons of gifted orators like Frederick Douglass, Ralph Waldo Emerson, Wendell Phillips, Henry David Thoreau, and Daniel Webster.

Hosting such events was difficult in an era without reliable communication and transportation, and over time the difficulties inherent to booking speakers, advertising, renting halls, and pricing and printing tickets wore on devout reformers; yet members considered themselves part of an imagined moral community, forging a collective identity that in times of frustration and despair provided sustenance.

In addition to holding meetings and sponsoring lectures, antislavery societies relied on a number of tactics to convince others of the sin of slavery. In the Great Postal Campaign of 1835, more than 1 million pieces of antislavery literature were distributed throughout the United States. Signed petitions were also forwarded to the United States Congress and state legislatures, requesting such things as the abolition of the internal slave trade and the limiting of slavery's expansion into Western territories. Petition drives are symbolic for their grassroots nature, with women taking the lead in traveling door-to-door, often miles at a time to obtain signatures. In one year alone, 415,000 signatures on antislavery petitions were forwarded to Washington, and within two years there were more than 2 million. In spite of these successes, the peaceful movement of moral suasion was short-lived. Southerners destroyed antislavery mail and convinced Congress to institute a Gag Rule in 1836, thus tabling all abolitionist petitions. Increasingly, antislavery lecturers and audience members risked their lives when they attended a public event. In Boston, Garrison was pulled off a stage and dragged down the street with a noose around his neck, and in Illinois, Elijah Lovejoy, the editor of an antislavery newspaper was shot to death by a rabid pro-slavery mob.

Abolitionists, many of whom had learned about the evils of slavery as youngsters on their parents' knees, underestimated the difficulty of moral suasion in converting others. New tactics were required. In 1840, prominent abolitionists who disagreed with some of Garrison's radical ideas, among them his refusal to embrace the American political system and his advocacy of women's rights, bolted the American Anti-Slavery Society and formed the American and Foreign Anti-Slavery Society. That same year they organized the Liberty Party, the first political party in the United States expressly devoted to the abolition of slavery. The party ran James G. Birney for president in 1840, but he received only 7,000 votes. Abolitionism was faltering

Nevertheless, committed reformers—especially free blacks—refused to give up. Feelings of racial solidarity motivated these men and women to maintain

the struggle. Many had been slaves themselves and were in constant danger of being reenslaved, and most had loved ones still in bondage. Although they were in general less economically positioned to fight slavery than white abolitionists, free black abolitionists led by Samuel Cornish, Martin Delany, Frederick Douglass, James McCune Smith, and John B. Vashon, worked as lecturers, writers, newspaper editors, and agents, and established and attended national Negro Conventions in order to keep slavery on the national agenda. Slaves, who continually demonstrated a willingness to fight and even die for liberty, convinced them that their efforts were not in vain.

Slaves had always resisted, and whether taking part in day-to-day acts of resistance, running away, or revolting, they responded to a higher law when seeking liberty. White masters and local officials did not easily detect the most common acts of defiance. Slaves broke tools, feigned sickness, slipped poison into the owners' drinks, and burned buildings to the ground. These actions occurred without warning, and at times, the most plaintive and acquiescent slave was culpable; for Southern whites, they were both unpredictable and unstoppable.

Slaves also ran away. In the Upper South, they ran away from farms and plantations in search of either the Mason–Dixon line or the Ohio River—important geographic thresholds separating free from slave soil. In the Lower South, fugitives sought heavily populated seaports like New Orleans or Charleston, or absconded to hard-to-reach forests, mountains, and swamps where they lived on the largess of other fugitives as well as the crops and livestock of local communities. The most well-known group of American fugitive slaves were those who joined with militant Creek Indians and together, known as the Runaway, or Seminole Indians, fought a series of brutal wars with the United States government.

Violent resistance was uncommon for American slaves, for in a region where they were outnumbered, unarmed, and under constant surveillance, such methods were tantamount to suicide. Nonetheless, throughout the nineteenth century, slaves acting alone and in groups resorted to violence in an effort to be free. Two instances of violent slave resistance in particular kept the spirit of abolitionism alive in the 1840s. In July 1839, captives on a Spanish slave ship named the *Amistad* revolted against the white crew and murdered the captain. The *Amistad* eventually sailed into New York outside of Long Island where the United States Navy apprehended its black passengers and then delivered them to Connecticut for trial.

LUCRETIA COFFIN MOTT (1793–1880)

Born on January 3, 1793, in Nantucket, Massachusetts, Lucretia Coffin grew up in Boston, where she attended public school for two years in accordance with her father's wish that she become familiar with the workings of democratic principles. A Quaker, she studied and taught at a Friends school near Poughkeepsie, New York. It was then that her interest in women's rights began. She was paid only half the salary male teachers were receiving simply because of her gender. In 1811, she married James Mott, a fellow teacher from the school, and the couple moved to Philadelphia, Pennsylvania.

After 1818, Lucretia Mott became known as a lecturer for temperance, peace, the rights of labor, and the abolition of slavery. In 1821, she was accepted as a minister of the Friends and joined the Hicksite (Liberal) branch of the Society when a rift occurred in the 1820s. She aided fugitive slaves, and following the initial meeting of the American Anti-Slavery Society in 1833, she organized the Philadelphia Female Anti-Slavery Society. She met opposition within the Society of Friends when she spoke of abolition, and attempts were made to strip Mott of her ministry and membership. In 1837, she helped organize the Anti-Slavery Convention of American Women, and in May 1838 her home was almost attacked by a mob after the burning of Pennsylvania Hall, Philadelphia, where the convention had been meeting.

Refusal by the World Anti-Slavery Convention in London (1840) to recognize women delegates led Mott to champion the cause of women's rights. Mott still managed to make her views known. While there, she met Elizabeth Cady Stanton and became a mentor to the younger activist. In 1848, taking up the cause of women's rights, she and Stanton called a convention at Seneca Falls, New York, the first of its kind, "to discuss the social, civil, and religious rights of women." The Woman's Rights Convention issued a "Declaration of Sentiments" modeled on the Declaration of Independence; it stated that "all men and women are created equal." From that time Mott devoted most of her attention to the women's rights movement.

Mott wrote articles ("Discourse on Woman" appeared in 1850), lectured widely, was elected president of the 1852 convention at Syracuse, New York, and attended almost every annual meeting thereafter. At the organizing meeting of the American Equal Rights Association in 1866, she was chosen president. The following year she joined Robert Dale Owen, Rabbi Isaac M. Wise, and others in the organization of the Free Religious Association.

After passage of the Fugitive Slave Law in 1850, Mott and her husband had also opened their home to runaway slaves escaping via the Underground Railroad. After the Civil War, she worked to secure the franchise and educational opportunities for freedmen; she continued to be active in the causes of women's rights, peace, and liberal religion until her death. Mott died on November 11, 1880, in her home outside Philadelphia.

James G. Lewis

There antislavery groups provided for the legal defense of the fifty-three slaves in a celebrated case that eventually went to the U.S. Supreme Court. Defended by the ex-president and long-time abolitionist John Quincy Adams, the high court ruled in favor of the rebellious slaves, setting them free. In November 1841, more than 100 American slaves being transported from Virginia aboard the Brig *Creole* to the slave markets of the Deep South, overtook the crew and sailed the ship to the British Bahamas, where islanders aided in their escape. The Northern press followed both cases closely and reported on them in great detail; in antislavery circles the leaders of the two revolts, Joseph Cinque and Madison Washington, became causes celebres.

Notwithstanding the efforts to keep abolitionism a vibrant cause in the 1840s, interest waned and membership in antislavery societies declined. Slavery was a divisive issue and many simply chose to avoid conflict. But the issue would not go away, and when the Fugitive Slave Act became law in 1850, interest in abolitionism revived instantly. Congress passed the law in response to the increasing numbers of runaway slaves to the North and as part of a compromise to settle the issue of whether to allow slavery in the territories ceded to the United States by the Mexican government following the Mexican-American War. According to the controversial law, harsh punishments including imprisonment and fines awaited those found guilty of assisting fugitive slaves, federal funds would be used to return fugitives, and federal judges were to be paid ten dollars when they found suspected fugitives guilty of running away and five dollars when they set them free. The Fugitive Slave Act gave rise to a new era of antislavery resistance, one that was both more militant in its outlook and more willing to use violent tactics than its predecessor.

GROWING MILITANCY AGAINST SLAVERY

Throughout the North, black and white abolitionists mobilized, forming Vigilance Committees to protect free blacks, and on numerous occasions they battled with slave catchers and officers of the law to aid runaway slaves. The most notorious case occurred in Boston in May 1854 when an armed and angry antislavery mob stormed the local courthouse to free Anthony Burns, a fugitive slave from Virginia who was awaiting trial. It took federal marshals, soldiers, and companies of state troops to repulse the attack, but not before one deputy fell dead from a gunshot. In June, black drapes and inverted American flags, which hung from the buildings lining Boston's streets, greeted soldiers as they marched Burns to the wharf where they placed him on a ship and returned him to slavery. To Northerners the point was clear: the United States government aided and abetted slaveholders. In opposition to the Fugitive Slave Act, Northern states passed personal liberty laws that forbade state officials from assisting in the capture and return of suspected runaways, Garrison publicly burned a copy of the Constitution on the Fourth of July, and free blacks petitioned the Massachusetts legislature to sanction the formation of a black military company.

Abolitionists' increasing militancy, the willingness of slaves to risk it all by running away, and the enforcement of the Fugitive Slave Act gave rise to the legendary Underground Railroad. Ironically, the Underground Railroad was neither underground nor a railroad. It was, instead, a clandestine and loosely organized network run by ordinary Americans—black and white, male and female, Northern and Southern, rich and poor—who risked fine, imprisonment, and the loss of their lives by assisting fugitive slaves, providing them with food, shelter, clothing, money, medical care, and at times guns and other weapons for self-defense. In the three decades before the American Civil War, it is estimated that as many as 1,000 slaves per year "rode its rails" to freedom.

Heroic tales of conductors and passengers on the Underground Railroad resulted in a culture of protest in the North, one evidenced most clearly by the explosion of popular interest in the topic of slavery in the region's print culture, in newspapers, almanacs, and pamphlets. Slave narratives and fictional accounts of American slavery became especially popular. Solomon Northrop's *Twelve Years a Slave* (1853)

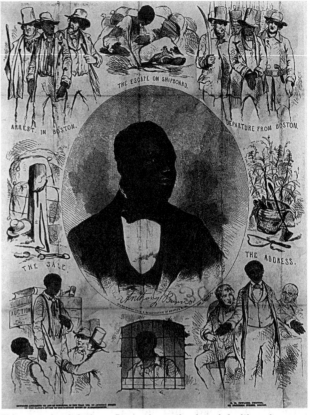

This portrait of Anthony Burns shows the famed fugitive slave surrounded by key incidents in his life, including his sale at auction, his arrest in Boston, his escape from Richmond on shipboard, his forced departure from Boston, and his imprisonment. *(Library of Congress)*

sold more than 8,000 copies within a month of its publication, while Harriet Beecher Stowe's *Uncle Tom's Cabin*, first published as a serial in 1851–1852, sold a million copies in less than a year-and-a-half after being published in book form in 1852. Publications of these books made instant celebrities of their authors, and the printed and visual images of abused and defenseless slaves they evoked became ubiquitous throughout Northern popular culture, in poems, songs, and material items like badges, boxes, and clothing. These images were meant to weigh on the consciences and influence the hearts and minds of those who deemed antislavery an unworthy cause, but they likewise served as a source of abolitionists' inspiration and collective consciousness.

As the movement culture of abolitionism increasingly engulfed Northern lives, the United States Congress passed the Kansas-Nebraska Act in 1854. The law allowed settlers in the territories of Kansas and Nebraska to decide on whether these territories would allow slavery to exist. In essence, the new law repealed the Missouri Compromise, which for more than twenty years had limited the expansion of slavery. When Northern abolitionists and pro-slavery Southerners rushed to Kansas to participate in upcoming elections, the sectional conflict turned violent. After pro-slavery Southerners destroyed property in the free soil town of Lawrence, radical abolitionists under the leadership of John Brown pulled five pro-slavery settlers from their beds in the middle of the night and murdered them in the streets. Three years later, Brown and more than twenty followers attacked the federal arsenal at Harper's Ferry, Virginia, in an attempt to launch the first salvo of a large-scale slave insurrection. The raid failed, and while five of Brown's men escaped, the others were either killed or executed. Brown, who survived several gunshot wounds, was arrested, tried, convicted, and hanged to death on December 2, 1859.

Brown's detractors labeled him insane, but this religious devotee was foremost a committed opponent of human bondage. He had witnessed the abuse of slaves first-hand and become disenchanted with both the tactics of moral suasion and the American political process. He insisted that abolition would come only through bloodshed, and he gave his own for the cause. His raid provides a dramatic example both of the tactical shift that had taken place among abolitionists in the decades leading up to the Civil War and of the extremism that came to characterize the sectional crisis in general.

The Civil War erupted in April 1861, but abolitionists' work was still incomplete. They wanted to make the war about slavery, a difficult task considering that throughout the first year of the war, President Abraham Lincoln repeated his pledge to leave slavery intact where it already existed. But just as they had done before, antislavery activists mobilized. They formed new groups to raise funds for the writing, publication, and distribution of antislavery literature, and again petitioned the United States Congress to emancipate Southern slaves. In just one year during the war, the Massachusetts Anti-Slavery Society published 100,000 emancipationist pamphlets. Throughout the duration of the war, abolitionists collectively forwarded approximately 400,000 signatures to Washington. A number of abolitionists played a prominent part in the war as soldiers in white units and officers of black troops. Others raised money, made clothing and blankets for the freedmen, or went south to work as teachers or healthcare providers.

In spite of their passion and commitment, abolitionists' war efforts would have been doomed were it not for the actions of the slaves themselves. During the first two years of the Civil War, slaves by the tens of thousands simply walked away from the farms and plantations on which they lived in search of Union lines, and by their sheer numbers forced Lincoln to act. On the grounds of military necessity, Lincoln issued the Emancipation Proclamation on January 1, 1863, freeing slaves in the territories in rebellion. The Proclamation said nothing about slaves in the Border States and Southern territories controlled by the Union Army. Nevertheless, it symbolized Lincoln's shifting attitude towards abolition and led ultimately to the ratification of the Thirteenth Amendment in December 1865, which forever abolished slavery.

With the end of slavery, abolitionists joined other movements of the late nineteenth century to reform labor and municipal governments, and secure women's rights. Many continued to fight for the civil rights of African Americans, who after the Civil War still needed assistance in overcoming the daunting obstacles of racial discrimination, economic dislocation, and social segregation. The antislavery movement ended, but today the memories of its interracial and cross-class character, and of its ultimate success, serve as important reminders of the ability of ordinary American to effect change.

Matt Clavin

BIBLIOGRAPHY

Freehling, William W. *The Road to Disunion*. New York: Oxford University Press, 1990.

Horton, James Oliver, and Lois E. Horton. *In Hope of Liberty: Culture, Community, and Protest Among Northern Free Blacks, 1700–1860*. New York: Oxford University Press, 1997.

Jeffrey, Julie Roy. *The Great Silent Army of Abolitionism: Ordinary Women in the Antislavery Movement*. Chapel Hill: University of North Carolina Press, 1998.

Kraut, Alan M., ed. *Crusaders and Compromise: Essays on the Relationship of the Antislavery Struggle to the Antebellum Party System*. Westport, CT: Greenwood Press, 1993.

McKivigan, John R., and Stanley Harrold, eds. *Antislavery Violence: Sectional, Racial, and Cultural Conflict in Antebellum America*. Knoxville: University of Tennessee Press, 1999.

McPherson, James M. *Battle Cry of Freedom: The Civil War Era*. Vol. 6, Oxford History of the United States. New York: Oxford University Press, 1988.

———. *Ordeal by Fire: The Civil War and Reconstruction.* 3d ed. Boston: McGraw-Hill, 2001.

Steward, James Brewer. *Holy Warriors: The Abolitionists and American Slavery.* New York: Hill and Wang, 1997.

Still, William. *The Underground Rail Road.* Philadelphia: Porter & Coates, 1872.

Walters, Ronald G. *The Antislavery Appeal: American Abolitionism after 1830.* Baltimore, MD: Johns Hopkins University Press, 1976.

NORTH–SOUTH REACTIONS TO ANTISLAVERY

Few white Americans, in the North or the South, sympathized with the abolitionists when their movement first appeared in the 1830s. Their attempts to promote racial equality and appeals for the immediate emancipation of all slaves in the United States stirred fears throughout the country, regardless of the level of personal involvement with slavery. Predictably, Southerners were hostile to what they saw as an attack on their property, safety, and general way of life. They fought the spread of abolitionist sentiment by espousing a more militant pro-slavery ideology, destroying literature sent through the mails, and pushing for a gag rule that tabled all discussion of the slavery issue in Congress. Despite their residence in states that had provided for the end of slavery, Northerners also saw abolition as a threat. Fears of racial amalgamation, disunion, and social instability contributed to a strong, often violent, anti-abolitionist sentiment in the North throughout the 1830s. Only at the end of the decade, when Southern "slave-power" attempts to curb abolitionist agitation seemed a bigger threat to the American social fabric than the abolitionists themselves did Northern opinion shift slowly to a more supportive stance on abolition and American unity on the subject begin to fragment along sectional lines.

THE RISE OF ABOLITION

The sectional division of the United States—half-free and half-slave—had largely existed since the end of the American Revolution. On a state-by-state basis Northerners gradually did away with the institution of slavery in their region during the first decades of independence. Antislavery sentiment thus was not a new phenomenon that arose with the abolitionism of the 1830s. Many Americans, especially those in the Northern states, had long recognized slavery's inconsistency with the ideals of natural rights that had fostered the new republic. At the same time, however,

most citizens accepted the notion that slavery was a state issue and therefore tolerated the perpetuation of the institution in the South. The compromise on slavery and the delegation of policy on the subject to the states was necessary to American political unity from the very inception of the nation. It was built into the Constitution.

Even for those who opposed slavery, the unity and stability of the new American republic trumped any desire to attack the institution. Early antislavery advocates were gradualists who focused on actions that would bring an eventual end to slavery without disrupting the American social structure. Many worried about the effect that a large free black population would have on this structure and proposed a policy of "colonization"—sending free blacks out of the United States to Africa or the Caribbean in order to maintain social order. The American Colonization Society, organized in 1816 and made up of citizens from both Northern and Southern states, promoted this effort and formed the backbone of antislavery efforts before the rise of abolition.

The abolitionists therefore represented a real departure from the antislavery advocates of previous years. Not only did they plead for the unconditional, immediate end of slavery but they also opposed colonization and insisted on racial equality in American society. In addition, the new movement became a biracial one, with black and white reformers working together to pursue common goals.

Abolitionism was a strain of a larger reform impulse of the 1830s that included such issues as temperance, social welfare, pacifism, and women's rights. This impulse grew, in great measure, as a response to developments associated with the market revolution, which transformed Northern society in the years after the War of 1812. Population growth, industrialization, technical innovation, and the growing commitment to a free-labor system produced a combination of anxiety

The "gag rule," in effect from 1836 to 1844, barred members of the House of Representatives from introducing petitions or documents relating to abolition. In this 1839 lithograph, Massachusetts representative John Quincy Adams, chief opponent of the gag rule, lies prostrate on a pile of antislavery petitions, an abolitionist newspaper, and a resolution to recognize Haiti. Above him stands South Carolina representative Waddy Thompson, Jr., a gag-rule advocate, who says, "Sir the South loses caste whenever she suffers this subject to be discussed here; it must be indignantly frowned down." *(Library of Congress)*

and optimism in Northern society. Reformers felt the need to address dislocations in the social order brought about by this revolution, but they also remained optimistic that all problems could be surmounted in an innovative, modernizing society. In addition, the Second Great Awakening, a religious revivalism that had spread throughout the Northern states in the 1820s, stressed the idea of one's ability to lift both himself and his society up out of sin and contributed to this spirit of reform. Individuals began to feel they had the power, and therefore the responsibility, to improve society.

Abolitionism grew, in part, out of the optimistic strain of this reform impulse. Theodore Dwight Weld, Arthur and Lewis Tappan, Elizur Wright, and William Lloyd Garrison—all of whom had been touched by revivalism—emerged in the 1830s as leaders of the drive for immediate emancipation. During the 1830s, they promoted a policy of "moral suasion," believing that they could appeal to the conscience of the nation, both in the Northern and Southern states, to provoke an end to slavery. By educating the populace about the evils of slavery, they believed they could convince most Americans to support their goal. In 1831, Garrison began publishing *The Liberator*, a newspaper dedicated to the promotion of abolition. In 1833, he joined with the Tappans and other abolitionists to create the American Anti-Slavery Society (AAS). Throughout the remainder of the decade, this society promoted lectures, circulated petitions, and organized the dissemination of printed materials opposing slavery. The AAS became the abolitionists' central vehicle in the use of moral suasion to promote an immediate end to slavery.

Immediatism, however, was not a white invention. Free blacks, encouraged by the emancipations of the Revolutionary era but disheartened by the gradualism and centrality of colonization in contemporary white antislavery efforts, organized their own institutions of protest. Frustration at the continued subjugation of the black race rather than optimism about human perfectibility fostered their involvement in the abolition movement. Free blacks operated newspapers, held conventions, produced tracts, circulated petitions, and made speeches advocating emancipation and black equality well before Garrison and other white abolitionist leaders were drawn to the cause. Four years before Garrison started his antislavery newspaper, John Russwurm and Samuel E. Cornish began publishing *Freedom's Journal*, a black abolitionist newspaper. Free Northern blacks organized National Negro Conventions annually throughout the early 1830s to discuss issues affecting their race, and white abolitionists later incorporated many of the opinions put forth at these meetings on colonization, segregation, and the importance of black education into their own ideology.

Perhaps the most influential early black abolitionist was David Walker, a free black man who lived in Boston and wrote for *Freedom's Journal*. In 1829, after touring the Southern states, Walker published his *Appeal to the Colored Citizens of the World*. In this work, he depicted the miseries of slavery and called for black unity in defying both slavery and racism. Walker took a strong stand against colonization and sanctioned the notion of a racial uprising, as a last alternative, in order to achieve freedom and equality. White abolitionists rejected the proposition of violent resistance, but the arguments of Walker's *Appeal* resonated with them. His work, along with other black abolitionist efforts, persuaded white abolitionists to commit to abolition not just as a means of lifting up white society but as a necessary attack on the constraints placed on black individuals, both within and outside of slavery.

The campaign for abolition therefore became a biracial one. Free blacks were the largest supporters of Garrison's newspaper, and both black and white reformers were represented in the AAS. Nevertheless, white and black abolitionists did tend to operate separately. Many black reformers continued to work through black institutions and organizations, while "mainstream" white organizations often included only a few blacks. These reformers, however, worked toward common goals: the end of slavery and black equality. Despite their tendency to self-segregate, their

unity on these goals seemed quite radical to the majority of the American population during the 1830s.

PRO-SLAVERY IN THE SOUTH

Nowhere did the abolitionists seem more radical, or more of a threat, than in the Southern states. Southern slave owners had long defended the "peculiar institution" of slavery as a regrettable but necessary component of Southern society. They believed that immediate abolition of the institution would destroy their economic base. Slave owners would lose the huge investments that they had put into their slaves and would be hard-pressed to find an alternative form of labor to feed the plantation economy. In addition, white Southerners worried that the liberation of slaves and creation of a large free black population would at best lead to mass social dislocation and at worst foster race war.

Much of the emotion behind the Southern response to abolition in the 1830s arose from this fear of violent black retribution. Although slaves rarely rose up in rebellion, the possibility of insurrection had always haunted the white Southern psyche; the fears extended across white Southern society, encompassing poor whites as well as slave owners. Fresh in the memory of many Southerners was the Denmark Vesey conspiracy of 1822. Vesey, a free black from Charleston, was rumored to have gathered up to 9,000 black followers in preparation for a large-scale revolt. Although whites suppressed it before it ever took place, news of the planned rebellion reminded many Southerners of the precarious nature of their region's race relations.

The distribution of David Walker's *Appeal*, which advocated black unity and sanctioned slave rebellion, heightened Southern fears. After its publication in 1829, black sailors who worked along the Atlantic coast spread the pamphlet into the Southern states. Free blacks passed it along informal inland communication networks until, by 1831, the pamphlet had permeated much of the South. The widespread dispersal of Walker's words exposed the sophisticated communication networks among free blacks in the South. Whites tried to suppress the spread of the incendiary pamphlet when they became aware of its existence, and several states, fearing slave rebellion, passed harsher slave codes as a result of its distribution. Many of these new slave codes placed heavier social controls on slave access to education.

The white South's discovery of this black communication network coincided with the beginnings of organized abolition in the North. When Garrison started publication of *The Liberator* in 1831, slave owners began to fear a possible alliance between Northern abolitionists and organized Southern blacks in a rebellion against slavery.

Another event in 1831 intensified Southern white anxieties. Nat Turner, a Virginia slave, led an uprising that left approximately sixty whites dead in August 1831. Turner was a slave preacher who believed that God ordained him to lead his people out of slavery. With no clear plan, Turner and five followers went from farm to farm in Southampton County, killing most of the white people they encountered. As they progressed, nearly eighty more slaves joined the rebellion. The militia eventually suppressed the uprising, and white vigilantism broke out, resulting in the murder of approximately 100 black Virginians.

Although no evidence exists that Turner had read either Walker's *Appeal* or *The Liberator*, many Southerners connected the uprising to the distribution of abolitionist materials among free blacks and slaves. They blamed abolitionists for the rebellion, and they charged them with deliberately encouraging insurrection. Because perceived black militancy in the South grew contemporaneously with the emergence of Northern abolitionist activism, the two became linked in the Southern mind.

Following the events of 1831, citizens throughout the South held meetings to discuss the abolitionist threat. They passed laws forbidding the distribution of literature that could foment slave rebellion. Southern authorities offered rewards for suspected abolitionists, and those who were turned in faced fines, lashings, or imprisonment. Southern leaders also issued demands to Northern authorities that they silence the abolitionist leaders. In Georgia, the state legislature offered a $5,000 bounty to anyone who would bring Garrison to the state to stand trial.

In Virginia, the Turner episode led to a resolve to address the slavery problem in a different way. Throughout 1831 and 1832, the Virginia legislature debated a bill calling for the gradual, compensated emancipation of slaves in the state. Those who pressed for the initiative cited the economic impracticality of slavery and the superiority of a free-wage system of labor. Those against the motion refuted slavery's economic impracticality. They alluded to the benign, paternalistic relationship between Southern masters and slaves and argued that emancipation would too severely upset the Southern social structure. In the end, a substantial majority in the Virginia legislature defeated the motion for gradual emancipation. This defeat signaled the end of any discussion of Southern state-led emancipation and the beginning of a more explicit Southern defense of slavery.

The first to advance this defense was Thomas Roderick Dew, a professor from William and Mary College. In 1832, Dew published *Review of the Debate in the Virginia Legislature*, cataloguing his reactions to issues that had been discussed in the Virginia legislature's debates on gradual emancipation. Dew argued that the abolitionists' desire to end slavery was impractical. He believed that social institutions changed slowly over time and that any idealistic attempt to intervene and restructure those institutions too quickly would cause mass disorder. He recommended that Southerners commit to the social order that they were a part of and come down firmly on the side of pro-slavery rather than rely on the concept of slavery as a "necessary evil."

A number of even more vehement Southern pro-slavery writers followed Dew in the decades before the Civil War. Among these writers were newspaperman James Henry Hammond, whose writings offered a biblical defense of and sociological rationalizations for slavery; politician William Harper, who attacked the idea of natural rights and insisted that some men were born to subordinate roles in society; and the most famous pro-slavery advocate, George Fitzhugh, who argued that slave labor was superior to the free-labor system of the North. These polemicists were joined by other ministers, politicians, and scholars in developing a more radical pro-slavery stance that not only defended slavery on practical grounds but argued that it was a positive good. They refuted the idea of racial equality, condemned outside interference with Southern institutions, criticized the Northern social structure and labor system as inferior to that of the South, and cited biblical support and historical precedent as a justification of slave labor.

For the first few years after Dew's argument, however, the South remained relatively quiet on the subject of slavery. A desire to avoid conflict, protect Southern honor, and avoid nurturing any impulse toward slave insurrection drove this period of restraint. Southern leaders remained anxious about abolitionist rhetoric, but they avoided the subject of slavery in order to avoid feeding the debate. Instead they began to focus their attention on the idea of "states' rights," a concept that fueled the nullification controversy of 1832–1833.

The nullification controversy involved a conflict between President Andrew Jackson and South Carolina senator John C. Calhoun over the South Carolina legislature's desire to nullify a federal tariff. Issues of sovereignty were at stake. Calhoun argued that state legislatures were the true voice of the people. They were responsible for the creation of the federal government and had ceded only limited powers to that government. When the federal lawmakers passed laws that overstepped their bounds, state legislatures could reject the validity of those laws within the state. Furthermore, states had the right to secede from the union in order to protect their rights.

Although economic reasons drove the dispute, many Southerners seized upon the concept of states' rights as a way to protect slavery. If they established the precedent of state power over federal legislation, then they could avoid the possibility of any future federal interference with slavery. In addition, the states' rights doctrine emphasized the rights of the community over those of the individual and thus fed Southern arguments that the need to preserve the stability of the Southern social structure eclipsed the natural rights of slaves. In 1835 and 1836, as abolitionists used new strategies to further their cause, this concept of sacrificing individual rights for the good of the community became central to the Southern defense of slavery. Furthermore, Southern argument extended this concept beyond the right to enslave to encompass the circumscription of white rights.

NATIONAL CONTROVERSIES OVER ABOLITIONIST INITIATIVES

During the mid-1830s, two abolitionist initiatives led to major national debates over abolition, government power, and individual rights. The postal campaign of 1835–1836 and the simultaneous intensification of petitioning Congress for antislavery measures both helped lead to Southern demands for the circumscription of abolitionist rhetoric and Northern recognition of the movement's subversive potential.

In 1835, the executive committee of the AAS embarked on a postal campaign to spread abolitionist literature throughout the South. The abolitionists flooded the mails with antislavery tracts addressed to Southern ministers, public officials, and newspaper editors. The campaign was part of the abolitionists' larger strategy of moral suasion, and their intent was to attract white Southerners to the cause and persuade slave owners to free their slaves. Southerners, however, were convinced that abolitionists were aiming their literature at Southern slaves and free blacks in an attempt to foment rebellion.

A violent reaction to the campaign spread through the South. In some areas, those caught with abolitionist materials received the death penalty, and in other areas vigilance committees relieved the courts of their prisoners and stoned, beat, or even killed their victims. Tighter controls on the Southern free black population were applied everywhere in fear that the abolitionist literature would incite race war.

John C. Calhoun warned Northern leaders that antipathy toward the North was spreading throughout the Southern states and that further antislavery agitation could lead to disunion. Southern governments made demands for Northern extradition of abolitionist agitators to the South to be tried for inciting uprising and violating state laws forbidding the distribution of antislavery literature. In addition, they requested that Northern states pass legislation curbing the rhetoric of abolitionists who were operating within their boundaries.

Southern protests led to a growing awareness of the abolition movement in the North. Most Northerners were unsympathetic to abolition and resented the divisive nature of the movement. Northern state governments, however, did not respond positively to Southern demands for Northern laws restraining abolitionists. Although the threat of disunion disturbed them, they would not pass laws infringing on free speech.

The mail campaign became a national issue in July 1835 when a mob stormed the U.S. Post Office in Charleston and burned mailbags that were filled with abolitionist tracts. The contradiction between state laws prohibiting the circulation of abolitionist literature and federal protections of the United States mail brought up questions not only about state or federal sovereignty but also about individual rights to free speech versus a community's right to preserve social stability.

In August 1835, U.S. Postmaster General Amos Kendall declared that he had no authority to inhibit the delivery of abolitionist literature but that he also could not force delivery. Local authorities should therefore decide on whether to withhold abolitionist literature based on their own state laws concerning the circulation of the material. This solution, he felt, should be a temporary one, and he recommended that the United States Congress take up the issue for the sake of the union.

President Jackson echoed this recommendation. In December 1835, arguing that the U.S. mail was intended to unite and not divide the country, Jackson recommended that Congress pass a law preventing use of the mail for distributing "incendiary publications" that were meant to promote slave rebellion. Senator Calhoun opposed Jackson's proposal that Congress control the mails because this gave the federal government the power to decide what materials should be considered incendiary. Instead, he argued that no law should be passed regulating the U.S. postal service but that the states should be allowed to exercise police power over the mails with no federal intervention. Other senators, such as Daniel Webster from Massachusetts, opposed any legislation that would limit free speech.

In July 1836, after continued debate on the issue, Congress passed a measure reorganizing the Post Office and requiring that the postmaster deliver all written matter that was addressed to a specific location. The slave states, however, made little effort to cooperate with this law. They continued to suppress abolitionist materials that arrived in the South. Lawmakers, fearing sectional division, let the issue alone.

At the same time as the dispute over the postal campaign was occurring, Congress faced a similar controversy over the proper handling of antislavery petitions that were submitted to the legislature. The petitioning of Congress for measures against slavery had long existed in the United States, but in 1835, owing to the organization of the AAS, the petitioning intensified. The main objectives of the petitions submitted at this time were the closure of the internal slave trade and the abolition of slavery and the slave trade in Washington, D.C. The federal government could be construed to have some control over both of these measures. Abolitionists argued that it could act on the slave trade through its power over interstate commerce and its jurisdiction over matters in Washington, D.C., gave it the authority to attack slavery in that locale. Opponents of the petitions argued that the states maintained exclusive control over slavery and that the federal government had no right to take any action against it at all. Debates in Congress over the issue leaned toward the latter view.

In 1836, at the urging of Southern representatives, Congress passed a gag rule that automatically tabled any petitions concerning slavery. Because the body claimed that it had no authority over the issue of slavery, there was no reason to discuss the petitions. Northern congressmen cooperated with the gag rule in order to preserve both party and sectional unity, and so the rule was renewed each year throughout the rest of the decade.

Abolitionists only increased the volume of petitioning in response to this policy, and they called attention to the fact that the protection of slavery was now leading not only to the denial of black rights but to the infringement of white civil rights as well. In order to appease what was increasingly referred to as "the Southern slave-power," freedom of speech was dangerously curbed.

ANTI-ABOLITION IN THE NORTH

These major controversies drew Northerners' attention to the abolitionists. Many Northern journalists and politicians criticized the movement, and between 1834 and 1838, rioting frequently broke out throughout the North protesting abolitionist activities.

Like the Southern population, most of the Northern public initially viewed abolition as a threat to the stability of the existing social order. Unlike the response of the South, however, that of the North had little to do with any dedication to the institution of slavery itself. It was grounded more in "anti-abolition" than in any "pro-slavery" sentiment. Northern anti-abolitionist sentiment radiated from a variety of concerns. Anxieties about race, economic and social status, foreign threats, and the preservation of the Union all contributed to Northern hostility towards abolition.

Paradoxical fears concerning both racial conflict and racial amalgamation drove much of the Northern opposition. The end of slavery in the North did not mean the end of racism, and a majority of white Northerners rejected the abolitionist push for racial equality. Doubts that blacks could successfully, and peacefully, assimilate into white society coexisted with irrational fears of "miscegenation," interracial sexual relations, corrupting the white race. Citizenship and equality for blacks had not followed Northern emancipation, nor had Northern manumissions added great numbers of free blacks to society. The abolitionists' attack on both racial inequality and their attempts to free the masses of black slaves in the South therefore unsettled many Northern whites.

Some Northerners also viewed the abolition movement as a threat to their economic and social status. The economic connections between Northern merchants and bankers and the Southern plantation system remained strong during this period, and an attack on slavery would therefore affect more than the Southern economy. It would hurt many Northerners' economic status as well.

In addition, many Northern leaders felt that abolitionists were, in part, responsible for the deterioration of tradition and their own authority in society. Abolitionists criticized various church denominations for accepting slavery. They drew women out of their traditional domestic sphere and into the public realm.

SOUTHERN IDEAS OF LIBERTY.

Sentence *passed upon one for supporting that clause of* our *Declaration viz. All men are born free & equal.*
" *Strip him to the skin! give him a coat of Tar & Feathers!! Hang him by the neck, between the Heavens and the Earth!!! as a beacon to warn the* Northern Fanatics *of their danger!!!!* "

This 1835 lithograph printed in the North shows an imaginary scene of southerners' violent opposition to abolitionism and those who opposed slavery. Holding a whip, a judge, drawn with the ears of an ass, sits on bales of cotton and tobacco. With the Constitution lying trampled underfoot, the judge sentences an abolitionist to execution, while a cheering crowd surrounding the gallows awaits the condemned man's arrival. Beyond can be seen a cauldron filled with hot tar, boiling over an open fire. Genuine instances of the tarring, feathering, and hanging of antislavery advocates in Georgia, Louisiana, and Mississippi in the early 1830s may have inspired this lithograph. *(Library of Congress)*

They brought whites and blacks together to work for a common cause. Abolitionists attacked the compromises of the Constitution, property rights, church authority, and the safety of the American Union; and their definitions of equality threatened existing social hierarchies. Many prominent doctors, lawyers, merchants, bankers, clergymen, judges, and politicians therefore vehemently opposed abolition, seeing it as a threat not only to the social order but also to their positions of authority within that order.

Other groups also feared that abolitionist agitation might bring a loss of social and economic status. Although they opposed slavery in principle, many

Northern laborers believed that the criticism of slavery deflected attention from the problems of free-wage labor in the North, which many abolitionists —in their attack on slavery—idealized as a system of labor. Some also feared the increased job competition that would result if slaves were freed and brought into the market economy.

Recent immigrants from Ireland, who filled the least desirable jobs in the Northern economy, were particularly hostile to abolition. An inundation of free blacks in the market economy would threaten their jobs first. These immigrants therefore began to make a concerted effort to differentiate themselves from free blacks, emphasizing the political and social privileges due to them as members of the white race. Members of the Irish Catholic community also believed that abolitionists were hostile to their own group interests. They associated abolition with nativism and anti-Catholicism, which grew out of the same evangelical impulse as did antislavery; many abolitionists were, in fact, outspoken critics of the Irish Catholic community. Both antiblack and anti-abolitionist impulses thus ran strong throughout this sector of Northern society.

Other Northern anxieties included the suspicion that abolitionists were instruments of foreign interference in the affairs of the United States. A strong American nationalism existed in the 1830s, and connections between English and American abolitionists led to protests against "meddling outsiders" who passed judgment on American society and threatened American unity. When prominent English abolitionist George Thompson made a speaking tour in the Northern states in 1835, he consistently faced hostile, often violent, crowds. Newspaper reports on his activities emphasized his nationality and denounced English ignorance of the complicated American situation concerning slavery. Many of these articles also asserted that abolitionists were part of a foreign plot to weaken the United States.

The American nationalism of the period contained a strong element of concern for the Union. Sectional interests were diverging as the Northern states became more industrial and the South became more committed to the plantation economy. A strong desire to protect the Union and overcome sectional rifts existed in both the North and the South, and both sections viewed the abolitionists' crusade against slavery as a real danger to this effort.

This Northern hostility to abolition was expressed in the anti-abolitionist mobbing that occurred frequently throughout the region. In July 1834, mobs attacked Arthur Tappan's home in New York City. In October 1835, a convention to create an antislavery society was forcibly broken up in Utica, New York. Mobs repeatedly harassed the Tappans, Garrison, Weld, and other antislavery speakers on lecture tours.

Initially, most Northerners blamed the abolitionists themselves for the disorder. They characterized the reformers as fanatics whose actions would lead to mass social upheaval and eventually destroy the nation. As the violence continued, however, negative opinion began to shift away from the abolitionists and toward those who attacked their efforts. Two particularly destructive acts in May 1838 solidified this shift: the burning of Pennsylvania Hall, an antislavery meeting place in Philadelphia; and the murder of abolitionist editor Elijah Lovejoy in Alton, Illinois, during a mob attack on his printing press.

THE NORTHERN SHIFT FROM ANTI-ABOLITION

Abolitionists had long publicized the pacifist nature of their movement, and the escalating violence of the anti-abolitionist opposition convinced much of the Northern population that the blame for disorder rested on the shoulders of the attackers and not the victims of attack. In addition, during the late 1830s some abolitionists—recognizing that racism was as entrenched in the North as in the South—began to emphasize the danger that the protection of slavery posed for white civil liberties rather than focusing on appeals for racial equality.

Both the Northern anti-abolitionist violence and the Southern assault on individual rights led to a growing acceptance of the abolitionists throughout the North. Northern hostility shifted away from abolitionist activity and onto those who violated American ideals in their responses to it. Ironically then, support for the abolitionists grew in a circular way, in reaction to the Southern pro-slavery and Northern anti-abolitionist measures against the movement. These reactionary elements now represented a more dangerous threat to the Northern social order than did the abolitionists.

Like the initial opposition to abolition, Northern acceptance of the movement had little to do with slavery itself. It represented neither a condemnation of unfree black labor nor an acceptance of black equality. Instead, the shift occurred out of conservative concerns about the maintenance of social order and the preservation of white rights. These concerns now fed the sectional rift that was growing between the Southern and Northern states. As this rift expanded throughout the antebellum era, Northern hostility toward the South remained grounded in resistance to Southern attempts to dominate U.S. policy and circumscribe white rights. This hostility did, however, eventually lead in the 1860s to civil war and the culmination of one of the abolitionists' goals—the end of slavery in the United States.

The achievement of emancipation, however, was a qualified victory for the abolitionists. They had helped to force a confrontation between the North and the South that led to the end of slavery. They failed, however, in their campaign of moral suasion. The hearts and minds of Americans remained unchanged, in both the North and the South, and most white citizens remained unconcerned about black rights or racial equality. War forced white Southerners to accept an end to slavery, but they found other ways of exploiting black labor and limiting black freedoms. Northern support for black freedom and equality, which had grown more from hostility toward the South than out of a belief in those causes, eroded as soon as sectional hostility abated. Another century would have to pass, and another generation would have to wage their own campaign for change, before most Americans would adequately address the full agenda of the abolitionists and provide guarantees of racial equality to all citizens of the United States.

Angela Murphy

BIBLIOGRAPHY

Barnes, Gilbert. *The Antislavery Impulse, 1830–1844*. Gloucester, MA: Peter Smith, 1933.

Dew, Thomas Roderick. *Review of the Debate in the Virginia Legislature of 1831 and 1832*. 1832. Reprint, Westport, CT: Greenwood Press, 1970.

Faust, Drew Gilpen, ed. *The Ideology of Slavery: Proslavery Thought in the Antebellum South, 1830–1860*. Baton Rouge: Louisiana State University Press, 1981.

Foner, Eric. "Abolitionism and the Labor Movement in Antebellum America." In *Anti-Slavery, Religion and Reform*, eds. C. Bolt and S. Drescher. Hamden, CT: Archon Books, 1980.

Freehling, Alison Goodyear. *Drift Toward Dissolution: The Virginia Slavery Debate of 1831–1832*. Baton Rouge: Louisiana State University Press, 1982.

Freehling, William W. *The Road to Disunion: Secessionists at Bay, 1776–1854*. New York: Oxford University Press, 1990.

Grimsted, David. *American Mobbing, 1828–1861: Toward Civil War*. New York: Oxford University Press, 1998.

Harrold, Stanley. *The Abolitionists and the South, 1831–1861*. Lexington: University Press of Kentucky, 1995.

———. *American Abolitionists*. New York: Pearson Education, 2001.

Litwack, Leon F. *North of Slavery: The Negro in the Free States, 1790–1860*. Chicago: University of Chicago Press, 1961.

Nye, Russel B. *Fettered Freedom: Civil Liberties and the Slavery Controversy, 1830–1860*. East Lansing: Michigan State College Press, 1949.

Ratner, Lorman. *Powder Keg: Northern Opposition to the Antislavery Movement, 1831–1840*. New York: Basic Books, 1968.

Richards, Leonard L. *"Gentlemen of Property and Standing": Anti-Abolition Mobs in Jacksonian America*. New York: Oxford University Press, 1970.

Roediger, David R. *The Wages of Whiteness*. New York: Verso, 1991.

Roediger, David R., and Martin H. Blatt, eds. *The Meaning of Slavery in the North*. New York: Garland, 1998.

Simms, Henry H. *Emotion at High Tide: Abolition as a Controversial Factor, 1830–1845*. Baltimore, MD: Moore, 1960.

Sorin, Gerald. *Abolitionism: A New Perspective*. New York: Praeger, 1973.

Stewart, James Brewer. "The Emergence of Racial Modernity and the Rise of the White North, 1790–1840." *Journal of the Early Republic* 18 (Spring 1988): 181–236.

———. *Holy Warriors: The Abolitionists and American Slavery*. Revised ed. New York: Hill and Wang, 1996.

Tise, Larry E. *Proslavery: A History of the Defense of Slavery in America, 1701–1840*. Athens: University of Georgia Press, 1987.

Walker, David. *David Walker's Appeal*. 3d ed. Baltimore, MD: Black Classic, 1993.

Wyatt-Brown, Bertram. *Lewis Tappan and the Evangelical War against Slavery*. Cleveland, OH: Press of Case Western Reserve University, 1969.

2

CIVIL RIGHTS MOVEMENT

INTRODUCTION

The civil rights movement ranks at the forefront of epochal events in American history, including the Revolutionary War and the Civil War. This section focuses on the scope and complexities of the U.S. civil rights movement, from the 1865 post–Civil War Reconstruction period through the 1960s upsurge in mass protest and civil unrest. The enactment of transformative civil rights legislation and shifts in racial-ethnic political power and leadership during the twentieth century are highlighted and grounded in major historical conflicts, outlining more than a hundred years of intense struggle for racial justice.

HISTORY OF THE MOVEMENT

Color-based bondage, spanning the American colonial period through the end of the Civil War in 1865, was constitutionally inscribed, universally institutionalized, and ingrained in the fabric of American society. Against this backdrop of slavery, the antebellum period of American racial history and nearly 100 years of Jim Crow legalized segregation against African Americans set the stage for the civil rights movement. When viewed as a continuum of interrelated events, leaders, and ideologies, the civil rights era defies simple chronological categorization. However, for the purposes of accessibility of information, contributors have suggested major historical groupings, including pre–World War I, World War I to World War II, post–World War II, and the 1960s protest period, also known as the modern civil rights era.

The post–Civil War system of racial control and separation, cast in the mold of slavery, was frequently punctuated by public lynchings of blacks, race riots, random acts of violence, and harsh political repression against both blacks and progressive whites who organized resistance and rebellion throughout the twentieth century. Thus, the seeds of the civil rights movement took root in centuries of blood-soaked oppression, fertilized anew by ongoing injustice.

Among the antecedent root causes of the movement were the unresolved contradictions of racism and exploitation embedded in both the system and legacy of chattel slavery, the American Revolution, the abolitionist movement, and the Civil War. America's racial caste system was never eliminated and created deep historical conditions, giving rise to peonage, convict labor, superexploitation of industrial labor, color codes, and waves of African-American migration, in which blacks fled from the oppressive South to the less than welcoming North. The mass civil rights movement reached a crescendo during the 1960s protest period, as millions of people viewed and were influenced by events such as the 1955 murder of Emmett Till, the 1963 assassination of Medgar Evers, the Birmingham church bombing killing four black girls, Dr. Martin Luther King Jr.'s march from Memphis to Montgomery, desegregation of public schools in places like Little Rock, Arkansas and "Old Miss," and the integration of Chicago's Rainbow Beach.

The public stage occupied by luminaries and founders of the movement such as W.E.B. Du Bois, Ida B. Wells, Dr. Martin Luther King Jr., Rosa Parks, Malcolm X, Paul Robeson, Adam Clayton Powell, Angela Davis, A. Philip Randolph, Ella Baker, James Meredith, Jesse Jackson, Thurgood Marshall, Fanny Lou Hamer, Roy Wilkins, thousands of other civil rights leaders, and millions of unsung masses of followers was constructed over generations of resistance and sacrifice. The movement, at its base, was composed of common folk fighting the dehumanization and degradation of racism and segregation.

Historians and analysts have characterized the civil rights movement as revolutionary because it fundamentally altered the political, legal, social, educational, and cultural landscape of twentieth-century America. The movement consciously sought, through ideology, protest, and social policy, to promote racial equality by systematically removing the social, political, economic, and legal barriers imposed on black Americans, Native Americans, women, immigrants, and other people of color. Both the means and methods of struggle were subject to constant ideological, philosophical, and practical debate and internal conflict. The articles in this section reveal major fault lines and individual battles within the larger battle.

The movement made significant gains but was not, however, linear: It ebbed and flowed with historical tides of progress and reaction, advance and retreat, terror and self-defense, revolution and counterrevolution. The legal-constitutional arena, highlighted by various civil rights acts and amendments to the U.S. Constitution—from the Reconstruction Acts of the 1860s to the Civil Rights Act of 1964 and the Voting Rights Act of 1965—are among the most obvious and enduring legal victories won through mass pressure and direct action.

The civil rights epoch is most closely associated with the 1960s' overt and covert battles, marches, boycotts, demonstrations, sit-ins, strikes, pickets, and rallies, many of which were locally based and nationally organized by an array of organizations, coalitions, and activists. Places and events are indelibly etched in the annals of history: Selma, Alabama; Jacksonville, Florida; the Montgomery Bus Boycott; the March on Washington; Attica; and the Watts rebellion. These events were frequently at odds with each other, and leaders differed over the path the movement should take in order to advance the struggle. Although many of the great battles were fought in the Southern states, the movement also engulfed the Northern, Eastern, and Western states, attracting young and old, male and female, rich and poor, black and white, Latino and Asian people.

Although predominantly comprised of African Americans, Jewish, Italian, and other supporters and activists played an important role in the movement, particularly in the early stages of the struggle.

Major civil rights groups founded included the Niagara Movement and its progeny, the National Association for the Advancement of Colored People (NAACP), Universal Negro Improvement Association (UNIA), African Blood Brotherhood, Brotherhood of Sleeping Car Porters (BSCP), National Negro Congress (NNC), March on Washington Movement (MOW), Abraham Lincoln Brigade, Congress of Racial Equality (CORE), Southern Christian Leadership Conference (SCLC), Mississippi Freedom Democratic Party (MFDP), the Student Nonviolent Coordinating Committee (SNCC), Coalition of Black Trade Unionists (CBTU), Angela Davis's Che-Lumumba Club

(CPUSA), Black Panther Party (BPP), and Young Lords Party (YLP). These and others carried the torch to illuminate the civil rights struggle and to fend off attacks on African Americans from the likes of the Ku Klux Klan, Southern racist Democrats known as Dixiecrats fighting for "states rights," and assorted American Fascists.

The movement had close organizational and ideological ties with the women's movement from the time of its inception and became closely aligned with the anti-Vietnam War movement of the 1960s and 1970s. Hundreds of smaller local, grassroots-oriented civil rights efforts stimulated the rise of antiwar protests, the organization of senior citizens as manifested by the emergence of the Gray Panthers, a militant multiracial senior citizens organization, and La Raza, the Mexican-American farm workers movement under the leadership of Cesar Chavez.

The late twentieth century witnessed many "events," including "white backlash," racial polarization, attacks on Affirmative Action, adverse legal rulings since the 1970s linked to the rise of neoliberalism, conservative, and neoconservative Republicans opposed to the civil rights agenda in national, state legislative, executive, and judicial branches of government, and continuing racist resistance from politicians like Alabama governor George Wallace, Georgia governor Lester Maddox, Senator Strom Thurmond (R-SC), Senator Trent Lott (R-MS), and their local states rights followers. The convergence of these virulently hostile forces and the wrenching domination of political power contributed to the decline of the civil rights epoch.

Articles in this section denote a complex movement with numerous, evolving ideological strains and tendencies, including radical and reformist, separatist and integrationist, Black Muslim, Jewish, Catholic, liberal, conservative, Gandhi-style nonviolent philosophy, Socialist, Communist, and capitalistic.

Tensions between competing ideologies and organizations were manifested by relations ranging from active coalitions to violent internal organizational opposition. The evolving interplay between resistance and change within U.S. social institutions characterized and contextualized the civil rights era. Thus, as the movement transformed elements of society, civil rights organizations were particularly subject to the intense, frequently overwhelming forces of internal and external change.

ITS IMPACT

The removal of most of the overt, racially offensive and formerly legal manifestations of Jim Crow segregation, including the desegregation of public accommodations like transportation, lunch counters, and workforces in commercial stores like Woolworth's, constituted significant and enduring civil rights victories. Black and white children attending public schools together, in the North and South, came to symbolize the movement's impact and hope for the nation. The movement also substantially achieved the integration of federal employment, the armed forces, entry-level corporate employment, and most industrial trade unions, with the skilled trades lagging in terms of integrated membership.

The movement's aspiration for America was implanted and imparted as hope for the world as tens of millions of Indians, Chinese, Soviets, Africans, and Europeans watched news clips, listened to radio reports, and read local papers covering the unfolding dramas with riveted fascination. International political leaders closely watched the U.S. civil rights struggles, as common folk around the world, many engaged in their own anticolonial struggles, were inspired. In this sense, the civil rights movement helped set the stage for the international human rights struggles that followed. The American civil rights movement had a profound international impact. This influence was played out in U.S. foreign policy, as issues of freedom and democracy reverberated globally, influencing anticolonial and African struggles for independence, the anti-apartheid and nonaligned movement, and the establishment of institutions like the United Nations, which was in no small measure aided by the African-American civil rights activist Dr. Ralph Bunche.

In the political and electoral realm, by the end of the twentieth century more than 5,000 African Americans had been elected to federal, state, and local governments, far surpassing the number of blacks elected during Reconstruction after the Civil War. However, African Americans elected to office did not necessarily translate into their holding meaningful political power, as economic and social bastions of privilege still dominated American life.

In terms of economic relations, indices of poverty, unemployment, labor and housing discrimination, and business ownership, the impact of the modern civil rights movement was far less successful. The legacy of slavery in America stymied generations of ameliorative social policies, including Reconstruction's never-delivered promise of "40 acres and a mule" for every African American, President Franklin D. Roosevelt's New Deal, Truman's Fair Employment Practices Committee (FEPC), and Lyndon Johnson's Great Society and War on Poverty. Equality remained elusive, and African Americans were polarized by the underlying economic system. Although some blacks entered the middle class, the majority was mired in poverty and despair.

Ironically, Dr. King's most famous "I have a Dream" speech at the 1963 March on Washington for Jobs and Justice, resonating against the backdrop of the Lincoln Memorial, coincided exactly with the death of W.E.B. Du Bois, solemnly announced to the throngs of marchers from the dais, and followed by a moment of silence. This marked both the pinnacle and the beginning of the decline of the civil rights movement and the nation's failure to resolve its racial history.

Community control movements like Brooklyn's Ocean Hill Brownsville and the multicultural education movement based largely in America's urban public schools, calling for the inclusion of people of color, women, and immigrants in the K-12 curriculum, of late twentieth and early twenty-first century America had as their impetus the spirit and philosophy of the civil rights movement, the ongoing work of activists, and the furthering of the unfinished agenda of dismantling the racial caste system in America. The movement also gave rise to black and women's caucus movements in unions, churches, and political parties, and spawned African-American, Latino, and ethnic studies programs and curricula that soon sprouted up in many American colleges and universities, including "Open Admissions" policies massively integrating the City University of New York, the nation's largest urban higher education system.

Although the impact of the civil rights movement continues in myriad ways, the modern civil rights era, according to most observers, has drawn to a close. This demise resulted from a complex combination of forces, including divisions between radical and liberal leaders, ideological splits among nationalists and integrationists, those supporting passive nonviolent resistance and self-defense, and, not least importantly, setbacks created by government-orchestrated repression, dirty tricks, sabotage, and the assassinations of Dr. King, Malcolm X, Medgar Evers, and others.

By the end of the twentieth century, civil rights laws and policies were severely tested. Many of the once powerful civil rights organizations, especially at the local level, withered or disintegrated in political and generational countercurrents. Clarence Thomas, the conservative African-American jurist, replaced his pioneering predecessor, Thurgood Marshall, on the U.S. Supreme Court, symbolizing a reversal of the Court's civil rights trajectory and producing a chill in America's liberal political climate. The trend of limiting or reversing civil rights law was reflected in the U.S. Supreme Court's narrow 5–4 ruling in *Grutter v. Bollinger* (June 2003), upholding the University of Michigan's right to the "forward looking" practice of considering diversity and the critical mass of minorities admitted to its law school as a "compelling state interest." However, in a mixed signal within the same ruling, the Court struck down the university's point system, which allowed extra consideration of applicants based on race, a policy more closely related to Affirmative Action as a "backward looking" remedy for past wrongs.

Future generations have been left to grapple with the complex and contentious economic, political, and legal issues of race and diversity, thus setting the stage for a new phase of civil rights struggles in the twenty-first century.

Joseph Wilson

CIVIL RIGHTS MOVEMENT 1865–1910

Although whites often influenced black life both legally and practically in the forty-five years following the abolition of slavery, it was through millions of everyday trials that African Americans struggled for justice. Using political, economic, cultural, and social means towards ends ranging from full access to white-dominated institutions to total control of their own, separate communities, blacks fought to define their own experiences amidst oppression.

THE CONSTITUTIONAL AMENDMENTS

Ratified between 1865 and 1870, a series of three constitutional amendments promised 4.5 million African Americans previously banned from citizenship (about one-ninth of whom had never been slaves) all the civil rights guaranteed by the Constitution of the United States. The Thirteenth Amendment (1865) declared, "Neither slavery nor involuntary servitude . . . shall exist within the United States, or any place subject to their jurisdiction." The Fourteenth Amendment (1868) made "All persons born or naturalized in the United States . . . citizens of the United States and of the State wherein they reside." The Fifteenth Amendment (1870) pledged, "The right of citizens of the United States to vote shall not be denied or abridged by the United States or by any State on account of race, color, or previous condition of servitude."

Legal measures nullified the U.S. Supreme Court's *Dred Scott v. Sandford* (1857) decision, which mandated that all blacks, whether free or slave, "are not included, and were not intended to be included, under the word 'citizens' in the Constitution, and can therefore claim none of the rights and privileges which that instrument provides for and secures to citizens of the United States." In reality, African Americans battled individually and collectively to gain these legal protections, often unsuccessfully in the face of overwhelming white power. In the years following these constitutional amendments, the Supreme Court narrowly defined civil rights legislation, and the federal government's commitment to black freedom waned.

Following the end of the Civil War in 1865, defeated Confederate states ratified the Thirteenth Amendment but refused to approve the Fourteenth Amendment. Instead, Southern states passed laws called Black Codes that placed major restrictions on newly emancipated African Americans. Black Codes limited the areas where blacks could live and hold property. Blacks could not testify or be jurors in court cases involving whites. These restrictions varied locally, but most included vagrancy laws that drafted unemployed blacks into forced labor if they failed to pay a $50 fine. On the basis of race, Black Codes imposed curfews, denied voting rights, prevented the ownership of alcohol, livestock, and firearms, banned intermarriage, and restricted travel.

In 1866 and 1867, Congress responded to the Black Codes. It extended the life of the Freedmen's Bureau, a federal agency that was originally set to expire after a year, and passed a Civil Rights Bill. In addition to providing medical, educational, and economic support to former slaves, the Freedmen's Bureau protected black civil rights. It enforced contracts between black labor and white employers and created new courts wherever it deemed local judicial authorities to be prejudiced against African Americans. The Civil Rights Bill banned the denial of citizenship rights according to color and presaged the Fourteenth and Fifteenth Amendments. Congress also passed the Reconstruction Act, which imposed military rule on Confederate states, called for new Southern governments, and required each Southern state to ratify the Fourteenth Amendment or lose political representation. Black men had the right to vote, but their doing so depended on federal policing of former Confederates.

African Americans organized politically during

this period and gained power in some Southern states. Churches were integral to this purpose, as were more specialized creations like the Lincoln Brotherhood and the Heroes of America. Following the Civil War, the largest black political organization was the Union League, which had ties to the Freedmen's Bureau and the Republican Party. Blacks played important roles in the governments of South Carolina and Louisiana. In Alabama, Florida, and North Carolina, black representation was marginal. In Mississippi, unchecked white violence and intimidation prevented blacks from capitalizing on their numerical majority at the polls. In some states, black voting strength backed by federal authority led to increased African American political representation and power. Others, like Georgia, more successfully resisted this possibility.

Despite white intransigence, African Americans never let their oppressors fully delimit their political vision. When the Georgia legislature barred its black members in 1868, for example, the ousted men fought for their seats and regained them following federal military intervention. Even in states where they lacked meaningful government representation, the blacks' assertiveness encouraged civil rights legislation. From 1869 to 1873, South Carolina, Texas, Mississippi, Florida, and Louisiana passed civil rights laws in response to black demands.

By the late 1870s, the Supreme Court's narrow constitutional interpretations and the federal government's decreasing commitment to fighting a guerrilla war against antiblack terrorist organizations like the Ku Klux Klan marked the end of the period known as Reconstruction (1865–1877). In the *Slaughter-House Cases* (1873) decision, the U.S. Supreme Court separated state and national citizenship, nearly nullifying the Fourteenth Amendment by declaring almost all rights the product of state citizenship. In *United States v. Cruikshank* (1876), the Court ruled that the Fourteenth Amendment empowered the federal government to punish states, but not individuals, for depriving citizens of their rights. In *United States v. Reese* (1876), it determined that the Fifteenth Amendment barred the denial of suffrage on the basis of race but did not guarantee citizens the right to vote, allowing injudiciously applied poll taxes and literacy tests to circumvent the law and disfranchise most blacks. With neither the Court's help nor the protection of Northern soldiers, who left the South in 1877, black civil rights gains were compromised.

From the 1830s until nearly the twentieth century, the Convention Movement developed black middle-class leadership on the grassroots level. Conventions were made up of delegates who were chosen locally. Both nationally and within their states, these leaders held meetings to propose solutions to black problems. In October 1864, about 150 black men met in Syracuse, New York, to organize the National Equal Rights League, which demanded African-American political equality. Perhaps because they were dominated by elites, however, many conventions proposed more conservative means for black advancement. For example, conventions in 1865 and 1866 in North Carolina, Alabama, and Kentucky stressed education, morality, and industry as the keys to black success. Nevertheless, federal protection in the South in the 1870s led to an increased focus on political strategies for racial equality. The largest of the Reconstruction-era national conventions, held in Washington, D.C., in December 1873, was devoted entirely to civil rights agendas. Once Reconstruction ended, however, conventioneers generally returned to more conservative programs endorsing race-based economic separatism to further black causes.

DIVERGENT AFRICAN-AMERICAN PERSPECTIVES

Like the diverse people they represented, African-American leaders possessed varied visions of black empowerment. Some were black nationalists who believed that African-American success depended on economic and/or political racial unity and the maintenance of autonomous black social, cultural, and spiritual spheres. Others were integrationists who called for full access to white-dominated institutions and stressed black participation in all aspects of American life. The dialogue, ideological intersection, and conflicts between black nationalists and integrationists have fundamentally marked African-American political and intellectual history since the eighteenth century.

Of the black nationalists who proposed that African Americans emigrate to Africa, the most influential in the United States near the end of the nineteenth century was Henry McNeal Turner, an African Methodist Episcopal bishop who had been one of the legislators sacked in Georgia's 1868 purge of its black politicians. Turner believed that black Americans needed to run their own governments in newly established African colonies. There was also a religious mission to Turner's plan. Like the Harvard-educated physician Martin Delany and the Episcopalian missionary Alexander Crummell, Turner

SPEECH BY BISHOP HENRY M. TURNER
June 22, 1867

Bishop Henry M. Turner (1834–1915), of the Methodist Episcopal Church, a leading African-American opponent of slavery, became a member of the Georgia legislature following the Civil War and appealed to African Americans in Georgia to become active in political life.

. . . Many of our fellow citizens in the country, and even in the towns and villages, are far from being awake to their own interests and to the interests of prosperity; not because they are disinterested at all, but because many cherish the foolish idea that they had better not have anything to do with political matters; thus leaving it, as they say, to their white friends and colored leaders to manage—misapprehending as you see, that they are individually responsible and connected to the weal or woe of our future civil and political status. The result is that hundreds declared they will not register; others say, they do not care to either register or vote until things are more settled; others again, say they cannot lose the time just now, crops are being laid by, and for every day they lose, from three to five dollars are deducted from their wages; while still others declare it is useless to register, for they have already been told that if they ever vote in harmony with Congress, or old Joe Brown, their throats will be cut from ear to ear, consequently, they are determined not to register,

or vote, in the face of such events; especially, when they would be sure to vote to sustain the power that gave them freedom. . . .

The question then resolves itself into [a] plan by which the fore-going evils may be remedied, and the liberties of our race preserved. This can only be done by organizing associations in the above named cities, where a weekly or monthly fee can be collected for the purpose of salarying intelligent men to traverse the rural regions of our State, and deliver such lectures to them as will inform them that their inactivity now is an unpardonable crime. . . .

Let the people of our cities rise in the majesty of their strength and the more correct knowledge and send the true alarm like thunder crashes through the country, towns and hamlets, until every man shall see his duty, and be forced to do it. If the country districts vote wrong, our cities will be no more than a drop in the bucket. If the men are too indifferent to take action on this matter, I must respectfully appeal to the ladies. Ladies! form yourselves into societies; gather all the funds you can and employ as many colored speakers (or white either) as you can, and send them in the field to teach our people what to do, and how to do it. Your destiny is ours; ours is yours. We rise and fall together. . . .

Source: The Loyal Georgian, [Augusta], July 6, 1867.

---

believed that Africa's salvation depended on the exportation of Protestantism and Western mores to that continent.

In part, Turner's success in returning blacks to Africa was determined by their lack of faith in the United States and its institutions. For example, when in 1883 the U.S. Supreme Court declared the 1875 Civil Rights Act to be unconstitutional, Turner expanded his campaign to transplant black Americans to Liberia. Although he was able to convince only a small group of African Americans to leave, Turner's plan had symbolic importance because of the level of black independence it proposed. Historians have argued that poverty and lack of transportation rather than disinterest kept many blacks from relocating to Africa during this period.

Although it had been in existence for decades before the Civil War, the American Colonization Society (ACS) also responded to the immediacy of the post-Reconstruction era. By the late 1880s, the white-

controlled ACS, which many blacks distrusted, had declined in popularity but still sent about a hundred colonists to Liberia annually, in part owing to the impact of Henry McNeal Turner, who served for a time as one of its vice presidents.

Perhaps the ACS's most famous emigrant was Edward Wilmot Blyden, whose trip to the United States in 1889 brought national attention to the Back-to-Africa movement and sparked congressional debate about funding the repatriation of dissatisfied American blacks. Born in the Dutch West Indies, Blyden had been educated by an American missionary before completing his schooling in Liberia with assistance from the ACS. While a resident of Liberia, Blyden had founded that country's national college and served as its minister to Great Britain.

Blyden, who had visited the United States several times previously, was by 1889 at the peak of his influence on Americans because of the publication of his 1887 book, *Christianity, Islam and the Negro Race*, and because of contemporary political and socioeconomic conditions. Although a Presbyterian, Blyden sensed that Islam fostered racial pride and was potentially more attractive to blacks than sectarian Christianity, which often equated blackness with evil. Blyden asserted that if American blacks formed new churches in Africa, they could save the continent from total submission to Islam. Although Blyden was more ambivalent toward modernizing Africa than were Crummell, Delany, and Turner, he shared their desire to Christianize it.

In late 1889, Blyden found support for his Back-to-Africa movement both popularly and in Congress. According to some Southern ministers, Blyden could have mustered 500,000 black people to emigrate from the region immediately if there had been ample transportation and money to do so. Before the 1888 election, Republicans had tried to retain black support with promises of lasting civil rights legislation. In his State of the Union Address the next year, President Benjamin Harrison proposed that Congress pass a law calling for federal supervision of elections. Because this measure would greatly increase black political power, some white Southern leaders saw emigration as more desirable than a strong black voting bloc. Senator Matthew Butler of South Carolina proposed a bill that would provide transportation for all Southern black persons who agreed to certify their wish to become citizens of their destined country. Senator R.L. Gibson of Louisiana called for the investigation of acquiring or designating territory in Africa for black expatriates. The introduction of these measures reveals the relative popularity of Back-to-Africa movements and their parallel meanings to blacks and whites following Reconstruction. Importantly, however, most African Americans, whether black nationalists or integrationists, criticized these programs and preferred to remain in the United States. Some historians also argue that black nationalists who supported the emigration movement viewed separatism as only a temporary means to eventual incorporation into American life.

In the face of massive civil rights rollbacks, migration within the United States also became an attractive option for ex-slaves. During a matter of weeks in 1879, thousands of freed people from Mississippi, Louisiana, and Tennessee, terrorized by antiblack legislation and attracted by promises of farmland in Kansas, boarded steamships to St. Louis, Missouri. This rush, known as the Kansas Fever Exodus or Exoduster Movement, saw nearly 15,000 African Americans come to Kansas over the next year. About three-

quarters of these migrant families wound up owning their own homes. Another 35,000 blacks moved to Missouri, Indiana, and Illinois from the South during this period. In these areas, migrants formed all-black towns that resonated with the self-help economic separatism proposed by conservatives. Most migrants were poor, rural folk. Middle-class and urban-based blacks were less likely to leave the South during this period.

AFRICAN-AMERICAN LABOR
Although black Americans have generally turned toward self-help, racial unity, and economic advancement when faced with oppressive conditions, there are always those, like leading black journalist and newspaper editor T. Thomas Fortune, who have championed political protest, if not the immediate integration of all American institutions. Fortune understood the importance of race unity and pride in political and economic, if not social, matters.

A critic of the Senate's colonization efforts and the emigration movement, Fortune formed the Afro-American League, which had its first national convention in Chicago in 1890. Also during that year, a group of 445 men, including most leading black politicians of the time, met in Washington, D.C., to discuss the barriers blocking first-class African-American citizenship. The Citizens' Equal Rights Association became the organizational offshoot of this meeting. Fortune believed that African Americans should split their votes in ways designed to make both major parties compete for them. Too long, Fortune argued, blacks had sold short their power at the polls to the Republican Party. Fortune also believed that economic influence would ultimately ensure civil rights, and later he devoted increased energy to industrial rather than political efforts.

Like many African Americans, Fortune encouraged black participation in labor unions in the 1880s and the politics of radical agrarianism in the 1890s. Although the United Mine Workers and the Knights of Labor were relatively unbiased during the 1880s, the National Labor Union, founded in 1866, and the American Federation of Labor, founded in 1886, took longer to freely admit African Americans. African Americans also formed their own groups like the Colored National Labor Union in 1869, but they attracted few members. Blacks gravitated toward populism in the 1890s. At its peak, the Colored Farmers Alliance, with many of its advocates loyal to the Populist Party, claimed over one million members. Before it eventually capitulated to racism, the Populist Party through

The abolition of slavery did not significantly improve the conditions of African Americans, who, under Jim Crow laws, now became contract laborers for former white slaveowners, subject to oppressive conditions and denied freedom of movement. *(Brown Brothers)*

its focus on interracial political cooperation won the support of many blacks seeking to weaken the Democratic Party's control of the South.

ROLLING BACK BLACK RIGHTS

By custom and by law, private citizens and public officials in the North and the South restricted black civil rights gains. All over the country, Jim Crow laws forced racial segregation. Courts in Ohio and Massachusetts ruled that separate schools for blacks and whites were constitutional. In Indiana, laws banned intermarriage. West Virginia, Virginia, Delaware, Kentucky, and Mississippi laws limited juror status to adult white males. The Supreme Court of the United States upheld the constitutionality of such statutes in

Plessy v. Ferguson (1896), which maintained that forced racial separation on railway carriages did not violate the Fourteenth Amendment if facilities for blacks and whites were equal. Because of racism and the unequal distribution of power, however, black accommodations were almost always inferior. Nevertheless, the federal government rarely intervened in such situations.

Lynching was the era's predominant sign of racial inequality. These ritualized killings, which were public displays designed to terrorize blacks from asserting power, sometimes involved the complicity of local law enforcement agents that allowed white vigilante groups to remove blacks falsely accused of crimes from jail cells. Whites were almost never punished for

RACIAL DISCRIMINATION AT WORK
1878

After the Civil War and the end of slavery, exclusion from training programs leading to skilled occupations was a means to discriminate against African Americans and to keep workplaces segregated.

There is something in America, commonly called prejudice that so opposes the progress of the colored people, as to render it well nigh impossible for them to make any headway at all.....

We have a great number of young men that would like to become skilled workmen; but hardly can there be a locality picked out in the whole country where it is possible for the colored parent to get a mechanic on any terms whatever, to take his boy and learn him a trade.

If you go to the brick mason or plasterer and try to get your boy in, he will tell you, yes we will take him to make mortar or carry brick; but we can't take and learn him a trade. And so, if he would learn any other trade he is refused—and the boy dispirited, comes to the conclusion that every avenue for his advancement is blocked. Yes, blocked by caste prejudice, and so with our young ladies. If an advertisement is read in our daily papers, that apprentices are wanted to learn dress-making, or bonnet-making, or trimming, and a young colored lady makes application for the place, she is told that the kitchen is supplied with a cook and the main shop is only to be filled with white girls. If a clerk is wanted in a grocery house, or a dry goods store, and a young colored man of good education and pleasant address makes application for the place, he is told that they have a man on their delivery wagon now, and that behind the counter they have only white boys, not that their qualifications are not all sufficient, but their faces are not white enough, that's all. So there is in every avocation, except the lower ones in life. If we look at the educational advantages offered in most localities, we will find the same prejudice exists.

Source: The Colored Citizen [Fort Scott, Kansas], November 23, 1878.

these murders, in which black corpses were usually mutilated, even when photographs illustrating their involvement in such acts circulated as post cards or novelty items. While most common in the Deep South, lynching was a nationwide problem, occurring

Ida B. Wells, African-American freedom fighter and opponent of white violence in the Jim Crow era, led a life-long struggle against lynching. A prolific writer on white oppression of African Americans, Wells published *Red Record*, a study of lynching in America. *(© Bettman/CORBIS)*

as far north as Duluth, Minnesota, and often drawing thousands of white spectators. Lynching of African Americans increased greatly following the Civil War. From 1889 to 1918, over 2,500 blacks were lynched. In the overwhelming majority of the cases, the victims were male. Local judicial, political, and law enforcement officials allowed lynching and Congress never passed an antilynching bill, leaving blacks on their own to deal with this form of terrorism.

By the late 1890s, African-American clubwomen were one of the nation's strongest antilynching forces. In addition to forming local leagues and committees that constituted the black clubwomen's movement, several leaders also created the National Association of Colored Women's Clubs (NACW) in 1896. Promoting women's rights, racial uplift, and antilynching protest and legislation, the NACW attracted a spectacular group of members and supporters, including investigative journalist Ida B. Wells and organizer Mary Church Terrell. Women from reform groups na-

IDA BELL WELLS-BARNETT

(1862–1931)

Born in Holly Springs, Mississippi, on July 16, 1862, Ida Wells was the daughter of slaves and the oldest of eight. She was educated at Rust University, a freedmen's school in Holly Springs, and at fourteen years of age began teaching in a country school. With the death of her parents and three siblings from yellow fever in 1878, she worked to keep her family together. She continued to teach after moving to Memphis, Tennessee, in 1884 and attended Fisk University during several summer sessions.

In 1884, Wells challenged the rule of segregated seating on railroads and filed suit against the Chesapeake & Ohio Railroad for having been forcibly removed from her seat after she had refused to give it up for one in a "colored only" car. In 1887, the Tennessee Supreme Court, reversing a circuit court decision, ruled against Wells. In the late 1880s, she began writing articles for her local church newspaper that were then reprinted in black-owned and operated newspapers around the country. In 1891, Wells also wrote some newspaper articles critical of the education available to African-American children. Her teaching contract was not renewed because of her writings. She then turned to journalism full time, buying an interest in the *Memphis Free Speech* and working as an editor at that publication from 1891 to 1892.

After three of her friends were lynched by a mob in 1892, Wells began an editorial campaign against lynching that quickly led to the sacking of her newspaper's office. Warned to stay out of town, she went to the Northeast and became a renowned antilynching activist. She continued her antilynching crusade, first as a staff writer for the *New York Age* and then as a lecturer and organizer of antilynching societies. She spoke in a number of major U.S. cities and twice visited Great Britain for the cause.

In 1895, she married Ferdinand L. Barnett, a Chicago lawyer, editor, and public official, and adopted the name Wells-Barnett. From that time she restricted her travels to raise her family, but she was very active in Chicago affairs. Wells-Barnett contributed to the *Chicago Conservator*, her husband's newspaper, and to other local journals; published a detailed look at lynching in *A Red Record* (1895); and was active in organizing local African-American women in various causes from the antilynching campaign to the suffrage movement. She founded what may have been the first black woman suffrage group, Chicago's Alpha Suffrage Club.

From 1898 to 1902, Wells-Barnett served as secretary of the National Afro-American Council, and in 1910 she founded and became first president of the Negro Fellowship League, which aided newly arrived migrants from the South even over the objections of middle-class urban blacks. She was militant in her demand for justice for African Americans and in her insistence that it was to be won by their own efforts. Although she took part in the 1909 meeting of the Niagara Movement, she would have nothing to do with the less radical National Association for the Advancement of Colored People that sprang from it. She ran for state senator in 1930 but came in third in the primary election. Undeterred, she continued her work while writing her autobiography. Wells-Barnett died in Chicago, Illinois, on March 25, 1931. Her autobiography, *Crusade for Justice*, was published posthumously in 1970.

James G. Lewis

---

tionwide contributed to the magazine *Women's Era*, which discussed socioeconomic and political issues like healthcare, education, and community development. A number of NACW members would continue their antilynching work throughout the twentieth century through the National Association for the Advancement of Colored People (NAACP).

Members of the clubwomen's movement tended toward conservative, self-help strategies for improvement. The president of the National Federation of Afro-American Women, which merged with the Colored Women's League to form the NACW, was Margaret Murray Washington, the wife of Booker T. Washington. Like her husband, Washington endorsed black nationalist industrial education, which urged blacks to learn trades that would give them economic power and to avoid participation in politics or integrated social functions. The NACW slogan, "Lifting as we climb," revealed the class-consciousness of the clubwomen's movement. Most clubwomen were from the middle-class or elite and saw as their goal the improvement of rank-and-file blacks. They felt that integration and social equality could be achieved once common folk were trained in bourgeois ways of life. Programmatically, local clubs reflected this idea by providing welfare benefits for less fortunate black citizens. Some focused on prison reform; others set up orphanages; and several provided free legal services for the poor.

FREDERICK DOUGLASS

By the Civil War, Frederick Douglass was black America's leading spokesperson, a status he would maintain until his death in 1895. Born a slave in 1818, Douglass escaped to freedom as a young adult. He gained national attention after his first autobiography, *Narrative of the Life of Frederick Douglass, An American Slave, Written by Himself*, was published in 1845. An abolitionist and women's rights advocate, Douglass related the elimination of sexism to African American advancement, like members of the clubwomen's movement would at the turn of the century. Elizabeth Cady Stanton, the white women's rights activist, called Douglass "the only man I ever saw who understood the degradation of the disfranchisement of women." Douglass realized the different challenges facing black and white women, and addressed them in his pro-feminist speeches and writings, but he generally advocated for women's rights in nonracial terms. Douglass shared the clubwomen's desire for assimilation while eschewing race pride per se. He believed that blacks sometimes had to organize along racial lines, but he felt that such groups were routes to integration and citizenship rather than autonomous ends. Unlike most clubwomen, however, Douglass argued for the immediate integration of all American institutions and equal political and civil rights for blacks and whites. In this regard, he was perhaps the most militant of the post-Reconstruction era's black spokespersons.

Douglass did not reject entirely the black economic sphere as a site for gaining power. He believed that learning trades and acquiring property would bring African Americans closer to full citizenship rights. During this period, Douglass felt that classical education was not sufficient and called for industrial education. Unlike conservatives, however, Douglass believed that blacks would succeed economically on the open market rather than through all-black commercial and industrial networks. Douglass wanted blacks to compete with whites for money, resources, and employment rather than operate within separate communities. In an 1886 speech, he told a Boston audience, "I think the blacks are in a position in some respects more favorable to progress than the whites. They, at least, can work. They have hard hands, strong frames, and are accustomed to toil, and the toilers of any country will, in the end, be uppermost." More than any other leader of the period, Douglass believed that blacks could gain social, political, and economic equality to whites through full participation in all American institutions. Although he understood the usefulness of certain tenets of black nationalism, Douglass rejected separate black and white spheres as both ends and means to solving racial problems.

BOOKER T. WASHINGTON

Booker T. Washington became America's most influential black man following an 1895 speech in which he endorsed racial segregation. This "Atlanta Compromise" address proposed black disfranchisement and a repudiation of black political power in the South in return for a share of the economic growth that came with post-Reconstruction Northern investment in the former Confederacy. The speech epitomized Booker T. Washington's leadership. It eschewed racial pride, and it urged blacks to be humble. It implied that black ignorance rather than white racism was the key barrier to black success. It also proposed that blacks and whites inhabit separate social spheres, and it called for a retreat from political protest and for a focus on economic advancement. To Washington, civil rights were meaningless without the protection of wealth.

Born a slave in 1856, Washington was first educated shortly after emancipation. As a teen, he received secondary training at Hampton Institute, a white-run industrial school. Hampton's program molded Washington's belief that liberal arts courses like reading, philosophy, grammar, history, and arithmetic were useful only in conjunction with job skills and training in trades like sewing, carpentry, construction, and printing. Washington's outstanding record as a student and then a teacher at Hampton earned him a recommendation from the school's white headmaster for a position as the principal of a newly chartered black normal school in Tuskegee, Alabama in 1881.

Washington's leadership and expansion of Tuskegee Institute centered on territorial possession, ownership of property, and land control, making the school into a model of independence that anticipated future black nationalist ideas involving economic solidarity and racial separatism. In particular, Tuskegee's brick-making enterprise materialized Washington's philosophies. Washington believed that a brickyard would boost Tuskegee's income, beautify the town, prove the school's usefulness to the community, and teach students an industry. Brick making also gave Washington control over the construction of new

Emancipation Day Parade in Richmond, Virginia, on April 3, 1905. The parade celebrates the fall of Richmond, when African Americans of the city became free. *(Library of Congress)*

buildings on campus. Furthermore, it asserted black discipline and modernity to racist whites, because producing brick from start to finish was difficult, demanding, scientific work.

Although Tuskegee was Washington's home base, it was not the only site from which he wielded influence. Another vehicle he used to bolster black economic strength was the National Negro Business League (NNBL). In 1915, the year of Washington's death, NNBL membership was estimated to be as high as 40,000, with 600 local chapters in thirty-six states and West Africa. The NNBL was an alliance of property-owning blacks whose total resources could help overcome problems faced by individual investors, most notably lack of capital and difficulties getting loans from white bankers. The organization also endorsed "buy-black" campaigns.

Washington's promotion of all-black towns typified his balancing act: black autonomy on the one hand, accommodation of white racists on the other. Washington declared self-segregated places like Mound Bayou, Mississippi, a town founded in 1867 by Isaiah Thornton Montgomery, a former slave, to be "the finest possible concrete argument that the Negro is ready for citizenship." He claimed that white racial separatism "has frequently been to create for the Negro a special business opportunity." However, Washington ignored the political aspects of all-black towns and did not celebrate publicly their self-governance.

Despite these all-black institutions and their focus

on self-help, positioning Booker T. Washington as a black nationalist is a curious proposition because of his accommodationism, deference to white norms, gradualism, and assuaging of white racists. Historians and contemporary observers have been conflicted about whether or not Washington's refusal to confront whites in exchange for the smooth operation of the Tuskegee machine and his acquisition of personal power ultimately benefited or harmed black Americans. Although Tuskegee's success refuted the basest claims of black inferiority, it also willingly accepted white limitations on the scope of black achievement and autonomy. Washington's overall impact on American race relations until his death in 1915 remains a source of considerable scholarly debate.

W.E.B. Du Bois

W.E.B. Du Bois was one of Washington's staunchest critics during the early twentieth century. In his classic 1903 book, *The Souls of Black Folk*, the thirty-five-year-old college professor Du Bois challenged the consensus that Washington spoke for all African Americans. According to the Massachusetts-born Du Bois, "Mr. Washington's program practically accepts the alleged inferiority of the Negro races." Du Bois doubted Washington's belief that civil and constitutional rights would evolve from black wealth and thought that Washington's refusal to focus on politics made his economic vision unreliable.

In July 1905, Du Bois brought together thirty black men in Ontario, Canada, for what would become known as the Niagara Movement. This movement centered on leadership by college graduates, whom Du Bois referred to as the Talented Tenth. The Niagara Movement championed voting and civil rights protest as the means to increase black opportunity in the United States. The Niagarites saw Washington as the greatest obstacle to their goals.

Although the all-black Niagara Movement folded after four years, it gave birth to the interracial National Association for the Advancement of Colored People (NAACP), which became one of the most powerful black sociopolitical organizations in the twentieth century. The integrated nature of the NAACP challenged Washington's call for racial separatism. NAACP members argued that civil rights were fundamental to black freedom and economic independence. W.E.B. Du Bois became the NAACP's director of publicity and research in July 1910 and founded the organization's official journal, *The Crisis*. From his position as its editor, Du Bois opposed Washington's

policies and called for increased black political protest.

From emancipation to the twentieth century, African Americans proposed a variety of strategies to achieve first-class citizenship. Many, most notably the emigrationists, believed that such a condition was impossible within the United States, and urged blacks to return to Africa to form new governments and societies. Most, however, insisted that the battle for freedom be contested in America. Some, like Booker T. Washington, believed economic advancement to be a harbinger of equal protection under the law. Others, including Frederick Douglass and W.E.B. Du Bois, insisted that blacks could best advance through political means and the immediate integration of white-dominated institutions. These debates resonated throughout twentieth-century intellectual history, reflecting the competing traditions of integrationism and black nationalism in African American life. In the 1960s, for example, these differences were demarcated by the emergence of the Black Power movement in response to the civil rights movement. The longevity of these dialogues suggests the permanence of the struggle by blacks for equal opportunity in the United States.

Michael Ezra

Bibliography

Altschuler, Glenn C. *Race, Ethnicity, and Class in American Social Thought, 1865–1919*. Arlington Heights, IL: Harlan Davidson, 1982.

Angell, Stephen Ward. *Bishop Henry McNeal Turner and African-American Religion in the South*. Knoxville: University of Tennessee Press, 1992.

Blassingame, John W., and John R. McKivigan, eds. *The Frederick Douglass Papers: Volume 5, 1881–1895*. New Haven, CT: Yale University Press, 1992.

Blyden, Edward Wilmot. *Christianity, Islam, and the Negro Race*. 1887. Reprint, Chicago: Aldine, 1967.

Brown, Mary Jane. *Women in the American Anti-Lynching Movement, 1892–1940*. New York: Garland, 2000.

Du Bois, W.E.B. *The Souls of Black Folk*. 1903. Reprint, New York: Penguin Books, 1989.

Finkelman, Paul, ed. *Dred Scott v. Sandford: A Brief History with Documents*. Boston: Bedford Books, 1997.

Foner, Philip S., ed. *Frederick Douglass on Women's Rights*. Westport, CT: Greenwood Press, 1976.

Franklin, John Hope. *Reconstruction after the Civil War*. Chicago: University of Chicago Press, 1961.

Franklin, John Hope, and Alfred A. Moss. *From Slavery to Freedom: A History of African Americans*. 7th ed. New York: McGraw-Hill, 1994.

Harlan, Louis R. *Booker T. Washington: The Making of a Black Leader, 1856–1901*. New York: Oxford University Press, 1972.

———. *Booker T. Washington: The Wizard of Tuskegee, 1901–1915*. New York: Oxford University Press, 1983.

Henretta, James A., et al. *America: A Concise History, Volume 2: Since 1865*. Boston: Bedford Books, 1999.

Lewis, David Levering. *W.E.B. Du Bois: Biography of a Race, 1868–1919*. New York: Henry Holt, 1993.

Logan, Rayford. *The Betrayal of the Negro: From Rutherford Hayes to Woodrow Wilson*. New York: Da Capo, 1954.

Lynch, Hollis R. *Edward Wilmot Blyden: Pan-Negro Patriot*. London: Oxford University Press, 1967.

———, ed. *Selected Letters of Edward Wilmot Blyden*. Milwood, NY: KTO Press, 1978.

Meier, August. *Negro Thought in America, 1880–1915*. Ann Arbor: University of Michigan Press, 1963.

Meier, August, and Elliot Rudwick. *Along the Color Line: Explorations in the Black Experience*. Urbana: University of Illinois Press, 1976.

Moses, Wilson Jeremiah. *The Golden Age of Black Nationalism, 1850–1925*. New York: Oxford University Press, 1978.

Nieman, Donald G. *To Set the Law in Motion: The Freedmen's Bureau and the Legal Rights of Blacks, 1865–1868*. Millwood, NY: KTO Press, 1979.

Norton, Mary Beth., et al. *A People and a Nation: A History of the United States*. 3d ed. Boston: Houghton Mifflin, 1990.

Painter, Nell Irvin. *Exodusters: Black Migration to Kansas after Reconstruction*. Lawrence: University Press of Kansas, 1976.

Redkey, Edwin S. *Black Exodus: Black Nationalist and Back-to-Africa Movements, 1890–1910*. New Haven, CT: Yale University Press, 1969.

Redkey, Edwin S., ed. *Respect Black: The Writings and Speeches of Henry McNeal Turner*. New York: Arno, 1971.

Richardson, Heather Cox. *The Death of Reconstruction: Race, Labor, and Politics in the Post-Civil War North, 1865–1901*. Cambridge, MA: Harvard University Press, 2001.

Royster, Jacqueline Jones., ed. *Southern Horrors and Other Writings*. Boston: Bedford Books, 1997.

Smock, Raymond W., ed. *Booker T. Washington in Perspective: Essays of Louis Harlan*. Jackson: University of Mississippi Press, 1988.

Stampp, Kenneth M. *The Era of Reconstruction, 1865–1877*. New York: Vintage Books, 1965.

Thomas, Brook, ed. *Plessy v. Ferguson: A Brief History with Documents*. Boston: Bedford Books, 1997.

Thornburgh, Emma Lou. *T. Thomas Fortune: Militant Journalist*. Chicago: University of Chicago Press, 1972.

White, Horace. *The Life of Lyman Trumbull*. Boston: Houghton Mifflin, 1913.

MOVEMENT TO ABOLISH CONVICT LABOR

Convict labor was a facet of American criminal justice from the colonial period and usually took the form of temporary enslavement or indentured servitude. Significantly, it was individualized. Similarly, efforts to reform and humanize criminal justice began at least as early as William Penn and his Pennsylvania Quakers. Later reformers, including Benjamin Rush, Thomas Jefferson, Louis and Theodore Dwight, Edward Livingston, Dorothea Lynde Dix, and Charles Sumner helped create in the United States what, despite numerous and obvious flaws, was hailed by such European observers as Gustave de Beaumont, Alexis de Tocqueville, and Nicholas Julius as the very model of enlightened criminal justice. As George Washington Cable, a noted Southern social reform advocate, wrote in *The Silent South* (1885), however, "[c]ommunities rarely allow the prison its rightful place among their investments of public money for the improvement of public morals and public safety. Its outlays are begrudged because they do not yield cash incomes equal to their cash expenses."

PENITENTIARY MODELS

For Americans in general, and the voters of the South in particular, taxpayer support of a state prison was an unpopular proposition almost from the start. As the potential for capitalist profit from convict labor became clear, movements to maintain the reformatory ideals of the penitentiary, protect prisoners from exploitation, and prevent the unfree labor of convicts from negatively impacting free workers faced a constant struggle with both state and local authorities and the enterprises that profited from convict labor. These movements lasted well into the twentieth century and face new challenges in the twenty-first.

By the early nineteenth century, the concept of reformative penitentiaries had taken hold throughout the United States. The "Auburn System," pioneered at the New York penitentiary in the 1820s, provided for separate cells for each prisoner and a congregate work area, managed by private contractors. This combination of the perceived educational value of hard work for convicts and the very real potential of profitable manufacturing had a broad appeal throughout the country in these early years of industrial capitalism. Consequently, the Auburn model was widely mimicked and, by mid-century, every state with any sort of central prison, except Pennsylvania and New Jersey (which relied on expensive Quaker-inspired solitary confinement and largely symbolic labor), had adopted variations on the Auburn penitentiary. In states with no penitentiary before the Civil War, such as Florida and the Carolinas, individual convicts were leased to individual bidders in a manner not unlike a slave auction (the crucial difference, of course, was that the service of convicts was temporary in most cases).

A logical extension of the penitentiary-as-factory model, in fact, was the "convict lease," in which either the entire penitentiary facility was leased to a private contractor or, in some cases, inmates were remanded to individual bidders for work outside the walls of the prison. This notion, too, was quickly adopted across the country. Although convicts labored in all antebellum American penitentiaries, and labored for private contractors in many facilities under the "contract system," the notion of leasing either the entire facility or its inmates was most appealing in the South and West. This idea did not take hold in most of the North and Northeast, in part, because the emergence of penitentiaries coincided, in these regions, with the growth of the industrial economy. Clearly, convicts who worked for private interests were in competition with free laborers. The relatively broad franchise in the North and Northeast, combined with the strength and influence of workers' movements, made convict leasing politically unattractive. The relatively slow emergence of significant private industry in the South and West, on the other hand, opened the door for private interests to employ convicts. In the South, in particular, the pervasiveness of slavery (and the relatively restricted franchise for even free white men) made convict leasing politically more palatable.

RACIALIZATION OF CONVICT SYSTEM IN POST–CIVIL WAR ERA

After the Civil War and the end of chattel slavery, race became a prominent issue in the penal systems of the United States in general, and the South in particular. The code of race relations that dictated day-to-day life in the late nineteenth-century South forbade the equal treatment of African-American and white prisoners. This repressive social system, combined with the fact that the former slaves, or "freedmen," represented a new group of potential convicts, made the exploitation of convict labor far easier to defend than during the antebellum period. Concern for any failure of the system to reform and redeem the convict was blunted by the widespread belief in the inherent inferiority of African Americans. Furthermore, the safety and health of the convicts was not an issue for white society since the general welfare of the black race was rarely considered important in white public discourse. Thus, the expanded practice of leasing convicts to private contractors stemmed in part from an overall decrease in public concern for the welfare of its prisoners commensurate with an increase in the number of African Americans in the system. These factors, combined with the very real potential for substantial profits for government agencies and cheap labor for lessees, perpetuated convict leasing in the United States well into the twentieth century.

RESISTANCE TO CONTRACT LABOR

Several Southern states, including Georgia and Mississippi, began limited leasing programs almost immediately after the end of the Civil War, and the direct leasing of convict labor soon became common throughout the South, and the Deep South in particular. In fact, by the end of Reconstruction, all of the former slave states with the exception of Delaware used some form of leasing system to maintain their convict populations. Outside the South, however, only Nebraska, New Mexico, and Washington leased convicts after the Civil War. The Southern prisoners, increasingly and overwhelmingly African Americans, were employed on cotton and sugar plantations, in railroad, levee, and dock construction and maintenance, in the timber and lumber industries, in the turpentine industry, and in coal mining. Although it was

not until the 1930s that convict leasing and contract labor were finally brought down in most states, numerous local and national movements had organized explicitly to oppose the practices, including the Louisiana Prison Reform Association, various state branches of the national Central Howard Association (named for eighteenth-century British reformer John Howard), the National (later, American) Prison Association, the (North) Carolina Prisoner's Aid Society, the Texas Society for the Friendless, the Ex-Prisoners' Aid Society of Virginia, the Anti-Convict League and Union of Alabama, and the State Campaign Committee for the Abolishment of the Convict Contract System (also of Alabama). By the 1870s, in fact, there was already a strong movement afoot to combat the increased use of convict labor for private profit. The movement in opposition to convict leasing was diverse and the emphasis of the reformers differed in every state, but criticism of the system centered around a few common themes.

The primary concern was humanitarian. Even in the increasingly intense Jim Crow environment of the late nineteenth century, reformers were able to gain support for their attacks on leasing by pointing to the horrible conditions often faced by the convicts. Investigations in Georgia in the 1870s, for example, revealed frequent and brutal whippings of inmates, often for trivial reasons. Texas convicts were discovered to be shoeless and ill clad, even in winter, and to be fed insufficient and often rancid rations, and Tennessee investigators decried the poor health and sanitary conditions in the prison work camps. In Alabama, a startling 41 percent of all leased convicts died in 1869. In all leasing states, moreover, the public decried the use of very young, very old, and female inmates in work programs. Such early humanitarian concerns were easily laid to rest by authorities, however. Restructured leases limiting the nature and amount of corporal punishments, increasing and better regulating the food, lodging, and clothing of convicts, and mandating a general improvement in the sanitary conditions of work camps did much to defray criticism. More importantly, state and local governments coupled these minor reforms with increased charges to the lessees, thereby increasing the flow of money into public coffers and muting much of the criticism.

Several critics focused on questions of penology. Booker T. Washington, for example, argued that the lease system provided no mechanism for the improvement or reform of convicts and that, in fact, the harshness of the system made many convicts worse than they had been before their confinement. One Alabama convict inspector wrote, in his 1882 report, that the notion that the state prison system was at all reformatory was "one of the grandest farces, and one of the most sublime humbugs that human intelligence could possibly imagine." The alternative, as supporters of the lease did not hesitate to note, was increased public funding of the penal system, and concerns for the improvement of prisoners were again denied their "rightful place."

Just as supporters of convict leasing (and contract labor in general) emphasized financing in their argument for continuing the system, critics pointed to the negative economic results in their calls for reform. The most basic argument was that convicts, like slaves, served as unfree, low-cost, and therefore unfair competition with free laborers. The Farmers' Alliance, Populist movement, and labor groups, including the Knights of Labor, rallied in state after state to argue on these grounds. In Tennessee, in 1891 and 1892, the conflict between free workers and the exploiters of convict labor came to a head when free miners, in a replay of similar actions in Kentucky five years earlier, assaulted and took possession of several coal mines employing prisoners.

The convicts were then either set free or, in a powerful act of symbolism, shipped by rail to the state capital in Nashville. The free miners were emboldened by the recent political success of Populist and Alliance candidates, and then embittered and driven to action by the still-slow pace of change. By 1895, the Tennessee miners, like their colleagues in Kentucky, succeeded in removing the last convict from direct competition with free labor in the state. Free miners in other states were never as aggressive (or as successful) as those in Tennessee or Kentucky, but between 1881 and 1900 over twenty strikes, with convict labor as a central bone of contention, occurred throughout the Southern coalfields. According to historian Karin Shapiro, the failure of free miners to win the fight in Georgia was due in part to the relatively small size of the coal industry in the state. In Alabama, it was not the size but the makeup of the workforce that may have hampered the miners: the coal mining workforce in that state was almost half African American, and the powerful racism of the era made cooperation between the miners and their winning of sympathy from the broader public more difficult.

THE PROFIT MOTIVE AND GROWING PUBLIC AWARENESS

Sympathy for free labor was, of course, not the only economic weapon in the arsenal of lease critics. In Alabama, for example, it was argued that each convict robbed the merchants of the Birmingham area (where the state's coal mines and, therefore, convict laborers were concentrated) of a family of potential consumers. Similarly, Rebecca Latimer Felton of Georgia argued that the system's increasingly racial bias might encourage African Americans to leave the state and thereby deprive employers of cheap free labor. Furthermore, in these states and others, it became clear that police and judges often arrested and convicted men (and women) for no reason other than to bring in fees from leasing. In Birmingham, this situation became so severe that local iron and steel mills protested that many of their best workers were unfairly hauled off to the convict coal mines after carousing on payday. They were then unavailable for their legitimate jobs the next morning.

Indeed, the massive amounts of money the lease systems brought into state and local coffers engendered widespread corruption, which was also vigorously criticized by opponents of leasing. By 1900, Mississippi critics (most prominently, the editor of the Jackson *Clarion Ledger*) managed to convince the state government to take sole custody of convicts and work them on a 12,000-acre plantation in the Delta. This success came after decades of manipulation of the system by contractors who had become enormously wealthy on the backs of convict laborers. Removing private profit from the equation, reformers argued, would not only benefit the state treasury but would eliminate the often corrupt bidding wars for leases. Louisiana, under pressure from the influential citizens of the Louisiana Prison Reform Association, followed Mississippi's lead in 1900.

Virginia and West Virginia, never keen on leasing, had focused instead on the contract labor of convicts inside prison factories. By the 1910s, the good roads movement had largely succeeded in drawing convict labor out of private contracts and into public improvement work. In the early years of the twentieth century, North and South Carolina gradually shifted from for-profit leasing to a system that gave counties control of convicts for the purpose of road construction and maintenance. North Carolina returned to the lease system during World War I and continued it, on a limited basis, until finally outlawing it in 1929. State convicts thereafter were concentrated almost entirely in road work. South Carolina, on the other hand, continued limited contracts on prison labor while also operating "state-use" industries in the penitentiary. Georgia ended convict leasing and contract labor in 1909, and Texas did the same in 1912. In both states, as in Mississippi and Louisiana before them, it was exposure of the widespread brutality and corruption of the system that finally forced change. Similar scandals rocked Arkansas, but the finances of penal slavery were seemingly too strong to prompt rapid reform. Finally, in an effort to bolster reform efforts, in 1912 Governor George W. Donaghey pardoned 360 state convicts. The move earned him praise from voters and antileasing activists, as well as Theodore Roosevelt and Socialist and labor militant Eugene V. Debs. Finally, in 1913, the state abolished leasing.

Although humanitarian groups, penal theorists and reformers, labor unions, and hundreds of politicians of various stripes (not least the Populists) had long struggled to effect change, it was ultimately negative publicity that broke the power of what was often called the "penitentiary rings" of Florida and Alabama. The two states' systems were quite different in most respects—Florida had little central penal authority and leased most of its convicts to turpentine camps, plantations, and lumber mills, whereas Alabama's large and complex penal system was financed through widespread (and quite profitable) contracts with coal mining companies. The two states' final shifts to new penal practices were prompted by very similar scandals. In Florida, the fate of Martin Talbert, a young North Dakotan, caused such an uproar that the state legislature ended leasing in 1923. In Alabama, similarly, the deaths of Hoote Taylor and James Knox, in 1925, added impetus to reform calls, which finally succeeded in 1928.

Over the years, thousands upon thousands of men and women had died in the custody of various states, but Talbert, Taylor, and Knox were all victims of a combination of brutal beatings and brutal work. In addition, they were all from outside the states in which they died. Most importantly, they were all white men in a system that functioned predominantly, if not solely, as a means of controlling black men. To the detriment of lease supporters, these factors all combined to attract the attention of Joseph Pulitzer's *New York World*, which ran detailed exposes of the South's penal systems. For Southern boosters, even those who favored leasing in principle, "bad press" was the last straw.

CONCLUSION

In many ways, American penal history, particularly as regards convict labor, can be seen in microcosm in Alabama. In the early 1840s, the state adopted a variation on the Auburn system, was one of the first states to lease its prison to an outside contractor, and was one of the first to lease convicts outside the walls of the penitentiary. After the Civil War, state convicts worked on state-owned and private plantations, in state and private factories, on railroads, docks, levees, and roads, and in timbering camps and lumber mills. Moreover, coal mining made the state's penal system one of the most profitable (and corrupt) in the nation. Opponents of the lease system pointed to the stunning racism (often between 80 and 90 percent of the state's convicts were African American), deep corruption (which nearly brought down a governor) and, increasingly, outrageous dangers it engendered (over 120 black convict miners died in one explosion in 1911). Religious reformers (including the state Baptist Convention), labor groups (including the Knights of Labor and United Mine Workers), Progressive-era business groups (including the Jaycees and, eventually, the United States Steel Corporation), and women's groups (including the League of Women Voters) were among the many who campaigned against the system. This eclectic group of reformers was not unlike others throughout the country, since convict labor (particularly for private profit) impacted upon so many facets of society. Alabama was also typical in that the fight against convict leasing and contract labor drew the attention of some of the state's most prominent citizens (including Booker T. Washington, Julia S. Tutwiler, Amelia Worthington Fisk, Pattie Ruffner Jacobs, and Hugo Black).

The lease system essentially died with Talbert, Taylor, and Knox, but convict labor continued. For example, in response to the 1892 miners' rebellion, Tennessee built its own mining prison at Brushy Mountain with little public outcry. It functioned until 1938 but was gradually supplanted in importance by state-operated light industry. In fact, well into the twentieth century, Rhode Island, Connecticut, Delaware, Iowa, and several other states outside the South maintained a contract labor system for state and local convicts. In the country as a whole, the life blood of the contract and leasing systems, and the reason for their survival in the face of mounting protest, was profit. Even as these systems declined in popularity, at least thirty-five states employed convicts in manufacturing goods for state use. By 1928, contract (and some lease) labor on the part of convicts was still legal (if not always employed) in thirty-one states, but the trend was toward curtailment of such activities.

Contract labor and leasing emerged in the mid-nineteenth century because state and local governments were unwilling to pay to support reformative penitentiaries and were attracted by the notion that, rather than being a drain on public coffers, penal facilities could be made profitable. The desire for profit (or at least sustainability) continued to motivate politicians and influenced the decision to convert prisons into publicly owned and operated factories and plantations. This fixation on income from prison labor made prisoners into a commodity and, ironically, encouraged authorities (if only subconsciously) to desire more convicts. It also discouraged any efforts (such as education, parole, or other reformative measures) that might hasten individual convicts' departure from the system. In the late twentieth century, the notion of private, for-profit penal administration made a dramatic comeback, and a new generation of reformers began to attack this "innovation" in terms that are almost as old as the American penitentiary itself.

Gregory L. McDonald

BIBLIOGRAPHY

Ayers, Edward L. *Vengeance and Justice: Crime and Punishment in the Nineteenth Century South.* New York: Oxford University Press, 1984.

Bodenhamer, David J. *The Pursuit of Justice: Crime and Law in Antebellum Indiana.* New York: Garland, 1986.

Cable, George Washington. *The Silent South.* 1885. Reprint, Montclair, NJ: Patterson Smith, 1969.

Carper, N. Gordon. "Martin Talbert, Martyr of an Era." *Florida Historical Quarterly* 52 (October, 1973).

Cvornyek, Robert Louis. "Convict Labor in the Alabama Coal Mines, 1874–1928." Ph.D. diss., Columbia University, 1993.

Dyer, Joel. *The Perpetual Prisoner Machine: How America Profits from Crime.* Boulder, CO: Westview Press, 2000.

Friedman, Lawrence M. *Crime and Punishment in American History.* New York: Basic Books, 1993.

Gollaher, David. *Voice for the Mad: The Life of Dorothea Dix.* New York: Free Press, 1995.

Lichtenstein, Alex. *Twice the Work of Free Labor: The Political Economy of Convict Labor in the New South.* New York: Verso Books, 1996.

McDonald, Gregory Lewis. "Satisfying the Claims of Offended Justice: Politics, Profit, and Change in the Alabama Penal System, 1819–1928." Master's thesis, University of Southern Mississippi, 1998.

McGinn, Elinor Myers. *At Hard Labor: Inmate Labor at the Colorado State Penitentiary, 1871–1940.* New York: Peter Lang, 1993.

Morris, Norval, and David J. Rothman, eds. *The Oxford History of the Prison: The Practice of Punishment in Western Society.* New York: Oxford University Press, 1995.

Oshinsky, David. *Worse Than Slavery: Parchman Farm and the Ordeal of Jim Crow Justice.* New York: Free Press, 1997.

Rafter, Nicole Hahn. *Partial Justice: Women in State Prisons, 1800–1935.* Boston: Northeastern University Press, 1985.

Sellin, J. Thorsten. *Slavery and the Penal System.* New York: Elsevier, 1976.

Shapiro, Karin A. *A New South Rebellion: The Battle against Convict Labor in the Tennessee Coalfields, 1871–1896.* Chapel Hill: University of North Carolina Press, 1998.

Taylor, William Banks. *Brokered Justice: Race, Politics, and Mississippi Prisons, 1798–1992.* Columbus: Ohio State University Press, 1993.

Thomas, Mary Martha. *The New Woman in Alabama: Social Reforms and Suffrage, 1890–1920.* Tuscaloosa: University of Alabama Press, 1992.

Walker, Donald R. *Penology for Profit: A History of the Texas Prison System, 1867–1912.* College Station: Texas A&M University Press, 1988.

Ward, Robert David, and William Warren Rogers. *Convicts, Coal, and the Banner Mine Tragedy.* Tuscaloosa: University of Alabama Press, 1987.

Wheeler, Marjorie Spruill. *New Women of the New South: The Leaders of the Woman Suffrage Movement in the Southern States.* New York: Oxford University Press, 1993.

Woodward, C. Vann. *Origins of the New South, 1877–1913.* 1951. Reprint, Baton Rouge: Louisiana State University Press, 1971.

Anti-Lynching Movement

Lynching, lynch law, or "Lynch's Law" as it was originally known, originated during the Revolutionary War as a form of frontier justice, occurring most frequently in areas that lacked routine access to law enforcement. In most cases where "lynch law" was employed, members of the community, in the absence of recognized court officers, would use their own interpretations of the law, serving as judge, jury, and executioner. Over time, vigilante justice became integrated into American life, occupying a fringe space in the competition for social, political, and economic dominance. Although images of men and women hanging from trees are the most familiar manifestations of this "strange fruit," attacks ranged from tar and feathering to burning, beating, and dragging individuals to their death. Whether carried out in secret or before a crowd of thousands, these violent, extralegal attacks left members of the community with vivid memories of the brutality of lynching.

THE COLOR OF LYNCHING

In the antebellum period, lynching was used to punish those involved in slave insurrection both black and white, but for the most part those held in bondage were exempt from the penalty of death for two reasons: first, because of their monetary value, and second, because murder of a slave at the hands of "parties unknown" undermined the authority of the slave owner. Extralegal means were often used to punish challenges to social boundaries by European, Asian, and Mexican immigrants, as well as native-born whites. It was only after the Civil War that African Americans became the primary target of lynch mobs.

White Southerners feared the newly freed millions who gained not only the protection of the federal government but also the power of the vote. Groups like the Ku Klux Klan and the Knights of the White Camelia launched guerrilla attacks against African Americans, Republicans, and sympathetic whites who favored the ideological death of the Old South. In this hostile atmosphere, African-American calls for social and racial equality were interpreted freely as demands for interracial sexual relationships between black men and white women. Public proclamations by white Southerners against "race amalgamation" masked the fear that African Americans would turn on their former owners and expressed the resentment over the demise of the slave system. During the next several decades, the anti-lynching movement worked to undermine and ultimately eradicate these long-held attitudes in the pursuit of racial justice. Between 1889 and 1932, more than 3,700 people were lynched in the United States. The majority of these lynchings occurred in the South, and most of the victims were African-American men.

AFRICAN-AMERICAN ANTI-LYNCHING MOBILIZATION

Ida B. Wells-Barnett, journalist and activist, stands as one of the first and most outspoken opponents of lynching. Her most important publication, *A Red Record: Tabulated Statistics and Alleged Causes of Lynching in the United States, 1892–1893–1894* (1895), carefully documents where and why African Americans were lynched during this period. Wells-Barnett's findings challenged the claims made by white men that African-American men brought the wrath of the mob on themselves by sexually assaulting white women. Although there were incidences of rape, Wells-Barnett found that less than one-third of all lynchings occurred because of this crime. Instead, black men and women were murdered for reasons as varied as theft, arson, or for simply being related to a person accused of a crime. In addition, lynchers targeted African Americans who owned their own farms and businesses, those who were outspoken, and individuals

SOUTHERN HORRORS
LYNCH LAW IN ALL ITS PHASES, 1892

Ida B. Wells was a leading African-American opponent of lynching in the post–Civil War era. In this pamphlet, she argued that white men justified the practice as retribution against black men's alleged rape of white women.

PREFACE

The greater part of what is contained in these pages was published in the *New York Age*, June 25, 1892, in explanation of the editorial which the Memphis whites considered sufficiently infamous to justify the destruction of my paper, *The Free Speech*.

Since the appearance of that statement, requests have come from all parts of the country that "Exiled" (the name under which it then appeared) be issued in pamphlet form. Some donations were made, but not enough for that purpose. The notable effort of the ladies of New York and Brooklyn Oct 5 have enabled me to comply with this request and give the world a true, unvarnished account of the causes of lynch law in the South.

This statement is not a shield for the despoiler of virtue, nor altogether a defense for the poor blind Afro-American Sampsons who suffer themselves to be betrayed by white Delilahs. It is a contribution to truth, an array of facts, the perusal of which it is hoped will stimulate this great American Republic to demand that justice be done though the heavens fall.

It is with no pleasure I have dipped my hands in the corruption here exposed. Somebody must show that the Afro-American race is more sinned against than sinning, and it seems to have fallen upon me to do so. The awful death-roll that Judge Lynch is calling every week is appalling, not only because of the lives it takes, the rank cruelty and outrage to the victims, but because of the prejudice it fosters and the stain it places against the good name of a weak race.

The Afro-American is not a bestial race. If this work can contribute in any way toward proving this, and at the same time arouse the conscience of the American people to a demand for justice to every citizen, and punishment by law for the lawless, I shall feel I have done my race a service. Other considerations are of minor importance.
New York City, Oct. 26, 1892.
    Ida B. Wells

Source: Ida B. Wells, *Southern Horrors: Lynch Law in All Its Phases* (1892). Reprinted in Jacqueline Jones Royster, ed., *Southern Horrors and Other Writings: The Anti-Lynching Campaign of Ida B. Wells, 1892–1900* (Boston: Bedford Books, 1997).

who failed to acknowledge their place as second-class citizens.

In the postbellum South, white male fears of political, economic, and social emasculation were hidden behind the myth of the black rapist. Southern obsession with this fiction was deeply entrenched, even though by the 1930s, more than fifty women were lynched. In addition to *A Red Record*, Wells-Barnett's other publications, including *Southern Horrors: Lynch Law in All Its Phases* (1892), and *Mob Rule in New Orleans: Robert Charles and His Fight to the Death* (1900) stripped away the veneer claims that lynching was a chivalrous act in defense of white womanhood. Instead, mob violence was identified as a form of social control intended to keep African Americans in their place as second-class citizens. As their political rights were being stripped away by Southern Democrats, so too were blacks denied freedom of association, equal access to education, and full protection under the law. Wells-Barnett's studies, along with her numerous news articles and lectures that challenged the mythology supporting lynching, served as the foundation for anti-lynching campaigns through the mid-twentieth century.

In 1890, T. Thomas Fortune, a contemporary of Wells-Barnett, organized the National Afro-American League, a nationwide organization opposed to lynching. At the first meeting, held in Chicago, the group called for an end to mob violence and the prosecution of lynchers. The enthusiasm of this meeting could not be sustained, and Fortune's organization was unable to foster widespread support. However, local leagues were formed, and the message of the failed league inspired others to speak out on lynching. One of the more notable voices was that of emigration supporter Bishop Henry M. Turner, who called for a convention to discuss the problem of mob violence. From this meeting, the National Equal Rights Council was formed. The ERC program incorporated both political and legal campaigns to secure the eradication of lynching. Its plans included investigating and publicizing episodes of mob violence, along with lobbying federal and state officials for legislation to aid the victims of vigilante justice and their dependents. The ideas from these conventions in the early 1890s formed the basis of the anti-lynching movement's two-pronged campaign that aimed to draw attention to these extralegal attacks and to secure federal legislation.

Perhaps the most sustained social and political activity came from black women through a series of local women's clubs. African-American women's groups, like the National Association of Colored Women (NACW), also adopted the anti-lynching cause as part of their campaigns. At the September 1897 meeting of NACW in Nashville, Tennessee, the group's agenda included the eradication of lynching, in addition to the promotion of temperance. Local women's clubs were also active in the fight against mob violence. For example, the Ida B. Wells chapter in Chicago launched a campaign against vigilante justice by writing to President William McKinley, Congress, and the governor of Illinois, with the goal of securing official statements against recent lynchings.

The National Afro-American League, reconvened by T. Thomas Fortune as the Afro-American Council in September 1898, again called for the eradication of lynching in its crusade for racial justice. Mary Church Terrell, the first president of the NACW, served as the director of the Anti-lynching Bureau. Booker T. Washington, founder and president of Tuskegee Institute, was noticeably silent on the lynching issue. Known for his program of accommodation, Washington refused to condemn Republican leaders and southern whites for their inability, and in some cases refusal, to halt attacks on African Americans. Although he occasionally made anonymous contributions to the struggle against mob violence, both to organizations and to individuals, Washington's position on this issue placed him at odds with many African-American leaders. By the turn of the century, the split in the anti-lynching movement was obvious. On one side were outspoken activists like Ida B. Wells, who advocated a confrontational approach, including self-defense, to secure an end to mob violence. On the other side were supporters of Washington, who advocated a less overt program of change to the status of African Americans in the South.

By the 1890s, whites joined interracial organizations that advocated an end to racial discrimination. The National Civil Rights Association, founded by Albion Tourgee in October 1891, was ardently opposed to segregation laws and discrimination. In addition, Tourgee served as Homer A. Plessy's attorney in the 1896 landmark U.S. Supreme Court case, *Plessy v. Ferguson*, which legalized racial segregation in the South.

The turn of the century marked the first documented meeting of white southerners opposed to lynching. Those present at the Montgomery Race Conference of 1900 discussed the impact of mob violence on southern society. Much of the focus was on the way lynching undermined the authority of elected officials and amplified racial discord. These issues discussed in 1900 would resurface again among white southern anti-lynching groups after World War I. The conference concluded without any significant resolutions, solutions, or reflections on the underlying causes of mob violence.

W.E.B. DU BOIS AND THE NAACP

The next major chapter in the anti-lynching crusade led by African Americans took place in 1905, when W.E.B. Du Bois invited a group of African Americans to Niagara Falls, Canada, to form an organization that would stand in opposition to Booker T. Washington. For Du Bois and many others, Washington's public message of accommodation could not be reconciled with the continuing attacks on African Americans and their status in the South. This group of twenty-nine argued that African Americans needed protection from mob violence and that Washington's program of hard work, thriftiness, and patience did not lead to increased tolerance and warm feelings between the races. The events of the following year, including the Atlanta Race Riot and the national responses to the Brownsville Affair, laid plain the need for a more aggressive plan of action among the Du Bois supporters. These two crises can be seen as a watershed marking a shift in anti-lynching tactics, as well as an increase in interest in the anti-lynching movement and in interracial cooperation to fight against mob violence. The Niagara Movement dissolved by 1908, but it laid the groundwork for a new national organization to fight against racial bias.

The idea for the National Association for the Advancement of Colored People (NAACP) was sparked by the 1908 race riot in Springfield, Illinois. In 1909, a multi-racial group of liberals called for a national conference to discuss the recent outbreaks of mob violence, black disfranchisement, and racial discrimination. Three African-American activists who were involved with the formation of the NAACP—W.E.B. Du Bois, Mary Church Terrell, and Ida Wells-Barnett—brought with them a history of anti-lynching organizing and ensured that lynching would be at the top of the group's agenda. The platform of the NAACP attacked all areas of discrimination, from legal segregation and disfranchisement to access to equal education and enforcement of the Fourteenth and Fifteenth Amendments. During its first year, the association called for more protection of African Americans in the South and an end to racial bias and lynching. Unlike many of the post-Reconstruction black organizations, the NAACP was able to capitalize on the experience and networks of its members. In addition, the organization, through its publication *The Crisis*, was able to engage with the increasingly literate and professional African-American population on the issue of lynching.

The NAACP used every available resource to publicize outbreaks of mob violence, including collecting its own statistics, providing information to newspapers, conducting its own investigations of mob violence, organizing lectures and conventions, and performing dramatic interpretations of famous cases. Both James Weldon Johnson and Walter White, two of the most important leaders of the association, began their careers investigating lynchings as field secretaries for the organization. By 1921, the organization could claim 400 branches throughout the United States. Although the NAACP program attacked racial discrimination on a variety of fronts, one of the main tenets of the NAACP was the use of the courts to bring about racial equality. In the early years of the group's existence, the NAACP's Legal Defense was one of the most successful departments in the organization.

Between 1901 and 1920, fifteen measures were introduced against the lynching of foreign nationals. Although these victims' dependents received almost $1 million in compensation, there was no discussion about African Americans who suffered at the hands of lynchers. The majority of congressional representatives exhibited concern only when there was an increase in the numbers of white victims of mob violence. During this same period, sixteen bills were introduced to investigate and prosecute those who participated in lynchings; all sixteen perished in committee. The first major anti-lynching bill to be seriously considered by Congress was the 1922 Dyer Bill, introduced by Representative Leonidas Dyer (R-MO). Dyer was a strong advocate for the passage of federal anti-lynching legislation and had proposed measures as early as 1911. Moved by the 1917 race riot in his home state, Dyer once again introduced anti-lynching legislation in 1918. The bill, which defined lynching as the murder of a United States citizen by a group larger than three people, set forth to punish not only the mob participants but also the law officers who failed to carry out their assigned duties. Thus, sheriffs who failed to protect their prisoners or failed to arrest the mob participants faced a fine up to $5,000 and up to five years in prison, and those convicted of colluding with the mob faced sentences of five years to life imprisonment. In addition, the bill charged the federal government with responsibility for prosecuting those who participated in the lynching in the event that the state apparatus failed to do so. Finally, compensation of $10,000 would be provided to the victim's dependents by the county where the lynching occurred. The legislation received support from both the National Association of Colored Women (NACW) and the NAACP. The association drew upon the relationship forged between African Americans and the U.S. government during Reconstruction and envisioned federal intervention and a national solution, rather than local and regional solutions. This difference produced a deep divide between the NAACP and other groups based in the North and southerners who opposed lynching and favored states' rights.

ANTI-LYNCHING ACTIVISM AMONG AFRICAN-AMERICAN WOMEN

In anticipation of the bill, the Anti-Lynching Crusaders, a female-based offshoot of the NAACP, organized a campaign to enroll 1 million female members and raise $1 million to push for the passage of this legislation. The underlying goal of this group, led by Mary B. Talbert, board member of the NAACP and president of the NACW, was to motivate women to participate in the anti-lynching campaign. Several hundred black women, all volunteers, fanned out across their respective states, handing out anti-lynching pamphlets and calling on religious and community leaders to take a public stance against lynching. Talbert herself traveled across the United States to raise funds and support.

One of the most shocking points for the female audience was that women were the victims of lynching along with men. The crusaders tapped into preexisting women's networks, and they succeeded in securing endorsements from prominent white women, including the executive committee of the National Council of Women. The Anti-Lynching Crusaders failed to create an interracial organization with southern white women, but the group was successful in publicizing the anti-lynching campaign in both the black and white press. Although these women did not openly challenge the mythology behind mob violence, later activists would follow the path laid out by the crusaders, using religion, as well as traditional ideas of respectability and womanhood, to call for an end to lynching.

Initially, African-American and Northern-based interracial associations were optimistic about passage of the Dyer Bill. Yet, while the legislation successfully passed through the House of Representatives, it succumbed to a Democratic filibuster in the Senate. Using the power of the polls, African Americans in the North were able to express their displeasure by voting against opponents of the bill in the 1922 election. The measure would come up for consideration again in 1925 but was again defeated by Southern Democrats. Although the Dyer Bill was finished, the ideas encapsulated in the legislation continued to be put forth time and time again during the next decade.

Federal legislation was so difficult to secure in part because southern members of Congress were skillful in their application the states' rights argument. States like Georgia, Tennessee, Texas, and the Carolinas enacted laws to protect prisoners, compensate victims' families, and punish lynchers. This wave of post-Reconstruction anti-lynching legislation was a result of the struggle between the remaining African Americans in state governments and southern white Democrats fearful of interracial unity among the remaining Republicans, Populists, and groups like the Knights of Labor and the Farmers' Alliance. Across the region, laws were enacted to protect prisoners and punish the instigators and participants in mob violence. These laws coincided with the disfranchisement of African Americans. Those opposed to federal anti-lynching legislation used these laws, though seldom enforced, as proof that white southerners were not unsympathetic to the plight of African Americans; to refute these arguments, those who supported federal intervention pointed to the fact that these laws were rarely applied.

COMMISSION ON INTERRACIAL COOPERATION

Between 1917 and 1921, a wave of mob violence erupted that extended from Texas to Illinois and reflected the post–World War I intolerance of blacks and political radicals. African-American-sponsored organizations sprouted up rapidly to combat what they perceived to be an attack on black communities across the nation. Many of these organizations had ties to either the Socialist or Communist Party, as more blacks began to integrate a class analysis into their understanding of the persistence of racial hatred and violence. The African Blood Brotherhood, founded in

1919 by Cyril V. Briggs, included the end of lynching and mob violence among its concerns. Friends of Negro Freedom, organized by A. Philip Randolph, Chandler Owen, and Nevil Thomas, also denounced lynching. Organizations like the Negro American Political League, which later became the National Equal Rights League, held forums, lectures, and debates publicizing the problem of lynching. By 1928, the Communist Party (CP) and its legal wing, the International Labor Defense (ILD), had become active in the struggle for African-American rights. The International CP identified African Americans in the South as an oppressed nation, and as such the Communists in the United States began an intensive campaign to recruit black members for their challenge to the structures of economic, political, and social injustice in the United States. Offering a critique of capitalism, the CP argued that lynching and mob violence were just more ways to subordinate an already exploited black worker.

In 1919, Will W. Alexander and Willis D. Weatherford formed the Commission on Interracial Cooperation (CIC), in the midst of attacks against African Americans, immigrants, and leftists. Believing that lynching was at the heart of racial conflicts, the commission campaigned for an end to mob violence, peonage, and police brutality. At the same time, it sought to address the racial inequities in areas such as education and public service. Underlying the foundation of the commission was a strong belief in religion and the fellowship of Christians regardless of race. Its goal was racial peace and stability, not racial equity; thus, the CIC had no desire to attack the underlying cause of racial bias or to challenge the established practices of racial segregation. In fact, in its beginning, the group held separate meetings for its black and white members.

To eradicate mob violence, the CIC followed the NAACP in publicizing lynchings, encouraging prominent citizens to influence state and local officials, and rallying support for politicians who spoke out against mob violence. Reaching back to the findings of Ida B. Wells, the Commission agreed that rape was not the root cause of most lynchings. The CIC tried to intervene before hostilities could escalate into violence, and interracial pairs were sent into communities to mediate racial tensions. The group was not afraid to confront those groups, like the Ku Klux Klan, that they considered to bring blight to the region. The commission had the advantage of being based in the South, rendering legitimacy to the claim that indeed some whites in the region did not support lynching and were willing to work with African Americans to improve relations between the races. The CIC supported state legislation against mob violence and applauded sheriffs who protected their prisoners in the face of an angry mob. Unlike its northern counterpart, the NAACP, the commission refused to support federal anti-lynching legislation as a means to end mob violence. It took the position that the actions of a few should not taint the reputations or affect the wallets of the majority, as they would in the Dyer Bill. Fining entire counties would only serve to increase racial hostility; therefore, interference from Washington would not end the enmity between the races. The commission believed that its goal could be reached only by enforcement of existing state legislation, education, and promotion of tolerance and respect.

In addition to its lobbying efforts and community activities, the CIC published a periodical, *Southern Frontiers*, and numerous pamphlets on the state of race relations and on lynchings. Serving as a clearinghouse for information, the group sent reports of mob violence to newspapers, along with positive depictions of African Americans, featuring heroic acts and intellectual achievements. It was also outspoken about the biased representations of African Americans in school textbooks and encouraged college forums and courses on race relations. Starting in 1925, the commission awarded medals to local law enforcement officials for the successful prevention of mob violence. Most effectively, the organization sponsored the Southern Commission on the Study of Lynching in 1930, which published several significant studies, including *Lynchings and What They Mean*, and *The Tragedy of Lynching*. As sociologists and investigators, scholars interviewed local residents to uncover the motivations of mob participants. In these scholarly projects, the CIC promoted research into the underlying economic and social influences at play in episodes of racial violence.

ALLIANCE WITH WHITE WOMEN

Initially, the CIC and its women's auxiliary, known as the Women's Work Department, were on the same path. Each emphasized gradual reform, a scholarly understanding of lynching, and production of publications. The women's auxiliary offered women an opportunity to take a more active part in the anti-lynching campaign, though they were limited to the role of observers rather than militant activists. The scholarly approach to the lynching crisis allowed the participation of respectable white women, who could take comfort in their educational pursuits. Like

their parent organization, the Women's Work Department focused on undermining the myth that lynching was justified because of rape.

The Association of Southern Women for the Prevention of Lynching (ASWPL), founded by Jessie Daniel Ames in 1930, was an offshoot of the CIC. In the midst of the Great Depression and an increase in racial violence, Ames believed that another anti-lynching movement was needed to deal a final blow to mob violence. A new group would also allow Ames more control over the direction of an anti-lynching campaign, ending the gendered work of the CIC. Taking a leave of absence as director of the Women's Work Department, Ames created this new volunteer organization that claimed the eradication of lynching as its only goal. Returning to Wells's evidence that most lynchings did not occur as a result of a sexual assault, the ASWPL sought to break down the myths surrounding racial violence. Ames understood that she was fighting against a double standard that characterized white women as fragile individuals who needed to be protected and confined to the home. Meanwhile, under the guise of protecting the virtue of white women, white men could roam with impunity, using the myth of the immoral black woman to engage in unsanctioned sexual relationships and the myth of the black rapist to murder black men without fear of punishment.

By forming an organization limited to white women, Ames avoided the controversies of race and gender equality. The ranks of the ASWPL were made up of respectable, prominent, middle-class, white women who were often involved in a variety of organizations, both religious and secular, including the Young Women's Christian Association (YMCA) and the Methodist Women's Missionary Council. Their profile led Ames to claim that her members were uniquely positioned to challenge common assumptions on the motivations for racial violence.

Membership in the organization grew quickly, and by the 1940s, the ASWPL could claim access to more than 4 million women through their participation in other clubs and organizations. The ASWPL organized around a three-point program that denounced the idea that lynching was essential to the protection of white women; argued that mob violence undermined the Constitution, the legal process, and law enforcement; and insisted that lynching undermined the moral authority of its members' Christian missionary campaigns. Each supporter signed a pledge committing to the prevention of lynchings in their respective communities. The group also offered

A huge crowd in Owensboro, Kentucky, watches Rainey Betha minutes before his execution on August 14, 1936. Like lynchings, public hangings were popular events witnessed by thousands from the late nineteenth century through the mid-twentieth century. *(Brown Brothers)*

a class-based analysis of lynching, turning attention from the poorest members of the community to the most prominent.

The ASWPL supporters were charged with the moral responsibility to eradicate lynching in their communities. Ames argued that mob violence occurred only when communities did not stand in opposition, and it was the duty of respectable, southern white women to lead the way. Like the CIC, the association held lectures, criticized editors for publishing inflammatory stories on black crime and impending lynchings, and lobbied state officials. In addition, supporters were encouraged to write letters and visit local law officers as a way to persuade these men to use their official powers to defuse any poten-

tial for mob violence. A telephone tree was implemented so that at the first whisper of trouble, ASWPL women could alert local law enforcement and any other person necessary to defuse a potentially violent situation. Like the NAACP, the association supporters traveled to the scenes of recent lynchings to conduct their own investigations, interviewing both whites and blacks.

For years African-American women in the CIC argued that lynching would end when white women took a prominent position in the movement. However, the ASWPL's racial exclusion was difficult for many to accept. In 1931, the association met with African-American women of the CIC to discuss common problems with their male counterparts. Emerging from this meeting, Association participants concluded that lynching did not make white women more secure; instead, they were used as political pawns by white men. In addition, the group called for the protection of black women. By 1938, Ames argued that without the vote African Americans were vulnerable to numerous abuses by the local authorities and by the mob. Although Ames had contact with the NAACP's Walter White and the NACW's Mary McLeod Bethune, Ames's attitudes toward the black masses were paternalistic. She spoke publicly on her belief that blacks could not end mob violence. In her opinion, white liberals should be solely responsible for social reform because they could control the speed at which change was adopted.

Ames, as the dominant force in the organization, saw the ASWPL as a regional organization. She refused to support any federal anti-lynching legislation, believing that it was not necessary, and instead she focused her efforts on education and the enforcement of state and local laws to prevent mob violence. Just as the CIC had refused to support the Dyer Bill, the ASWPL refused to support the Costigan-Wagner proposal in 1934. Co-sponsored by Senator Edward Costigan (D-CO) and Senator Robert Wagner (D-NY), this legislation was the second attempt to pass a major anti-lynching bill through Congress. In many ways the Costigan-Wagner Act was similar to the Dyer Bill, with two significant differences. First, there was no specific provision that allowed the federal government to prosecute the members of the lynch mob. Second, federal prosecution of law officers found to be derelict in their duty could take place only if, after thirty days, a state failed to prosecute the officers. This bill gave states some time to marshal their forces, but those who opposed any type of federal intervention still saw this as an infringement on states' rights.

When the NAACP organized support for the Costigan-Wagner Bill, Ames's support as the executive director of the ASWPL was noticeably absent. Rather than support the federal legislation, Ames actively worked behind the scenes to undermine Walter White and the NAACP campaign. Her staunch opposition to federal intervention ultimately caused a split in the association, with the Methodist Woman's Missionary Council siding with the NAACP. Both publicly and unofficially, other ASWPL member organizations moved toward supporting federal legislation. African-American women in the CIC expressed their disapproval of both Ames and the official stance of the ASWPL. Even the commission, which had staunchly opposed the Dyer Bill, came out in support of the Costigan-Wagner Act. Polls taken at the time suggest that 70 percent of Americans and 65 percent of southerners supported federal anti-lynching legislation. Nevertheless, the Costigan-Wagner Bill, in several variations, did not pass.

Although the anti-lynching debate moved forward, Ames and the ASWPL remained mired in her refusal to support federal anti-lynching legislation. The association was disbanded in 1942, with Ames returning briefly to her post as Director of Women's Work in the CIC. In her opinion, the ASWPL had served its purpose, yet Ames failed to see that the civil rights movement was moving on to the next phase.

CONCLUSION

As the anti-lynching movement built up support for the eradication of race-based violence, it destroyed long-standing myths promoted by white southerners. Although these organizations failed to secure the passage of federal anti-lynching legislation, international attention began to focus on the United States government and its failure to protect the rights of African Americans. The newspaper coverage of segregation, race riots, and lynchings showed how the United States' promotion of international democracy was undermined by its failures to secure democratic freedoms for all its citizens at home. After World War II, the tide slowly turned in favor of civil rights organizations.

Lynching continued throughout the second half of the twentieth century with the murder of Emmett Till in August 1955, the kidnapping and assassination of the three civil rights workers James Chaney, Andrew Goodman, and Michael Schwerner in June 1964, and the dragging death of James Byrd in June 1998. While these were high-profile events, the symbolic significance of lynching had decreased as issues of voting and civil rights became central to the campaigns for racial justice in the United States. There is one coda, however: campaigns against police brutality may bring aspects of the anti-lynching crusade into the twenty-first century.

Prudence Cumberbatch

BIBLIOGRAPHY

Ames, Jessie Daniel. *The Changing Character of Lynching*. Atlanta: Commission on Interracial Cooperation, 1942.

Brown, Mary Jane. *Eradicating This Evil: Women in the American Anti-Lynching Movement*. New York and London: Garland, 2000.

Dray, Philip. *At the Hands of Persons Unknown: The Lynching of Black America.* New York: Random House, 2002.

Grant, Donald L. *The Anti-Lynching Movement, 1883–1932.* San Francisco: R and E Research, 1975.

Hall, Jacqueline Dowd. *Revolt Against Chivalry: Jessie Daniel Ames and the Women's Campaign Against Lynching.* New York: Columbia University Press, 1979.

Shapiro, Herbert. *White Violence and Black Response: From Reconstruction to Montgomery.* Amherst: University of Massachusetts Press, 1988.

Southern Commission on the Study of Lynching. *Lynchings and What They Mean.* Atlanta: The Commission, 1931.

———. *The Tragedy of Lynching.* Chapel Hill: University of North Carolina Press, 1933.

Wells, Ida B. *Southern Horrors: Lynch Law in All Its Phases.* New York: New Age, 1892.

Wells-Barnett, Ida B. *Mob Rule in New Orleans: Robert Charles and His Fight to the Death.* Chicago: Ida B. Wells-Barnett, 1900.

———. *A Red Record: Tabulated Statistics and Alleged Causes of Lynching in the United States, 1892–1893–1894.* Chicago: Donohue & Henneberry, 1895.

White, Walter. *The Fire in the Flint.* New York: Knopf, 1924.

———. *Rope and Faggot: A Biography of Judge Lynch.* New York: Knopf, 1929.

Williamson, Joel. *The Crucible of Race: Black-White Relations in the South Since Emancipation.* New York: Oxford University Press, 1984.

Zangrando, Robert L. *The NAACP Crusade Against Lynching, 1909–1950.* Philadelphia: Temple University Press, 1980.

CIVIL RIGHTS MOVEMENT 1910–1930

The years between 1910 and 1930 encompass a critical but often overlooked era of civil rights activism in the United States. These twenty years, considered by many as the nadir of race relations in the United States, built the foundations on which a later civil rights movement would thrive. During this time, a varied and crucial group of movements, individuals, and organizations would wrest from white elites the responsibility for initiating activism on their own behalf. Legislative and political victories would be the gains of a later era, but civil rights activists between 1910 and 1930 would provide this later movement with tactics, precedents, and ideologies.

As the first decade of the twentieth century drew to a close, relations between black and white Americans could hardly have been worse. In 1895 Booker T. Washington, in his "Atlanta Compromise" speech, had spoken as the leader of black America in the South. Washington renounced social and political activism, urging blacks instead to adopt a life of industrious work, thrift, and docility. Only after proving their merit to whites would blacks be ready for the responsibilities of political rights such as voting. Essentially, voicing black acceptance of segregation, Washington declared: "In all things that are purely social we can be as separate as the fingers, yet one as the hand in all things essential to mutual progress." The next decade would see increased segregation as Jim Crow laws solidified the boundary between blacks and whites.

The economic gains and social calm promised by the compromise failed to appear. Mired in sharecropping, Southern blacks found themselves unable to escape the cycle of debt. Lynching, long a terror in the South, gradually spread across the entire country. At the turn of the century, a rise in lynching began, which by its decline at the outbreak of World War I had claimed more than 1,100 lives. Frustrated with and outraged by Washington's leadership, a group of

African Americans, led by the activist intellectual W.E.B. Du Bois, met at Niagara Falls in 1905. The Niagara Movement hoped to take from Washington the leadership of the African American community. In the process, the Niagara Movement aimed to redirect energies from occupational training toward a movement that would acquire for African Americans the political and social equality they deserved. The Niagara Movement would soon disappear, but Du Bois and others would redefine black life in America.

THE NAACP

In August 1908, a riot erupted in Springfield, Illinois. A white mob lynched two African American men just miles from the resting place of Abraham Lincoln. Racism and violence could no longer be said to be limited to the South. Dismayed by the dismal state of race relations, a group of progressive white Americans, including journalist Mary White Ovington and Oswald Garrison Villard (a descendant of abolitionist William Garrison), called for a conference in 1909 with the goal of gaining equal rights for African Americans. This group made sure to invite the radical Du Bois, a leading advocate of anti-Washington sentiment, to the conference. The attendees agreed to form a permanent organization to fight for the cause of civil rights. By 1910, this organization was incorporated as the National Association for the Advancement of Colored People (NAACP). Du Bois, renowned for his academic scholarship, became the director of publicity and research. The only African American among the NAACP's officers, Du Bois described himself as a propagandist and took charge of *The Crisis*, the official NAACP magazine, which documented the organization's achievements and, increasingly, Du Bois's own civil rights agenda.

The NAACP began its civil rights efforts by exposing injustices and violence done to African Americans. The organization soon launched a dual crusade

W.E.B. DU BOIS (1868–1963)

William Edward Burghardt Du Bois was born in Great Barrington, Massachusetts, amidst the turmoil of Southern Reconstruction. Over the next hundred years Du Bois would shape the civil rights movement in the United States and African identity worldwide. Devoting his life to the social, political, and economic liberation of African Americans—and later all Africans—Du Bois pioneered a historical and scientific approach to solving the problem of race. As an undergraduate, Du Bois attended Fisk University in Nashville, Tennessee, and then Harvard University. His education continued at the University of Berlin in Germany and again at Harvard, where he would earn a Ph.D. in history. Helping to pioneer the discipline of sociology in the United States, Du Bois accepted a professorship at Atlanta University.

In 1903, Du Bois published *The Souls of Black Folk*, a collection of essays in which he declared that "the problem of the Twentieth Century is the problem of the color line." *The Souls of Black Folk* established Du Bois as the leading African-American intellectual of his time and pitted him against the reigning leader of the race: Booker T. Washington. Rejecting Washington's doctrine of accepting political disfranchisement and social segregation in exchange for economic progress, Du Bois demanded immediate and full equality for African Americans.

To this end, Du Bois founded the Niagara movement in 1905. Five years later, he left Atlanta University to help found the National Association for the Advancement of Colored People (NAACP) in New York City. Aside from the militant Du Bois, the group's only African-American officer, the NAACP consisted of white intellectuals sympathetic to the African-American cause. Du Bois became the director of publicity and immediately began production of the NAACP's official magazine, *The Crisis*. In this position Du Bois had an outlet that allowed him to communicate with black and white America. When monthly circulation of the magazine reached 100,000 in 1918, Du Bois had already succeeded Washington as the leader of African America.

Du Bois's writings in *The Crisis* varied from news items to art criticism to political polemics to personal quarrels. Each word aimed at guiding white and African Americans toward his vision of civil rights: full equality and total freedom. As Du Bois's reputation ascended around the world, his vision of black freedom broadened as well. Increasingly, Du Bois advocated Pan-Africanism, the solidarity of purpose and identity among all the Africans of the world. In 1919, Du Bois began a series of Pan-African Congresses that advocated the colonial liberation of the African continent.

By the mid-1930s, Du Bois grew frustrated with the NAACP's tactics and leadership. He quit the organization and returned to Atlanta University. Having already completed two careers of remarkable achievement, Du Bois continued to achieve new heights of brilliance. In 1935, he published *Black Reconstruction in America*, a masterful work whose thesis—that the African American was the central actor of Reconstruction—defines today's historical interpretation of that era.

As progress in racial relations failed to keep up with his leadership, Du Bois moved further to the political left. As an advocate of international causes, including the antinuclear and peace movements, Du Bois embraced Communism as the means of uplifting the African people. Du Bois left the United States in 1961, personally manifesting his goal of Pan-Africanism by relocating to the newly independent African nation of Ghana. There he worked on his lifelong dream of an *Encyclopaedia African*—an epic reference book of the African diaspora. Du Bois became a citizen of Ghana where he died in 1963 and remains interred.

Paul Rubinson

to defend African Americans deprived of their legal rights and to oppose lynching. The earliest victory for the organization occurred in 1911 when it successfully lobbied to have William H. Lewis restored to the American Bar Association (ABA). Lewis had been thrown out of the all-white ABA when its members discovered that he was black. In 1914, the NAACP presented the White House with a petition of 20,000 signatures protesting segregation within the federal bureaucracy. After the presentation, the Treasury Department began to reverse its segregationist policies.

The organization also successfully lobbied against segregationist bills in the U.S. Congress in 1915.

Legal battles proved the most effective of the NAACP's early tactics. The first legal challenge from the NAACP resulted in the U.S. Supreme Court decision in 1915 in favor of the NAACP. *Guinn* v. *United States* centered on the constitutionality of the so-called grandfather clauses in Southern states. Ex-Confederate states promulgated these clauses during the late 1890s and early 1900s to prevent African Americans from voting, and in 1910 Oklahoma passed

Prolific scholar, author, historian, and editor, W.E.B. Du Bois helped launch the Niagara Movement and found the National Association for the Advancement of Colored People in the early twentieth century. His militant stance on race relations directly challenged the accommodationist position of Booker T. Washington. *(© Underwood Photo Archives, Inc.)*

had been unfairly influenced by mob domination. In 1923, the Supreme Court ruled in favor of the NAACP that federal courts must review claims of mob-dominated trials. The *Moore* decision resulted in greater scrutiny of state criminal trials by the Supreme Court.

NAACP antilynching efforts originally focused on state governments. After an NAACP activist was attacked in Austin, Texas, while lobbying the state government, the organization's leaders decided in 1911 that only a national antilynching law could confront the widespread antipathy to blacks in Southern states. Accordingly, the organization began lobbying the federal government in 1921 on behalf of Missouri Representative L.C. Dyer's antilynching law. Appearing at congressional hearings, NAACP members lobbied effectively enough that the Dyer bill passed the House of Representatives. Filibustering Southern senators thwarted the bill, but the organization declared a moral victory, since the Dyer bill had gotten farther in Congress than any civil rights legislation in the twentieth century. Relative success with the tactics of court challenges and legislative lobbying would ensure their adoption as standard NAACP methods in the following decades and would result in resounding success during the 1950s and 1960s.

THE CRUSADE AGAINST *BIRTH OF A NATION*

The NAACP did not limit its activism to court cases and lobbying. The crusade against the film *Birth of a Nation* proved that the organization could mobilize against any event or situation. Released in 1915 and instantly redefining the motion picture industry, D.W. Griffith's *Birth of a Nation* proved more popular than any movie to that point. The epic film was so successful that, by one historian's judgment, its gross revenues were not surpassed until the 1980s. The film contained a virulent racism commensurate with its success. Focusing on the Reconstruction era, Griffith portrayed blacks as brutish, savage, and libidinous heathens intent on destroying civilization; only through the heroic efforts of the Ku Klux Klan is the South saved. Far from creating this vision of Reconstruction, Griffith merely presented it in a captivating new genre. President Woodrow Wilson uttered after a private viewing, "It is like writing history with Lightning. And my only regret is that it is all so terribly true."

Alerted by its office in Los Angeles, where *Birth of a Nation* premiered (under its early title of *The*

a permanent one. The *Guinn* ruling overturned Oklahoma's grandfather clause, declaring such clauses to be in violation of the Fifteenth Amendment. The NAACP celebrated an important victory, though the victory was mostly symbolic, as Southern states had allowed grandfather clauses to lapse long before and had found other ways to prevent African Americans from voting.

During the early 1910s, many cities enacted segregation ordinances that prevented blacks from moving into white neighborhoods. With African Americans prevented from relocating, ghettos emerged in cities across the nation. The NAACP challenged a Louisville, Kentucky, ordinance of 1914 and in the 1917 *Buchanan v. Warley* decision the U.S. Supreme Court ruled again in favor of the NAACP, declaring such ordinances to be in violation of the property rights of both white and black Americans. The third celebrated victory for the organization came when the U.S. Supreme Court ruled on the *Moore v. Dempsey* case. The NAACP alleged that a 1919 Arkansas trial resulting in the death sentence for six blacks

Clansman), the NAACP mobilized against the film's appearance in New York. The nascent film industry in 1915 was subject to censorship laws, and the NAACP hoped to take advantage of these laws. Basing its argument on the fact that a stage production of *The Clansman*, a stage production of the Thomas Dixon novel on which Griffith based his film, resulted in riots, the NAACP won some cuts from the censorship committee. The film nevertheless premiered to huge crowds and great acclaim. NAACP activists marched and distributed pamphlets against the film, though some felt their efforts only increased public interest in the film. Other civil rights activists, including Booker T. Washington's protégé Emmett Scott, insisted that African Americans' energies would be better spent creating films of their own. The NAACP continued to fight *Birth of a Nation* well into the 1930s, arguing that the film was not art but rather mob incitement. By the 1930s, the organization had met little success in its campaigns against the film. In later decades, NAACP efforts would shift to lobbying Hollywood studios for more substantial roles for African Americans and better portrayals of black people.

DU BOIS AND *THE CRISIS*

As the NAACP waged legal and political battles on behalf of African Americans, W.E.B. Du Bois symbolized to many the civil rights movement itself. While connected to the NAACP through *The Crisis*, Du Bois adopted a militant stance and often clashed with the leadership of the organization. In the pages of *The Crisis*, Du Bois attacked his enemies, pressured political and social elites, and most importantly attempted to guide the opinion of African Americans to his vision of civil rights and black identity. Espousing full political and social rights for blacks (and women), Pan-Africanism, and Socialism to some extent, Du Bois soon replaced Washington as the most prominent African-American leader in the United States. In 1915, the year of Washington's death, circulation of *The Crisis* averaged some 30,000, and by 1918, it soared to 100,000 a month. Black and white readers delighted in Du Bois's polemics, which raged against racism in education, counseled blacks on presidential elections, and decried lynching, to highlight just a few of the issues on which he wrote. One reader was buried with a copy that he had not had time to read before his death. By 1921, the NAACP counted 400 branches. Thanks largely to James Weldon Johnson, the organization's first African-American executive secretary, many branches even began to appear in Southern cities.

As lynching and low wages drove African Americans away from the South, the National Urban League appeared to aid them in their transition from the country to the city. Formed in 1911, the Urban League eventually set up branches in every industrial Northern city. The Urban League fought discrimination in labor unions, federal programs, and the military. It boasted a magazine entitled *Opportunity*. African-American newspapers in Chicago, Boston, Philadelphia, and Baltimore voiced the concerns of a growing black population.

WORLD WAR I AND THE FIGHT FOR DEMOCRACY

Congress approved Woodrow Wilson's request for a declaration of war against Germany in April 1917, bringing the United States into World War I. Inspired by patriotism and the hope of gaining political equality and social acceptance, blacks responded with gusto. Because Wilson framed American entry into the war as a fight to make the world "safe for Democracy," many African Americans felt that by fighting—and dying—for their country, white America would no longer be able to deny them their rights.

Early activism focused on the right of African Americans to take part in the war effort. Racism and discrimination barred African-American participation from the beginning. The NAACP had to lobby Secretary of War Newton D. Baker merely to include African Americans in the conscription act passed in the spring of 1917. African Americans soon discovered that the military had no plans to train them as officers. Agitation began which divided civil rights activists between those who lobbied for separate training camps and those who felt separate camps would inhibit postwar social equality. In October 1917, the military opened a separate training facility for African-American officers in Des Moines, Iowa. Despite this, African Americans would primarily fill labor positions during the war rather than be given fighting roles.

Hostility from white citizens and insults from white superiors made life in the military exceptionally difficult and tense for African-American soldiers. In August 1917, residents of Houston, Texas, began harassing African-American soldiers. The soldiers then erupted and killed seventeen whites. After a cursory trial, thirteen soldiers were hanged. After another incident in South Carolina, the military soon sent the black regiments overseas rather than face another riot. In October 1917, Secretary Baker appointed Emmett

Five police officers and a soldier patrol a Chicago neighborhood after days of violence racked the city. The summer of 1919 ushered in the bloodiest wave of racial disturbances the nation had ever seen. Some twenty-five riots broke out across the country, the most serious one in Chicago, where thirty-eight people were killed, more than 500 injured, and more than 1,000 families left homeless. *(Chicago Historical Society)*

Scott as special assistant to the secretary of war. Scott's role consisted of advising Baker on matters involving African-American servicemen and investigating racial issues in the military.

Once overseas, African-American soldiers proved themselves excellent fighters when given the chance. Members of the 369th Infantry, nicknamed the Harlem Hellfighters, distinguished themselves by spending 191 consecutive days under fire, the longest of any U.S. troops. After the armistice, the French Army asked the Hellfighters to lead them into German-occupied territory. Two African-American soldiers were honored with the *Croix de Guerre* after capturing a German patrol. Astoundingly, U.S. officials nevertheless prohibited the Hellfighters from marching in the Allied victory parade through Paris.

THE HOMEFRONT

As the war raged in Europe, the battle over civil rights continued at home. The contrast between the war for democracy and the conditions of African Americans became frighteningly magnified in the city of East St. Louis, Illinois, in early July 1917. Whites, angered by competition for jobs from blacks, erupted in violence after suspicious blacks shot at an unmarked police car. After four days of rioting, thirty-nine African Americans and eight whites lay dead. On July 28, Du Bois led the NAACP Silent Parade through New York City. Between 8,000 and 10,000 African Americans marched, with women dressed in white and men in black. The demonstrators marched silently to the rhythm of muffled drums. Banners asked, "Mr. President, why not make America safe for democracy?" and "Mother, do lynchers go to heaven?" Widely publicized, the Silent Parade demonstrated the NAACP's size, strength, and ability to mobilize quickly. Race riots also erupted in Chicago and some two dozen other cities throughout the nation.

Although most African Americans supported the war, few could overlook the hypocrisy of the U.S. claim to fight for democracy while a huge segment of the population languished without voting rights and in fear of lynching. A segment of the African-American population questioned the value of fighting on behalf of a government that denied them basic human rights. Du Bois had recently written an article castigating the European powers for starting the war based on the colonial carving of the African continent. Du Bois then shocked many Americans when, in the July 1918 issue of *The Crisis*, he published his now-infamous "Close Ranks" editorial. The usually militant Du Bois declared, "Let us, while this war lasts, forget our special grievances and close our ranks shoulder to shoulder with our white fellow citizens and the allied nations that are fighting for democracy. We make no ordinary sacrifice, but we make it gladly and willingly with our eyes lifted to the hills."

In 1919, Du Bois journeyed to Paris hoping to influence the proceedings surrounding the Treaty of Versailles. He spent most of his time investigating the conditions of African-American troops in Europe. Many had been ill-treated, he found, suffering base-

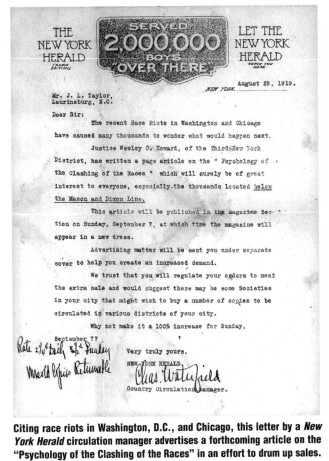

Citing race riots in Washington, D.C., and Chicago, this letter by a *New York Herald* circulation manager advertises a forthcoming article on the "Psychology of the Clashing of the Races" in an effort to drum up sales. *(Rare Book, Manuscript, & Special Collection Library, Duke University)*

less charges of incompetence and rape. Du Bois amassed countless pages of evidence for a planned book on African Americans in World War I. As he returned to the United States, African Americans anticipated seeing their participation in the fight for democracy abroad result in newfound freedoms at home.

THE GREAT MIGRATION

World War I also helped spark the widespread migration of African Americans out of the South and into the North. This exodus, known as the Great Migration, transformed the fundamental nature of life for many African Americans. Migrants left farms for work in urban industries and in the process escaped the rigid social hierarchy of the Jim Crow South. African Americans expressed profound joy at earning good money and voting for the first time. This sharp increase in population in Northern cities provided the civil rights movement with a mass base that awaited mobilization in cities like Chicago, Detroit, and especially New York. The Great Migration also shaped the social, economic, and geographic patterns of African Americans for most of the twentieth century. Bursting with promise, the Great Migration allowed millions of African Americans to experience wealth, community, equality, and education, helping them to realize the promise and vision of America that they had long been denied.

The Numbers

Out of the roughly 8 million African Americans living in the United States in 1910, about 7 million of them lived in the South. Between 1916 and 1930, more than 1 million African Americans left the South at a rate of 500 per day. Those who remained behind stood agape as entire neighborhoods and even towns were left abandoned. At the end of the line for these migrants lay the great modern cities of the North, beckoning them with a seemingly endless amount of well-paying jobs. The African-American populations of these cities skyrocketed almost overnight. During the decade ending in 1920, the African-American population of Detroit, Michigan, jumped from a mere 5,741 to 40,838—an increase of more than 600 percent. The population in Cleveland, Ohio, grew by some 300 percent; in Chicago, Illinois, it grew by almost 150 percent. Newark, New York, Indianapolis, Philadelphia, and Cincinnati each saw the Great Migration increase their African-American populations by more than 50 percent. Migration lagged during the years of the Great Depression, but only by 1960 did it really cease, after some 5 million African Americans had relocated in the North. By the time the Great Migration ended, African-American life had been as drastically altered as it had after Emancipation.

The Impulse

With Emancipation, African Americans took the first step in their search for equal status in America. The Great Migration continued this quest, spurred by several different factors. Despite the promise of the New South, by 1910 the former states of the Confederacy remained isolated and rural. Northern industry had managed to spur some activity in the urban centers of the South, but agriculture continued to dominate the region's economy. Most African Americans earned their living as farm laborers on cotton farms. In 1910, however, a boll weevil infestation began that ruined much of the South's cotton crop. Since cotton was the primary crop of the region, many farm owners could no longer afford to hire laborers. Other farmers began

to switch from agriculture to livestock, which required less labor. Out of work, some African Americans looked to the North for jobs. Many, however, moved to the cities of the South, where burgeoning industry held some promise of work.

Between 1910 and 1920, African Americans swelled cities like Atlanta, Norfolk, Baltimore, and Houston. When they arrived, they soon learned that there was little work for them to do. Although it proved true that the nascent industries needed workers, white supremacy ensured that the best jobs went to white laborers. When African Americans did find jobs, they were usually the most unpleasant and lowest paying. The African Americans already living in Southern cities and working as artisans also found that industrialization ended their livelihood; the billowing smoke of the factories quickly made their craft obsolete.

At the same time, black and white relations reached despairing levels. Jim Crow laws rigidly enforced a racial hierarchy, leaving African Americans economically powerless, socially subservient, and politically silent. Brutal lynchings punished anyone who stepped outside of the caste system. African Americans had their freedom, but racism prevented them from attaining the status that was their right as Americans. A song from the time expressed the feeling that they had every reason to leave the South: "Boll weevil got the cotton/ Cut worm in the corn/ Debil in the white man/ We's going on." The North, where abolition had begun and the Underground Railroad had headed, beckoned as a better home.

Despite these factors, millions of African Americans might not have headed North if there had not been plenty of jobs available. The outbreak of World War I in 1914 created the final impulse. Just as Northern industries increased wartime production, European immigration slowed to a trickle. Since immigrants provided the main labor source for urban factories, owners had to look elsewhere for workers. They looked South and saw African Americans looking North. Thus began the African-American transformation from rural agricultural worker to urban industrial worker.

Making the Move

Northern companies directly encouraged migration. Companies hired agents to roam the South and advertise jobs in Northern factories. For each worker eventually hired by the company, the agent received a small fee. Agents found entire African-American communities eager to board trains bound for the

North. More than just publicists for a company, the agents spread the word to hundreds of thousands of African Americans that the North eagerly awaited their arrival.

The Great Migration was primarily a family event. Migrants who found work up North would tell their friends and families, who would soon join them. Once they relocated, the Urban League and other voluntary associations helped families get settled, find work, and build communities. The African-American press, most notably the *Chicago Defender,* also encouraged the Great Migration. The *Defender* blared headlines urging African Americans northward and at the same time printed advertisements from industries seeking workers.

White Southerners at first rejoiced as African Americans departed. Many felt it would end the so-called Negro Problem. Soon, however, some Southerners began to worry about the loss of such a huge segment of the population. Some authorities tried to arrest the agents of Northern industry and prevent African Americans from leaving, though this had little effect on the exodus.

While relocating to Northern urban-industrial centers, African Americans settled into vibrant neighborhoods bursting with culture. This massive influx of people sparked artistic and political movements, including Black Nationalism and the Harlem Renaissance during the 1920s. In time, however, Northern racism disillusioned African Americans about the Great Migration. The vibrant communities of the 1920s would later grow into ghettos as white Northerners resisted integration. Poverty would menace black ghettos during much of the twentieth century, and some African Americans actually moved South during the Sunbelt migration of the 1970s.

Black Nationalism

Another aspect of civil rights activism during the 1920s focused on black nationalism, also called Pan-Africanism or Negro Zionism. Black nationalists espoused a separatist doctrine, declaring that whites had proven untrustworthy and a hindrance to black progress worldwide. Instead of striving toward equality, black nationalists advocated the solidarity of the African diaspora, the freedom of Africa from colonial rule, and an eventual return of Africans worldwide to Africa.

During the antebellum era, some abolitionists advocated the creation of an independent African state where blacks could live. When the West African nations of Sierra Leone and Liberia were established

in the late eighteenth and early nineteenth centuries, respectively, a modest number of blacks relocated there. After Emancipation, however, African Americans anticipated and worked for full political and social rights. As their plight worsened, African Americans again became receptive to the idea of a return to Africa. In 1915 Alfred Sam, from Ghana, led a small group of African Americans from Oklahoma to Ghana, although conflict with British authorities quickly ended his endeavor.

Marcus Garvey and the Universal Negro Improvement Association

Born in Jamaica, Marcus Garvey would become the most renowned advocate of black nationalism. After a time studying in London, Garvey returned to Jamaica convinced that blacks must rely only on themselves for progress. He later recalled his epiphany:

> I asked, "Where is the black man's government?" "Where is his King and his kingdom?" "Where is his President, his country, and his ambassador, his army, his navy, his men of big affairs?" I could not find them. . . . My brain was afire. There was a world of thought to conquer. . . . All day and the following night I pondered over the subject matter of that conversation, and at midnight, lying flat on my back, the vision and thought came to me that I should name the organization the Universal Negro Improvement Association and African Communities (Imperial) League. Such a name I thought would embrace the purpose of all black humanity.

Garvey founded his visionary organization—usually known simply as the Universal Negro Improvement Association (UNIA)—in Jamaica in 1914.

Modeled loosely after Booker T. Washington's Tuskegee Institute, the UNIA in Jamaica focused on teaching trades to blacks. Frustrated there, Garvey moved to New York, the heart of black America, in 1916. New York's blacks regarded Garvey with suspicion at first, but after a triumphant speaking tour across the country, he returned to New York lauded by the city. A charismatic and impassioned speaker, Garvey appealed to New York's large community of West Indian blacks as well as the large numbers of working-class African Americans recently arrived in New York. Garvey gave many blacks a sense of pride in their race, equating their color with strength and beauty. Darker-skinned blacks, who felt alienated by the lighter skinned, seemingly aristocratic blacks of the NAACP, felt particularly uplifted by Garvey's message.

Garvey's doctrine left many others aghast, however, because it overturned many conventions of African-American intellectual thought. He scoffed at so-called benevolent whites, declaring his affinity for the overt racists of the U.S. South, including the Ku Klux Klan. Bald and honest racism, Garvey argued, drove blacks to form their own institutions, ideas, and identity. Oppression, according to Garvey, only encouraged empowerment. Garvey thus turned the intellectual impetus of the NAACP on its ear, winning the hearts and imaginations of the black masses as he alienated the African-American cultural elite.

By 1919, more than thirty branches of the UNIA had been established in the United States, with hundreds more forming around the world. The movement in the United States published its own newspaper, The Negro World, as well as most of the trappings of an independent nation: a flag, a medical organization, a military, and a shipping line. The Black Star Line aimed to establish an all-black commercial endeavor and, it was hoped, eventually return blacks to their ancestral African homeland. Elaborate, regal costumes resembling the raiments of imperial Europe clothed the leaders of the movement, offering a challenge to traditional notions of political power and race. A constitution dictated the political structure of the eventual nation, with Garvey as the provisional president-general of Africa. The movement called for a unity of purpose, culture, and religion among the world's blacks, expressed in the UNIA's slogan "One God, One Aim, One Destiny." Garvey's popularity soared, particularly among blacks disillusioned with Du Bois and the NAACP's support of American involvement in World War I. At the movement's height in 1923, Garvey estimated his legion's numbers at 6 million; the more recent assessments place the number in the hundreds of thousands, although millions worldwide surely heard Garvey's message and embraced his spirit.

Living and agitating so near to each other, a conflict between Du Bois and Garvey seems to have been all but inevitable. Garvey reached a large percentage of African Americans, creating the first true mass movement among African Americans in the United States. African Americans sent the UNIA hundreds of thousands of dollars during the 1920s in order to finance the organization's various ventures. Stock had to be sold to get the Black Star Line running, and money had to be provided for an arrangement between the UNIA and the Liberian government. Gar-

vey's popularity allowed him to challenge Du Bois for leadership of African Americans, igniting a bitter feud between them.

DU BOIS AND PAN-AFRICANISM

A rivalry between Du Bois and Garvey ruined what might have been a remarkable partnership. Garvey had called on Du Bois upon his arrival in New York in 1916, but the editor of The Crisis was out of town and made no followup effort to contact the young man. Despite their personal enmity, the two leaders shared strikingly compatible views on the role of Africa in African-American life. Foreshadowing Garvey's message, Du Bois stated in 1919 that "Amelioration of the lot of Africa tends to ameliorate the conditions of colored peoples throughout the world." The two nevertheless pursued their own avenues toward Pan-Africanism.

As the NAACP engaged in legal battles, Du Bois forged his own way toward black nationalism independent of the organization. Since at least 1900, Du Bois had envisioned a civil rights movement encompassing blacks beyond the borders of the United States. In 1919, during the conference ending World War I, Du Bois journeyed to Paris to attend the first of six Pan-African Congresses. The fate of colonial Africa formed the main subject matter of these summits, although squabbling between delegates marred many of the sessions. The representatives of French colonies in Africa made loyalty to France a sticking point regarding many of the agreements.

At the second Pan-African Congress in 1921, Du Bois crafted a declaration that intoned that the world must fully assimilate blacks with complete equal rights, or remove all colonial bonds from Africa, leaving the continent free and independent. The Congress eventually drafted a manifesto directed at the League of Nations. The manifesto asked the League to address the needs of black workers, assign a black member to the League's Mandates Commission, and formally declare "the absolute equality of races." The League produced minimal action on these demands. Nevertheless, Du Bois had begun a concerted political effort to unite blacks around the world.

As Du Bois enlisted the black elites of many nations for his vision of Pan-Africanism, Marcus Garvey mobilized the black masses. Du Bois scoffed at Garvey's ostentation and expressed skepticism at his separatist philosophy. Du Bois's perceived snobbery angered Garvey, creating a rivalry unseen since the days of the Washington–Du Bois split. Although the previous power struggle had been over the mantle of

African-American spokesmen, this new cleavage centered on the mobilization of an entire race. Garvey's actions would soon end the rivalry, resulting in his organization's demise.

THE DEMISE OF GARVEY

As the UNIA rose in popularity, government scrutiny of the organization increased as well. The centerpiece of the UNIA, the Black Star Line, invited investigation. Having raised over $600,000 in stock share sales in just one year, the shipping line never materialized into the strong business Garvey had promised. The line featured a paltry three ships only barely in seaworthy condition. Incompetence, mismanagement, and a casual atmosphere plagued the company's finances. In 1922, the government indicted Garvey and other Black Star Line officials for fraudulently using the mails to solicit money for the company. Acting in his own defense, Garvey was found guilty and was sentenced to five years in prison in February 1925. Deported to Jamaica in 1927, Garvey died in London thirteen years later.

Garvey's movement flickered just a short while, but it presaged a number of later black movements. Although African Americans proved reluctant to move to Africa because America was, after all, home, millions of blacks worldwide embraced their connection to the African diaspora. His message of "African redemption" and African fundamentalist religion was absorbed into the Rastafarian faith. In 1930, W.D. Fard established the Black Muslims, a black nationalist religion that identified the Islamic faith as the medium through which blacks would attain justice from whites. Future leaders Malcolm X, Louis Farrakhan, and Stokely Carmichael drew heavily on Garvey's philosophies of Black Pride and separatism. The differing ideologies, actions, and attitudes of Garvey and Du Bois anticipated some of the conflicts of later civil rights eras.

SOCIALISM, COMMUNISM, AND AFRICAN-AMERICAN LABOR

By the 1920s, African Americans had long decried the American labor movement's refusal to support them. They believed that the forces of capital had long pitted African-American workers against white workers, using the former as scabs. Resentment continued in the twentieth century when blacks began to compete with whites for jobs. African-American leaders, including Du Bois, pondered the merits of socialism in helping blacks gain equal rights. The American So-

cialist Party, under the leadership of Eugene V. Debs, displayed little inclination toward courting African Americans as members. Rebuffed by the American radical left and inspired in part by the Bolshevik Revolution of 1917 and Vladimir Lenin's declaration of support for them, African Americans formed a burgeoning Socialist movement of their own.

A. Philip Randolph and Chandler Owen in 1917 founded *The Messenger*, a publication devoted to the goals of radical socialism and black freedom. A year later the African Blood Brotherhood (ABB) appeared, a militant, black nationalist organization. Advocating armed defense against lynching, equal rights, and an end to segregation, the Marxist ABB eventually merged with Marcus Garvey's UNIA. By the end of the 1920s, the Communist Party of the United States of America openly sought black membership; Du Bois himself visited the Soviet Union in 1926 and expressed admiration for that nation's social system. The most influential outgrowth of this relationship with the far left appeared in 1925 when Randolph organized the first major African-American labor union—the Brotherhood of Sleeping Car Porters (BSCP)—which mobilized African-American employees of the Pullman rail company. Although African-American efforts toward socialism would wax and wane in later decades, the BSCP and Randolph would ascend to preeminence in the labor and civil rights movements.

THE HARLEM RENAISSANCE AND THE "NEW NEGRO"

Universally hailed as a glorious artistic movement, the Harlem Renaissance has recently been the subject of reinterpretation, placing it near the heart of the social and political debate of the 1920s. The explosion of talented African-American novelists and poets spurred further definition of the civil rights movement and the role of the arts in African-American life. Although many African Americans would see the Renaissance as a celebration of aesthetic achievement, some civil rights leaders, Du Bois most notably, would press for a more purposeful goal for the artistic movement.

At first Du Bois and the NAACP heartily backed the movement, as did other civil rights organizations. Du Bois attended a March 1924 ceremony sponsored by the National Urban League's journal *Opportunity* celebrating African-American writers and poets. Many point to the *Opportunity* ceremony as the birth of the Harlem Renaissance. Both *Opportunity* and

Du Bois's *Crisis* encouraged the movement by publishing the latest essays, short stories, novels, and poems by African Americans. Du Bois himself often provided criticism of recent works. Soon *The Crisis* offered cash awards for the best works. James Weldon Johnson exemplified the connection between the civil rights movement and the Harlem Renaissance by simultaneously working as the NAACP's executive secretary and becoming one of the greatest writers of the Renaissance.

Rooted in the social upheaval of the Great Migration, black writers found themselves in Harlem, where black culture thrived and evolved thanks in large part to Marcus Garvey's cultural revolution. Dubbed "the New Negro," a new generation of African Americans created a new and vibrant social world during the 1920s, as did much of America. Claude McKay, Langston Hughes, Countee Cullen, and Zora Neale Hurston, among many others, led the revolution of black letters. For Du Bois and Charles S. Johnson, the editor of *Opportunity*, the artistic achievements of African Americans, though culturally pleasing, would help attain the most essential goals of political and social equality. Financial support of the movement created a new front on which to wage the battle for civil rights. Du Bois posited that if white America accepted the African American on artistic terms, social acceptance could not be far behind.

Du Bois's political definition of the movement irritated many artists. Many of the Renaissance's artists believed that art was for its own sake, but Du Bois refused to tolerate any diversion of energies from the cause of civil rights. Du Bois also maintained a seemingly snobbish allegiance to "higher" art forms as the Harlem Renaissance grew to include what he saw as a *declasse* musical fervor. By 1926, Du Bois grew weary of the movement and its failure to embrace a political dimension. The novels of the late Renaissance, he argued, presented to white readers a caricature of the black lower class rather than reality. A novelist in his own right, Du Bois decried the lack of a commercial market for the free thoughts and experiences of African Americans. As the decade progressed, more and more whites began visiting Harlem to see the sensual new movement for themselves. Lacking a political purpose, Du Bois saw the Renaissance devolve into what he felt was bawdy entertainment for gawking whites.

END OF AN ERA

At the close of the 1920s, Du Bois grew increasingly frustrated. *The Crisis* had entered a period of decline in readership and influence; Du Bois himself had seen his stature challenged by upstarts like Marcus Garvey. Frequent clashes with the leadership of the NAACP eventually led to his retirement from the organization he helped guide. "The world will not give a decent living to the persons who are out to reform it," he counseled in 1929.

A great many African Americans, however, beamed optimism at the end of the decade. The Great Migration had provided them with jobs and communities in Northern cities and saved many from the lynching terror of the South. The Harlem Renaissance enlivened the race, and the various movements for equal rights had found tactics, direction, and support. The NAACP continued its lobbying efforts, thwarting the federal appointment of a racist North Carolina judge in 1930. Soon, however, the country would be riven by the Great Depression, creating new challenges, new needs, and new directions for the civil rights movement.

African-American activism would yield greater results in the future. The tactics, leaders, and philosophies of the later movement all demonstrate a direct descent from an earlier civil rights era. NAACP efforts would produce the landmark *Brown v. Board of Education* decision in 1954; protest marches would secure civil and voting rights acts; and economic clout would result in several successful boycotts. The phrases "Black is beautiful," "Freedom now," and "By any means necessary" echo the urgency of the years between 1910 and 1930.

Paul Rubinson

BIBLIOGRAPHY

Berry, Mary Frances, and John W. Blassingame. *Long Memory: The Black Experience in America*. New York: Oxford University Press, 1982.

Harrison, Alferdteen, ed. *Black Exodus: The Great Migration from the American South*. Jackson: University of Mississippi Press, 1991.

Kelley, Robin D.G. *Freedom Dreams: The Black Radical Imagination*. Boston: Beacon, 2002.

Lewis, David L. *W.E.B. Du Bois: Biography of a Race, 1868–1919*. New York: Henry Holt, 1993.

———. *W.E.B. Du Bois: The Fight for Equality and the American Century, 1919–1963*. New York: Henry Holt, 2000.

Marks, Carole. *Farewell—We're Good and Gone: The Great Black Migration*. Bloomington: Indiana University Press, 1989.

Stein, Judith. *The World of Marcus Garvey: Race and Class in Modern Society*. Baton Rouge: Louisiana State University Press, 1986.

Trotter, Joe William, Jr. *The Great Migration in Historical Perspective: New Dimensions of Race, Class, and Gender*. Bloomington: Indiana University Press, 1991.

Zangrando, Robert L. *The NAACP Crusade Against Lynching, 1909–1950*. Philadelphia: Temple University Press, 1980.

GARVEY'S UNIVERSAL NEGRO IMPROVEMENT ASSOCIATION MOVEMENT

Much criticized in its own day and often reductively referred to as a "Back-to-Africa" movement, the Garvey movement was arguably the most influential grassroots black movement of the twentieth century. The movement sprang out of the activities of the Universal Negro Improvement Association (UNIA) and had strong international appeal among peoples of the African diaspora. The UNIA was based at its height in the early 1920s in headquarters in New York and later in Kingston, Jamaica, and London, England. The movement achieved a high public profile in the years immediately following World War I, largely through the dynamism of its founder and leader, Marcus Garvey, and the popular attraction of his message of pride and Pan-Africanism to disenfranchised people of color. The strength of that message, and the controversies it engendered, garnered backlashes from African Americans of the left and the intellectual elite, as well as political suppression on the part of the U.S. government and colonial officials. Despite this repression, the influence of Garveyism was profound—in the United States, the Caribbean, and Africa.

FOUNDING AND HEYDAY

The UNIA, with its unique and complex economic, cultural, spiritual, and political platform, was the brainchild of Marcus Garvey, who was born in Jamaica in 1887 and died in London in 1940. Under Garvey's leadership and dominance, the movement had both radical and reactionary elements. Garvey was strongly influenced by the intellectualism of his peasant father, the oratorical skills of powerful Jamaican pastors, and the political apprenticeship in unionization and organizing he obtained while working as a young man in the printing trade. After working in Central America and studying and meeting African intellectuals in London, he formed the fledgling UNIA in Kingston in 1914 along with his then-girlfriend (and later first wife) Amy Ashwood. She shared his interest in racial uplift and oratory, and remained throughout her lifetime a supporter of the Pan-Africanist cause.

Garvey originally planned the UNIA as a benevolent and educational association. Booker T. Washington's Tuskegee Institute served as an inspiration, as did the tradition of black neighborhood associations and the lessons of collective action of the trade union movement. The organization was radically reformulated, however, in 1916–1918, when Garvey traveled to the United States and was welcomed into the highly energized postwar New Negro scene of Harlem. Garvey was mentored in New York by fellow West Indian activists and leftist intellectuals, including Cyril Briggs, W.A. Domingo, and Hubert Harrison. Garvey readily took on the mantle of New Negro militancy. He drew crowds as a street speaker and urged identification with Zionist, Irish, and Indian nationalist movements. His message of defiance, with its emphasis on black manhood, self-defense, and authority, had particular resonance for blacks who wished to react boldly to the postwar climate of racial violence, including former African-American soldiers who had fought to protect democratic rights in Europe that they themselves did not have at home.

Garvey quickly proved himself an able showman and organizer, as well as a master of propaganda. Annual UNIA conventions and frequent parades and demonstrations, complete with marching men and women in uniforms, helped the Garvey movement achieve a recognizable presence in Harlem. Garvey spread the word through weekly mass meetings at New York's Liberty Hall and through the *Negro World* newspaper, which featured front-page Garvey editorials and reprints of major speeches, as well as international news and coverage of UNIA programs and activities. The paper soon reached an international distribution and served as the organ of the Garvey movement for many years. French- and Spanish-language pages were added for a time, and the paper reached audiences throughout the Afro-Caribbean and many regions of Africa.

Garvey assembled around him a group of colleagues and advisers who served as national and regional UNIA officers, including Henrietta Vinton Davis, who was instrumental in building a national following for Garveyism in early organizing tours. Together, these leaders built a multifaceted program. Black business enterprise was fostered through the founding of several small businesses through the commercial wing of the UNIA, the African Communities League (ACL), and the Negro Factories Corporation. Meanwhile, the UNIA's highly ritualized meetings and social functions, along with elaborate titles and uniforms, borrowed much from the black Masonic tradition. Self-culture was promoted among members, many of whom did not have the benefit of advanced formal education, and an Afrocentric curriculum was manifested in the many different educational efforts the organization undertook over the years. Afrocentricism was also encouraged in religious faith as Garveyite meetings functioned on a model familiar to followers active in the black church, including the use of prayers and anthems. Garvey encouraged the recognition of black heroes and of a black Madonna, and spoke of the future liberation of Africa from white colonial domination ("Africa for the Africans" was a familiar UNIA refrain). The Black Star Line, the UNIA and ACL's shipping company, was conceived to help create black-controlled trade of products and resources between the Caribbean and the United States, and eventually, it was hoped, to supply passenger transportation and trade to Africa. Like other UNIA businesses, it was also seen as a potential employer of a skilled black labor force, with opportunities for black managers and leadership. Most importantly, it functioned as a powerful propaganda and fundraising tool, as thousands of black people of meager income invested in Black Star Line stock, and thus shared in the dream of black global enterprise and repatriation to Africa.

Hundreds of local UNIA divisions were founded in the United States, the West Indies, and abroad, including in strongholds of British and European colonialism. The movement attracted women as well as men, and UNIA auxiliaries, including the uniformed Motor Corps, Universal African Legion (male) and Black Cross Nurses (female), and juvenile divisions of children, all of which were based on military models,

offered opportunities for UNIA activism. The UNIA convention in 1920 marked an early apex of the movement, when mass parades of Garveyites wound their way through the streets of New York and crowded meetings at Madison Square Garden while Black Star Line vessels plied the waters of the Atlantic and offered excursions on the Hudson River. At that convention, the UNIA proclaimed a radical anticolonial platform in its landmark Declaration of Rights of the Negro Peoples of the World. Over the next few years, the UNIA engaged actively in international diplomacy. UNIA delegations held negotiations with Liberia over potential colonization plans there and went to the League of Nations to petition on behalf of African independence.

REPRESSION AND DECLINE

The Garvey movement succumbed slowly to a combination of internal and external forces. Garvey jealously guarded power. The movement was rife with charges of corruption and splintered by factionalization. Differences sometimes blossomed into violence, as in the 1923 assassination of James Eason, a former Garvey lieutenant turned rival. A continual problem with undercapitalization doomed Garveyite businesses, including the Black Star Line, which sank into disrepair and bankruptcy, leaving employees unpaid along with an organization saddled with steep debts for operating costs and unfulfilled purchase payments. Garvey was also attacked politically by black leftists who believed he was defrauding working people, and by W.E.B. Du Bois and other Talented Tenth leaders, a group who disagreed with his segregationist tactics and separate institution building. Relations with Liberia soured, as the Liberian leadership came to doubt Garvey's intentions and succumbed to lucrative counteroffers of development deals from the Firestone Tire and Rubber Company.

Meanwhile, there was the constant fact of political repression. From the beginning, the UNIA was subjected to intensive surveillance, and Garvey soon became a particular target of J. Edgar Hoover, who worked with State Department officials and within what was then known as the Bureau of Investigation. The distribution of the *Negro World* was suppressed in Africa and banned in areas of Central America and the Caribbean. Undercover agents regularly reported on Garvey's activities and UNIA functions. Restrictions were placed on Garvey's ability to travel to Africa, and attempts were made to bar his reentry into the United States when he went to the Caribbean in 1921. Things came to a head

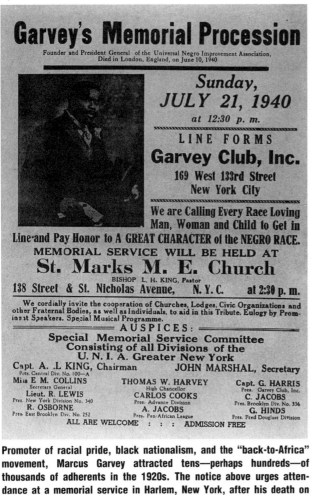

Garvey's Memorial Procession

Founder and President General of the Universal Negro Improvement Association,
Died in London, England, on June 10, 1940

**Sunday,
JULY 21, 1940**
at 12:30 p. m.

LINE FORMS
Garvey Club, Inc.
169 West 133rd Street
New York City

**We are Calling Every Race Loving
Man, Woman and Child to Get in
Line-and Pay Honor to A GREAT CHARACTER of the NEGRO RACE.**
MEMORIAL SERVICE WILL BE HELD AT
St. Marks M. E. Church
BISHOP L. H. KING, Pastor
138 Street & St. Nicholas Avenue,   N. Y. C.   at 2:30 p. m.

We cordially invite the cooperation of Churches, Lodges, Civic Organizations and
other Fraternal Bodies, as well as Individuals, to aid in this Tribute. Eulogy by Prominent Speakers. Special Musical Programme.

AUSPICES:
**Special Memorial Service Committee
Consisting of all Divisions of the
U. N. I. A. Greater New York**

Capt. A. .L KING, Chairman   JOHN MARSHAL, Secretary
Pres. Central Div. No. 100—A
Miss E. M. COLLINS   THOMAS W. HARVEY   Capt. G. HARRIS
Secretary General   High Chancellor   Pres. Garvey Club, Inc.
Lieut. R. LEWIS   CARLOS COOKS   C. JACOBS
Pres. New York Division No. 340   Pres. Advance Division   Pres. Brooklyn Div. No. 336
R. OSBORNE   A. JACOBS   G. HINDS
Pres. East Brooklyn Div. No. 252   Pres. Pan-African League   Pres. Fred Douglass Division
ALL ARE WELCOME   :   :   :   ADMISSION FREE

Promoter of racial pride, black nationalism, and the "back-to-Africa" movement, Marcus Garvey attracted tens—perhaps hundreds—of thousands of adherents in the 1920s. The notice above urges attendance at a memorial service in Harlem, New York, after his death on June 10, 1940. *(Manuscripts, Archives, and Rare Books Division, Schomburg Center for Research in Black Culture, The New York Public Library)*

when Garvey was arrested on mail-fraud charges stemming from the sale of Black Star Line stock in 1922. Free on bail, and in an apparent effort to politically appease government officials, he responded by taking the UNIA on a decided turn to the right. Eschewing coalition politics with other black organizations, he scheduled a meeting with leaders of the Ku Klux Klan in Atlanta in the summer of 1922 to discuss mutual opposition to race mixing and the integrationist policies of the National Association for the Advancement of Colored People. This earned him additional ire from black activists, who joined in a "Garvey Must Go" campaign.

Garvey was tried and convicted in 1923. Denied appeal in 1925, he was imprisoned in Atlanta Federal Penitentiary. His second wife, Amy Jacques Garvey, the former manager of UNIA headquarters in Har-

lem, was instrumental in the leadership of the movement in these years, as well as in the lobbying and public relations efforts for his release. It was through her that the two influential volumes of the *Philosophy and Opinions of Marcus Garvey* were produced and distributed (in 1923 and 1925). President Calvin Coolidge commuted Garvey's sentence in late 1927, and Garvey was subjected to immediate deportation, whereupon the Garvey movement entered a new phase.

LATTER YEARS

Soon after his release, Garvey embarked on a speaking tour of England and France and entered the political arena in Jamaica. He founded the People's Political Party there and ran for office under its reform auspices. He built a UNIA cultural center in Kingston, but it failed financially with the deepening Depression, and in 1934 he relocated to London, where he produced and published the *Black Man* magazine. Meanwhile, the UNIA dwindled in these years but continued to function in local divisions. Garvey presided at conventions held outside U.S. borders in Jamaica and Canada. The Garvey movement's last major controversies came in the latter half of the 1930s with the Italo-Ethiopian War (Garvey published editorials critical of Haile Selassie and his policies, while UNIA activists in Harlem rallied to Ethiopia's defense) and, in 1938, with the UNIA's massive grassroots petitioning support for the Greater Liberia Bill, repatriation legislation sponsored by the rather infamous Theodore Bilbo of Mississippi.

Garvey, who in his final years expressed admiration for rising Fascist leaders, died in relative obscurity in 1940. His bold nationalist and Pan-Africanist legacy has far eclipsed the controversies that embroiled his movement in his time, and in 1964 he was proclaimed Jamaica's first national hero. The philosophies of the Garvey movement in many ways set the stage for resurgent waves of black nationalism in the latter part of the twentieth century, and helped shape Rastafarian and Black Muslim belief. Garveyism also served as direct inspiration to successful leaders of anticolonial independence movements. The cultural impact of the movement, especially its emphasis on racial pride and identification with Africa, has proven pervasive.

Barbara Bair

BIBLIOGRAPHY

Clarke, John Henrik, ed. *Marcus Garvey and the Vision of Africa.* New York: Vintage Books, 1974.

Garvey, Amy Jacques. *Garvey and Garveyism.* New York: Collier, 1976.

Hill, Robert A., et al., eds. *The Marcus Garvey and Universal Negro Improvement Association Papers.* 8 vols. Berkeley: University of California Press, 1983–1995.

Lewis, Rupert. *Marcus Garvey: Anti-Colonial Champion.* Trenton, NJ: Africa World, 1988.

Vincent, Theodore. *Black Power and the Garvey Movement.* San Francisco: Ramparts, 1972.

BROTHERHOOD OF SLEEPING CAR PORTERS

A. Philip Randolph and Milton P. Webster organized the Brotherhood of Sleeping Car Porters (BSCP) in 1925. The BSCP remained an independent union for its first three years, eventually affiliating with the American Federation of Labor (AFL) in 1928. Randolph remained president of the BSCP until 1968; in 1978, the BSCP merged with the Brotherhood of Railway and Airline Clerks. Over the course of its fifty-year history, the BSCP and A. Philip Randolph voiced the concerns of black workers nationwide. Randolph never relented in pressuring the AFL to best represent the interests of its black members, despite much resistance on the part of the AFL leadership.

Randolph and other BSCP members spearheaded many of the major civil rights battles of the 1940s, 1950s, and 1960s. Randolph, for example, organized both the 1941 and 1963 Marches on Washington, the first of which resulted in the creation of the Fair Employment Practices Committee and the second of which became one of the defining moments of the civil rights movement. E.D. Nixon, a member of the BSCP, helped organize the Montgomery bus boycott in 1955. The boycott not only ended the practice of segregation in Montgomery's public transportation system, but it also helped launch the career of Martin Luther King Jr., one of the foremost civil rights activists of the twentieth century.

Members of the BSCP launched movements in the 1940s, 1950s, and 1960s that formed part of an important economic and social movement for the rights of people of color. The black men and women working on the railroads as porters and maids suffered discrimination, low wages, and long hours and were always treated as subservient to white patrons. The BSCP, therefore, not only represented an economic movement to gain better working conditions for its members, but it also embodied a social movement designed to dismantle the racist assumptions upon which the job of "porter" had been based.

PULLMAN SLEEPING CAR PORTERS

Railroad magnate George Pullman officially created the occupation of "porter" in 1867. Just two years after the end of the Civil War, Pullman founded the Pullman Palace Car Company. Pullman considered that passenger comfort was the key to the company's profitability and success. A porter's mission, as conceived by Pullman and described by historian William Harris in his book, *Keeping the Faith: A. Philip Randolph, Milton P. Webster, and the Brotherhood of Sleeping Car Porters* (1977), was to "insure that passengers arrived at their destinations in the best physical and mental condition." With his customers' comfort in mind, Pullman decided to employ black men and women to attend to the needs of white passengers. Playing upon prevalent racial stereotypes of the era, Pullman contended that black men should be employed as porters because of "the elegance whites were said to experience in having black servants; the fact that blacks were cheap labor; and the accepted social distance between the races." George Pullman's philosophy contributed to the company's great success. By 1914, Harris finds, the company employed 12,000 porters, becoming the largest employer of black men in the country and, according to Harris, the "word porter became synonymous with black."

Working at Pullman provided black men with a steady income and the opportunity to travel across the country, but the assumptions upon which the job was based contributed to great resentment among porters. A. Philip Randolph voiced the porters' feelings throughout the 1920s—some sixty years after Pullman created the job. Randolph argued that because subservience was essential to the job and black men and women were consciously hired to wait on white passengers, the workers essentially became an extension of the "servant-master relationship that existed during slavery." Although Pullman countered that the company purposefully employed black men and women out of a concern for their welfare, porters responded by pointing out that they were not hired for any other job. Few, if any, black men were employed in the repair shop, as engineers, or as conductors, and few white men worked as porters. Further evidence of Pullman's differential treatment toward black employees can be found in how he set up his famous "model town." Pullman built his model town to provide housing for his white employees and expose them to his idea of a proper lifestyle; the community included churches and schools, and people's behavior was closely monitored. Pullman's overbearing paternalism came back to haunt him when his white workers went out on strike in 1894 to protest cuts in wages, raises in rent payments, and the general lack of control they were allowed to exert over their lives.

SUBORDINATION OF PULLMAN'S BLACK WORKERS

White workers, whether or not living in Pullman's model town, used their membership in the powerful railroad unions to make demands of Pullman; black porters, without a union, had no equivalent recourse. Although the railroad industry gave rise to the strongest labor unions in the United States in the late nineteenth and early twentieth centuries, none of the "big four" (the Brotherhood of Locomotive Engineers, the Brotherhood of Locomotive Firemen, the Brotherhood of Railway Trainmen, and the Order of Railway Conductors) admitted black workers as rank-and-file members. The nationally based American Federation of Labor (AFL), created in 1886, had by 1900 become what Harris calls, "a bastion in the development and maintenance of racism in the United States." Randolph and fellow organizers Milton P. Webster and Ashley Totten faced an enormous uphill battle when in the 1920s they embarked on a concerted organizing campaign to improve the wages and working conditions among black porters.

A STRATEGY FOR CHANGE

Most black porters readily acknowledged that working conditions were unacceptable. In addition to working for long hours at low wages, black porters were forced to remain on call for several hours per day without pay. Moreover, porters performed conductors' work at wages considerably below standards and had little bargaining power or job security. Despite substandard treatment, few porters agreed on a strategy to improve working conditions. To complicate matters, the Pullman Company instituted an in-house office known as the Employees Representation Plan (ERP) designed to address and quell worker grievances. ERP was formed by the Pullman Company to compete with the Pullman Porters and Maids Protective Association (PPMPA), formed in 1920. The ERP contended with the PPMPA for the support of workers. In the short-term, ERP proved more effective because it could resolve worker grievances with the company's support. Although most porters supported the PPMPA's demands, they also benefited somewhat from the increased representation ERP provided. Nevertheless, it was clear that ERP was, as Harris describes, a company union like many that emerged in the 1920s to prevent more radical employee-driven unions from gaining footholds in various industries throughout the United States. In 1924, frustrated porters decided to demand that ERP petition the company for a raise to $100/month (from an average of $67.50 for 400 hours of service). ERP responded by offering a much smaller, $5 wage increase. ERP served the company well: it allowed Pullman to assert that it was responsive to employee needs, even if the modest gains were on company rather than worker terms.

FORMING AN INDEPENDENT UNION

Although most porters accepted the agreement, a significant number still believed in developing a "real" union rather than continuing to rely on ERP. Porters' hours remained long. On average, workers traveled over 11,000 miles per month and were not paid while waiting in terminals. Moreover, Pullman deducted the cost of required uniforms and shoes from worker pay in addition to meals. Even after working at Pullman for fifteen years, the most a porter could earn was $94.50 a month (according to government estimates from 1926, the average family required $2,088/year, or $174/month, to live adequately). If any significant changes were to occur, porters realized they needed their own employee-run union.

In 1925, Ashley Totten, a disgruntled porter who worked for ERP, listened to a speech by A. Philip Randolph and immediately asked him to work on organizing a "real" union for porters and maids at Pullman. Randolph agreed. A series of secret meetings were held in New York, culminating in the establishment of the National Committee to Organize Pullman Porters into the Brotherhood of Sleeping Car Porters. Officers were elected. Randolph became the committee's general organizer, W.H. Des Verney (who had worked as a porter for thirty years) assisted Randolph, and Roy Lancaster (a former ERP official) took the job of secretary-treasurer. The new committee worked

ASA PHILIP RANDOLPH (1889–1979)

Born in Crescent City, Florida, on April 15, 1889, to a preacher and his wife, A. Philip Randolph moved to New York City in 1911 and worked during the day while attending the College of the City of New York at night. He read modern economic and political writers, including Karl Marx, which led him to believe that the black working class was the hope for black progress. In 1917, he and a friend established the black magazine *The Messenger*. As a writer and editor, Randolph criticized black and white leaders alike while further developing his interest in the labor movement. In 1917, he organized a small union of elevator operators in New York City. A member of the Socialist Party, he ran for public office several times but was never elected.

After the war, he devoted his energies to organizing the Pullman car porters, a group of black workers he had tried to organize earlier. He was elected president of the Brotherhood of Sleeping Car Porters when it was formed in 1925. Despite bitter opposition by the Pullman Company, Randolph won recognition for the union, pay increases, and shorter hours in 1937. An untiring fighter for civil rights, in 1941 he organized the March on Washington Movement to protest against job discrimination in the defense industry. This effort, although it did not culminate in a march, worried President Franklin D. Roosevelt enough that he established the Fair Employment Practices Committee during World War II. Using a similar technique, Randolph also succeeded in the fight against segregation in the armed forces. His election to a vice presidency of the American Federation of Labor-Congress of Industrial Organizations (AFL-CIO) in 1955 was, in part, in recognition of his efforts to eliminate racial discrimination and fight against communism in the organized labor movement.

In 1963, Randolph was director of the March on Washington for Jobs and Freedom, one of the largest civil rights demonstrations ever held in the United States. He hoped to obtain government sponsorship of black jobs through the march, but it was overshadowed by the demands of the Southern civil rights movement and Martin Luther King Jr.'s "I Have a Dream" speech. Within a year, the Civil Rights Act of 1964 was signed.

Randolph and others founded the A. Philip Randolph Institute in 1964 to serve and promote cooperation between labor and the black community. His understanding of the economic plight of urban blacks predated the riots of the 1960s that drew the nation's attention to them. Randolph retired from the presidency of the union in 1968, although he continued in his position as a vice president of the AFL-CIO. He died on May 16, 1979, in New York City. Though very successful in achieving his goals of integration and civil rights, his aloof and intellectual style kept him from becoming as well known a black leader as the more charismatic King or Malcolm X.

James G. Lewis

closely with black Socialist Frank Crosswaith, who had organized the Trade Union Committee for Organizing Negro Workers (TUC) earlier that year.

Randolph and the Committee, with Crosswaith's support, organized a rally in Harlem to launch the brotherhood. According to historian Philip Foner in *Organized Labor and the Black Worker, 1619–1973* (1974), the rally "was hailed by the *Amsterdam News* as 'the greatest labor mass meeting ever held of, for and by Negro working men.'" Those who attended generated a list of demands: recognition of the Brotherhood of Sleeping Car Porters, as opposed to the ERP, as the sole bargaining agent for porters; an increase in wages to $150 per month; a significant decrease in hours; and payment for the time spent preparing the train cars. Foner's *Organized Labor and the Black Worker* includes Frank Crosswaith's recollections of the rally eleven years later:

The soldiers of labor's cause must never be permitted to forget that fateful August night eleven years ago, when enveloped by the suffocating heat of a summer's night and the stifling smoke from a hundred cigars, cigarettes, and a few pipes, several hundred Pullman porters defiantly threw down the gauntlet of battle to the nation's mightiest industrial monarch.

A BUDDING MOVEMENT

Although some porters supported the BSCP, others feared they could not win a fight against Pullman, which was still the largest employer of black men in the county. Support from black communities across the nation was also slow to emerge. Local black leaders in Chicago, for example, were reluctant to support the nascent movement, arguing that the Pullman Company was a great benefactor of the Negro people and that—having employed so many black workers—

the company should not be attacked. The Pullman Company made sure all of its porters were made aware of the sentiment among black leaders opposed to unionization. For its part, the Pullman Company stated that the BSCP was spearheaded by a group of "derelicts," "morons," and "gripers," and that the organization was led by Randolph, an "outsider" and a "Communist agitator."

THE MOVEMENT GAINS SUPPORT

The BSCP gained much needed publicity when Perry Howard, who supported the company, challenged Randolph to a debate for the purpose of "blasting and demolishing the Brotherhood and its leadership once

and for all." But this tactic backfired as Howard was booed off the stage by the attendees. The debate was reported in *The Messenger* and generated a great deal of publicity for the budding BSCP. Shortly thereafter, Ashley Totten and A. Philip Randolph traveled the country to explain the case for an independent union for porters in Salt Lake City, San Francisco, Minneapolis, Kansas City, Oakland, St. Louis, and other cities. The two leaders noted that the ERP, a company-dominated organization, could not meet the needs of workers and that an independent union of black sleeping car porters would greatly benefit their interests. The movement had begun. Randolph and Totten's tour generated a number of converts as work-

Members of the Brotherhood of Sleeping Car Porters—the largest and most influential predominantly African-American union in the 1930s—march in support of integration, civil rights, and labor reform. *(Brown Brothers)*

ers decided that supporting BSCP efforts to form an independent union was worth the risk of losing their jobs.

Initially, the Pullman Company thought the BSCP would be short-lived. Once it was clear that more and more porters were interested in the union, the company hired thugs to attack BSCP organizers and fired porters active in the union—some who had worked for Pullman for twenty years or more. Pullman went so far as to pay black newspapers to write derogatory articles about the BSCP. The Chicago *Defender*, for example, advised readers, according to historian Philip Foner, "to 'align themselves with the wealthier classes in America' as their only hope of salvation." The Pullman Company also placed ads in the St. Louis *Argus*, a struggling newspaper that quickly rebounded as a result of Pullman's support. To counter this negative publicity, the BSCP organized conferences and labor institutes in major cities throughout the United States—especially in the North, where union activists discussed the benefits of organizing a bona fide union. To counter the BSCP's growing popularity, the Pullman Company granted porters an 8 percent increase in 1926 and began hiring Filipino, Chinese, and Mexican men to replace black porters.

By 1927, the company's anti-BSCP efforts seemed to be working, and many of the local chapters of the BSCP that had opened in various cities throughout the United States began to close. In the nick of time, large labor unions that had historically antagonistic relationships with Pullman and other railroad companies provided much needed support. Unions representing workers in the needle trades, the Chicago Federation of Labor, and even top officials from the AFL sent money to BSCP and publicly spoke out in support of the fledgling union. The BSCP also gained the support of leading civil rights organizations, including the National Association for the Advancement of Colored People (NAACP), the Colored Women's Economic Council, and the National Urban League (NUL). Emboldened, the BSCP attempted to use the government's Railway Mediation Board to force the Pullman Company to recognize the BSCP as the porters' sole bargaining agent. The attempt failed.

Once again, the BSCP's future looked bleak. Perhaps out of desperation, the BSCP threatened to wage a strike against the Pullman Company to demand that it finally recognize the union. Porters voted 6,053 to 17 to walk off the job, and yet, despite overwhelming support and great pre-strike publicity, Randolph began to have doubts. In June of 1928, the BSCP leadership called off the strike amid intense criticism from

porters, from the black press, and from some AFL-affiliated unions. Nevertheless, according to Philip Foner, Randolph argued that the strike served an important purpose. The strike "had 'reversed the concept of the American public stereotype of a shuffling, tip-taking porter to an upstanding American worker, demanding his right to organize a union of his own, as well as a living wage.'"

Even though the Pullman Company refused to recognize the BSCP, the union nevertheless applied for a charter with the American Federation of Labor. Despite strong opposition from powerful and more conservative national unions, AFL president William Green granted the BSCP a charter in 1928 and thirteen of the BSCP's largest chapters became AFL-affiliates. Although the BSCP had less influence than some of the AFL's more powerful unions because of the type of charter the BSCP was granted, affiliation with the AFL lent the BSCP some permanence and stability.

PULLMAN RECOGNIZES THE BROTHERHOOD OF SLEEPING CAR PORTERS

The Depression created grave challenges for the BSCP. The union barely survived as membership dropped to 658 in 1933. Union-friendly New Deal legislation prompted a resurgence in union membership, however and, just one year later, the BSCP had 2,627 members. All the while, A. Philip Randolph continued to press Pullman to recognize the BSCP. Finally, in 1937, with the support of favorable legislation in the 1934 Railway Labor Act and a series of well-negotiated mediated talks, Pullman finally recognized the BSCP as the sole bargaining agent for its porters and maids. According to William Harris, Randolph claimed that he and his fellow BSCP leaders had brought "Pullman to its knees." By 1937, Harris argues that the BSCP had "attained a position of prominence that marked it as a leader among black organizations." For the next forty years, its members, who referred to the BSCP as either "the union" or "the movement," would use their positions in the BSCP to both pressure the labor movement to respond to black workers' demands and to wage numerous civil rights struggles.

Lisa Phillips

BIBLIOGRAPHY

Foner, Philip. *Organized Labor and the Black Worker, 1619–1973.* New York: Praeger, 1974.

Harris, William H. *Keeping the Faith: A. Philip Randolph, Milton P. Webster, and the Brotherhood of Sleeping Car Porters*. Urbana: University of Illinois Press, 1977.

Pfeffer, Paula. *A. Philip Randolph: Pioneer of the Civil Rights Movement*. Baton Rouge: Louisiana State University Press, 1990.

Santino, Jack. *Miles of Smiles, Years of Struggle: The Untold Story of the Black Pullman Porter*. Urbana: University of Illinois Press, 1989.

Wilson, Joseph F. *Tearing Down the Color Bar: A Documentary History and Analysis of the Brotherhood of Sleeping Car Porters*. New York: Columbia University Press, 1989.

CIVIL RIGHTS MOVEMENT 1930–1953

As the United States entered the Great Depression, racial segregation remained "the law of the land" in all Southern states as well as some areas of the North. Both the national citizenship rights and due process guarantees of the Fourteenth Amendment (1868) and the voting rights protections of the Fifteenth Amendment (1870), enacted to ensure the civil rights of some four million former slaves, existed only on paper for the great majority of African Americans. In the South at the end of the nineteenth century, upper- and middle-class whites, through their legal arm, the Democratic Party, extralegal terrorist groups like the Ku Klux Klan (KKK), and sympathetic U.S. Supreme Court decisions, had moved toward a policy of disenfranchisement and segregation—a policy that destroyed the agrarian reform-oriented Populist Party's attempt to build an economic alliance of poor Southern white and black tenant farmers and sharecroppers. By the first decade of the twentieth century, de jure segregation had triumphed everywhere in the former Confederate states.

The new century saw increased pressure for blacks to leave the economically stagnant South for the North. The exodus was accelerated by mounting violence in the form of race riots and lynchings of African Americans who stayed in the South. The formation of the National Association for the Advancement of Colored People (NAACP) by progressives and Socialists, both white and black, in response to the spread of such violence in 1908, was one important expression of a developing civil rights consciousness. The black scholar W.E.B. Du Bois emerged as editor of the NAACP newspaper, *The Crisis*, which campaigned against racist defamation and exposed racist violence. Du Bois had earlier challenged Booker T. Washington's formal acceptance of racial segregation and disenfranchisement in exchange for financial support from white philanthropy for black vocational education and low-level patronage from the national Republican Party. Spearheading campaigns against segregation in federal offices in the Wilson administration and against the virulently racist film *Birth of a Nation* (1915), which glorified the KKK of Reconstruction, the NAACP emerged as the nation's major national civil rights organization by the end of World War I.

SEGREGATION AND GLOBAL EXPANSION

African-American involvement in segregated units and in Northern defense industries during World War I produced a schizophrenic response among U.S. government agencies. On the one hand, they sought to mobilize blacks for the war effort, and on the other, they kept them under surveillance as a potentially subversive factor, especially black troops in France, whose fraternization with the French population was a cause of great fear among military leaders. In the immediate postwar era, the Red Scare of 1919 launched against Socialists, Communists, and Anarchists in the wake of the Russian Revolution merged with a "Red Summer" of race riots against black urban populations, which saw seventy blacks lynched and thousands burned out of their homes as demobilized black troops returned to a segregated society in the midst of major strikes, rapid inflation, and both hopes and fears of revolutionary upheavals.

In the aftermath of the Red Scare and Red Summer, a number of trends that would influence the development of a civil rights movement after 1930 became visible. First, the outmigration of Southern blacks to the North, which began to gather force at the turn of the century and accelerated during the war, continued to grow rapidly. In the period 1920–1930, 749,000 blacks left the South. Whereas 93 percent of the black male workforce in 1890 had been in the agricultural sector, only 42 percent of black males were in agricultural work in 1930. With the shift from the South to the North and to urban areas even within the South, a black working class and a larger middle class living in cities with a much higher level of group solidarity and social organization were coming into existence. The working class and middle class (thrown together by residential segregation, with the middle class dependent entirely on the businesses of the working class) were keenly aware of the conditions they had escaped in the rural South and of the role of Southern segregation in serving as the political and ideological foundation for the oppression of African Americans everywhere, just as Southern slavery had served as the basis for institutional and ideological racism everywhere in the antebellum period.

Meanwhile, important national and global developments had made the questions of racism and colonialism more central to the post–World War I era. Although the colonial empires were reshuffled after the war, with England and France taking control of Turkish possessions in the Near East and German colonies in Africa, powerful anticolonial movements sprang up in India and China, and anticolonial activity grew in Africa. In the United States, a Communist Party was founded in fits and starts out of the left wing of the Socialist Party and the Industrial Workers of the World (IWW).

BLACKS AND THE COMMUNIST PARTY

Inspired by the Russian Revolution and serving as the left wing of the international Socialist movement, Communists on the world scene established a Communist International (CI) centered at Moscow and made organizing among the nonwhite peoples of the colonial world and oppressed nationalities and minorities a central task. The fact that a potential great power and revolutionary state was actively supporting antiracist and anticolonialist policies globally influenced such diverse non-Communist anticolonial fighters in the interwar era as the Indian Jawaharlal Nehru, the Ghanaian Kwame Nkrumah, and, initially, the Kenyan Jomo Kenyatta in a socialist direction and encouraged a much higher level of militancy among colonized peoples and oppressed minorities.

The Communist Party USA would soon take a position emphasizing the interdependent struggle against racism and colonialism. The party saw the "Negro question" as central to the liberation of the working class of the United States; in contrast, its Socialist Party competitors saw class in "color-blind" terms—that is, no working-class group had special needs, and all problems would be solved by socialism. Alone among the political groups, the Communists, from the 1920s on, made organizing work among Af-

rican Americans and against racism among white workers a very high priority.

Black radicals who formed the African Blood Brotherhood in the postwar period were to come into the ranks of the Communist Party, as were people drawn from both the marginalized poor and middle-class intellectuals in the campaigns party activists would launch. Among these campaigns were those against peonage in the South and lynching throughout the country, and for integrated unions through such early organizations as the Trade Union Educational League, the Trade Union Unity League, and the American Negro Labor Congress. In addition, A. Philip Randolph, active in the Socialist Party before the war and a lifelong opponent of Communism, would organize the Brotherhood of Sleeping Car Porters in the 1920s and connect trade union work with general civil rights activity in both the American Federation of Labor and the larger society.

At the same time, Marcus Garvey, a West Indian, emerged as the leader of the most significant Black Nationalist movement in U.S. history, mobilizing millions of blacks in parades and demonstrations under the banner of a Universal Negro Improvement Association (UNIA) with a back-to-Africa message that many contemporaries saw as Black Zionism. Garvey soon lost many of his left radical supporters when he sought to organize a black capitalism, eschewed alliances with labor, and even ask for some support for his back-to-Africa project from the KKK. Nonetheless, many of his grassroots supporters subsequently agreed to involve themselves in militant civil rights campaigns after the Coolidge administration largely destroyed Garvey's movement by prosecuting him for business fraud and deporting him to the West Indies in the mid-1920s.

Finally, the 1920s saw a wave of black artistic and intellectual ferment, symbolized by the Harlem Renaissance and the concept of a "New Negro." This cultural flowering would produce a generation of poets, musicians, novelists, journalists, historians, and social scientists with a much broader worldview than the assimilationist black bourgeoisie that had supported Booker T. Washington in the past and that in the 1920s was represented in both the conservative wing of the NAACP and various small-business and fraternal associations. These intellectuals, as liberals and radicals, would become important spokespersons for movements redefining "the Negro" individually and collectively and defining and demanding equality after 1930.

The work of Communists and those they mobilized was a key factor in both radicalizing and expanding civil rights activities during the Depression. In the summer of 1930, Communists organized grassroots unemployed councils to fight for work relief and home relief (public jobs and what today is called welfare) and against evictions in urban areas. Organizing white and black supporters to fight against the evictions of black families particularly was part of the campaign of the unemployed councils, which encouraged other left groups, the Socialist-supported Workers Alliance of America and Christian socialist A.J. Muste's American Workers Party, to undertake similar campaigns. Communist-led Hunger Marches involving white and black unemployed, as well as other forms of integrated protests for jobs and relief, became common in urban areas and were often met by extensive police violence. When three black youths, for example, were killed by police in such a demonstration in Chicago in the early 1930s, thousands of whites joined blacks for their funeral, a phenomenon never before witnessed in the history of Chicago or any other American city.

Outside of the African-American press, the Communist newspaper, the *Daily Worker*, its regional version, the *Southern Worker*, and various Communist-published factory "shop papers" highlighted the oppression of blacks in the South and actively criticized forms of racial discrimination in the workplace. Communists organized a black Share Croppers Union (SCU), centered in Alabama. In 1931, Socialists were active in establishing a Southern Tenant Farmers Union (STFU), which, though predominantly white, had both black and white members and leaders.

The formal Communist position favoring the right of African Americans (if they so chose) to live in a "black state" within the "black belt" (the large plantation region that cut across several Deep South states) as part of a larger Socialist America had limited interest for blacks. The Communist movement made a qualitative breakthrough when its workers' legal defense organization, the International Labor Defense (ILD), took the case of nine black youths and young men accused of raping two white women at Scottsboro, Alabama, in 1931. The Scottsboro case became the most important civil liberties/civil rights case of the 1930s and the first case involving African Americans that, rivaling the Sacco-Vanzetti case of the 1920s, saw international protests from Hamburg to London, Paris to Capetown, Moscow to Shanghai.

The case also led the NAACP, which had shied away from rape cases in the past, to involve itself in the Scottsboro defense and to broaden its general civil rights activity. Finally, the campaign for the Scottsboro boys, as they were commonly referred to, helped spark a national antilynching movement, which included both the ILD and the NAACP, and represented a precursor of the informal alliances between liberals and radicals that would characterize the New Deal period.

THE NEW DEAL, WAR, AND SEGREGATION

In the 1930s, the New Deal government of President Franklin D. Roosevelt marked the first time that a Democratic administration reached out to African Americans on the national level. Among the most prominent was Mary McLeod Bethune, an educator whom Roosevelt appointed administrative assistant for Negro Affairs and director of the Division of Negro Affairs in the National Youth Administration. Civil rights advocates became increasingly active, as nationalist radical and liberal black militants, with Communists taking the most important initiative, established the National Negro Congress (NNC) in 1936, which sought to create an organization that would advance the struggle for civil rights by coordinating support for the labor movement and the New Deal government among blacks and support for civil rights issues within the New Deal government and the labor movement. It would be a casualty of global politics in the aftermath of the German-Soviet Non-Aggression Pact of 1939, when members divided sharply over Communist support for the Soviet position. The NNC was in part an attempt to bring to the United States an organization similar to the anticolonial Indian National Congress of Mohandas Gandhi and Jawaharlal Nehru and the African National Congress of South Africa, to both raise the consciousness of blacks and create an alliance among blacks, labor, and the New Deal. Adam Clayton Powell, the Harlem minister who would lead boycotts against employment discrimination at Harlem stores and would later become the first black elected to Congress from New York and only the third black congressman since Reconstruction (and the most influential congressperson in drafting Great Society legislation in the 1960s) worked closely with the National Negro Congress.

A. Phillip Randolph, the National Negro Congress's first president, while denouncing its Communist leaders and withdrawing from the NNC in 1940, drew on its commitment to national political action when he threatened a national march on Washington to protest discrimination in the war production industries in 1941. Randolph's threat spurred President Roosevelt, who had failed to support antilynching

MARY McLEOD BETHUNE (1875–1955)

Mary Jane McLeod was born on July 10, 1875, in Mayesville, South Carolina, and was the daughter of former slaves. She began her life picking cotton, but a scholarship to Scotia Seminary in North Carolina in 1888 launched her long and distinguished career as educator and activist. She graduated from Scotia Seminary (now Barber-Scotia College) in 1893 and attended the Moody Bible Institute in Chicago in 1894 in hopes of becoming a missionary in Africa. Rejected for that position, she became a teacher and held a succession of positions in the South. She married Albertus L. Bethune in 1898 and settled in Savannah, Georgia.

In 1904, Bethune moved to Daytona Beach, Florida, where, in October, she opened a school of her own, the Daytona Normal and Industrial Institute for Negro Girls. Over the next two decades she worked tirelessly to build the school into a leading institution. She also helped lead a voter registration drive that proved unpopular with local whites but demonstrated her resolve to overturn Jim Crow laws. In 1923, the school was merged with the Cookman Institute for Men, then in Jacksonville, Florida, to form what from 1929 was known as Bethune-Cookman College in Daytona Beach. Bethune was president of the college from 1923 to 1942 and again from 1946 to 1947. Under her administration, the college won full accreditation and grew to an enrollment of more than one thousand.

An activist, Bethune mobilized thousands of black women as leader and founder of the National Association of Colored Women and the National Council of Negro Women. A national figure, she first advised Presidents Calvin Coolidge and Herbert Hoover on child welfare issues. Bethune's efforts on behalf of education and improved racial relations led to her appointment in 1936 by President Franklin D. Roosevelt as administrative assistant for Negro Affairs (her title changed in 1939 to director of the Division of Negro Affairs) of the National Youth Administration, a post she held until 1944. In 1935, she founded the National Council of Negro Women, of which she remained president until 1949, and she was vice president of the National Association for the Advancement of Colored People from 1940 to 1955. She was an adviser on minority affairs to Roosevelt and assisted the secretary of war in selecting officer candidates for the U.S. Women's Army Corps (WAC).

President Harry Truman sent her to San Francisco where she consulted with organizers of the United Nations (UN) about the concerns of black Americans and people of color from Europe, Africa, and the Caribbean. Along with W.E.B. Du Bois and others in her contingent, she argued for increased attention to the plight of minorities worldwide in the wake of colonialism. Although the white members of the UN ignored their ideas, Bethune did not waver. Afterward, she continued working for the needs of black Americans until her death in Daytona Beach, Florida, on May 18, 1955.

Through her efforts to promote full citizenship rights for all African Americans and her feminist perspective, she came to symbolize the dual role black women played as activists for the rights of blacks and women.

James G. Lewis

---

legislation or to give Southern unionists in textiles and agriculture the support his government had provided for Northern industrial workers, to issue an executive order barring discrimination in war production industries and establishing a Fair Employment Practices Committee (FEPC) to supervise the antidiscrimination policy. The subject of intense controversy during the war, the FEPC would be abolished in 1945 but would return in 1964 in the form of the Equal Employment Opportunity Commission (EEOC), a vital part of the Civil Rights Act of that year.

The National Negro Congress also sparked the Southern Negro Youth Congress (SNYC), a Communist-led youth group with a broad, nonsectarian political approach that brought together black religious and fraternal organizations around campaigns to enact antilynching legislation and social legislation to as-sist the poor. At its New Orleans meeting in 1940, the SNYC instituted a regional voter registration campaign and focused its energies on individual cases of police brutality against blacks in the South. The SNYC also organized African-American art exhibits and poetry readings by Langston Hughes and others, and it established, in the tradition of the Works Progress Administration (WPA)'s Federal Theater, "people's theaters" in Richmond, Birmingham, and New Orleans, as well as roving political puppet shows throughout the rural South.

An important precursor of the mass civil rights movement of the 1950s and 1960s, the SNYC fought discrimination at army bases in the South during the war around the slogan "Fight Fascism Abroad and K-K-K ism at Home." Although it would be a casualty of both the Cold War and a postwar segregationist backlash (at its last annual conference in Birmingham, Alabama, in 1948, delegates were subjected to relentless harassment and arrests under the orders of Birmingham chief of police Eugene "Bull" Connor), the SNYC was the first political activity for many later black Southern civil rights activists.

At a time when mainstream media, movies, and radio portrayed the United States as a lily-white society and were filled with demeaning racist stereotypes, Communist-led cultural publications like *The New Masses* and New Deal projects like the WPA's Federal Theater and Federal Arts Project, along with labor theaters and book clubs, helped bring a new generation of politically conscious African-American writers and artists to a wide multiethnic audience.

In pro–New Deal newspapers like the *New York Post*, *Philadelphia Record*, and *Chicago Sun Times*, sympathetic portrayals of black struggles against discrimination began to appear by the late 1930s. Black cultural figures participated in campaigns to raise funds to aid Republican Spain, and the Abraham Lincoln Brigade, the American volunteer group fighting on the side of the Spanish Loyalists, became the first fully and formally integrated military force in American history.

The Harlem of the 1920s that housed the Cotton Club became the Harlem of mass protests against Benito Mussolini's invasion of Ethiopia in 1935, boycotts against discrimination, labor organizing, and the election of Adam Clayton Powell to the House of Representatives and African-American Communist Party leader Benjamin Davis to New York's City Council during World War II. Through the work of WPA photographers like Dorothea Lange, both the suffering and dignity of black and white Southern sharecroppers began to reach large audiences. Such images could sometimes even be found in *Life* magazine. In addition in these years, the WPA was to help train the great African-American social realist painter, Jacob Lawrence.

Whereas African-American culture had served as an exotic, separate, and sexually liberating alternative to mainstream America in the 1920s (itself a deeply condescending expression of racism), black artists were in the forefront of the struggle against exploitation and oppression, which concerned the growing number of people in the larger society in the 1930s.

Professional baseball remained segregated, and professional football, relatively new and minor at the time, had become segregated by the end of the 1920s. Paul Robeson, for example, had been a professional football player before the game was segregated in the

early 1920s. However, the changes produced by the center-left politics and the urban-liberal-labor world of the 1930s could be seen in professional boxing. Before World War I, heavyweight champion Jack Johnson had been demonized and had become the target of sports promoters' crusades to find a "great white hope" to bring back the championship to "the white race." In stark contrast, Joe Louis met with Franklin D. Roosevelt at the White House before he fought the German Max Schmeling in 1938, and Lewis's victory was universally seen as a symbolic victory for the United States against Hitler's Nazism. When Louis fought the Irish-American boxer Billy Conn in 1941, this was seen as a battle between two champions, both representing "common man" values, rather than as a battle between a white and a black.

Richard Wright was often at odds with his fellow Communists on artistic and cultural matters, and subsequently, like his party colleague Ralph Ellison, he left the Communist Party and repudiated its politics. Wright's *Native Son*, published in 1940, sold 250,000 copies in three weeks and became a Book-of-the-Month Club selection. Not since the abolitionists had promoted the narratives of escaped slaves in the antebellum period had politically significant work by an African-American writer reached such an audience. Bigger Thomas, the central character of *Native Son*, came to symbolize for a generation the social cataclysm that the dehumanizing system of segregation and the ideological racism that sustained it might bring.

In the late 1930s, the NAACP also began to mount a set of legal challenges to Southern segregation, first attacking the fraudulent nature of its "separate but equal" doctrine in circumstances where the per capita funding of segregated public facilities was always grossly unequal. In *Gaines v. Missouri* (1938), the U.S. Supreme Court ruled against Missouri's failure to provide law school facilities for black citizens under the system of school segregation. African-American lawyers such as Charles Hamilton Houston and his protégé Thurgood Marshall played a major role in the early assault on racist laws in the South.

The liberalizing of the federal judiciary that the Roosevelt administration would begin as it struggled against the conservative-dominated Supreme Court in the late 1930s would eventually produce a Supreme Court that would reverse *Plessy v. Ferguson* (1896) and enact a series of decisions in the 1950s and 1960s that would assert and protect the civil rights and civil liberties of political dissenters and religious and ethnic minorities. In that sense, a Supreme Court and a fed-

CHARLES HAMILTON HOUSTON
(1895–1950)

Born on September 3, 1895, in Washington, D.C., Charles Hamilton Houston litigated and participated in the resolution of critical civil rights cases in U.S. history, including the *Brown v. Board of Education* (1954) decision that ended the legal practice of racial segregation in public schools. Houston graduated Phi Beta Kappa from Amherst College in 1915. He then entered the U.S. Army during World War I, where he became an officer in the Black Army Corps and was commissioned a second lieutenant. The discrimination and contempt that Houston experienced as a black officer in the segregated U.S. Army were a primary motivation for him to pursue a legal career as a civil rights activist. He would later write, "The hate and scorn showered on us Negro officers by our fellow Americans convinced me that there was no sense in my dying for a world ruled by them. I made up my mind that if I got through this war I would study law and use my time fighting for men who could not strike back."

Houston then entered Harvard University in the fall of 1919 where he went on to become the first African American to edit the *Harvard Law Review*. After graduating from Harvard University in 1922, Houston joined the faculty of Howard University Law School in 1924 and became vice-dean in 1929. Houston played a critical role in educating young African-American law students. At Howard, he cultivated, encouraged, and inspired African-American law students who would go on to renowned legal careers.

Houston was the primary legal architect and tactician who organized the *Brown* legal team before the U.S. Supreme Court for the National Association for the Advancement of Colored People (NAACP). This case was initially several separate civil rights cases ultimately combined into the historic *Brown* decision. Houston died on April 26, 1950, shortly before the decision was rendered, but at a point in time when eventual victory seemed certain. Between 1935 and 1948, Houston won seven of eight cases he argued before the Supreme Court. Leading academics, lawyers, and judges recognized Houston's crucial role. A year before his death, Houston's position as a civil rights leader was commended by Harvard Law School Dean Erwin Griswold, who awarded him the NAACP's Spingarn Medal for his legal contribution to the cause. Houston is considered to be the legal inspiration behind subsequent civil rights–era legislative and judicial decisions. In 1993, Federal Circuit Judge A. Leon Higginbotham Jr. wrote: "You must understand this: without *Brown* there would have been no civil rights movement, no civil rights act, and no voting rights act. Without Houston there would have been no *Brown*."

Immanuel Ness

eral judiciary forged in large part out of the struggles of the 1930s would become the most important government ally of the civil rights movement of the 1950s and 1960s.

World events in the 1930s would help shape the American civil rights movement. The victory of Adolf Hitler's Nazi Party in Germany in 1933 saw the establishment of a dictatorship committed to an ideology and policy of extreme racism, nationalism, and militarism. Segregating and terrorizing Germany's Jewish religious minority—using it, in effect, as a guinea pig for its policies of dominating "non-Germans" by brute force based on the pseudoscientific theory of Aryan superiority—the Nazi movement both inspired its right-wing imitators throughout the world and stimulated a coalition between liberal and radical forces internationally dedicated to fighting the Fascist state and increasingly attacking racist ideas in education and racist institutions.

At the 1936 Olympics in Berlin, U.S. Olympic Committee chief Avery Brundage attempted to appease Nazi leaders and to vent his own prejudices by removing Jewish-American athletes from key events and seeking, unsuccessfully, to downplay the contribution of African-American athletes. In the late 1930s, rightist enemies of the industrial union drives condemned the Congress of Industrial Organizations (CIO) and the New Deal as dominated by Communists, Jews, and "Negroes." And in the late 1940s, the House Un-American Activities Committee routinely asked its unfriendly witnesses whether or not they opposed laws in the South against miscegenation. But Nazi Germany's growing threat of world war and the growing connection between domestic racist ideology and policies with opposition to the New Deal and its urban-liberal-labor coalition (a connection that became more significant by 1938 as many segregationist Southern Democrats joined Republicans in a conservative congressional coalition) undermined the legitimacy and normality of racist ideas and practices for millions of Americans.

WAR, SEGREGATION, AND INEQUALITY

Where the United States was on civil rights questions on the eve of World War II can be better grasped when we look at where the nation was on the eve of World War I. Whereas the Wilson administration had intensified segregation and the president himself had been used in advertising that praised *Birth of a Nation* in 1915, Eleanor Roosevelt, in a highly publicized event in 1939, resigned from the Daughters of the American Revolution when that conservative group refused to rent Constitution Hall for a concert featuring African-American singer Marian Anderson. Mrs. Roosevelt was instrumental in arranging a concert for Anderson at the Lincoln Memorial, where many thousands of blacks and whites in effect protested racism.

In 1914, blacks were demonized in the South politically and were invisible everywhere else, except as crude caricatures in minstrel shows, newspaper cartoons, and on food and other commercial packaging. In 1939, the Democrats in particular were developing outreach programs to Northern blacks, the new CIO industrial unions had been founded on nonracist, inclusionary principles, and campaigns for state and local antidiscrimination legislation and commissions were being mounted by liberal and labor forces in Northern urban areas.

During the war years, the most important radical movement of the time, the Communist movement, was committed centrally to antiracist policies. Although the combined membership of the Communist Party USA (CPUSA) and the Young Communist League (YCL) peaked at only about 100,000 in 1939 (significantly less than the prewar Socialist Party), the institutional influence of Communist-oriented radicals, through alliances with New Deal liberals in reform and social protest movements, in which such radicals routinely fought racism, was far greater than that of any other radical movement since the antebellum abolitionists.

The German-Soviet Non-Aggression Pact of 1939 weakened the Communist movement and undermined the liberal-radical alliances that had characterized progressive politics in the late 1930s. The Communists pointed to Neville Chamberlain's appeasement of Hitler at Munich in 1938 and his complete failure to join the Soviets in supporting the Spanish Republic against Generalissimo Francisco Franco's Fascist forces as evidence that the European

non-Fascist capitalist states were appeasing Nazi Germany in order to allow Hitler to destroy the Soviet Union, thus necessitating the pact. Communist opposition to Roosevelt's military preparedness program around the slogan "The Yanks Are Not Coming" destroyed Communist credibility among many New Deal liberals. The CPUSA's position also led to a wide variety of attacks on Communists in the unions and on many of the organizations in which they had played leading roles as organizers and activists, like the National Negro Congress.

Nonetheless, the Communists maintained their focus on antiracist campaigns in the unions and communities and, in line with Communist parties throughout the world, became more militant critics of global colonialism. (In the late 1930s, Communist campaigns against colonialism in Europe and North America had been muted as Communists worked to build support for anti-Nazi collective security alliances with the British and French empires, the largest colonial empires in the world.). As the war began in the autumn of 1939, early Axis victories accelerated the New Deal's rearmament program, leading Roosevelt to provide aid to an encircled Britain after the German conquest of Western Europe, institute the nation's first peacetime draft, and define U.S. policy so as to transform the United States into an "Arsenal for Democracy." By the winter of 1941, as Roosevelt had established a lend-lease program to provide direct aid to keep Britain in the war, A. Philip Randolph's threatened March on Washington led to Executive Order 8802—abolishing discrimination in the new defense industries and establishing the FEPC.

BLACKS IN THE NORTH

Black migration to the North, which dipped from its 1920s highs to 349,000 in the 1930s, now rose sharply again as the war industries began to open. Of the 1.5 million blacks who came north in the 1940s, more than three-fourths would settle in the industrial Northeast, Middle West, and California, whose industrial base and population grew rapidly during and after the war. More than 500,000 of these migrants were to become members of the new, inclusive CIO industrial unions. As the war and Cold War economies strengthened conservative politics generally and the Republican Party particularly, African-American voters in the urban North were to become crucial to the success of the Democratic Party, making Franklin D. Roosevelt's policy of juggling the interests of Northern liberals and Southern segregationists impossible to sustain in the long run. In the process, the

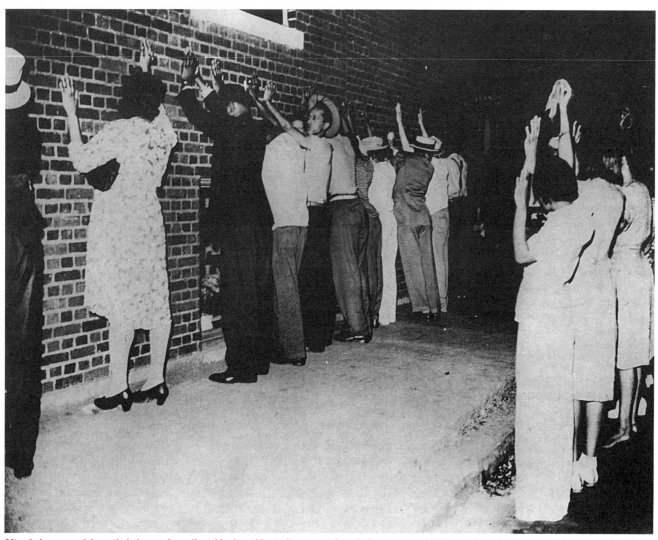

After being gassed from their homes by police, black residents line up against their apartment building in Detroit. The city's race riot of June 1943 proved the bloodiest domestic uprising of World War II, leading to thirty-four deaths. President Franklin D. Roosevelt declared a state of emergency and sent 6,000 soldiers to restore order. *(Brown Brothers)*

combined labor movement, which had fewer than 3 million members in 1933, reached nearly 15 million in 1945, a fivefold increase. Black membership, which was about 150,000 at the start of the New Deal, had reached 1,250,000 by the end of the war, a nearly tenfold increase.

More than 3 million black males were to register for the draft, and more than 500,000 were to be stationed abroad, serving in a military that remained segregated, as it had been since free blacks were barred from joining the army in the administration of George Washington. More than 1 million black men and women entered industrial labor, producing most dramatically racist wildcat strikes among white work-

ers, particularly white migrants from the South. In 1943, as war production mounted, more than 250 wildcat strikes and violent outbreaks of whites attacking blacks took place. In Detroit, a major riot occurred in June, which cost the lives of twenty-five blacks and nine whites. In Philadelphia in 1944, a wildcat strike on the cities' streetcars against the introduction of black conductors led the administration to send 5,000 troops to defend the rights of the black employees and keep the public transportation system working.

Yet, the fierce racist backlash, and the polls showing that large numbers of Northern whites were indifferent to segregation and believed that blacks were responsible for their own problems, belied important wartime progress. First of all, civil rights protests against "normal racism" were growing, from condemnations of the Red Cross policy of separating blood donations by race to the organization of support groups made up of servicemen's wives, both white and black, to oppose discrimination on military bases. In the industrial unions of the CIO, left militants fought more actively to promote blacks into leadership positions, contending that only an integrated leadership could seriously reflect an integrated membership and eliminate long-established racist practices. These campaigns initiated in limited form the ideas and policies that would be picked up by the civil rights movement in the 1950s and would come to be called affirmative action.

NEW DEAL FOR WHOM?

Membership in the NAACP, which had been only 50,000 in 1940, grew to 450,000 by the end of the war, marking a spectacular increase in the direct involvement of blacks in civil rights activities. In 1942, a new, more militant civil rights organization, the Congress of Racial Equality (CORE), was established, committing itself to the tactics of "nonviolent direct action" associated with Mohandas Gandhi and the Indian national independence movement. Launching sit-ins at de facto segregated theaters and restaurants in the North, CORE was initially sponsored by the Fellowship of Reconciliation (a Christian pacifist social action group led by the Reverend A.J. Muste, the Christian Socialist and pacifist active earlier in Depression protests). Although the group remained small and was to suffer from the reaction against all forms of militant political action in the early Cold War years, CORE would become a major force in the Northern civil rights movement of the 1960s. The tactics it pioneered were to be developed by Martin Luther King Jr. in leading the main battle against Southern segregation in the 1950s and 1960s.

The "Double V" campaign, which the African-American newspaper the *Pittsburgh Courier* declared in early 1942, reunited the liberals and radicals of the 1930s on a program to "defeat Hitler, Mussolini, and Hirohito by Enforcing the Constitution and Abolishing Jim Crow." A two-front war against the Fascist Axis abroad and American racism at home made powerful sense, since racism was clearly a major part of the enemy's ideological arsenal. One cartoon set in a redneck Southern byway summed it up perfectly: "Hitler doesn't like Negroes either."

In the South itself, New Deal politician Ellis Arnall was elected governor of Georgia, a state previously dominated by the race-baiting Tallmadges, and the militant labor liberal politician Claude Pepper of Florida served as a harbinger of possible alternatives to conservative coalition segregationist politicians. In *Smith v. Allwright* (1944), the U.S. Supreme Court, in response to civil rights challenges, abolished the white primary, thus establishing the possibility that blacks in areas of the upper South who had sustained the right to vote could now influence the Democratic Party. Also, blacks joined with white Southern opponents of segregation to form the liberal Southern Regional Council, committed to reform the oppressive aspects of Jim Crow policy and gradually remove segregation from Southern life.

It is true that most Southern New Deal politicians avoided direct opposition to segregation, as did Roosevelt himself. Roosevelt associated segregation in the South with economic backwardness, and so he looked to the region's economic development, stimulated by the expansion of such programs as the Tennessee Valley Authority, as the long-term solution to all of its problems.

Yet the president's many concessions to powerful Southern Democrats during his administration undermined even this policy. State differentials in minimum wages and unemployment benefits, largely tolerated to enable such legislation to get through congressional committees chaired by Southern Democrats, kept Southern labor cheap. Although the Southern labor movement made significant gains in the 1930s and 1940s, it lagged well behind the national labor movement, given both the lower level of industrialization and urbanization and the force of both segregation and right-wing Bible Belt religious influence in supporting both police and vigilante violence against union organizers and strikers.

The contradictions within New Deal policy could be seen most forcefully when the conservative coalition in Congress forced the resignation of Farm Security Administration (FSA) director Clarence Benham "Beanie" Baldwin for allegedly permitting FSA funds to be used to help blacks and poor whites pay their poll tax. Baldwin, an ardently antiracist Southern white and a champion of labor–civil rights alliances, became the director the CIO's new Political Action Committee, which had been established to fight against the conservative coalition's attempt to use the war situation to undermine the gains made by both the New Deal and labor.

As the war entered its final phase, moving toward the total defeat of the Fascist Axis, the war against Jim Crow and its supporters remained far more problematical. Franklin Roosevelt, who had de-emphasized New Deal social commitments in favor of a "win-the-war" unity policy, seemed to return to Depression-era militancy when on the eve of the 1944 presidential campaign he called for a "new bill of rights." Dubbed the Economic Bill of Rights by the press, this legislation would provide employment, education, housing, and health care as fundamental citizenship rights.

Meanwhile, an alliance of Northern machine and Southern conservative Democrats struck at the New Deal by seeking to oust from the national ticket in 1944 Roosevelt's vice president, Henry A. Wallace, who had spoken against the 1943 riot in Detroit and had clearly made civil rights, along with strengthening labor and maintaining cooperation with the Soviet Union, central to the administration's postwar policy. Although both the CIO and the NAACP strongly supported Wallace, with Roosevelt's reluctant approval, he was replaced with Senator Harry Truman of Missouri, a compromise candidate whose record made him acceptable to all factions, including regular Democrats, labor, and civil rights supporters. (Truman, a machine Democrat, had cultivated African-American support in his Senate campaigns.)

Before he left the vice presidency to assume the position of secretary of commerce, Henry Wallace reflected a common theme among New Dealers that the war was revolutionizing the world and that the United States could not safely move right while the rest of the world was moving left. Seeing the revolutionary movements struggling for social justice as worthy of support, Wallace warned that a policy of "force without justice"—a return to the old imperialism abroad and pre–New Deal politics at home, which conservative publisher Henry Luce had called for in 1941 in his advocacy of an "American Century"— "would make us into everything we have hated in the Nazis."

AMERICAN RACISM ON A WORLD STAGE

Revelations in 1945 that the Nazis' racist anti-Semitism had resulted in genocide—the murder of more than 6 million European Jews, nearly two-thirds of Europe's Jewish population and more than one-third of the Jewish population of the world, stood as stark testimony to the effects of institutional and ideological racism. Although England and France sought to reestablish their colonial empires as far as they could, greatly expanded resistance movements in the colonies along with the colonial powers' economic and political decline made that impossible. France

withdrew from its Near Eastern colonies by the end of the war and began a policy of withdrawing from its African colonies, although it fought long, disastrously unsuccessful colonial wars in Indochina and Algeria in the postwar era. By 1947, England withdrew from India, its most important, and the world's largest, colony, and over the next two decades it would relinquish its Near Eastern and African colonies as well. After initially attempting to restore their Indonesian empire, the Dutch withdrew in 1948. In its wake, colonialism left wars without end between Jewish settlers and Arabic populations and states in Palestine; Muslim separatists and defenders of a united India on the Indian subcontinent; and fierce conflicts between those elites installed by the retreating colonial powers and their rivals. However, the doctrines of European and white supremacy, and the interrelated "scientific racism" that had remained respectable in the prewar era, were now at least in the open; these sentiments were associated with fringe elements, neo-Nazis, colonialist diehards, and white settler dictatorships in Rhodesia and South Africa, and American segregationists by the middle 1950s.

Although the U.S. government's involvement in fighting the Cold War would make many of these groups its unofficial allies, the Cold War pushed U.S. policy in two contradictory ways—toward supporting and strengthening rightist racist elements in the South and internationally in the name of global anti-Communism, and toward recognition that the anti-racist credentials of its Soviet and Communist rivals were far more appealing to the world's nonwhite majority than its defense of a "Western free world alliance" of the former colonial and Axis powers, much less its own policies of segregation. Nonwhites, because of the American segregation model, could not be effectively portrayed simultaneously as indivisible and as demonizing minorities in Africa, Asia, and Latin America, where they were the overwhelming majority. By the middle 1950s, the rise of an "Afro-Asian bloc" in the new United Nations, defining itself formally as a loose association of "nonaligned nations" and informally as a "Third World" (outside the U.S.- and Soviet-led European blocs and including both capitalist-oriented nations and the new People's Republic of China), highlighted these problems and provided some political space for a civil rights movement to grow in spite of far-reaching Cold War repression.

The early Cold War years were to set back the movement for civil rights by targeting many of its most militant defenders, black and white, as agents of the new Soviet and Communist enemy. The right-wing slogan "every liberal is a Socialist, every Socialist is a Communist, every Communist is Moscow's spy" was an example of the mind-set that, with the coming of the Korean War and the emergence of Senator Joseph McCarthy in 1950, would transform the antiradicalism of the post–World War I Red Scare and the conservative coalition's House Un-American Activities Committee into a long-term system of institutionalized political exclusion modeled after segregation.

BLACKS IN THE ANTI-COMMUNIST ERA

As a result, the center–left alliance in labor and government that had nurtured the civil rights movement of the 1930s and 1940s was largely shattered. The first defeat civil rights forces suffered was congressional elimination, with the end of the war, of the Fair Employment Practices Commission, which all civil rights activists fought to make permanent. A wave of lynchings and other attacks against returning African-American servicemen in the South was met by demonstrations in Washington (which J. Edgar Hoover, in reports to President Truman, attributed to Communist activity). When Paul Robeson, a world-renowned scholar, singer, and actor, led a delegation to the White House to protest the racial violence in the South and the elimination of FEPC, he was met coldly by President Truman, who told him that he and all blacks should remain loyal to the "democracy" of the United States and Britain. When Robeson responded that Britain at that very moment was depriving hundreds of millions of Indians of their democratic rights, the president angrily walked out.

Inflation, strikes, and Truman's failing leadership permitted anti–New Deal Republicans to win control of both houses of Congress in 1946, the first time that they had done so since 1928. Over President Truman's veto, they passed the Taft-Hartley Act (1947), a series of amendments to the National Labor Relations Act of 1935, which substantially tilted the act back toward employers and enabled states to in effect enact anti-union shop "right-to-work" laws that would greatly restrict organizing drives. The act also barred Communists from holding union office and called upon all union officials, from shop steward on up, to annually sign an affidavit that they were not members of the Communist Party.

The effect of the Taft-Hartley law, upheld by the courts over the years except for its crudely unconstitutional anti-Communist clause (the Communist Party

PAUL ROBESON   (1898–1976)

The son of a runaway slave who became a minister, Robeson was born in Princeton, New Jersey, on April 9, 1898. Only the third black student to attend Rutgers University, he graduated first from Rutgers in 1919, where he was an All-American football player and class valedictorian, and then from Columbia University law school in 1923. He married Eslanda Goode, who urged him to pursue acting.

With a resonant voice and the ability to project a humane spirit, Robeson won roles that were previously off-limits to blacks. He garnered wide acclaim with his creation of the title role on stage in Eugene O'Neill's *Emperor Jones* in 1923; he later starred in the film version (1933). Other outstanding dramatic performances include Crown in DuBose Heyward's *Porgy* (1928) and *Othello* (in London, 1930, and New York, 1943–1944). In 1925, he made his debut as a concert singer. Possessing a magnificent bass voice, he became known especially for his rendition of "Ol' Man River" in Jerome Kern's play *Show Boat* in 1926 (and a decade later in the film) and for his interpretations of spirituals.

Increasingly frustrated with the racism he faced even as a popular entertainer, Robeson turned to political involvement. In the 1930s, he developed an interest in Pan-Africanism. Then, following a series of visits to the Soviet Union, where he first felt free of racism, he formed close ties with American Communists in part because of their campaign for equal rights for black Americans. Robeson's widely publicized criticisms of the Truman administration's Cold War policies, his association with Communist causes, and his winning of the International Stalin Peace Prize in 1952 made him a controversial figure in the United States during the McCarthy-era repression. At one point, the U.S. State Department suspended his passport, preventing him from traveling abroad. He quickly paid the price for his candor and could not find work in the United States. After his passport was returned, he moved to England in 1958 and continued to appear in concerts in Europe and the Soviet Union. He returned to live in the United States in 1963 but remained largely out of the public eye until his death on January 23, 1976.

James G. Lewis

was technically legal, and the affidavit constituted a bill of attainder against its members), was to both contain the labor movement and undermine its relationship to civil rights activists.

In the CIO, the act stimulated anti-Communist purges, which would remove those most committed to integrated inclusionary unionism, both black and white. In addition, Southern states were quick to adopt "right-to-work" laws, and the CIO, which had prepared for an ambitious Southern organizing drive, abandoned that drive in 1948, leaving Southern black and white labor very weak. Federal Bureau of Investigation (FBI) agents now began asking government employees whether they owned Paul Robeson records, and anyone who was a member of a civil rights group was placed on the lists that the HUAC, the FBI, and a variety of business and veterans organizations were circulating and cross-referencing. As a result, black militants in labor and their white radical allies found themselves fighting to defend their own civil rights to engage in political action as much as to extend civil rights in the larger society. As an example of the changing political climate, Coleman Young, who had distinguished himself as combat pilot in the segregated army air corps flying unit the Tuskegee Airmen during the war, found himself a victim of the Taft-Hartley-induced purge of radicals in the Michigan state CIO in 1948. Decades later, Young would become Detroit's first African-American mayor. Overwhelmingly, African-American activists were disproportionately the targets of the labor purges and blacklists. Although many would continue to struggle and eventually make comebacks, in the 1950s they constituted a "political lost generation" unable to provide direct and open leadership to the new civil rights movement they continued to support.

The early postwar era saw a significant erosion of black economic gains. During the war, as the incomes of the general workforce increased sharply, per capita black income rose from 40 percent of white income in 1940 to 60 percent in 1945, only to drop significantly in the postwar era. Twenty years later, at the dawn of the Great Society's War on Poverty and civil rights legislation, it was 54 percent of white income.

Yet, some gains would be sustained. By 1946, there were more than two dozen blacks serving in various Northern and even some border state legislatures. Truman continued Roosevelt's policy of appointing some blacks to high-profile positions, most importantly William Hastie, who was appointed U.S. governor of the Virgin Islands in 1946. Ralph Bunche,

a founder of the National Negro Congress, served in State Department and United Nations capacities for the U.S. government. Furthermore, the president established a national commission to study race relations. Strongly influenced by antiracist ideals and staffed by both African-American and white social scientists, the commission's 1947 Report, *To Secure These Rights*, was the most advanced statement in defense of equal citizenship rights ever taken by an official U.S. government group. In the South, with border state and upper South communities playing the leading role, the number of blacks registered in the South rose from 2 percent in 1940 to 12 percent in 1947.

Black teachers in Florida, Alabama, Virginia, and Arkansas had also won decisions in federal courts, overturning unequal public school pay schedules for black and white teachers in segregated school systems. The huge increase in unionized black workers went hand in hand with a substantial increase in the funding of black education, and black school attendance improved significantly. As early as 1946, the U.S. Supreme Court ruled that segregated interstate bus carriers, mandated by state law in the South, were not constitutional.

CONSERVATIVE FORCES

In the early postwar period, it was possible, but very difficult, to launch major attacks against both de jure and de facto segregation in the economy and the larger society through protests, union actions, and legislation. African-American activists in the North and their labor and progressive allies were in place to carry forward such campaigns against a collapsing system of Southern segregation in the midst of a global antiracist upsurge. The purges in labor and in the general society inspired by the Cold War would blunt these campaigns for the greater part of a decade and by the mid-1950s would change the nature of civil rights activism by taking leadership away from Northern urban labor and political activists and giving it to Southern black ministers.

The story of Coleman Young's struggle to continue to fight for civil rights generally and to defend himself from McCarthyism was repeated thousands of times in the late 1940s and early 1950s as trade union and mass protest activists found themselves on a variety of blacklists and as an anti-Communist political consensus took a heavy toll. Except for the end of segregation in the military, the U.S. government would not implement any recommendation of Truman's special commission until the 1960s.

By the end of 1947, Communists, other radicals, and alienated popular front liberals launched a campaign to challenge the Truman administration, its Cold War orientation, and its failures to advance New Deal policies domestically, outside of the Democratic Party.

This campaign resulted in the creation of the Progressive Party, which ran former vice president Henry Wallace and Senator Glen Taylor of Idaho for president and vice president, respectively. The Progressive Party actively challenged segregation in the Deep South, as its members braved assaults and arrests for holding integrated meetings. Many observers believe that in response to the Progressive Party, which made full racial equality a major campaign issue, the liberal Democrats were able to put a strong civil rights plank into the Democratic Party platform in 1948. This move sparked a walkout by Southern segregationists, who proceeded to nominate Governor Strom Thurmond of South Carolina and Governor Fielding Wright of Mississippi for president and vice president, respectively, and made the constitutional defense of segregation their major campaign theme. The challenge of the Progressive Party also encouraged the Truman administration to respond to A. Philip Randolph, who, though strongly opposed to the Progressive Party, had created the Committee Against Jim Crow in Military Service and Training in 1947. With Randolph threatening to lead a march on Washington (as he had against discrimination in the defense industries in 1941), Truman issued an executive order integrating the armed services—an order that would initially be resisted by many in the military, including General and later President Dwight D. Eisenhower, and not really implemented until the Korean War.

The defeat of the Progressive Party, which garnered a little more than 1 million votes, and Truman's surprise election, intensified the political purges and blacklists already in existence and led the administration to largely abandon the domestic program that it had run on, including support for civil rights legislation, in order to gain support for the North Atlantic Treaty Organization (NATO) military alliance and other policies expanding the Cold War. Although supporters of the Progressive Party were especially targeted by the blacklists and both Henry Wallace and Glen Taylor were driven from political life, Strom Thurmond and many of his Dixiecrat supporters would be welcomed back into the Democratic Party. By 1952, the Democrats had nominated John Sparkman of Alabama, both a moderate New Dealer and a segregationist, for vice president, and substantially weakened its 1948 civil rights plank.

CIVIL RIGHTS AND RACIST VIOLENCE

The NAACP supported the Truman administration and, in actively withdrawing from its wartime militancy, lost many of its younger activists. When CORE launched a Journey of Reconciliation to challenge segregation on interstate busses in the South, the NAACP gave it no support and the Freedom Ride of eight whites and eight blacks was harassed by Southern authorities and not publicized in the media. Conservative NAACP president Walter White also barred members of the national staff (a majority of whom supported the Progressive Party campaign) from open advocacy of the Wallace campaign and ousted W.E.B. Du Bois, the organization's most prominent African-American founder, as research director for his support of the Progressive Party in 1948. In the face of mounting racist violence in the North, the NAACP counseled moderation, soft-pedaled criticism of the Truman administration, and focused exclusively on its legal challenges to Southern segregation.

The late 1940s also saw a rising tide of racist violence as KKK organizing grew in the North in response to the black migration. When Paul Robeson, who had been a leading supporter of the Progressive Party in 1948, was alleged to have said at an International Peace Conference in Paris, of which Communists were the most important initiators, that American blacks would not "fight" for the United States in a war against the Soviet Union, he faced a firestorm of criticism in the United States and had his passport seized in 1950. The U.S. government even barred his going to Canada, where a passport was not required. When Robeson sought to sing at a concert to raise funds for the Civil Rights Congress at Peekskill, New York, in 1949, threats of violence forced a postponement. Subsequently, with thousands of members of left-led New York City labor unions working security, the concert was held. However, New York State police barred concert security from protecting the concertgoers, whose busses were attacked by racist mobs as they left. Connecting rabid racism and Cold War anti-Communism, the Peekskill riot, which New York State blamed on the concert organizers, was seen by many as a coming of lynch law, if not Fascism, to the North.

With the coming of the Korean War, attacks against both black and white radicals intensified. W.E.B. Du Bois, the most prominent African-American scholar in the nation for nearly half a century, found himself arrested and handcuffed at the age of eighty-two by federal agents for his involvement in an anti–Korean War organization, which the government considered "an agent of a foreign power" (the Soviet Union). Although international protests finally led the government to drop the charges, Du Bois's passport was lifted and his books were systematically removed from libraries across the country. The African-American press, black colleges in the South, and the NAACP generally supported the purges of black activists, failing to defend either Du Bois or Robeson, and fired suspected radicals within their own ranks. Attempts by blacklisted African-American trade unionists to organize a National Negro Labor Council in 1951 to revive the militancy of the 1930s and 1940s would also become a casualty of Cold War political repression. Perhaps the most telling act of discrimination involved Henry Winston, an African American who was one of the national leaders of the Communist Party convicted of "conspiring to teach or advocate the violent overthrow of the government" under the Smith Act. Winston lost his eyesight when prison officials, ignoring repeated protests from his family and attorneys, denied him medical treatment until it was too late. Benjamin Davis, an African American, former New York City councilman, and another Smith Act political prisoner, was placed in a specially segregated unit at the federal prison at Terre Haute, Indiana, in spite of legal protests.

The history of the Civil Rights Congress (CRC), a Communist-led group created through a merger of the International Labor Defense, the defunct National Negro Congress, and a small National Federation of Constitutional Liberties group in 1946, highlighted the Cold War political climate. Seeking to revive the mass protests of the 1930s, the CRC spent much of its time fighting attempts by HUAC, the FBI, and the Subversive Activities Control Board (created by the McCarran Internal Security Act of 1950) to destroy it. In its most famous case, one that was reminiscent of Scottsboro, the CRC launched an international campaign to defend Willie McGee, a Mississippi truck driver accused of raping a married white woman. Although there was important evidence that McGee had been having a consensual affair with the woman, who cried rape when her husband discovered the affair, he was nevertheless executed in the political atmosphere that reigned during the Cold War. The CRC played a more positive role in the defense of the Trenton Six, African-American youths accused of murdering a white secondhand store owner in Trenton, New Jersey.

Although police had held the youths for days without any access to attorneys and had threatened to use "truth serum" and other forms of coercion to force confessions from them, they were convicted and sentenced to death. While New Jersey judicial authorities removed CRC attorneys from the appeals, the campaign for the Trenton Six eventually produced a new trial at which three were acquitted and, in a bizarre Cold War compromise, the others convicted with a jury recommendation for early parole. Disbanded in 1956 in part in response to intensified government harassment stemming from the Communist Control Act of 1954, even in its last year the CRC was to play a significant role in 1955 in mobilizing African-American communities to protest the murder of Emmit Till, a Chicago teenager bludgeoned to death while visiting relatives in Mississippi because he was heard saying "hey, baby" to a white female store clerk.

Disowned publicly by the NAACP, in the early 1950s the CRC filed a study, *We Charge Genocide*, with the United Nations detailing the immiseration and oppression of African Americans. Although mainstream media in the United States either ignored or condemned the study, it was published in many languages and was received sympathetically in many quarters, including non-Communist, nonradical circles, in the countries emerging from colonialism.

McCarthyism was at high tide as the Korean War ended in 1953, and the new Eisenhower administration seemed completely oblivious to civil rights questions—so much so that the U.S. government refused to sign the United Nations Covenant against Genocide, responding to the fears of segregationists that it might somehow be used to interfere with segregation. Both domestic and international developments, however, would soon see a revival of civil rights activities.

RETURN OF CIVIL RIGHTS ACTIVISM

The NAACP's long-term legal campaign against segregation would bear fruit in the U.S. Supreme Court's 1954 *Brown v. Board of Education* decision, which barred school segregation, and, in principle, segregation generally, as inherently unequal. The emergence of the new nations of Africa and Asia made U.S. segregation and racism front-page news and constituted a continuing reproach to U.S. attempts to portray its foreign policy as a defense of "freedom and democracy." Federal court decisions compelled a reluctant Eisenhower administration to "enforce" the law of the land against segregationist obstructionism and violence. The postwar repression had created a political vacuum in many Northern black communities; the vacuum would be filled counterproductively by the black separatist group the Nation of Islam (Black Muslims), which nevertheless would continue to develop through the 1950s in the North. The growing urban black populations would begin to address such questions as substandard housing and police brutality, with calls for police civilian review boards and demands for the appointment of blacks to police forces and the judiciary.

In 1955, Rosa Parks, a secretary in Montgomery, Alabama, long involved in civil rights activities, would in effect continue the civil rights movement of the 1930s and 1940s when she refused to sit at the back of a segregated bus, sparking what was in effect a mass strike or boycott against the bus system of the city. E.D. Nixon, a veteran organizer for A. Philip Randolph's Brotherhood of Sleeping Car Porters and representing a community without either elected political leaders or an effective labor movement, convinced a young black minister, Martin Luther King Jr., to serve as the rallying point and spokesperson for the boycott. The boycott's success would usher in a revitalized civil rights movement which, within a decade, would not only destroy de jure segregation in the South, but would also stir up a politics of mass protest that seemed to have been dissipated by the Cold War.

Norman Markowitz

BIBLIOGRAPHY

Anderson, Jervis. *A. Philip Randolph: A Biographical Portrait.* Berkeley: University of California Press, 1986.

Duberman, Martin. *Paul Robeson.* New York: New Press, 1996.

Foner, Philip S. *Organized Labor and the Black Worker.* New York: International Publishers, 1973.

Foner, Philip S., ed. *Paul Robeson Speaks.* New York: Citadel Press, 1982.

Ginger, Ann Fagan, and David Christiano, eds. *Cold War Against Labor.* 2 vols. Berkeley, CA: Meiklejohn Civil Liberties Institute, 1987.

Goodman, James. *Stories of Scottsboro.* New York: Pantheon Books, 1994.

Horne, Gerald. *Black Liberation/Red Scare: Ben Davis and the Communist Party.* London: Associated University Presses, 1994.

———. *Communist Front? The Civil Rights Congress, 1946–1956.* London: Associated University Presses, 1988.

Kelley, Robin D.G. *"Hammer and Hoe" Alabama Communists During the Depression.* Chapel Hill: University of North Carolina Press, 1990.

Lawson, Steven F. *Black Ballots: Voting Rights in the South, 1944–1969.* New York: Columbia University Press, 1977.

Layton, Azza Salama. *International Politics and Civil Rights Policies in the United States, 1941–1960.* Cambridge: Cambridge University Press, 2000.

Lewis, David Levering. *W.E.B. Du Bois.* Vol. 2. New York: Henry Holt, 2000.

———. *When Harlem Was in Vogue.* New York: Oxford University Press, 1981.

Marable, Manning. *Race, Reform, and Rebellion.* Jackson: University of Mississippi Press, 1991.

Meier, August, and Elliott Rudwick. *CORE; A Study in the Civil Rights Movement, 1942–1968.* New York: Oxford University Press, 1973.

Naison, Mark. *Communists in Harlem During the Depression.* Urbana: University of Illinois Press, 1983.

Robeson, Paul. *Here I Stand.* Boston: Beacon, 1958.

Sitkoff, Harvard. *A New Deal for Blacks: The Emergence of Civil Rights as a National Issue.* New York: Oxford University Press, 1978.

Urquhart, Brian. *Ralph Bunche: An American Life.* New York: W.W. Norton, 1993.

Weiss, Nancy J. *Farewell to the Party of Lincoln: Black Politics in the Age of FDR.* Princeton, NJ: Princeton University Press, 1983.

Zangrando, Robert. *The NAACP and the Crusade Against Lynching: 1909–1950.* Philadelphia: Temple University Press, 1980.

CIVIL RIGHTS MOVEMENT 1954–1970

The years between 1954 and 1970 stand as a legacy in the history of social movements. During these years, the civil rights movement mobilized African Americans on a national scale, wrenching from the federal government ground-breaking legislation and support. African Americans elevated themselves out of second-class citizenship in the United States, winning legal equality with whites and bringing the races closer to social and economic equality than ever before. By 1970, the movement had asserted a positive self-identity for African Americans, grounded in bonds of ancestry and experience. Using political and economic tactics of devastating efficiency, the civil rights movement destroyed legal segregation and discrimination in the United States. Social movements have mimicked its tactics ever since. The movement wrought such great change, especially in the South, that participants and witnesses hailed it as a second Reconstruction.

The numbers and status of African Americans helped make the movement possible. In 1950, the African-American population totaled 15.8 million; by 1960, it was 19 million, just above 10 percent of the entire U.S. population. The slow development of an African-American middle class helped as well: college students made up one of the more innovative and resourceful groups of the movement. The shape of discrimination had also changed. As the 1940s ended, lynchings in the South became less common. Jim Crow laws remained, drawing a barrier between the races which was crossed at one's peril. After lynchings began to disappear, these laws became the primary grievance of African Americans. Discrimination became less wrathful and more institutionalized, giving African Americans legal recourse against injustice. Before 1954, civil rights activism consisted mostly of the ideas and expressions of organizations and individuals. After 1954, events and actions against discrimination crashed like waves upon the United States.

The movement during this most important era consisted of two phases. From 1954 to 1965 the movement, located primarily in the South, sought true integration in the United States, aiming to remove race as an advantage or disadvantage for all people. The movement featured an interracial constituency seeking fairness from state governments, support from the federal government, and moral empathy from the public at large. As demands for equality outpaced social progress, the movement changed. After 1965, African-American activists became more militant, formulating as their goal an empowered African-American identity separate from white society.

THE MOVEMENT TAKES SHAPE 1954–1960

The *Brown* Decision

Near the middle of a decade often described as bland and conformist, the U.S. Supreme Court announced a landmark decision that helped to spawn the civil rights revolution. Since 1896 segregation had ruled the South, curtailing the political, economic, and social rights of African Americans. Jim Crow laws enforced these restrictions on freedom. Segregation was justified by the Court's ruling in *Plessy v. Ferguson* (1896) that "separate-but-equal" facilities satisfied the demands of the Fourteenth Amendment's equal protection clause. Whites and African Americans used separate water fountains, bathrooms, restaurants, and schools in the South. African Americans enjoyed few, if any, voting rights. The unanimous *Brown v. Board of Education of Topeka* decision in May 1954 turned *Plessy* on its head, declaring segregation unconstitutional. A combined force of grassroots activists, lawyers from the National Association for the Advancement of Colored People (NAACP), and federal authority created the watershed decision, anticipating the structure of the mass civil rights movement that followed.

The U.S. Supreme Court case known as *Brown v.*

Board of Education began as five separate lawsuits against segregated schools in various parts of the country. These lawsuits initially argued that the separate, black-only schools compared miserably to much better-funded white schools. During the 1940s, Southern states spent four times as much on white schools as they did on African-American schools. In addition, teachers at white schools were paid 30 percent more than teachers at African-American schools; this disparity in spending severely limited African Americans' education. In Clarendon County, South Carolina, young African Americans had to walk miles to school as the state refused to provide them with a school bus. Once at school, the students crowded into a tiny, dark room. There they awaited their turn for instruction, as only one or two teachers had to teach several classes at once. African-American students across the South faced similarly stifling conditions. Later, the NAACP would focus on *Plessy* and attack the doctrine of segregation itself.

Gradually, African-American communities took action against segregationist school boards. Encouraged by the NAACP, African-American parents in Clarendon braved harassment from local whites and filed a lawsuit to fight for decent schools. In Farmville, Virginia, sixteen-year-old Barbara Johns called for a student strike in protest of the local school board's refusal to provide adequate educational resources. The strike began on April 23, 1951, when Johns lured the school's principal off campus with a diversionary phone call. This spontaneous movement soon turned into another NAACP lawsuit against segregated schools. In Topeka, Kansas, segregation dictated that Oliver Brown send his eight-year-old daughter to an all-black school more than twenty blocks from his house. When Brown tried to register his daughter at the white-only school just seven blocks from his home, she was denied. Brown then sued the state board of education. Later, the NAACP combined these suits and two others from Washington, D.C., and Delaware into the *Brown v. Board of Education* that it presented before the U.S. Supreme Court.

Decades before *Brown*, the NAACP had begun a concerted effort aimed at tearing down school segregation. The organization chose the Fourteenth Amendment as its main weapon. Led by civil rights lawyer Thurgood Marshall, the NAACP first targeted graduate schools. In 1936, Marshall and his mentor, Charles Houston, won a lawsuit integrating the University of Maryland law school. After World War II, the pace of desegregating graduate schools increased. In *Sweatt v. Painter* (1950), the U.S. Supreme Court ordered the desegregation of the University of Texas law school on the grounds that the school's prestige and resources made it vastly superior to—and thus unequal with—any of the black-only law schools hastily built by the state.

With the *Sweatt* ruling as precedent, Marshall and other NAACP lawyers presented the *Brown* case to the U.S. Supreme Court in December 1952. Although past rulings, including *Sweatt, had* resulted in desegregated graduate schools, attorneys had avoided challenging the basic premise of *Plessy*. During the *Brown* arguments, however, Marshall charged that segregated schools were inherently unequal, independent of actual resources. To support this claim, NAACP lawyers presented psychological evidence gathered by social scientists, proving that young African Americans in segregated schools suffered low self-esteem.

The Court took no action on the case for nine months. Justice Felix Frankfurter delayed a decision, hoping to eventually produce a unanimous verdict, which he felt would be easier to enforce. Chief Justice Fred Vinson, who Frankfurter considered a barrier to a unanimous decision, died suddenly in September 1953. President Dwight Eisenhower replaced Vinson with California governor Earl Warren who, to the president's chagrin, immediately endeavored to make the *Brown* decision a unanimous one overturning *Plessy*. On May 17, 1954, the U.S. Supreme Court ruled nine to zero, declaring "We conclude, unanimously, that in the field of public education the doctrine of 'separate but equal' has no place."

The Court's decision proved easier to declare than to enforce. The decision ordered states to comply with "all deliberate speed," a vague reference that, combined with Eisenhower's refusal to endorse the decision, resulted in uneven, reluctant, and often elusive desegregation. Schools in Kansas, Missouri, West Virginia, Maryland, and Delaware quickly desegregated, while the states of the Deep South took a stand of "massive resistance" against the ruling. Officials in some Virginia counties chose to close their schools for years rather than desegregate. Although massive resistance was clearly unconstitutional, it was also time-consuming to challenge and overturn. Thus, by the late 1950s, many Southern schools remained segregated in fact if not by law. The ruling nevertheless created momentum to integrate not just schools, but public places across the South. As pressure to integrate escalated, so did resistance, culminating in a military "invasion" of Little Rock, Arkansas. Before this confrontation, two events in the Deep South galvanized African Americans against the injustices of

BROWN V. BOARD OF EDUCATION OF TOPEKA (1954)

The U.S. Supreme Court ruled in Brown v. Board of Education of Topeka *(1954) that racial segregation based on the principle of "separate but equal" violated the U.S. Constitution's equal protection and due process provisions. Subsequently, racial segregation in public places was ruled illegal. Though legally not permissible, racial segregation continues through discriminatory practices that evade the spirit of the law.*

The plaintiffs contend that segregated public schools are not "equal" and cannot be made "equal," and that hence they are deprived of the equal protection of the laws. Because of the obvious importance of the question presented, the Court took jurisdiction. Argument was heard in the 1952 Term, and reargument was heard this Term on certain questions propounded by the Court.

Reargument was largely devoted to the circumstances surrounding the adoption of the Fourteenth Amendment in 1868. It covered exhaustively consideration of the Amendment in Congress, ratification by the states, then existing practices in racial segregation, and the views of proponents and opponents of the Amendment. This discussion and our own investigation convince us that, although these sources cast some light, it is not enough to resolve the problem with which we are faced. At best, they are inconclusive. The most avid proponents of the post-War Amendments undoubtedly intended them to remove all legal distinctions among "all persons born or naturalized in the United States." Their opponents, just as certainly, were antagonistic to both the letter and the spirit of the Amendments and wished them to have the most limited effect. What others in Congress and the state legislatures had in mind cannot be determined with any degree of certainty.

An additional reason for the inconclusive nature of the Amendment's history, with respect to segregated schools, is the status of public education at that time. In the South, the movement toward free common schools, supported by general taxation, had not yet taken hold. Education of white children was largely in the hands of private groups. Education of Negroes was almost nonexistent and practically all of the race were illiterate. In fact, any education of Negroes was forbidden by law in some states. Today, in contrast, many Negroes have achieved outstanding success in the arts and sciences as well as in the business and professional world. It is true that public school education at the time of the Amendment had advanced further in the North, but the effect of the Amendment on Northern States was generally ignored in the congressional debates. Even in the North, the conditions of public education did not approximate those existing today. The curriculum was usually rudimentary; ungraded schools were common in rural areas; the school term was but three months a year in many states; and compulsory school attendance was virtually unknown. As a consequence, it is not surprising that there should be so little in the history of the Fourteenth Amendment relating to its intended effect on public education.

In the first cases in this Court construing the Fourteenth Amendment, decided shortly after its adoption, the Court interpreted it as proscribing all state imposed discriminations against the Negro race. The doctrine of "separate but equal" did not make its appearance in this Court until 1896 in the case of *Plessy v. Ferguson* . . . involving not education but transportation.

In approaching this problem, we cannot turn the clock back to 1868 when the Amendment was adopted, or even to 1896 when *Plessy v. Ferguson* was written. We must consider public education in the light of its full development and its present place in American life throughout the Nation. Only in this way can it be determined if segregation in public schools deprives these plaintiffs of the equal protection of the laws.

Today, education is perhaps the most important function of state and local governments. Compulsory school attendance laws and the great expenditures for education both demonstrate our recognition of the importance of education to our democratic society. It is required in the performance of our most basic public responsibilities, even service in the armed forces. It is the very foundation of good citizenship. Today it is a principal instrument in awakening the child to cultural values, in preparing him for later professional training, and in helping him to adjust normally to his environment. In these days, it is doubtful that any child may reasonably be expected to succeed in life if he is denied the opportunity of an education. Such an opportunity, where the state has undertaken to provide it, is a right which must be made available to all on equal terms.

We come then to the question presented: Does segregation of children in the public schools solely on the basis of race, even though the physical facilities and other "tangible" factors may be equal, deprive the children of the minority group of equal educational opportunities? We believe that it does.

Source: Brown v. Board of Education of Topeka, *347 U.S. 483-96 (1954).*

Jim Crow, providing them with hope that change was possible and with the tactics to bring it about.

Emmett Till's Lynching

To residents of the Mississippi Delta, the historic *Brown* decision might as well have been announced on a different planet. In the Delta, among the nation's poorest areas, a rigid social hierarchy dominated white and black society during the 1950s. If an African-American male so much as glanced suggestively at a white woman, pride and caste dictated that he could expect a white gang to punish him. Mamie Till Bradley, an African American born in the Delta's desolate Tallahatchie County, Mississippi, moved to Chicago sometime before 1941 which, compared to Mississippi, stood as a paradise of equality. In Chicago, large African-American communities allowed young children to grow up free from the subservient nature of the residents of the Delta.

On July 25, 1941, Bradley gave birth to a son, Emmett Till, nicknamed "Bobo." In 1955, after completing the seventh grade, Till journeyed to Tallahatchie County in late August to visit relatives. Staying with his uncle, Moses Wright, the fourteen-year-old Till quickly earned a reputation among his country relatives as a dapper, cocky city-slicker, and the distant worlds of the South and North collided. Till showed his cousins a photograph of a white female, bragging that she was his girlfriend. Till's bravado thrilled and terrified his relatives, since such a willful violation of the color line would surely have meant death for any of them in Mississippi.

Perhaps emboldened by his relatives' amazement, Till accepted a dare that would soon lead to his death. Riding with cousins and friends on August 24 to the town of Money, Mississippi, the group arrived at a small grocery store owned by Roy and Carolyn Bryant, two white residents of the town. With Mrs. Bryant left alone tending the store, Till's friends dared him to approach her and ask for a date. Till accepted the challenge, though accounts vary on what exactly transpired in the store. Mrs. Bryant later testified that after asking for a date, Till grabbed her waist and said, "Don't be afraid of me, baby. I ain't gonna hurt you. I been with white girls before." Mrs. Bryant claimed she fetched a pistol and watched as Till snapped "Bye, baby," and whistled at her as he walked out the door. A witness outside the store claimed Till said nothing but "Bye, baby" during the entire exchange.

The specifics matter little, for Till had in any case violated the mores of the Deep South. Mrs. Bryant initially said nothing about the incident to her hus-

band, Roy, but local African Americans, aghast and perhaps impressed with Till's actions, made sure Bryant found out. The customs of the South demanded retribution. Bryant and his half-brother J.W. Milam set out a few days later to find Till. Arriving at Moses Wright's cabin, they demanded Wright produce the boy. As they left with their prisoner, they threatened to kill Wright if he told anyone about their visit.

Milam and Bryant took Till to an abandoned barn, fully intending to punish and injure—but not kill—him. Till's refusal to cower to their threats, however, infuriated the men. Apparently still boasting of his exploits with white women, Till incurred the fatal wrath of Milam. "Chicago boy, I'm tired of 'em sending your kind down here to stir up trouble. Goddam you—I'm going to make an example of you," Milam yelled. The men drove Till to the Tallahatchie River, where they shot him in the head. Tying a cotton gin to his neck as a weight, they threw Till into the river. Bloated and grotesque, Till's body floated to the surface a few days later, recognized by Moses Wright only because the body wore a ring with Till's initials. A storm of publicity quickly burst over tiny Tallahatchie County.

Till's mother demanded her son's body be returned to Chicago, where thousands attended an open casket funeral. The entire nation thus saw the brutality of the Jim Crow South. "Have you ever sent a loved son on vacation," she erupted, "and had him returned to you in a pine box, so horribly battered and water-logged that someone needs to tell you this sickening sight is your son—lynched?"

While much of the nation reacted with outrage, residents of the Mississippi Delta were surprised to learn that Bryant and Milam would have to stand trial, as most crimes against African Americans went unprosecuted. During September, reporters invaded Sumner, Mississippi, where the trial took place. In a segregated courtroom, an all-white jury listened as Mrs. Bryant described Till's actions, beginning with the date request and ending with the infamous "wolf whistle." The crucial moment of the trial occurred when Moses Wright took the witness stand. Few in the African-American community expected Wright to challenge Bryant and Milam because of their earlier death threat. Wright took the stand nevertheless, and, when asked to identify the men who took Till, Wright pointed at Milam, declared "Thar he," and then pointed at Bryant.

Wright's bold testimony gained the praise of many across the nation, but it had little impact on the trial's outcome. Bryant and Milam's defense attorney

ROSA PARKS (1913–)

Rosa Louise McCauley was born in Tuskegee, Alabama, on February 4, 1913. Memories from her childhood in rural Alabama included such disparate episodes as her mother encouraging her to get an education, and also cowering in her bedroom at night while Ku Klux Klansmen on horseback rode past her house. She graduated from Alabama State Teachers College (now Alabama State University), married Raymond Parks, and moved to Montgomery and made her living as a seamstress because of the few opportunities afforded black women in that era. In 1943, she and her husband became members of the Montgomery (Alabama) chapter of the National Association for the Advancement of Colored People (NAACP), and Parks served as its secretary until 1956. Parks was still working as a seamstress in Montgomery, a strictly segregated city, when she sparked the civil rights movement.

On December 1, 1955, she was arrested and fined for refusing to relinquish her seat on a public bus to a white man, a violation of the city's racial segregation ordinances. Under the guidance of the Montgomery Improvement Association and the leadership of the young pastor of the Dexter Avenue Baptist Church, Martin Luther King Jr., a boycott of the municipal bus company was begun on December 5. The boycott caused a national sensation and helped launch the civil rights movement. It lasted until December 20, 1956, when the U.S. Supreme Court upheld a lower court's decision declaring Montgomery's segregated seating unconstitutional. For her role in initiating the successful campaign, which brought King to national prominence, Parks became known as the "mother of the civil rights movement."

In 1957, Parks and her family moved to Detroit, where she was employed on the staff of U.S. Representative John Conyers from 1965 until her retirement in 1988. She remained active in public service through the NAACP and the Rosa and Raymond Park's Institute for Self-Development, a youth self-esteem and jobs program she created in 1987. The Southern Christian Leadership Council established the annual Rosa Parks Freedom Award in her honor.

James G. Lewis

---

appealed to the "Anglo Saxon" courage of the all-white jury, urging them to free the accused. The jury complied, returning a not guilty verdict which, a juror commented, would have been returned even quicker had they not lingered over soda pop. After the trial, Moses Wright, fearing for his life, moved to Illinois.

While the acquittal stunned and angered many Northern residents, ensuing events only increased public fury. In January 1956, journalist William Huie published Milam and Bryant's personal account of the evening of Till's death. Huie convinced the men that, since they had been tried and acquitted, they could not be tried again for the murder. For about $4,000 the two men openly told Huie the grisly details of how and why they had killed Till. To many observers, including future activist Anne Moody, the Till lynching revealed the need for a concerted civil rights movement as well as the violence and recalcitrance that would define white resistance.

The Montgomery Bus Boycott

Although the *Brown* decision and the Till lynching ignited mass uproar against segregation, the movement did not arise spontaneously. When African Americans in Montgomery, Alabama, unleashed a successful boycott against the city's segregated bus system in 1956, the movement drew upon established networks of community activism and legal support. In Montgomery, the movement brought together African-American churches, nonviolent tactics, and the charismatic Martin Luther King Jr. Joined during the Montgomery Bus Boycott, these three ingredients shaped the specific leaders and methods the civil rights movement would follow during the first half of the 1960s.

Montgomery's city busses concretely embodied segregation, reinforcing the racist structure of society any time an African American rode the bus. On the busses, front seating was reserved for whites. African Americans sat in the rear and could sit in a middle section until there were no seats left for whites in the front. If this occurred, African Americans were obliged to surrender their seats to whites. The city's laws codified this system of segregation. Nearly all of Montgomery's African Americans relied on the busses for transportation to and from work. E.D. Nixon, Montgomery's NAACP representative, had long hoped to challenge the segregated bus system. In May 1955, when a young African-American woman was arrested for violating the bus segregation laws, Nixon considered filing a lawsuit. He soon scuttled the plan when it turned out that the young woman was pregnant; Nixon wanted a plaintiff of unimpeachable moral character.

Nixon soon had his lawsuit when Rosa Parks, a Montgomery seamstress and NAACP secretary, was arrested on December 1 for violating the segregation laws. Parks had often been ejected from busses for the same violation during the 1940s. She had also spent time in Tennessee at the Highlander Folk School, a center advocating social change and racial equality. Parks headed the local NAACP Youth Council, guiding young African Americans to challenge segregated city institutions, including the library and busses. She knew Nixon well and was aware of his wish to launch a lawsuit against Jim Crow. Although Parks probably did not intend to become the plaintiff in Nixon's lawsuit, she was no stranger to civil rights activism. The night of her arrest, Nixon filed a lawsuit with Parks's consent against the segregated bus system.

Meanwhile, a local group of African-American women, known as the Women's Political Council (WPC), took the opportunity to launch an economic attack on the bus system in concert with Nixon's lawsuit. Jo Ann Robinson and Mary Fair Burks worked all night composing and mimeographing leaflets calling for a one-day boycott of the busses on December 5. A budding movement soon grew out of the local churches, reflecting the connections in the South between African-American religious life and social activism. When African Americans founded the Montgomery Improvement Association (MIA) to coordinate the efforts against segregation, the organization elected the recently arrived preacher Martin Luther King Jr. as its president.

A preacher possessed of a powerful eloquence, King helped inspire the Montgomery community to turn the WPC protest into a year-long boycott aimed at crippling the segregated bus system. At a mass meeting announcing the start of the boycott, King preached "If we are wrong—the Supreme Court of this nation is wrong. If we are wrong, God almighty is wrong!" Nightly meetings at King's Dexter Avenue Baptist Church boosted the morale of the walking residents of Montgomery with powerful sermons and spirituals including "We Shall Overcome," which later became the unofficial theme song of the entire civil rights movement. The nightly meetings also raised money and established tactics for the movement. The MIA organized car pools to get people to and from work. Many chose to walk despite cold days, rainy nights, and the seeming eternity of the boycott. An elderly woman known as Mother Pollard summarized

the sentiment of the marchers when she said, "My feets is tired, but my soul is rested."

King based the boycott movement in the philosophy of nonviolence. Although Mohandas K. Gandhi often receives credit for inspiring King's embrace of nonviolence, King actually acquired his conceptions of moral justice and social change from the writings of Reinhold Niebuhr during his seminary studies. More than a mere tactic, King envisioned nonviolence as at once a moral and an economic tool of justice. By actively accepting the oppressor's threats and violence, nonviolent activists hoped to draw moral witness to the inherent wrongs of segregation. White oppressors would see the depravity of their own immoral actions, leading to a moral uplift of the entire society. Any unjust laws, such as Jim Crow laws, could be broken since they lacked moral validity. At the same time, nonviolence had strong economic effects. Empty, ghost-like buses rumbled through Montgomery streets, threatening the economic solvency of the company and some downtown businesses as well.

For a year the boycott continued. The white residents of Montgomery refused to give in to the demands of the MIA, and maneuvered at first through political actions to thwart the boycott. Alabama banned the NAACP from the state in 1956. As the boycott dragged on, Montgomery whites became more confrontational. Montgomery police arrested King at one point, and in early 1956 a bomb exploded outside his home.

In November 1956, the U.S. Supreme Court ruled that Montgomery's bus segregation ordinances were unconstitutional, and on December 20, the boycott ended. Long disdainful of grassroots activism, some NAACP officials, including Thurgood Marshall, scoffed at the boycott, quipping that the walkers ought to have merely waited for the lawsuit to be settled. Tensions between the NAACP, led by Roy Wilkins, and the grassroots activists of the civil rights movement would grow in the following years. King's leadership of a successful movement made him a minor celebrity; the movement's tireless efforts inspired several boycotts across the South. Nevertheless, after the Montgomery boycott, King faced a crossroads. Skeptics charged that the MIA had not integrated schools, businesses, or local government. Although the boycott worked against busses, King pondered how to apply his nonviolent tactics against other institutions such as restaurants, where African Americans were not even allowed in.

MARTIN LUTHER KING JR.

(1929–1968)

Martin Luther King Jr. was born in Atlanta, son of the pastor of Ebenezer Baptist Church. As a Morehouse College student in Atlanta, Crozer Theological Seminary in Pennsylvania, and Boston University, he deepened his understanding of theological scholarship and Mahatma Gandhi's nonviolent strategy for social change. Ordained in 1948, King received a Ph.D. in theology in 1955 and became pastor of Dexter Avenue Baptist Church in Montgomery, Alabama. By that time he was married to Coretta Scott.

In December 1955, during the Montgomery bus boycott, King was elected president of the Montgomery Improvement Association and gained national prominence for his oratorical skills and courage. King's house was bombed in 1956, and, along with other boycott leaders, he was convicted of conspiring to interfere with the bus company's operations. In December 1956, the boycott achieved a major victory when the U.S. Supreme Court ruled Alabama's law sanctioning the segregation of buses and other public services unconstitutional.

In 1957, building on the Montgomery victory, King and other black ministers founded the Southern Christian Leadership Conference (SCLC), as a base to expand civil rights activities, in the South and nationwide. As president, King emphasized black voting rights. In 1957, King visited Ghana to celebrate the country's independence and then India, to deepen his understanding of Gandhi's ideas of nonviolent resistance. Two years later, King resigned as pastor of Dexter, returning to his father's church in Atlanta, headquarters of SCLC.

King's transformation from spokesman for civil rights to protest did not occur instantaneously. In 1960, King was criticized for not doing more to support black college student sit-ins and the Student Nonviolent Coordinating Committee (SNCC). Even after October 1960, when King joined a student sit-in and was arrested, disputes between SCLC and SNCC continued during the movement's campaign of mass protests in Albany, Georgia, during 1961–1962.

After achieving few objectives in Albany, Georgia, King initiated a major campaign in Birmingham, Alabama, against white police officials who discriminated against African Americans. In 1963, clashes between unarmed black demonstrators and police with attack dogs and fire hoses generated newspaper headlines throughout the world. King was arrested and, while in jail, composed his refutation against conservative critics in his classic work, "Letter from a Birmingham Jail." On August 28, 1963, black economic demands and the Southern civil rights movement congealed in a march of more than 250,000 protesters. There, from the steps of the Lincoln Memorial, King delivered his famous "I Have a Dream" speech.

The following year, in 1964, King received the Nobel Peace Prize for his leadership in the nonviolent civil rights movement. He then went to Selma, Alabama, to lead a voter-registration campaign, culminating in the Selma-to-Montgomery Freedom March. Despite success and accolades, however, King faced challenges to his leadership from the Black Muslim Movement and other critics. Malcolm X's black nationalist radicalism articulated the anger of Northern urban blacks more effectively than King's moderate position, and in 1966 King was criticized by Stokely Carmichael, proponent of "black power." Shortly afterward, in the summer of 1966, King went to Chicago to launch a slum-rehabilitation and open-housing program that captured the imagination of African Americans. During an uprising, white counter-protesters physically assaulted King, who vowed to return and accomplish his goals.

In 1967, King declared his opposition to the Vietnam War, asserting the United States to be "the greatest purveyor of violence in the world." The position was intended to link the antiwar and civil rights movements, but was criticized by the National Association for the Advancement of Colored People and the Urban League. Early in 1968, King initiated a "poor people's campaign" to confront economic problems not addressed by civil rights reforms, calling for national boycotts and a guaranteed family income. However, King's antiwar and economic positions triggered opposition from the Johnson administration, which used the Federal Bureau of Investigation to harass him.

King interrupted his plans for a Poor People's March to Washington for a trip to Memphis, Tennessee, in support of striking sanitation workers. When delivering his last speech in Memphis, he admitted, "We've got some difficult days ahead, but it really doesn't matter with me now, because I've been to the mountaintop." On April 4, 1968, he was shot and killed on the balcony of the motel where he was staying. His death touched off riots in several major cities, an outpouring of grief and anger from the black community that ironically found expression through violence.

After his death, King remained a controversial symbol of the civil rights struggle, revered for his martyrdom on behalf of nonviolence and condemned by others for his insurgent views. In 1986, King's birthday, January 15, became a federal holiday. It is celebrated on the third Monday of January.

James G. Lewis

The Little Rock Nine

Soon after the end of the Montgomery Bus Boycott, a crisis erupted in Arkansas that set a pattern for Southern states resisting integration and a precedent for intervention by the federal government in civil rights incidents. Despite the efforts of "massive resistance," school desegregation was all but inevitable after the *Brown* decision. Moderate Southerners focused on how to implement desegregation with as little turmoil as possible. Across the South, many communities expected the peaceful town of Little Rock, Arkansas, to serve as a model of desegregation.

In 1957, the Little Rock school board began selecting a small group of African-American high school students that would integrate the school system. With the help of Daisy Bates, the president of the state NAACP, nine African-American students enrolled for the fall semester at Central High School in Little Rock. As the beginning of the school year approached, some white residents began to actively oppose integration. White Citizen's Councils (WCC), pro-segregation groups of prominent local leaders growing throughout the South, appeared in Little Rock. Pledging themselves to prevent integration, the Little Rock WCC also challenged Orval Faubus, the moderate governor of Arkansas, to make a stand against federal intervention. The WCC convinced Georgia governor Marvin Griffin, a renowned racist, to visit Little Rock. Threatened by this challenge and hopeful of winning reelection, Faubus shifted his stance and vowed to oppose desegregation.

Claiming that the enrollment of the nine African-American students would cause a riot, Faubus ordered the Arkansas National Guard to Central High on September 4. Daisy Bates brought eight of the students to school, where they were turned away by the National Guard's bayonets. Bates had forgotten to pick up the ninth student, Elizabeth Eckford, who arrived at Central High by herself. A mob quickly surrounded her, threatening to kill her as the National Guard watched. A local woman, observing the scene, helped Eckford onto a nearby bus, rescuing her from serious harm.

For days the Little Rock Nine returned, only to be forced away by a mob. Television cameras carried footage of the events across the nation, giving life to the nascent genre of nightly television news. In Washington, D.C., President Eisenhower wanted to avoid intervening in civil rights issues. Reluctantly, he agreed to meet with Faubus. During the meeting, Faubus seemed to agree that he would allow admittance to the students, but when he returned to Little Rock, Faubus simply removed the National Guard from around the school. On September 23, Bates escorted the students to Central High and hurried them into the school through a side entrance. At the front of the school, an angry throng of whites attacked a group of reporters covering the scene. As the mob grew more intense, local police removed the African-American students from the school. Infuriated by Faubus's duplicity, Eisenhower ordered the 101st Army Paratroopers to Little Rock and nationalized the Arkansas National Guard a day later. Federal troops—the first in the South since Reconstruction—marched the Little Rock Nine into Central High. Faubus's popularity soared.

With the threat of overt physical violence mollified, some fifty white Central High students launched a campaign of harassment and intimidation inside the school. The African-American students suffered insults, minor assaults, and stolen books. One of the Nine was quickly expelled after retaliating against her tormentors. The other eight graduated at the end of the school year.

The Movement and Politics

With the federal intervention at Little Rock, civil rights activists noted that the gross violations of constitutional rights, combined with media exposure, could pressure the federal government into action. With the precedents of overturning segregation in the *Brown* decision, the outrage over Emmett Till, the activist strategies of Montgomery, and federal intervention in Little Rock, the civil rights movement erupted in the 1960s.

Martin Luther King Jr. stood at the center of the movement. To coordinate his efforts at social change, he founded the Southern Christian Leadership Conference (SCLC) with Ella Baker as its executive director. Although the small organization struggled at first, King's growing reputation would add prestige and funding to the SCLC. Political leaders began to notice King and the potential African-American votes he might bring them. The 1960 presidential candidates Richard Nixon and John F. Kennedy both courted a King endorsement. King hesitated to commit, but when he was arrested during a 1960 demonstration at an Atlanta department store, Kennedy called King's wife Coretta in a sympathetic gesture. Nixon, even though he was possibly closer to King than Kennedy, remained aloof. In the days before the election, Kennedy campaign workers publicized Kennedy's phone call among African-American communities. African Americans responded overwhelmingly in favor of

ELLA JOSEPHINE BAKER (1903–1986)

Granddaughter of slaves, Ella Josephine Baker was born on December 13, 1903, in Norfolk, Virginia, to Blake Baker, a steamship waiter, and Georgianna (Ross) Baker, a schoolteacher. Due to the absence of schools for African Americans in her hometown of Littleton, North Carolina, Baker went to school in Raleigh, North Carolina, attending Shaw boarding school and Shaw University, where she graduated with a degree in sociology in 1927. In 1927, Baker moved to New York City and soon after became an activist for civil rights, women's equality, and economic justice. In 1930, Baker joined the Young Negroes Cooperative League, a Harlem-based organization seeking to harness the economic power of the black community. She became the national director in 1931. During the Depression era, Baker worked in the Works Project Administration as a literacy teacher and as a labor educator in the Workers Education Project. She later became active as a journalist in local black newspapers.

Baker was at the vanguard of the civil rights movement, rejecting the status quo and embracing the necessity for militancy and direct action to challenge white institutionalized racism in the United States. She became an active member of the National Association for the Advancement of Colored People (NAACP) in 1940, serving as a field secretary until 1946, when she left the organization, frustrated by the failure of the organization to embrace a more proactive strategy for change. However, in 1954, after unsuccessfully running for the New York State Assembly as a Liberal Party candidate, Baker returned to the NAACP as chair of the New York City branch.

In the late 1950s, as the civil rights movement expanded, Baker found that the mainstream African-American organizations were frequently too complacent and moderate. Again, Baker chose more radical, direct action tactics, such as sit-ins and street protests, both of which were critical to the achievements of the civil rights movement in the 1960s. In the late 1950s, after joining and actively participating in the Southern Christian Leadership Council, Baker chose to join forces with younger, radical forces. In 1960, she became a key adviser and strategist for young students, forming the Student Nonviolent Coordinating Committee (SNCC), a militant civil rights organization. In 1964, she helped launch the Mississippi Freedom Democratic Party, a grassroots political organization that threatened the established, all-white Mississippi Democratic Party. She was also a close adviser to the Black Panther Party, a militant social justice organization advocating economic equality for African Americans.

From the 1970s until her death on her birthday in 1986, Baker was committed to advancing the cause of racial equality, advising key organizations in the United States, and helping advance the struggle against apartheid in South Africa.

Immanuel Ness

Kennedy, helping him win key states, including Pennsylvania, Michigan, and Illinois, in an election that saw Kennedy win the popular vote nationwide by a razor-thin margin of about 100,000 votes.

The federal government and the American public would learn to take the civil rights movement seriously during the turbulent 1960s. As the decade began, a group of students unleashed a ground-breaking series of demonstrations across the South. Soon after, a volatile mix of activists, white racists, and federal troops exploded across the South.

NONVIOLENCE TRIUMPHS IN THE SOUTH
1960–1965
The Sit-ins

As the 1960s began, direct action tactics took the civil rights movement on a new and powerful course. The sit-in became a potent symbolic and economic weapon against segregation. The first recorded sit-ins took place sporadically between 1957 and 1960, primarily in North Carolina and Oklahoma. African Americans simply entered segregated parks, hotels, waiting rooms, and restaurants, and peacefully demanded service. On February 1, 1960, the movement escalated when students at North Carolina A&T University decided to launch sit-ins at segregated lunch counters in Greensboro.

Legend has it that the North Carolina students began the movement spontaneously. Scholars of the movement, however, have shown that the student movement began as an organized, planned effort against Jim Crow laws. The students involved were active in their local NAACP Youth Council and had direct involvement with leaders of the earlier sit-ins. The NAACP refused to sanction the demonstrations, though by the time the movement began, the sit-in students had a well-established activist network of their own. By April, sit-ins had occurred in over seventy Southern cities, including Durham, Birmingham, Little Rock, New Orleans, and Atlanta. At first, sit-ins disrupted the economic activity on a small scale. As African-American students took places at white-only lunch counters, white patrons and employees became nervous and confused. Most often, the manager would simply close the restaurant for the day. Sit-ins thus threatened the economic health of the targeted businesses.

The sit-ins swept across the South, but nowhere was their impact more drastic and influential than in Nashville, Tennessee. Building on the social connections between the four African-American universities in Nashville, students formed a network of activism dedicated to destroying segregation. Inspired by the North Carolina sit-ins, local students launched a movement in February 1960 that not only desegregated much of Nashville, but also created leaders and organizations instrumental to the success of the national civil rights movement. The leaders of the Nashville movement made manifest the Gandhian ideal of nonviolence. James Lawson, schooled in Gandhian principles in India, educated the volunteer activists in the meaning and practice of nonviolence. Diane Nash (later Nash Bevel), a student at Fisk University, coordinated volunteers at the downtown demonstrations in the afternoon after sitting through her college courses in the morning. John Lewis, James Bevel, and Marion Barry, soon to become leaders of national prominence, helped lead the movement as well.

As the demonstrations spread, so did resistance to them. Sit-ins in Nashville and most other cities unfolded in predictable ways. Groups of angry whites would surround the demonstrators, taunting and shouting at them, and often burning them with cigarettes or dousing them with ketchup and mustard. In Nashville, Lawson taught the activists not to respond or retaliate if provoked. As the students willfully received insults and blows, their antagonists grew increasingly angry. Often the crowds would attack the students, hitting them, throwing them on the ground, and kicking them. Police then usually arrested the demonstrators. In Nashville, Nash's group coordinated the sit-ins with precision. The volunteers descended on businesses in waves, and as they were removed, harmed, or arrested, replacements would arrive to continue the demonstration.

Inspired by the resolve of the city's youth, adult and community leaders in Nashville exerted pressure of their own on the white establishment. Churches held mass meetings and collected money for the demonstrations, and adults began to boycott the segregated downtown businesses. This economic pressure combined with the sit-ins to force the business owners to concede to African-American demands. With students crowding the city's jails and a boycott and sit-ins slowing the economy, African Americans managed to cripple Nashville's segregated downtown. By May 1960, restaurants integrated their lunch counters, and businesses began to hire African-American workers.

The efforts of the students in the Nashville movement marked a new beginning in the civil rights movement. College students across the nation formed the vanguard of the civil rights movement. Veterans of the Nashville movement, with the help of Ella Baker, the former coordinator of Martin Luther King's SCLC, created the Student Non-Violent Coordinating Committee (SNCC). Rejecting formal leadership and bureaucracy, SNCC would soon harness the fervor of the students into a dramatic force for change in the South. Nash, Lewis, and Bevel helped bring the civil rights movement some of its most dramatic triumphs during the early 1960s. Also inspired by the Nashville movement, the Congress of Racial Equality (CORE), a small social equality organization, incorporated students into its leadership. Roughly one year after the desegregation of Nashville, CORE began the explosive Freedom Rides, which would lead the movement, the South, and the federal government into a maelstrom of activism and violence.

The Freedom Rides

By 1961, civil rights activists had come to expect some form of violence to occur during a demonstration. Most Americans, however, experienced the violence indirectly through sporadic events that grabbed media attention. The Till lynching, the Little Rock Nine, and the sit-ins exposed to some extent the brutality unleashed on civil rights demonstrators in the South. Still, the movement competed with other events for attention from the general public and the federal government. Crises such as the successful flight of the Soviet satellite *Sputnik* and the Bay of Pigs easily captivated the nation's attention. Civil rights activists began to act not only to change laws, but to draw the nation's attention to the constitutional violations and crimes against African Americans in the South. The Freedom Rides launched in the summer of 1961 publicized Southern violence to an entirely new degree.

This violence was not entirely accidental. Activists knew that images of violence stirred public reaction and the federal government more than any demonstration, protest, or plea. James Farmer, CORE's director, announced in early 1961 that his organization would send seven African-American and six white volunteers on bus rides from Washington, D.C., to New Orleans, Louisiana. Project Freedom Ride would test legal compliance with the recent *Boynton v. Virginia* (1960) decision, in which the U.S. Supreme Court declared segregation involving interstate transportation unconstitutional. The Freedom Riders planned to stop at bus stations in the Deep South and integrate the waiting and dining areas. At the same time, CORE hoped to spur federal intervention in the enforcement of desegregation. The riders fully expected some resistance and quite possibly violence, which would, they predicted, force the federal government into action in support of civil rights. The rides came at a difficult time for the new president, John F. Kennedy. Initially pledging quick and decisive action on civil rights, Kennedy found himself caught between activist demands and the entrenched Southern wing of the Democratic Party. Any support offered the activists, Kennedy knew, would erode his support in his own party and thus his efforts on behalf of civil rights slowed.

Two buses of Freedom Riders roared out of Washington, D.C., on May 4, 1961. The rides unfolded relatively uneventfully until the first bus arrived in Anniston, Alabama, on May 14. A mob of racists awaited the bus as it pulled into the station. As the riders stepped off the bus, 200 whites attacked, unleashing a minor riot. As the riders retreated to the bus, rioters attacked the bus itself, slashing its tires. The bus pulled off with the mob in pursuit, only to sputter to the side of the road after six miles because of its flattened tires. This time the mob surrounded the bus and set fire to it, trapping the riders inside. An undercover Alabama policeman, planted on the bus earlier in the trip, forced the door open by threatening the attackers outside with a gun. As the riders escaped, the bus burst into flames. News photographers captured the fiery image, which covered the front page of national newspapers the next day. The mob later attacked the second bus as it pulled into Anniston.

On May 14, riders on the second bus were also attacked at Anniston and then again at Birmingham. Earlier that day, Birmingham Sheriff Bull Connor, fully aware that a mob awaited the bus, gave his police officers the day off, ostensibly in honor of Mother's Day. That night the Freedom Riders huddled in the Reverend Fred Shuttlesworth's church as yet another mob menaced on the streets outside. Local African Americans greeted the Freedom Riders as heroes, though many of the riders could not enjoy their adoration. Severely beaten, most of the riders needed serious medical attention, which local hospitals were reluctant to provide. The riders faced a premature death. Officials in the Kennedy administration discussed intervening but refused to use federal troops to protect the riders. Such a move would enrage segregationist state officials, who viewed federal intervention as an invasion. Meanwhile, Greyhound officials refused to supply a driver for the dangerous trip. Exasperated, the president sent Attorney General Robert Kennedy's aide John Seigenthaler to Alabama on behalf of the Justice Department.

Horribly battered (one rider became paralyzed for life as a result of the beatings), the original Freedom Riders flew out of Alabama. In Nashville, Diane Nash and John Lewis of the SNCC recruited volunteers to continue the Freedom Rides. On May 17, eight blacks and two whites arrived in Birmingham, where Connor promptly apprehended them, escorting them to the Tennessee border the next day. Undeterred, the new volunteers sneaked back to Birmingham. Recognizing the riders' refusal to quit, Robert Kennedy worked to make their trip as safe as possible. Kennedy forced Greyhound officials to provide a driver for the Birmingham-to-Montgomery journey, and on May 20 the bus arrived in Montgomery.

Angry whites ambushed the riders at the Montgomery bus terminal, savagely beating them with fists, feet, and anything they could find, including soda crates. Seigenthaler had followed the bus to Montgomery and attempted to protect the riders as the riot erupted, but whites attacked him as well. That evening the riders huddled with 1,200 local African Americans in Reverend Ralph Abernathy's church. King led a mass meeting as the ubiquitous mob assembled outside to menace the African Americans inside. Federal marshals, dispatched by the White House, protected the church from possible destruction by the mob.

The rides continued. The riders begged King to join them, but he refused. Farmer, recently arrived in Montgomery, decided at the last minute to join the ride into Jackson, Mississippi. Kennedy secured a martial escort for the ride out of Alabama, but danger still threatened in Mississippi. Striking a bargain with U.S. senator James Eastland (D-MS), Kennedy promised to allow state officials to arrest the riders to prevent mob violence. Safe from the deadly violence of Alabama, the riders then entered the haunting Mississippi prison system. As Freedom Rides continued, some 400 riders would be arrested in Mississippi. Embracing a "jail, no bail" vow, many riders filled the local prisons, straining law enforcement and draining government funds to feed and house the prisoners. As the cells filled, some riders were transferred to the Parchman state penitentiary where they suffered abuse and starvation.

Not all riders remained in jail, and bail and court costs slowly drained the CORE treasury. After the emotional and financial drain of the Freedom Rides, CORE nearly dissolved. By September 1961, Robert Kennedy quietly exerted pressure on the Interstate Commerce Commission and state and local officials, resulting in stricter enforcement of desegregation. CORE had helped end segregation in interstate travel by late 1962. After the turmoil, the White House urged civil rights activists to pursue voting rights rather than integration, as the administration faced less political risk and had greater constitutional leverage in that area. To the movement's dismay, the Kennedy administration had shown a preference to act reluctantly and quietly, a response that would repeat itself in Mississippi during the integration of Ole Miss.

Civil Rights in Mississippi

For most of the country, the crisis at Central High School in Little Rock seemed to be the culmination of the *Brown* decision, but in some ways it was a small-scale preview for the final stand of the bastion of segregated education in the South: the University of Mississippi. Ole Miss flaunted a racist attitude and a proud Confederate past, boasting "Colonel Reb" as its mascot. Civil rights advocates had long hoped to integrate the institution but were thwarted time and time again. Ole Miss officials considered the idea of enrollment of African-American students at the school a simple absurdity. When African-American Clennon King applied to Ole Miss in 1958, state officials used this act as proof of his insanity and had him committed to Mississippi's Whitfield Asylum. King was later found sane and released with the aid of his brother, C.B. King, who was active in the Albany, Georgia, movement.

In January 1961, an African-American student at Jackson State named James Meredith contacted the NAACP about starting a lawsuit to gain him entrance to Ole Miss. Meredith, a U.S. Air Force veteran, discussed the lawsuit with Mississippi NAACP field secretary Medgar Evers, as well as Thurgood Marshall. The lawsuit began, and in September 1962 a federal judge ordered Ole Miss to enroll Meredith. Mississippi governor Ross Barnett fully intended to make a stand against forced integration. A virulent segregationist, Barnett, like Orval Faubus in Little Rock, felt that resisting school desegregation would improve his

political career. Although some moderate Mississippi whites supported Meredith's enrollment, Barnett appealed to the racists of the state, appearing at football games pledging to resist the tides of change.

Despite his tirades, Barnett understood that he had no legal case against desegregation. He quickly worked to frame the issue as one resulting from the federal authorities' excessive trampling on states rights. Secretly bargaining with President Kennedy on September 30, 1962, Barnett suggested that a military escort draw weapons on him and force him to integrate the university, allowing him to save face with the state's ardent racists. Kennedy refused Barnett's deal and ordered a force of federal marshals to bring Meredith to the city of Oxford and Ole Miss later that evening. A mob, consisting of some students but mostly local whites, surrounded the registration building while federal agents secretly whisked Meredith into a dorm on campus.

As darkness fell, the crowd grew and violence soon followed. Rioters threw rocks and broke windows, threatening the nervous, outmanned, and poorly armed group of U.S. marshals. The violence escalated when Barnett told the state highway patrol, which had been on the scene to keep order, to disperse. As Kennedy gave a speech in Washington claiming that the Ole Miss standoff had been settled, gunshots shattered the night air in Oxford. The marshals fired tear gas to quell the riot. Soon a reporter and a local observer lay dead, victims of random shootings. During the melee, Barnett took to the radio airwaves, declaring, "I call on Mississippi to keep the faith and courage. We will never surrender." Federal officials worried that the mob might soon discover Meredith, with his murder sure to follow.

In the early hours of the morning, Kennedy ordered military units to Oxford. Arriving at about 4 A.M., federal troops smothered the rebellion, and five hours later escorted James Meredith to the registration building. Roughly five years after the Little Rock Nine, federal troops again enforced school desegregation by escorting an African American past a would-be lynch mob. After the outburst surrounding his arrival on campus, Meredith's college career passed relatively peacefully. In the summer of 1963, he graduated from Ole Miss with a degree in political science.

Mississippi African Americans, long despairing of any progress in civil rights, were now filled with new hope as they pondered Meredith's successful integration of Ole Miss. Considered by many as the state most egregiously in violation of civil rights, Mississippi witnessed in the following years a new bout of activism. Medgar Evers consulted with Meredith frequently and helped lead these efforts. In Jackson, Mississippi, students launched a wave of sit-ins at local restaurants in 1963. Although the national NAACP generally disapproved of direct action measures, Evers could not ignore the proven efficacy of such tactics. Evers chose not to take part in the sit-ins but led meetings protesting the arrest of demonstrators. At an NAACP rally Evers vowed: "Freedom has never been free . . . I love my children and I love my wife with all my heart. And I would die, and die gladly, if that would make a better life for them."

On June 12, as Kennedy addressed the nation on civil rights, a white sniper shot Evers in the back outside of his home, quickly killing him. Evers's death came to be described as a political assassination rather than a lynching. After his funeral 1,000 young African Americans marched through downtown Jackson, ending at a tense standoff with local law enforcement officials. The confrontation ended when John Doar, a Justice Department official calmed the crowd. President Kennedy met with Evers's widow and children after his burial at Arlington National Cemetery. The slaying of the well-known Evers inspired many activists to set their sights on Mississippi as a future center of concerted action.

Albany

After the Montgomery Bus Boycott, King felt pulled in different directions. In demand as a speaker, he gave numerous speeches. He journeyed to India to learn from the disciples of Gandhi. In New York City, he survived an assassination attempt while publicizing his book on the Montgomery movement. By 1961, some critics argued that King had done little actual work for the cause of civil rights. Soon King found himself drawn into a budding movement to integrate the town of Albany, Georgia.

In 1961, a drive began against the entrenched segregationist laws of Albany. With the help of SNCC, local students organized protests at bus terminals that had yet to be integrated, and they demanded biracial discussions with the town leaders. After an energetic start, the Albany movement sputtered as demonstrators were arrested and white officials ignored African-American demands. King arrived in December, and the hero of the Montgomery movement helped mobilize a large number of Albany's African Americans.

As King increased the Albany movement's activism, white city officials adapted to meet the rising challenge. Albany Police Chief Laurie Pritchett knew

that the activists wanted to be arrested and that by filling the local jails they hoped to create a logistic and economic logjam for the city government. Violent treatment of demonstrators and overflowing jails would make headlines in the North, possibly bringing federal intervention. Pritchett ordered his officers to treat demonstrators gently while arresting them. He also made arrangements with prison officials in neighboring counties to imprison activists, enabling him to avoid crowding Albany's jails.

In July 1962, King went to jail in order to bring greater attention to the conflict in Albany, but city officials set him free, knowing that by being in prison King would only strengthen the movement. After over a year of work, the Albany movement had little progress to show for its efforts. The movement showed signs of strain. SNCC and the Albany students who began the movement resented the intrusion of King and the SCLC. As the Albany movement faded, King began to plan for a project that he would coordinate from the beginning, rather than showing up only as the movement needed outside support. He set his sights on the city of Birmingham, Alabama.

Birmingham

After the Albany debacle, King faced criticism and pressure to re-create his success in Montgomery. Steadily losing momentum, King's SCLC needed a successful movement in order to bring federal and public attention to civil rights. The SCLC chose Birmingham as its next target because of that city's blatant violations of civil rights. The notorious Sheriff Bull Connor, who had allowed thugs to pummel activists during the Freedom Rides, personified the racism of the city. The movement in Birmingham would begin with a boycott during the Easter shopping season, when African Americans usually filled the cash registers of downtown department stores. Demonstrations would complement the boycott, and arrests would fill the jails. King asked SCLC official Fred Shuttlesworth, who had harbored the Freedom Riders in his Birmingham church, to create a plan for the movement, and then embarked on a speaking tour to raise money for the project.

Sit-ins and marches began on April 3, 1963, but the number of demonstrators and arrests fell far short of King's expectations. For a week the movement dragged on. Birmingham police arrested marchers but not in the drastic numbers needed to fill the jails. At the Sixteenth Street Baptist Church, King led nightly mass meetings to build support. The actions gained scant attention even within Birmingham, though of-

LETTER FROM BIRMINGHAM JAIL
MARTIN LUTHER KING JR.   April 16, 1963

*Martin Luther King's famous "Letter from Birmingham Jail"
to clergymen is emblematic of his dedication to nonviolent
civil disobedience. King's letter is cited as a philosophic and
strategic turning point in the modern civil rights movement.*

My Dear Fellow Clergymen

While confined here in the Birmingham city jail, I
came across your recent statement calling my present
activities "unwise and untimely." . . .

. . . I am in Birmingham because injustice is here. . . .

Moreover, I am cognizant of the interrelatedness of
all communities and states. I cannot sit idly by in Atlanta and not be concerned about what happens in Birmingham. Injustice anywhere is a threat to justice
everywhere. . . . Whatever affects one directly, affects all
indirectly. Never again can we afford to live with the
narrow, provincial "outside agitator" idea. . . .

In any nonviolent campaign there are four basic
steps: collection of the facts to determine whether injustices exist; negotiation; self-purification; and direct
action. We have gone through all these steps in Birmingham. There can be no gainsaying the fact that racial injustice engulfs this community. Birmingham is
probably the most thoroughly segregated city in the
United States. Its ugly record of brutality is widely
known. Negroes have experienced grossly unjust treatment in the courts. There have been more unsolved
bombings of Negro homes and churches in Birmingham than in any other city in the nation. . . . On the basis of these conditions, Negro leaders sought to
negotiate with the city fathers. But the latter consistently refused to engage in good-faith negotiation. . . .

We will reach the goal of freedom in Birmingham
and all over the nation, because the goal of America is
freedom. Abused and scorned though we may be, our
destiny is tied up with America's destiny. Before the
pilgrims landed at Plymouth, we were here. Before the
pen of Jefferson etched the majestic words of the Declaration of Independence across the pages of history, we
were here. For more than two centuries our forebears
labored in this country without wages; they made cotton king; they built the homes of their masters while
suffering gross injustice and shameful humiliation—
and yet out of a bottomless vitality they continued to
thrive and develop. If the inexpressible cruelties of
slavery could not stop us, the opposition we now face
will surely fail. . . .

Before closing I feel impelled to mention one other
point in your statement that has troubled me pro
foundly. You warmly commended the Birmingham police force for keeping "order" and "preventing violence." I doubt that you would have so warmly
commended the police force if you had seen its dogs
sinking their teeth into unarmed, nonviolent Negroes. I
doubt that you would so quickly commend the policemen if you were to observe their ugly and inhumane
treatment of Negroes here in the city jail; if you were
to watch them push and curse old Negro women and
young Negro girls; if you were to see them slap and
kick old Negro men and young boys; if you were to
observe them, as they did on two occasions, refuse to
give us food because we wanted to sing our grace together. I cannot join you in your praise of the Birmingham police department. . . .

I wish you had commended the Negro sit-inners and
demonstrators of Birmingham for their sublime courage,
their willingness to suffer and their amazing discipline in
the midst of great provocation. One day the South will
recognize its real heroes. They will be the James Mere-
diths, with the noble sense of purpose that enables them
to face jeering, and hostile mobs, and with the agonizing
loneliness that characterizes the life of the pioneer. They
will be old, oppressed, battered Negro women, symbolized in a seventy-two-year-old woman in Montgomery,
Alabama, who rose up with a sense of dignity and with
her people decided not to ride segregated buses, and
who responded with ungrammatical profundity to one
who inquired about her weariness: "My feets is tired, but
my soul is at rest." They will be the young high school
and college students, the young ministers of the gospel
and a host of their elders, courageously and nonviolently
sitting in at lunch counters and willingly going to jail for
conscience' sake. One day the South will know that when
these disinherited children of God sat down at lunch
counters, they were in reality standing up for what is
best in the American dream and for the most sacred values in our Judaeo-Christian heritage, thereby bringing
our nation back to those great wells of democracy which
were dug deep by the founding fathers in their
formulation of the Constitution and the Declaration of
Independence. . . .

Yours for the cause of Peace and Brotherhood,
Martin Luther King Jr.

ficials passed a law outlawing demonstrations. Hoping to galvanize the movement, King willfully violated this injunction and was instantly arrested. King entered a Birmingham prison on Good Friday, April 12. While locked in solitary confinement, King read a smuggled newspaper. One article enraged him. The article described white religious leaders in Birmingham criticizing the movement's demands. The moderate clergy counseled King to patiently wait for justice. On the same newspaper (and on subsequent sheets of paper smuggled inside), King scrawled his "Letter from Birmingham Jail." In the letter, King confronted such criticisms:

> I have almost reached the regrettable conclusion that the Negro's great stumbling block is not the White Citizen's Council—or the Ku Klux Klanner, but the white moderate who is more devoted to "order" than to justice, who prefers a negative peace which is the absence of tension to a positive peace which is the presence of justice, who constantly says "I agree with you in the goal you seek, but I can't agree with your methods of direct action," who paternalistically believes that he can set the timetable for another man's freedom.

King also countered the notion that the civil rights movement needlessly created turmoil and conflict and disrupted peaceful communities.

> Actually, we who engage in nonviolent direct action are not the creators of tension. We merely bring to the surface the hidden tension that is already alive. We bring it out in the open, where it can be seen and dealt with. Like a boil that can never be cured so long as it is covered up but must be opened with all its ugliness to the natural medicines of air and light, injustice must be exposed, with all the tension its exposure creates, to the light of human conscience and the air of national opinion before it can be cured.

The SCLC sent King's letter to religious leaders and publications across the country. Although the letter inspired some activism among American clergy, notably the arrival of a group of rabbis to support the Birmingham movement, King's essay remained relatively ignored until after the Birmingham settlement.

On Easter Sunday King left his prison cell only to find the movement facing collapse. The SCLC leaders pondered a bold move to reignite the movement. With adults reluctant to go to jail, high school children volunteered to march instead. King refused this idea, but

James Bevel, a veteran of the Nashville sit-in movement, convinced King that they should be allowed to march, reasoning that segregation affected African Americans of any age. High school students and then even younger children lined up to march on May 2. As their nervous parents watched, the children marched, stunning Bull Connor's men. As police arrested one group of marchers, another made its way toward a protest at city hall. Soon the jail cells were filled with children as young as six years old.

The next day more children—and adults inspired by the sacrifice of the youth—assembled in the Sixteenth Street Church to march. Connor's men surrounded the church, having received instructions to prevent any marches. When marchers left the church, the police unleashed high-pressure fire hoses on the demonstrators, sending young and old bodies tumbling backward on the streets. Snarling police dogs chased children, sinking their fangs into several of them. A picture of a vicious dog, its jaws clamped on a young boy's stomach, landed on the front page of newspapers across the country the next day. The police attacked the demonstrators with clubs, leaving the streets of Birmingham littered with blood and battered bodies.

Connor's brutal reaction to the children's march turned public sentiment toward the movement. City officials worked with Shuttlesworth and King to reach an agreement. Northern industrialists, upon whom city leaders counted on for investment, began to criticize the city government. Demonstrators flooded downtown, ruining the economic health of local businesses. No African Americans spent any money downtown, and many whites, alarmed by the racial disturbances, also stayed away from Birmingham's business district. On May 10, Shuttlesworth announced that "The City of Birmingham has reached an accord with its conscience." City officials agreed to the movement's demands of integration of sitting rooms, restrooms, water fountains, and lunch counters, as well as a biracial committee to investigate the further needs of African Americans in the city.

Violence threatened to destroy the fragile agreement. Alabama governor George Wallace denounced the settlement, and bombs erupted across the city. Angry African Americans threw rocks at police; state troopers responded by beating African Americans. On May 12, President Kennedy ordered army units to the city which eventually calmed the rioting. The dramatic, gruesome scenes from Birmingham shocked the nation and troubled its conscience. Never had the mistreatment of African Americans been covered by so many media. The conflict troubled John Kennedy as well. Soon after the settlement was ratified, the president announced that he would send a civil rights bill to Congress.

The March on Washington

King's celebrity soared after the SCLC's victory in Birmingham. Numerous periodicals and journals reprinted his "Letter from Birmingham Jail." The man who toppled the most segregated city in the nation became a hero to millions. His popularity transcended the South. In June 1963, King spoke in Detroit as a crowd of 125,000 nearly exploded in adoration. President Kennedy summoned King for a meeting in the White House. In the summer of 1963 the time was right, King felt, for a grand display of the movement's strength.

After a brief discussion with his advisers, King agreed that the display should take the form of a giant march in the nation's capital. Other civil rights organizations, including SNCC and the NAACP, offered their participation. The idea of a march on Washington resonated with the older leaders of the movement. A. Philip Randolph, an elder statesman of the civil rights movement, had proposed a march on Washington during World War II in order to pressure President Franklin D. Roosevelt to integrate the defense industries. When Roosevelt agreed to this integration, Randolph called off the march. In 1963, Randolph planned a march for jobs in Washington, and he agreed to combine this with King's idea of a march for freedom. Randolph later agreed to take charge of the March on Washington for Jobs and Freedom, though most of the organization efforts fell to King's associate Bayard Rustin.

On August 28, 1963, an integrated mass of some 250,000 marchers gathered at the Washington Monument. From there they descended on the Lincoln Memorial, where various civil rights leaders, including Randolph and John Lewis of SNCC, addressed the crowd. The televised march marked a turning point for the American civil rights movement. Speakers, basking in the newfound attention from the federal government, expressed support for Kennedy's civil rights bill. The movement changed symbolically as well. The day before the march, W.E.B. Du Bois died in Ghana. For the first half of the twentieth century, Du Bois had led the civil rights cause as an NAACP founder and one of the country's most prominent and outspoken intellectuals. The day after his death a new generation of civil rights leaders celebrated their ascent into the nation's history.

In the final speech of the day, King gave his most famous oration, expressing themes of interracial harmony and justice grounded in the Bible and the Declaration of Independence. Abandoning his prepared remarks in the middle of his speech, King extemporized:

> I have a dream that one day on the red hills of Georgia, sons of former slaves and the sons of former slave owners will be able to sit down together at the table of brotherhood. I have a dream that one day even the state of Mississippi, a state sweltering with the heat of injustice, sweltering with the heat of oppression, will be transformed into an oasis of freedom and justice. I have a dream that my four children will one day live in a nation where they will not be judged by the color of their skin, but by the content of their character. . . .
>
> And when this happens and when we allow freedom to ring, when we let it ring from every village and every hamlet, from every state and every city, we will be able to speed up that day when all God's children, black men and white men, Jews and Gentiles, Protestants and Catholics, will be able to join hands and sing in the words of the old Negro spiritual: "Free at last. Free at last. Thank God Almighty, we are free at last."

Across the nation viewers praised King's eloquence. The dignified behavior of the marchers impressed many whites who had felt that a mass gathering of African Americans would only degenerate into raucous behavior. The march convinced many liberal politicians and average Americans that they could embrace the aims of the movement.

King's SCLC was but one of many organizations directing the movement, but the general public recognized King as its leader. King's stature impressed many, including Kennedy. At the same time, however, Federal Bureau of Investigation (FBI) director J. Edgar Hoover initiated a program of surveillance against King, suspecting the movement to be a Communist plot. FBI wiretaps recorded King's private meetings and phone conversations, as Hoover hoped to find evidence of Communist infiltration. The Kennedy administration agreed to Hoover's wiretaps, though Hoover never found any ties to the Soviet Union.

The triumph of the March on Washington displayed the size and eloquence of the movement, but violence continued in the South. Just three weeks after the march, a bomb devastated the Sixteenth Street Baptist Church in Birmingham, killing four young

I HAVE A DREAM
MARTIN LUTHER KING, JR.

Civil rights leader Martin Luther King Jr. delivered his "I Have a Dream" speech on the steps of the Lincoln Memorial in Washington, D.C., on August 28, 1963. The speech was crucial in expanding the civil rights struggle into a national movement that could not be ignored in either the South or the North.

Five score years ago, a great American, in whose symbolic shadow we stand signed the Emancipation Proclamation. This momentous decree came as a great beacon light of hope to millions of Negro slaves who had been seared in the flames of withering injustice. It came as a joyous daybreak to end the long night of captivity. But one hundred years later, we must face the tragic fact that the Negro is still not free.

One hundred years later, the life of the Negro is still sadly crippled by the manacles of segregation and the chains of discrimination. One hundred years later, the Negro lives on a lonely island of poverty in the midst of a vast ocean of material prosperity. One hundred years later, the Negro is still languishing in the corners of American society and finds himself an exile in his own land.

So we have come here today to dramatize an appalling condition. In a sense we have come to our nation's capital to cash a check. When the architects of our republic wrote the magnificent words of the Constitution and the Declaration of Independence, they were signing a promissory note to which every American was to fall heir. . . .

Let us not wallow in the valley of despair. I say to you today, my friends, that in spite of the difficulties and frustrations of the moment, I still have a dream. It is a dream deeply rooted in the American dream.

I have a dream that one day this nation will rise up and live out the true meaning of its creed: "We hold these truths to be self-evident: that all men are created equal." I have a dream that one day on the red hills of Georgia the sons of former slaves and the sons of former slaveowners will be able to sit down together at a table of brotherhood. I have a dream that one day even the state of Mississippi, a desert state, sweltering with the heat of injustice and oppression, will be transformed into an oasis of freedom and justice. I have a dream that my four children will one day live in a nation where they will not be judged by the color of their skin but by the content of their character. I have a dream today.

I have a dream that one day the state of Alabama, whose governor's lips are presently dripping with the words of interposition and nullification, will be transformed into a situation where little black boys and black girls will be able to join hands with little white boys and white girls and walk together as sisters and brothers. I have a dream today. I have a dream that one day every valley shall be exalted, every hill and mountain shall be made low, the rough places will be made plain, and the crooked places will be made straight, and the glory of the Lord shall be revealed, and all flesh shall see it together. This is our hope. This is the faith with which I return to the South. With this faith we will be able to hew out of the mountain of despair a stone of hope. With this faith we will be able to transform the jangling discords of our nation into a beautiful symphony of brotherhood. With this faith we will be able to work together, to pray together, to struggle together, to go to jail together, to stand up for freedom together, knowing that we will be free one day.

This will be the day when all of God's children will be able to sing with a new meaning, "My country, 'tis of thee, sweet land of liberty, of thee I sing. Land where my fathers died, land of the pilgrim's pride, from every mountainside, let freedom ring." And if America is to be a great nation, this must become true. So let freedom ring from the prodigious hilltops of New Hampshire. Let freedom ring from the mighty mountains of New York. Let freedom ring from the heightening Alleghenies of Pennsylvania! Let freedom ring from the snowcapped Rockies of Colorado! Let freedom ring from the curvaceous peaks of California! But not only that; let freedom ring from Stone Mountain of Georgia! Let freedom ring from Lookout Mountain of Tennessee! Let freedom ring from every hill and every molehill of Mississippi. From every mountainside, let freedom ring.

When we let freedom ring, when we let it ring from every village and every hamlet, from every state and every city, we will be able to speed up that day when all of God's children, black men and white men, Jews and Gentiles, Protestants and Catholics, will be able to join hands and sing in the words of the old Negro spiritual, "Free at last! free at last! thank God Almighty, we are free at last!"

CIVIL RIGHTS ACT OF 1964
TITLE VII, SECTION 703

The Landmark Title VII of the Civil Rights Act of 1964 bans discrimination on the basis of race, color, religion, sex, pregnancy, or national origin. Title VII was originally intended to defeat race discrimination in employment. Ironically, opponents of the ban on racial discrimination included the prohibition of sex discrimination as a means of defeating the legislation.

Unlawful Employment Practices

(a) It shall be an unlawful employment practice for an employer—

(1) to fail or refuse to hire or to discharge any individual, or otherwise to discriminate against any individual with respect to his compensation, terms, conditions, or privileges of employment, because of such individual's race, color, religion, sex, or national origin; or

(2) to limit, segregate, or classify his employees or applicants for employment in any way which would deprive or tend to deprive any individual of employment opportunities or otherwise adversely affect his status as an employee, because of such individual's race, color, religion, sex, or national origin.

(b) It shall be an unlawful employment practice for an employment agency to fail or refuse to refer for employment, or otherwise to discriminate against, any individual because of his race, color, religion, sex, or national origin, or to classify or refer for employment any individual on the basis of his race, color, religion, sex, or national origin.

(c) It shall be an unlawful employment practice for a labor organization—

(1) to exclude or to expel from its membership, or otherwise to discriminate against, any individual because of his race, color, religion, sex, or national origin;

(2) to limit, segregate, or classify its membership or applicants for membership, or to classify or fail or refuse to refer for employment any individual, in any way which would deprive or tend to deprive any individual of employment opportunities, or would limit such employment opportunities or otherwise adversely affect his status as an employee or as an applicant for employment, because of such individual's race, color, religion, sex, or national origin; or

(3) to cause or attempt to cause an employer to discriminate against an individual in violation of this section.

Source: U.S. Equal Employment Opportunity Commission. *Title VII of the Civil Rights Act of 1964 (Pub. L. 88–352) (Title VII), amended, in volume 42 of the United States Code,* Washington, D.C., 2000.

---

girls. So many bombs had exploded there that activists nicknamed the city "Bombingham." Two blacks were murdered on the street that same day. In Mississippi whites shot at African Americans who tried to register to vote. Violence seemed omnipresent, culminating in the assassination of John Kennedy in November 1963, which was unrelated to the civil rights movement. With Lyndon Johnson, a Southerner, as president, African Americans wondered what the fate of the civil rights bill would be. As 1964 unfolded, white violence created new tactics and demands in the movement. Once again, the movement descended upon Mississippi to confront the forces of discrimination, hatred, and terror.

Freedom Summer

Lyndon Johnson thrilled civil rights activists when he announced, soon after taking office, his intention to push Kennedy's civil rights legislation through Congress. The federal government thus mobilized behind a bill outlawing segregation in the United States. Dedicating the legislation to the slain president's legacy, Johnson impressed African Americans even further when he vowed not to accept any changes to the bill. Johnson knew the bill faced the block of Southern Democrats in the Senate who might filibuster it to death. He also feared that his actions might turn the Deep South against the Democratic Party, a prediction that proved true in the 1964 presidential election.

Johnson used his considerable powers of persuasion to sway Republican and Democratic congressmen alike to support the civil rights bill. At one point, he courted the support of Senate Minority Leader Everett Dirksen (R-IL), telling him, "you're worthy of the Land of Lincoln. And the Man from Illinois is going to pass the bill, and I'll see that you get proper attention and credit." The bill passed in the Senate, and on July 2, with King in attendance, Johnson signed the Civil Rights Act of 1964. The act outlawed segregation in restaurants, hotels, and all the other areas targeted by the sit-in movement years earlier.

One month earlier, SNCC and CORE had begun

FANNIE LOU TOWNSEND HAMER (1917–1977)

Born in Ruleville, Mississippi, on October 6, 1917, Fannie Lou Townsend was the youngest of twenty children. By the time she was six, she was working the fields with her sharecropper parents. She dropped out of school at age twelve to work the land full-time with her family.

In 1942, she married Perry ("Pap") Hamer. Her civil rights activism began in August 1962, when she answered a call by the Student Nonviolent Coordinating Committee (SNCC) for volunteers to challenge voter registration procedures that excluded African Americans. On one of her attempts to register, she was shot at by an angry white racist. Her family was forced off the land and lost their work because of her activism. In 1963, she and several others were imprisoned and violently attacked while in their cells for challenging Mississippi's discriminatory voting laws. A young civil rights worker named Andrew Young traveled to Mississippi to bail her out of jail. Young then sent Hamer to Atlanta to meet with Martin Luther King Jr., who referred her to the United States Department of Justice. U.S. Attorney General Robert F. Kennedy, outraged by what he learned, filed criminal charges against the police officers that had carried out the beatings. An all-white, all-male jury acquitted the lawmen of all charges. She then became a field secretary for SNCC and a registered voter in 1963, and she also began working for the Southern Christian Leadership Conference.

In 1964, Hamer became vice chairperson of the Mississippi Freedom Democratic Party (MFDP), established after unsuccessful attempts by African Americans to work with the all-white Mississippi Democratic Party. As the spokesperson of the MFDP, she gave a nationally televised address to the Credentials Committee at the 1964 Democratic National Convention in which she described incidents of violence and injustice suffered by civil rights activists, including her own experience of a jailhouse beating that left her crippled. Although President Lyndon B. Johnson tried to block the telecast by calling a press conference during her testimony, network television executives aired her testimony later that evening, allowing the American television audience to hear firsthand of the horrors inflicted upon blacks in the Deep South. A year later, President Johnson signed the Voting Rights Act of 1965, which ensured that all blacks of eligible age would be permitted to vote.

As a member of the Democratic National Committee for Mississippi (1968–1971) and the Policy Council of the National Women's Political Caucus (1971–1977), Hamer actively opposed the Vietnam War and worked to improve economic conditions in Mississippi. Her bid for the Mississippi State Senate in 1971 failed, but she kept working on behalf of her fellow impoverished blacks. She died on March 14, 1977, in Mound Bayou, Mississippi.

James G. Lewis

Freedom Summer in the state of Mississippi. More violent than any other state, Mississippi was also guilty of the worst violations of African Americans' voting rights. During the 1950s, although African Americans constituted a majority in some areas, only 5 percent were registered to vote in the entire state. To register, African Americans had to take a test reading and interpreting the state constitution; registrars failed them arbitrarily. Attempts to register brought harassment and sometimes murder upon the individual.

Robert Moses and James Forman of SNCC developed a large-scale summer project, called Freedom Summer, to liberate African Americans from Mississippi's oppression. SNCC needed large numbers of volunteers to implement Freedom Summer, and they found recruits among white college students of the North. On June 20, the first Freedom Summer workers arrived in Mississippi; in all over 1,000 students, most of them white, headed South. Freedom Summer fo-

cused on increasing the political and educational strength of African Americans. Most volunteers worked to register African-American voters, while many others set up Freedom Schools to alleviate the failings of Mississippi's woefully inadequate school system. At the Freedom Schools, the volunteers taught subjects, including African-American history, literacy, theater, and creative writing, to young and old alike. Volunteers also organized community centers for local African Americans.

White residents and law officials of Mississippi perceived Freedom Summer as an invasion, envisioning Communist, white college radicals commingling with African Americans. This encounter replayed the cultural clash of the Emmett Till lynching on a grand scale. White Mississippians attempted to repel the volunteers with violence. Ku Klux Klan members burned churches that hosted Freedom Schools and bombed buildings where SNCC volunteers worked. Racists

Evicted from her land, jailed, and savagely beaten for trying to register to vote, Fannie Lou Hamer riveted the nation with her life story and description of white brutality. She is shown here speaking at the 1964 Democratic National Convention, where she led a delegation of the Mississippi Freedom Democratic Party, which sought to represent the state. *(AP Wide World Photos)*

shot at those attempting to register to vote. The most notorious incident occurred just as the first wave of volunteers arrived. On June 21, civil rights workers James Chaney, Andrew Goodman, and Michael Schwerner disappeared outside the small town of Philadelphia. Mississippi law enforcement officials claimed that the workers were hiding to create publicity, but on August 4 FBI agents discovered the three bodies buried under an earthen dam. By the end of the summer, four volunteers had been killed, 1,000 arrests had been made, and nearly seventy churches, homes, and businesses had been burned or bombed.

Moses had pictured the voting registration campaign as the most important theme of Freedom Summer. Out of 17,000 attempted registrations, only 1,600 were accepted, driving Moses to shift his focus. He then decided to help African Americans in Mississippi create their own political party. With the help of Fannie Lou Hamer, a local sharecropper, Moses created

the Mississippi Freedom Democratic Party (MFDP), which represented some 80,000 African-American Mississippians. The MFDP elected delegates to the Democratic National Convention that August in Atlantic City. There they presented themselves as the true representatives of Mississippi.

The MFDP quickly caused controversy at the convention. President Johnson insisted on seating the white, Democratic delegates from Mississippi, though many Northern Democrats supported the MFDP. Johnson assigned Senator Hubert Humphrey (D-MN) to reconcile the convention. Humphrey proposed seating the entire delegation of Mississippi Democrats along with two representatives from the MFDP. Outraged and unwilling to associate with African Americans, all but three of the Mississippi Democrats stormed off the convention floor. The MFDP voted among themselves to reject the compromise, and over the next few nights the entire MFDP used borrowed passes to gather on the convention floor where they led prayer demonstrations and sang freedom songs. By the end of the Freedom Summer of 1964, the civil rights movement had redefined its purpose and its tactics. The Civil Rights Act outlawed segregation, granting the goal of the early activism, but also making its direct action tactics such as the sit-in and the boycott relatively obsolete. At the next major battleground of civil rights, a march for voting rights would again spur the federal government into action.

Selma

After Lyndon Johnson's landslide election victory in 1964, his administration began to consider a voting rights bill. Grassroots activism worked simultaneously to break down barriers to voting and draw national attention to the problem. For years Diane Nash Bevel, an African American civil rights activist, had advocated a voting rights movement in Alabama.

SNCC had long been working on a small voting rights campaign in Dallas County, and in December 1964 King announced his intention to visit the town of Selma. As in Birmingham, King led protest marches and demonstrations, leading to violent arrests carried out by Sheriff Jim Clark. King himself was arrested on February 1, 1965; three days later, the Islamic militant Malcolm X arrived in Selma to give a speech.

Over the next two weeks, demonstrations continued. On February 18, a night-time march took place in Marion, a small town near Selma. Police, state troopers, and an angry white mob surrounded the marchers. Suddenly the streetlights went out and chaos erupted. Ordinary civilians and law enforcement officials attacked the marchers. During the brawl, a state trooper shot Jimmie Lee Jackson in the stomach; a week later he died. Friends of Jackson threatened to march from Marion to Montgomery

A police officer forcibly restrains Dr. Martin Luther King Jr., during a demonstration in Mississippi in 1966. (© Underwood Photo Archives, Inc.)

where they would present his body to Governor Wallace. Wallace announced that he would use the highway patrol to resist any such march.

King surprised many by endorsing the march. SNCC officials declined to participate because of the threat of violence, though many members including chairman John Lewis took part as individuals. The march began on Sunday, March 7, with King out of the state, having received threats on his life. Six hundred African Americans gathered in Selma and started the 50-mile journey to Montgomery. Marchers noticed the absence of the usual white antagonists. Six blocks from the church, the march approached the Edmund Pettus Bridge above the Alabama River. A sea of blue-helmeted, club-toting state troopers awaited the marchers. When Major John Cloud ordered them to retreat, the marchers bowed their heads in prayer but did not move. The state troopers then turned into a vigilante posse, attacking the marchers ruthlessly. Troopers on horseback clubbed marchers' heads and fired tear gas into the fleeing crowd. Unconscious marchers were trampled in the confusion. At the end of "Bloody Sunday," seventy African Americans were hospitalized.

King returned to Selma immediately, where SNCC activists wanted to attempt the march again. A federal judge issued an injunction against marches, however, and King worried that defying a federal court order might threaten the voting rights bill taking shape in Washington. Relations between King's SCLC and other civil rights organizations, especially SNCC, had always been tense, but during the Selma conflict the two groups became nearly irreconcilable. King encouraged marchers to gather on the following Tuesday but decided that they would not defy the court order against marches. Leading 1,500 African Americans back to the Pettus Bridge, King halted the march even though state troopers stood aside at the bridge. The march broke into song and turned around, returning to the church where the march started. Infuriated SNCC members dubbed the day "Turnaround Tuesday."

In the White House, Johnson watched the events in Selma unfold. Less than a year after risking his political career for a civil rights bill, Johnson again took action in support of African Americans. On March 15, Johnson addressed Congress demanding new federal legislation for voting rights. Referencing the events in Selma, Johnson said; "Their cause must be our cause, too. Because it is not just Negroes, but really all of us who must overcome the crippling legacy of bigotry and injustice. And," he concluded, referencing the

movement's most famous spiritual, "we shall overcome." Johnson's speech allegedly moved King to tears, while some SNCC members denounced it as a hollow gesture.

Soon after Johnson's speech, the federal injunction against the march was overturned. Over 4,000 white and African-American pilgrims began the Selma-to-Montgomery march on March 21. Over the next five days the number if marchers swelled to 25,000. Gathering in front of the state capitol, the marchers presented a petition to Governor Wallace asking for the enforcement of voting rights in Alabama. The march had been remarkable for its lack of violence, though as the marchers dispersed, Ku Klux Klansmen killed Viola Liuzzo, a volunteer from Michigan, as she ferried marchers back to Selma. On August 6, Johnson signed the Voting Rights Act into law, allowing Justice Department officials to intervene wherever voting discrimination occurred.

TRANSITION TO MILITANCE 1965–1970

The legislative victories of the Civil Rights Act and the Voting Rights Act sent Jim Crow to his grave. By 1967, African Americans had achieved unprecedented political standing: Cleveland elected an African-American mayor, and Johnson appointed Thurgood Marshall to the U.S. Supreme Court. Although these laws brought a freedom to African Americans not seen since emancipation, they also threatened to end the movement. The movement had met its goals and faced a crisis of what to do next. Without specific legislation to demand, the movement began to confront the more insidious and less tangible problems of poverty and racism. Federal legislation could only tear away segregation in the law books of the South; it could not change entrenched attitudes.

Activists and observers alike grew weary of the struggles for change. After countless beatings, arrests, and murders, African Americans began to discard the nonviolent tactics of the movement. Racism and discrimination dominated Northern cities in fact, though not in law, and African Americans raged against this invisible oppression. Moderate whites who supported the Southern movement proved reluctant to help African Americans in the North, feeling that they should be pleased with the new legislation. The years between 1965 and 1970 saw the mainstream movement focus its criticisms against capitalism and the distribution of wealth in the United States. This new criticism often led to direct defiance of the state. The movement's student wing

VOTING RIGHTS ACT OF 1965

The Voting Rights Act, perhaps the most important part of civil rights legislation, was adopted in 1965 and extended in 1970, 1975, and 1982 as a means to give voting rights to African Americans and other ethnic minorities disenfranchised by Jim Crow legislation in the South and other states. The Act enforces the Fifteenth Amendment, which guarantees that no person be denied the right to vote on account of race or color.

AN ACT To enforce the fifteenth amendment to the Constitution of the United States, and for other purposes.
Be it enacted by the Senate and House of Representatives of the United States of America in Congress [p*338] assembled, That this Act shall be known as the "Voting Rights Act of 1965."

SEC. 2. No voting qualification or prerequisite to voting, or standard, practice, or procedure shall be imposed or applied by any State or political subdivision to deny or abridge the right of any citizen of the United States to vote on account of race or color.

SEC. 3.
   (a) Whenever the Attorney General institutes a proceeding under any statute to enforce the guarantees of the fifteenth amendment in any State or political subdivision the court shall authorize the appointment of Federal examiners by the United States Civil Service Commission in accordance with section 6 to serve for such period of time and for such political subdivisions as the court shall determine is appropriate to enforce the guarantees of the fifteenth amendment (1) as part of any interlocutory order if the court determines that the appointment of such examiners is necessary to enforce such guarantees or (2) as part of any final judgment if the court finds that violations of the fifteenth amendment justifying equitable relief have occurred in such State or subdivision: Provided, That the court need not authorize the appointment of examiners if any incidents of denial or abridgement of the right to vote on account of race or color (1) have been few in number and have been promptly and effectively corrected by State or local action, (2) the continuing effect of such incidents has been eliminated, and (3) there is no reasonable probability of their recurrence in the future. . . .

SEC. 4.
   (a) To assure that the right of citizens of the United States to vote is not denied or abridged on account of race or color, no citizen shall be denied the right to vote in any Federal, State, or local election because of his failure to comply with any test or device in any State with respect to which the determinations have been [p*340] made under subsection (b) or in any political subdivision with respect to which such determinations have been made as a separate unit, unless the United States District Court for the District of Columbia in an action for a declaratory judgment brought by such State or subdivision against the United States has determined that no such test or device has been used during the five years preceding the filing of the action for the purpose or with the effect of denying or abridging the right to vote on account of race or color: Provided, That no such declaratory judgment shall issue with respect to any plaintiff for a period of five years after the entry of a final judgment of any court of the United States, other than the denial of a declaratory judgment under this section, whether entered prior to or after the enactment of this Act, determining that denials or abridgments of the right to vote on account of race or color through the use of such tests or devices have occurred anywhere in the territory of such plaintiff. . . .
Approved August 6, 1965.

Source: South Carolina v. Katzenbach (1966), appendix.

fractured into factions of increasingly militant groups, and the concept of Black Power rejected the integrationist goals of the earlier movement. In its place a new black nationalism reshaped the movement into an assertion of African-American identity and cultural change.

The Nation of Islam and Malcolm X

As the mainstream civil rights movement took shape during the 1950s, the Nation of Islam grew as well. Often referred to as the Black Muslims, the Nation rejected the integrationist goals of the civil rights movement. Started in the 1930s, the Nation espoused a racial cosmology in which God was a black man and whites were devils. Led by Elijah Muhammad, the Nation created a new self-image for African Americans, stressing economic self-reliance, a withdrawal from white politics, and the teachings of the Nation's unique vision of Islam. Members opened small businesses, sold copies of Muhammad's newspaper, and

MALCOLM X (1925–1965)
(also known as el-Hajj Malik el-Shabazz)

Born on May 19, 1925, in Omaha, Nebraska, Malcolm Little was the son of a Baptist preacher who was an avid supporter of Marcus Garvey's United Negro Improvement Association. When he was a child, his family moved to Lansing, Michigan. Shortly thereafter his father was killed and his mother was institutionalized. Malcolm dropped out of school after the eighth grade and headed for New York City. Living and working in Harlem, he became involved in drug dealing and burglary, was arrested, and was sentenced to a ten-year prison term in 1946.

He was introduced to the philosophy of the Lost-Found Nation of Islam, popularly known as the Black Muslims, while serving his prison term and converted to its utopian and racist point of view that the white man is the devil with whom blacks cannot live. Malcolm adopted X—symbolic of a stolen identity—as his last name. He became a Muslim minister upon his release in 1952 and quickly became very prominent with a following perhaps equaling that of the Black Muslims' leader, Elijah Muhammad. His controversial denunciations of white society and his call for vengeance polarized the civil rights movement; yet he found sympathy among many white college students who found ugly truths in his condemnations. Malcolm became increasingly frustrated with the Nation of Islam for failing to join the civil rights movement and with Muhammad personally for turning a blind eye to the corruption at the highest levels of his organization. In December 1963, Elijah suspended Malcolm after a speech in which Malcolm suggested that President John F. Kennedy's assassination was a matter of the "chickens coming home to roost."

In 1964, upon a pilgrimage to Mecca he discovered that orthodox Muslims preached equality of the races. He announced his conversion to orthodox Islam and his new belief that there could be brotherhood between blacks and whites. He changed his name to el-Hajj Malik el-Shabazz but remained convinced that racism was still a major problem in the United States. In his Organization of Afro-American Unity, formed after his return in June 1964, the tone was still that of militant black nationalism but no longer of separation. In February 21, 1965, he was shot and killed in a public auditorium in New York City. His assassins were identified as Black Muslims sent by Elijah Muhammad, but this is a matter of controversy. He foreshadowed his own death and martyrdom in *The Autobiography of Malcolm X* (1965), which traced his journey from childhood to his conversion to orthodox Islam. Both his book and his rhetoric directly influenced the Student Nonviolent Coordinating Committee's embrace of black power in 1966.

James G. Lewis

replaced their surnames with an "X" to symbolize their identity stolen by slavery.

During the 1950s and 1960s, Muhammad's most trusted and talented minister, Malcolm X, spurred the Nation to its greatest growth. Malcolm forcefully advocated black self-reliance and the pursuit of freedom "by any means necessary." Members of the Nation armed themselves for self-defense, creating the perception among many whites that they were preparing for a race war. Malcolm drew thousands of converts to the Nation and quickly became the most visible of the Nation's members. He also criticized the goals and tactics of the nonviolent civil rights movement, arguing that freedom could never be attained without bloodshed.

Malcolm grew frustrated with the Nation's censure of political activism, straining his relationship with Muhammad. When Malcolm commented that the Kennedy assassination was a result of white America's fundamentally violent nature, Muhammad ordered Malcolm to cease public speaking. Malcolm remained the Nation's most recognized figure, however. In 1964, he welcomed the young heavyweight boxing champion Cassius Clay's conversion to Islam. Disturbed by the Nation's refusal to act for social change and disillusioned with Muhammad after allegations of adultery surfaced, however, Malcolm left the Nation of Islam in 1964. After a pilgrimage to the Holy Land, Malcolm returned to the United States and rejected the separatism of his earlier philosophy. Instead, he stressed African-American unity and seemed to say that reconciliation with whites was possible.

His feud with Muhammad continued, and on February 21, 1965, assassins from the Nation gunned Malcolm down in New York City. After death, Malcolm's ideas inspired legions of African Americans to reassess notions of their cultural and ethnic heritage. The Nation of Islam thrived during the 1960s, boasting 500,000 members and reaching millions more through its positive reinforcement of African-American identity.

An eloquent and electrifying orator, Black Muslim leader Malcolm X preached racial pride and black separatism. He is shown here at a rally in New York City on July 27, 1963. He was assassinated two years later. *(AP Wide World Photos)*

Chicago: The Nonviolent Movement Dwindles

In 1966, Martin Luther King Jr. took his movement to the North. Hoping to re-create his successes at Birmingham and Selma, King knew that Chicago would be different. Racism existed almost as a part of the city's infrastructure. African Americans lived in ghettos, and Mayor Richard Daley ruled the city like a pharaoh. Unlike Birmingham, the Chicago government featured several African-American representatives. Although these representatives aimed to please the Daley machine, local African-American residents and the press held faith in these officials and felt King's actions would not necessarily help them. The sheer size and diversity of the city threatened to overwhelm the movement. Rival churches and the Nation of Islam, headquartered in Chicago, opposed the SCLC's actions. King's close friend and colleague Ralph David Abernathy later wrote: "We should have known better than to believe we could come to Chicago and right its wrongs with the same tactics we had used in Montgomery, Birmingham, and Selma. We entered a different world when we came to this northern city in 1966, a world we didn't fully understand."

Undeterred, King moved into a Chicago slum to begin a campaign against housing discrimination. King's celebrity assured at least a decent turnout to his meetings. Working with ghetto dwellers, King encouraged them to fight delinquent landlords by refusing to pay rent and spending the money on improvements to their property. King then demanded that Daley produce a housing ordinance against real estate agents who perpetuated the division of Chicago into racial and ethnic enclaves. Vowing to integrate Chicago's lily-white neighborhoods, King led a march on August 5 where white demonstrators, waving Confederate and Nazi flags, hurled bricks, rocks, and bottles at the marchers. King later commented that the white mobs in Chicago were far more vicious than those in the South.

King pledged to continue the marches, and promised that they would extend into the white suburb of Cicero, famous for a recent murder of an African American in search of a job. Daley and other officials, agreeing that a march into Cicero could turn into a mass murder, agreed to meet with King. On August 26 the two men met, with Daley agreeing to the SCLC's demands of housing ordinances and an end to discrimination. Such an agreement mattered little, since it was only upon Daley's actions that the agreement could ever be enforced. After King left Chicago Daley took no action on his promises. Chicago proved to King that he would have to refocus his efforts.

Riots

The federal government desegregated the South by the mid-1960s but did little to calm the rising aggravations of police brutality, unemployment, and poverty ravaging African-American communities in Northern cities. With no faith in public officials, African Americans felt the oppression of racism more than ever. In the summer of 1964, riots broke out in Philadelphia, Harlem, and Paterson and Elizabeth, New Jersey. By 1966 rioting had spread to thirty-eight cities including Chicago, Cleveland, and San Francisco. The next year 164 riots threatened to tear major cities apart, including Newark and Detroit in July. Observers noted that these were not race riots in the traditional sense. Instead, African Americans destroyed white-owned businesses and property, acting out their rage against the economic and racial oppression suffered by African Americans.

Because the main activity was looting and not killing, observers dubbed these "commodity riots." Johnson dispatched a commission led by Illinois governor Otto Kerner to investigate the causes of the riots. The Kerner Commission found that America was two societies separated by race and poised in direct opposition to each other. The roots of violence, the commission argued, sprang from white racism entrenched in every area of life, including employment, education, and housing. By 1968, however, the Viet-

nam War had gutted Johnson's Great Society, and most white Americans had no patience for furthering the program on behalf of African Americans whom they feared as rioters.

Black Power

Civil rights activism continued in the South in 1966, and whites continued to mar demonstrations with violence. It seemed that every Southern city would have to be the site of demonstrations and violence before whites accepted African-American civil rights. In June, James Meredith began a March Against Fear from Memphis to Jackson. Along the way a white man fired a shotgun at Meredith, causing minor wounds to his face. The new SNCC chairman Stokely Carmichael erupted at the news. Continuing Meredith's march, Carmichael thundered "The only way we gonna stop them white men from whuppin' us is to take over. We been saying freedom for six years and we ain't got nothing. What we gonna start sayin' now is Black Power!"

To Carmichael, Black Power meant an affirmation of black identity and active responsibility in decision making. Across the nation, young African Americans chanted "Black Power," creating a cultural wave that continues to this day. African Americans came to reject the term "Negro," instead referring to themselves as "blacks." In the process, blackness came to represent the fundamental identity of African Americans. In the political realm, Carmichael and other Black Power advocates criticized the compromises with whites fashioned by the NAACP and SCLC.

African Americans of all social and geographic status embraced Black Power. An expression rather than an organization, Black Power inspired African Americans to embrace their African heritage and create a sense of cultural unity based on that heritage rather than their status as Americans. On college campuses, African-American students mobilized to create Black Studies departments and black student unions, as well as cultural heritage programs and activities. Black Power revolutionized American sports as well. College and professional athletes grew angry at the lack of African-American coaches and managers. Muhammad Ali (formerly Cassius Clay) refused to fight in Vietnam, which he disdained as a white man's war. At the 1968 summer Olympics in Mexico City, African-American sprinters Tommie Smith and John Carlos bowed their heads and raised gloved fists in the Black Power salute as they received their gold and bronze medals.

Black Power reconceptualized the war in Viet-

FLORYNCE RAE "FLO" KENNEDY (1916–2000)

Florynce Rae Kennedy, the second of five daughters, was born on February 11, 1916, in Kansas City, Missouri. Her father was a Pullman porter and later owned a taxi business. He once stood up with a shotgun to members of the Ku Klux Klan who wanted to drive him from a home he had bought in a mainly white neighborhood. Within a few years of graduating high school, Kennedy had opened her own business and became involved in her first political protest, helping organize a boycott when the local Coca-Cola bottler refused to hire black truck drivers. She moved to New York City in 1942 and earned her B.A. at Columbia University. She applied to Columbia Law School but was rejected because she was female. After threatening a discrimination suit, she was admitted and was one of the first black women to graduate in 1951.

After a brief stint at a law firm, she opened her own practice in New York. One of her cases involved representing the estates of the jazz greats Billie Holiday and Charlie Parker to recover money owed them by record companies. Even though she won the cases, she became increasingly disillusioned with the racism she saw in the justice system. She turned to political activism.

After that, Kennedy's legal cases were almost always political. In 1966, she represented H. Rap Brown, the civil rights leader. In 1968, she sued the Roman Catholic Church for what she viewed as interference with abortion. In 1969, she organized a group of feminist lawyers to challenge the constitutionality of New York State's abortion law, an action credited with helping influence the Legislature to liberalize abortion the next year. In 1969, she helped represent twenty-one Black Panthers on trial in Manhattan for conspiracy to commit bombings, among other things. They were eventually acquitted, but during the trial she used them to draw attention to a restaurant that did not admit blacks or Jews.

Broadening her approach, in the 1960s and 1970s, Kennedy spoke out forcefully in many forums on behalf of African Americans but also women, the poor, homosexuals, prostitutes, and minorities. She ignored grassroots efforts, saying they moved too slowly. Her strategy was to go after the biggest targets possible. To fight racism in the media, she founded the Media Workshop in 1966, and she formed the Feminist Party when she grew impatient with the National Organization of Women. Its first act was to nominate Representative Shirley Chisholm (D-NY) for president of the United States.

In the 1970s, Kennedy became particularly active in promoting women's right to abortions. Noted for her often outrageous outspokenness, she published her autobiography, *Color Me Flo: My Hard Life and Good Times* (1976), and worked the college lecture circuit with Gloria Steinem. In 1957, Kennedy married Charles Dye, a writer, who died a few years later. She died on December 23, 2000.

James G. Lewis

nam. African Americans blamed the war for bankrupting the Great Society programs that promised a relief from poverty. They also saw the Vietnamese as fighting a war of liberation against the United States; African Americans could empathize with a people fighting for freedom against American oppressors. Many resented the administration's claim of supporting freedom and democracy in Vietnam, since the same government had been reluctant to support freedom and democracy in the Deep South.

The Black Panthers

In December 1966, SNCC ousted its white members; CORE took the same action eight months later. This move alienated moderate African Americans and whites, drying up funding for both organizations. H. Rap Brown, Carmichael's successor at SNCC, advocated militant resistance to police and whites. The Black Panthers, whom Carmichael joined in 1967, quickly became the most visible new organization of the Black Power era. Founded in Oakland in 1966, the Black Panther Party became the most vocal advocate of African-American militancy since Malcolm X. Its founder, Huey P. Newton, formed the Black Panthers to encourage self-defense and self-reliance among Oakland's African Americans. The Panthers formed school breakfast programs for children, clothing and shoes distribution, and a free medical clinic.

The notoriety of the Panthers centered around their self-defense program. Panthers carried weapons for protection, a right protected by law in California at the time. Regardless of its legality, the vision of armed African-American militants patrolling Oakland terrified whites. The Panthers argued that self-defense was an essential right, given Oakland's history of police brutality. In October 1967, Newton was arrested following a shoot-out with police where an officer was killed. Across the country thousands flocked to the Black Panthers in the "Free Huey" movement. By 1970, most major U.S. cities featured a branch of the Black Panther Party, whose members were constantly arrested, imprisoned, or in shoot-outs with police. Among those who defended them in court was Florynce Rae "Flo" Kennedy, one of the most prominent civil rights and feminist attorneys in the country. By 1973, more than thirty Panthers had been killed. The Panther Party was constantly in disarray. Members argued with each other, and the FBI constantly sabotaged the organization. The Black Panther Party lingered through the 1970s, but infighting and violence had rendered all of the militant African-American organizations politically dead.

The Assassination of King

In the years following his setback in Chicago, King came to believe that the fundamental inequities of American capitalism caused racial injustice. He began to concentrate on the eradication of poverty as the road to freedom for African Americans. King joined others in denouncing the Vietnam War for ruining the Great Society's antipoverty programs. In March 1968, King traveled to Memphis in support of a sanitation workers' strike. The workers wanted recognition of their own, African-American labor union. The usual nonviolent approaches broke down, and violence broke out at demonstrations. On April 4, a sniper's bullet shattered King's jaw, killing the civil rights leader who had often expressed acceptance and serenity at the thought of dying for his cause. Riots erupted across the nation that night in over 130 cities, resulting in forty-six deaths.

Although King's tactics had lost much of their efficacy, he remained the undisputed figurehead of the movement until his death. His charisma, oratory, and willingness to suffer continued to draw many to his demonstrations; after his assassination, the civil rights movement never approached the influence seen under his leadership. Abernathy succeeded King as head of the SCLC and in May launched the Poor People's Campaign. Bringing together a coalition of poverty-stricken minorities, the campaign gathered in Washington, D.C., to pressure Congress into further legislation against poverty. The centerpiece of the campaign was Resurrection City, a shantytown on the national mall that symbolized the plight of America's poor.

Short-sighted planning and a lack of organization hindered the Poor People's Campaign. The hastily built Resurrection City lacked water, sanitation, and

A youthful Jesse Jackson, who had been with Dr. Martin Luther King Jr., the night he was assassinated in Memphis, Tennessee, in 1968, arrives home in Chicago carrying a copy of the *Chicago Defender*. (© Robert A. Sengstacke)

electricity. Heavy rains turned the mall grounds into mud. Fewer than 2,500 demonstrators turned out, and many who did bickered and fought between themselves. Although few poor people were drawn to the campaign, the general public exhibited even less interest in the movement. After the perceived excesses of the Great Society and the social strife of riots, no one was very enthusiastic about supporting further government expenditures against poverty. In June, as the demonstrators at the Poor People's Campaign straggled home, the SCLC and the civil rights movement faded from prominence.

THE END OF AMERICA'S SECOND RECONSTRUCTION

After King's death, no African-American leader rose to guide the movement. In 1969, James Forman, formerly of SNCC, announced a demand that whites pay reparations for centuries of slavery and racism. An era had ended: instead of appealing to basic biblical and constitutional rights, activists focused on feelings of white guilt to seek redress for past and present wrongs. After 1970, demands for integration continued for a time, primarily in the form of mandatory school busing, but resistance slowed these efforts. Federal actions took the form of preferences and entitlements such as Affirmative Action to counter subtle and invisible forms of discrimination as well as the support network established over centuries of social, economic, and racial oppression giving whites an inherent advantage in business and education.

The civil rights movement spawned volatile progeny. The student movement of the late 1960s drew inspiration and experience from the civil rights movement: many members of the New Left cut their teeth during SNCC's Freedom Summer. Many women felt sexism dominated the civil rights and student movements and initiated a women's movement of their own. Chicanos and Native Americans learned from the civil rights movement the tactics they would use in their own fights for freedom during the late 1960s and 1970s. No social movement before or since the civil rights movement has mobilized moral, political, and grassroots power on such a scale, influencing countless people outside itself, including generations unborn.

Paul Rubinson

BIBLIOGRAPHY

Abernathy, Ralph David. *And the Walls Came Tumbling Down.* New York: HarperPerennial, 1989.

Beschloss, Michael R., ed. *Taking Charge: The Johnson White House Tapes, 1963–1964.* New York: Simon and Schuster, 1997.

Blossom, Virgil T. *It HAS Happened Here.* New York: Harper & Brothers, 1959.

Branch, Taylor. *Parting the Waters: America in the King Years, 1954–63.* New York: Simon and Schuster, 1988.

———. *Pillar of Fire: America in the King Years, 1963–65.* New York: Simon and Schuster, 1998.

Burner, Eric. *And Gently He Shall Lead Them: Robert Parris Moses and Civil Rights in Mississippi.* New York: New York University Press, 1994.

Button, James W. *Black Violence: Political Impact of the 1960s Riots.* Princeton, NJ: Princeton University Press, 1978.

Chesnut, J.L., Jr. *Black in Selma: The Uncommon Life of J.L. Chesnut, Jr.* New York: Farrar, Straus and Giroux, 1990.

Cleaver, Eldridge. *Soul on Ice.* New York: Laurel, 1968.

Collier-Thomas, Bettye, and V.P. Franklin. *My Soul Is a Witness: A Chronology of the Civil Rights Era, 1954–1965.* New York: Henry Holt, 1999.

Halberstam, David. *The Children.* New York: Random House, 1998.

———. *The Fifties.* New York: Fawcett Columbine, 1993.

Huckaby, Elizabeth. *Crisis at Central High: Little Rock, 1957–58.* Baton Rouge: Louisiana State University Press, 1980.

Jeffries, Judson L. *Huey P. Newton: The Radical Theorist.* Jackson: University Press of Mississippi, 2002.

Kluger, Richard. *Simple Justice: The History of* Brown v. Board of Education *and Black America's Struggle for Equality.* New York: Alfred A. Knopf, 1987.

Malcolm X, and Alex Haley. *The Autobiography of Malcolm X.* New York: Ballantine Books, 1965.

McAdam, Doug. *Freedom Summer.* New York: Oxford University Press, 1988.

Meier, August, and Elliott Rudwick. *CORE: A Study in the Civil Rights Movement, 1942–1968.* New York: Oxford University Press, 1973

Moody, Anne. *Coming of Age in Mississippi.* New York: Laurel, 1968.

Morris, Aldon D. *The Origins of the Civil Rights Movement: Black Communities Organizing for Change.* New York: Free Press, 1984.

Pearson, Hugh. *The Shadow of the Panther: Huey Newton and the Price of Black Power in America.* Reading, MA: Addison-Wesley, 1994.

Perry, Bruce. *Malcolm: The Life of a Man Who Changed Black America.* New York: Station Hill, 1991.

Ravitch, Diane. *The Troubled Crusade: American Education, 1945–1980.* New York: Basic Books, 1983.

Robnett, Belinda. *How Long? How Long? African-American Women in the Struggle for Civil Rights.* New York: Oxford University Press, 1997.

Steele, Shelby. *The Content of Our Character: A New Vision of Race in America.* New York: St. Martin's, 1990.

Tushnet, Mark V. *Making Civil Rights Law: Thurgood Marshall and the Supreme Court, 1936–1961.* New York: Oxford University Press, 1994.

Van Deburg, William L. *New Day in Babylon: The Black Power Movement and American Culture, 1965–1975.* Chicago: University of Chicago Press, 1992.

Weisbrot, Robert. *Freedom Bound: A History of America's Civil Rights Movement.* New York: W.W. Norton, 1990.

Whitfield, Stephen J. *A Death in the Delta: The Story of Emmett Till.* New York: Free Press, 1988.

Wilkins, Roy. *Standing Tall: The Autobiography of Roy Wilkins.* New York: Viking, 1982.

Williams, Juan. *Eyes on the Prize: America's Civil Rights Years, 1954–1965.* New York: Viking, 1987.

NONVIOLENT DIRECT ACTION

Popularized by African-American activists during the 1960s, nonviolent direct action became the most successful protest strategy in the modern civil rights movement. The sit-in movement and the Freedom Ride epitomized this active form of nonviolent resistance, which dramatized the plight of African Americans and forced white America to confront the reality of segregation and discrimination. Rooted in the pacifist activism of the 1930s and 1940s, the nonviolent direct action campaigns of the 1960s are credited with contributing to the passage of the federal civil rights legislation of 1964 and 1965.

ROOTS AND EARLY ACTIVISM

Although African Americans had responded to discrimination and segregation with nonviolent protest in the past, there was no tradition of nonviolence in the black community at the beginning of the twentieth century. Isolated incidents of nonviolent activism such as boycotts of segregated streetcars or peaceful demonstrations against discriminatory statutes in the nineteenth and early twentieth centuries never developed into a black mass movement. In the 1920s and 1930s, several African-American intellectuals became interested in the nonviolent anticolonial struggle in India that civil rights activist Mohandas Gandhi had initiated against Britain. The black press reported extensively about Gandhi's campaigns of civil disobedience, such as the famous Salt march of 1931, and many black intellectuals traveled to India to meet Gandhi and to acquaint themselves with his philosophy of nonviolence. Influenced by Hindu traditions and Western philosophy, Gandhi had formulated his philosophy of *Satyagraha*, which can be translated as "truth seeking." Nonretaliation and positive goodwill toward the opponent were the essence of this approach that attempted to appeal to the conscience of the oppressor by suffering and dramatizing the issue at stake. If this plea failed to bring about meaningful change, protestors would employ strategies of nonviolent coercion such as noncooperation and civil disobedience.

Inspired by Gandhi's philosophy, A. Philip Randolph was one of the first black civil rights activists to suggest that nonviolent activism could be successfully applied to the African-American freedom struggle. Randolph founded and led the all-black March on Washington Movement (MOWM) in 1941, which he considered a modified version of Gandhi's nonviolent principles. Calling his approach "non-violent good-will direct action," Randolph threatened President Franklin D. Roosevelt with bringing 100,000 African Americans to Washington, D.C., if he refused to ban discrimination against black Americans in the defense industry. Afraid of embarrassing the United States in its fight for democracy against Nazi Germany, Roosevelt yielded to Randolph's demands and issued Executive Order 8802, which outlawed racial discrimination in the defense industry. Together with the newly created Fair Employment Practices Committee (FEPC), the president's measure effectively created new job opportunities for African Americans in the booming industry. Although Randolph's vision of a nonviolent mass demonstration in the national capital would not be achieved until 1963, the MOWM had indicated the potential of collective nonviolent resistance.

Like Randolph, members of the pacifist Fellowship of Reconciliation (FOR) were devout admirers of Gandhi. In 1942, an interracial group of college students, most of whom were FOR members, founded the Congress of Racial Equality (CORE), an organization that espoused nonviolent interracial activism to challenge discrimination and segregation. Coming from a primarily white and middle-class background, small groups of CORE activists staged numerous "sit-down" campaigns in several Northern cities in 1942 and 1943, successfully desegregating restaurants and

FRED HAMPTON (1948–1969)

Fred Hampton was born in Chicago and raised in the nearby suburb of Maywood. He was a gifted student and athlete while in high school. Following graduation, he enrolled at Triton Junior College, majoring in pre-law. While in college, he became president of the local chapter of the National Association for the Advancement of Colored People (NAACP) in Maywood. As youth director, he built a comparatively large, racially integrated, and well-organized youth group of around 500 members in a community of 27,000. He led a drive for the establishment of more and better recreational facilities and improved schooling for Maywood's black youths, all the while embracing nonviolent activism to achieve his goals.

Coincident with Hampton's activities the Black Panther Party for Self-Defense started its rise to national prominence. Hampton was attracted to the Black Panthers because of their ten-point program of black self-determination. He joined the party and moved to downtown Chicago, where he helped launch the party's Illinois chapter in November 1968. His outstanding organizational skills served him well. He got inner city street gangs to agree to a nonaggression pact. He forged the alliance by emphasizing that racial and ethnic conflict between the white, black and Puerto Rican gangs would only serve to keep its members mired in poverty. In May 1969, Hampton called a press conference to announce that a truce had been declared among this "rainbow coalition," a phrase he coined that was later adopted and popularized by Jesse Jackson.

Hampton also took up the Black Panthers' efforts in community services while reaching out to white radical groups like the Students for a Democratic Society (SDS). In April 1969, he noted in a speech that the Panthers' ten-point program was being altered because "we used the word 'white' when we should have used the word 'capitalist.' " Despite such efforts, the Chicago chapter of the Panthers and the SDS split over ideology, and Hampton denounced the more militant faction known as the Weathermen who sought out violent confrontations with police. He saw no purpose in gratuitous violence since it worked against his larger goal of forming a common cause with as many groups as possible. Around November 1969, Hampton learned he was soon to become chief of staff, a high-profile position that would make him a major spokesperson for the Panthers and possibly lead to national prominence.

Meanwhile, Mayor Richard J. Daley, the Chicago Police, state attorney Edward V. Hanrahan, and the Federal Bureau of Investigation (FBI) targeted the Black Panthers and Hampton for surveillance and harassment. Characterizing the Black Panthers as just another criminal gang causing trouble, the police made raids and arrests in an attempt to discredit and destroy them. On December 4, 1969, the police and FBI raided the Panther party headquarters yet again as part of this plan. Working from information provided by an informant, the raid took place at 4:45 in the morning. During the ten minutes of furious gunfire, Mark Clark, a Panther leader from Peoria, Illinois, and Hampton, who had been drugged by the informant and who slept through the entire event, were killed and four others seriously wounded. A special commission investigated the shootout and found that the raid more closely resembled an execution than a legitimate police action. While Hampton had been shot multiple times while in bed, his pregnant girlfriend lying beside him was left unharmed.

Hampton's funeral was attended by more than 5,000 people, and black leaders including Jesse Jackson and Ralph Abernathy, the head of the Southern Christian Leadership Conference, gave eulogies. The officers involved in the raid were cleared of charges, but the families of the slain men filed civil suits and won a large undisclosed amount of money. Jackson and Abernathy set up a scholarship fund in Hampton's name to help keep his name and cause of social change through education alive. Hampton's son, Fred, Jr., born after his father's death, has followed his father into political activism.

James G. Lewis

public accommodations. Another example of CORE's nonviolent strategy was the Journey of Reconciliation in 1947, designed to test the U.S. Supreme Court's recent *Morgan v. Virginia* decision, which had declared segregation in public transportation unconstitutional. Traveling by bus and train across the upper South, activists encountered less white resistance than ex-pected, but a violent mob in North Carolina eventually stopped the Journey. Although CORE had successfully used the nonviolent direct action technique, the organization together with the MOWM remained the lone spearhead of nonviolent activism in the 1940s.

In fact, chances for a black nonviolent mass

Fred Hampton, chairman of the Black Panther Party of Illinois, was killed at the age of twenty-one in a gun battle, after police entered a Chicago apartment to search for weapons. *(CORBIS)*

movement seemed slim in the aftermath of World War II. Many African-American newspapers severely criticized Randolph's organization, considering his advocacy of nonviolence "suicidal." The majority of blacks doubted that Gandhian nonviolence could be successfully adapted to the specific circumstances of blacks in the United States. While Indian activists had fought their nonviolent battle in their own country against a small British colonial elite, African Americans were vastly outnumbered by unsympathetic whites. Moreover, in a society that cherished masculine qualities of self-defense, nonviolence was an alien concept to both white and black Americans. Pacifist CORE members were usually laughed at or considered insane when attempting to explain Gandhi's concept of nonretaliation, and hundreds of violent racial clashes during World War II served as a reminder that African Americans were far from espousing nonviolent activism. Rather, an increasing number of black Americans—particularly thousands of black soldiers who returned to the United States— refused to accept white violence passively. Many African Americans were determined to fight back when attacked by whites.

ACTIVISM IN THE EARLY CIVIL RIGHTS MOVEMENT

Only the Montgomery bus boycott of 1955–1956 prepared the ground for the future nonviolent assault against segregation and discrimination. The successful nonviolent boycott against segregated seating in Montgomery's city buses thrust a young minister named Martin Luther King Jr. upon the national stage. Although later considered an icon of philosophical nonviolence, King's espousal of Gandhi was a result of joint efforts by older FOR and CORE activists, who tutored the young minister in the abstract concept of *Satyagraha*. Prior to becoming a national celebrity, King was unfamiliar with Gandhian nonviolence and could hardly be considered an advocate of pure nonviolence. During the early days of the Montgomery boycott, armed black men guarded King's brightly lit house against white terrorists, and visitors were amazed to find pistols and shotguns in the living room. However, under the influence of pacifist activists Bayard Rustin and Glen Smiley, King eventually banned all guns from his house and gradually came to formulate a philosophy of nonviolence that fused Gandhian nonviolence with traditions of a distinct Afro-Christianity. King's emerging philosophy of nonviolence found institutional expression in the Southern Christian Leadership Conference (SCLC), organized by King and other black ministers with the assistance of Rustin in 1957. Dedicated to confronting Southern racial practices with nonviolent direct action, the SCLC became one of the most prominent civil rights organizations of the 1960s.

However, not King's organization but a spontaneous student-led sit-in movement in early 1960 ushered in the heyday of nonviolent protest. Sparked by four black college students in Greensboro, North Carolina, on February 1, 1960, the sit-in movement spread within a few months into almost every Southern state. Effecting the desegregation of lunch counters and restaurants across the South, the student sit-ins epitomized the essence of nonviolent direct action. Beaten and intimidated by vicious white mobs, sit-in protestors did not retaliate when attacked and actively forced a change of the racial status quo by dramatizing the injustice of segregation. That same year, several sit-in leaders founded the Student Nonviolent Coordinating Committee (SNCC), another organization that was determined to challenge the racial status quo with nonviolent resistance.

On May 14, 1961, white racists set fire to this Greyhound bus in Anniston, Alabama, and then attacked passengers as they escaped from the bus. Some of the passengers were members of the "Freedom Riders" group sponsored by the Congress of Racial Equality. (© *Underwood Photo Archives, Inc.*)

MAJOR SUCCESSES IN THE 1960S

In 1961, CORE staged yet another audacious direct action project: the Freedom Ride. Modeled after the Journey of Reconciliation, the Freedom Riders this time tested the *Boynton v. Virginia* U.S. Supreme Court decision, which had officially desegregated public transportation facilities such as waiting rooms and restrooms. Unlike the 1947 protest, however, the Freedom Ride led activists in the most dangerous areas of the Deep South. White Southerners reacted with an unprecedented level of violence to this challenge of traditional racial practices. In Anniston, Alabama, white mobs bombed one of the buses and beat the Freedom Riders with chains and clubs. The next day, whites in Montgomery besieged the activists in a local church and had to be held at bay by federal troops.

Pictures that showed the burning bus and activists covered with blood became front-page news across the world. Nonviolent direct action had exposed American racism in front of the world, a fact that deeply embarrassed the United States in its fight for democracy in the Cold War struggle against the Soviet Union. Although it had severely limited black activism in the 1950s, the Cold War now gave African-American activists enormous political leverage, making nonviolent direct action an even more effective weapon in the black freedom struggle. In an attempt to prevent additional international bad press, President John F. Kennedy ordered an entourage of heavily armed soldiers along with several helicopters to protect the buses.

The nonviolent demonstrations that Martin Luther King's SCLC staged in Alabama in 1963 and 1965 unquestionably proved the efficacy of nonviolent direct action. Having learned from its failed nonviolent campaign in Albany, Georgia, in 1962, where local police had thwarted activists' efforts with a nonviolent tactic of their own, SCLC had opted to use a different strategy in Birmingham. Assisted by thousands of black teenagers, activists deliberately provoked a violent response by local police, creating a crisis that neither local nor federal authorities could simply ignore. Commanded by Birmingham's police chief, Eugene "Bull" Connor, firefighters fought nonviolent black children with high-pressured water hoses, while policemen arrested and jailed thousands of young protestors. Like the Freedom Ride, the brutality that Birmingham's authorities used to crush the nonviolent demonstrations triggered a national and international public outcry and exposed Southern racism in the eyes of the world. White Americans and international observers were similarly appalled by the pictures of Alabama state troopers who attacked nonviolent protestors with clubs and tear gas on the Edmund Pettus Bridge in Selma, Alabama, in 1965. The subsequent Selma-to-Montgomery march became a tribute to nonviolent activism. The Birmingham and Selma demonstrations along with the nonviolent March on Washington in 1963 contributed to passage of the Civil Rights Act of 1964 and the Voting Rights Act of 1965.

LIMITATIONS AND DEMISE

Although these carefully planned nonviolent direct action projects had successfully exposed segregation and discrimination, the efficacy of nonviolence was limited. The success of nonviolent direct action depended largely on the wide media attention that these violent crises received. In addition, only federal intervention could restrain white violence against civil rights activists. In the hundreds of small Southern communities, where activists attempted to implement the federal civil rights legislation, violence against African Americans remained virtually unrestrained. Trying to convince blacks in Mississippi, Louisiana, and other states in the Deep South to register to vote, CORE and SNCC activists together with local blacks quickly became targets for a campaign of terror and intimidation. Between 1960 and 1968, white supremacist terrorists—in particular, members of the Ku Klux Klan—shot into black homes, bombed black churches, and murdered dozens of civil rights activists in an attempt to stop civil rights activities. Neither appeal-

ing to the conscience of white Southerners nor staging local nonviolent protests could curb white brutality.

Faced with constant violent threats, many local African Americans relied on armed self-defense to protect their communities from white terror. In virtually every local community where CORE and SNCC members were organizing in the 1960s, blacks protected themselves and civil rights workers with pistols, rifles, and shotguns. By 1965, armed protection had become a simple necessity for both local black Southerners and Northern activists. In many Southern civil rights projects, nonviolent protest and armed self-defense worked hand in hand. In fact, for numerous activists, it became common to stage nonviolent demonstrations during the day and to rely on armed protection at night. Their experience in the rural South led many CORE and SNCC activists to question the efficacy of pure nonviolence and contributed to the radicalization of both organizations.

Moreover, nonviolent protest could not affect the wretched condition of poor African Americans in the black ghettos of the urban North. Neither the Civil Rights Act nor the Voting Rights Act had altered the socioeconomic roots of poverty in American cities, a fact that caused much frustration among young blacks in the North and West. Unsurprisingly, many of these black teenagers rejected the nonviolent philosophy of Martin Luther King and felt drawn to the militant message of black nationalist Malcolm X, who had rejected nonviolence as an obstacle to developing an affirmative black identity. The influence of black nationalism along with activists' day-to-day experience in the Deep South and their frustration with the federal government's inaction led most SNCC and CORE members to abandon the ideal of integration and nonviolence. The James Meredith March of 1966 became the stage for the new slogan Black Power, which called for economic and political power for African Americans and the right of armed self-defense. That same year, SNCC and CORE officially embraced Black Power and the concept of armed resistance, thus conspicuously abandoning their nonviolent roots. Only Martin Luther King's organization and the National Association for the Advancement of Colored People (NAACP) continued to support nonviolence and severely criticized the new slogan.

In the ensuing years, many African Americans, frustrated with the slow pace of change, opted to use violence to express their anger. Between 1965 and 1968, hundreds of civil disorders rocked black ghettos in American cities, during which African Americans protested their condition by destroying white property and battling police. After 1967, black nationalist groups such as the Black Panther Party for Self-Defense and the Republic of New Africa enjoyed a considerable increase in membership. The assassination of Martin Luther King in 1968 marked the definitive end of a decade-long era of nonviolent protest.

ASSESSMENT

Nonviolent direct action proved to be the most successful protest strategy in the African-American freedom movement. By exposing and dramatizing discrimination and oppression in the American South, black activists were able to rouse sympathy among white Americans and around the world. For a minority that never constituted more than 12 percent of the American population, nonviolence provided African Americans with a powerful tactic that could be successfully used to pressure local and federal authorities into yielding to activists' demands. The Cold War gave African Americans additional leverage in their struggle for civil rights. Embarrassed by international criticism of American racial practices in their fight for democracy, the American government was forced to ponder how to respond to the numerous crises that black nonviolent protest had provoked. Thus, the nonviolent demonstrations in Birmingham, Selma, and Washington, D.C., contributed to passage of the Civil Rights Act of 1964 and the Voting Rights Act of 1965.

The power of nonviolence was limited, however. Implementing federal civil rights legislation in the Deep South proved far more difficult than lobbying for its passage. Organizing in hundreds of small rural Southern communities, civil rights workers quickly learned that nonviolent protest did little to stop white supremacist violence. Their calls for federal intervention ignored, Southern African Americans had to rely on their own ability to protect themselves. Thus, armed self-defense and nonviolent direct action frequently operated in symbiosis in Southern civil rights projects. Furthermore, nonviolent protest could not challenge the socioeconomic basis of black poverty in the urban ghettos of the north. Frustration with the limitations of nonviolence among African Americans, along with the militant message of black nationalism, led to the gradual abandonment of the nonviolent protest and its demise at the end of the 1960s.

Simon Wendt

BIBLIOGRAPHY

Bondurant, John H. *Conquest of Violence: The Gandhian Philosophy of Conflict.* Princeton, NJ: Princeton University Press, 1958.

Carson, Clayborn. *In Struggle: SNCC and the Black Awakening of the 1960s.* Cambridge, MA: Harvard University Press, 1995.

Dudziak, Mary L. *Cold War Civil Rights: Race and the Image of American Democracy.* Princeton, NJ: Princeton University Press, 2000.

Garrow, David J. *Bearing the Cross: Martin Luther King Jr., and the Southern Christian Leadership Conference.* New York: Morrow, 1986.

Kapur, Sudarshan. *Raising Up a Prophet: The African-American Encounter with Gandhi.* Boston: Beacon, 1992.

Meier, August, and Elliot Rudwick. *CORE: A Study in the Civil Rights Movement, 1942–68.* Urbana: University of Illinois Press, 1975.

Pfeffer, Paula F. *A. Philip Randolph, Pioneer of the Civil Rights Movement.* Baton Rouge: Louisiana State University Press, 1990.

Van Deburg, William L. *New Day in Babylon: The Black Power Movement and American Culture, 1965–1975.* Chicago: University of Chicago Press, 1992.

Congress of Racial Equality

Founded in 1942, the Congress of Racial Equality (CORE) became one of the most prominent civil rights organizations in the 1960s. Using interracial nonviolent activism, CORE spearheaded some of the most daring nonviolent direct action campaigns, most notably the Freedom Ride in 1961. Although CORE's early members were committed to the nonviolent philosophy of Indian activist Mohandas Gandhi, debates over nonviolence intensified in the mid-1960s. By the end of the decade, CORE had abandoned its moderate nonviolent roots and had embraced black nationalism and armed self-defense.

Early Years

The small group of black and white college students that gathered in Chicago in 1942 to found the Committee of Racial Equality—the name was later changed to Congress of Racial Equality—had deep roots in religious pacifism. The majority of these early members were members of the Fellowship of Reconciliation (FOR), a pacifist organization that had originated in England. Organized in the United States in 1915, FOR was dedicated to ending warfare and integrating minorities into American society.

The small band of young activists consisted of devout believers in the nonviolent philosophy of civil rights activist Mohandas Gandhi, who had led a nonviolent struggle against Great Britain's colonial rule in India. Activists such as CORE's white first executive secretary George Houser, viewed Gandhi's concept of nonretaliation and redemptive suffering as more than merely a tactic; they considered it a philosophy of life. A. Philip Randolph's nonviolent March on Washington movement in 1941 gave confidence to early CORE that future nonviolent mass-activism was possible in the United States.

Although some members—in particular former black divinity student James Farmer—envisioned CORE to be an interracial mass organization, the organization remained confined to a few chapters in the North and Midwest for almost two decades of its existence, which were characterized by a predominantly white middle-class membership. In the years 1942 and 1943, these small cadres of pacifist activists launched numerous successful "sit-down" campaigns in Chicago, New York, and Washington, D.C., forcing restaurants and public accommodations to end their policy of de facto segregation.

The sit-in movement of the 1960s would propel this form of nonviolent direct action to international prominence. Despite these encouraging beginnings, CORE's early chapters were characterized by instability and financial crises. In addition, persuading white and black Americans of the power of Gandhi's abstract concept of nonviolence proved difficult. Potential recruits responded mostly with contempt or mockery to CORE members' attempts to explain the idea of nonretaliation. Even in some CORE chapters, activists debated whether activists should rely on armed self-defense to protect black homes from white assaults. In a society that cherished traditions of manly self-defense, nonviolence seemed to remain confined to a small elite of committed activists, trained in Gandhian nonviolence.

In 1947, CORE launched its first national project— the Journey of Reconciliation. Testing the recently passed *Morgan v. Virginia* (1946) U.S. Supreme Court decision, which had declared segregation in interstate travel unconstitutional, interracial teams of CORE and FOR activists traveled the upper South by bus and train. Surprisingly, during their trip through Virginia, Kentucky, Tennessee, and North Carolina, riders encountered less white resistance than expected. However, in Chapel Hill, North Carolina, a violent white mob finally stopped the Journey. Several activists were later sentenced to short jail terms and fines, while black pacifist Bayard Rustin and another white activist had to serve an additional 30 days on a road gang. CORE considered their campaign a great success, but the American public had barely noticed the Journey. At the end of the 1940s, CORE continued to operate in obscurity but was laying crucial groundwork for future activism. The Journey of Reconciliation would later become a model for CORE's Freedom Ride in 1961.

The first half of the 1950s was the low point of CORE's history. An attempt to establish additional chapters in the South failed, and the anti-Communist hysteria that gripped the United States at the end of the 1940s compounded the organization's problems. Confronted with accusations of being infiltrated by Communists, CORE was preoccupied with defending itself against the mostly unfounded allegations. Only the Montgomery bus boycott in 1955 and 1956 seemed to promise the beginning of a brighter future for the weakened organization. CORE member and long-time pacifist Bayard Rustin assisted the Montgomery movement and tutored young leader Martin Luther King Jr. in Gandhian nonviolence. The successful boycott popularized nonviolent activism, and with the anti-Communist scare waning, CORE was prepared to concentrate on its scheme for a nonviolent mass movement. By the end of the 1950s, CORE had established several chapters in the South.

EXPANSION IN THE 1960S

In February 1960, a spontaneous student-led sit-in movement spread quickly across the South and ushered in CORE's heyday. Members of the organization assisted the student movement, offering workshops in nonviolent direct action and forming new chapters in the South. Gradually, the outlines of a mass organization began to take shape. The Freedom Ride of 1961 finally propelled CORE into the national spotlight, and proved the efficacy of nonviolent activism. This time testing the U.S. Supreme Court's *Boynton v. Virginia* (1960) decision, which had extended desegregation to all terminal facilities in interstate travel, two interracial teams of activists set off for the Deep South from Washington, D.C. White mob violence in Anniston and Birmingham, Alabama, served CORE's goal to focus national and international attention on southern injustice. Pictures of the burning bus that white hoodlums had bombed in Anniston became front-page news around the world. As a result, the federal government could no longer ignore the Freedom Ride and dispatched federal troops to protect the Freedom Riders and local blacks from white assaults.

Although CORE had planned to terminate the campaign in Birmingham, young activists from the Student Nonviolent Coordinating Committee (SNCC) took up the Freedom Ride and convinced CORE activists to rejoin. In Jackson, Mississippi, the journey was finally stopped when local authorities arrested the Freedom Riders for violating the local segregation laws, but similar Freedom Rides spread in the ensuing months. In September 1961, the Interstate Commerce Commission (ICC) finally mandated all interstate travel facilities desegregated. The following year, CORE launched "Freedom Highways," another direct action project that targeted segregation in restaurant chains along major highways. In the aftermath of the Freedom Ride, CORE experienced an unprecedented increase in membership and staff in the North and South. By 1964, CORE had 50,000 members in over 120 chapters across the country.

RADICALIZATION AND DEMISE

The organization used its newly acquired popularity to make new inroads into the Deep South. Working primarily in Louisiana, Mississippi, Georgia, and South Carolina, CORE launched voter registration campaigns and nonviolent direct action projects. Organizers also established numerous new chapters in the former confederacy. But CORE workers quickly learned that redemptive suffering did little to affect segregation and discrimination in the Deep South. Their attempts to implement the Civil Rights Act of 1964 and the Voting Rights Act of 1965 on the local level were met by a campaign of white violent terror. Especially in Louisiana and Mississippi, the organization's nonviolent commitment was put to the test. The barrage of violent harassment, shootings, and bombings that rained down on CORE members and local activists led many civil rights workers to doubt the efficacy of the nonviolent philosophy. The fact that Southern African Americans not only rejected nonviolence but relied on armed self-defense in the face of white violence triggered additional debates over the nonviolence, and plunged many CORE organizers into moral conflict. By 1963, few members viewed nonviolence as a way of life but adhered to it merely because of tactical considerations. Especially in the aftermath of the murder of three civil rights activists in the summer of 1964 in Mississippi, many CORE members abandoned their belief in pure nonviolence.

Although field workers eventually accepted and even welcomed local blacks' armed protection, the issue of armed self-defense posed a serious predicament for CORE's national office. In particular, the Deacons for Defense and Justice, a black self-defense organization that had come out of a CORE project in

CORE, the Congress of Racial Equality, became increasingly militant during the 1960s. On March 9, 1965, members in San Francisco present U.S. Attorney Cecil Poole with a petition demanding that the Department of Justice indict Alabama governor George Wallace and Selma sheriff James Clark on charges of murder. *(AP Wide World Photos)*

Jonesboro, Louisiana, in 1964, seemed to contradict CORE's professed nonviolent ideal. National director James Farmer assured the concerned national media that CORE would never abandon its long-standing belief in nonviolent activism. However, the organization's doctrine was already crumbling. Many of CORE's new predominantly African-American members came from a working-class background and were unfamiliar with nonviolence. In addition, many Northern CORE chapters were strongly influenced by the militant rhetoric of black nationalists such as Malcolm X. By 1966, both Southern and Northern CORE members had concluded that armed self-defense was a simple necessity in the organization's civil rights projects. That year the organization's annual convention officially embraced the concept of self-defense and Black Power.

Even before calls for Black Power could be heard in the urban ghettos of the North, CORE had paid increasing attention to the plight of poor African Americans in Northern cities. Moreover, although the organization formed numerous Southern chapters in the aftermath of the Freedom Ride, the majority of CORE chapters had remained outside the South. Concerned with the socioeconomic roots of poverty, CORE members in cities such as New York, Chicago, or Los Angeles concentrated on decent housing, job opportunities for blacks, and police brutality. Few African Americans in the North had experienced tangible gains from the civil rights legislation of 1964 and 1965. Similarly, many of them felt that blacks would benefit little from coalitions with whites, who were believed to dictate rather than assist the black freedom struggle. This growing animosity between white and black activists had made CORE a virtually all-black organization by the end of 1966. Responding to this changed mood among its members, national CORE began to advocate Black Pride, black political empowerment, and black economic advancement. Floyd B. McKissick, who had become CORE's new national director in 1966, in particular called for black capitalism to advance African Americans' economic position.

The organization's increasing militancy, together with its vocal criticism of the United States' role in the escalating Vietnam War, cost CORE much of its white support. Lacking contributions from white sympathizers, the organization's already critical financial situation worsened. Illustrating CORE's ongoing radicalization, the 1967 convention voted to remove the word "multiracial" from the organization's constitution. In 1968, Roy Innis succeeded McKissick as head of CORE and attempted to commit the organization to a more militant form of black nationalism, calling upon blacks to build "a nation within a nation." However, by the end of the 1960s, CORE had disappeared from the forefront of the civil rights movement. The organization still exists today, but it never regained the vanguard position it held in the early 1960s.

ASSESSMENT

The Congress of Racial Equality was crucial to the success of the African-American civil rights movement. In the 1940s, CORE pioneered the cautious beginnings of nonviolent activism, introducing Gandhi's protest technique to the American scene. Moreover, experienced in nonviolent protest, CORE members were essential in assisting and guiding new generations of civil rights leaders and activists that emerged in the 1950s and 1960s. Martin Luther King Jr. as well as many student activists learned the essentials of nonviolent direct action from veteran CORE members. Finally, CORE spearheaded the nonviolent movement of the 1960s, exposing Southern injustice in the eyes of the world and inspiring thousands of future civil rights activists.

The organization's rise to national prominence in the early 1960s simultaneously planted the seeds for its radicalization and demise. Thousands of new African-American members who joined CORE in the 1960s felt no deep commitment to nonviolence, let alone redemptive suffering. In addition, CORE's goal to assist local southern movements, rather than dominate them, left national CORE little room to influence protest strategies among its growing membership. When armed self-defense began to complement nonviolent direct action in many Southern projects, CORE confronted a tragic dilemma. Though committed to its local constituents, the organization's national leadership also had to sustain desperately needed financial contributions from Northern white supporters. These contributions dwindled when CORE abandoned nonviolence and interracial activism. Eventually, CORE could no longer endure this balancing act between its local black membership and Northern white supporters. Mirroring the mood of its black membership, CORE's espousal of black nationalism and armed self-defense toward the end of the 1960s was an ironic result of its success.

Simon Wendt

BIBLIOGRAPHY

Anderson, Jervis. *Bayard Rustin: Troubles I've Seen*. Berkeley: University of California Press, 1998.

Bell, Inge Powell. *CORE and the Strategy of Nonviolence*. New York: Random House, 1968.

Farmer, James. *Lay Bare the Heart: An Autobiography of the Civil Rights Movement*. New York: Arbor House, 1985.

McKissick Floyd. *Three-Fifths of a Man*. Toronto: Collier-Macmillan, 1969.

Meier, August, and Elliot Rudwick. *CORE: A Study in the Civil Rights Movement*. Urbana: University of Illinois Press, 1975.

Van DeBurg, William. *New Day in Babylon: The Black Power Movement and American Culture, 1965–1975*. Chicago: Chicago University Press, 1992.

Wendt, Simon. " 'The Spirit, the People, the Courage, and the Shotguns:' The Southern Black Freedom Struggle, Armed Resistance, and the Radicalization of the Congress of Racial Equality." Master's thesis, University of Wisconsin-Madison, 2000.

CIVIL RIGHTS MOVEMENT 1970–1990

As the 1970s began, the civil rights movement had both expanded and fragmented, spawning and sharply influencing a variety of new social movements inspired by its tangible victories and its ability to mobilize millions. From the mid-1960s, the political slogan "Black Power" and the cultural slogan "Black Is Beautiful" sheltered a variety of new groups, from the Black Panther Party, seeking to adopt strategies drawn from the Cuban and Chinese revolutions, to U.S. slum ghettoes, to champions of "Black capitalism" and entrepreneurs of clothing, hairstyles, art, and furniture drawn from African culture. In large and middle-size cities, a generation of African-American politicians began to emerge, as Irish Americans had at the end of the nineteenth century, as leaders of coalitions of people of color, gaining mayoral and other leadership positions. Vague concepts of cultural pride and identity, community control, and group empowerment influenced Puerto Ricans on the East Coast, Chicanos (Mexican Americans) in the Southwest, Asian Americans, and Native Americans, who organized mass protest campaigns of liberals and radicals, sought to study the history, culture, and art of their various groups, and to share the gains and protections of the civil rights legislation and policies of the mid- and late 1960s.

The upsurge had also expressed itself powerfully among African-American trade unionists who had formed a rank-and-file movement in the United Auto Workers (UAW), represented by the Dodge Revolutionary Union Movement (DRUM) in 1968 and a larger left-led League of Revolutionary Black Workers in 1969. Both organizations were led by far-left militants. With older leaders like A. Philip Randolph and Bayard Rustin supporting the Johnson administration in its Vietnam War policies and turning sharply against the young black labor radicals, militant black trade unionists, both liberals and radicals, established the Coalition of Black Trade Unionists, which contin-

ues to this day as the major organized civil rights force in the labor movement, out of a conference in Chicago in 1972.

THE ELECTORAL ARENA

The achievements of the civil rights movement were registered in the count of elected officials. By 1975, the country had 135 black mayors, 82 of whom were in the South. Of the 3,069 blacks holding municipal, educational, and law enforcement positions, 1,702 were in the South. As the number of blacks in Congress increased to eighteen, newly elected members, including former Congress of Racial Equality (CORE) activists William Clay of St. Louis and self-proclaimed Socialist Ron Dellums of the San Francisco Bay area, played the leading role in establishing a Black Congressional Caucus, which would function largely through the Democratic Party. In March 1972, over 12,000 people and a wide variety of black organizations, ranging from moderate liberal to revolutionary nationalist, met at Gary, Indiana, to seek to develop a united political strategy, the largest and broadest political convention of African Americans in U.S. history. Richard Hatcher, the African-American mayor of Gary, Representative Charles Diggs of Detroit, and playwright and critic Amiri Baraka, at the time a revolutionary nationalist, served as cochairs of the meeting, which sought to develop black political independence and influence in U.S. politics and was itself an example of the continued vitality of the radical currents of the 1960s and their influence among African Americans and other minorities.

EDUCATION AND STUDENT ACTIVISM

Civil rights activism had also inspired a variety of university liberal and radical activists to launch student strikes and other actions in the late 1960s for the inclusion of various ethnic and woman's studies programs in the university curriculum and for minority admission to universities. After strikes led by African-American and Puerto Rican students at the City University of New York (CUNY), the university instituted a controversial open admissions policy in August 1970.

By 1970, these demonstrations had involved feminists, Mexican Americans, Native Americans, Asian Americans, gay men and lesbians, and others who echoed both the civil rights movement's call for equal rights and black radical-influenced calls for "empowerment," community control, and the search for historical roots, group identity, and cultural pride. They had also produced a complex and multifaceted opposition, which conservative politicians sought to manipulate as a "white backlash."

In 1968, for example, an experimental program of the New York City Board of Education to establish community-controlled school districts (a tradition in the United States generally) led to a strike by the United Federation of Teachers (UFT) when the board in one of the three districts, Ocean Hill-Brownsville, an overwhelmingly African-American slum neighborhood in Brooklyn, New York, sought to transfer nineteen teachers seen as disruptive to the community control experiment. The ensuing conflict divided labor and civil rights activists, saw the distribution of crude anti-Semitic leaflets and slurs, which UFT leader Albert Shanker sought through the principle of guilt by association to attribute to the leadership of the district, and eventually led the New York State legislature in 1969 to enact legislation that ended the project.

Although both Jewish-American and African-American teachers united to denounce Albert Shanker's and the general media's attempt to define the dispute in terms of the influence of antiwhite and anti-Semitic black separatists, the conflict became the beginning of and the model for subsequent media portrayals, if not creations, of black-Jewish tensions and conflict in which future generations of whites and blacks saw the two most prominent victims of racism in modern history and, in the United States, the most important allies in the campaigns for civil rights, as bigoted enemies of each other.

When students representing the "Third World liberation front," a broad coalition of African-American, Mexican-American, Asian-American, and Native-American activists, shut down San Francisco State College in 1969, calling for open admissions, a school of ethnic studies, and an upgrading of the black studies program, college president S.I. Hayakawa emerged as a man on horseback who, with the support of California governor Ronald Reagan, used police and the National Guard to suppress the student strike. A Japanese American, Hayakawa emerged as a conservative hero and won election to the U.S. Senate in 1970 as a Republican.

THE RIGHT-WING BACKLASH

Although civil rights groups continued to proliferate through the mid-1970s, political power had clearly passed to the opponents of the movement, whose campaigns against "compulsory school" bussing, the "reverse racism" of Affirmative Action, and, most of all, "law and order," were portrayed by the mass media as representing the new spirit of the times. As early as 1966, California conservatives had countered a campaign to establish open housing through a state referendum with an anticrime referendum. In 1968, Richard Nixon used the concept of a return to "law and order" as the central theme in his presidential campaign and pledged to appoint a "Southerner"— by which he meant an opponent of civil rights—to the U.S. Supreme Court.

Although the conservative "support your local police" campaigns and attacks on the judicial activism of the Supreme Court, highlighted by the far-right "impeach Earl Warren" campaigns, were a reaction to radical cultural and political movements of all kinds, the classic white American fear of rampaging blacks, highlighted by the urban riots of the late 1960s, stood at the center of these attacks. Although his administration was to extend Affirmative Action for women and, ironically, institute in its Philadelphia Plan for minority set-asides in federally supported construction projects the sort of "quotas" that he routinely condemned, Richard Nixon cultivated anti–civil rights constituencies and helped create a political climate hostile to civil rights and civil liberties.

Nixon's pledge to appoint a "Southerner" to the U.S. Supreme Court was initially thwarted when the Senate rejected Clement Haynesworth and Harold Carswell, his first nominees. Although a number of his appointees, Lewis Powell and Harry Blackmun particularly, were later to be considered liberals when compared to the Reagan and Bush nominees, Nixon did appoint William Rehnquist to the Court, along with Warren Burger as chief justice, and generally moved the Court in a more conservative direction. The administration also worked closely with Senator Strom Thurmond, the former leader of segregationist Democrats who had joined the Republican Party in 1964, increasing Thurmond's power in the Republican Senate minority.

More important, Nixon unleashed the Federal

On trial for supplying weapons to prisoners at a California county courthouse, Angela Davis defiantly raises her fist on March 16, 1971. She was later acquitted. *(AP Wide World Photos)*

Bureau of Investigation (FBI) and other federal agencies against the Black Panther Party and other black militants and played what came to be known as the "race card" in politics more actively against civil rights than any president in decades.

The wave of violence against black militants grew massively in the Nixon years. Angela Davis, an African-American member of the Communist Party and ally of the Black Panther Party, was arrested in 1970 for allegedly supplying arms to Jonathan Jackson, brother of imprisoned Black Panther leader and prisoners rights advocate George Jackson, which he used in a courtroom shootout, leading to his death and the death of the courtroom judge. After an international campaign to free her, Davis was acquitted of all charges in 1972 and became a leader of the National Alliance against Racist and Political Repression, a left-led civil rights group.

George Jackson, whose book, *Soledad Brother* (1970), had given him an international following, was killed by San Quentin prison guards in August 1971,

with the fantastic cover story that Jackson had hidden a pistol in his afro haircut. Demonstrations in and out of prisons against Jackson's death spread throughout the country, the most important taking place at the Attica state prison in New York, when a multiracial alliance of prisoners seized the jail, took guards as hostages, and demanded reforms in prison living conditions. Governor Nelson Rockefeller's order to National Guard and local police forces to attack the prison with tear gas and grenades resulted in the death of twenty-nine prisoners and ten guard hostages, as the police implemented savage reprisals against surviving leaders of the prison rebellion.

CARTER AND THE CIVIL RIGHTS MOVEMENT

As the decade progressed, the prison population of the country more than doubled, and young black males, caught in a decade of economic "stagflation" (high inflation and relatively high unemployment) and political stagnation were the most likely to be arrested and imprisoned. By 1976, most civil rights groups found themselves fighting defensive battles in and through the Democratic Party, as Coretta Scott King, John Lewis, and Andrew Young campaigned for the former governor of Georgia, Jimmy Carter, who gained the democratic nomination for president as the most conservative of a field of Democratic nominees. Although Carter was to appoint more members of minority groups and women to federal office than any president before him, he moved away from advancing the War on Poverty. For some students of contemporary history, the Carter years saw the beginning of "post–civil rights politics."

The late 1970s also witnessed an intensification of divisions among blacks. At the top was an expanding black "middle class" of college-educated technical and professional employees who had benefited tremendously from the educational opportunities and entry-level employment created by the Affirmative Action policies inspired by the civil rights movement. Large numbers of these African Americans and members of other minorities experienced incomes and unemployment rates fairly close to those of their white professional counterparts.

These visible gains of the new, significantly expanded black middle class had diverse and contradictory effects on U.S. politics. Some whites viewed these achievements as the result of "reverse racism," quotas that were providing jobs for unqualified people. Although civil rights activists challenged these views rationally with statistics showing that Affirmative Action policies worked in providing entry-level positions in education and employment for members of minorities who were roughly equal in skills to whites, such arguments had limited effects, given the deep racist assumptions that underlay the "reverse racism" contention, that is, blacks were unable to compete with whites and, without Affirmative Action policies, would return to their "place" as "invisible" providers of service labor.

For other whites, the visible black middle class was evidence that civil rights had triumphed and that the society could now honor Martin Luther King Jr. and the other civil rights martyrs with appropriate ceremonies, accepting uncritically a new "status quo" in which segregation was over and discrimination was marginal. Such complacent thoughts ignored the deepening urban and rural poverty that blacks and other minorities faced with the abandonment of the Great Society's War on Poverty and the urban fiscal crisis of the inflationary 1970s, which led cities in particular to reduce funding for education, social services, and public assistance programs in real dollars.

BACKLASH

Everywhere minorities turned in the "post–civil rights era" their successes and their failures would be held against them by conservatives who preached a recycled doctrine of self-reliance and personal responsibility in a "color-blind" society. When William Junius Wilson's *The Declining Significance of Race: Blacks and Changing American Institutions* (1978) saw the existence of a large "underclass" rather than race as the central question facing blacks, conservative media and think-tanks seized upon the concept to attack existing Affirmative Action and antidiscrimination policies, ignoring totally Wilson's subsequent calls for federal programs to raise the living standards of the "underclass."

Allen Bakke's successful U.S. Supreme Court challenge to Affirmative Action in 1978 (Bakke, a white man, argued that "Affirmative Action policies" kept him from gaining admission to medical school at the University of California at Davis, which, he claimed, admitted less-qualified blacks) brought the concept of "reverse racism" to a broad national audience. Meanwhile, the sharp increase in violent crimes, particularly homicide, among African Americans, was blamed not on the sinister interaction of drugs and poverty, but on the moral character of individuals, who had to be incarcerated in a rapidly growing prison system. That most of the victims of violent crimes committed by African Americans were other African Americans was often rationalized to defend increased incarceration as in the interest of African Americans. As the nation spent hundreds of billions of dollars in the last third of the twentieth century on "the war on drugs," which routinely channeled white drug users into rehabilitation programs and blacks and Latinos into jails and prisons, the jail and prison population increased nearly ten times, producing what critics called a racially biased "prison industrial complex," with over 600,000 employees and nearly 2 million inmates.

Meanwhile, African-American mayors in big cities like Atlanta, Detroit, and Los Angeles found themselves routinely slashing social services and firing public employees, many of whom were African Americans and other minorities, while they provided tax benefits in unsuccessful attempts to keep corporations from fleeing their communities. Increased political representation also did little to prevent a sharp increase in racist crimes and police brutality cases.

Perhaps the most extreme case of "police action" took place in Philadelphia in 1985 against a small communitarian group, MOVE, whose members all took the surname Africa. The MOVE group had been a source of conflict in the neighborhood because of their refusal to conform to standards of garbage collection, their keeping of animals, and other acts that had led to clashes with the police. In 1977–1978, police had unsuccessfully blockaded the MOVE commune in a conflict that led to the death of one police officer and numerous injuries. Faced with repeated complaints and clashes in May 1985, Mayor Wilson Goode, Philadelphia's first African-American mayor, authorized a police attack on the commune, which had been fortified by its members. What happened then was a Vietnam War–style search-and-destroy attack. As the Philadelphia police commissioner shouted the command, "Attention MOVE: This is America," police fired thousands of rounds of ammunition into the MOVE house, followed by a state police helicopter dropping a fire bomb that destroyed the MOVE building and spread to sixty-one other houses in the neighborhood, killing eleven of the thirteen MOVE members in the House, including five children.

Although few weapons and no explosives were found in the debris, Mayor Goode defended the attack as follows: "We cannot permit any terrorist group, and revolutionary group in this city, to hold a whole neighborhood or a whole city hostage." In the 1980s, the vague concept of "terrorism," both domestic and international, began to replace "international communism" as a permanent enemy.

REAGAN AND THE CHALLENGE TO CIVIL RIGHTS

African-American males in particular were increasingly the victims of what may be viewed as a "state terrorism" enforced by local police. Regardless of how many members of minorities had gained political office, statistics showed that in 1980, twenty-two blacks were likely to be killed in confrontations with police for every one white. Nor were the outbreaks of violence against blacks being addressed as they had been in the 1960s. In 1980, a major ghetto riot suppressed by the National Guard left 18 dead and 400 injured in the Liberty City district of Miami, an African-American slum neighborhood with a 50 percent unemployment rate. In the midst of the "Iran hostage crisis" and the presidential election year, the general

response of the mass media was to treat the incident as trivial.

Indifference was also the response to a series of brutal murders and mutilations in a variety of places, from Mississippi backwaters to major cities like Buffalo, New York, and Atlanta, Georgia. When 28 black youths were murdered in Atlanta, Georgia, between 1979 and 1982, the arrest of a black man for the crime prompted general feelings of relief. The Los Angeles Police Department's aggressive police policies led to the deaths of over 300 African Americans in the 1970s, 15 of which were attributed to "legitimate" choke holds. Faced with massive criticism and calls for his removal, Police Chief Darryl Gates commented in 1979 that "we may be finding that in some blacks when the carotid choke hold is applied the veins or arteries do not open up as fast as they do on normal people."

By 1980, a second shock wave of inflation and the U.S. embassy hostage crisis put ardent conservatives in a position to gain the presidency for the first time since Calvin Coolidge's election in 1924. Ronald Reagan, former motion picture actor and governor of California, launched his campaign for the presidency after his nomination by the Republican Party in August of 1980 with a speech at Philadelphia, Mississippi, scene in 1964 of the murder of three civil rights workers, Andrew Goodman, Michael Schwerner, and James Chaney. Reagan chose this place to announce his commitment to a restoration of "states' rights." When Jimmy Carter cited Reagan's opposition to the Civil Rights Act of 1964 in their televised presidential debate, the former actor reminisced that when he was a boy in rural Illinois he didn't even know that there was such a thing as a race problem.

Reagan's appeal to an America that had existed in the Hollywood movies of the 1930s, all white, except for occasional black servants and ethnic comedy relief characters, with strong Anglo-American heroes fighting off domestic and foreign villains, played well to a suburban electorate whose principal response to inflation was to support tax cuts for themselves and budget cuts that disproportionately harmed urban working-class and minority communities.

The civil rights movement also suffered from the unintended consequences of its successes. Inspired by the political atmosphere created by the civil rights movement, the 1965 Immigration Act repealed the "national origins" quota system for immigrants that had heavily favored people from Western Europe and the British Isles over people from Eastern and Southern Europe and largely excluded non-Europeans. By the late 1980s, more than 80 percent of new legal immigrants were non-Europeans. Although some brought with them professional skills and education that would give them positions in technical and professional work, from the expanding health maintenance organizations (HMOs) to various research and development positions, a much larger number came to function as cheap service labor working for minimum wages in "gentrified" urban areas. Both at the top and bottom of the "labor market," they provided competition for African Americans, Latinos, and other traditional U.S. minorities, taking jobs that colleges were preparing U.S. minorities to hold at the top and taking jobs at the bottom at wages and conditions below what many African American and Latino workers would tolerate.

The effects of deindustrialization undermined unions like the United Steelworkers and the United Automobile Workers, which had been the center for major economic gains of African Americans and other minorities. As the Reagan administration froze minimum wages, packed the NLRB and other agencies dealing with unions with conservatives, and launched the most aggressive anti–trade union campaign of any administration since the 1920s, blacks, Latinos, and other minorities often suffered the brunt of these attacks. Although 20 percent of African-American workers were in professional and managerial positions in 1990, as against 5 percent in 1950, these substantial middle-class gains were offset by the loss of well-paying union jobs in basic industry and by the relative decline in the living standards of lower income groups, particularly those among the bottom 20 percent of income earners. By the late 1980s, one-third of all black families earned incomes below the official poverty line, and unemployment for black youth reached as high as 43 percent. In addition, minorities were hugely overrepresented in the statistics of female heads of households, who accounted for two-thirds of those officially poor.

Although many of these trends were evident in the late 1970s, the Reagan administration intensified them quantitatively. In opposition to the Great Society's "welfare statism" and long-abandoned "War on Poverty," the Reagan administration sought to eliminate many programs that directly assisted the poor and racial minorities. Reagan tax cuts, defined as an attempt to increase investment and consumption at the top in order to "trickle down" wealth through the private sector to lower income groups, transferred over $25 billion in subsidies from the lowest 20 percent to the highest 20 percent of income earners, a policy that one critic called "reverse Robin Hood." The Reagan administration proceeded to eliminate surviving Great Society public service job programs, remove over 500,000 recipients from the food stamp plan, and reduce funding for housing and urban development by 80 percent, including a crusade to eliminate all forms of federally supported rent controls and either sell off or destroy federally supported public housing.

Although military budgets experienced their greatest rise in peacetime in U.S. history, Medicaid benefits for working low-income people were removed, child nutrition programs were cut 27.7 percent, the low-income energy assistance program was cut 8.3 percent, and unemployment benefits were cut 6.9 percent. Aid to Families with Dependent Children, Medicaid, Supplemental Security Income (SSI) for the disabled, along with food stamps, were the favored targets of the administration, whose tax cuts and spectacular rise in military spending saw a near tripling of the federal deficit.

The Reagan administration also made clear its opposition to Affirmative Action programs and its commitment to change the enforcement of those programs by federal agencies while challenging them in the courts. Reagan's appointees to the Civil Rights Commission (CRC) and the Equal Employment Opportunity Commission (EEOC), particularly EEOC director Clarence Thomas, a conservative Republican whose admission to Yale Law School was directly related to Affirmative Action, openly opposed Affirmative Action. They were also far less sympathetic, if not obstructionist, to enforcement of civil rights grievances on questions of discrimination in employment, housing, and education. Issues of continuing school segregation and violations of voting rights were usually met with the response that the legislation of the 1960s had already taken care of those problems.

THE DEATH PENALTY

The Reagan administration also strongly supported the institution of the death penalty, which the U.S. Supreme Court, reversing a 1973 decision, had declared legal once more in 1977. People of color were disproportionately much more likely to be sentenced to death than were whites convicted of homicide. Homicides continued to rise despite the institution of the death penalty. One factor is the Reagan administration's support for a substantial weakening of existing gun laws, catering to the politically powerful National Rifle Association.

By the 1980s, the death penalty had been abolished in virtually all other developed countries. One case, however, which has lasted twenty years, was to become an international cause celebre.

In Philadelphia in 1981, Mumia Abu-Jamal, a former Black Panther and radio commentator known for his criticisms of police brutality against blacks, was accused of killing a Philadelphia police officer when he found the officer in an altercation with his brother in a slum neighborhood. Although ballistics evidence was inconclusive and although Abu-Jamal himself was shot and beaten, the major witnesses against him had criminal records, and the judge was criticized by many for acting in a biased manner, Abu-Jamal was convicted and sentenced to death. After spending twenty years on death row and becoming the subject of a global campaign to free him and expose the injustice of the U.S. use of the death penalty, Abu-Jamal saw a federal judge throw out the death penalty conviction in 2001 but sustain the murder conviction. However, Abu-Jamal remains in jail for life. In the 1980s and 1990s, the application and implementation of the death penalty grew sharply, with Texas and Florida, the two great centers of post–civil rights Sunbelt conservatism, leading the way.

REVERSALS TO AFFIRMATIVE ACTION AND REVIVAL OF ACTIVISM

The Justice Department's assistant attorney general for civil rights, William Bradford Reynolds, launched a number of high-profile cases in the 1980s to attack local Affirmative Action programs, most significantly a program enacted by a Republican mayor of Indianapolis, Indiana, to increase the number of minorities and women in public service. The Reagan administration's failure to win these cases in what was an increasingly conservative-dominated Supreme Court was due, it has been argued, to their extreme and sweeping attacks on Affirmative Action policies, along with the cogent defense of Affirmative Action policies directed by the National Association for the Advancement of Colored People (NAACP)'s chief counsel, Lani Guinier. Yet, the long-term effects of the appointment of conservatives to the federal judiciary have placed not only Affirmative Action but the antidiscrimination machinery of the federal government, along with the reproductive rights of women, in serious jeopardy. Finally, Reagan unsuccessfully opposed the campaign by civil rights activists to have Martin Luther King Jr.'s birthday declared a national holiday, declaring that such a holiday would be too expensive.

But the 1980s were fraught with contradictions. Jesse Jackson, who had been a young activist with Martin Luther King Jr. at the time of his murder in 1968, and the leader of the activist Operation PUSH (People United to Serve Humanity) in Chicago in the late 1960s and 1970s, established the Rainbow Coalition, seeking to revive the poor people's movement that King was leading at the time of his assassination. Running in Democratic primaries against Walter Mondale and Gary Hart in 1984, Jackson, opposed by many elected African-American politicians, made a strong showing. Four years later, he garnered over 7 million votes from minorities and progressive whites to become the leading challenger to Michael Dukakis, the Massachusetts governor who emerged as the candidate of the Democratic establishment. Jackson repeatedly called for a new coalition of minorities, youth, gay men and lesbians, and working-class whites, in effect a grand civil rights coalition, to "win back America."

In Chicago in 1983, such a coalition appeared to triumph with the election of Harold Washington, an African-American congressman, in what had been the premier Democratic machine city since New York mayor Fiorello La Guardia ousted Tammany Hall in the 1930s. Benefiting from minority voter registration drives, Washington defeated both incumbent mayor Jane Byrne and Richard Daley, the son of the legendary mayor and machine leader. Washington then built a model reform administration, winning a second term in 1987. A fatal heart attack ended his administration, which, in the tradition of coalitions held together by strong leaders, soon fragmented. Power struggles led to the restoration of an updated version of the machine, under the leadership of Richard Daley, whom Washington had defeated in 1983.

Similar increases in black and Latino voting led to the victory in the New York City Democratic primary of David Dinkins, a long-time progressive African-American Democrat over three-term mayor Edward I. Koch, a more conservative Democrat, in 1989. An economic recession and violent confrontations between blacks and Hasidic Jews would help defeat Dinkins in a close election against law-and-order Republican Rudolph Giuliani in 1993, whom he had narrowly defeated in the 1989 general election. The fragility of new multiethnic urban coalitions was seen most pointedly in New York City, where a slight drop in the Latino vote for Dinkins constituted his margin of defeat.

Civil rights activism also revived in the 1980s to frustrate the Reagan administration's attempt to "im-

JESSE LOUIS JACKSON (1941–)

Jesse Louis Burns was born on October 8, 1941, in Greenville, South Carolina, to an unwed mother and raised in poverty. He took his stepfather's last name at around age fifteen. Jackson's success as a student and athlete won him a scholarship to the University of Illinois. When he learned that he would not be allowed to play quarterback on the football team because of his race, he transferred to North Carolina Agricultural and Technical College (A&T). He then attended the Chicago Theological Seminary (1963–1965) and was ordained a Baptist minister in 1968.

While at A&T in Greensboro, North Carolina, Jackson and his future wife, Jacqueline Davis, became active in the civil rights movement. He served as the point man for the Greensboro sit-ins that helped to integrate city restaurants. In 1963, Jackson joined the Southern Christian Leadership Conference (SCLC) and quickly gained a reputation as an effective organizer, working in Chicago to integrate schools and housing while in the seminary. Two years later he became an associate of Martin Luther King Jr. and was present when King was assassinated in Memphis in 1968.

During the years following King's death, Jackson emerged as the inheritor of King's followers. Jackson served as executive director (1966–1971) of Operation Breadbasket, a program of the SCLC that addressed the economic problems of blacks in Northern cities. In 1971, he broke with the SCLC and founded Operation PUSH (People United to Save Humanity), an organization to pressure large corporations to provide jobs and economic opportunities for blacks and other minorities. Through the 1970s, Jackson emphasized economic empowerment rather than traditional civil rights issues. Drawing on his preaching background, he combined messages of uplift ("I *am* somebody!") with militancy ("It's nationtime!") to attract a large following. He also made controversial forays into international politics, including a meeting in 1979 with the head of the Palestine Liberation Organization. In 1983, he secured the release of a captured navy pilot during a trip to Syria.

That same year, many, but not all, black political leaders endorsed the idea of a black presidential candidate to create a "people's" platform, increase voter registration, and have a power base from which there could be greater input into the political process. Working from that position, Jackson launched the first serious presidential candidacy by a black politician.

Jackson ran his largely symbolic campaign in 1984 with the support of the Rainbow Coalition, an umbrella organization of minority groups. During the race, he faced renewed charges of anti-Semitism because of his association with the controversial Nation of Islam leader Louis Farrakhan, and for his reference to New York City as "Hymietown." Jackson apologized repeatedly for this remark and has since emphasized his distaste for all forms of bigotry, but the stigma remains. Black support was divided between Jackson and former vice president Walter Mondale, who had a long history of civil rights activism. Mondale won the nomination but lost by a large percentage of electoral votes in the general election.

Jackson's 1988 campaign for president differed dramatically from the earlier one. He proved to be a potent candidate, finishing a strong second to the eventual nominee, Michael Dukakis. He avoided controversy and went into the convention a threat to Democratic leaders. His campaign forever changed the notion that a black president in America was unimaginable. After the convention, Jackson stepped aside and watched as Dukakis lost in a landslide to the Republican candidate, George H.W. Bush.

After the 1988 election, Jackson returned to his activist roots. Since 1986, he has been president of the National Rainbow Coalition, an independent political organization aimed at uniting disparate groups including racial minorities, the poor, peace activists, and environmentalists. In 1989, he moved with his Rainbow Coalition from Chicago to Washington, D.C., hoping that the coalition could be more effective in the nation's capital. He has also campaigned for statehood for the District of Columbia. Jackson continued to write, speak, and lead protests for social change.

In the 1990s, Jackson surprised many supporters by not running for the presidency in 1992 or 1996, citing family commitments and fatigue. He also returned to international politics. In 1991, he traveled to Iraq and convinced Saddam Hussein to begin releasing Americans held hostage after Hussein's invasion of Kuwait. In 1994, Jackson met with Fidel Castro in Cuba, and, later that year, President Bill Clinton sent him on a peace mission to Nigeria. Jackson briefly hosted a television program on which public issues are discussed. In 1996, he returned to Chicago to resume leadership of PUSH and has continued speaking out on racial issues.

James G. Lewis

prove" relations with the apartheid government of South Africa under the banner of "constructive engagement." Blacks and whites in communities and in universities campaigned to have local governments, universities, and religious and other institutions divest funds from companies doing business with South Africa as long as apartheid remained in place. The movement also focused on having the United States join other nations in imposing sanctions on South Africa, which Congress, overriding Reagan's veto, did in 1986. The victory was perhaps the most important expression of African-American and civil rights influence on U.S. foreign policy and economic policy in history.

As the 1980s ended, the depth of the divisions over civil rights and the lack of either a liberal or conservative policy consensus were clear. In the 1988 presidential campaign, Jesse Jackson appeared to be a major force within a Democratic Party in which people of color were more visible in leadership positions than at any time in U.S. history. Those who had not lived through the 1970s might at first believe that Richard Nixon's "Silent Majority" rhetoric had long been vanquished by a civil rights consensus that had made Martin Luther King Jr.'s "I Have a Dream" speech at the 1963 March on Washington a reality.

But a closer look would reveal something very different. In 1989, over 600,000 black males between the ages of twenty and twenty-nine, nearly one-fourth of the African-American male population in that age category, were either in prison or on parole or probation—about a third more than all African Americans enrolled in institutions of higher education.

The rapidly expanding use of the death penalty also stood at the pinnacle of a criminal justice system that routinely provided much higher numbers of convictions and incarcerations for people of color than for whites for comparable offenses. In *McCleskey v. Kemp* (1987), involving the death sentence of a black Georgia man convicted of killing a white police officer, the U.S. Supreme Court, in a five-to-four decision, rejected the plaintiff's argument to set aside the death penalty on the grounds that the Georgia criminal justice system was four times more likely to apply the death penalty to a black convicted of killing a white than vice versa, with the following Catch-22 contention by Justice Lewis Powell: "apparent discrepancies in sentencing are an inevitable part of our criminal justice system. . . . If we accepted McCleskey's claim that racial bias has impermissibly tainted the capital sentencing decision, we would soon be faced with

similar claims as to other types of penalty. . . . Studies already exist that allegedly demonstrate a racial disparity in the length of prison sentences." By the mid-1980s, black Americans became a prime component of the prison-industrial complex.

In 1989, the U.S. Supreme Court ruled that states had the right to execute juvenile criminals at least sixteen years old and mentally retarded criminals. By the end of the 1980s, blacks were the primary victims of both crime and a criminal justice system committed to punishment rather than rehabilitation, as well as longer periods of incarceration as a way to improve crime statistics. That many states denied those convicted of felonies the right to vote and other important civil rights made the criminal justice policies of the 1970s and 1980s a mechanism for disenfranchisement of hundreds of thousands of African Americans and other people of color.

These many contradictions could be seen in a number of dramatic developments at the end of the 1980s. First Jesse Jackson's remarkable run in the Democratic presidential primaries of 1988 represented the most serious political challenge by an African American in presidential politics in U.S. history. Still, Jackson, who had nominated George McGovern sixteen years earlier, was dogged by an anti-Semitic remark he had made to an African-American reporter during the campaign, referring to New York City as "Hymietown." Jackson's remark received wide coverage, which served to highlight African-American–Jewish-American conflict, while the far more disturbing anti-Jewish references uttered by the Reagan administration's Patrick Buchanan and the anti-Semitic commentaries that frequently surfaced from released documents of Richard Nixon received less coverage.

During the 1988 presidential election, Republicans used what was perhaps the crudest expression of racism in modern presidential politics when they showed an ad denouncing Democratic candidate Michael Dukakis for releasing, as governor of Massachusetts, "Willie" Horton, an African American, on a prison furlough program. Horton, whose first name was William, subsequently raped a white woman. Many critics believed that the ad's purpose was to portray Dukakis as a weak-hearted liberal who would release criminals to run rampant if he were president. The use of "Willie" and the highlighting of the crime of rape, those critics contended, left no doubt as to what group and what fear the successful Bush campaign was appealing to.

The U.S. Supreme Court, which had been the

most important governmental ally for racial equality in the 1950s and 1960s, weakened support for civil rights in the late 1980s, with the Reagan administration's appointment of conservatives Antonin Scalia and Anthony M. Kennedy to the Court, along with its promotion of the Court's most militant conservative, Nixon appointee William Rehnquist, to the post of chief justice. In *Patterson v. McClean Credit Union* (1989), the Court ruled that civil rights legislation against discrimination in employment did not cover on-the-job harassment. In *Martin v. Wilkes* (1990), the Court ruled that there was no time limit on white employees challenging Affirmative Action consent decrees, thus creating the possibility that Affirmative Action decisions in favor of minorities could be tied up in challenges and undone long after they had been made. In *Wards Cove Packing Company v. Antonio* (1989), the Court ruled that grievants had to prove not only that specific business policies discriminated against them, but that the policies did not constitute a "legitimate business goal," providing the attorneys for private sector defendants with a potentially open-ended loophole. In condemning these decisions as representing a policy of "retrenchment" on questions of civil rights, Justice Thurgood Marshall observed that "history teaches that when the Supreme Court has been willing to shortchange the equality rights of under-represented groups, other basic personal civil liberties like the rights to free speech and to personal security against unreasonable searches and seizures are also threatened."

CONCLUSION

As the 1990s began, the successes and failures of the civil rights movement were everywhere to be seen. Four decades after Harry Truman integrated the U.S. Army, President Bush appointed General Colin Powell to lead the Joint Chiefs of Staff. An African American, Powell with the help of Affirmative Action had reached the highest position in the U.S. military and was seen by some as a future Republican presidential candidate, a "Black Eisenhower" who exuded a military-organization-man mentality and gained fame in the Gulf War of 1991. (Powell was appointed secretary of state in the administration of George W. Bush in the early 2000s.)

Faced with the retirement of Thurgood Marshall, Bush, who had seen liberal Democrats block the nomination of conservative judge Robert Bork at the end of the Reagan administration, appointed an African American and conservative, Clarence Thomas, as his replacement. Although the Thomas nomination became a cause celebre owing to charges that Thomas had sexually harassed a subordinate, Anita Hill, during his leadership of the EEOC, the fact that a black so thoroughly opposed to everything the civil rights movement stood for could be more easily nominated for the Supreme Court than a white with similar views had stood Affirmative Action on its head, although few enemies of Affirmative Action accused Bush of "reverse racism."

By the 1990s, the civil rights movement had transformed U.S. society but not necessarily as its activists had hoped. As the last decade of the twentieth century began, both the opponents and proponents of civil rights were locked in something like World War I trench warfare—a stalemate in which fierce battles raged over issues of Affirmative Action, inclusion and social diversity, the relationship of gays and lesbians to civil rights—a "culture war" with little chance of victory in the short run by either side.

Norman Markowitz

BIBLIOGRAPHY

Abu-Jamal, Mumia. *Live from Death Row.* Reading, MA: Addison-Wesley, 1995.

Carter, Dan. *From George Wallace to Newt Gingrich: Race and Conservative Counter-revolution.* Baton Rouge: Louisiana State University Press, 1996.

Cole, David. *No Equal Justice.* New York: W.W. Norton, 1999.

Davis, Mike. *City of Quartz.* New York: Vintage Books, 1992.

Dudzak, Mary. *Cold War Civil Rights.* Princeton, NJ: Princeton University Press, 2000.

Edsall, Thomas, and Mary Edsall. *Chain Reaction: The Impact of Race, Rights and Taxes in American Politics.* New York: W.W. Norton, 1991.

Harry, Margot. *Attention Move: This Is America!* New York: Banner, 1990.

Irons, Peter. *A People's History of the Supreme Court.* New York: Viking, 1980.

James, Joy, ed. *The Angela Y. Davis Reader.* Oxford: Blackwell, 1998.

Klinkner, Philip, and Roger Smith. *The Unsteady March: The Rise and Decline of Racial Equality in America.* Chicago: University of Chicago Press, 1999.

Marable, Manning. *Race, Reform and Rebellion: The Second Reconstruction in Black America, 1945–1990.* Jackson: University of Mississippi Press, 1991.

Wilson, William Junius. *The Declining Significance of Race: Blacks and Changing American Institutions.* Chicago: University of Chicago Press, 1978.

RACIAL VIOLENCE AND THE CIVIL RIGHTS MOVEMENT

Standing primarily for racist violence against African Americans, racial violence was a major impediment in the African-American struggle for civil rights in the twentieth century. However, an increasing number of blacks refused to passively accept mob violence and racist terror. Especially in the aftermath of World War I, many African Americans protected their communities against white violence. Similarly, numerous black World War II veterans fought back in the face of white assaults. During the civil rights movement of the 1960s, white terrorism again erupted but was frequently prevented by black armed protection. Toward the end of the decade, traditional forms of southern antiblack mob brutality had waned, while northern cities experienced a wave of violent unrest in African-American ghettos.

LYNCHING AND THE BLACK RESPONSE

By 1900, lynching had become a common means of racial control in the American South. Frequently watched by thousands of jeering spectators, this ritualized form of mob violence was part of white America's design to keep African Americans "in their place." The majority of white men in the South believed that lynchings were necessary to protect Southern women from reputed black rapists. However, economic and political motivations lay at the root of this primarily Southern phenomenon. Using violence to enforce the racial status quo, whites were determined to confine African Americans to a status of simple laborers stripped of their political rights. Punishing blacks for violating the traditional Southern racial etiquette, white tormentors frequently tortured and mutilated their black victims. In many cases, whites castrated the accused black man or severed his fingers and ears. Between 1880 and 1952, white Americans lynched almost 3,500 black Americans, although many other murders went unreported.

The majority of African Americans were struck with fear in the face of this reign of terror. Between 1915 and 1930, many Southern blacks attempted to escape white violence and oppression by migrating to Northern cities such as New York and Chicago. Some black Southerners relied on armed self-defense to protect themselves from white violence. Occasionally, armed African Americans confronted white lynch mobs that intended to kidnap black defendants from their prison cells. Outspoken black journalists such as Ida B. Wells and Thomas Fortune advised blacks to repel white attackers with arms. As early as 1892, in a pamphlet entitled "Southern Horrors: Lynch Law in All Its Phases," Wells had concluded "that a Winchester rifle should have a place of honor in every black home, and it should be used for that protection which the law refuses to give."

Before World War II, however, most black defense efforts resulted in the death of the defender, whom whites vastly outgunned and outnumbered. In the 1920s and 1930s, violent altercations between black farmers and their white landlords sometimes ended in fierce gun battles, but these isolated incidents of individual resistance did little to challenge the entrenched system of white supremacy. Only in the 1930s, due to widely publicized antilynching campaigns by the National Association for the Advancement of Colored People (NAACP) and the Association of Southern Women for the Prevention of Lynching, did the worst forms of mob violence subside. However, covert lynchings persisted until the end of the 1960s.

RACE RIOTS AND BLACK MILITANCY AFTER WORLD WAR I

In the aftermath of World War I, Northern cities in particular became a stage for another form of racial violence: the race riot. Triggered mostly by a violation of Northern de facto segregation or rumors of rape and compounded by economic competition between black and white workers, whites invaded African-American neighborhoods, destroying property and terrorizing the black community. Although Northern cities had experienced white mob violence before, the numerous riots that took place during the so-called Red Summer of 1919 did not conform to the traditional pattern of black passivity. This time, many African Americans fought back when whites attacked their community. Spearheaded by the combat experience of black veterans, the defenders of black neighborhoods frequently welcomed their white assailants with volleys of disciplined gunfire. Black intellectuals spoke of the emergence of a "New Negro," who would refuse to be intimidated by white terror. Expressing this increasing militancy in 1919, the *New York Times* quoted W.E.B. Du Bois as counseling blacks: "When the armed lynchers gather, we too must gather armed." That same year, armed African Americans in Chicago and Washington, D.C., battled white invaders and police in riots that lasted several days.

White authorities frequently thwarted these protection efforts by disarming African Americans, while whites continued to launch violent forays into black neighborhoods. Despite this resistance, the majority of victims killed during the riots were black. Sometimes, as in the Tulsa race riot of 1921, black armed opposition resulted in the obliteration of the entire black neighborhood, forcing the surviving blacks to leave the town. However, the postwar riots had demonstrated that an increasing number of African Americans would sell their lives as dearly as possible. White reaction to the news of this black militancy bordered on the paranoid. During the postwar riots, rumors about looming black armed revolutions circulated among terrified white city-dwellers.

RACIAL VIOLENCE DURING AND AFTER WORLD WAR II

During World War II, Northern cities and Southern army camps again became the front lines for violent skirmishes between black and white Americans. The stationing of black soldiers in army camps located in the Deep South triggered hundreds of violent melees with white military policemen and local Southerners. During several race riots in the North—particularly in Chicago in 1943—numerous blacks fought back when attacked by white mobs. In many Southern states, rumors spread among white Southerners that African Americans were planning armed insurrec-

tions after the war, during which they would murder the white population. Although racial violence never reached as high a level as in the aftermath of World War I, racial clashes continued to erupt in the postwar South.

In 1946, in Columbia, Tennessee, hundreds of black veterans armed themselves to protect the African-American community. Reflecting the attitude of African-American veterans across the South, black Columbian men returned to the South with a new determination to challenge the racial status quo. In the wake of an altercation between a black woman and a white radio repairman, word reached the black community that a lynch mob was about to invade the neighborhood. When a group of police officers approached the black section of town at night, the defenders mistook them for the mob and injured several officers in the ensuing shootout. White police reacted swiftly and violently, destroying black businesses and arresting hundreds of black Columbians. Only after an extended court battle did lawyers of the NAACP manage to free those blacks indicted for the shooting.

The beginning of the modern civil rights movement in 1955 in Montgomery, Alabama, together with the *Brown v. Board of Education* U.S. Supreme Court decision one year earlier, sparked a new upsurge in racial violence. In particular, the prospect of having to desegregate public education as mandated by *Brown* led many white Americans to rely on force to discourage blacks from challenging Jim Crow. In opposition to this threat to traditional racial practices, white Southerners organized the White Citizens Council and revived terrorist groups such as the Ku Klux Klan.

The murder of Emmett Till in 1955 was a tragic reminder that Southern African Americans still lived in constant fear of death when violating the traditional racial etiquette. However, in sharp contrast to lynchings in the past, the two white men who murdered young Till for whistling at a white woman were not cheered by large white crowds in bright daylight. Rather, they dragged the boy from his uncle's home in the middle of the night and later attempted to hide his dead body in the Tallahatchie River. Moreover, scrutinized by national and international media, Mississippi authorities were forced to bring the murder case to court. Never before had members of a lynch mob been indicted in Mississippi. Despite the unsurprising acquittal of the two men by an all-white jury, the Till murder indicated that racial violence would now trigger a national and international outcry along with a critical look at Southern racial practices. The murder of Mack Charles Parker in 1959 in Mississippi sparked a similar clamor and can be considered the last example of this "traditional" form of lynching.

ANTI–CIVIL RIGHTS VIOLENCE AND THE BLACK RESPONSE

Civil rights activism sparked a fierce response from white Southerners. During the Montgomery bus boycott in 1955 and 1956, whites bombed the house of civil rights leader Martin Luther King Jr., impelling him to post armed guards around his house. Even after Montgomery blacks had won their fight for the desegregation of the city's bus lines, whites continued to shoot at buses and houses of local activists. As the civil rights movement gained momentum, so did white resistance. In 1957, when nine high school students in Little Rock, Arkansas, attempted to test the *Brown* decision, hostile white mobs welcomed them. For the first time since Reconstruction, President Dwight D. Eisenhower dispatched federal troops to the South to protect African Americans from mob violence. However, once the Little Rock crisis was over, local leader Daisy Bates was at the mercy of white hoodlums who regularly fired their guns into her house. Consequently, armed blacks began to guard the Bates residence, while bright floodlights blinded potential assailants. That same year, Robert F. Williams, a local NAACP activist in Monroe, North Carolina, organized a black self-defense group that protected the local movement from Ku Klux Klan attacks. In 1959, the national NAACP suspended Williams as president of the Monroe chapter for calling upon African Americans to "meet violence with violence."

In the 1960s, white terrorists repeatedly attempted to stop the civil rights movement with violent terror. In 1960 and 1961, respectively, white mobs beat and harassed nonviolent sit-in demonstrators and Freedom Riders, triggering vociferous protest from national and international audiences. Police brutality against protestors in Birmingham, Alabama, in 1963 and in Selma, Alabama, in 1965 had a similar effect. In fact, the public violence that white supremacists used to stop civil rights demonstrations was crucial to activists' success in exposing southern injustice in front of the world.

The majority of civil rights projects, however, took place outside the national spotlight, and attempts to launch voter registration drives and to desegregate public accommodations in the Deep South were far more dangerous than staging widely publicized non-

violent direct action projects. Without federal protection, activists and local African Americans became a constant target for violent reprisals. In particular, civil rights workers from the Student Nonviolent Coordinating Committee (SNCC) and the Congress of Racial Equality (CORE) along with local black activists became victims of racial violence during their campaigns in Louisiana, Mississippi, Alabama, and other southern states. Local and state branches of the Ku Klux Klan increased their membership considerably in the early 1960s and launched a campaign of terror against the movement. In the years 1960–1968, white supremacists bombed numerous black churches, torched the homes of local civil rights leaders, and shot into civil rights offices and black homes in nightly attacks.

Dozens of civil rights activists and local African Americans fell victim to this upsurge in white brutality. In 1963, four black teenage girls died when a group of Klansmen bombed a local church in Birmingham, Alabama. A year later, during SNCC's Mississippi Freedom Summer project, white supremacists murdered three civil rights activists. Primarily because two of the dead activists were white northerners from influential families, the federal government launched a large-scale FBI investigation, leading to the indictment of the killers. Eventually, however, an all-white jury acquitted the men involved in the murder. Only in 1965 and 1966 did the federal government begin to take decisive steps to curb Klan terrorism.

Confronted with the government's inaction, many African Americans concluded that they had to rely on their own ability to defend themselves against racial violence. Numerous blacks across the South protected themselves with guns. In many Mississippi counties, local African Americans guarded their homes with rifles and shotguns at night. In some parts of the South, local men organized informal defense groups that protected black churches and the homes of civil rights leaders. In 1964, in Jonesboro, Louisiana, African Americans organized the Deacons for Defense and Justice, a self-defense unit that patrolled the black section of town at night and guarded nonviolent activists. One year later, blacks organized another branch of the defense organization in Bogalusa, Louisiana, where blacks engaged in several shootouts with Ku Klux Klan members. Later establishing branches in Mississippi and several northern cities, the Deacons became widely known for their uncompromising stance on protecting the civil rights movement from white violence. Although these protection efforts could not stop white violence entirely, they thwarted many white assaults.

RACE RIOTS IN THE 1960s

Although the worst forms of racist terror began to subside by 1967, a new form of violence had emerged in the black ghettos of the urban North and West. Frustrated with the unaltered condition of poor blacks in the North, some African Americans began to express their protest violently. Though frequently termed race riots, these urban upheavals differed significantly from the riots in the aftermath of World War I. In 1967 and 1968, there were no white invaders who attempted to attack blacks and their property. Rather, these disorders were frequently sparked by an unjust incident of police brutality against blacks. To protest this injustice and their wretched condition, blacks destroyed white property in the black section of town, frequently burning large parts of the ghetto to the ground.

Accompanied by looting and sporadic shootouts between black snipers and police officers, most of these riots lasted several days. In reaction to the violence, city and state authorities dispatched large contingents of National Guardsmen to quell the disturbances. While the 1965 Watts riot in California had foreshadowed the violence to come, the hundreds of urban upheavals that rocked American cities in 1967 and 1968 left an unprecedented trail of destruction. Some of the worst rioting took place in the aftermath of the assassination of Martin Luther King Jr. in April 1968, when observers counted 230 riots in at least 125 cities across the country. In the aftermath of the riots, 46 people lay dead while 2,600 had been injured, the vast majority of whom were African-American. Property worth $45 million lay in waste. Although government officials studied the underlying causes of the violence and concluded that socioeconomic conditions coupled with racist discrimination were at the root of the problem, the plight of the urban black population remained practically unchanged.

ASSESSMENT

Until the end of the 1960s, racial violence served as a constant reminder that white Americans were determined to stop African Americans' quest for civil rights by any means. Although lynchings waned toward the end of the 1930s, racist violence against black Americans remained rampant. However, World War I constituted a turning point in racial violence.

An increasing number of blacks—in particular, war veterans—began to fight back when attacked by white mobs. World War II further radicalized African Americans and prepared the ground for the modern civil rights movement. Racial violence during the black freedom struggle of the 1960s both impeded and assisted the movement. Although harassment and numerous murders of civil rights activists slowed down the pace of change, white brutality against black activists also helped expose Southern racism in the eyes of the world. Hence, many Americans as well as international observers called upon the federal government to protect African Americans and to acknowledge their grievances.

Until the administration finally took steps to stop white supremacist terror, however, African Americans had to protect themselves. During the civil rights movement in the South, a considerable number of blacks relied on armed protection, thus preventing many white attacks. Toward the end of the 1960s, the character of racial violence changed. Rather than defending themselves against white invaders, blacks now protested by destroying white property and by battling white police in northern ghettos. By the end of the decade, the worst forms of antiblack violence had waned.

Simon Wendt

BIBLIOGRAPHY

Boshin, Joseph, ed. *Urban Racial Violence in the Twentieth Century.* 2d ed. Beverly Hills, CA: Glencoe, 1976.

Brundage, W. Fitzhugh, ed. *Under the Sentence of Death: Lynching in the South.* Chapel Hill: University of North Carolina Press, 1997.

Ellsworth, Scott. *Death in a Promised Land: The Tulsa Race Riot of 1921.* Baton Rouge: Louisiana State University Press, 1982.

"For Action on Race Riot Peril." *New York Times*, October 5, 1919, p. X10.

Horne, Gerald. *Fire This Time: The Watts Uprising and the 1960s.* New York: Da Capo, 1997.

O'Brien, Gail Williams. *The Color of the Law: Race, Violence, and Justice in the Post–World War II South.* Chapel Hill: University of North Carolina Press, 1999.

Shapiro, Herbert. *White Violence and Black Response: From Reconstruction to Montgomery.* Amherst: University of Massachusetts Press, 1988.

Tyson, Timothy B. *Radio Free Dixie: Robert F. Williams and the Roots of Black Power.* Chapel Hill: University of North Carolina Press, 1999.

Wade, Wyn Craig. *The Fiery Cross: The Ku Klux Klan in America*. New York: Simon & Schuster, 1987.

Waskow, Arthur I. *From Race Riot to Sit-In, 1919 and the 1960s: A Study in the Connections Between Conflict and Violence*. Garden City, NY: Doubleday, 1966.

Wells, Ida B. "Southern Horrors: Lynch Law in All Its Phases." *On Lynching*. 1892. Reprint, New York: Arno, 1969.

Whitfield, Stephen J. *A Death in the Delta: The Story of Emmett Till*. Baltimore, MD: Johns Hopkins University Press, 1988.

BLACK NATIONALISM AND THE CIVIL RIGHTS MOVEMENT

On a formal level, the Civil War and Reconstruction had established the freedom of African Americans. The Thirteenth Amendment abolished slavery, and the Fourteenth and Fifteenth amendments established the rights of African Americans to due process and equal protection and prohibited the denial of the right to vote on the basis of race, color, or previous condition of servitude. In Congress, as Eric Foner's *Reconstruction* (1988) has shown, the triumph of the Radical Republicans, dedicated to the creation of a biracial democracy in the South, meant that African Americans were able to join in coalitions with poor whites to be elected or to elect individuals sympathetic to their desires for education and employment.

This golden moment lasted only until 1876, when the Hayes-Tilden election standoff and recession in the North contributed to a dismantling of the radical effort to develop a biracial democracy. In return for granting the Republicans the presidency, federal troops were withdrawn from the South, permitting voter intimidation by merchants and paramilitary groups to reduce the numbers of African-American voters. Those who persisted in exercising their vote despite these obstacles were further winnowed down by means of various legal devices: poll taxes, grandfather clauses, and literacy tests, which had a devastating impact on the eligibility of African-American voters. As McMillen's *Dark Journey* (1989) illustrates, three years after the conclusion of the Civil War, in 1868, 96.7 percent of the eligible African-American voting-age population was registered; between 1892 and 1899, the number dropped to between 5.9 and 9.1 percent and skidded to a low of 0.4 percent in 1940.

The position of African Americans was ensured by a hysterical scrutiny of passing and the misrepresentation of African Americans in ways meant to convey to the outside world that African Americans were happy with their lot, unworthy of investment in their education, childish, or dangerous and in need of control by authorities as documented in Marlon Riggs's film *Ethnic Notions*. What these images cloaked was the extreme exploitation of African-American labor by the sharecropping system and the use of police repression to shore up the power of growers who benefited from the enforcement of vagrancy laws. These laws, which made it possible for police to jail individuals with less than the prescribed sum, then turn them over to people who agreed to pay their bail, imposed severe limits on African-American mobility.

Given disfranchisement and police control, it is remarkable that African Americans perhaps had one strength that the other ethnic movements in America lacked: slavery in conjunction with the constitutional limit on the importation of slaves had created a Pan-ethnic community with an identity more firmly in place and earlier than that of the other ethnic movements.

THREE PROTOTYPICAL RESPONSES: SEGREGATION, CIVIL RIGHTS, AND NATIONALISM IN THE EARLY TWENTIETH CENTURY

How to respond to repression was a subject of heated debate, as symbolized by the contrasting approaches of the major African-American leaders of the late nineteenth and early-twentieth centuries: Booker T. Washington, W.E.B. Du Bois, and Marcus Garvey. Southern-born and noticeably darker than Du Bois, Booker T. Washington urged accommodation while working to improve the lot of the mass of Southern African Americans. In his "Atlanta Compromise" speech delivered at the Cotton States and International Exposition in Atlanta in 1895, Washington urged African Americans to "cast down their buckets" where they may and to learn industrial skills and pull themselves up by their bootstraps until they had earned the respect of white America. Washington's pronounced creed was that African Americans should not seek social equality. The Harvard-educated and lighter-skinned W.E.B. Du Bois (1868–1963) called for the "Talented Tenth" of the African-American community to prove themselves the equals of white Americans while fighting legally through the National Association for the Advancement of Colored People (NAACP) for civil rights. Marcus Garvey (1887–1940) was Jamaican-born, noticeably dark-skinned, and a global traveler who had left the British colony for England and then America. Born later than the others, he would temporarily fill the void left by Washington's death and advocated a distinctly Pan-African, nationalist approach, separatism, inspired intriguingly in part by the democratic rhetoric of President Woodrow Wilson. Garvey's emphasis on black pride and rejection of miscegenation would be echoed in the Nation of Islam of the 1960s. In particular, Garvey asserted that Africans had a glorious past that was denied by whites. He encouraged the African diaspora to focus their energies on freeing Ethiopia and going "Back to Africa" to make their contribution to the world. To achieve his ends, he established the Universal Negro Improvement Association in 1914, and the organization soon spread to cities in New York, Pennsylvania, Ohio, Michigan, and Illinois, which had gained African-American population as a consequence of the first great migration North for war jobs.

Garvey's movement emerged in the tense atmosphere of the World War I and immediate postwar years. A violent atmosphere, including 38 lynchings in 1917 and 58 in 1918, 24 bombings of homes in Chicago where African Americans pushed outside the boundaries seen as their own, and the East Saint Louis, Illinois, and Chicago riots coincided with Woodrow Wilson's call for self-determination of all peoples. The fact that African Americans had spilled their blood in the war years to make the world safe for democracy helped spread the black nationalist message among the masses for the first time. However, by the 1920s, Garvey's charismatic appeals to his fellow African diaspora were disrupted by a mail fraud conviction and questions about his Black Star Steamship Line, which, run by whites, was seen as ridiculing his claims for developing a self-sufficient and separate African-American economy. Garvey's deportation effectively ended his major influence.

BLACK NATIONALISM IN TEMPORARY DECLINE: THE 1920S TO THE 1960S

From the 1920s through the 1960s, black nationalism and the black pride that accompanied it were weak at best. Ralph Ellison's (1914–1994) fictional *Invisible Man* (1952), published in part soon after World War II, illustrates this tension, despite the presence of Marcus Garvey and his successor, the Nation of Islam, in espousing Black Pride. Pausing at the scene of the eviction of an elderly African-American couple, the Invisible Man's survey of the remnants of the couple's life reveals the conflicting pressures on African-American families, who are drawn to and away from an affirmation of pride in their ethnic past. Among the litter are images affirming both a desire to assimilate and a desire to assert a pride in the African-American's difference: an image of Abraham Lincoln and emancipation papers, a straightening comb symbolizing the desire to conform to white standards of beauty, an Ethiopian flag, and an article on Marcus Garvey.

Ellison's personal life, which was filled with discrimination, illustrates the difficulty inherent in the African-American's quest for social change. Tainted by association with Communism, African Americans found themselves hobbled in the fight for civil rights immediately after World War II. And thus, it awaited the emergence of a younger generation to take the lead following the U.S. Supreme Court's historic 1954 decision. World War II nonetheless proved a major turning point for African Americans, paving the way for the civil rights and later black power movements of the 1960s. The fact that African Americans, though treated as second-class citizens, gave their lives to the war effort made them restive and at the same time made many mainstream Americans receptive to the blacks' fight for equality at home and abroad.

Urbanization was crucial to the development of this new political identity: James C. Davies' J-curve theory, relayed in Wolfenstein's *The Victims of Democracy* (1981), notes that "rising and declining satisfactions" foment rebellion. "Revolution [or rebellion] is most likely to take place when a prolonged period of rising expectations and rising gratification is followed by a short period of sharp reversal during which the gap between expectations and gratifications quickly widens and becomes intolerable." Incomes had risen as African Americans left the South for defense jobs and as the decline of cotton prices and mechanization of cotton farming pushed others out. All this movement stalled, however, during the Korean War. In the 1960s, the federal government's commitment to raising African Americans' economic status also increased as African Americans moved north, transforming them into marginal but crucial swing voters who could decide presidential elections. And the winds of decolonization in Africa and Asia began to inspire a spirit of rebellion in America's blacks who connected the independence movements to the civil rights struggle here at home.

The influence of the broader foreign policy environment is seen most clearly in the young Dr. Martin Luther King Jr. (1929–1968). In 1955, a year after the Supreme Court officially desegregated schools in *Brown v. Board of Education* and the same year that Rosa Parks refused to give up her seat on a Montgomery, Alabama, bus, King was catapulted to leadership of the national civil rights movement when he led a freedom walk of 125,000 people in Detroit, Michigan, and a 250,000 person rally in Washington, D.C. As Marable's *Race, Reform, and Rebellion* (1991) suggests, King's "Letter from Birmingham Jail" cites the influence of decolonization in spurring him on. In his historic letter, King insisted that African Americans needed to assert their rights immediately because they had "waited for more than 340 years for [their] constitutional and God-given rights" and while "the nations of Asia and Africa [were] moving with jetlike speed toward political independence," African Americans had crept "at horse-and-buggy pace toward gaining a cup of coffee at a lunch counter."

Those who could not wait won achievements that further raised expectations. The 1957 Civil Rights Act guaranteed the voting rights of African Americans and empowered the Justice Department to sue state and local interests favoring school segregation and restricting voting; the 1960 Civil Rights Act allowed federal judges to appoint referees to register voters in place of local judges; the 1964 Civil Rights Act outlawed Jim Crow in public accommodations at the local and state level; and the Voting Rights Act of 1965 placed federal examiners in the South to safeguard voter registration. By 1968, one of the last vestiges of voter discrimination, the poll tax, was finally abolished. Thus, by 1968, African Americans had won the right to an integrated cup of coffee, and yet some members of the black nationalist movement rejected that right as irrelevant.

BLACK NATIONALISM, MUSLIM STYLE: THE NATION OF ISLAM

After a nearly forty-year absence, Marcus Garvey's *Philosophy and Opinions* was reissued in the 1960s. The renewed interest in Garvey confirmed an awakening among African Americans of Black Pride, which was also reinvigorated by the growth of the Nation of Islam. Although the Nation of Islam had been around in the 1930s and 1940s, it experienced remarkable growth only with the national emergence of Malcolm X (1925–1965), the son of a murdered follower of Marcus Garvey. Unlike the Black Panthers, a militant African-American civil rights organization, the Nation of Islam's recruits were so deeply immersed in the lower class that they lacked so-called real jobs. The Nation of Islam's recruits instead habituated a world where members supported themselves with crime, including prostitution, numbers running, and drugs, which often led to incarceration. Former prisoners, impressed by the Nation of Islam's emphasis on Black Pride, dignity, self-determination, and the language of victimization, reformed their behavior once they became members of the Nation, leaving drugs and prostitution behind. The Nation of Islam trained both men and women in separate roles; for example, it emphasized women's duties as mothers, wives, and homemakers. Black Muslims asserted pride in their heritage by rejecting forced assimilation, and as part of their politicization they renamed themselves. Thus it was that Malcolm Little became Malcolm X, thereby rejecting the name imposed on the family by slavemasters. And like Garvey's earlier movement the Nation of Islam rejected economic assimilation, proposing to establish a separate economy, though it pushed further than Garvey in demanding a separate state in America. In order to facilitate the creation of an imagined community centered around Muhammad's conception of Islam, the Nation of Islam published a newspaper *Muhammad Speaks*, issued statements over radio stations, and established two universities of Islam, one in Detroit and another in Chicago, to impart the Nation's conception of Africa's glorious past. The paramilitary Fruit of Islam defended the community.

The Nation of Islam originated in 1931 when a man named Elijah Poole (1897–1975) was visited by a mysterious figure, Wallace D. Fard, considered by many to be the founder of the Black Muslim movement. Poole's meeting with the silk and yard goods peddlar convinced him that blacks were descended from Muslims, lost in America, and would be "redeemed" by Islam. Poole also insisted that the white

ELIJAH MUHAMMAD (1897–1975)
(originally Elijah Poole)

Born near Sandersville, Georgia, on or about October 7, 1897, Elijah Poole was the son of former slaves and sharecroppers. He quit school after finishing the third grade to work in the fields to help his family make ends meet. He left home at sixteen, married, and moved his family to Detroit in 1923 to find work.

Around 1930, Poole joined the Nation of Islam, a movement founded by Wallace D. Fard that preached black separatism, and he quickly moved up in the organization. When Fard mysteriously disappeared in 1934, Poole took over, changed his name, and made a national movement out of the Black Muslims, arguing for separation of the races, and scorning attempts of the civil rights movement to bring about integration. In addition to establishing religious centers of worship, Muhammad stressed the need for African Americans to establish their own economic power base and to become economically self-sufficient. He encouraged the establishment of black businesses to foster economic development that focused on buying and selling between and among black companies.

Muhammad required strict obedience to certain tenets of Islam. He and many other members of the organization were arrested during World War II for refusing to serve in the military. After his release from prison, he moved to Chicago and established the headquarters for the Nation of Islam. The movement bene-fited directly from the pent-up frustrations of the black masses and offered those frustrations a militant, if avowedly nonviolent, expression. Soon there were mosques in all larger cities with sizable black populations.

Muhammad welcomed Malcolm X as a minister after Malcolm X's release from prison in 1952, and in 1955, Louis Walcott, who soon changed his name to Louis Farrakhan, joined. But Muhammad soon found Malcolm X eclipsing his own popularity. Malcolm left the Nation of Islam in a very public philosophical split regarding the separation of the races. After Malcolm's assassination in 1965, Muhammad dispatched Farrakhan to New York to rebuild the temple there and promoted him to National Representative.

In his later years, however, Muhammad moderated his antiwhite tone and stressed self-help among blacks rather than confrontation between the races. When he died on February 25, 1975, his son Wallace took over, leading the movement closer to traditional Islam and changing its name to the World Community of Islam in the West. In 1985, he dissolved the organization in order that its members might become a part of the worldwide orthodox Islamic community. A splinter group based in New York City and under the leadership of Louis Farrakhan retained both the name and the founding principles of the Nation of Islam.

James G. Lewis

race was a source of evil, produced from the original, black race by an evil scientist. In 1931 Poole changed his name to Elijah Muhammad and began proselytizing. He was arrested in 1942 for draft-dodging despite his age (he was forty-four) and served in federal prison between 1942 and 1946. It was also in prison that Muhammad found many of his recruits, including the young Malcolm X, who was serving for burglary charges in the same prison as Elijah Muhammad and converted to Islam in 1952.

Malcolm X blended many of the black nationalist Garveyite teachings to which he had been exposed as a young man with the Nation of Islam's teachings. Malcolm X echoed Garvey's emphasis on the beauty of blackness through his constant references to rejecting the practice of conking (i.e., straightening) kinky hair to look white as self-degrading. In this connection, Malcolm X expressed particular admiration for the actors Lionel Hampton and Sidney Poitier, both of whom refused to tamper with their natural looks.

More importantly, however, Malcolm X's life experiences were shared by many others in the ghetto and across the color spectrum: like Native American activists, he noted how the welfare system divided up his family; he cringed at stereotypes, particularly those in *Gone With the Wind*; and he decried the imposition of limited opportunities when a high school teacher advised him to avoid trying to become a lawyer and settle for being a carpenter. As a result of these experiences, Malcolm X rejected integration, refused service in America's wars, affirmed with others that African Americans had a glorious past denied to them by whites, and stereotyped whites as murderers, rapists, and kidnappers. As the charismatic minister of Harlem's Temple Number Seven, he convinced others to follow his path.

Malcolm X's pilgrimage to Mecca in 1964 altered his ideas on what place Islam had in changing the African Americans' position. In Mecca he learned that Islam drew together worshippers from all races, including whites. Astonished, Malcolm X noted the unity of people who encompassed all races and all colors. This experience encouraged him to admit and then abandon his "sweeping indictments of *all* white people," as he noted in *The Autobiography of Malcolm X* (1965). In 1964, Malcolm X established the Organization of Afro-American Unity (OAAU) and Muslim Mosque Inc., and it was at this time that he shifted his emphasis from black separatism to black nationalism. The OAAU promoted political participation, opposition to housing discrimination, cultural centers, and self-defense. To symbolize the change, Malcolm X changed his name once again: now he became El-Hajj Malik El-Shabazz. Malcolm X's cooperation with non-African Americans in the Nation of Islam, however, conflicted intensely with the Nation of Islam's policies and may have been one of the factors in his assassination by Nation of Islam members in 1965.

Several weaknesses soon began to undermine the Nation of Islam: anti-Semitism as expressed in Malcolm's work and carried on in the Nation of Islam by Malcolm X's effective replacement Louis Farrakhan was one major source of weakness. Malcolm X's advocacy of adopting any means necessary, including violence, similarly constrained his movement, although the threat of violence was intended more as a deterrent. Although black nationalism may have recruited many of the disaffected masses, over 300 years of slavery had exposed African Americans to the dominant culture, including Christianity, which made a break from such traditions infeasible. As a result of the Nation's position, a *New York Times* poll in 1964 found that only 6 percent of those polled felt Malcolm X was advancing the cause of African Americans, leaving him trailing King at 75 percent by a wide margin. Malcolm X and the Nation of Islam reached an audience unrepresented by the "middle-class" "Uncle Toms" they decried, but in some ways Malcolm X's movement was less widely respected than these more moderate movements.

THE BLACK PANTHERS

The Black Panthers burst upon the national scene in October 1966, shortly after the assassination of Malcolm X. The party's minister of defense, Huey Newton (1942–1989), and chairman, Bobby Seale (1936–), were college students, representing a slightly different black nationalist constituency. Other prominent officials of the Black Panthers included Stokely Carmichael, an opponent of assimilation, and Eldridge Cleaver (1935–1998), the party's minister of information.

STOKELY CARMICHAEL (1941–1998)
(also known as Kwame Ture, after 1969)

Born in Port-of-Spain, Trinidad, on June 29, 1941, to a carpenter and his wife, Carmichael emigrated to the United States in 1952 at age eleven, and was shocked by the racism he encountered. He felt no reassurance when he attended the Bronx High School of Science and encountered white liberals who adopted him as a "mascot."

While attending Howard University (1960–1964), Carmichael joined the Congress of Racial Equality (CORE) in its efforts to integrate public accommodations in the South. He participated in the Freedom Rides in 1961 and the voter registration drive known as Freedom Summer in 1964. After graduation, he joined and was elected leader of the Student Nonviolent Coordinating Committee (SNCC), and changed the group's focus from peaceful integration to "black liberation." He quickly emerged as the leading spokesman for Black Power, a phrase he helped popularize. The position drove a wedge into the civil rights movement, and the phrase became a symbol of violence to whites who feared uprisings in American cities. In 1967, Carmichael joined with Charles Hamilton to write the book, *Black Power*. Carmichael resigned from SNCC and became a Black Panther. He differed with its leader, Eldridge Cleaver, because Carmichael favored forging alliances with radical whites. This led to his resignation from the Panthers in 1968.

He and his wife, Miriam Makeba, moved to Guinea, West Africa, in 1969, where he supported Pan-Africanism, and changed his name to Kwame Ture (after Kwame Nkrumah of Ghana and Sekou Toure of Guinea). In 1972, he briefly returned to the United States to promote his Pan-African ideology, which he described as an increased awareness and acceptance by American blacks of the culture, heritage, and ideals of Africans. He stressed that it was the ultimate extension of Black Power. He helped to establish the All-African People's Revolutionary Party and worked as an aide to Guinea's prime minister, Sekou Toure. After the death of Toure in 1984, Carmichael was arrested by the new military regime and charged with trying to overthrow the government. However, he only spent three days in prison before being released. He died of cancer on November 15, 1998.

James G. Lewis

Members of the Black Panthers guard the speakers' platform during a conference at Temple University in Philadelphia on September 7, 1970. *(AP Wide World Photos)*

Cleaver illustrated the link between the Nation of Islam and the Black Panther Party, as well as some of their most glaring differences. Like many Black Muslims, Cleaver became a convert to Black Muslim while in prison, drawn as he was to the tenets of the religion as well as to Malcolm X's charismatic leadership. Similarly, Panther Bobby Seale was radicalized when he heard Malcolm X speak. However, like Malcolm X who changed his policy on separatism toward the end of his life, the Panthers moved toward a position of working with other races on their issues, while maintaining that the African-American community was colonized and deserved an independent state based upon socialist principles.

Eldridge Cleaver's *Soul on Ice* (1968) illustrates many of these themes. Cleaver faced the same self-hatred, instilled by the majority society's media, although he insisted that this was a product not of diabolical design but of the fact that the majority society inundated the black community with the standards of white beauty on a daily basis. Cleaver's racial consciousness was aroused as a result of *Brown v. Board of Education* (1954) and the ensuing conflict over integration. That conflict forced him to question the price of Americanization and his place in America. According to Cleaver, at Soledad Prison, the prisoners "cursed everything American—including baseball and hot dogs" as they watched leaders "callously compromising over [issues] of right and wrong." Cleaver's attitude also drew from the Muslim movement.

Yet the Black Panther Party was amenable to co-operation with whites: *Soul on Ice* is dedicated to Cleaver's white lawyer Beverly Axelrod. When Malcolm X changed his position, Cleaver noted that "there were those of us who were glad to be liberated from a doctrine of hate and racial supremacy." In addition, Cleaver favorably remarked on the changing attitudes of white youth as signs of potential cooperation.

Self-determination, education, full employment, decent housing, an end to police brutality, fair trials, decriminalization, and fair rates of military service and reinvestment of community resources in the community were the keynotes of the Panthers demands. They were made by working-class and middle-class African Americans, many of them students, in a context in which civil rights had been achieved, welfare was assumed as a state obligation, and the Vietnam War was sending disproportionate numbers of African Americans to die for their country.

The Panthers' demand, "We want all black men to be exempt from military service," also had other overtones. Panther member Cleaver conceived of the Black Power struggle and opposition to American neo-imperialism as inextricable. In *Soul on Ice,* he noted that 16 percent of American troops were composed of African Americans and that the struggle for decolonization had promoted civil rights. According to Cleaver, the end of the Vietnam War would allow the United States to return to repressing blacks much as had happened at the end of the Civil War. As a result, Cleaver insisted in *Soul on Ice* that "the black man's interest lies in seeing a free and independent Vietnam" because "[i]f the nations of Asia, Latin America, and Africa are strong and free, the black man in America will be safe and secure and free to live in dignity and self-respect." He also argued that decolonization had created a window for African Americans to assert their rights.

Lyndon Johnson's War on Poverty played a role in raising expectations for reform that were never fully realized. Ultimately, the federal government suppressed both the Nation of Islam and the Black Panthers; in addition, the organizations were wrest apart by factions and by the influence of their violent tactics. A gun battle with police in 1968 led to Cleaver's return to jail. After his release in 1966, he ran as the presidential candidate of the Peace and Freedom Party, but when he was required to return to jail, he decided to flee to Cuba. His travels within totalitarian Communist countries soon diluted his faith in Communism. By 1971, the Black Panther Party's top officials, Cleaver and Newton, were running competing organizations in New York and California, respectively. In addition, the Federal Bureau of Investigation began targeting the Black Panther Party and other nationalist organizations for infiltration. The murder of Black Panther Party member Fred Hampton in a police raid in December 1969 has come to symbolize the ruthless suppression of nationalist groups by the Federal Bureau of Investigation's COINTELPRO, an acronym for the organization's domestic "counterintelligence program."

Throughout the twentieth century, black nationalism ebbed and flowed as a response to the civil rights movement's demands for integration. In response to the subordinate position of African Americans in American society, black nationalism did not demand access to mainstream institutions; instead, it demanded the space to carve out a separate sphere in which black talent and leadership could develop, black-owned businesses could flourish, and racial pride would increase. The proponents of this black nationalism followed no particular religious sect: Garvey's movement was an answer to Christian precepts but not Islamic like the Nation of Islam, and the Black Panthers lacked a religious identity. In addition, the constituencies of the Nation of Islam and Black Panthers ranged from workingclass to underclass to college-students as they emerged during the teens and the twenties and the fifties and the sixties. In each case, however, earlier ideologies provided core concepts for the later movements as seen in the works of Malcolm X and Eldridge Cleaver.

On the whole, black nationalism's most enduring legacy was to provide a more radical alternative to integrationism, an alternative that may have swayed leaders to cooperate with more moderate leaders, to encourage attention to the way American history was presented, and to shed a light on the problems of African Americans who fell outside the middle and upper classes. The movement was not without problems, however—from Garvey's accommodation of the KKK, to the Black Muslim's paramilitary Fruit of Islam and rabid anti-Semitism, and to the Black Panthers' embrace of violent rhetoric and poor choice of methods to demonstrate their rights, including entering the California Legislature with weapons to highlight their right to bear arms.

Anne Woo-Sam

BIBLIOGRAPHY

Anderson, Benedict R. O'G. *Imagined Communities: Reflections on the Origin and Spread of Nationalism.* Rev. ed. London and New York: Verso, 1991.

Churchill, Ward, and Jim Vander Wall. *Agents of Repression: The FBI's Secret Wars against the Black Panther Party and the American Indian Movement.* Corrected ed. Boston: South End, 1990.

Cleaver, Eldridge. *Soul on Ice.* New York: McGraw-Hill, 1968.

Dudziak, Mary L. *Cold War Civil Rights: Race and the Image of American Democracy.* Princeton, NJ: Princeton University Press, 2000.

Ellison, Ralph. *Invisible Man.* New York: Vintage Books, 1947.

Ethnic Notions. Written, produced, and directed by Marlon T. Riggs. California Newsreel, 1987. Videocassette.

Foner, Eric. *Reconstruction: America's Unfinished Revolution, 1863–1877.* New York: Harper & Row, 1988.

Freedom on My Mind. Written and edited by Michael Chandler. Produced and directed by Connie Field and Marilyn Mulford. Clarity Educational Productions, 1994. Videocassette.

Garvey, Marcus. *Philosophy and Opinions of Marcus Garvey, or, Africa for the Africans.* Comp. Amy Jacques Garvey. 2d ed. London: Cass, 1967.

Grossman, James R. *Land of Hope: Chicago, Black Southerners, and the Great Migration.* Chicago: University of Chicago Press, 1989.

Lemann, Nicholas. *The Promised Land: The Great Black Migration and How It Changed America.* New York: Alfred A. Knopf, 1991.

Levine, Lawrence W. *Black Culture and Black Consciousness: Afro-American Folk Thought from Slavery to Freedom.* New York: Oxford University Press, 1977.

Lincoln, C. Eric. *The Black Muslims in America.* Boston: Beacon, 1961.

Magida, Arthur J. *Prophet of Rage: A Life of Louis Farrakhan and His Nation.* New York: Basic Books, 1996.

Malcolm X. Warner Bros., 40 Acres and a Mule Filmworks, 1993. Videocassette.

Malcolm X. *The Autobiography of Malcolm X as Told to Alex Haley.* New York: Grove, 1965.

Marable, Manning. *Race, Reform, and Rebellion: The Second Reconstruction in Black America, 1945–1990.* 2d ed. Jackson: University Press of Mississippi, 1991.

McMillen, Neil R. *Dark Journey: Black Mississippians in the Age of Jim Crow.* Urbana: University of Illinois Press, 1989.

Moody, Anne. *Coming of Age in Mississippi.* New York: Dell, 1968.

Morrison, Toni, ed. *Race-ing Justice, En-gendering Power: Essays on Anita Hill, Clarence Thomas, and the Construction of Social Reality.* New York: Pantheon Books, 1992.

Nash, Gerald D. *The American West Transformed: The Impact of the Second World War.* Bloomington: Indiana University Press, 1985.

Richard Wright: Black Boy. Produced by Mississippi Educational Television/BBC. California Newsreel [distributor], 1994. Videocassette.

Takaki, Ronald T. *A Different Mirror: A History of Multicultural America.* Boston: Little, Brown, 1993.

Wolfenstein, E. Victor. *The Victims of Democracy: Malcolm X and the Black Revolution.* Berkeley: University of California Press, 1981.

Wright, Richard. *Black Boy (American Hunger): A Record of Childhood and Youth.* New York: HarperPerennial, 1993.

Anti-Apartheid Movement

The anti-apartheid movement in the United States encompassed a broad coalition of organizations operating on governmental and nongovernmental levels. While varying widely in method and degree of intensity, they all shared the goal of ending racial oppression in South Africa. In order to get a clear understanding of this movement, it is helpful to place it in a historical context.

Historical Background

The struggle for racial justice in South Africa began at the end of the eighteenth century as the indigenous inhabitants resisted British and Dutch colonialism. Britain's involvement in South Africa began in 1795 as it sought to establish a military base in what is now Cape Town. Britain's mission was to control the shipping routes to and from India, its most valued colonial possession, as well as to prevent rival European nations from challenging British supremacy in the region. What began as a limited, military operation quickly turned into an increasingly imperial one after British naval authorities learned that the potential existed for several deep harbor ports in addition to the one in Cape Town. In order to prevent their European rivals from securing any of these ports, the British government decided to expand its authority into the hinterland using Dutch immigrants (Afrikaners, or Boers) for this purpose.

Conflict developed as white colonists, especially Afrikaners, began to move inland and secure the most fertile lands, which had been the ancestral homeland to the Xhosa and Zulu ethnic groups. The increasing friction between the British and Boer populations added significantly to what would later shape segregationist policy in South Africa. The Boers, having as their aim the permanent occupation of the land, developed much more intense and racist views of Africans than the British, who still saw their mission as limited and strictly military.

To deal with the growing conflict between the Dutch settlers and Africans, the British government settled on a system of racial separation (apartheid) as the most cost-effective strategy to control these groups. Similar to their approach in Java to control various ethnic groups, the British placed the different African ethnic groups on reserves (Xhosastands). The policy of establishing Xhosastands to restrict the contact between Boers and the indigenous populations failed. The failure was caused primarily by the Afrikaners' ever-increasing desire to own and control more ancestral lands. Afrikaner expansion culminated in the establishment of their own republic of Natal in 1838.

British consternation over the Boer colonial expansion was further evidenced by their annexation of the Natal republic in 1843. This annexation came about because the British saw the potential for two unfavorable developments that could jeopardize Britain's overall military objectives. First was the continued conflict between the Boers and indigenous groups, which grew in intensity when gold and diamonds were discovered on native lands, lands that were supposedly reserved for indigenous peoples. The Afrikaners' aggression had the potential for uniting the various African ethnic groups and resulting in a costly nationwide war. The second possibility that Britain feared was a union between Holland and the Boers. If the British were to allow Afrikaners increasing power, the likelihood of their securing a military alliance with Holland was too great to chance.

The culmination of Afrikaner resistance to British demands led to the Boer War, 1899–1902. Although this war ended in defeat for the Afrikaners, it set the stage for the more modern notion of apartheid. An uneasy power-sharing arrangement between the defeated Boers and British colonists existed until the 1940s, when the Afrikaner National Party was able to gain a majority in Parliament. Ideologues of the National Party, looking forward to eventual victory, began to work out the most extreme and austere form of apartheid in order to secure control over the economic and social systems of the country. In 1948, the Afrikaner Nationalist Party came to power after winning a majority victory in Parliament, which in turn simultaneously ushered in one of the most racist systems ever devised and one of the greatest resistance movements against it.

APARTHEID

Apartheid (defined as "apartness" in the Afrikaners' language) is a strict system of racial segregation and discrimination instituted by white South Africans against black South Africans. Racial discrimination in South Africa was institutionalized with the passage of the 1948 apartheid laws. Race laws touched every aspect of social life, including a prohibition against mixed-race marriages and the sanctioning of "white only" jobs. In 1950, the Population Registration Act required that all South Africans be racially classified into one of three categories: white, black (African), or colored (mixed decent). The colored category included major subgroups of Indians and Asians. Classification into these categories was based on such arbitrary characteristics as appearance, social acceptance, and descent. For example, a white person was defined as "in appearance obviously a white person or generally accepted as a white person." A person could not be considered white if one of his or her parents was nonwhite. The determination that a person was "obviously white" would take into account his or her "habits, education and speech and deportment and demeanor." A member of an African tribe or race was considered black, and a colored person was one who was not white or black. The Department of Home Affairs (a government bureau) was responsible for the classification of citizenry. Noncompliance with the race laws was dealt with harshly. All Africans were required to carry "pass books" containing fingerprints, photo, and information to gain access to nonblack areas.

RESISTANCE TO APARTHEID IN THE UNITED STATES

The origins of U.S. resistance to apartheid in South Africa date back to as early as 1912 when the National Association for the Advancement of Colored People (NAACP) helped to organize the African National Congress. Another African-American organization involved in the early resistance to apartheid in South Africa was the Council on African Affairs. A third organization that participated in the early phase of

the American-led anti-apartheid movement was the American Committee on Africa, which was established in 1953. All of these organizations were led by African Americans, highlighting the obvious connection between racial oppression at home and its equivalents abroad.

The early organizing around resistance to apartheid (1912–1953) played a very important role in creating a foundation from which later efforts were built. During this time, anti-apartheid movements in the United States grew, as other struggles in the region, such as the wars for independence in Angola, Mozambique, Zimbabwe, and Zambia, escalated.

In the second half of the twentieth century, specific acts of violence committed by the South African government bolstered the movement as well. The Sharpeville incident on March 12, 1960, when sixty-nine unarmed protesters were brutally shot to death by the South African police, sparked a worldwide outcry for justice. In 1976, the uprising in Soweto, where over a thousand students were killed for protesting against state educational policies that implied black inferiority, drew attention again to the injustices of the apartheid system. Finally, the murder of the popular Black Consciousness leader Steve Biko while in police custody in 1977 ignited international outrage at the South African government.

THE TWO APPROACHES OF THE ANTI-APARTHEID MOVEMENT

The Governmental Approach

The anti-apartheid movement in the United States can be divided into two broad categories: governmental-business and nongovernmental efforts. The United States' governmental policy did not pay much attention to South Africa until the 1960s, when several internationally publicized injustices of the apartheid regime forced it to do so. Following this, U.S. government policy fluctuated between adopting a close relationship with the South African government and applying mild sanctions against it. The most punitive measures came with the Carter administration's support of the 1977 international arms embargo of South Africa. However, even though the U.S. government officially condemned the apartheid regime, it never attempted or even threatened to end it with the use of force. The closest embrace between the U.S. government-business interests and the South African government came under the Reagan administration's policy of "constructive engagement," a form of quiet

On April 19, 1985, students at Columbia University in New York denounce the South African government's policy of racial segregation known as apartheid. *(AP Wide World Photos)*

diplomacy seeking incremental rather than comprehensive change. This policy was instituted to provide continued U.S. military access to the Cape of Good Hope in the event of a military confrontation with the former Soviet Union.

U.S. businesses, particularly lending institutions and import-export and manufacturing firms, were even more reluctant to curtail relations with the apartheid system than the U.S. government because of the potential for high rates of return on their investments. In fact, business pressure to secure such an outcome sometimes culminated in the U.S. government's sponsorship of companies doing business in South Africa. Some of the U.S. government institutions that fell under these pressures were the Export-Import Bank of the United States, the Department of Agriculture, and

the Commerce Department. Another indication of the strong business ties between the United States and South Africa is seen in investment figures. For example, in 1950 U.S. businesses invested a total of $140 million in South Africa. By 1982, that number had increased to $2.5 billion. It is for these reasons that U.S. government policy and U.S. businesses became the primary targets of the nongovernmental anti-apartheid movement until apartheid's end in 1992.

The Nongovernmental Approach

In their attempt to end apartheid in South Africa, nongovernmental anti-apartheid organizations focused their efforts on four methods aimed at overturning apartheid. These methods included business sanctions, local and state divestment, and direct aid. A wide range of organizations participated in these efforts, including churches, universities, and large and small grassroots organizations.

Sanctions

The largest and most effective of these methods were economic sanctions. Sanctions against South Africa were designed to isolate the apartheid regime economically and culturally. A main thrust in the sanctions movement came from the United Nations (UN) in 1962 when the General Assembly first called for sanctions against South Africa due to pressure brought about by the anticolonial struggles taking place throughout the African continent. Then in 1963, the UN Security Council adopted a resolution for a voluntary embargo on military sales to South Africa. Following the Sharpeville incident, the death of Black Consciousness leader Steve Biko, and the continued repressive measures taken by the South African government against dissidents, the United Nations made the embargo mandatory in 1977.

Nongovernmental anti-apartheid groups in the United States called for sanctions against businesses involved directly and indirectly with the South African government. These groups used both direct and indirect sanction methods to pressure domestic businesses. Activists targeted institutions that had, indirectly, and often unknowingly, dealings with the apartheid regime. These dealings were often in the form of investments made by major lending institutions on behalf of such organizations as universities, foundations, labor unions, churches, and state and local governments. Anti-apartheid groups used some of these venues as key organizing centers, especially churches and universities.

Activists also targeted corporations with a shareholder responsibility and divestment strategy. Anti-apartheid activists argued that corporations were responsible not only for the conditions of their own workers but also for those of their trading partners. Because the South African regime allowed business to blatantly disregard human rights, many anti-apartheid organizations found limited support for their efforts even in this traditionally conservative environment. Perhaps the greatest sponsor of the corporate shareholder responsibility approach was the Reverend Leon Sullivan, who developed what has become known as the "Sullivan Principles." The Sullivan Principles list six guidelines that firms doing business in South Africa should follow. They include among other things nonsegregation of the races in all eating, comfort, and work facilities; increasing the number of blacks and other nonwhites in management and supervisory positions; and equal pay for all employees doing equal or comparable work. If these measures were not followed, he advocated that shareholders introduce resolutions at stockholder meetings to curtail their dealings with the South African government.

The most direct form of action launched by the anti-apartheid movement was in the form of divestment. Whereas shareholder responsibility sought a more enlightened investment policy, the divestment movement wanted to stop all current and future investment. Churches and universities were the primary driving force behind this movement. Churches were one of the first targets of divestment and rapidly became major supporters of the movement itself. Banks also were among the first organizations to be targeted for divestment. In 1966, student protesters demanded that eleven banks, including Citibank, withdraw $23 million in loans to the South African government. Although banks remained a constant target of the anti-apartheid movement, a minority of them still found ways to get loans to the South African government until the end of the apartheid regime in 1994.

State and Local Governments

The anti-apartheid movement began to target state and local governments in earnest in the early 1970s. Their goal was to prevent these institutions from investing any further in South Africa. Because state legislatures and city councils controlled millions of dollars in employee pension funds and university endowments, anti-apartheid activists saw a tremendous opportunity to put pressure on the South African government by lobbying them to divest from South Africa. Hampshire College in Amherst, Massachusetts, was the first American university to divest from South Africa in 1976, and the first comprehensive bill affecting all state investments was passed in Connecticut in 1980 and 1981.

The decision by anti-apartheid activists to apply pressure on the apartheid regime by targeting state and local governments was crucial in terms of both short-term tactics and long-term strategy. Anti-apartheid activists proved that in the short term it was possible to make a strong statement of condemnation by having millions of dollars cut off from the South African government. This was no small victory considering that most divestment efforts in the 1980s ran counter to U.S. foreign policy that actually supported efforts to invest under its policy of "Constructive Engagement."

State and local divestment actions helped the broader strategic aim of the movement, which was to internationalize the anti-apartheid struggle by making opposition to apartheid part of the American national debate. Prior to legislative action on the state and local level, the majority of anti-apartheid actions were confined to the university and church organizations. By pressuring legislative bodies, the anti-apartheid movement became more mainstream and thus more effective in reaching its goal of abolishing apartheid in South Africa.

Direct Aid

The nongovernmental anti-apartheid movement in the United States also employed the method of direct aid in its fight to end apartheid in South Africa. This approach was the smallest in comparison to the other methods used and must be understood as part of a much broader and more intense international effort. Given the relatively conservative climate of official U.S. policy toward South Africa, anti-apartheid activists were forced to rely on grassroots efforts. Private organizations, churches, and universities carried out the vast majority of these efforts.

Aid for South African scholarships at American universities played an important role in educating the American public about the devastating effects of apartheid. This translated into a strong anti-apartheid movement on college campuses. Throughout the 1980s, several universities witnessed anti-apartheid demonstrations during which students took over administration buildings and teach-ins where professors canceled their regular classes to inform students about the history and impact of apartheid. Perhaps the most visual form of protest was the construction of "Shanty Towns" (poorly constructed huts on college campuses) to demonstrate the horrible living conditions most Africans were forced to endure.

Church organizations, especially African-American interdenominational groups, also played a significant role in directly aiding apartheid opponents. These organizations sponsored South African refugees who were either banned from their country or forced out because of their own anti-apartheid activities. These refugees lectured to congregations throughout the country, raising awareness among the American public as to the conditions of apartheid. In addition to raising awareness, these lectures raised monetary funds to support families and various organizations operating within South Africa.

Grassroots organizations also played a major role in the fight against apartheid in South Africa. These organizations ranged in size from well-known groups like the NAACP and TransAfrica to local community groups and the Mugabe Trust Fund. The larger organizations galvanized support in the form of scholarship funds, lecture tours, and donations to large South African–based groups like the African National Congress (ANC). The smaller grassroots organizations tended to support smaller self-help groups. For example, funds raised by SISA (Social Identities South Africa) went to a local collective of women in South Africa, who were learning how to make, market, and sell quilts to supplement their incomes.

CONCLUSION

The efforts of the anti-apartheid movement in the United States came to fruition when Nelson Mandela became president of South Africa in 1994. The election of Mandela as president also marked the end of the efforts of millions of people from across the world, many of whom gave their lives. The international struggle against apartheid lasted nearly 200 years from the early resistance fighters of the Xhosa and Zulu ethnic groups to the liberation struggles in neighboring Mozambique and Angola to the protests staged by college students in the United States.

The specific role of the United States in helping to end apartheid may be smaller in scale than that of other countries, but when one considers the close relationship shared by the U.S. government and the apartheid regime, the actions of thousands of activists played a leading role in the collapse of the regime. Although governmental applications of mild pressure were evident, it was the nongovernmental agencies that had the greatest impact on ending apartheid. Driven by a sense of justice, the anti-apartheid movement embodied a diverse group of people with various religious, ethnic, and class backgrounds. The diversity of the participants in the anti-apartheid movement was also reflected in the diversity of approaches employed to end apartheid.

The anti-apartheid movement in the United States focused its energies in three main areas: business sanctions; university and state and local government-sponsored divestment; and direct aid. Although each of these approaches targeted a different audience, they all shared a similar goal of both applying pressure on the South African government and raising the consciousness of Americans as to the horrible reality of life under apartheid. Activists involved in business sanctions forced major companies to be at least conscious of how their business practices affected South

African workers. This effort brought about the Sullivan Principles, the most comprehensive corporate guidelines for doing business in South Africa.

Universities were the site of both divestment and direct aid campaigns, employing a number of tactics and strategies. With these efforts a significant victory was won in 1976 when Hampshire College became the first institution of higher education to divest from South Africa. Similarly, campus activists working directly to aid South Africa were successful in pressuring institutions to sponsor scholarships for dissidents and hold teach-ins. Activists working for state and local government divestitures won a critical victory when Connecticut became the first state to pass a comprehensive bill affecting all state investments in 1980 and 1981.

Direct aid given by American activists to the struggle against the South African government played an incalculable role in the ultimate defeat of apartheid. South African dissidents sponsored by the anti-apartheid movement brought awareness about the hideous nature of apartheid to the American public, which in turn helped to strengthen the divestiture and sanction movements as well. Direct aid on the grassroots level by organizations like the NAACP also helped to build and strengthen both large and small organizations inside South Africa. The overall effect of the thousands of people participating in the anti-apartheid movement in the United States and abroad was a critical force in the collapse of the regime.

Ernest D. Green

BIBLIOGRAPHY

Cobbett, William, and Robin Cohen, eds. *Popular Struggle in South Africa.* Trenton, NJ: Africa World, 1987.

Eger, David, Caroline Cummings, and Cathy Keil. *District of Columbia Special Investment Study: South Africa Proposal.* Louisville, KY: Medinger Asset Planning Service, 1983.

Hauck, David, Meg Vorhees, and Glen Goldberg. *Two Decades of Debate: The Controversy over U.S. Companies in South Africa.* Washington, DC: Investor Responsibility Research Center, 1983.

Kline, Benjamin. *Genesis of Apartheid: British African Policy in the Colony of Natal 1845–1893.* New York: University of America Press, 1988.

Lazerson, Joshua. *Against the Tide: Whites in the Struggle Against Apartheid.* Boulder, CO: Westview Press, 1994.

Love, Janice. *The U.S. Anti-apartheid Movement: Local Activism in Global Politics.* New York: Praeger, 1985.

Mandela, Nelson. *Long Walk to Freedom.* Boston: Little, Brown, 1994.

Reddy, E.S. *Apartheid: The United Nations and the International Community.* New York: Advent Books, 1980.

Shepard, George. *Anti-apartheid: Transnational Conflict and Western Policy in the Liberation of South Africa.* Westport, CT: Greenwood Press, 1977.

CIVIL RIGHTS MOVEMENT 1990–2000

There is vigorous debate over the future direction of the civil rights movement as it moves into the new century. There are three main perspectives. The first group, whose views are articulated by such scholars as Stephan and Abigail Thernstrom, have suggested that our nation must "move beyond race." They argue that on many social and economic indicators, the gap between blacks and whites has become narrower and that public opposition to race-based policies indicates that a new approach is needed. The U.S. Supreme Court has endorsed this view by implementing a "color-blind jurisprudence" over a broad range of issues. The second group is represented by traditional civil rights activists and groups such as Jesse Jackson, the Congressional Black Caucus, and the National Association for the Advancement of Colored People (NAACP); they argue that the civil rights movement must continue to fight for the equality of opportunity by enforcing existing law and pushing for equality of outcomes by protecting and expanding racially targeted Affirmative Action programs and other policies that address racial inequality. These first two groups share the goal of racial equality and integration, but differ on how much progress has been made in achieving those goals. The final group does not support the goal of integration; instead, advocates of this view such as Louis Farrakhan and the Nation of Islam argue for African-American self-sufficiency and separation. They argue that African Americans can never gain equality within the repressive, white-dominated economic and political system.

A large majority of civil rights advocates endorse the second view. They argue that it would be a mistake to conclude that racial politics is no longer consequential in the twenty-first century in the United States or that the work of the civil rights movement is complete. They point to the resegregation of public schools, persistent gaps between whites and racial minorities in health and economic status, racial profiling, hate crimes, a backlash against immigrant groups, and continuing discrimination in employment and housing as ample evidence that the nation is not ready to "move beyond race." At the same time, this group rejects calls for racial separation as ultimately short-sighted and self-defeating.

THE CONTEXT OF RACIAL POLICY IN THE UNITED STATES SINCE 1990

Evidence for the persistent gaps between whites and blacks may be framed in terms of subjective interests (public opinion) and objective interests (indicators of socioeconomic status). Well-publicized public opinion surveys provide ample evidence of the racial divide in the 1990s. For example, racially divergent assessments of the fairness and legitimacy of law enforcement and the judicial system helped produce startling polls showing (according to a July 7, 1994, Gallup poll) that 60 percent of African Americans believed that former football star O.J. Simpson (who is black) did not murder his wife and Ronald Goldman (who were white) while 68 percent of white Americans believed he was guilty. Perhaps even more telling are the surveys that reveal many blacks believe in massive white conspiracies to kill them or keep them subjugated. A 1992 survey of 1,056 African Americans by the Christian Leadership Conference showed that 35 percent believed that AIDS was a form of black genocide and 30 percent said they did not know what to believe (implying that it was possibly true). Rumors about white supremacists tampering with soda pop to sterilize black males are quickly accepted by alienated urban blacks. Many whites view such beliefs as "black paranoia," but whites engage in similar rushes to judgment when they avoid black youths on the street or when a white cab driver refuses to pick up a well-dressed black businessperson. Political scientists have demonstrated that such racial stereotyping has a significant impact on perceptions of government assistance programs and violence and crime.

The racial divide is also evident in objective terms. More than three times as many black families are below the poverty line than white families (19.1 percent compared to 5.3 percent in 2000). Poverty rates for Hispanic families in 2000 (at 18.5 percent) were similar to those for black families. Furthermore, while black median household income in 1999 was only 66.2 percent of white family income, the gap in wealth is much more dramatic: the average white household has nearly seven times the assets the typical black family has (in 1993, the median household net worth was $49,030 for whites and $7,073 for blacks). Figures for Hispanics are somewhat better, but the gaps are still large. (Hispanic household income was 72.7 percent of white income, $33,400 compared to $45,900, while median Hispanic household wealth was $7,255, according to the U.S. Census Bureau.)

Other indicators show similar patterns. The rate of black, adult male unemployment has been about twice as high as that for white adult males for the past forty-five years (which is substantially higher than the nearly equal ratio of 1.26 in 1940). The other depressing statistic on the objective position of blacks is that only one-third of black children lived in two-parent households in 1995 (compared to 76 percent of white children). In 1940, two-thirds of black children and 91 percent of white children lived with two parents. Blacks are more likely than whites to be victimized by crime; for some crimes, such as murder of young black men, the figures are stunning. A black male between the ages of 18 and 24 is 10.5 times as likely to be murdered as a white male in that same age range. Also, on every imaginable measure of the quality of health—life expectancy, infectious diseases, infant mortality, cancer rates, heart disease, and strokes—the gaps between whites and blacks are large, and in many cases the gulf is growing. For example, in 1995, the life expectancy for blacks was about 10 percent shorter than that for whites (70 years compared to 77), the infant mortality rate was double for blacks (15.1 deaths per 100,000 births, compared to 7.6), and maternal mortality was more than triple (22.1 deaths per 100,000 life births for blacks compared to 7.1 for whites). Similar gaps exist for cancer rates, levels of diabetes, strokes, and heart attacks.

The greatest disparity between racial minorities and whites, however, may be in the criminal justice system. Racial profiling subjects many innocent blacks to intrusive searches, and recent studies have shown that blacks are more likely than whites to be convicted for the same crimes and that blacks serve longer sentences as well. In many large American cities, tensions between police departments and minority communities periodically boil over. The largest race riots since 1990 were in Los Angeles in 1992 following the acquittal of four white police officers who had been videotaped brutally beating a black man, Rodney King. The riots left 54 people dead and more than 2,000 injured, and caused more than $1 billion in damage, including about 800 businesses that were destroyed, many of them Korean-American businesses in the Central Los Angeles area. More recently, police officers killed unarmed black men in Cincinnati and New York City, which precipitated more violence. In an incident in New York in 1999, police killed Amadou Diallo, a law-abiding African immigrant, in a hail of forty-one bullets as he was standing in his own doorway. The four officers were looking for a black suspect, and when Diallo reached for his wallet, they assumed it was a gun. The African-American community was outraged when the officers were acquitted. A similar killing of an unarmed black man, nineteen-year-old Timothy Thomas, by police in Cincinnati in 2001 led to three days of rioting in which dozens of people were injured and more than 800 were arrested. The officer in this case was also acquitted. Civil rights advocates point out that such incidents are far too common.

African Americans and other minorities are also subjected to hate crimes much more frequently than whites. One especially gruesome murder that received national attention in 2000 (including during the presidential campaign) involved a black man, James Byrd, who was chained to the back of a pickup truck by three white men and dragged to his death in 1998. Two of the murderers were sentenced to death and the other received life in prison.

This backdrop of racial inequality, discrimination, and violence provides continued motivation for civil rights activists to push their agenda in the three branches of government: legislative, executive, and judicial. In some instances, issues are pursued in several arenas simultaneously; in others, redress is sought in one arena after alternative avenues are exhausted. The civil rights movement also continues to mobilize the grass roots. Even groups outside the traditional civil rights movement, such as the Nation of Islam, have used the tactics of mass protest. The "Million Man March," in October 1995, was organized by Louis Farrahkan and attracted about 400,000 to Washington, D.C. Traditional civil rights leaders had distanced

Race riots in Los Angeles following the acquittal of four white police officers accused of beating a black man left 54 dead and more than 2,000 injured. The violent 1992 uprising was the deadliest race riot in American history. Above, National Guardsmen remove sandbags placed to protect the Los Angeles Coliseum after the violence subsided. *(AP Wide World Photos)*

themselves from Farrahkan in the past because of his racist and anti-Semitic views. However, the Million Man March helped established Farrahkan as a political force that was difficult to ignore. Despite the continued use of this tactic, in recent years marches and civil disobedience have not played the central role that they did in the 1960s.

THE LEGISLATIVE ARENA

The bedrock of equal protection that exists today stems from landmark legislation passed by Congress in the 1960s, namely, the 1964 Civil Rights Act, the 1965 Voting Rights Act, and the 1968 Fair Housing Act. There have been many amendments of these laws since the 1960s, but the only significant change since 1990 was the 1991 Civil Rights Act. This legislation overruled or altered parts of twelve U.S. Supreme Court cases that had eroded the intent of Congress when it passed the civil rights legislation. As will be discussed below, the Supreme Court had moved in a "color-blind" direction that made it more difficult for employees to prove racial discrimination in the workplace. The 1991 law expanded earlier legislation and increased the costs to employers for intentional, illegal discrimination. Two of the central debates were over the "disparate impact standard" and where the bur-

On March 23, 1999, hundreds of protesters, including actress Ruby Dee (center), flanked by her husband Ossie Davis (left) and Al Sharpton (right), march to New York Police Headquarters to demand the arrest of the officers who killed Amadou Diallo, an unarmed West African immigrant. It was the eleventh day of protests. *(AP Wide World Photos)*

den of proof should lie in a discrimination case: the employer or the employee. President George H.W. Bush vetoed an earlier version of the bill in 1990, arguing that it was a "quota bill." The first Bush administration ultimately agreed that the burden of proof should be on the employer, so the central question was how to define the standard that would determine whether a practice that had a "disparate impact" (i.e., a disproportionate impact) on a racial minority was, in fact, not discriminatory. Democrats in Congress pushed for a relatively tough standard that it be "essential to business practice." That is, if a business practice was discriminatory in its effect, it had to be essential to the business. For example, if a university required all assistant professors to have a Ph.D., and if it could be shown that more white applicants had Ph.D.s than minority applicants, the uni-

versity would have the burden of proof to demonstrate that the Ph.D. was essential for doing the job. President Bush wanted a vaguer standard of "legitimate business objectives." Congress ended up adopting language that was somewhere in between: the employer must show that the practice is "job related for the position in question and consistent with business necessity."

The other significant civil rights legislation of the 1990s was not passed into law. The Racial Justice Act would have permitted minority inmates on Death Row to use statistical data on discriminatory application of the death penalty to appeal their sentences. Government studies and academic research have conclusively demonstrated unequal application of the death penalty based on the race of the *victim*. A murderer is much more likely to be put on Death Row if

After the acquittal of the officers accused of killing unarmed immigrant Amadou Diallo, protesters march down Broadway on April 5, 2000, denouncing both the verdict and police brutality. *(AP Wide World Photos)*

he killed a white person than if he killed a black person (ranging from 4.3 times more likely in Georgia to 84 times more likely in Texas). However, in 1987 the Supreme Court ruled in *McKlesky v. Kemp* that a pattern of discrimination could not be the basis for a death sentence appeal; rather actual discrimination in the specific case must be demonstrated. The Congressional Black Caucus pushed for the Racial Justice Act as part of the $33.4 billion crime bill in 1994. It passed the House by a 217 to 212 margin and was defeated in the Senate 58 to 41. The provision was dropped in conference committee when President Bill Clinton decided not to jeopardize the entire crime bill over the controversial act. Despite defeat on the specific provision, many political observers saw the 1994 crime bill as a victory for civil rights advocates because for the first time the federal legislation included

significant financial support for crime prevention measures ($9 billion), including some programs that were criticized by Republicans, such as "midnight basketball," aimed at keeping inner-city kids off the streets.

One other topic that Rep. John Conyers (D-MI) has pursued for years is reparations for slavery. This issue will be addressed in more detail below, but Rep. Conyers's efforts received a recent boost when Rep. Tony Hall (D-OH) introduced a resolution asking Congress to apologize for slavery. Rep. Hall introduced the measure again the next year (2000), but this time asked for funding to set up a commission to examine slavery's legacy, fund education programs to study slavery's effects, and establish a national slavery museum. The measure did not pass but is likely to receive more attention in the future.

In one of the largest demonstrations of the decade, some 400,000 people—primarily African-American men—gather at the Capitol Building in Washington, D.C., for the Million Man March on October 16, 1995. *(AP Wide World Photos)*

THE EXECUTIVE ARENA

The civil rights movement has also benefited greatly from presidential action, such as President Harry Truman's integration of the armed services in 1948 (Executive Order 9981), President Dwight Eisenhower's calling in the National Guard to enforce a court order to integrate Central High School in Little Rock, Arkansas, in 1957 (Executive Order 10730), and Executive Orders by Presidents John F. Kennedy and Lyndon Johnson that established Affirmative Action (#10925 in 1961 and #11246 in 1965). However, in recent years it is less likely that significant and dramatic change will come from unilateral action by the president. Instead, attention to civil rights concerns in the executive branch has primarily been in two areas in the past fifteen years: racial diversity in presidential

appointments and use of the bully pulpit to promote racial concerns and interests.

President Clinton excelled in both of these dimensions. In 1992, candidate Clinton promised a government that "looks like America." Clinton's cabinet, subcabinet, and judicial appointments achieved the greatest gender and racial balance of any in history. Fourteen percent of Clinton's first-year presidential appointments were African-American (compared to 12 percent of the population in 1992), 6 percent were Hispanic (compared to 9.5 percent of the population), and the percentage of Asian-American and Native American appointees was identical to their proportion in the population. Clinton truly delivered an administration that "looked like us."

Nonetheless, there were a few rough spots in Clinton's attempt to achieve racial diversity in his top-level appointments. The nomination of Lani Guinier, a civil rights lawyer and law professor whom Clinton nominated to be assistant attorney general for civil rights, was the most controversial. Guinier's academic writings proved to be her undoing. In various law review articles, she expressed doubts about the ability of our political system to represent the interests of blacks. Instead she called for a system of "proportionate interest representation" that would involve procedures such as veto power over certain legislation for minorities and different electoral institutions, such as cumulative voting. When a firestorm of protest erupted, Clinton hesitated, but then withdrew her nomination, saying that he was not familiar with some of her more controversial ideas when he made the nomination. This did not please civil rights activists, who argued that her ideas were misrepresented and that at the very least she should have been granted a hearing.

Discord also surrounded the rise and demise of Dr. Joycelyn Elders as surgeon general. The former head of the Arkansas Department of Health who served during Governor Clinton's tenure, Elders was well known for her bluntness and firmness in support of sex education and abortion. Throughout her tenure, Elders was a thorn in the side of conservative, fundamentalist, and Catholic groups. Clinton was finally forced to ask for her resignation in the controversy that followed Elder's response to a question about her views on masturbation.

Racial politics also figured prominently in Clinton's appointments to the Equal Employment Opportunity Commission (EEOC) and the most recent Civil Rights division head. The EEOC appointment was delayed for more than a year because Clinton wanted to find a Latino to fill the spot. Critics pointed out that leaving a Reagan/Bush administration holdover to run this important department may have been too high a price to pay for diversity.

Bill Lann Lee's appointment to the position that initially would have been Guinier's was also somewhat controversial. Lee was the first Asian American appointed to this important civil rights post, and organizations such as the NAACP saw the appointment as a movement away from recognizing the black/white divide as the central racial cleavage in our society. Others, however, saw the nomination as overdue recognition of the increasingly multiracial composition of our nation.

President Clinton also used the bully pulpit to advocate a civil rights agenda. For example, when Affirmative Action came under attack from the courts, he advocated an approach of "mend don't end." He also had a deep, personal connection to African Americans that was rooted in symbolic politics. Toni Morrison, the Nobel prize–winning author, developed this point in her well-publicized observation in *The New Yorker* in 1998 that, "White skin notwithstanding, this is our first black President. Blacker than any actual black person who could ever be elected in our children's lifetime. After all, Clinton displays almost every trope of blackness: single-parent household, born poor, working-class, saxophone playing, McDonald's-and-junk-food-loving boy from Arkansas."

There is no doubt that Clinton connected with blacks as no other president ever had. In addition to the life-connections noted by Morrison, there were other important symbolic gestures and policy stands. Many blacks greatly appreciated Clinton's trip to Africa when he apologized for slavery, the attention he drew to racial problems through his "National Conversation on Race," his record number of minority presidential appointments, and his support for Affirmative Action. One columnist echoed Morrison, saying that blacks have a "spiritual soul mate" in Clinton. "They like the fact that his golfing buddy is a brother, that his personal secretary is a sister, that he invites himself to black churches, that he prays with blacks and sings their songs without using a hymnal," wrote Bill Maxwell in the *St. Petersburg Times*. "He regularly brings black jazz musicians, rock stars, athletes, children and business owners to the White House."

This symbolic side of racial politics within the White House may be more important than it appears. While playing a saxophone or eating Big Macs may not translate into substantive policy change, the diversity of Clinton's appointments had substantive im-

pact that went beyond their symbolic importance. The other area that resided at the intersection of symbolic and substantive politics was Clinton's "National Conversation on Race" and the broader "Race Initiative." This eighteen-month-long effort is an excellent example of Clinton's attempt to use his charismatic leadership, the bully pulpit of the presidency, and his personal commitment to the issue to focus the nation's attention on the nation's race problem. Many critics dismissed the effort as empty symbolism, but the Race Initiative did help focus national attention on many of the problems faced by minorities.

Although President George W. Bush has not achieved the same level of diversity in his appointments as Clinton, his administration has been more diverse than that of other Republican presidents. Of the nineteen cabinet and cabinet-rank appointments, fifteen are men and four are women. There are two blacks (Secretary of State Colin Powell, who is Jamaican-American, and Secretary of Education Rod Paige, who is African-American), two Asian Americans (Secretary of Labor Elaine Chao and Secretary of Transportation Norman Mineta), one Cuban American (Secretary of Housing and Urban Development Mel Martinez), and one Arab American (Secretary of Energy Spencer Abraham). Condoleezza Rice has an important position on the White House staff as National Security Advisor. However, it is noteworthy that the rhetoric that surrounded these appointments was not couched in terms of Affirmative Action, but rather merit. Critics argued that gender and race played a central role in these decisions, just as they did with Clinton, even if the rhetoric had a different tone. Despite the different approach, President Bush has made more serious overtures to minorities, especially Latinos, in his effort to expand the base of the Republican Party.

THE LEGAL ARENA

Unlike the Warren Court, which produced several Supreme Court decisions that were crucial to the civil rights movement (most importantly *Brown v. Board of Education* in 1954), the Rehnquist Court of the 1990s and early 2000s has been unsympathetic to the cause. As noted above, the Court has been gradually imposing a "color-blind jurisprudence" over a broad range of issues. Four Supreme Court justices—William H. Rehnquist, Clarence Thomas, Antonin Scalia, and Anthony M. Kennedy—adhered to the color-blind perspective, while four others—David H. Souter, Stephen G. Breyer, John Paul Stevens, and Ruth Bader Ginsburg—were willing to consider race in a variety of contexts. The swing vote belonged to Sandra Day O'Connor, who tended toward the color-blind view but was willing to side with the liberals in some instances.

One area in which the color-blind approach had a big impact is in the racial redistricting that occurred in 1992 in which fifteen new U.S. House districts were specifically drawn to help elect African Americans and ten districts were drawn to provide an opportunity to elect new Latino members. This dramatic change in the number of minorities in Congress (the increase was greater than 50 percent) was rooted in the 1982 amendments to the Voting Rights Act. Instead of mandating a fair *process*, this law and subsequent interpretation by the Supreme Court in the 1980s mandated that minorities be able to "elect representatives of their choice" when their numbers and configuration permitted. This shift meant that the legislative redistricting process now had to avoid discriminatory *results* rather than only being concerned with discriminatory *intent*. However, in a series of decisions starting with the 1993 landmark case *Shaw v. Reno*, the Supreme Court's adherence to a color-blind jurisprudence has thrown the constitutionality of black majority districts into doubt (*Miller v. Johnson* 1995; *Bush v. Vera* 1996). There are at least five votes on the Court to uphold the Voting Rights Act, and Sandra Day O'Connor made it clear in *Bush v. Vera* that black majority districts are legal as long as they are "done right." But the Court has consistently held that if race is the predominant factor in drawing district lines, the districts are unconstitutional because they violate the "equal protection" clause of the Fourteenth Amendment. This line of cases struck down black majority districts in North Carolina, Georgia, Louisiana, Virginia, Texas, and Florida. The most recent case, *Easley v. Cromartie* (2001), upheld the redrawn 12th District in North Carolina (which no longer was black majority), arguing that when race and partisanship are so intertwined (as they are when 90 percent of African Americans vote for the Democratic candidate), plaintiffs cannot simply assume that African Americans were placed together for racial reasons. This opens the door for a greater consideration of race than had been allowed in the previous cases. However, racial redistricting remains an unsettled area of the law.

The racial redistricting cases illustrate a central concern in the institutional balance of power that is also of great importance to civil rights advocates: the U.S. Supreme Court has become increasingly activist in the area of civil rights. They are unwilling to defer to any other part of government if that branch disa-grees with their view of discrimination and "equal protection." Thus, the Court was willing to overturn state legislatures in racial redistricting, the U.S. Congress with the Violence Against Women Act and the Americans with Disabilities Act, the U.S. executive branch contracting policies in cases that subjected racial "set-aside" programs to the "strict scrutiny" standard (*Adarand Constructors v. Pena*, 1995), the Florida State Supreme Court in *Bush v. Gore* (2000), and California state law in a recent employment discrimination case (*Circuit City Stores v. Adams* 2001). This string of cases indicates that the central tendency of the Court is not one of preferring state power to national power, as some have argued. Rather, it is a consistent activist assertion of judicial power over the elected institutions.

One final area concerns hate crimes and hate speech. The Court ruled in *R.A.V. v. St. Paul* (1992) that speech could not be directly punished just because it was racist. This case overturned a St. Paul, Minnesota, ordinance that banned cross burning aimed at frightening or angering others "on the basis of race, color, creed, or gender." However the issue was once again before the Court to determine whether the decision applied to all bans on cross burning or just to poorly worded ones. This case will also attempt to define the line between hate speech (which is largely protected by the First Amendment as long as it is not a "direct incitement" to "imminent danger") and hate crimes, which under *Wisconsin v. Mitchell* (1993) allow additional penalties to be attached to a criminal verdict as long as guilt or innocence is determined separate from the racially motivated action.

CONTINUING AND FUTURE CIVIL RIGHTS ISSUES

Affirmative Action

Affirmative Action in higher education has been a hotly contested area of the law in recent years. This was not always the case. The 1978 *Bakke* decision struck down racial quotas but allowed race to be used in admissions decisions as a "plus factor" to promote diversity in the student body. This process was widely followed and largely unquestioned until 1996 when the Fifth Circuit Court of Appeals held that it was unconstitutional to consider race in law school admissions at the University of Texas. More recently, a circuit court in Washington reached the opposite conclusion. Even more puzzling were two conflicting cases from the University of Michigan. A December 2000 district court case held that race-conscious undergraduate admissions was acceptable, but a decision a few months later in the same district court held that considering race in law school admissions was not constitutional. The U.S. Supreme Court will have to sort out these conflicting lower court decisions and determine the extent to which race can be used as a consideration in admission decisions to institutions of higher education.

The crucial point of contention is "viewpoint diversity"—the claimed advantage of Affirmative Action is the diversity that it brings to classroom discussions. Advocates of Affirmative Action argue that viewpoint diversity is essential to learning and having racial diversity in the student body is likely to produce more viewpoint diversity than having an all-white student body. Furthermore, proponents argue, the courts are not the proper place to decide these issues. Instead, as with the complex and highly charged topics of racial redistricting, the political branches of government are where these decisions should be made. Advocates also make a very pragmatic argument that getting rid of Affirmative Action would almost certainly lead to a system that is *less* rooted in merit-based admissions than the current system—an odd position for political conservatives to hold.

Opponents reply that supporters of Affirmative Action have not provided convincing evidence that racial diversity in colleges has any beneficial effects. They also maintain that "viewpoint diversity" arguments assume that members of all racial minorities think alike, drawing a comparison to racial profiling in law enforcement. It is just as offensive, they say, that an admissions committee thinks that one black student has the same views as another black student as it is that a police officer may pull over a black teenage male just because he fits a certain criminal profile.

Slavery Reparations

Many people argue that one cannot tackle the issue of race without directly addressing slavery. From the earliest colonial experience and the introduction of slavery to debates at the Constitutional Convention about how slaves should be considered, the controversy over whether slavery would be allowed in the new states created during westward expansion in the early nineteenth century, and the bloody Civil War, slavery was at the core of American politics. The legacy of slavery was central during the Reconstruction period and the Jim Crow era in the South. Although some argue that the success of civil rights legislation in the 1960s finally allowed America to move out from

the shadows of slavery, others contend that those shadows still cast a darkness over our land. Proponents of the latter view insist that it is time to publicly recognize the long-term impact of slavery and make meaningful reparations for the toll that slavery has taken on the African-American population.

Critics of this view make several arguments against slavery reparations. Most important, even if there is a debt that should be paid for slavery, they say, it is not clear who owes that debt given that most Americans, white and black, are from families that immigrated to this country long after slavery ended. They also argue that American society has already paid substantial debts for slavery through various policies such as Affirmative Action and that any serious effort to implement reparations would harm race relations in this nation by promoting a "renewed sense of grievance" among African Americans. Several central legal questions must also be resolved: Who are the plaintiffs? Who are the defendants? Does a "statute of limitations" apply? Which legal arguments are likely to be most successful?

Proponents of reparations are pursuing their goal in both the legal and legislative arenas. In exploring these questions, many legal experts, including those who were involved in the successful tobacco litigation, argue that a class-action lawsuit would be on firm legal ground. In such circumstances, it may be in the interests of Congress (and the U.S. government) to pass legislation that would set the terms of reparations, rather than leaving it up to the courts.

Multicultural Issues

A host of issues involving the multicultural, multiracial nature of American society will assuredly become more important as whites will no longer constitute a majority of the U.S. population by the middle of this century. Two of these issues are English as the official language and immigration.

The decision by many states to adopt laws establishing English as the official language has had practical consequences. For example, the U.S. Supreme Court recently upheld an Alabama state law that required that the state driver's license test be conducted only in English. A Mexican immigrant, Martha Sandoval, sued under Title VI of the 1964 Civil Rights Act, saying that the state law had a disparate impact on non–English speaking residents. However, in 2001, the Court held in *Alexander v. Sandoval* that individuals may not sue federally funded state agencies over policies that have a discriminatory effect on minorities under Title VI. This decision could have far-reaching consequences for the use of the Civil Rights Act to fight patterns of discrimination. Two areas that could be affected are education policy (civil rights advocates, for example, have challenged the use of standardized testing because of its disparate impact on minorities) and environmental policy (lawsuits have been brought under Title VI alleging "environmental racism," such as siting hazardous waste dumps in predominantly minority areas).

Immigration was thrust back onto center stage in the wake of the terrorist attacks on September 11, 2001. In light of these attacks, some people see immigration as an outside threat that must be curtailed. In the past decade, other social welfare implications of immigration have been central in many political debates. In 1994, voters in California adopted Proposition 187, which denied most public benefits to illegal immigrants. The Republican governor, Pete Wilson, campaigned heavily in favor of Proposition 187, and the Republican candidate for president in 1996, Robert Dole, also ran ads in California warning about the negative effects of immigration. However, the measure was subsequently struck down by the courts. When Democrat Gray Davis's success in the 1998 gubernatorial race in California was attributed, in part, to the newly galvanized and growing Hispanic population, Republicans softened their position on immigration. President Bush has actively cultivated the Hispanic vote. However, anti-immigration sentiments still run strong in the United States, and the issue is likely to become even more controversial in the next decade.

David T. Canon

BIBLIOGRAPHY

Canon, David T. *Race, Redistricting, and Representation: The Unintended Consequences of Black-Majority Districts.* Chicago: University of Chicago Press, 1999.

Dawson, Michael C. *Behind the Mule: Race and Class in African-American Politics.* Princeton, NJ: Princeton University Press, 1994.

Grofman, Bernard. *Race and Redistricting in the 1990s.* New York: Agathon, 1998.

Hochschild, Jennifer L. *Facing Up to the American Dream: Race, Class, and the Soul of the Nation.* Princeton, NJ: Princeton University Press, 1995.

Kousser, J. Morgan. *Colorblind Injustice: Minority Voting Rights and the Undoing of the Second Reconstruction.* Chapel Hill: University of North Carolina Press, 1999.

Lublin, David. *The Paradox of Representation: Racial Gerrymandering and Minority Interests in Congress.* Princeton, NJ: Princeton University Press, 1997.

Morrison, Toni. "Talk of the Town." *The New Yorker*, October 5, 1998, p. 3.

Sapiro, Virginia, and David T. Canon. "Clinton and the Politics of Gender and Race." In *The Clinton Presidency*, ed. Colin Campbell and Bert Rockman, 197–231. Chatham, NJ: Chatham House, 2000.

Swain, Carol M. *Black Faces, Black Interests: The Representation of African Americans in Congress.* Cambridge, MA: Harvard University Press, 1993.

Thernstrom, Stephan, and Abigail Thernstrom. *America in Black and White: One Nation, Indivisible.* New York: Simon and Schuster, 1997.

U.S. Department of Health and Human Services. http://www.hhs.gov.

U.S. Department of Labor, Bureau of Labor Statistics. *Labor Force Statistics from the Current Population Survey.* http://www.bls.gov/cps.

CIVIL RIGHTS MOVEMENT
TWENTY-FIRST CENTURY

In the decades following the civil rights movement, problems of racial justice grew more subtle and insidious. After some limited narrowing of the gap during the 1960s and 1970s, inequality between white and black Americans (by income, wealth, education, employment, etc.) remained the same and by many measures grew worse during the 1980s and 1990s. The decline in manufacturing and the movement of many industries away from U.S. cities drove urban unemployment in the United States and sweatshop labor in developing nations, affecting people of color most severely. During the same period, the black middle class grew significantly, and the media focus on a few highly visible and wealthy black Americans from Oprah Winfrey to Clarence Thomas quietly obscured the inverse growth of the black underclass. Moreover, the rhetoric of mainstream America during this period successfully coopted Martin Luther King Jr.'s vision of equality into justification for a "color-blind" society, effective immediately, making it nearly impossible to talk about any problem of race, let alone devise and support solutions to it.

By the year 2000, several universities had been mandated by the courts to dismiss any consideration of race in their admissions processes. Continuous debate over school voucher programs, themselves capable of serving only a small portion of children, received attention and diverted national energy from improving public schools for all children, especially underserved urban schools where students of color were the overwhelming majority. The U.S. government effectively ignored the fact that 25 percent of sub-Saharan Africans were HIV positive and that black American infection rates were on the rise too. And as immigration trends continued to diversify the American populace, discrimination against and oppression of immigrant workers, children, and communities expanded. Following the events of September 11, 2001, the repression of immigrant rights and civil rights overall expanded.

How are people of color and those supportive of racial justice responding? New trends in black electoral politics, grassroots movement building, and national debate have emerged to address these and other challenges of twenty-first-century racial justice.

BLACK ELECTORAL POLITICS

Since the emergence of the first black mayoralty in 1967, black Americans have won the mayoralty in nearly every major U.S. city. Not all candidates came directly from civil rights activism, but nonetheless there was the sense early on that the struggle for civil rights had moved from the streets into local government. People of color and those involved in the civil rights struggle hoped this new arena would bring substantive change to the lives of black Americans, most of whom lived in major cities by this point. Unfortunately, vast institutional barriers and emergent economic and demographic shifts resulted in little substantive change and deep disappointment for city residents of color.

Nonetheless, by the dawn of the twenty-first century, two significant "generations" of black mayors had emerged, and a third was on its way. In the context of Newark, New Jersey, generational shifts in the black mayoralty can be seen through the cases of Mayors Kenneth Gibson and Sharpe James, and in the 2002 mayoral candidate Cory Booker. The first generation was embodied by Kenneth Gibson, elected in 1970, who benefited from the breakthrough to mayoral power, some remaining white electorate and tax base, and the breakdown of some tangible walls like the integration of the police force.

In the second generation, embodied by Mayor Sharpe James, elected in 1986, black mayors faced poorer cities that were more dependent on social services. In desperate need of immediate solutions, these

On March 1, 2003, hundreds of demonstrators rally in Detroit in support of Affirmative Action and the University of Michigan's admissions policy. Later in the year, the United States Supreme Court upheld the university's policy. *(AP Wide World Photos)*

mayors sought corporate funding in many cases. The framework of economic development shifted to a single-project focus, such as stadiums and casinos, but was unable to halt the growth of urban poverty during this time.

In the third generation, we have seen young individuals such as Kwame Kilpatrick and Cory Booker who have benefited from increases in black professional education and are now challenging their parents' generation in their efforts to effect urban change. The outlook of these individuals is far more politically independent and pragmatic, far less wedded to the traditional black community. As stated in Jonathan Tepperman's *New York Times Magazine* article (2002), Booker said, "I haven't divorced myself from the tradition of African-American politics . . . But I don't want to be a great *black* politician; I want to be a great politician."

Beginning in 2000, in cities like Atlanta, Houston, Detroit, Cleveland, and Newark, the third generation of black mayoral leadership has moved away from black unified support for one person to, as noted by

Ronald Walters, a specialist on African-American leadership, "everyone into the water." More specifically, these candidates, often raised and educated outside of the city, began crafting messages and policies that merge the need for "change" with standard appeals to black legitimacy. Many of these candidates receive significant funding from outside the city itself, in order to challenge strong incumbents. And there is some valid concern that these candidates will be the final step in urban residents' loss of agency over their lives and cities. On May 14, 2002, Cory Booker lost to incumbent Sharpe James, who had raised suspicion throughout the campaign about Booker's "outsider" status and true intentions. James's campaign slogan, on the other hand, "The Real Deal," affirmed his genuine commitment to civil rights struggle.

So in the context of the black mayoralty, a clear identification with and commitment to continuing the civil rights struggle remains primary to twenty-first-century black leadership and support. The mayoral races of Cory Booker vs. Sharpe James and others certainly testify to the continuing significance of race, and particularly black consciousness to local politics.

The black congressional leadership has also witnessed new trends, especially in relation to the attacks of September 11, 2001, and other global dynamics. Representatives Earl Hilliard and Cynthia McKinney, two prominent black Democratic incumbents with progressive civil rights agendas, lost primary elections to more moderate black challengers in the summer of 2002. In both cases, the incumbents publicly acknowledged critical connections between domestic racial justice struggles and the struggles of people of color abroad. For instance, in the midst of vast media attention to the Israeli-Palestinian conflicts, both incumbents had expressed views sympathetic to the plight of the Palestinian people and as a result were seen as unfriendly to Israel. Consequently, opponents emerged with the strong financial backing of some Jewish Americans and other Israel supporters.

Cynthia McKinney also spoke out on the events of September 11, questioning President George Bush's prior knowledge of the attacks and the massive human rights violations of his subsequent "War on Terrorism." Her vigilant dissent and commitment to racial justice during the post-9/11 era generated more staunch opposition and funding from individuals and organizations outside of her district. In sum, both races were decided in large part by concerns unrelated to the immediate problems of the candidates' constituents and were directly related to a post-9/11 squelching of dissenting voices.

GRASSROOTS MOVEMENT BUILDING

Activism and organizing are long-standing tools of racial justice, but they did not receive significant attention during the post–civil rights era. Mainstream media accounts of the racial justice struggle usually included little to no mention of ongoing activist efforts, focusing instead on the limited efforts of elected officials. Furthermore, the overwhelming media attention to the ostensibly successful *individuals* of the 1980s and 1990s, especially entertainers and athletes, perpetuated an illusion of progress and obscured the real need for *collective* analysis and organizing around continuing problems of race and poverty. Moreover, the end of the Cold War, the destruction of Social Democratic and Marxist social change models globally, and the decline of the union movement in the United States left few models with which to express alternate visions of social change. In response to this crisis, scholars such as Lani Guinier and Manning Marable, in partnership with activists, began noting the many constraints of electoral politics and leadership and calling for a return to grassroots strategies for racial justice.

Such scholars shared a standard critique of post–civil rights electoral leadership: that much of it is increasingly "symbol over substance" and is disconnected from the concerns of poor people of all colors. As they advocate for change in leadership, Guinier and Marable are talking about more than simply replacing leadership personalities, issues, or priorities. They are calling for a fundamental restructuring of our systems of democratic governance and participation. Indeed, Manning Marable made the following call to action in *Race and Class* (1994): "Through a renewed commitment to struggle, let our rejoicing begin. Through a vision of human equality and social justice, let the fight for democracy take place. The problem of the twenty-first century is the challenge of multiracial democracy."

With these words, Marable calls for a renewal of a *transformationist* vision of black politics and the pursuit of radical democracy. No longer concerned about winning a black mayoralty or separating from the system, Marable aligns his politics with individuals such as Patricia Williams, Kimberle Crenshaw, Angela Davis, bell hooks, James Jennings, and Cornel West, and distinguishes their perspective. The chief distinction of a *transformationist* perspective, as compared to *inclusionist* and *separatist* perspectives, is that it calls for the dismantling and destruction of *all* forms of inequality. Marable continues, "Often black people have begun with the objective of abolishing racism, but in the process of struggle have come to realize that wider power relationships must also be transformed to achieve full human equality," including inequalities rooted in gender, sexual orientation, religion, and globalization.

And so the theoretical stage was set for many grassroots activists and scholars to respond to the events and aftermath of September 11, 2001, with a nuanced understanding of the *dynamic* nature of multiple inequalities and oppression. Following the events of September 11, widespread violations of immigrant rights spurred grassroots activists into action. The recent USA Patriot Act passed by Congress deems all noncitizens, documented or not, as potential terrorists and subject to the expanded powers of local and state police, the Federal Bureau of Investigation (FBI), and the Immigration and Naturalization Service (INS). According to the American Civil Liberties Union, the USA Patriot Act confers unprecedented detention authority on the attorney general based on

M. Andrew Robinson-Gaither, a Methodist pastor from Los Angeles, demands reparations for slavery at a demonstration in Washington, D.C., on August 17, 2002. *(AP Wide World Photos)*

unspecified and vague national security threats. Specifically, it permits the detention of noncitizens facing deportation based solely on the attorney general's certification that he has "reasonable grounds to believe" the person endangers national security. As activists Jane Bai and Eric Tang wrote in *ColorLines* (2002), "Before September 11, a green-card holder could get a traffic ticket, pay a $50 fine, and their case was closed. Today, that same person can be racially profiled, stopped, turned over to the FBI and INS, and detained for up to six months without being charged with any crime or violation."

Mainstream media portrayed all Americans, including black Americans, as more patriotic than ever and eager to see Arab Americans as the new target of racial profiling. But many black Americans resisted this divide-and-conquer tactic, recognizing instead the linked fate of all people of color, in some cases with

poor whites as well. As activists Bai and Tang continued, "Today the language and imagery are 'terrorist,' 'immigrant,' and 'Arab,' but the infrastructure established in the process is a potent source of increased racism and repression against all people of color and indeed all who live in the U.S." These and other activists and scholars began noting the links between immigrant rights and racial justice movements, and the opportunities for sharing resources and action between the two.

NATIONAL DEBATE

With changing electoral politics and growing grassroots energy before us, what's the nation actually talking about at the turn of the century? Clinton's Dialogue on Race, Bush's retreat from the UN World Conference Against Racism, Affirmative Action, reparations, and September 11 have been at the forefront of national debate with regard to race. In 1997, President Bill Clinton launched a National Dialogue on Race. Four years later, even as evidence of racial profiling and other forms of institutional racism were rampant, the U.S. government under President George W. Bush refused to participate in the World Conference Against Racism in Durban, South Africa. The two actions together are highly symbolic of the U.S. government's resistance to understanding the implications of our past.

Although controversy over the World Conference Against Racism was quickly overwhelmed by the events of September 11, U.S. behavior in both instances was motivated by common problems of race and power. As organizer Rinku Sen wrote in *ColorLines* (2002), "Before and after September 11, the Administration has attempted to redefine the real racists and control the debate to build public support for its actions. Before and after September 11, activists have learned that the line between domestic and foreign policy is thinner than we thought, requiring us to take on new strategies."

By 2002, a number of African-American civil rights groups were also advocating for a national acknowledgment of the problem. In particular, the issue of reparations for African Americans has emerged since 1999, becoming a major topic of debate in the mainstream media. Such advocates for reparations reminded Americans that in January 1865, enslaved black Americans were promised "a plot of not more than (40) forty acres of tillable ground" in Special Field Order No. 15. Three months later, President Andrew Johnson rescinded the order. A century and a half later, continuing institutional racism has been met by little to no reparation, and race remains a strong and consistent indicator of economic and political outcomes. The issue of reparations has emerged as a major ideological divide between those who would like to shunt the issue of slavery into the past and those who believe the legacy of slavery remains embedded in U.S. institutions, policy, and practice.

CONCLUSION

In spite of the attempt to erase the significance of race in the twenty-first century—as reflected in the decline

of Affirmative Action, the emergence of a class of black electoral candidates unwilling to address race upfront, and the squelching of dissenting voices that challenge the white male establishment—the undeniable facts of HIV/AIDS across the African diaspora, and post-9/11 immigrant and civil liberties repression in the United States show that problems of race and power persist and remain deep. But the growth of strong, though quiet, grassroots multiracial mobilization since September 11 and the recent reparations movement are just two of many signals that efforts for racial justice live on.

In the United States and beyond, people of color and those committed to racial justice are striving to understand the evolving problems of race and power and to devise new and responsive strategies. Although visions of racial justice may be diverse and highly contested, there is a common unmet need among people of color for dignity and equality in daily life. For many, the recent events of September 11, 2001, have highlighted shared struggles for justice across color, citizenship, and community, producing new multiracial coalitions based not on pragmatism but on a shared fate.

Kendra Field

BIBLIOGRAPHY

Bai, Jane, and Eric Tang. "The War at Home." *ColorLines*, Spring 2002.

Colburn, David R., and Jeffrey S. Adler, eds. *African-American Mayors: Race, Politics, and the American City*. Chicago: University of Illinois Press, 2001.

Dawson, Michael. *Black Visions: The Roots of Contemporary African-American Political Ideologies*. Chicago: University of Chicago Press, 2001.

Guinier, Lani, and Gerald Torres. *The Miner's Canary: Enlisting Race, Resisting Power, Transforming Democracy*. Cambridge, MA: Harvard University, 2002.

Marable, Manning, and Leith Mullings. "The Divided Mind of Black America: Race, Ideology and Politics in the Post–Civil Rights Era." *Race and Class* 36:1 (1994).

Sen, Rinku. "Durban and the War." *ColorLines*, Spring 2002.

Tepperman, Jonathan. "Complicating the Race." *The New York Times Magazine*, April 28, 2002.

3
WOMEN'S MOVEMENT

INTRODUCTION

Women's activism is often characterized as occurring in "waves"; that is, it seems very strong at times, and then it seems to fizzle out, much like the crashing of waves in the ocean. The use of the waves metaphor is controversial because some historians see continuity between different periods of activism by women. However, many scholars use the wave concept because it is a useful way to describe women's activism throughout U.S. history. The period characterized as the first wave of women's activism began in 1848 at the Seneca Falls Convention and ended in 1920 with the passage of the Nineteenth Amendment. The major focus of the first wave was to expand not only women's rights, most notably that of suffrage, but also other legal rights, such as the right of married women to own and inherit property and the right to divorce. The period encompassed by the second wave of women's activism is far shorter, running from the 1960s to the early 1980s. The second wave also made legal gains for women, such as legalized abortion and federal legislation banning sexual discrimination, but it also sought equality for women in everything from a shared division of child care and household labor to equal pay for equal work. Finally, the third wave of women's activism is still occurring. While the first two waves of women's activism took a similar shape with large public demonstrations, the founding of national organizations, and a relatively focused agenda, the third wave is less direct, and for a good reason. Participants in the third wave see women's issues as only part of their social activism and are as likely to focus on cultural methods of change as they are on the political process.

1800–1865

In the early nineteenth century, the changes wrought by industrialization and then urbanization and immigration created the conditions that gave rise to the earliest social movements in the United States. These changing conditions did not impact men and women in the same way. As industrialization moved economic activity out of the household into the public arena, a division between the public world and the private home emerged. This public/private split impacted different groups of women in different ways. For white women in the emerging middle class, the ideology of separate spheres meant that women were defined by not working outside the home and were increasingly viewed as the moral guardians of society as they remained apart from the amoral world of capitalism. For immigrant women, this ideology obviously did not describe their existence as they were part of families that relied on all members to bring in wages to support the group. Gendered ideology, however, might determine what kind of work women took, for example, preferring to complete piecework within the home rather than working outside the home in a factory. Nonetheless, "not working" did not constitute womanhood for this group. For slave women, the ideology of separate spheres was even less relevant.

For middle-class white women, exclusion from the paid labor market left time for participation in philanthropy or social reform. Indeed, women comprised the backbone of these early social movements. Women became involved in utopian experiments, temperance, abolition, moral reform, health and dress reform, and labor movements. Gradually, as some women became involved in social movements, they realized that they needed more power to be able to change society. This realization led some women to ultimately demand the right to participate in politics through the vote. Furthermore, although many women entered social movements in order to improve life for others, as the essays in this section reveal, many women came to see that women needed to organize on behalf of themselves. The movement for women's rights grew, in part, out of women's participation in the abolition movement. As women became increasingly involved in the public world, some of them sought to transform their role in the private arena of the middle-class home. Other social movements, such as the cooperative housekeeping movement, represent a radical challenge to women's roles. Though small in scale, this movement is an important precursor to the efforts of women activists in the 1960s and 1970s and illustrates the extent to which involvement in social movements transformed some female participants.

1865–1920

Americans seeking to address the changes in society after the Civil War created many social movements. Women during this period became involved with a variety of issues, most notably suffrage, to elevate their status in society, as well as movements to help those less fortunate than themselves. Increasing access to education, at least for white middle-class women, provided a new justification for women's activism as young women, trained in the social sciences, began to make helping others a profession. Women became increasingly involved in politics through involvement in anti-imperialism and progressivism.

Although white, economically privileged women found it easiest to engage in reform, women from all areas of society became involved in social movements. Women of color could not work from a position of moral superiority because society often viewed them as "subhuman." The former slave Sojourner Truth aptly illustrated this point in a stirring speech, "Ain't I a Woman?" Nonetheless, women of color found ways to organize during the later part of the nineteenth century. These women might not organize single-sex groups, but rather worked as members of mixed-sex social movements. White working-class women also organized on their own behalf, creating strategic alliances based on class and at other times based on gender.

1920–1960

Historians long ignored the period between 1920 and 1960, believing that after securing the right to vote, women vanished from social movements until the resurgence of activism in the 1960s However, scholars have reexamined this epoch. As essays in the section explore, women continued to organize as constituencies, including the first national black women's organization. Women's political activism continued during this period in efforts to pass the Equal Rights Amendment. Efforts to expand women's rights continued in the work to legalize birth control. Women also continued to make inroads in politics, a direct outcome of their involvement in progressive social movements. Although World War II curtailed much activism on the home front, the organizations that remained active during this period, and those that ran and participated in them, became a crucial resource to women in the 1960s.

1960–1980

Indeed, the period following World War II saw a level of social activism in the United States that was so unprecedented that its images still mark out the national imagination. Mention of a single place such as "Selma" or "Kent State" immediately brings to mind these much-publicized events of the civil rights and antiwar movements. Although women actively participated in both, the period following World War II marked the emergence of the largest social movement dedicated to changing the status of women in American society. Activists attacked the issue of women's subordinate position from many different approaches. Though not an ideologically unified movement, the women's movement had a profound impact on American society, especially on the anti-rape movement, the abortion rights movement, and the establishment of women's studies.

1980–PRESENT

Initially, the 1980s and 1990s might seem to be a period of decreased activism by women, but scholars have now begun to acknowledge this period as a third wave. Central to the third wave's understanding of gender is sexuality. The story of women's participation in social movements is still being written. Across the country, young scholars are busily documenting the efforts of women to transform society, not only for themselves but also for others. The essays in this section serve as a rich introduction to the many ways in which women have participated in social movements and provide a point of departure for further investigation.

Michelle Moravec

WOMEN'S SOCIAL MOVEMENT
1800–1869

In the United States in the early nineteenth century, social movements were seen as primarily the province of men. However, the emerging concept of women's responsibility for the moral and spiritual well-being of the nation combined to create a growing culture of female reform. Beginning in the 1830s, women participated in a number of reform movements aimed at addressing social problems, including utopianism, temperance, abolitionism, moral reform, labor reform, health reform, and dress reform. The religious roots of reform and the ideal of women's moral authority meant that most early female activists focused their efforts on moral suasion—the ability of an individual to influence another through moral or spiritual arguments. However, as tactics shifted to encompass a narrowing definition of reform that emphasized legislative action, women fought to expand the definition of proper womanhood both within the context of individual social movements and through the organized women's rights movement.

In the first few decades of the nineteenth century, the ideology of separate spheres defined public associations and charitable work as belonging to the public world of men. At the same time, however, small groups of women were creating a space for themselves as "public women" through their participation in benevolent work and reform. Men were assigned control over the public sphere, which included government, the workplace, and the world beyond the home. Women, who were defined by what was termed the "cult of true womanhood," were understood to have authority over the private or domestic sphere, particularly for the family's spiritual well-being. This dichotomy between public and private life did not always hold true in day-to-day life, but it proved to be a powerful force that shaped the definition of both men and women throughout the antebellum period. Many women felt that gender as a category far overshadowed racial and class boundaries, and the presumption of shared life experiences among women contributed to the belief that a national (and international) community of women existed.

The assumption of women's concern for others and their innate virtue led many to feel that women were best suited to care for the poor and oppressed. Female moral authority was thought to have the potential to transform American society. Some women felt that this potential carried with it a responsibility to act in support of their convictions, and they used the ideology of female moral authority to justify their participation in a wide range of social and reform activities. Initially, the work of reform primarily used women's accepted power to influence others in order to rehabilitate individuals. However, as more and more women became comfortable in the world of public activism, and as reform activities became more collective in means and more legislative in ends, women moved into positions of leadership and began to use overtly political tactics. Although this transition did not occur without criticism, over time female reformers expanded the definition of womanhood to include a space for women in both the private and public spheres.

Of course, the idea of separate spheres could also be used as a conservative force. When women were thought to overstep their bounds, by wearing clothing that obscured gender boundaries, speaking before audiences of men, or petitioning in support of legislation, they faced harsh public criticism that questioned both their morality and their femininity. The decision to enter into and maintain public activism was not always easy, and women had to endure disparagement not only from the press, but also from their local communities, and sometimes even their families. Furthermore, the notion that bonds of gender transcended class and racial distinctions often concealed real differences among women. The majority of female reformers in the pre-Civil War era were white and middle class; their values dominated antebellum reform movements, and issues important to nonwhite activists were often ignored or even opposed by white reformers.

UTOPIANISM

A number of women were drawn to utopian movements during the antebellum period. In keeping with the idea that individuals had the power to change society simply by example, both religious and nonreligious groups attempted to remove themselves from society in order to create alternative social structures. For some women, utopian movements allowed them to live out their religious, social, and political ideals within a community of like-minded persons. Other women probably followed their husbands and families into utopian communities. Women's experiences within communal societies varied from group to group. Although some utopian communities attempted to equalize or at least reconsider conventional gender relations, others reinforced and even extended existing patriarchal structures.

Among the religious utopian communities of the pre-Civil War era, the Shakers and the Mormons attracted the largest number of followers. During their heyday in the 1840s, about sixty semi-autonomous Shaker communities comprising about 4,000 members existed across the United States. The Shakers of the antebellum era did not set out to create equality among the sexes, but to bring both men and women closer to God. Although women had a larger role in community government than in other contemporary Protestant sects and were considered responsible for the spiritual well-being of the members, men controlled the economic aspects of community life. Fundamental to Shaker life were the tenets of celibacy and the separation of the sexes. Women and men were segregated both in living and in working arrangements in order to free them to concentrate on their religious life.

Conversely, the Mormons were explicit in their patriarchal foundation. In contrast to prevailing gender definitions, men were considered to be spiritually and morally superior to women, and control over religious life remained firmly in male hands. Within the Mormon community, women were confined to domestic roles and encouraged to bear children. Although they represented a minority of family relations, polygamous marriages were considered the ideal within the Mormon community and must have had the greatest effect on individual women. Mormons often argued that polygamy meant less work for women, and indeed some women may have gained some measure of independence if wives maintained separate households. On the other hand, the first wife's consent for her husband to marry again was not always willingly given, and jealousy could follow if multiple wives lived under the same roof.

Nonreligious utopian movements proliferated in this period; the most notable communities were at New Harmony, Indiana, and Oneida, New York. In the 1820s, the New Harmonites set out to promote equality between men and women among other goals. In an effort to eliminate gender and class differences, leaders introduced a new costume for both men and women that would become the foundation of the dress reform movement. However, this attempt to visually equalize the sexes did not translate into a day-to-day reality. Women were still expected to perform domestic tasks, which were considered to hold less value than the work performed by men. Furthermore, the community's shared control over the governance of the family and household eliminated women's traditional base of power within the private sphere.

The Oneida Community did more to alter gender roles than any other utopian group of the pre-Civil War era. Leader John Humphrey Noyes promoted dress reform in order to minimize gender distinctions and to promote women's physical mobility. Some changes in gender relations did follow; not only did women work in traditionally male occupations, but some women even held positions of authority over men. Family arrangements were radically revised through the practice of "complex marriage," whereby all adults were considered to be married to the entire community. However, Noyes's strong influence over the community meant that the larger patriarchal community replaced the smaller patriarchal group of the family. Male leaders maintained strict control over who was and was not allowed to bear children, and men still dominated the income-producing occupations. Furthermore, the few women who occupied leadership positions were primarily limited to ceremonial roles.

TEMPERANCE

In the early nineteenth century, increased alcohol consumption was thought to be the primary cause of social disorder. The temperance movement that arose in response quickly garnered the support of women, who saw male drinking as the primary cause of domestic discord. Female temperance workers recognized that woman's subordinate role within the family meant that it was she and her children who suffered if the male head of household drank to excess. Reformers sought to protect women from the effects of male intemperance by attempting to control the behavior of men, first through moral suasion and later through legislative action.

As early as 1818, women's names had begun appearing on petitions opposed to the granting of tavern licenses. The American Temperance Society, founded in 1826, was the first voluntary association of any kind to attract large numbers of women from across the country. Women felt relatively comfortable participating in early temperance work because of its tactical focus on informal persuasion rather than political action. They distributed propaganda, ran temperance hotels, and attempted to persuade the men in their community to abandon alcohol. Although most women joined male-run societies, by the end of the decade women had begun to form their own independent organizations; twenty-four independent female temperance societies existed by 1831.

With the emergence of the Daughters of Temperance, sister organization to the Sons of Temperance, women were finally provided with a leadership vehicle within the temperance movement. The Daughters attracted large numbers of female activists, reaching their peak membership of 30,000 members in 1848. The association connected local auxiliaries and supported women's interest in the movement through the *New York Olive Plant*, the first temperance newsletter to be edited by women. Following the Maine Law crusades of the early 1850s, which sought to end alcohol consumption in that state through legislative means, women expanded their activism to include petitioning for temperance laws and canvassing voters in the North and South. Although they had little impact on the movement, a few scattered incidents of female vigilantism against saloons appeared during this period.

As women sought to broaden their role in the temperance movement, they forced issues of women's rights to the forefront of the movement. Many male temperance workers resisted the expansion of women's roles, fearing that the movement would lose respectability and momentum. When the leaders of the Sons of Temperance refused to allow women to participate equally in their 1852 convention, prominent women's rights advocates, including Susan B. Anthony, Elizabeth Cady Stanton, and Amelia Bloomer, walked out and formed the Woman's State Temperance Society of New York. However, independent female organizations only lasted a few years as

many activists shifted their focus to women's rights. Although women would come to dominate the movement in the post-Civil War era, by the 1860s the sex-integrated Templars remained as the only significant organization to support women's temperance work.

ABOLITIONISM

Given the prevailing belief in women's moral responsibility for the nation, no issue of the pre-Civil War era provoked greater female commitment than that of the abolition of slavery. For many women, slavery was a sin that simply could not be ignored. Many white women were sympathetic to the plight of slaves, and the idea of a national community of women meant that female reformers particularly identified with female slaves. However, for free African-American women, the issue of slavery was deeply personal and immediate. Free black women organized not only to eradicate slavery, but also in support of equal rights and increased access to education for their communities. Throughout the movement, female abolitionists attempted to influence those around them to support abolition through moral suasion, and in later decades they turned their attention to legislative and political action.

In spite of public criticism, women immediately began to join the nascent antislavery movement of the early 1830s, at first creating auxiliary groups to male organizations. One of the first groups to organize was the Boston Female Anti-Slavery Society, which was established as auxiliary to abolitionist leader William Lloyd Garrison's newly formed New England Anti-Slavery Society. When women were excluded from signing the "Declaration of Sentiments and Purposes" at the formation of the American Anti-Slavery Society in 1833, they responded by creating the biracial Philadelphia Female Anti-Slavery Society under the leadership of Lucretia Mott. Within a few years, both racially integrated and segregated female abolitionist organizations emerged across the Northeast. Early female efforts focused on petition drives opposing slavery. By 1837, enough women were participating in the movement to hold the first National Female Anti-Slavery Convention in New York, with eighty-one delegates attending from twelve states.

As women moved into leadership positions within the abolitionist movement, they faced mounting criticism for what was deemed unwomanly behavior. When sister activists Sarah and Angelina Grimké lectured in front of mixed-gender audiences, public opposition was fierce. Female abolitionists were criticized in the press and by the clergy, and they were even physically threatened. Crowds stormed a meeting of the Boston Female Anti-Slavery Society in 1835, and three years later the Anti-Slavery Convention of American Women was attacked by a mob of 10,000 that destroyed Pennsylvania Hall. By the late 1830s, tensions surrounding women's expanding activism precipitated a split within the movement as abolitionists faced questions of women's rights. Although this dissension caused a decline in the movement's adherents over the 1840s, women's activities continued to broaden in spite of their reduced numbers. New tactics moved beyond moral suasion and petition drives to include antislavery fairs and political party organization.

Growing public acceptance for the idea of abolition brought many women back to the movement in the 1850s. The changing political and social environment meant that lecture audiences were increasingly receptive to female speakers, and many women joined pioneers such as Mott and Sojourner Truth on the lecture circuit. Escalating momentum for the movement in the years prior to the Civil War allowed women to perform their work on a larger, more public scale. Women's petitioning efforts in support of emancipation grew so extensive that in 1863, they organized the Woman's National Loyal League to coordinate efforts at a national level. During the Civil War, African-American women established associations to aid the massive numbers of freed slaves streaming northward, and both white and black women organized to meet the needs of soldiers. The scope of abolitionism broadened during this period to include issues such as education and voting rights for free blacks. However, the movement lost energy after emancipation and the passage of the Fourteenth Amendment as female abolitionists transferred their commitment to other reform movements, including temperance and women's rights.

MORAL REFORM

In the early nineteenth century, many Americans viewed prostitution as being responsible for much of the perceived moral and social disintegration of society. New standards of morality emanating from the emerging middle classes, the growth of urban centers in the Northeast, and the flourishing culture of reform combined to create new standards for sexuality. Women linked prostitution to male dominance in economic, political, and social life, viewing women as the victims of an imbalance of power between the sexes. However, female moral reformers did not adopt the position of later women's rights activists. Instead,

they understood prostitution in terms of women's lack of protections rather than their lack of rights. Reformers first sought to reclaim "fallen women," creating asylums where prostitutes could repent and train for alternate employment. Later reformers shifted their tactics, attempting to foster public discussion of the moral dangers of prostitution and advocating for legal prevention.

Although men largely directed early attempts at moral reform, women soon began to participate in the movement. The Magdalen Society of New York, established in 1811, delegated the training and care of penitent prostitutes in the society's asylum to a committee of women. As a movement, moral reform gained few followers in the early part of the century, and it was not until the 1830s that a substantial following was established. Although men led the first significant moral reform organization, the New York Magdalen Society, women took the lead with that society's successor, the New York Female Benevolent Society. A split within the movement between reformers who advocated the reclamation of individual prostitutes and those who wanted to pursue moral education and the public exposure of prostitution led to the formation of the New York Female Moral Reform Society (FMRS) in 1834.

Although the FMRS was originally formed as an auxiliary to the all-male American Society for Promoting the Observance of the Seventh Commandment, it quickly came to dominate the moral reform movement. At its height in 1841, the FMRS had 555 auxiliaries and approximately 50,000 members. The *Advocate of Moral Reform* advised local groups on how to combat prostitution and created a sense of community among geographically separate auxiliaries. At first, the FMRS established an institution for repentant prostitutes, but this tactic was quickly abandoned. Following the trend toward legislative action prevalent in most reform movements of the period, the society began to organize petition drives aimed at creating laws that would punish seducers. Petition campaigns culminated in the passage of anti-seduction legislation in 1848, but laws proved difficult to enforce and few victims came forward to press charges. By the end of the decade, the FMRS had become truly national in scope and reflected this shift in its name change to the American Female Moral Reform Society.

Over the course of the 1840s, the FMRS shifted its focus to poor relief, which reformers had identified as the root cause of women's entry into prostitution. The society began to link its projects with those of other reform organizations that were working to address the plight of the poor, and in 1846 they founded an asylum for impoverished women and children. By the following decade, the society, now the American Female Guardian Society, had almost completely shifted its focus to poor assistance, and it downplayed its role in the moral reform movement in order to gain public support for its activities.

LABOR REFORM

The industrial revolution of the early nineteenth century brought women into the workplace, primarily in the textile industry. Textile mills recruited women both because of their traditional association with textile production and because they were a source of cheap labor. By the 1830s, women filled the New England mill towns, where they worked in sweatshop conditions, lived in substandard housing, and received far less pay than men. Early attempts to combat these problems were short-lived; women would strike for a few hours or days and then return to work. Working women had little experience at organizing, and associations such as the United Tailoresses Society of New York lasted only a few years. The economic depression of the late 1830s further undermined women's attempts at organization.

The Lowell Female Labor Reform Association of 1845–1846, however, proved that women were able to build a stable organization with strong leadership. Although the association was unsuccessful in its attempts to pass protective legislation, including a ten-hour workday, the organization became so prominent that its leaders became directors of the New England Labor Reform League in 1846. Over the course of the next decade, the influx of immigrants, who accepted even less pay than American-born workers and had little experience with trade unions, contributed to the lack of successful labor reform. However, the growing national momentum in favor of unionization in the 1860s led to a resurgence of female labor organization. Women joined the new national labor unions, including the National Labor Union and the Knights of Labor. At the same time, established male unions lent their support to working women, who formed numerous female trade associations. In addition, growing interest on the part of middle- and upper-class women in the plight of working women led to the formation of protective organizations, which offered legal and other services.

HEALTH REFORM

One of the primary tenets of the antebellum worldview was that women were sickly. Whether there was something in women's lifestyles that made them more prone to illness, or whether women's experiences were influenced by the prevailing acceptance of female infirmity, the health of women commanded attention throughout the nineteenth century. At the same time, the values of the emerging middle class stressed women's role in preventing sickness in her family, and many felt that disease could be prevented if women were properly educated. These trends combined to create a growing health reform movement that attracted many female followers.

Women made up a significant portion of the physiological societies that first appeared in the 1830s, and over the next few decades a number of female physiological societies were active throughout the Northeast. Interest in health led some women to pursue a career as physicians, and several unlicensed female doctors were practicing medicine by the 1840s. At the same time, alternative health movements allowed women the possibility of pursuing an interest in medicine outside of the established medical community. The hydropathic movement, which maintained that good health could be achieved through the internal and external application of water, counted many women among its supporters. In addition, many women became interested in phrenology, a "science" that studied the shape of the skull as a means of analyzing the brain and understanding personality.

DRESS REFORM

Chief among the culprits of women's ill health was clothing. Critics argued that women's restrictive clothing impaired the full functioning of internal organs and limited physical movement. Many health reformers adopted the dress reform costumes worn at the Oneida Community, particularly at hydropathic "water-cure" spas. The movement was given a brief burst of overwhelmingly negative publicity when leading women's rights advocates adopted dress reform in the early 1850s. The movement never recovered; the redefinition of gender identities proposed by dress reform costumes appeared to many Americans to be overly radical. In contrast to national trends favoring collective, legislative reform action, the movement always stressed the power of the individual. Their one concession to the growing spirit of cooperative action was to organize the National Dress Reform Association in 1855 as a means of promoting the movement. However, dress reform's lack of consolidation and exclusion of other reform issues led to its eclipse by the following decade.

WOMEN'S RIGHTS

The experiences of female reformers in a number of different reform movements over the course of the antebellum era convinced many of the need for organized action on their own behalf. Some women believed that female political rights were needed in order to achieve success in abolitionism, temperance, and other reform movements. For others, who were frustrated in their attempts to gain positions of leadership and to participate actively in the public sphere, equal rights for women became a necessity in and of itself. Following their exclusion from the World Anti-Slavery Convention in 1840, Elizabeth Cady Stanton and Lucretia Mott articulated the need for organized action in behalf of women's political and social equality. They organized the first women's rights convention in Seneca Falls, New York, in 1848, which was followed by yearly national conventions at which reformers debated the aims of the movement and formed an ideology.

At first, few advocates except Stanton were interested in the question of female suffrage, choosing instead to focus on issues of property and earnings control, divorce, educational and employment opportunities, and women's legal status. However, public criticism of women's rights advocates' experimentation with dress reform convinced many of the need for organized, collective action centered on one key issue. Suffrage emerged as the central focus for the movement, although during the post–Civil War era debates over the Fourteenth Amendment split the movement into those who supported African-American suffrage and those who held the voting rights of women to be more important. The latter camp united under Stanton and Susan B. Anthony's leadership in the National Woman Suffrage Association, which incorporated a broad vision of women's rights that extended beyond female suffrage. Those who believed that all other issues must be excluded in order to win the vote created the American Woman Suffrage Association, through which they concentrated on obtaining female voting rights at the state level.

Thus, by 1869, women had become active in numerous reform organizations attempting to address a broad range of social problems. Movements such as abolitionism had largely succeeded in achieving their primary aims; other movements, including moral re-

form and dress reform, had seen their support dwindle; while still others, such as women's rights, had only begun to gain momentum. Women had carved out a space for themselves in the public sphere, gaining the right to take political action, to lead public organizations, and to organize on their own behalf. The stage was set for women's ascendancy as a political force, and their work in the coming decades in the club movement, the settlement house movement, temperance, labor reform, and the women's rights movement would pave the way for women's political enfranchisement and the national reform agendas of the Progressive Era.

Kendra Van Cleave

BIBLIOGRAPHY

Berg, Barbara J. *The Remembered Gate: Origins of American Feminism: The Woman and the City, 1800–1860.* New York: Oxford University Press, 1978.

Blocker, Jack S., Jr. *American Temperance Movements: Cycles of Reform.* Boston: Twayne, 1989.

Cayleff, Susan E. *Wash and Be Healed: The Water-Cure Movement and Women's Health.* Philadelphia: Temple University Press, 1987.

Chmielewski, Wendy E., Louis J. Kern, and Marlyn Klee-Hartzell, eds. *Women in Spiritual and Communitarian Societies in the United States.* Syracuse, NY: Syracuse University Press, 1992.

Dorsey, Bruce. *Reforming Men and Women: Gender in the Antebellum City.* Ithaca, NY: Cornell University Press, 2002.

Fischer, Gayle V. *Pantaloons & Power: A Nineteenth-century Dress Reform in the United States.* Kent, OH: Kent State University Press, 2001.

Flexner, Eleanor, and Ellen Fitzpatrick. *Century of Struggle: The Woman's Rights Movement in the United States.* Cambridge, MA: Belknap, 1996.

Foster, Lawrence. *Women, Family, and Utopia: Communal Experiments of the Shakers, the Oneida Community, and the Mormons.* Syracuse, NY: Syracuse University Press, 1991.

Ginzberg, Lori D. *Women and the Work of Benevolence: Morality, Politics, and Class in the Nineteenth-Century United States.* New Haven, CT: Yale University Press, 1990.

Hobson, Barbara Meil. *Uneasy Virtue: The Politics of Prostitution and the American Reform Tradition.* New York: Basic Books, 1987.

Hoffert, Sylvia D. *When Hens Crow: The Woman's Rights Movement in Antebellum America.* Bloomington and Indianapolis: Indiana University Press, 1995.

Jeffrey, Julie Roy. *The Great Silent Army of Abolitionism: Ordinary Women in the Antislavery Movement.* Chapel Hill: University of North Carolina Press, 1998.

Morantz, Regina. "Making Women Modern: Middle Class Women and Health Reform in 19th Century America." *Journal of Social History* 10 (June 1977): 490–508.

Terborg-Penn, Rosalyn. *African American Women in the Struggle for the Vote, 1850–1920.* Bloomington: Indiana University Press, 1998.

Wertheimer, Barbara Mayer. *We Were There: The Story of Working Women in America.* New York: Pantheon Books, 1977.

Whiteaker, Larry. *Seduction, Prostitution, and Moral Reform in New York, 1830–1860.* New York: Garland, 1997.

Moral and Dress Reform Movement

1800–1869

The American dress reform movements of the nineteenth century attempted to use women's clothing to effect social and political change. In response to the tight waists and long skirts currently in vogue, reformers proposed a loose-fitting costume incorporating long pantaloons and short dresses. Advocates wore and promoted this reform costume for a number of reasons: because of spiritual and religious convictions, to improve women's health, and to expand women's social role and status. Although little attention was paid to early attempts at dress reform, the issue became highly charged when leaders of the emerging women's rights movement adopted and politicized reform dress.

WHY DRESS REFORM?

Dress reformers responded to both the realities and the social constructions of nineteenth-century middle-class women's clothing, which had long relied on shaping undergarments and draped fabric in order to mold the body into what was considered an attractive form. For a brief period at the turn of the nineteenth century, clothing followed the relatively lightweight, high-waisted "classical" style, which was believed to be more natural. This trend reversed itself in the 1810s as fashionable clothing began to incorporate a growing number of layers, and undergarments became more and more substantial. As the century progressed, it appeared that women's clothing was growing more and more extreme, as skirts grew wider, the ideal waist grew narrower, and decoration proliferated. During this period, religious leaders, the medical establishment, and a number of other cultural critics increasingly condemned women's fashions. Those who disapproved of women's clothing and the fashion industry blamed dress for a number of social and physical ills, including a host of diseases and medical disorders, and sins such as vanity and pride.

The ideological foundations of dress reform were drawn from this criticism and from the growing reform spirit of the early nineteenth century. A number of disparate social movements contributed to the genesis of dress reform, including utopianism, health reform, and women's rights. Reformers tended to be white, middle class, and female, although a number of key leaders were male. The movement as a whole was characterized by an individualistic approach rather than collective action; most dress reformers felt that personal example would lead to broader social and political change. Although different groups claimed to endorse different clothing, all of the reform costumes were influenced by popular representations of Middle Eastern women's dress and by children's clothing, featuring loose-fitting dresses ending at or below the knee, worn over loose-fitting pantaloons.

EARLY DRESS REFORM

Many utopian communities of the early nineteenth century advocated for simplified clothing, particularly for women. It was in this tradition that the communal society of New Harmony, Indiana, designed alternative styles of dress for both genders in 1824. The Harmonites, led by Robert Owen, aimed to eliminate class and gender differences by promoting a style of dress based on children's attire. Significantly, men and women's clothing was not the same; men were encouraged to wear loose-fitting pantaloons covered by jackets, while women were offered a knee-length coat over pantaloons. However, minimized visual distinctions between the genders did not translate to increased status for women, who were still relegated to domestic tasks of lesser value. This first experiment with dress reform, notable as the only one to include men's clothing, ended along with the New Harmony community in 1827.

Dress reform was next taken up at the Oneida Community, a religious revival community located in upstate New York. Oneida's leader, John Humphrey

Noyes, introduced a reform costume for women in 1848 that was remarkably similar in design to that worn at New Harmony. The Oneida dress reform movement did not aim to eliminate gender distinctions altogether, but to encourage equality among men and women and to purge women of the sin of vanity. Again, women wore a costume designed to emulate clothing worn by children, consisting of pantalets (an undergarment worn only by children in this period) covered by a below-knee-length dress; they also cut their hair short in a style that mimicked children. Under Noyes's influence, a majority of Oneida women adopted the reform costume, citing their increased ability to perform traditionally masculine tasks as the primary benefit. However, women continued to wear "long dress" when outside the Community to avoid harassment by crowds. Despite women's altered appearance, the ideal of gender equality symbolized by the reform costume was never achieved. When Noyes left the Community in 1879, dress reform was quickly abandoned.

The changes in women's clothing promoted at Oneida influenced others involved in the reform movements of the mid-century. Many dress reformers began as supporters of hydropathy, an alternative health movement that stressed physical well-being, achieved through the ingestion and physical application of water, above all other things. Dress reform corresponded well with the philosophy of hydropathy. Proponents emphasized personal example over collective action, believing that women must first achieve full health before any social or political changes were possible. Fashion had long been blamed for women's physical ills, both real and imagined, and health reformers saw clothing as an obvious area for reform. Numerous "water-cure" spas promoted a reform costume based on a short dress and pantaloons for patients, and many women were able to try out the new clothing within a secluded environment. Dress reform was also publicized in the *Water-Cure Journal*, a popular health reform journal. Hydropathic physicians such as James Caleb Jackson and Harriet N. Austin became staunch proponents of the new costume; Austin wore reform dress until her death in 1891.

Hydropaths were not the only ones to be influenced by the Oneida reform costume. Some utopian communities experimented with dress reform, including Hopedale, North American Phalanx, Brook Farm, Modern Times, and Ruskin Commonwealth. In addition, various religious groups tried out alternative clothing for women, including the Mormon community in Utah and the Strangite Mormon sect at Beaver Island, Michigan. However, little public attention was paid to these early experiments outside of reform communities.

DRESS REFORM AND WOMEN'S RIGHTS

The relative obscurity of dress reform changed radically in 1851 when key leaders of the emerging women's rights movement adopted and thereby politicized the reform costume. Women's rights dress reformers tied women's social and political role to their clothing, arguing that contemporary fashions enforced female passivity and were therefore a primary cause of women's oppression. Women's rights advocates believed that women themselves were partially to blame for their own subjugation and that if they gave up wearing clothing that restricted their movements and pandered to their vanity, they would become both physically and intellectually free. Calling their costume "freedom dress," women's rights advocates again endorsed short dresses over pantaloons (known to women's rights dress reformers as "Turkish trousers").

Elizabeth Smith Miller was the first to adopt the costume for everyday wear; Elizabeth Cady Stanton and Amelia Bloomer soon followed. When the three women walked through Seneca Falls, New York, in reform costumes, major newspapers, including the *New York Tribune*, *Boston Carpet-Bag*, and *Chicago Tribune*, covered the incident and a startling amount of public furor was unleashed. The popular press linked dress reform to women's suffrage, free love, and other currently unpopular reform movements, and women wearing the reform costume in public often found themselves at the mercy of hostile crowds. No matter how careful dress reformers were to point out that they were not wearing men's clothing, the image of women wearing trousers seems to have stirred deep fears about gender identity and the role of women in American society.

The public attention paid to dress reform did not necessarily detract from the movement; it actually helped to publicize it. Bloomer filled her journal *Lily* with articles endorsing dress reform; major national newspapers reprinted these articles, dubbing the costume "Bloomers." Eventually, many female reformers adopted the costume, including Susan B. Anthony, Paulina Wright Davis, Lucy Stone, Sarah and Angelina Grimké, Celia Burleigh, Charlotte Beebe Wilbour, Helen Jarvis, and Lydia Jenkins. However, these women and their supporters did not organize collectively or even lecture on dress reform. Believing that individual actions would have the greatest influence,

In commemoration of Amelia Bloomer's one hundredth birthday, farmers dressed in "bloomers" tend a vegetable garden in 1918. *(The Schlesinger Library, Radcliffe Institute, Harvard University)*

they simply wore the alternative clothing and hoped thereby to influence other women to make the same decision. Hydropath James Caleb Jackson proposed a national organization devoted to dress reform in 1851 but was turned down by Stanton and Bloomer in favor of personal example.

Eventually, however, the public ridicule attracted by the reform costume proved too much for women's rights advocates, who felt that the attention paid to their appearance detracted from their ideas on other issues. Stanton became the first to return to long dress in 1853, arguing in a letter to Lucy Stone (co-written with Anthony) dated February 16, 1854, "We put the dress on for greater freedom, but what is physical freedom compared with mental bondage?" By the following year, most women's rights leaders had given up dress reform, choosing to focus instead on issues such as suffrage, marriage reform, and education.

However, their experiences convinced these reformers of the necessity of organized, collective action centered on one key issue, a conviction that would influence the suffrage movement throughout its duration.

DRESS REFORM AFTER WOMEN'S RIGHTS

Hydropaths continued to support the cause of dress reform, and under the leadership of Dr. James C. Jackson they organized the National Dress Reform Association (NDRA) in 1855. Although the NDRA eventually expanded its constitutional objectives to include women's rights issues, the association often found itself in opposition to women's rights leaders who argued for collective action against legal and government institutions. Wearing the short dress and pantaloons outfit, which they called the "American costume," the members of the NDRA continued to advocate for individual action based on the belief that social change would follow. *The Sibyl: A Review of the Tastes, Errors & Fashions of Society*, published by Lydia Sayer Hasbrouck, became the unofficial voice of the NDRA, and the journal served to create a sense of community among geographically distant dress reformers.

By the 1860s, however, dress reformers had become isolated from much of the reform community, primarily because of their lack of collective action and their narrow focus. *The Sibyl* ceased publication in 1864 owing to lack of subscriptions, and the NDRA disbanded sometime that year or the next. There were scattered attempts to revitalize the movement, but they met with little success. Under the leadership of Ellen Gould White, the Seventh Day Adventists experimented with dress reform, but most female followers failed to embrace the reform costume. Dress reform as a social movement was largely abandoned, although some individual advocates continued to wear the reform costume.

In the 1870s, women's clubs in the urban Northeast revived interest in dress reform, although it was a movement of a very different nature. These advocates severed ties to the broader ideology of earlier movements that connected women's dress to their social and political roles. The new generation of dress reformers discarded the short dress and pantaloons costume that had proved so troublesome, instead promoting relatively small changes in women's undergarments. Some success was achieved, although it was due in large part to dress reformers' acceptance of prevailing gender definitions and notions of femininity. The New England Woman's Club of Boston and the Sorosis Club of New York City sponsored lectures on dress reform, and Mary Tillotson (a former leader of the NDRA) organized the short-lived American Free Dress League (1870–1873). Small-scale reform continued in this vein into the 1920s, but it remained disconnected from any larger ideological framework.

Dress reformers of the nineteenth century explored the relationship of clothing to gender identity, using alternative dress as a means to question and redefine women's social and political roles. They connected woman's visual appearance and physical mobility with her health and with her role and status in American society. Reformers believed that by wearing the reform costume, individual women would effect broader change. Although the movement attracted significant public attention and caused considerable debate, it ultimately failed to achieve many of its goals owing to its lack of collective action and its radical redefinition of seemingly fundamental gender truths. In spite of the efforts of dress reformers, most American women continued to dress as fashionably as possible.

Kendra Van Cleave

BIBLIOGRAPHY

Cayleff, Susan E. *Wash and Be Healed: The Water-Cure Movement and Women's Health.* Philadelphia: Temple University Press, 1987.

Donegan, Jane B. *"Hydropathic Highway to Health": Women and Water-Cure in Antebellum America.* Westport, CT: Greenwood Press, 1986.

Fischer, Gayle V. *Pantaloons & Power: A Nineteenth-century Dress Reform in the United States.* Kent, OH: Kent State University Press, 2001.

Kesselman, Amy. "The 'Freedom Suit': Feminism and Dress Reform in the United States, 1848–1975." *Gender and Society* 5 (1991): 495–510.

Kriebl, Karen J. "From Bloomers to Flappers: The American Women's Dress Reform Movement, 1840–1920." Ph.D. diss., Ohio State University, 1998.

Lauer, Jeanette C., and Robert H. Lauer. "The Battle of the Sexes: Fashion in 19th Century America." *Journal of Popular Culture* 13: 4 (1980): 581–589.

Leach, William. *True Love and Perfect Union: The Feminist Reform of Sex and Society.* New York: Basic Books, 1980.

Nelson, Jennifer Ladd. "Dress Reform and the Bloomer." *Journal of American & Comparative Cultures* 23:1 (2000): 21–25.

Riegel, Robert E. "Women's Clothes and Women's Rights." *American Quarterly* 15:3 (1963): 390–401.

Steele, Valerie. *Fashion and Eroticism: Ideals of Feminine Beauty from the Victorian Era to the Jazz Age.* New York: Oxford University Press, 1985.

Matilda Joslyn Gage and Woman Suffrage History

Matilda Joslyn Gage was one of the preeminent leaders of the nineteenth-century women's rights movement. As an activist, speaker, and historian, she dedicated efforts on behalf of women's rights, which in large part are responsible for both the success of the movement and the preservation of its history. With Elizabeth Cady Stanton and Susan B. Anthony, she was a co-founder of the National Woman Suffrage Association (NWSA) in 1869 and over the next twenty years dominated its highest offices as chair of the executive committee, vice president, and president. She also founded and served as the president of the New York State Woman Suffrage Association during the same years. In addition, she owned and published the NWSA newspaper, the *National Citizen and Ballot Box,* and co-edited and wrote, with Stanton and Anthony, the first three volumes of the multivolume *History of Woman Suffrage* (1881–1887). After leaving the NWSA in a dispute over the 1890 merger with the American Woman Suffrage Association (AWSA), she joined with Stanton to write *The Woman's Bible* (1895) and published what would later be known as *Woman, Church and State* (1893).

The Syracuse Convention of 1852

Gage's story begins at one of the first conventions, where as one of the youngest attendees, she gathered her courage, took her daughter by the hand, and approached the podium. Unscheduled to speak, she was determined, however, to add her voice to the demand for women's rights. Waiting at the side of the stage for an opportune moment, she was soon beckoned forward by Lucretia Mott. "Trembling in every limb," she strode to the center of the stage to deliver the speech that would launch her onto the national stage and to the forefront of the women's rights movement, a cause to which she devoted the next fifty years of her life. Thus, the September 1852 Syracuse Women's

Rights Convention marked the entrance of Matilda Joslyn Gage into the struggle for this new reform.

She began her speech, "This convention has assembled to discuss the subject of women's rights, and form some settled plan of action for the future." Although a newcomer to the organized women's rights movement, her roots in the reforms of the age were strong and deep. The only child of Dr. Hezekiah and Helen Leslie Joslyn, Matilda Electra Joslyn was born in Cicero, New York, in 1826 into a household bristling with the reform imperative. Upstate New York during those years was the center of the action. Called "the burned over district" because of its enthusiasm for the waves of religious revivals that swept along the newly opened Erie Canal, the area was a hotbed of social reform activity. In this fertile soil, abolition and women's rights grew deep roots.

Family Ties to Social Reform

The Joslyn home opened its doors to local abolitionists, served as a stop on the Underground Railroad, and was a hub of political organizing and publishing. Her father, along with Elizabeth Cady Stanton's husband, organized the antislavery Liberty Party, which later become one strand of the liberal political parties that would coalesce into the Republican Party. He was also the publisher of *The State League,* newspaper of the Carson League, the local temperance association. The young Matilda was encouraged to stay and listen to the lively strategy meetings, which came to be among the clearest memories of her childhood. As a child and young woman, she was educated at home by her father in such subjects as physiology, Greek, and mathematics. At sixteen she entered the Clinton Liberal Institute in Clinton, New York, to complete her education in anticipation of entering medical school. Dr. Joslyn himself petitioned his alma mater, the Geneva Medical School, in 1843 and 1844 on her behalf, but she was rejected both times because she was a woman. Only a few short years later, that barrier would finally yield to Elizabeth Blackwell. Frustrated by these rejections, however, at the age of eighteen, Miss Matilda Electa Joslyn chose a more conventional path and married Henry Hill Gage, a Cicero merchant, on January 6, 1845, and settled in Fayetteville, New York.

History Offers a Usable Past

Following in the footsteps of her parents, Gage combined devotion to her family and devotion to women's rights into a single seamless garment. In fact, much of her ardor stemmed from her determination to open for her daughters doors that had been closed to her. This also accounts in large part for the two-pronged vision she brought to the women's rights cause. The first was her focus on economic independence for women, and the second was her enduring belief that the key to unlocking women's future was a clear understanding of women's past. She brought both of these perspectives to her first speech. In her judgment, women's situation was an historic construct needing radical reconstruction. She rejected arguments that women should remain in a position akin to "the vassalage in which much of mankind had been kept" in previous centuries. Women's position was not and should not be considered any more static or immutable than the situation of other formerly dependent groups. Gage argued against the view that women occupied an ordained sphere because of their gender. She also argued against the prevailing wisdom that women occupied that position because they were incapable of occupying other spheres. Her historian's eye brought a usable past to the to the women's movement that gave witness to the many accomplishments of women in other times, in other places, and under other circumstances. To those who said women could not, she spoke of women who had governed nations from Queen Semiramis to Victoria, scientists like Helena Lucretia Corano and Caroline Herschell, and literary giants such as Sappho and Margaret Fuller. Evidence of women's genius could be found, she asserted, in every avenue of learning.

Her impatience with entrenched orthodoxy was clear as she asked, "How can this mental and moral lethargy, which so binds the generality of women, be shaken off?!" Her answer, "Self reliance is one of the first lessons to be taught our daughters; they should be educated with our sons and equally with them taught to look forward to some independent means of support." Explicitly, she gave witness to the idea that educated women could and must use, manipulate, and interpret the wisdom of the past in their own self-interest. To these ideals she would devote the rest of her life.

Mott was so impressed by Gage's speech that she included it with the other speeches printed and sold to support the cause. Further enhancing her reputation as a gifted new advocate, Gage capably defended the goals of the convention in the editorial pages of the Syracuse newspapers from the derisive venom of local clergyman, Rev. Bryon Sunderland, and others eager to ridicule it. As a result, she quickly moved to the forefront of the women's rights movement.

Civil War Unity and Reformer Division

Gage joined forces with the founder of the movement, Elizabeth Cady Stanton, and another newcomer at the 1852 convention, Susan B. Anthony. The three leaders (later referred to by their contemporaries as the "triumvirate") set the agenda, planned the strategies, and wrote the history of their movement. In the years prior to the Civil War, however, all three were active in a broad spectrum of reform causes, including abolition and temperance, as well as women's rights. The end of the war, however, brought schism to the reform associations. Many women, among them, Stanton, Anthony, and Gage, hoped that with the end of the war and the end of slavery the complete prewar reform agenda would be written into the Constitution. When it became clear that women's rights, including suffrage, were expected to yield to narrower constitutional change, they were outraged. People like Lucy Stone and her husband, Henry Brown Blackwell, argued that it was the "Negro's hour." Stanton argued back, "Do you think all Negroes are men?" Debate over support for the proposed amendments tore what turned out to be the last meeting of the American Equal Rights Association (AERA) apart. As Stone, Blackwell, and other like-minded reformers left Washington, Stanton, Gage, and Anthony gathered to form a new association—one that would be wholly dedicated to women's rights. Of course, there were charges from the Stone-Blackwell faction that the "triumvirate" had waited until they left to call their meeting to purposely leave them out. Anthony denied that was the case but the damage was done. The rancor of the AERA meeting and the perceived snub tore the reformers apart. Stone, Blackwell, and other Boston-area reformers responded by forming their own woman suffrage association, the American Woman

Suffrage Association (AWSA). The two groups remained estranged from and antagonistic toward one another for the next twenty years.

With the birth of the new association, Gage plunged back into the work with renewed vigor. Free of the divided mission of the AERA, she was able to devote all of her energies to the cause of women's rights. A talented organizer, Gage had as one of her first tasks to draw up a plan for organizing state auxiliaries of the NWSA. Historian Ellen Carol DuBois judged her plan for New York State in *Feminism and Suffrage: The Emergence of an Independent Women's Movement in America, 1848–1869* (1978) as "ambitious. It called for vice presidents from each of New York's sixty counties and an advisory council composed of one woman from each of the state's thirteen congressional districts. "Friends," Gage admitted, "this is work. . . ." Within a few years, however, Gage's plan became the pattern for suffrage associations throughout the country.

THE NATIONAL CITIZEN AND BALLOT BOX

The new association also turned its attention to publishing. The general circulation press was at best indifferent to their cause and at worst antagonistic. Throughout its short, stormy history, Gage was a regular contributor to the *Revolution*. After its demise, she became the proprietor of the new NWSA newspaper, the *National Citizen and Ballot Box (NCBB)*. Published monthly from May 1878 to October 1881, it was "the recognized exponent of the views of the National Woman Suffrage Association" and listed Susan B. Anthony and Elizabeth Cady Stanton on the masthead as corresponding editors and Gage as editor and publisher. Its stated mission was as follows:

> As the first process towards becoming well is to know you are ill, one of the principal aims of the *National Citizen* is to make those women discontented who are now content—to waken them to self respect, and a desire to use the talents they possess—to educate their consciences aright to quicken their sense of duty—to destroy morbid beliefs and make them worthy of the life with which their Creator has endowed them.

Each edition's news and articles can be organized under seven broad categories: NWSA news, national politics, New York State politics, Gage's editorials, news and commentary from Stanton and Anthony, foreign news and correspondence, and consciousness raising. NWSA news commanded the front page with calls to conventions, reports of testimony before con-

gressional committees, convention minutes and speeches, and other NWSA business. Convention reports were especially important to women who could not attend the conventions. These reports, filled with detailed descriptions of each session and speeches reprinted in full, gave women around the country a sense of being part of an important movement. Lists of delegates familiarized them with convention regulars and, perhaps, like-minded women from their own state or county.

Gage's editorials were the heart and soul of the *NCBB* and clustered around five themes—citizenship and government, women and religion, personal politics, suffrage victories, and agonizing suffrage defeats. From her first public debate with Rev. Sunderland in the Syracuse newspapers, Gage was famous for her well-crafted arguments on behalf of women's rights against all comers, especially the clergy, "boxing them around with their own theology." The *NCBB* would give her a regular forum. She purchased the paper from Sarah Williams and changed its name from the *Ballot Box* to the *National Citizen and Ballot Box*. This was to underscore her continued support for the position that under the definition of national citizenship and equal protection contained in the Fourteenth Amendment, suffrage had been conferred upon women as national citizens. Although this argument had been denied in *Minor v. Happersett* (1874), her first editorial revisited the Court's claim that the national citizenship created in the Fourteenth Amendment did not imply national suffrage for all citizens to question the four (later six and then nine) classes of federally empowered voters. "If," she demanded, "states' rights took precedence over federal law with regard to something so basic to citizenship as the right to vote, what rights then did national citizenship confer; for what was the Civil War fought?"

For Gage, a woman who had been raised to think for herself, any mindless reliance on the interpretations of others was heresy. Uncowed by pontiffs, prelates, or politicians, she authored three anti-church resolutions for the Thirtieth Anniversary Convention in Rochester, New York, and then defended them in the *NCBB*. The Rochester Resolutions stated, in sum, that woman's first duty was to herself, as was the first duty of every individual; that woman had the right to individual conscience, in the spirit of the great principle of the Protestant Reformation; and that the perversion of the religious element in woman by priestcraft and superstition was the reason for her subjugation. The resolutions raised the usual furor in the general circulation press and in pulpits around the

To promote feminist reforms, including a constitutional amendment granting women the right to vote, Susan B. Anthony, Elizabeth Cady Stanton, Matilda Joslyn Gage, and others founded the National Woman Suffrage Association in 1869. This illustration from *Harper's Weekly* shows a packed organizing meeting. *(Brown Brothers)*

country. To her readers she instructed, "Oh woman! Be wise; study for yourself, act for yourself, *interpret* for yourself."

NWSA had been forged in the white-hot furnace of abandonment in the battle over the Fifteenth Amendment, and Gage was determined that it would not happen again. "Women," she argued, "do not work for any party that does not recognize the exact and equal rights of women with men, industrial and political. Work for your *own* political rights!" Anticipating the contemporary women's rights movement by nearly a century, she argued against impolitic alliances with parties across the spectrum of the nineteenth-century political landscape. To overtures from the Labor Party she replied, "[The Labor Party] has no woman suffrage plank and it does not include among its concerns that woman is paid only one-half, sometimes one-third as much as man for equal work."

To Gage, the personal was political. On July 4, 1879, she decorated her home in Fayetteville, New York, with funeral bunting and a sign proclaiming in bold letters: GOVERNMENTS DERIVE THEIR JUST POWERS FROM THE CONSENT OF THE GOVERNED. WOMAN HAS NOT CONSENTED. Of her readers she asked, "How many of you thus protested? Such opportunity lies in the hands of all." Determined to make the women's movement move, she lent her guidance to the women of Fayetteville organizing and electing a full slate of pro-suffrage women to the local school board, including her daughter. The resulting editorial offered a winning model for political campaigning, including sending carriages to bring women without transportation to the polls.

ACTIVISM ON THE NATIONAL STAGE

As an activist, Gage's stature derived in part from her role in a number of NWSA's more publicly visible and dramatic moments. In 1872, a small group of highly placed Washington women led by the wives of General William Tecumseh Sherman and Admiral John A. Dahlgren began publishing tracts against woman suffrage and presented a proposal to Congress for a Sixteenth Amendment regulating marriage and restricting divorce. With NWSA's annual Washington convention approaching, Gage, as chair on Arrangement, immediately invited Mrs. Dahlgren, leader of the group, to come and debate the issues with them. "Nothing would afford the officers [of the NWSA] . . . greater pleasure than to hold a debate with yourself and your friends." She even promised Elizabeth Cady Stanton would enter the lists. As she expected, they demurred, citing their "female modesty" prevented them from so public an event. Congress was, apparently, less formidable a venue than a NWSA convention.

Later that same year, Anthony determined that the time had come to test a woman citizen's right to vote, and she did so in Rochester. Stanton disapproved of the notion, but Gage offered enthusiastic support. Anthony was prosecuted by the federal government, but her recognition as a public figure forced a change in trial venue to neighboring Ontario County. Gage wrote a speech for herself, and wrote Anthony's speech "Is It a Crime for a United States Citizen to Vote?" and the two embarked on a whirlwind canvas of Ontario County in the weeks leading up to the trial.

The year 1876 was the nation's centennial, but where was citizenship for women? What did women have to celebrate? NWSA determined to ask just such questions. After the organizers of the Philadelphia ceremonies denied them a place in the official program, the NWSA officers decided to present their petition unofficially. They waited for an apt pause in the program and saw their chance as the last strains of the Brazilian National Anthem faded into the hot July breeze. Together Gage, Anthony, Sara Spencer, and Phoebe Couzins hustled to the podium and presented their Woman's Declaration of Rights.

Gage was one of many New York State Woman Suffrage Association (NYSWSA) women who saw the irony involved in the iconography of the Statue of Liberty. It was, she stormed, "the sarcasm of the nineteenth century to represent liberty as a woman, while not one single woman throughout the length and breadth of the land is as yet in possession of political liberty." The Statue of Liberty was scheduled for dedication in 1886, and the organizers made it clear that the women of the New York State Woman Suffrage Association were not welcome. "There will be no women in the gathering on the island, at least it is hoped not." Needless to say, President Gage and Vice President Lillie Devereux Blake rented a steamship,

raised their NYSWSA banners, barged into the official flotilla, and delivered their speeches.

A much weightier part of Gage's importance, however, rests on her scholarship. Gage was a pioneering advocate of women's history and a woman's historian. From her first speech in 1852, to the publication of her life's work, *Woman, Church and State,* in 1893, the guiding principle supporting her work was her belief that if women were educated in women's history, the debilitating doctrines of both church and state toward women would be exposed and ultimately overthrown. As William Leach wrote in *True Love and Perfect Union: The Feminist Reform of Sex and Society* (1980), she was "perhaps the most important of all nineteenth century feminist historians [who] ceaselessly mined the past for material on gifted women." The nation's centennial marked the beginning of conversations among the three NWSA leaders toward producing a pamphlet-sized history of their movement. The initial pamphlet they envisioned, however, grew to become the three original volumes of the *History of Woman Suffrage.* Anthony shouldered the administrative duties, and Stanton and Gage did the writing. All three organized the documents and artifacts of the first thirty years of their work. Begun in earnest in 1877, the volumes commanded much of the ensuing ten years to produce them. Gage's unique contribution to the project was her series of research-based essays on women's past that anchored each of the volumes. In addition to her work on the *History,* Gage began chronicling NWSA's current work in the *NCBB* during this same time period. As a result of this dual publishing effort, fully the first third of Volume III of the *History* can be traced to the pages of the *NCBB*.

Gage left the NWSA, only a few short years after the third volume of the *History* was published, in a heated dispute with Anthony over merging NWSA with the American Woman Suffrage Association (AWSA). For Gage, merger with the AWSA was an anathema, due to the organization's embrace of groups like the conservative Woman's Christian Temperance Union (WCTU). The WCTU and other conservative women's groups wanted votes for women in order to restrict American freedoms. Best known for its temperance crusades, the WCTU also supported amending the Constitution in order to proclaim God as the founder of nations and to allow the federal government to regulate marriage and further restrict divorce. Conservative women's groups had found a comfortable home in the AWSA. Gage was determined they would find no such succor in NWSA and had no interest in creating a hybrid organization that would do just that. Unfortunately, despite her best efforts the merger was effected, leaving her no choice but to leave the association to which she had given so much of her life.

The years after leaving the NWSA until her death in 1898 were some of Gage's most productive years in a career noted for its productivity. Initially, she and her supporters founded a new women's rights association, the explicitly anti-church Woman's National Liberal Union (WNLU), and began publishing another newspaper, *The Liberal Thinker*. Although the excitement of a new organization was exhilarating and she thoroughly enjoyed attracting all the usual denunciations from the pulpit and press to which NWSA had become a stranger and the NAWSA would never know, she was drawn to the task of compiling a lifetime of research.

In a letter to her son, Thomas Clarkson Gage, she described the revelation that became the dominant theme of her work. "I did not at first think of attacking the foundations of the church itself, but I was thinking one day when a sudden light came into my mind, an illumination, which said *the church* and then I knew it was right. I thought it all carefully over and I knew I meant *the church* itself and I said so." The church's antagonism toward women's equality, she realized, was not incidental to its teachings but the very foundation of its beliefs, from which all its other teachings derived. This thesis, first expressed publicly in her speech "The Dangers of the Hour," delivered at the WNLU convention, articulated this idea. "Wherever we find laws of the state bearing with greater hardship upon woman than upon man, we shall ever find them due to the teachings of the church." In her analysis it was a universal truth and she used it as the foundation of her research. Freed from the demands of the NWSA and her own WNLU, she began her most important writing task.

Woman, Church and State stands alone. Although the woman suffrage movement moved on words; through its speeches, newspapers, petitions, and resolutions; *Woman, Church and State* is the only monograph written by a nineteenth-century suffragist. Gage had a twofold purpose in mind when she published it. First, she intended to disprove the conflicting myths promulgated by the church that decreed that "God designed the subjugation of woman, and yet that her position has been higher under Christianity than ever before." Second, she wanted to inspire women to "read history for [themselves], and having read it, dare to draw [their] own conclusions from its

premises." Published in the summer of 1893, it drew savage attacks. Anthony Comstock, noted crusader against vice, declared he would "prosecute any school board that put it in their library." Publicly Gage responded to his attack in a statement that reads in part, "I look upon him as a man who is mentally and morally unbalanced, not knowing right from wrong, or the facts of history from 'tales of lust.' " Privately, she thought it was "all right splendid for the book. All it now needs is to get into the *Papal Index Expurgetorius!*" A month before her death she was too ill to attend NAWSA's Fiftieth Anniversary celebration of the Seneca Falls convention but was delighted that her book was hailed by Anna Howard Shaw. "[Praise for *Woman, Church and State*] must have been a *bomb* in that pious convention!" Grounded in its own time, *Woman, Church and State* argued issues that remain remarkably current, anticipating all of the important issues of the twentieth-century women's movement.

The legacy of Gage's life can be found in the causes she espoused, the events she lived and chronicled, and the history she wrote. In arguments that are as relevant today as they were a century ago, she arrayed her evidence and encouraged women to read and interpret history for themselves and on their own behalf. By so doing, she transcended the limited reform agenda of woman suffrage to leave a map toward tomorrow for all women. As a historian, Gage was acutely aware that the past could unlock the future when she predicted, "A brighter day is to come for the world, a day when the intuitions of woman's soul shall be accepted as part of humanity's spiritual wealth; when force shall step backward, and love, in reality, rule the teachings of religion; and may woman be strong in the ability and courage necessary to bring about this millennial time."

Mary E. Corey

BIBLIOGRAPHY

Barry, Kathleen. *Susan B. Anthony: A Biography of a Singular Feminist.* New York: New York University Press, 1988.

Brown, Olympia. *Papers of Olympia Brown.* Women's Studies Manuscript Collections from the Schlesinger Library. Bethesda, MD: University Publications of America, 1988. Microfilm.

Corey, Mary E. *Matilda Joslyn Gage: Woman Suffrage Historian, 1852–1898.* Ann Arbor, MI: UMI, 1995.

DuBois, Ellen Carol. *Feminism and Suffrage: The Emergence of an Independent Women's Movement in America, 1848–1869.* Ithaca, NY: Cornell University Press, 1978.

Gage, Matilda Joslyn. *Papers of Matilda Joslyn Gage.* Women's Studies Manuscript Collections from the Schlesinger Library. Bethesda, MD: University Publications of America, 1988. Microfilm.

Griffith, Elisabeth. *In Her Own Right: The Life of Elizabeth Cady Stanton.* New York: Oxford University Press, 1984.

Holland, Patricia G., and Ann D. Gordon, eds. *Papers of Elizabeth Cady Stanton and Susan B. Anthony.* Wilmington, DE: Scholarly Resources, 1989. Microfilm.

Leach, William. *True Love and Perfect Union: The Feminist Reform of Sex and Society.* New York: Basic Books, 1980.

Records of the National American Woman Suffrage Associations, Manuscript Division, Library of Congress, 1975. Microfilm.

Stanton, Elizabeth Cady, Susan B. Anthony, and Matilda Joslyn Gage, eds. *History of Woman Suffrage.* Vols. 1–4. Reprint ed. Salem, NH: Ayer, 1985.

POPULAR HEALTH MOVEMENT

As in many social movements, the Popular Health movement was not one coherent movement with a definitive beginning or ending. Rather, it was composed of several health belief systems that shared a strong antipathy to the elitism of regular medicine, a belief that people could and should make a difference in their own health, and an emphasis on both preventative care and more gentle treatments. The anti-elitist philosophy opened the doors for alternative practitioners as well as alternative practices, and women quickly moved into the ranks of lecturers, healers, authors, and teachers. Although certain individual women such as Harriot Kezia Hunt, Paulina Wright Davis, and Lydia Folger Fowler have been placed in historical record, the majority of women who participated in the Popular Health movement remain nameless. Further research into their contributions would be immensely valuable in understanding how this movement affected the lived experiences of American families during the 1830s and 1840s.

The specific movements included Thomsonian Botanics, homeopathy, Grahamites, and hydropathy, and shared many ideologies even while differing in philosophies concerning the role of the trained practitioner. The separate movements overlapped in time, reaching a critical mass in the 1830s and 1840s. The Popular Health movement resisted the increasing elitism of medical knowledge, urging instead that the public be taught about good health practices and the causation of disease. Although regular medicine demanded "heroic" treatments such as bloodletting and purging, many Popular Health movement healers emphasized the belief that citizens could heal themselves through a healthier lifestyle, regular exercise, a vegetarian diet, and the restorative power of water.

AMERICAN CULTURE IN THE 1830s AND 1840s

To understand the acceptance and drive for the Popular Health movement, it is helpful to understand several cultural shifts in the United States and, more specifically, within the American medical establishment during the 1830s and 1840s. The period in general was dominated by an anti-elitist sentiment as well as the belief in romantic reform and differing responses to modernization, including a new view of motherhood as serving a "Republican" role in raising patriot citizens.

During this period in history, the twin forces of modernization and industrialization were changing the average community and household. More married and single youth moved into urban centers, while increased immigration changed the "face" of America. For some reformers, nostalgia for close-knit rural communities, combined with a fear of the new commercialism, may have given extra urgency to their call for tight control over the health of "the body." This control, however, was located internally rather than externally. Echoing the move from monarchy to democracy, a theme of self-governance and freedom from the control of those "above" dominated this time period.

The anti-elitism of this era found its most prominent example in the presidency of Andrew Jackson (1829–1837), who was known as the "people's president." History has clearly shown that Jackson did not believe in freedom for all in the United States, but his overt rhetoric was one of full citizen participation. A large population explosion, combined with subsequent legal and social changes, brought greater opportunity to citizens: the right to vote, or "suffrage," was granted to all white men during the 1820s and 1830s; labor forces began to form proto-unions, gaining the first workhour reduction in 1835; and education supported by the state began to spread to children, especially in Northern states. The dream of an equal voice for all citizens seemed more possible than ever before in the United States.

ROMANTIC REFORM AND DISEASE ETIOLOGY

Large-scale migration and modernization often led to a feeling of being disconnected from what went before. There was a feeling of presentism, of immediacy, and of the empowerment of individuals; no longer were the elite or communal bodies the only ones able to enact change. Many of the leaders of the Popular Health movement were simply individuals from a variety of economic and social backgrounds who vigorously advanced an idea of better health for all. This philosophy, coupled with a population disillusioned about the possibility of healing from regularly trained physicians, formed the genesis of the health reform movement. In addition, the new belief that disease was not sent from God—that it was determined by human action and therefore could be prevented or alleviated through human action—allowed for greater focus on preventative care a century before sweeping changes were seen in hygienic practices around water and sanitation.

The history of American medicine has often been one of conflict over who was qualified to heal, echoing the debate between the Founding Fathers about whether the American people were fit to govern themselves or if an educated elite should "care" for them. The needs of a new country necessitated that healing be done by whoever was available—ministers, Native American herbalists, midwives, and the few doctors who had been educated before immigrating. The sharp distinctions in European societies between physician, surgeon, and apothecary were lost because most communities were too small to have separate healing practitioners, and resident healers were called upon to perform all three services. As the colonies gained in wealth, some practitioners were able to go abroad for training, teaching others when they returned. The first formal medical school did not open until 1765, in Philadelphia, and by 1830, only twenty-two medical schools were available to students.

This democracy born of necessity was quickly challenged. Those who could afford training, whether domestically or in Europe, began to distinguish themselves from other healers. A drive for licensure began in the mid-1700s, and by 1800, many states had licensing laws for physicians, creating the first official distinction between healers with formalized training, known as "regulars," and herbalists, home healers, midwives, and other domestic healers who came to be known as the "irregulars." At their extremes, regulars and irregulars differed in philosophy, diagnosis, and, most often, in treatment.

One characteristic of regular medicine was a focus on aggressive treatment of disease, known as "heroic medicine." Lynn Payer, in her work *Medicine and Culture: Varieties of Treatment in the United States, England, West Germany, and France* (1988), speaks of this style of healing made popular by Benjamin Rush—"the Father of American Medicine"—as related to the "toughness" required to "conquer" the wilderness of a "new frontier." As Americans were more able to withstand the hardships of creating a country, so their bodies should be more capable of withstanding harsher, more aggressive treatments. Bloodletting, or "bleeding" a patient, was common, as was induced vomiting or purging. A misunderstanding of the volume of blood held in the human body often caused the physician to allow up to a third of the patient's blood to flow out through cuts or leeches. This and the harsh drugs used to purge the patient sometimes precipitated the patient's death. In contrast, the more gentle treatments of the Popular Health movement did little to harm patients, while encouraging a building up of health through preventative measures such as diet reform and exercise.

THE POPULAR HEALTH MOVEMENT

The Popular Health movement is most commonly seen as comprising four philosophies: the teachings of Sylvester Graham, Thomsonian botanics, homeopathy, and hydropathy. In addition, individual health reformers who lived in the middle of these established theories combined elements of two or more of these philosophies to create their own local, eclectic system of healing. Several themes mark them as part of "the Popular Health movement": a rejection of heroic medicine and an emphasis on more gentle treatment; a belief in the body's ability to heal itself if properly cared for; a passion for educating the public about their own health and fitness; and, for most, a focus on patients from the lower to middle class. The final element that characterized the movements was a tendency to split into subgroups once the movement had gained a larger following. Differences in theory on whether to remain completely separate from regular medicine or to incorporate some of the more moderate regular treatments diluted the original tenets of "alternative" healing, but may also have permitted elements of the theory to survive the end of the Popular Health movement by being absorbed into the practices of regular doctors.

Best remembered today for the "graham cracker" named after him, Sylvester Graham (1794–1851) was an early and controversial figure in nineteenth-century health reform. His lectures promoting vegetarianism, a strict regimen of whole bran bread and plain drink, often led to riotous protests by local butchers, bakers, and grain-growers, while others dismissed his views as excessive and old-fashioned. Following a new social emphasis on sexual purity, he lectured for control both inside and outside of marriage, preaching that any form of sexual stimulation would lead to debility. It was Graham who wrote the first in a long American tradition of tracts detailing the dangers of masturbation on young people's bodies and characters in his "Lecture to Young Men" (1834).

Graham himself died at a relatively young age and became a figure of some ridicule for the extremity of his beliefs. Nonetheless, he popularized many health concepts which are widely accepted today: the health benefits of regular bathing, well-ventilated living areas, regular exercise, a diet high in vegetables and fiber and low in meat intake, and clothing that is not excessively confining. His ideas also had a great influence on subsequent movements, several of which simply modified his more radical ideas and created a more "palatable" health regimen.

Basically a refined system of herbalism, Thomsonian Botanics became an immensely popular method for citizens to heal themselves and their families. Samuel Thomson learned herbalism from a local unnamed female healer who attended his family. His studies with her convinced him of the healing properties of simple combinations of herbs, which he turned into a patented system of healing. In 1806, he began to sell "family rights" to his ideas for the price of $20; by 1813, he had patented his system, and by 1820, he had issued a publication called "New Guide to Health," which he also published in German for recent immigrants. Scholar Ronald Numbers reports in his 1977 essay on sectarian medicine that "by 1840 approximately 100,000 Family Rights had been sold, and Thomson estimated that about three million persons had adopted his system."

What set Thomson apart from most other sectarians was his genuine desire to educate the public in such a way that they would no longer need the aid of regular doctors. The Thomsonian mantra of "every man his own physician" illustrated his belief that citizens should be equipped to think and to care for themselves.

As was often the case, however, a split in theory developed. Although Thomson believed that each person could be his or her own doctor, other practitioners of Thomsonian Botanics felt that a formally educated medical practitioner was a necessary addition to the home health guides. Amidst bitter debate, these practitioners opened their own Botanic medical schools in the late 1830s. Despite the advantages of safety, cost-effectiveness, convenience, and the modesty afforded women in caring for themselves, the movement became divided and eventually began to lose popularity in the 1840s.

HOMEOPATHY AND HYDROPATHY

First refined in Germany by Samuel Hahnemann (1755–1843), homeopathy followed two laws: the law of similars (like cures like) and the law of infinitesimals (the more dilute the dose, the stronger the effectiveness of the drug). Highly popular in Germany, it was brought to the United States in 1825 by Hans Gram, an American medical student who had studied in Denmark, and it was later expanded by Gram's disciple John F. Gray. Early practitioners were either converted by Gram and Gray or were themselves German homeopathic physicians who immigrated to treat the large German population in Pennsylvania and the Midwest. Domestic kits containing instructions and diluted formulas of medicines were available for sale by the early 1830s. During the period of the Popular Health movement, homeopathy was utilized largely by the lower economic classes. The reason may have been that they were more able to afford treatment or that, as recent German immigrants, they preferred a healing system that was probably more familiar to them. As a national phenomenon, homeopathy did not begin to attract large numbers of practitioners until the 1850s, when it began to move into the middle classes. By the 1870s and 1880s, scholar Hans Baer believes that it had become the most influential heterodox medical system in the United States.

Homeopathy was especially popular with women because the medicines were considered extremely safe for both babies and older children. Even allopathic doctors agreed that homeopathic remedies would do little to no harm to patients; at the very most they might slow healing if the home practitioner took the wrong medicine. The slow healing alone made it preferable to the regular medical practice of the day. However, some homeopathic practitioners began to believe that at times more active treatment of a patient might be advantageous. This belief split the movement into two distinct ideologies: "mixers" or "low-potency" (less dilute) practitioners who advocated combining homeopathy with more allopathic diagnoses and treatments, and the "purists" or "high-potency" (more dilute) practitioners who maintained Hahnemann's original theory of using only extremely dilute homeopathic treatments.

The latest of the sects in the Popular Health movement, hydropathy, did not arrive in the United States until the mid-1840s. Three prominent health practitioners—two regularly trained physicians, Joel Shew and Russell Trall, and one female health reformer, Mary Gove Nichols—opened water cure businesses in New York City in the early 1840s. Gove Nichols set the stage for the active involvement of women in hydropathy; eventually, a large percentage of practitioners were female. A cross-fertilization of ideologies also drew in feminists interested in dress reform and in demolishing the monopoly of health provision by male doctors.

Hydropaths provided water cure clinics, books, and the *Water Cure Journal*, a periodical dedicated to spreading hydropathy to those who were unable to access a clinic. Like the early Thomsonians, many leaders in the hydropathic sect, including those who were regularly trained doctors, hoped eventually to make doctors obsolete except in treating the most extreme cases.

Another distinction of hydropathy is that it survived the demise of the Popular Health movement. When Ellen G. White, the prophetess of the Seventh-Day Adventist Church, found that hydropathy cured her two young sons of their high fevers and sore throats, she began to spread the message throughout the church. Out of this came the Battle Creek Sanitarium presided over by one of White's protégés named John Harvey Kellogg, brother to the cereal business czar.

LADIES' PHYSIOLOGICAL SOCIETIES

Beginning during the Popular Health movement, Ladies' Physiological Societies held "conversationals" about various health topics, including anatomy and physiology, nutrition, exercise, personal hygiene, dress reform, the evils of "self-pollution" (a Victorian codeword for masturbation), drug-free childbirth, midwifery and limiting family size. They were attended primarily by white, married or widowed, nonemployed women who could afford to pay the annual dues to attend. A wide variety of speakers, ranging from doctors to health reformers to the women themselves, presented information, answered questions, and took part in discussions. Although limited to the middle class, these conversationals contributed to the health education of women and set a precedent for the consciousness-raising groups of the 1970s Feminist Women's Health movement.

CONCLUSION

The Popular Health movement formed the first of what scholar Ruth Engs has called "Clean Living movements"—large-scale social movements, often tied into moral belief systems, which run in roughly eighty year cycles to decrease substance abuse and increase health and fitness in the population. The first Clean Living movement, which Engs places from 1830 to 1860, includes the Popular Health movement and focuses on temperance, tobacco, fitness, eugenics, nativism, diet, and Christian physiology.

In extending the date beyond the Popular Health movement, Engs includes the reform movements of the Seventh-Day Adventists led by Ellen G. White in promoting the Water Cure movement (1860s), spiritism (1850s), and osteopathy (1860s). Post–Civil War healing movements such as the systems of New Thought healing groups (1880s and 1890s), Mary Baker Eddy and Christian Science (1880s and 1890s), and chiropractics (1890s) also shared in the Popular Health movement's concern that health be made available to all.

Paula Jayne

BIBLIOGRAPHY

Baer, Hans A. *Biomedicine and Alternative Healing Systems in America: Issues of Class, Race, Ethnicity, and Gender.* Madison: University of Wisconsin Press, 2001.

Cassedy, James H. "Why Self Help? Americans Alone with Their Diseases, 1800–1850." In *Medicine Without Doctors: Home Health Care in American History,* eds. Guenter B. Risse, Ronald Numbers, and Judith Walzer Leavitt. New York: Science History Publications, 1977.

Engs, Ruth Clifford. *Clean Living Movements: American Cycles of Health Reform.* Westport, CT: Praeger, 2000.

Morantz, Regina. "Nineteenth Century Health Reform and Women." In *Medicine Without Doctors: Home Health Care in American History,* eds. Guenter B. Risse, Ronald Numbers, and Judith Walzer Leavitt. New York: Science History Publications, 1977.

Morantz-Sanchez, Regina. "Chapter Two: The Middle-Class Woman Finds Health Reform." In *Sympathy and Science: Women Physicians in American Medicine.* New York: Oxford University Press, 1985.

Nissenbaum, Stephen. *Sex, Diet, and Debility in Jacksonian America: Sylvester Graham and Health Reform.* Westport, CT: Greenwood Press, 1980.

Numbers, Ronald L. "Do-It-Yourself the Sectarian Way." In *Medicine Without Doctors: Home Health Care in American History,* eds. Guenter B. Risse, Ronald Numbers, and Judith Walzer Leavitt. New York: Science History Publications, 1977.

Payer, Lynn. *Medicine and Culture*: *Varieties of Treatment in the United States, England, West Germany, and France.* New York: Henry Holt & Company, 1988.

Rothstein, William. *American Physicians in the Nineteenth Century: From Sects to Science.* Baltimore, MD: Johns Hopkins University Press, 1972.

Shryock, Richard. "Sylvester Graham and the Popular Health Movement." *Mississippi Valley Historical Review* 19 (1931): 172–183.

Sokolow, Jayme. A. *Eros and Modernization: Sylvester Graham, Health Reform and the Origins of Victorian Sexuality in America.* Rutherford, NJ: Fairleigh Dickinson University Press, 1983.

Verbrugge, Martha H. "The Social Meaning of Personal Health: The Ladies' Physiological Institute of Boston & Vicinity in the 1850's." In *Health Care in America: Essays in Social History*, eds. Susan Reverby and David Rosner. Philadelphia: Temple University Press, 1979.

Walters, Ronald G. "Introduction: The Body and Beyond." *American Reformers: 1815–1860.* New York: Hill and Wang, 1978.

Weisman, Carol. "The Women's Health Megamovement." In *Women's Health Care: Activist Traditions and Institutional Change.* Baltimore, MD: Johns Hopkins University Press, 1998.

Whorton, James C. *Crusaders for Fitness: The History of American Health Reformers.* Princeton, NJ: Princeton University Press, 1982.

Women's Cooperative Housekeeping Movement

Cooperative Housekeeping is one of the major women's social reform movements that transformed American culture from the nineteenth century into the twentieth century by making it acceptable within the dominant gender ideology for women to have public professions, institutions, and businesses. Reformers made these new women's professions and public cooperative housekeeping enterprises acceptable in the dominant gender ideology by claiming that they were natural extensions of women's household roles. Women's public-domestic professions and institutions changed the gender system by conflating and combining the supposedly separate female domestic sphere with the male public sphere. Public cooperative housekeeping enterprises materially increased the visibility of women on public landscapes and showed that women could contribute to the public good as citizens before female suffrage was attained.

In the public cooperative housekeeping movement reform, women transformed private unpaid domestic tasks into paid public professions in institutions and businesses founded and operated by women for women. Housekeeping cooperatives replaced women's individual repetitive performance of housework in isolated male-dominated homes with shared performance of housework by a group of women in public institutions or businesses. Household tasks were more efficiently performed through cooperation, in some cases through division of women's labor into different specialized tasks.

FOUNDING

Public housekeeping cooperatives were founded by women for economic and political reasons. The main goal of public housekeeping cooperatives was to transform private unpaid household labor into new women's public professions that would be equivalent in status and remuneration to men's professions. New female professions created in public cooperative housekeeping institutions by reform women included nurses, dieticians, nutritionists, social workers, public health workers, kindergarten teachers, day care providers, kitchen garden teachers, playground supervisors, domestic science teachers, home economics teachers, and librarians.

The professionalization of women's domestic tasks was symbolized and implemented with professional training courses and schools that used special, often scientific, equipment. Professional schools employed women *in* the professions to educate other women *for* those professions. The need to professionally educate women was an instrumental argument for founding women's colleges and opening up federally funded institutions of higher education to women.

Educated middle-class women created housekeeping cooperatives so that they would have time for intellectual and reform activities. They also sought to alleviate working women's double burden of work and housework by founding child-care and cooking cooperatives for working families.

Some community cooperatives were organized by middle-class women to facilitate their own housekeeping. The most numerous type of middle-class community cooperative was the dining club, in which ladies volunteered in organizing paid servants to produce meals for club members that were either eaten at the dining club house or delivered to members' homes. The latter were usually called cooked-food delivery services, and in a few cases were organized by working-class women.

FORMS OF COOPERATIVE WORK

Most public cooperative housekeeping enterprises were organized by middle-class reformers to assist working-class women and their families. Many of these cooperatives were housed in social settlements, where unmarried reformers lived cooperatively while

One of the goals of the women's cooperative housekeeping movement was to break down barriers that blocked women from entering various professions. This early-twentieth-century photograph shows women working as telephone switchboard operators, a job formerly dominated by men. *(Brown Brothers)*

offering a variety of programs to the surrounding poor, usually immigrant, and urban community. Housekeeping cooperatives organized by reform women and offered to working-class families included day nurseries, kindergartens, kitchen gardens, playgrounds, and public kitchens.

Day nurseries that provided physical care for young infants first appeared in the United States in New York City in 1854. Kindergartens were children's educational cooperatives initially founded by and for middle-class women. But more kindergartens were soon founded for working-class women, usually in settlements. Kindergartens used special toys to assist children in discovering the scientific order of nature. The kindergarten movement was founded in 1838 in Germany by Friedrich Froebel and in the United States in 1860 by Elizabeth Peabody of Boston.

Kitchen gardens were founded by Emily Huntington in 1875 in New York City to teach poor children middle-class housekeeping practices. Parents who perceived kitchen gardens as training for domestic service usually refused to send their daughters to be trained for this stigmatized profession. However, kitchen gardens were usually presented as training children of both sexes to help with housework at home, which was welcomed by most poor working parents.

The American playground movement developed out of a playground for young children founded in 1885 in Boston by the women of the Massachusetts Emergency and Hygiene Association. The playground for small children had a large sand box that was called a sand garden after those in Berlin visited by association member Dr. Maria Zakrzewska. Playgrounds offered cooperative child play supervised by kindergarten teachers. Photographs show that many playgrounds established in the yards of women's social settlements were racially integrated.

Public kitchens offered scientifically cooked food at cheap prices to the urban poor. Inspired by German Volkskitchens, the U.S. public kitchen movement was founded by Ellen Swallow Richards, the first female student and professor at the Massachusetts Institute of Technology. At public kitchens, reformers had to change their original Yankee menu and offer more ethnic foods to be patronized by poor immigrants for more than hot water and broth.

The most widespread type of cooperatives founded by middle-class women for working women were the cooperative homes for single working women, which offered a safe and pleasant alternative to boarding houses that charged high rents and offered single women no protection against the advances of male boarders in nearby rooms. The increasing number of single working women in cooperative homes indicated that women valued the cooperative facilities, such as laundries, libraries, gymnasiums, classes, and social clubs, as well as the lower costs compared to many commercial boardinghouses. At the same time, a number of single working women objected to restrictive rules imposed in some cooperative homes for working women, especially religious ones. In Chicago, middle-class reform women maternalistically running YWCAs responded to the objections of resident working women by loosening some rules, permitting more socialization with men in parlors, establishing resident governance bodies, and building more private single rooms.

The municipal housekeeping movement involved even larger-scale socialized housekeeping at the level of the entire community. Reform women made an analogy between the household and the community, and argued that women were needed as moral housekeepers and mothers for the entire community, to clean up the dirt in streets and factories that endangered their families, especially children, with a dirty and therefore unhealthy environment as well as corrupted products such as adulterated milk and butter.

The professionalization of women's domestic roles in the municipal housekeeping movement led male public officials to appoint women as municipal playground commissioners, board of education members, street inspectors, garbage inspectors, factory inspectors, juvenile justices, and juvenile probation officers.

Playgrounds were cooperative housekeeping spaces also founded by women's organizations for municipal housekeeping purposes because they were considered orderly natural green spaces associated with women and God. Therefore, playgrounds were considered a higher moral influence over children that could prevent them from falling into juvenile delinquency as a result of contact with the corrupting temptations on the streets of men's "sinful cities of stone," as reformers called them.

ORIGINS OF PUBLIC COOPERATIVES

The roots of women's public cooperative housekeeping institutions include traditions of family and neighborhood cooperation. The earliest predecessors to the movement are probably cooperative agrarian practices in which neighboring farm women worked together to accomplish tasks such as husking corn (called husking bees), sewing quilts (sewing bees), and spinning thread. The most popular nineteenth-century domestic manual, *The American Woman's Home*, by Catherine Beecher and Harriet Beecher Stowe, further advised women to organize their children to cooperate in housekeeping.

Other roots of women's public cooperative housekeeping institutions include communitarian ideologies and practices. People who felt they could not reform the entire society and culture withdrew to form perfect cooperative societies in miniature, sometimes with the hope they would be emulated by the society at large.

Early ideologies supporting cooperative housekeeping advocated communal living, including the ideal elite commune dependent on slave labor that was designed by Plato in *The Republic* in the fourth century B.C.E. and reproduced in St. Thomas More's *Utopia* (1516). Christian communal living ideals drawn from the apostolic commune in the Bible supported the development not only of monasteries but also of abbeys and nunneries in which women cooperated in housework as early as the eleventh century. Nuns and monks operated the earliest charitable community cooperatives, including almshouses and orphan asylums.

The communitarian ideology of Christianity became codified in law in the American colony of Puritan New England, which was a religious state. Laws against the sins of usury and price gouging were based on biblical principles. As men increasingly participated in the development of capitalism in the eighteenth century, the values and practices required for capitalistic success, including the sins of usury and unfair pricing, drew men away from the church.

The majority of church members became women, who maintained communitarian cooperative values and practices in the domestic sphere. Women came to be considered innately more pious and moral than men because their domestic sphere was closer to nature and God and removed from participation in sinful capitalistic practices. Thus, cooperative housekeeping and communal living were widely associated with Christian morality and with women.

In America, women's charitable organizations founded and operated cooperative housekeeping organizations to raise orphaned girls, called female orphan asylums, starting in the early nineteenth century. Women's charitable organizations also founded cooperative homes for poor or unemployed working-class women and elderly women.

Religious communes were often viewed by their members as the perfection of society—heavens on earth. A number of Christian heretical communes with cooperative housekeeping fled persecution in Europe to establish communes in America. Nineteen Shaker communes were established under the leadership of Ann Lee between 1774 and 1826, three Rappite Harmony society towns were founded by George Rapp between 1805 and 1824, seven Amana Inspirationist communes were established after 1854, and three communes of Oneida Perfectionists were founded by John H. Noyes between 1847 and 1878.

Many nineteenth-century communes were based on the European nonsectarian philosophy of communitarian socialism, which was inspired by the American Revolution. In the late eighteenth century, the idea that equality should apply to women as well as men was argued by feminists on the eve of the French Revolution, including Judith S. Murray in the United States in 1790, Olympe de Gouges in 1791 in France, and Mary Wollstonecraft in 1792 in England. Communitarian Socialists Count Henri de Saint-Simon and Charles Fourier argued that equality of the sexes could be attained through socialization of private housework into public cooperatives, as well as cooperative factory labor by workers. Charles Fourier stated that "The degree of emancipation of women is the natural measure of general emancipation."

Fourier's ideas, translated into English and inter-preted by his disciple Albert Brisbane, were implemented in a variety of what were called "Associationist experiments" or "Fourierist Phalanxes" in the United States and Europe, predominantly 1840 to 1860. The most impressive was the Familistere or Social Palace at Guise, France, erected by Fourierist Jean-Baptiste-André Godin starting in 1859. The complex of buildings housed several hundred iron workers and their families in apartments with private kitchens, but also included a cooperative dining hall, cooperative child-care center, and café. The most renowned Socialist communitarian experiments in America included fifteen Owenite communes (1820s–1830) founded by the wealthy industrialist John Owen, the racially integrated Nashoba commune (1827) founded by feminist Frances Wright, Brook Farm (1841–1846) founded by unitarian minister George Ripley, and thirty Fourierist Associations (1840–1960), which combined science and religion.

In communes, cooperative housekeeping was often facilitated by inventions. The Shakers invented a washing machine, the common clothespin, an apple peeler and corer, a pea sheller, a cheese press, a round oven, and a conical stove for heating irons. At the Social Palace in Guise, France, reformers created bathtubs with adjustable bottoms for children or adults, laundry tubs that expelled water by spinning, and innovations in heating, lighting, and ventilation. The Oneida perfectionists used the latest heating, lighting, and sanitation devices, and invented an improved washing machine, a mop wringer, an institutional potato peeler, and a "lazy susan" to facilitate food service.

Outside of communes, women reformers proposed and implemented cooperative housekeeping businesses and institutions in communities. Women's public cooperative housekeeping enterprises comprised the first pay-for-housework movement. The reformers advocated removing aspects of housework from the home and transforming them into paid public professions and businesses.

In America, community cooperative housekeeping was proposed in 1834 in Caroline Howard Gilman's book *Recollections of a Housekeeper*, which advocated the professionalization of housekeeping services, including cooking establishments to provide families with prepared food. In 1865, Harriet Beecher Stowe, in her story "Christopher Crowfield" in *House and Home Papers*, proposed a Model Christian Neighborhood of ten to twelve families with a shared laundry and bake house. In an 1868 article for the suffrage journal *The Revolution*, Stowe sketched "A Model Village of New England" with a town laundry, bakery, and cook-house. She described her experience living in Europe and obtaining multicourse dinners from a neighborhood cook-shop. Stowe's Model Christian Neighborhood reappeared in 1869 in *The American Woman's Home*. In their manual, the Beecher sisters also designed a school that included instruction and participation in cooperative housekeeping by the elementary school's pupils.

THE CAMBRIDGE COOPERATIVE HOUSEKEEPING SOCIETY

In the United States, the earliest effort at implementing cooperative housekeeping ideas outside of a commune appears to be the Cambridge Cooperative Housekeeping Society (CCHS) in Cambridge, Massachusetts, founded in 1869 by Melusina Fay Peirce, wife of Harvard professor Charles Peirce, who founded the philosophy of pragmatism. Melusina had gained an unusual scientific education at the Agassiz Young Ladies' School founded by Elizabeth and Louis Agassiz, who was a geology professor at Harvard. After Melusina Fay met Charles Peirce, who was also a student of Louis Agassiz, and married him in 1862, Melusina "joined him [Charles] in his early scientific work," according to one biographer, and was "something of a scientist in her own right," according to another. This context elucidates why Zina, as she was called, rebelled at the "costly and unnatural sacrifice" of women's wider talents to "the dusty drudgery of house ordering."

A number of factors influenced Zina's interest in founding housekeeping cooperatives. First, she had personally experienced the widespread modern conflict between woman's role as housekeeper and her desire to express her intellectual talents. Second, during her childhood, Zina had seen neighborhood women cooperatively organize to perform her mother's sewing tasks so she could develop her strong musical talents. Zina believed that her mother's life had been ended prematurely by hard domestic labor. Third, Zina's writings show the influence of her great aunt Caroline Howard Gilman's book *Recollections of a Housekeeper* (1834), which advocated the professionalization of housekeeping services, including cooking establishments to provide families with prepared food. Zina's earliest article on cooperative housekeeping in the *World*, July 11, 1864, imagined an association of fashionable ladies who voluntarily supervised lower class women in producing and distributing food to families who paid for the service.

In 1869, Zina proposed the Cambridge Cooperative Housekeeping Society, according to ideas in her ground-breaking series of articles in the *Atlantic Monthly* from November 1868 to March 1869. The CCHS prospectus stated that it would follow the practices of the famous cooperative store established in England by the workman's organization, the Rochdale Equitable Pioneers, which sold store subscriptions to raise money to buy goods that were then sold to members at retail prices. The profits were then divided among the members according to the amount of their purchases.

The CCHS lost money and was disbanded in 1871 for a number of reasons, which Zina Peirce detailed in her final report as CCHS treasurer, and in her 1884 book *Cooperative Housekeeping: How to Do It and How Not to Do It*. The main reason the cooperative laundry, bakery, and store failed was the interference of the husbands of the cooperating women, who were predominantly Harvard professors. In her book, Zina recorded comments by husbands who objected to their wives cooperating for the comfort of other men; some husbands complained that wives who went to meetings of the CCHS inconvenienced them inasmuch as they were therefore unavailable for their household duties, such as sewing on a button. Zina pointed out with some irony that husbands who were abolitionists had no compunction about enslaving their wives to housework.

A number of husbands allowed their wives to join the CCHS only on condition that they would never actually use the cooperatives. This meant that the loads of clothes were too small to permit the large machines bought for the laundry to be run profitably. And groceries rotted on the cooperative store's shelves because many families were afraid to risk the loss of their regular suppliers of groceries. Furthermore, the cooperative bakery produced a batch of bread that went stale on the shelves for lack of a delivery man and wagon. Following the dominant gender ideology that limited women to the domestic sphere of the home, wives and their female servants expected goods to be delivered from the public sphere to their homes, even though in this case most of the members' homes were within a fifteen-minute walk of the cooperative building.

Zina made the mistake of creating a board of husbands to oversee the CCHS, with the idea that she would be able to manipulate them. Instead, the husbands reorganized the CCHS. They replaced Zina's egalitarian cooperative organizational structure commonly associated with women, in which three different committees of women organized each cooperative, with a male-hierarchical organizational power structure that put Zina in charge of all the cooperatives, discouraging the cooperation she sought among women in the CCHS.

Despite the failure of the Cambridge Cooperative Housekeeping Society, Zina Peirce was famous in the reform community for her theoretical articles and designs for community cooperative housekeeping. Her ideas and designs of a community cooperative in a neighborhood of kitchenless houses strongly influenced Charlotte Perkins Gilman and later reformers who proposed neighborhoods of middle-class kitchenless houses and community cooperative kitchens, dining clubs, and child-care facilities.

Women as well as men designed cooperative neighborhoods and communes, These women ranged from Melusina Fay Peirce to Charlotte Perkins Gilman and Alice Constance Austin, who in 1916 designed kitchenless houses and cooperative facilities for the Socialist commune of Llano del Rio in Antelope Valley, California.

CONCLUSION

Cooperative housekeeping and municipal housekeeping were major social movements of the nineteenth and twentieth centuries that transformed American culture with new women's gender ideology, public professions, institutions, and businesses. The professionalization of women's domestic tasks in the public sphere further justified women's higher education for these professions. Women's access to higher education and new women's public professions were major culture-change processes that were instrumental to the movement for female suffrage.

Suzanne M. Spencer-Wood

BIBLIOGRAPHY

Beecher, Catherine E., and Harriet B. Stowe *The American Woman's Home, or Principles of Domestic Science*. 1869. Reprint, Hartford, CT: Stowe-Day Foundation, 1975.

Hayden, Dolores. *The Grand Domestic Revolution*. Cambridge, MA: MIT University Press, 1981.

———. *Seven American Uptopias: The Architecture of Communitarian Socialism 1790–1975*. Cambridge, MA: MIT University Press, 1976.

Peirce, Melusina Fay. *Cooperative Housekeeping: How to Do It and How Not to Do It*. Boston: James R. Osgood & Co, 1884.

Scott, Anne F. *Natural Allies: Women's Associations in American History*. Urbana: University of Illinois Press, 1991.

Spencer-Wood, Suzanne M. "Diversity in 19th Century Domestic Reform: Relationships Among Classes and Ethnic Groups." In *Those 'Of Little Note" Gender, Race and Class in Historical Archaeology*, ed. Elizabeth M. Scott, pp. 175–208. Tucson: University of Arizona Press, 1994.

———. "Feminist Historical Archaeology and the Transformation of American Culture by Domestic Reform Movements, 1840–1925." In *Historical Archaelogy and the Study of American Culture*, ed. L.A. De Cunzo and B.L. Herman, pp. 397–446. Knoxville: Winterthur Museum and University of Tennessee Press, 1996.

———. "A Survey of Domestic Reform Movement Sites in Boston and Cambridge, c. 1865–1905." *Historical Archaeology* 21:2 (Fall 1987): 7–36.

———. "Towards an Historical Archaeology of Materialistic Domestic Reform." In *The Archaeology of Inequality*, eds. Randall M. McGuire and Robert Paynter, pp. 231–286. Oxford: Basil and Blackwell, 1991.

———. "Turn of the Century Women's Organizations, Urban Design, and the Origin of the American Playground Movement." *Landscape Journal* 13:2 (Fall 1994): 125–138.

———. "The World Their Household: Changing Meanings of the Domestic Sphere in the Nineteenth Century." In *The Archaeology of Household Activities: Gender Ideologies, Domestic Spaces and Material Culture*, ed. Penelope M. Allison, pp. 162–189. London: Routledge, 1999.

Stowe, Harriet Beecher. *House and Home Papers*. Boston: Fields Osgood and Co., 1865.

WOMAN SUFFRAGE MOVEMENT
1848–1920

Before the early 1970s, when women's history became a legitimate academic pursuit and women began writing their own history, suffrage was barely mentioned in textbooks, let alone militant activism by suffragists. Few know that it was women seeking the vote who *first* picketed the White House for a political cause and that these courageous women faced jail, hunger strikes, and forced feedings. Few know about the groups and leaders who fought for and against suffrage, and about the years of strategizing and education in their seventy-two-year struggle for enfranchisement.

"We hope the contribution we have made may enable some other hand in the future to write a more complete history of the most momentous reform that has yet been launched on the world—the first organized protest against the injustice which has brooded over the character and destiny of one-half the human race." So stated suffrage pioneers Elizabeth Cady Stanton, Susan B. Anthony, and Matilda Joslyn Gage in the introduction of Volume I of the six-volume series, *The History of Woman Suffrage* (1887).

In the nineteenth century, two great reforms were rapidly pressing forward, propelled by the controversy of earnest, consecrated protagonists on the one hand and bitter, hostile antagonists on the other—the antislavery and antiliquor movements. Both appealed strongly to the humanitarian sympathies of educated women. Whether the effort of women had any appreciable effect on either movement between 1800 and 1850 may be debated, but it is certain that these reforms furnished the most impelling motive leading women to emerge from their seclusion to take part in public affairs.

They came timidly at first, but, with the discovery that the majority of men not only did not want their help but expressed their antagonism in phrases and tones of bitter contempt, the spirit of many women was stung into resentment. They chafed at the restraint of individual liberty, and the bravest boldly defended the right of any woman to give service to any cause and in any manner she chose. Thus, the stage was set in the fight for woman suffrage.

Stanton and her friend, devout Quaker Lucretia Mott, began their activism as abolitionists, as did many of the early suffragists. They deeply resented the male abolitionists who would not allow them to speak at the World Anti-Slavery Convention in London in 1840. Women were excluded from participation and forced to sit in a curtained balcony as the men debated. Stanton's new husband, Henry B. Stanton, was an abolitionist leader. She seethed as her male colleagues conducted "the crucifixion [of woman's] pride and self-respect, the humiliation of [her] spirit."

The first women's rights convention, called by Stanton, Mott, Martha C. Wright, Mary Ann McClintock, and Jane Hunt, was held in 1848 at the Wesleyan Church in Seneca Falls, New York. Stanton described the meeting in the *History of Woman Suffrage* (1887) as follows:

> It had been decided to have no men present, but as they were already on the spot, and as the women who must take the responsibility of organizing the meeting and leading the discussions shrank from doing either, it was decided, in a hasty council around the altar, that this was an occasion when men might make themselves pre-eminently useful.
>
> James Mott, tall and dignified, in Quaker costume, was called to the chair; Mary McClintock appointed secretary, Frederick Douglass, Samuel Tillman, Ansel Bascom, E.W. Capron, and Thomas McClintock took part throughout the discussions. Lucretia Mott, accustomed to public speaking in the Society of Friends, stated the object of the Convention, and in taking a survey of the degraded condition of woman the world over, showed the importance of inaugurating some movement for her education and elevation.

ELIZABETH CADY STANTON

(1815–1902)

Born on November 12, 1815, in Johnstown, New York, Elizabeth Cady was educated at the Troy Female Seminary (now Emma Willard School) in Troy, New York. Intellectually gifted, she excelled in Greek and read law informally in the office of her father, Daniel Cady, a U.S. congressman and later a New York Supreme Court judge, before marrying. While studying law, she learned of the discriminatory laws under which women lived and determined to win equal rights for her sex.

In 1840 she married Henry Brewster Stanton, a journalist and abolitionist, and they attended the international slavery convention in London while on their honeymoon. The exclusion of women delegates from the floor of the convention angered Stanton and Lucretia Mott, who became a mentor to the younger Stanton, and led them to organize women to win greater equality. She and Mott called the first Woman's Rights Convention in the United States in 1848 at Seneca Falls, New York. Stanton drafted the Seneca Falls Convention's Declaration of Sentiments and argued forcefully for a suffrage clause to be included in the bill of rights for women that was drawn up at the convention. She became a frequent speaker on the subject of women's rights and circulated petitions that helped secure passage by the New York legislature in 1848 of a bill granting married women's property rights.

In 1851, she met Susan B. Anthony, and they formed a lifelong working relationship. Stanton, the better orator and writer, was perfectly complemented by Anthony, the organizer and tactician. Among their earliest targets were the laws that discriminated against married women, denying them the right to hold property, or wages, or guardianship of their children. In 1854, Stanton received an unprecedented invitation to address the New York legislature; her speech resulted in new legislation in 1860 granting married women the rights to their wages and to equal guardianship of their children.

During the Civil War, Stanton worked for abolitionism. In 1863, she and Anthony organized the Woman's National Loyal League, which gathered more than 300,000 signatures on petitions calling for immediate emancipation. The movement to extend the franchise to African-American men after the war, however, reemphasized the disenfranchisement of women and led her and her colleagues to redouble their efforts for woman suffrage.

Stanton helped organize and was president of the National Woman Suffrage Association (1869–1890). After it merged with a rival group to become the National American Woman Suffrage Association, she served as president from 1890 to 1892 of the new organization. With Anthony as publisher, she and Parker Pillsbury edited (1868–1870) *The Revolution*, a women's rights magazine. In 1878, she drafted a federal suffrage amendment that was introduced in every Congress thereafter until women were granted the right to vote in 1920. As a writer and lecturer she strove for legal, political, and industrial equality of women and for liberal divorce laws. She compiled with Susan B. Anthony and Matilda Joslyn Gage the first three volumes of the six-volume *History of Woman Suffrage* (1887) and wrote an autobiography, *Eighty Years and More* (1898). Stanton died in New York City on October 26, 1902.

James G. Lewis

They saw parallels between their lives as women and those of the slaves. Thus, they planned the convention intending to give the Seneca Falls gathering of 300 activists (including 40 men) the focus they needed to change their legal and political status. This was the first public protest of women's political, social, and economic inequality. They used the Declaration of Independence, a document ratified seventy-two years earlier, in 1776, which had failed to include women, as the basis for the Declaration of Sentiments. The Seneca Falls signers held "these truths to be self-evident, that all men *and women* are created equal."

Stanton first introduced the "radical" concept of votes for women as part of the Declaration of Sentiments. "It is the sacred duty of the women of this country to secure for themselves their sacred right to the elective franchise," declared Stanton.

Indeed, it might just as easily be argued that the struggle for women's rights in America really began with the Revolution itself. Certainly, women were fired by the revolutionary rhetoric of human rights and political liberties. And the war profoundly affected women's lives, changing forever their sense of themselves as citizens of the republic. A review of women's status in the American colonies, and the changes wrought and hopes unrealized by the Revo-

THE DECLARATION OF SENTIMENTS,
1848

In 1848, women's rights advocates gathered at a convention in Seneca Falls, New York. The Declaration of Sentiments, modeled after the U.S. Declaration of Independence, demands equal rights for women in society. It was signed by a committee of one hundred: sixty-eight women and thirty-two men.

When, in the course of human events, it becomes necessary for one portion of the family of man to assume among the people of the earth a position different from that which they have hitherto occupied . . . a decent respect to the opinions of mankind requires that they should declare the causes that impel them to such a course.

We hold these truths to be self-evident: that all men and women are created equal; that they are endowed by their Creator with certain inalienable rights; that among these are life, liberty, and the pursuit of happiness; that to secure these rights governments are instituted, deriving their just powers from the consent of the governed. Whenever any form of government becomes destructive of these ends, it is the right of those who suffer from it to refuse allegiance to it, and to insist upon the institution of a new government, laying its foundation on such principles . . . as to them shall seem most likely to effect their safety and happiness. Prudence, indeed, will dictate that governments long established should not be changed for light and transient causes; and accordingly all experience hath shown that mankind are more disposed to suffer while evils are sufferable, than to right themselves by abolishing the forms to which they are accustomed. But when a long train of abuses and usurpations, pursuing invariably the same object, evinces a design to reduce them under absolute despotism, it is their duty to throw off such government, and to provide new guards for their future security. Such has been the patient sufferance of the women under this government, and such is now the necessity which constrains them to demand the equal station to which they are entitled.

The history of mankind is a history of repeated injuries and usurpations on the part of man toward woman, having in direct object the establishment of an absolute tyranny over her. . . .

He has never permitted her to exercise her inalienable right to the elective franchise.

He has compelled her to submit to laws, in the formation of which she had no voice.

He has withheld from her rights which are given to the most ignorant and degraded men . . .

Having deprived her of this first right of a citizen, the elective franchise, thereby leaving her without representation in the halls of legislation, he has oppressed her on all sides.

He has made her, if married, in the eye of the law, civilly dead.

He has taken from her all right in property, even to the wages she earns.

He has made her, morally, an irresponsible being, as she can commit many crimes with impunity, provided they be done in the presence of her husband. In the covenant of marriage, she is compelled to promise obedience to her husband, he becoming, to all intents and purposes, her master . . .

He has so framed the laws of divorce . . . and in case of separation, to whom the guardianship of the children shall be given, as to be wholly regardless of the happiness of women—the law, in all cases . . . giving all power into his hands.

After depriving her of all rights as a married woman, if single, and the owner of property, he has taxed her to support a government which recognizes her only when her property can be made profitable to it.

He has monopolized nearly all the profitable employments, and from those she is permitted to follow, she receives but a scanty remuneration. He closes against her all the avenues to wealth and distinction which he considers most honorable to himself. As a teacher of theology, medicine, or law, she is not known.

He has denied her the facilities for obtaining a thorough education, all colleges being closed against her.

He allows her in church, as well as state, but a subordinate position, claiming apostolic authority for her exclusion from the ministry, and, with some exceptions, from any public participation in the affairs of the church.

He has created a false public sentiment by giving to the world a different code of morals for men and women . . .

He has usurped the prerogative of Jehovah himself, claiming it as his right to assign for her a sphere of action, when that belongs to her conscience and to her God.

He has endeavored . . . to destroy her confidence in her own powers, to lessen her self-respect, and to make her willing to lead a dependent and abject life.

Now, in view of this entire disfranchisement of one-half the people of this country, their social and religious degradation . . . and because women do feel themselves aggrieved, oppressed, and fraudulently deprived of their most sacred rights, we insist that they have immediate admission to all the rights and privileges which belong to them as citizens of the United States.

Source: Elizabeth Cady Stanton, *A History of Woman Suffrage,* vol. 1 (Rochester, NY: Fowler and Wells, 1889).

SENECA FALLS RESOLUTIONS, 1848

The Seneca Falls Resolutions of 1848 represent the first elocution of women's equality with men in the United States and set the stage for nationalizing the expansion of the women's rights movement.

Whereas the great precept of nature is conceded to be, "that man shall pursue his own true and substantial happiness." Blackstone, in his Commentaries, remarks, that this law of Nature being coeval with mankind, and dictated by God himself, is of course superior in obligation to any other. It is binding over all the globe, in all countries, and at all times; no human laws are of any validity if contrary to this, and such of them as are valid, derive all their force, and all their validity, and all their authority, mediately and immediately, from this original;

Therefore, Resolved, That such laws as conflict, in any way, with the true and substantial happiness of woman, are contrary to the great precept of nature, and of no validity; for this is "superior in obligation to any other."

Resolved, That all laws which prevent woman from occupying such a station in society as her conscience shall dictate, or which place her in a position inferior to that of man, are contrary to the great precept of nature, and therefore of no force or authority.

Resolved, That woman is man's equal—was intended to be so by the Creator—and the highest good of the race demands that she should be recognized as such.

Resolved, That the women of this country ought to be enlightened in regard to the laws under which they live, that they may no longer publish their degradation, by declaring themselves satisfied with their present position, nor their ignorance, by asserting that they have all the rights they want.

Resolved, That inasmuch as man, while claiming for himself intellectual superiority, does accord to woman moral superiority, it is pre-eminently his duty to encourage her to speak, and teach, as she has an opportunity, in all religious assemblies.

Resolved, That the same amount of virtue, delicacy, and refinement of behavior, that is required of woman in the social state, should also be required of man, and the same transgressions should be visited with equal severity on both man and woman.

Resolved, That the objection of indelicacy and impropriety, which is so often brought against woman when she addresses a public audience, comes with a very ill-grace from those who encourage, by their attendance, her appearance on the stage, in the concert, or in feats of the circus.

Resolved, That woman has too long rested satisfied in the circumscribed limits which corrupt customs and a perverted application of the Scriptures have marked out for her, and that it is time she should move in the enlarged sphere which her great Creator has assigned her.

Resolved, That it is the duty of the women of this country to secure to themselves their sacred right to the elective franchise.

Resolved, That the equality of human rights results necessarily from the fact of the identity of the race in capabilities and responsibilities.

Resolved, therefore, That, being invested by the Creator with the same capabilities, and the same consciousness of responsibility for their exercise, it is demonstrably the right and duty of woman, equally with man, to promote every righteous cause, by every righteous means; and especially in regard to the great subjects of morals and religion, it is self-evidently her right to participate with her brother in teaching them, both in private and in public, by writing and by speaking, by any instrumentalities proper to be used, and in any assemblies proper to be held; and this being a self-evident truth, growing out of the divinely implanted principles of human nature, any custom or authority adverse to it, whether modern or wearing the hoary sanction of antiquity, is to be regarded as a self-evident falsehood, and at war with the interests of mankind.

Seneca Falls Resolutions
Seneca Falls Conference
Seneca Falls, New York 1848

Source: Seneca County Courier, July 14, 1848. http://www.memory.loc.gov/cgi-bin/query/r?ammem/nawbib:@field(NUMBER+@band(rbnawsa+n7548)).

THE RIGHTS OF WOMEN
BY FREDERICK DOUGLASS, 1848

Antislavery leader Frederick Douglass, in a July 1848 editorial in The North Star, *expresses his strong support for the women's rights movement and the Seneca Falls Declaration of Sentiments.*

One of the most interesting events of the past week, was the holding of what is technically styled a Woman's Rights Convention at Seneca Falls. The speaking, addresses, and resolutions of this extraordinary meeting were almost wholly conducted by women; and although they evidently felt themselves in a novel position, it is but simple justice to say that their whole proceedings were characterized by marked ability and dignity. No one present, we think, however much he might be disposed to differ from the views advanced by the leading speakers on that occasion, will fail to give them credit for brilliant talents and excellent dispositions. In this meeting, as in other deliberative assemblies, there were frequent differences of opinion and animated discussion; but in no case was there the slightest absence of good feeling and decorum. Several interesting documents setting forth the rights as well as the grievances of women were read. Among these was a Declaration of Sentiments, to be regarded as the basis of a grand movement for attaining the civil, social, political, and religious rights of women. We should not do justice to our own convictions, or to the excellent persons connected with this infant movement, if we did not in this connection offer a few remarks on the general subject which the Convention met to consider and the objects they seek to attain. In doing so, we are not insensible that the bare mention of this truly important subject in any other than terms of contemptuous ridicule and scornful disfavor, is likely to excite against us the fury of bigotry and the folly of prejudice. A discussion of the rights of animals would be regarded with far more complacency by many of what

are called the *wise* and the *good* of our land, than would be a discussion of the rights of women. It is, in their estimation, to be guilty of evil thoughts, to think that a woman is entitled to equal rights with man. Many who have at last made the discovery that the negroes have some rights as well as other members of the human family, have yet to be convinced that women are entitled to any. Eight years ago a number of persons of this description actually abandoned the anti-slavery cause, lest by giving their influence in that direction, they might possibly be giving countenance to the dangerous heresy that woman, in respect to rights, stands on an equal footing with man. In the judgment of such persons, the American slave system, with all its concomitant horrors, is less to be deplored than this *wicked* idea. It is perhaps needless to say, that we cherish little sympathy for such prejudices. Standing as we do upon the watch-tower of human freedom, we cannot be deterred from an expression of our approbation of any movement, however humble, to improve and elevate the character of any members of the human family. While it is impossible for us to go into this subject at length, and dispose of the various objections which are often urged against such a doctrine as that of female equality, we are free to say that in respect to political rights, we hold woman to be justly entitled to all we claim for man. We go farther, and express our conviction that all political rights that it is expedient for man to exercise, it is equally so for woman. All that distinguishes man as an intelligent and accountable being, is equally true of woman; and if that government only is just which governs by the free consent of the governed, there can be no reason in the world for denying to woman the exercise of the elective franchise, or a hand in making and administering the laws of the land. Our doctrine is that "right is of no sex." We therefore bid the women engaged in this movement our humble Godspeed.

Source: The North Star, *[Rochester], July 28, 1848.*

lution, rendered the expressed frustration of the women at Seneca Falls understandable.

During the Revolutionary War, women had proven themselves adept at running businesses and family farms. Abigail Adams, who was married to a prominent member of the Continental Congress, ran their farm and produced the entire family income while her husband, John, engaged in politics. Yet, when she wrote to him in Philadelphia and expressed

her desire that he remember women in constructing the new nation's laws, he treated her request as a joke.

Early American culture prescribed specific tasks and subordinate status to women. Women managed the domestic-sphere duties, which included, in addition to child rearing, cooking, cleaning, washing, spinning, weaving, gardening, raising poultry, tending cattle, and trading in the local market. Under English common law, a married woman was "covered" by her

RESOLUTIONS OF THE FIRST NATIONAL WOMAN'S RIGHTS CONVENTION
WORCESTER, MASSACHUSETTS,
October 23–24, 1850

Two years after the Seneca Falls Resolutions, the National Woman's Rights Convention was held in Worcester, Massachusetts, in October 1850. The convention is considered to be a critically important moment in the struggle for women's rights in the United States.

WHEREAS, The very contracted sphere of action prescribed for woman, arising from an unjust view of her nature, capacities, and powers, and from the infringement of her just rights as an equal with man,—is highly injurious to her physical, mental, and moral development; therefore,

RESOLVED, That we will not cease our earnest endeavors to secure for her political, legal, and social equality with man, until her proper sphere is determined, by what alone should determine it, her Powers and Capacities, strengthened and refined by an education in accordance with her nature.

RESOLVED, That every human being of full age, and resident for a proper length of time on the soil of the nation, who is required to obey law, is entitled to a voice in its enactments; that every such person, whose property or labor is taxed for the support of government, is entitled to a direct share in such government.

RESOLVED, That women are clearly entitled to the right of suffrage, and to be considered eligible to office; the omission to demand which, on her part, is a palpable recreancy to duty; and the denial of which is a gross usurpation, on the part of man, no longer to be endured; and that every party which claims to represent the humanity, civilization, and progress of the age, is bound to inscribe on its banners, Equality before the law, without distinction of sex or color.

RESOLVED, That political rights acknowledge no sex, and therefore the word "male" should be stricken from every State Constitution.

RESOLVED, That the laws of property, as affecting married parties, demand a thorough revisal, so that all rights may be equal between them;—that the wife may have, during life, an equal control over the property gained by their mutual toil and sacrifices, be heir to her husband precisely to the extent that he is heir to her, and entitled, at her death, to dispose by will of the same share of the joint property as he is.

RESOLVED, That as women alone can learn by experience, and prove by works, what is their rightful sphere of duty, we recommend, as *next steps*, that they should demand and secure

1. *Education* in primary and high schools, universities, medical, legal, and theological institutions, as comprehensive and exact as their abilities prompt them to seek, and their capabilities fit them to receive;
2. *Partnership* in the labors, gains, risks, and remunerations of productive industry . . . ;
3. *A co-equal share* in the formation and administration of law, Municipal, State, and National, through legislative assemblies, courts, and executive offices;
4. Such unions as may become the guardians of pure morals and honorable manners—*a high court of appeal* in cases of outrage which cannot be and are not touched by civil or ecclesiastical organizations . . .

RESOLVED, That a Central Committee be appointed by this Convention, empowered to enlarge their numbers: on (1) Education; (2) Industrial Avocations; (3) Civil and Political Rights and Regulations; (4) Social Relations; who shall correspond with each other and with the Central Committee, hold meetings in their respective neighborhoods, gather statistics, facts, and illustrations, raise funds for purposes of publication; and through the press, tracts, books, and the living agent, guide public opinion upward and onward in the grand social reform of establishing woman's co-sovereignty with man. . . .

RESOLVED, That since the prospect of honorable and useful employment, in after life, for the faculties we are laboring to discipline, is the keenest stimulus to fidelity in the use of educational advantages, and since the best education is what we give ourselves in the struggles, employments, and discipline of life; therefore, it is impossible that woman should make full use of the instruction already accorded to her, or that her career should do justice to her faculties, until the avenues to the various civil and professional employments are thrown open to arouse her ambition and call forth all her nature.

RESOLVED, That every effort to educate woman, until you accord to her rights, and arouse her conscience by the weight of her responsibilities, is futile, and a waste of labor.

RESOLVED, That the cause we are met to advocate,—the claim for woman of all her natural and civil rights,—bids us remember the million and a half of slave women at the South, the most grossly wronged and foully outraged of all women; and in every effort for an improvement in our civilization, we will bear in our heart of hearts the memory of the trampled womanhood of the plantation, and omit no effort to raise it to a share in the rights we claim for ourselves.

Source: Resolutions of the First National Woman's Rights Convention. As reported in the Proceedings at Worcester, Massachusetts, October 23–24, 1850.

husband. The name given to her legal status was *femme covert*, which meant that she had virtually no rights at all. Everything she owned and everything she earned belonged to her husband. She did not even have legal claim to her own children.

For more than 200 years, women complained about their lot—about their exclusion from participating in public affairs, about being denied education, about religious rules that oppressed them, about their subordinate status in the community, and about their dependence on undependable men. Such protests, however, were likely to be infrequent, private, and voiced only when some particular humiliation compelled a woman to violate the stricture that she remain silent and subservient.

Two years after Seneca Falls, in 1850, the first national convention for women's rights was held at Worcester, Massachusetts, with nine states represented. The call had been signed by sixty-one men and women, among whom were Wendell Phillips, Lucy Stone, Ralph Waldo Emerson, Abby Kelly Foster, William Lloyd Garrison, Harriot K. Hunt, William H. Channing, Lucretia and James Mott, A. Bronson Alcott, and Samuel May. Before the meetings ended, an association was formed with Paulina Wright Davis of Rhode Island, the editor of *Una*, a magazine for women, at its head. Throughout the 1850s, national women's rights conventions were held annually, as were numerous local and regional meetings. By the 1860s, efforts for women's rights had become a movement.

ANTHONY MEETS STANTON

Susan B. Anthony, the other towering figure of the woman suffrage movement, did not meet Stanton until three years after Seneca Falls. They met in 1851 through Amelia Bloomer, who edited a temperance newspaper, the *Lily*. A member of a Massachusetts Quaker family, Anthony had resigned a teaching position in a bitter protest over discrimination against women and joined the temperance movement, an experience that taught her "the great evil of woman's utter dependence on man for the necessary means to aid reform movements." Initially, Anthony was not convinced that woman suffrage was really needed. Stanton had to persuade the younger Anthony that no reform movement would be successful as long as women were denied the ballot. Anthony's conviction was strengthened in 1852 when she was denied the right to speak at a temperance rally because of her sex.

Under the tutelage of Stanton, whose exceptional writing and inventive thinking complemented her own organizational and political skills, Anthony began her lifelong devotion to woman suffrage and securing legal equality for women. Anthony and Stanton had a remarkable working relationship for more than fifty years, each supplying abilities the other lacked. Henry Stanton once described it this way to his wife: "You stir up Susan, and she stirs the world."

In many ways, the two women were polar opposites. Anthony never married, while Stanton was the mother of seven. While Stanton was tied down with domestic duties, she counted on her friend to represent her in meetings she could not attend. She resented the constant household and child-rearing obligations and her dependence on her father and husband.

Along with Stanton and Anthony, Lucy Stone, one of the movement's greatest orators, played vital leadership roles in the women's rights movement for more than half a century despite their differences. Gage, another important early suffragist, was a staunch supporter of the movement when she attended the 1852 convention in Syracuse, New York. Her writings against slavery and in favor of women's rights were prolific. She spent many years as a close ally of Stanton and Anthony until they fell out in their later years over differing philosophical approaches to obtaining women's rights.

It took a long time for women's rights to win any popular support, even among women. Most people, male and female, approved separate spheres for men and women. Anthony was convinced that women failed to support suffrage because they did not realize what its absence cost them.

To its critics, woman suffrage was a very radical demand, threatening the very foundations of society. Ministers, journalists, and social commentators dismissed women's rights advocates. Anti-suffragists associated suffrage with divorce, promiscuity, child neglect, and as the source of all social evils. One of the most prominent churchmen of the time, the Rev. Horace Bushnell of Hartford, Connecticut, was horrified at the idea of women voting. His tract, *Women Suffrage: The Reform Against Nature*, is a tour de force of the anti-suffragists' argument: a woman's power lay in her beauty and her dependence. Any attempt to assert authority violated her nature, so it must inevitably fail. The indictment of Christianity in 1893 with Matilda Joslyn Gage's *Woman, Church and State* and Stanton's *The Woman's Bible* in 1895 also brought derision for the movement. One book, originally published in 1897, argued against woman suffrage as being antithetical to both democracy and progress. Its premise, intended to be an answer to the arguments made in the multivolume *History of Woman Suffrage* was that women could progress only in relation to the general progress of humanity.

CIVIL WAR AND SUFFRAGE EFFORTS

With the outbreak of the Civil War in 1861, women suspended their activities on their own behalf to devote all their energies to the "noble purpose" of freeing the slaves. Stanton and Anthony formed the Woman's National Loyal League in May 1863, launching a massive petition drive that delivered some 400,000 signatures to Congress the following year in support of the Thirteenth Amendment to the U.S. Constitution prohibiting slavery.

Once its ratification in 1865 was accomplished, Stanton, Anthony, Stone, Mott, and others formed the American Equal Rights Association (AERA) to press for universal adult suffrage, combining demands for African-American and woman suffrage into a single campaign. From the beginning of the movement, abolitionists encouraged the equality of women, but they did not think the public was ready for the idea and that the association of the two could doom the franchise for blacks.

The Fourteenth Amendment, adopted in 1868, created fresh difficulties for the suffragists by introducing the word "male" into the Constitution, thereby explicitly repudiating woman suffrage. Difficulties were increased by the Fifteenth Amendment, prohibiting federal and state governments from denying the vote to anyone "on account of race, color, or previous condition of servitude," submitted to the states in 1869. Stanton and Anthony felt intense betrayal, renounced their male collaborators, and argued for the development of an independent political position for women's rights.

In 1869, the American Equal Rights Association split into two warring factions after deep philosophical differences surfaced on the best strategy to achieve woman suffrage. Lucy Stone, Henry Blackwell, Julia Ward Howe, Henry Ward Beecher, Antoinette Brown Blackwell, and others formed the "more moderate" American Woman Suffrage Association (AWSA), which supported suffrage laws at the state level and believed the cause of the newly freed slaves came first and women could wait. Stanton, Anthony,

and Gage disagreed, believing the cause of women's rights was paramount. Their group, the National Woman Suffrage Association (NWSA), committed itself to a progressive platform of sweeping social change in women's status and a constitutional amendment on their own behalf. Their motto was: "Men their rights and nothing more; women their rights and nothing less."

The NWSA opposed the Fifteenth Amendment and pushed for a Sixteenth Amendment that would enfranchise women. Their short-lived publication, *The Revolution*, was the movement's first paper of national scope and promoted a wide variety of reforms. With financier George Francis Train and David M. Mellis, financial editor of the *New York World*, as backers, the paper appeared on January 8, 1868. Parker Pillsbury, one of three men who supported NWSA's formation, edited the paper for two years with Stanton. Anthony was publisher, while Gage was a major editorial contributor. By challenging the sincerity of both political parties in their attitude on suffrage, it became at once a power in the political field. In the words of Stanton: "Some denounced it, some ridiculed it, but all read it."

In 1872, Anthony attempted to vote and sought arrest to test the validity of the Fourteenth and Fifteenth Amendments which she, Stanton, and Victoria Woodhull insisted applied to women. She was indicted for "knowingly wrongfully and unlawfully voting for a representative to the Congress of the United States." She was found guilty and fined; she insisted she would never pay. Virginia Minor, a suffragist from St. Louis, succeeded in getting the issue before the U.S. Supreme Court, but, in 1875, the Court ruled unanimously that citizenship did not automatically confer the right to vote and that the issue of woman suffrage should be decided within the states.

NWSA and AWSA competed for leadership of the women's movement for twenty-one years. Both engaged in massive organizing and educational efforts, by traveling and lecturing, distributing leaflets and pamphlets, petitioning state legislatures to support suffrage referenda, and securing thousands of signatures on petitions. Anthony also lobbied the U.S. Congress diligently, but only one congressional vote was held before 1890 and it failed.

The suffrage movement gained a valuable ally when noted temperance leader Frances Willard, president of the Woman's Christian Temperance Union, led her organization to support suffrage in 1880. The state WCTU chapters endorsed suffrage and distributed suffrage literature. Even though Willard was an

SUSAN B. ANTHONY (1820–1906)

Along with her long-time friend and political collaborator, Elizabeth Cady Stanton, Susan B. Anthony is probably the most widely recognized women's rights activist. Remembered for her political genius and persistence, Anthony devoted her life to the campaign for women's equality and succeeded in improving women's economic, domestic, and educational status.

Born on February 15, 1820, in Adams, Massachusetts, Anthony grew up in a progressive Quaker atmosphere, where women participated in church affairs on an equal basis with men, and young girls were encouraged to pursue advanced education. Anthony was taught at home until age seventeen, when she attended the Friend's Boarding School in Philadelphia. One year later, she took a teaching job to support her family, who lost the cotton mill business they owned. After a series of further business losses, the Anthony family moved to the Rochester, New York, area to farm. In 1846, she became head of the Girls' Department of the Canajoharie Academy in Canajoharie, New York. Three years later, disillusioned with unequal pay and lack of opportunities for advancement for women teachers, Anthony left to help manage the family farm. Despite leaving teaching, Anthony never abandoned her belief in education for women. In 1881, she organized a campaign to admit female students to the all-male University of Rochester. Although it took nearly twenty years, women were finally admitted, but only after Anthony put up $2,000 of her own meager funds to finance housing for female students.

The Anthony family home was a popular gathering place for liberal intellectuals and social reformers and was engulfed in discussions about antislavery, temperance, and the budding women's rights movement. As leader of the local Daughters of Temperance in Canajoharie, Anthony showed a talent for public speaking and fundraising, and later became the president of the Rochester branch. Despite hard work for temperance, in 1852, Anthony was prevented from speaking at a rally because of her sex. Undaunted, Anthony founded the Woman's State Temperance Society of New York. Throughout the 1850s, Anthony worked for a variety of social reforms, serving as speaker for the American Anti-Slavery Society; advocating for equal voting rights for women members of the New York State Teachers' Association; demanding equal pay for women teachers; and organizing for passage of the Married Women's Property Act (1860), giving married women in New York State possession of their own earnings and guardianship of children in the case of divorce.

From the day they met on the streets of Seneca Falls, New York, in 1851, the friendship and political alliance between Anthony and Elizabeth Cady Stanton developed into an unstoppable force. Linked by outrage at social injustice and their desire to be part of reform, they worked together on abolitionist and temperance causes, forming in 1869 the National Woman Suffrage Association, the era's driving force for women's rights. Stanton and Anthony launched a fifty-year campaign to secure the right to vote for women through an amendment to the U.S. Constitution. Anthony was a tireless advocate, traveling to virtually every state and territory in the Midwest and West to educate and organize women and in support of women's suffrage. Anthony often averaged more than one hundred speaking engagements in a single year and testified at numerous congressional hearings.

Anthony did much more than just talk about women's right to vote–she voted! In 1872, protesting women's exclusion from the ballot box, Anthony organized a group of friends to attempt to cast their votes in Rochester, New York, planning to sue election officials when the women were turned away from the polls. To her surprise, their votes were accepted. Several weeks later, U.S. marshals arrested Anthony and charged her with illegal voting. At her trial in June 1873, Anthony was not allowed to speak in her own defense and was found guilty by the jury and fined $100. Despite her refusal to pay the fine, she was never imprisoned and the fine remained uncollected.

In 1889, Anthony helped organize the International Council of Women in London, and in 1904 she founded with Carrie Chapman Catt the International Woman Suffrage Alliance in Berlin. She preserved thousands of documents chronicling the women's movement in the multivolume *History of Woman Suffrage*, edited with leading women's rights activists.

Anthony died in Rochester on March 13, 1906, fourteen years before the Nineteenth Amendment to the U.S. Constitution, granting women the right to vote, was ratified. Although Anthony did not live to cast a legal vote, she left a legacy of social, political, legal, and educational reforms that improved the status of all the women who came after her. She also left them with a role model for the tireless pursuit of a dream, buoyed by her conviction that "failure is impossible."

Linda Czuba Brigance

AWSA member, she invited Anthony to speak before the group. This helped create support for suffrage among women who might never have become involved in the movement. The unintended consequence of this new alliance was that a powerful enemy of suffrage emerged—the liquor industry. This alliance caused great concern for Stanton and Gage, who saw the suffrage movement becoming more conservative and moving away from their broader agenda for women's rights. Anthony felt that the only important issue was the vote and that any woman who supported suffrage for whatever reason was an ally.

By 1889, the fierce animosity between the two suffrage groups was slowly abating due to younger members. Anthony met Stone secretly to discuss a merger. Gage found the idea absurd. The two groups were quite different. Stanton and Gage considered the real issues to be women's oppression by the church, the state, the capitalist, and the home. This was not the way AWSA saw it. When NWSA members committed civil disobedience by voting, the AWSA spoke out against the tactic. But Gage, as chair of the NWSA Executive Committee, was not consulted since her opposition was so fierce. Anthony called a meeting when Gage was out of town and proceeded to ram through the merger, which caused great consternation for numerous NWSA members since it was not put to a vote of the membership. The AWSA and NWSA combined into the NAWSA, and Gage, who felt deeply betrayed, went off to form her own group, the Woman's National Liberal Union. Stanton, who had been indifferent to the merger, was elected NAWSA president, Anthony became vice president, and Stone was head of the executive committee. Anthony took command of the organization and became president in 1892 and remained in office until 1900 when her protégé Carrie Chapman Catt, took over.

The pioneering work of Lucy Stone, combined with the intellectual and organizational partnership of Stanton and Anthony, dominated the drive for woman suffrage from the mid-nineteenth century until their deaths in 1893, 1902, and 1906, respectively. Despite their unflagging efforts and Anthony's rallying cry, "Failure is impossible!" uttered at her last public appearance shortly before her death, success did not come in their lifetimes. But their legacies inspired others to keep fighting.

Perhaps the most significant legacy of the suffrage struggle was the creation of a new political culture. Before victory was achieved in 1920, it was the suffragists who led the debate with banners, placards,

Despite harassment, arrest, and public ridicule, Susan B. Anthony spearheaded the feminist movement from the 1850s until her death in 1906. A passionate advocate of equal rights, her motto was "Failure Is Impossible." The Nineteenth Amendment to the Constitution, ratified in 1920 and granting women the right to vote, is often called the "Anthony Amendment." *(Library of Congress)*

and buttons—all items seen in political campaigns today, but unheard of and unused before the suffrage debate. The suffragists used color to denote political symbolism. The colors of the united suffrage movement were purple (for the royalty of womanhood), white (for purity in politics and in the home), and yellow or gold representing the crown of victory. Yellow had been a particularly important color because it represented enlightenment, and so yellow flowers, such as sunflowers and roses, were prevalent in suffrage imagery. Anthony was also identified with the yellow rose of suffrage. Supposedly her mother planted a yellow rose bush at their home in Rochester, New York, and she embraced the yellow rose as a suffragist symbol. The sun's rays symbolized the dawn of a new day for women. Tricolor sashes, banners, and "Votes for Women" buttons were worn during parades and other public appearances and have become much sought after memorabilia.

WOMAN SUFFRAGE AND THE RACE QUESTION

In the early 1900s, hundreds of small local women's groups consolidated into large federations like the General Federation of Women's Clubs, the National Council of Jewish Women, and the National Association of Colored Women, with many of their members supporting suffrage. Black women occasionally joined clubs dominated by white women but were, by and large, not made to feel welcome. Sojourner Truth early on had recognized the link between racism and sexism and became an eloquent spokesperson for civil rights and women's rights.

Black women, as victims of both racial and gender prejudice, had different reform agendas, which included a strong emphasis on racial uplift, as well as gender equality. Black women started clubs around the country to address their communities' most pressing needs—establishing settlement houses for blacks migrating to urban areas, funding libraries and schools, pushing legislation against lynching, protesting aspects of Jim Crow segregation, and working to win the vote. Soon, they became aware, as white women had, of the importance of a national network. They organized themselves into the National Association of Colored Women (NACW), a coalition of affiliated clubs numbering over 50,000 members.

Among the leadership in the black women's suffrage movement were Ida B. Wells (Barnett), who founded the Alpha Suffrage Club in Chicago in 1913, the first black women's suffrage organization, and Mary Church Terrell, who founded the Colored Woman's League in 1892 and was founding president of the NACW in 1896. Wells, a friend of Anthony, and Terrell, who reminded white women of black women's double oppression, were the only two women invited to the NAACP's organizational meeting and became charter members.

Terrell addressed the 1890 NAWSA convention in Washington, D.C., and spoke out from the floor: "As a colored woman, I hope this Association will include a resolution on the injustices of various kinds of which colored people are the victims. . . . My sisters of the dominant race, stand up not only for the oppressed sex but also for the oppressed race!"

Regrettably, the schism that developed after the Fourteenth and Fifteenth Amendments put the early suffragists at odds with their long-time allies from the abolitionist movement. NAWSA used racist and nativist arguments extensively as it plotted its "Southern Strategy" to garner support. Henry Blackwell, Lucy Stone's husband, crafted an argument that woman suffrage, far from endangering white supremacy in the South, could actually strengthen it. Woman suffrage with educational or property restrictions would disqualify most black women without "having to disenfranchise black men and risk congressional repercussions." Catt and Anthony went on speaking tours and held their 1895 convention in Atlanta where they bowed to their southern hosts' insistence that they keep Frederick Douglass, their long-time suffrage ally, away. He died later that year. Still, they pursued the strategy of distancing themselves from black supporters until 1903 when the region's politicians failed to be swayed and resisted "petticoat government."

Although the Nineteenth Amendment did not differentiate as to which women would gain the right to vote with its passage, many black women, particularly in the South, were systematically denied enfranchisement due to literacy tests, poll taxes, and other forms of intimidation. Prior to 1920, black women were often denied full participation in the suffrage movement because suffrage leaders feared they would lose the support of the white southerners. After the Nineteenth Amendment's passage in 1920, the fate of back women's voting rights remained an important political issue within the women's movement.

Adella Hunt Logan, a Tuskegee faculty member, wrote in the NAACP publication, *The Crisis*, that if white women needed the vote to protect their rights, then black women needed the ballot even more. Alice Paul, another prominent suffrage leader, publicly advocated the right for all women to vote. Yet her actions often contradicted this view. In 1913, Paul became the leader of the Congressional Union for Woman Suffrage, which in 1917 became the National Woman's Party. She urged NAWSA to change its state-based strategy and throw its power behind the effort to secure a federal suffrage amendment. Historians view her leadership as crucial to the successful congressional passage of the Suffrage Amendment in 1919 and its ratification in 1920.

However, this achievement was not reached without some sacrifice of black women's rights. Many southern white women did not support universal women's suffrage. Opposing black suffrage, they advocated educated suffrage, a strategy that erected barriers to nonwhite voters—women as well as men. Some southern white women endorsed state suffrage for white women only. Because of the power of white southern politicians in the federal government, northern white women who advocated a constitutional amendment realized that they needed the support of white southern women if they were to get the federal amendment passed. As a result, anti-black suffrage sentiments developed among northern suffragists, who felt that it was expedient to ignore black women, as well as among southern white women, who believed in white supremacy.

In 1913, Paul organized a suffrage parade outside the White House. Before the parade, she expressed sympathy for black women's suffrage, but when the parade began, suffrage leaders asked Wells not to march with the Chicago delegation and Terrell's Washington, D.C., contingent was asked to march at the end of the parade. Wells angrily refused, but Terrell's group agreed to do so. Paul and other leaders were more concerned about offending southern white women. Moreover, Paul would not publicly state that she endorsed black female suffrage.

In 1919, Paul described her goal as "removing the sex qualification from the franchise regulations . . . to see to it that the franchise conditions for every state were the same for women as for men." This statement was a subtle way of telling the white population that black women could be just as easily disenfranchised by state laws as black men had been. She was forewarning black women even before suffrage was passed that she would do little to tamper with the right of states to disenfranchise black women.

In the South after 1920, black women who tried to vote experienced physical and economic intimidation, poll taxes, and educational and character requirements. Paul and the NWP did nothing to stop this. Stating that the enfranchisement of black women was a race issue, not a women's issue, Paul argued that black women should address the people who blocked their access to the vote rather than the NWP.

Black women were often denied the right to speak at NWP meetings; Paul said there was no room on the schedule for them. However, when black women did speak before the NWP, their opinions were severely criticized. Black women became increasingly frustrated by the lack of attention to their needs. Addie W. Hunton led a delegation of sixty black women from fourteen different states to urge Paul to make the race question a prime concern. Hunton believed that Paul was hostile to the cause of black women. When the suffrage victory celebration was held in Washington, D.C., in 1921, Terrell asked Paul whether she endorsed enforcement of the Nineteenth Amendment for all women, and Paul refused to say that she did.

Thus, the two principal arguments involving race that characterized the movement were that white women ought not to be the political inferiors of black men and that woman suffrage would not threaten white supremacy.

WOMAN SUFFRAGE BECOMES MAINSTREAM

After Catt took the helm of NAWSA, she molded the organization into a tightly controlled lobbying machine. She considered the liquor industry the invisible enemy and charged that its corrupt practices in American politics delayed the woman suffrage victory. However, other changes at the turn of the century, outside the suffrage movement, were aiding the cause.

During the Progressive Era of the late nineteenth and early twentieth centuries, the quest for woman suffrage started to become more of a mainstream issue. More activists joined the movement as women's roles in society expanded, and they saw the need for reforms strengthened by legislation. Around the country, men and women who supported Progressive reforms, such as workers' protection, and an end to child labor, political corruption, and unsafe food and drugs, recognized that women's votes could help secure these efforts.

Middle-class reformers such as Jane Addams, founder of Hull-House in Chicago, Florence Kelley, executive secretary of the National Consumers League, Rose Schneiderman, labor organizer with the Women's Trade Union League, and Agnes Nestor, president of the International Glove Workers Union, worked diligently for suffrage as a way to achieve improved conditions for workers.

Harriot Stanton Blatch, Stanton's daughter, returned to New York in 1902 after many years of living in England where she observed the radical and innovative British suffrage movement. She was determined to bring more working-class women into the suffrage movement to improve their economic status. She organized the Equality League of Self-Supporting Women in 1907, which became the Women's Political Union. Blatch excelled at pulling together political alliances between middle-class reformers and working-class women to rally for suffrage, infusing the campaign with new life and broadening its constituency.

After Catt stepped aside from the NAWSA leadership after four years to care for her dying husband,

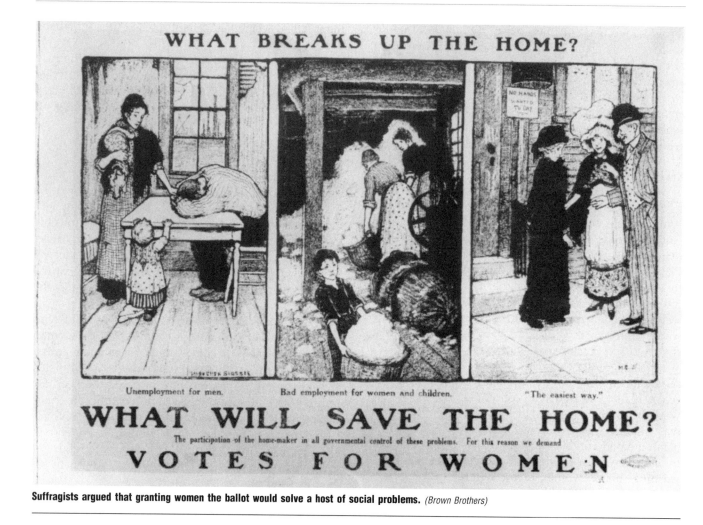

Suffragists argued that granting women the ballot would solve a host of social problems. *(Brown Brothers)*

Dr. Anna Howard Shaw took over. A veteran suffragist, medical doctor, and Methodist minister, Shaw embodied the essence of an emancipated woman. While her compelling oratory championed suffrage in every state in the Union, Shaw lacked Catt's vision and organizational skills, and she struggled to steer NAWSA for eleven years until Catt returned in 1914 after her husband's death. In that capacity, Catt, who was a brilliant and effective organizer, speaker, and fundraiser for the cause, spearheaded the final ratification effort in Tennessee in 1920.

Paul, who had studied and been active in the British suffrage movement, which stressed holding "the party in power responsible" for the amendment's fate, infused a new element of political imagery and street theater into the suffrage debate. She led a parade of 8,000 through the streets of Washington to draw attention to the cause and in protest of Woodrow Wilson's inauguration in 1913. The massive suffrage

parade was led by a tall, stunning young woman in flowing white robes on horseback. Thousands of women assembled in costumed marching units, holding colorful banners, and marched toward the White House accompanied by suffrage bands and floats. One Baltimore newspaper described the parade scene, as recalled in *The Perfect 36: Tennessee Delivers Woman Suffrage* (1998):

> Eight thousand women, marching in the woman suffrage pageant today, practically fought their way foot by foot up Pennsylvania Avenue, through a surging throng that completely defied Washington police, swamped the marchers, and broke their procession into little companies. The women, trudging stoutly along under great difficulties, were able to complete their march only when troops of cavalry from Fort Myers were rushed into Washington to take charge of Pennsylvania Avenue. No inauguration has ever

WHY WOMEN SHOULD VOTE
BY JANE ADDAMS, 1915

Jane Addams explains the importance of a leader in the women's suffrage as a means of alleviating the social ills of society. In the pamphlet, excerpted here, Addams explains that women both serve as primary caregivers in the family and take responsibility for the broader public health and educational needs of society.

This paper is an attempt to show that many women to-day are failing to discharge their duties to their own households properly simply because they do not perceive that as society grows more complicated it is necessary that women shall extend her sense of responsibility to many things outside of her own home if she would continue to preserve the home in its entirety.... A woman's simplest duty, one would say, is to keep her house clean and wholesome and to feed her children properly. Yet if she lives in a tenement house ... she can not fulfill these simple obligations by her own efforts because she is utterly dependent upon the city administration for the conditions which render decent living possible. Her basement will not be dry, her stairways will not be fireproof, her house will not be provided with sufficient windows to give light and air, nor will it be equipped with sanitary plumbing, unless the Public Works Department sends inspectors who constantly insist that these elementary decencies be provided....

If women follow only the lines of their traditional activities, here are certain primary duties ... which no one woman or group of women can adequately discharge unless they join the more general movements looking toward social amelioration through legal enactment.

The first of these ... is woman's responsibility for the members of her own household that they may be properly fed and clothed and surrounded by hygienic conditions. The second is a responsibility for the education of children: (a) that they may be provided with good books; (b) that they may be kept free from vicious influences on the street; (c) that when working they may be protected by adequate child-labor legislation.

(a) The duty of a woman toward the schools which her children attend is so obvious that it is not necessary to dwell upon it. But even this simple obligation cannot be effectively carried out without some form of social organization, as the mothers' school clubs and mothers' congresses testify, and to which the most conservative women belong because they feel the need of wider reading and discussion concerning the many problems of childhood....

(b) But women are also beginning to realize that children need attention outside of school hours; that much of the petty vice in cities is merely the love of pleasure gone wrong, the over-restrained boy or girl seeking improper recreation and excitement.... Women traditionally have had an opportunity to observe the plays of children and the needs of youth, and yet in Chicago, at least, they had done singularly little in this vexed problem of juvenile delinquency until they helped to inaugurate the Juvenile Court movement ...

(c) As the education of her children has been more and more transferred to the school, so that even children four years old go to the kindergarten, the woman has been left in a household of constantly narrowing interests, not only because the children are away, but also because one industry after another is slipping from the household into the factory.... The clothing and household linen are not only spun and woven, but also usually sewed by machinery; the preparation of many foods has also passed into the factory and necessarily a certain number of women have been obliged to follow their work there ... Because many thousands of those working in factories and shops are girls between the ages of fourteen and twenty-two, there is a necessity that older women should be interested in the conditions of industry. The very fact that these girls are not going to remain in industry permanently makes it more important that some one should see to it that they shall not be incapacitated for their future family life because they work for exhausting hours and under insanitary conditions....

In closing, may I recapitulate that if woman would fulfill her traditional responsibility to her own children; if she would educate and protect from danger factory children ...; if she would bring the cultural forces to bear upon our materialistic civilization; and if she would do it all with the dignity and directness fitting one who carries on her immemorial duties, then she must bring herself to the use of the ballot—that latest implement for self-government. May we not fairly say the American women need this implement in order to preserve the home?

Source: Jane Addams, *Why Women Should Vote* (New York: National American Woman Suffrage Association, 1915).

Patriotic images, slogans, and official documents are all invoked in this massive sign sponsored by the National Progressive Woman Suffrage Union.
(Brown Brothers)

produced such scenes, which in many instances amounted to nothing less than riots.

The mistreatment of many socially prominent women in the parade was embarrassing to the new Wilson administration. Congress held hearings into police failure to protect them, and the police chief was fired. Paul got exactly what she wanted: the issue of woman suffrage squarely on the front pages.

She continued to agitate. She and her followers chained themselves to the White House gates, where they were spat on and ridiculed. After several months of protest, in June 1917 more than 200 of her followers were arrested for "obstruction of sidewalk traffic" and put in Occoquan Workhouse in Virginia and the

Washington, D.C., jail. But for every protester arrested, there was another to take her place. They endured hunger strikes and forced feedings in jail to draw attention to their belief that they were political prisoners and, also, to embarrass the Wilson administration into supporting the Nineteenth Amendment.

Even though Catt and Paul vehemently disagreed with one another and their strategies differed on achieving the ultimate goal of a federal amendment, the movement needed both to succeed. While Paul and news about World War I were capturing national headlines, NAWSA suffragists continued to quietly win support state by state, city by city.

Catt's "Winning Plan" bolstered grassroots democracy as she urged NAWSA leaders in the states to

Huge crowds, including many children, line Fifth Avenue in New York City to watch a suffrage parade in 1916. *(Brown Brothers)*

support state referenda. She believed that once a state passed some form of woman suffrage, its congressional representatives and senators would become de facto supporters of a federal amendment. As more states passed woman suffrage, support in Congress increased, making passage of a constitutional amendment more likely.

NAWSA's lobbyists, led by Maud Wood Park, were collectively known as the "Front Door Lobby" because they were up front and aboveboard in their tactics. By keeping detailed cards on every legislator's promise as to how he would vote, they pioneered grassroots lobbying. In January 1917, Paul and her National Woman's Party began "Silent Sentinels" in front of the White House, hurling President Wilson's words in support of democracy in Europe back in his face on their banners and placards. Paul knew how to orchestrate political dissent for maximum effect, often to the dismay of NAWSA. This served to keep the

issue before the public and persuade elected officials to act.

When President Wilson finally endorsed the Nineteenth Amendment on January 9, 1918, and it passed Congress on June 4, 1919, the battleground shifted to the states, where thirty-six of the then forty-eight states were needed for ratification. Wisconsin became the first state to ratify on June 10, 1919.

A string of victories followed. By the summer of 1920, thirty-five states had ratified, eight had rejected it, and, with no other state even close to ratifying, the pro-suffrage forces looked to Tennessee. Tennessee became known as "The Perfect 36"—the last state that could possibly ratify the Nineteenth Amendment and make it law.

COUNTDOWN IN TENNESSEE

The fight in Tennessee began on June 19, when Tennessean Sue Shelton White, a close colleague of Alice

By demonstrating in front of the White House, woman suffrage leaders sought to showcase the hypocrisy of President Woodrow Wilson, who was fighting World War I "to make the world safe for democracy" and yet was denying democracy to half of all Americans. *(Brown Brothers)*

Paul, sent Governor Albert H. Roberts, a Democrat, a letter requesting a special session of the legislature. Other prominent Tennesseans requested the governor call a special session so women could vote in the August 5, 1920, state primary. The opposition was so vociferous that Governor Roberts called the special session for August 9 (conveniently after his party primary, which had been particularly fierce).

NAWSA leader Catt knew this final battle in Tennessee was going to be tougher than any other. She came to Tennessee in July expecting to stay a few days, but was there for nearly six weeks at the Hermitage Hotel in downtown Nashville. She wrote on August 15: "I've been here a month. It is hot, muggy, nasty, and this last battle desperate. Even if we win, we who have been here will never remember it with anything but a shudder."

What became known as "The War of the Roses" began with the anti-suffrage forces wearing the American Beauty red rose depicting their femininity and their efforts "to save Southern womanhood." The pro-suffrage forces countered with the yellow rose. Legislators arriving by train at Union Station in Nashville for the special session wore the rose reflecting their position on suffrage pinned to their lapels. One noncommittal legislator sported a talisman rose (a yellow rose with red stripes).

The Tennessee Senate voted 25–4 in favor of the Nineteenth Amendment on August 13; the House of Representatives was poised to change the course of American history during that hot, sultry summer of 1920.

After the Senate's overwhelming vote in favor, Catt wrote NAWSA headquarters: "We are one-half of one state away from victory." There were staunch supporters in the House, starting with Memphis Democrat Joe Hanover, who was the second youngest member of the General Assembly and a Polish immigrant who came to the United States as a child. Distressed that his mother could not vote, he ran for the House so he could cast his vote in favor of the Nineteenth Amendment because he believed so strongly in the right to vote for all Americans. He was known as "the man who took democracy seriously." He became the floor leader, a strong ally of Catt's, and kept the pro-suffrage forces together, which was no easy task.

The seventy-two-year struggle had come down to one last vote in the Tennessee House of Representatives. Representative Hanover led a united Memphis/Shelby County delegation with Representative T.K. Riddick of Memphis, who introduced the amendment, emphasizing that refusal to enfranchise women was "a relic of barbarism."

After all the parliamentary maneuvering, vote trading, and the devastating defection of Speaker Seth Walker to the anti-suffrage side, debate began on Wednesday, August 18.

Oration after oration reviewed seventy-two years of familiar arguments until, abruptly, a self-assured Speaker Walker turned over his gavel to Representative William Overton, another staunch anti-suffragist, then made his way down to the House floor and asked to be recognized. With melodramatic flourish, he was making it known that the "Antis," just as suffragists had calculated, had at least forty-nine sure votes, a majority of those present and voting.

"The hour has come. The battle has been fought and won, and I move you, Mr. Speaker, that the motion to concur in the Senate action go where it belongs—to the table!" And now his strategy was clear. As double insurance, Walker was moving to kill the amendment by tabling it. Any still uneasy fence-sitters could more easily justify a vote to table than an outright vote against.

Antis chorused, "Second the motion." Suffragists clamored for recognition. Overton ordered the roll call to begin. There were no surprises. Harry Burn's name came early in the roll; he voted in favor of tabling. Other members answered according to expectations until the name Banks Turner was called . . . The roll call went on, but before the final vote could be announced, Turner rose. "I wish to be recorded as against the motion to table." Suffragists gasped in joy. On a tie vote, 48–48, the motion was defeated. The Nineteenth Amendment was still alive in Tennessee.

But not for long. The motion to table had failed on a tie vote. It seemed certain that the original motion to concur in the Senate's ratification would do likewise. Realizing this, Walker immediately called for a vote on the original motion. Once more the agony of the roll call began. And this was the vote that counted.

The first two recorded votes were "aye" followed by four "nays." Harry Burn, a Republican who was the youngest member of the General Assembly, had been counted as a sure "Anti" since he wore the red rose. But he had not told anyone of a letter he had received that morning from his mother, Febb Ensminger Burn, of Niota in East Tennessee. She had written:

> Dear Son: Hurrah, and vote for suffrage! Don't keep them in doubt. I noticed some of the speeches against. They were bitter. I have been watching to see how you stood, but have not noticed anything yet. Don't forget to be a good boy and help Mrs. Catt put the 'rat' in ratification.
> Signed, Your Mother.

When his name was called, Harry Burn said "aye" so quickly that many did not realize what had happened. Banks Turner decisively shouted his "aye," and the resolution was carried 49–47. Seth Walker immediately jumped to his feet and cried out, "I change my vote from 'nay' to 'aye' and move to reconsider." It was too late.

Pandemonium prevailed. Women were screaming, weeping, singing. They threw their arms about each other and danced in the jam-packed aisles. Suffragist legislators tore off their yellow boutonnieres and threw them in the air to meet the gentle rain of yellow rose petals floating down from the galleries above!

The next day, Representative Burn rose on the floor of the House and responded to critics: "I want to take this opportunity to state that I changed my vote in favor of ratification because: 1) I believe in full suffrage as a right, 2) I believe we had a moral and legal right to ratify, 3) I know that a mother's advice is always safest for her boy to follow, and my mother wanted me to vote for ratification."

REFLECTIONS ON THE SUFFRAGE MOVEMENT

In 1923, Catt wrote in her book, *Woman Suffrage and Politics*:

> To get the word "male" in effect out of the Constitution cost the women of this country 52 years of pauseless campaign. . . . During that time they were forced to conduct 56 campaigns of referenda to male

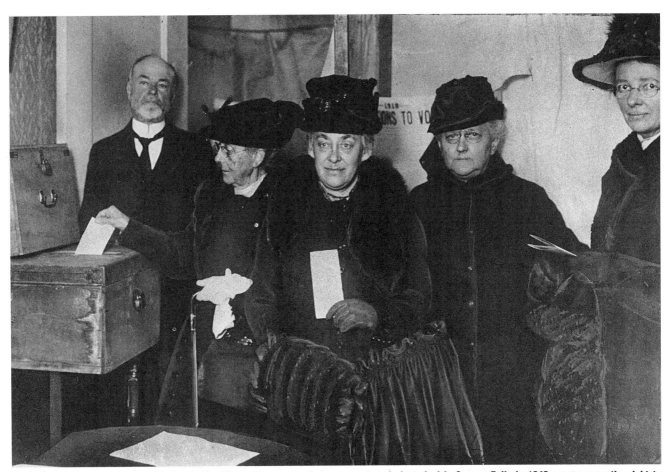

New York women cast their ballots for the first time. After a seventy-two-year struggle launched in Seneca Falls in 1848, women won the right to vote nationwide following ratification of the Nineteenth Amendment to the Constitution in 1920. *(Brown Brothers)*

voters; 480 campaigns to get Legislatures to submit suffrage amendments to voters; 47 campaigns to get State constitutional conventions to write woman suffrage into state constitutions; 277 campaigns to get State party conventions to include woman suffrage planks; 30 campaigns to get presidential party conventions to adopt woman suffrage planks in party platforms, and 19 campaigns with 19 successive Congresses.

Millions of dollars were raised, mainly in small sums, and expended with economic care. Hundreds of women gave the accumulated possibilities of an entire lifetime, thousands gave years of their lives, hundreds of thousands gave constant interest and such aid as they could. It was a continuous, seemingly endless, chain of activity. Young suffragists who helped forge the last links of that chain were not born when it began. Old suffragists who forged the first links were dead when it ended. . . .

It is doubtful if any man, even among suffrage men, ever realized what the suffrage struggle came to mean to women before the end was allowed in America. How much time and patience, how much work, energy, and aspiration, how much faith, how much hope, how much despair went into it. It leaves its mark on one, such a struggle.

The suffragists, who maintained their dedication and perseverance over the years, proved that peaceful revolution works. Whenever issues of equality for women are studied and debated, knowledge of woman suffrage history is always helpful. It shows that nothing is new. Every argument ever used to defeat equality was first used in the struggle for woman suffrage.

Paula F. Casey

BIBLIOGRAPHY

Barry, Kathleen. *Susan B. Anthony: A Biography of a Singular Feminist.* New York: Ballantine Books, 1988.

Catt, Carrie Chapman, and Nettie Rogers Shuler. *Woman Suffrage and Politics.* New York: Charles Scribner's Sons, 1923.

DuBois, Ellen Carol. *Feminism and Suffrage: The Emergence of an Independent Women's Movement in America, 1848–1869.* Ithaca, NY: Cornell University Press, 1978.

DuBois, Ellen Carol, ed. *The Elizabeth Cady Stanton–Susan B. Anthony Reader: Correspondence, Writings, Speeches.* Boston: Northeastern University Press, 1981.

Evans, Sara M. *Born for Liberty: A History of Women in America.* New York: Free Press, 1989.

Library of Congress. American Memory Historical Collections. http://memory.loc.gov/ammem/ammemhome.html.

Scott, Ann Firor. *Natural Allies: Women's Associations in American History.* Urbana: University of Illinois Press, 1991.

Scott, Ann Firor, and Andrew M. Scott. *Half the People: The Fight for Woman Suffrage.* New York: J.P. Lippincott, 1975.

Sims, Anastasia. *Powers That Pray and Powers That Prey: Tennessee and the Fight for Woman Suffrage.* Nashville: Tennessee Historical Society, 1991.

Stanton, Elizabeth Cady, Susan B. Anthony, and Matilda Joslyn Gage, eds. *History of Woman Suffrage.* Rochester, NY: Charles Mann, 1887.

Stevens, Doris. *Jailed for Freedom: American Women Win the Vote.* Ed. Carol O'Hare. Troutdale, OR: NewSage, 1995.

Wagner, Sally Roesch. *She Who Holds the Sky.* Aberdeen, SD: Sky Carrier, 1998.

Yellin, Carol Lynn. "Countdown in Tennessee." *American Heritage,* December 1978.

Yellin, Carol Lynn, and Janann Sherman. *The Perfect 36: Tennessee Delivers Woman Suffrage.* Oak Ridge, TN: Iris, 1998.

WOMEN'S MOVEMENT AND SOCIAL ACTIVISM 1865–1920

The nineteenth-century United States witnessed widespread organizing among white, middle-class women. Activists participated in religious, moral reform, antislavery, suffrage, and educational campaigns to elevate their status as well as to help those less fortunate than they, Taking their activism seriously, they wrote constitutions and by-laws, elected officers to oversee proceedings, circulated petitions to change laws, and gave public lectures to promote their goals. With the approach of the Civil War, however, women's reform took a back seat to the sectional conflict between the North and South. Now Union and Confederate women used their skills and energies to aid the Cause. They served as nurses, worked as camp followers, created the Sanitary Commission and other patriot organizations, and went into public school teaching, for many men, who had traditionally instructed children, were caught up in the war effort.

In many ways, the sectional confrontation between the North and South benefited women by broadening their societal role, by creating new work opportunities, and by freeing over 2 million female slaves. The struggle for women's emancipation, however, suffered, splitting the movement into two ideological camps. One side argued for universal suffrage, proclaiming that the time was ripe for blacks and women to receive the inalienable right to vote. Others asserted that it was the "Negro's Hour" and that women should temporarily take a back seat and focus on obtaining the vote for black men, who had been denied basic civil and political rights for centuries. Despite this setback in the women's rights campaign, the war opened up new opportunities and avenues for women's civic and political involvement.

Americans were noted for their volunteer enthusiasm, with the last third of the nineteenth century witnessing an even greater outpouring of associations. The growth in urbanization, industrialization, and immigration brought tremendous changes in the lives of women and men, poor and rich alike. The public and domestic landscapes took on unfamiliar sights as poverty swelled, child and female labor became norms, tenements towered over polluted cities, and factories bellowed their stacks in unprecedented numbers. Intellectuals, politicians, journalists, and social reformers expressed grave concern over the plight of the worker, often newly immigrated from southeastern Europe. Women, no less than men, led the march to cure these social ills.

At this time, women were increasingly gaining access to higher education, with many not marrying. Since the early nineteenth century, society had viewed women as inherently morally superior to men. Accordingly, women would naturally strive for the best interests of others and would restore purity and bring moral clarity to societal problems. Women had a special civic duty and mission to care for those less fortunate, especially women and children. College-educated women seized this opportunity to step into the public sphere and organize around a plethora of issues. Women's clubs, temperance societies, labor associations, settlement houses, birth control groups, suffrage organizations, and educational institutions blossomed. And as we will see, such involvement led women into political and government matters.

EDUCATION

In the nineteenth century, educational opportunities grew dramatically. The aftermath of the American Revolution gave rise to the notion that "citizens" needed to be educated for the newly created democratic nation to succeed. One result of this phenomenon was the education of young girls. As mothers, middle-class, white women now had the responsibility of raising virtuous, patriotic-spirited sons, the future leaders of tomorrow. Such a formidable shift in attitude opened the doors of education for both boys and girls. Even more importantly for women, not only

EMMA WILLARD (1787–1870)

Emma Willard was born Emma Hart in Berlin, Connecticut, on February 23, 1787, and was the next-to-last of seventeen children. Encouraged by her father, she began to acquire an education beyond the ordinary from an early age. In 1802, she enrolled in the Berlin Academy, her first school, where her progress was so rapid that by 1804 she was teaching in it; in 1806 she had charge of it for a term. In 1807, she taught briefly in an academy in Westfield, Massachusetts, and then became the principal of a girls' academy in Middlebury, Vermont, where in 1809 she married John Willard, a physician twenty-eight years her senior, and briefly stopped teaching to raise his children and her new baby.

Her husband's son lived with them while attending Middlebury College, and from him Emma learned of the vast difference in the education of men and women. Women were discouraged from learning mathematics, geometry, and the sciences because such subjects were thought to be beyond a woman's comprehension. Borrowing the young man's textbooks, she learned such subjects as philosophy and geometry. In 1814, with the family in financial difficulties, she opened a school in her home where she taught these and other subjects.

Inspired by her success, in 1818 she sent the New York legislature a plan for improving female education. The institution she envisioned would not be a private academy, such as already commonly existed, but a publicly endowed seminary supervised by a board of public men, precisely as the best institutions for young men were governed. At her expense, the plan was published and sent to some of the most prominent men in

the country. President James Monroe, Thomas Jefferson, and John Adams all read the document and approved its philosophy. The state legislature dismissed Willard's ideas as nearly heretical, but Governor DeWitt Clinton invited her to move to New York State. She opened her school in 1819 at Waterford even before receiving funding. The promised financial support never materialized.

In 1821, after receiving funding from the Troy, New York, town council, which had raised money to build a school for girls, Willard founded the Troy Female Seminary. The school pioneered the teaching of science, mathematics, and social studies to girls, and offered collegiate education to women and new opportunity to women teachers. It antedated Mary Lyon's Mount Holyoke Seminary (later College) by sixteen years and the first public high schools for girls (in Boston and New York City) by five years. The school attracted students from families of wealth and position and by 1831 had an enrollment of over 300, more than 100 of whom were boarding students.

Willard wrote a number of textbooks on such diverse subjects as biology, geography, and history, a journal of her investigative trip abroad in 1830, and a volume of poems. In 1838, she retired from the school, by which time hundreds of graduates, many of them teachers and all of them shaped by her philosophy, had carried her vision across the country. She devoted the remainder of her life to the improvement of common schools and to the cause of woman's education. Willard died in Troy on April 15, 1870. The Troy Female Seminary was renamed the Emma Willard School in 1895 and has remained a women's-only college preparatory school.

James G. Lewis

did female training include the domestic activities of cooking, cleaning, and decorative arts but educators also introduced the traditionally academic topics of science, history, government, and civic affairs. By 1850, numerous schools had sprung up with the explicit idea of creating a female educational standard equivalent to that found in elite male schools. Mirroring contemporary thought, rigorous studies should not interfere with a woman's ultimate goal of being a good wife and mother.

Emma Hart Willard, born in 1787 on a farm in Connecticut, was a pioneer in female education. As a child Willard displayed a precocious mind and with the encouragement of her father cultivated independent thinking. By the age of thirteen, she had not only

had the young girl's typical education of ornamental subjects but had also taught herself more academic topics such as geometry. She quickly became a favorite in her community as a tutor to both girls and boys, and in the spring of 1807 she had gained employment as an assistant at the academy in Westfield, Massachusetts. Willard, with her appetite for teaching and learning, worked in a variety of academies, and after unsuccessful lobbying for state funds to support female education, she opened the Troy Female Seminary in 1821. Under Willard's direction the school flourished, emphasizing rigorous studies on par with the best male schools. Troy graduates worked as teachers throughout the United States, and those who came into contact with them admired their manners and grace, a reflection of the tone that Willard had set for her pupils. Even though she had energetically sought to provide her students a solid, traditional education, she maintained that boys and girls should not receive exactly the same instruction, for marriage and motherhood were paramount in a woman's life. Nevertheless, Emma Willard and her Troy Seminary cultivated intellectual curiosity among young women, and in many ways she and her academy became prototypes for others interested in female training such as educational pioneers Catharine Beecher and Mary Lyons and their nineteenth-century ventures into women's education in the Northeast.

Oberlin College

In 1833, the opening of Oberlin College provided another critical step in the advancement of women's education. From its inception Oberlin welcomed women, and in 1835 it opened its doors to African Americans. Oberlin, an evangelical community founded to train teachers and preachers, established a precedent in coeducation. To make the college affordable to a broad base of pupils, all students were required to perform chores, with the women cleaning, laundering, cooking, and ironing, and the men tilling the soil, planting the food stuffs, and caring for animals. Such cost-cutting techniques allowed for women to receive education at a time when many families viewed a girl's training limited to household studies and her higher learning not worth the expense. In spite of the inviting and encouraging environment, female students were still treated differently than their male peers.

Oberlin educators set up a "Female Department" to oversee the curriculum and welfare of the young women. The young female scholars were closely guarded with a house mother in their sleeping and living quarters, but they could decide for themselves whether to pursue a rigorous, traditional academic curriculum or to concentrate on one that emphasized the domestic arts. Many coeds took advantage of this opportunity and studied the more demanding curriculums. Female graduates such as Lucy Stone, abolitionist and women's rights advocate, and Lucretia Mott, a leader in the abolitionist movement, matriculated at Oberlin and provided role models for future generations of young girls who dared to envision lives outside of the private sphere.

Female Education

By the end of the Civil War, female education had grown dramatically. The emerging trend in public education, the impact of the war, and the expansion of universities with passage of the Morrill Land Grant Act in 1862, all contributed to the expansion and acceptance of public and private education. The meaning of education and the type of training that sprang up took on an array of forms, ranging from learning the bare rudiments of literacy to acquiring technical knowledge to earning advanced degrees in universities. Most importantly, however, the growth in public education created a need for teachers, and young women, both black and white, filled this gap.

For some young women, the limited instruction provided in teacher training schools was not enough, and they started filling the ranks of the new universities, especially in the West and Midwest. For many proponents of female education, a woman's true education would not be found in these coeducational establishments. Often admitted only to help cut costs and relegated to traditional female programs, college administrators did not have serious intentions of providing quality studies for women, even barring them from certain courses such as anatomy. All-female colleges provided the answer to this void. Here young women would have access to curriculums that rivaled those of the best male colleges such as Harvard and Yale. Perhaps even more importantly, the female enrollees lived and studied in environments conducive to cultivating a sense of self, community, identity, and confidence.

After the founding of Vassar in 1861, considered the first of these female-centered schools, a string of well-endowed, rigorously academic female colleges emerged. From 1865 on, the colleges, known as the "seven sisters," (Barnard, Bryn Mawr, Mount Holyoke, Radcliffe, Smith, Vassar, and Wellesley) often had female professors and encouraged a sense of pride in their student populations. Despite such support, these early educational pioneers had a difficult hill to climb. Many contemporaries viewed a woman's intellect as inferior and education as a detriment to her health. For example, Edward Clarke, a leading opponent of women's higher learning, argued adamantly against women's education. In his widely read and received book, *Sex in Education* (1873), Clarke maintained that a woman did not have the physical or emotional stamina to withstand rigorous studies. He asserted that intellectual pursuits would weaken the brain, sometimes driving a woman to mental breakdown and ultimately destroying her reproductive capacity. These early schools therefore had to prove that females possessed the capability and the physical strength for intellectual achievement. The question persisted: How were these all-female colleges to combine the traditional tenets of womanhood with intellectualism?

One way to overcome these hurdles was to design a curriculum specific to women. Following the beliefs of M. Carey Thomas, pioneer in women's education and long-time president (1894–1922) of Bryn Mawr College, one of the "seven sisters" founded in 1885, women's educators proved to be innovators in this area. Convinced, like Thomas, that women and men had the "same love of abstract truth," the women's colleges designed curriculums tailored to a woman's particular needs. In addition to providing quality liberal arts programs, instruction also included traditional female courses such as art, music, and domestic science, with an intensive physical activity component. To make the schools more palatable for the female sex and their families, educators crafted a home-like atmosphere with the girls sleeping and eating together, as well as performing domestic chores such as cleaning. The mission of the schools still remained ambivalent. Just what was the purpose of a woman's advanced instruction? But under the veil of this domestic atmosphere, fewer and fewer opponents challenged the validity of women's colleges.

The establishment of the all-female colleges was a turning point in the history of women. At the least, the women-centered schools boosted self-esteem and confidence, provided an experience outside the home, and proved that women possessed the ability for higher learning free of mental or physical repercussion. No matter how much the founders and school organizers tried, these young women's experiences created a feeling of sorority in which they identified with one another, encouraging a female culture that allowed them the opportunity to develop and shape new roles and choices in society, not only for themselves but also for generations of women to come.

THE CLUB MOVEMENT

As previously noted, women and men had a long, rich history in association. In the last decades of the nineteenth century, following in the footsteps of past generations, women energetically organized and established women's clubs in unprecedented numbers. Middle- and upper-class black and white women comprised the majority of the membership, and the groups generally followed formal organizational rules patterned after parliamentary procedures, including officers, minutes, and regular reports. Most of the participants came from similar class backgrounds, but on the whole racial prejudices and tensions kept members from forming integrated clubs. Exclusion prevailed, with blacks being welcomed in name only and more often than not barred from activities. Such discriminatory actions, however, did not deter black women from founding their own clubs and incorporating race-specific issues into their agendas.

In 1868, Jane Croly, journalist and magazine editor, founded Sorosis. Croly was born in 1829 in England, and in 1841 her father moved his family to the United States. Upon her father's death in 1854, Croly was left virtually penniless. The following year she came to New York City and was quickly accepted into the newspaper world. For the next several years Croly, under the pen name of "Jennie June," worked at several papers writing columns for the "ladies" department. Even though she wrote columns devoted to fashion, gossip, and the domestic arts, she did not hesitate to criticize the limiting societal position of women. From the beginning, she lamented the crippling long, heavy, and hooped dress style and complained that the middle-class housewife lived a life of restless leisure. To alleviate some of these ills, Croly advocated women's education, but she recommended limited instruction for woman's main responsibilities, which should revolve around her duties as wife and mother. In a somewhat ambiguous tone she also expressed a special concern for what she believed to be the plight of the unemployed, middle-class working girl. Through her writings, she provided a type of career network informing young women of newly created jobs and directing them to employers where available positions existed.

In 1868, a chance occurrence spurred Croly to form the famous woman's club Sorosis. The New York Press Club had put together a dinner honoring Charles Dickens, and members did not invite women because the club was exclusively male. Inspired by this event, "Jennie June" organized a club for women, calling it Sorosis. Because of the highly visible nature of Sorosis's origins, it is often viewed as the beginning of the modern women's club movement. That same year Caroline Severance and Julia Ward Howe, both antebellum reformers, professional women, and women's rights advocates, began another club, the New England Woman's Club (NEWC). The establishment of these groups reflects the growing interest of women in joining in activities outside their homes, while remaining devoted to domestic ideals. For their participants, the clubs served as cultural and social centers, and they embodied a variety of purposes. Sorosis, for example, focused on traditional issues, while NEWC took on a more activist role, including women's rights concerns in its agenda. In the last quarter of the nineteenth century, clubs for middle-class, middle-aged women quickly caught on, growing in popularity and springing up throughout the United States.

Club Activities

These associations allowed women to explore non-domestic matters without challenging their traditional roles. Unlike the temperance or suffrage movements, the agendas of most clubs were vague, permitting women to associate in the public realm in a nonpoliticized way. Club activities often had literary overtones and served as sources of education for its members, many of whom, unlike their daughters, had had limited access to scholarly instruction. By the early twentieth century, in an atmosphere of and belief in change for the betterment of society, clubs now included more potentially controversial issues. The official statement of the national umbrella organization, the General Federation of Women's Clubs, emphasized the need to concentrate "on our own social order." Working on the local level, groups supported libraries, hospitals, playgrounds, women's education, social settlements, women's suffrage, and health services, to name only a handful of their successful programs. Still, the majority of women's clubs retained a noncontroversial tone, mirroring the interests of its local chapters. By World War I, club membership had swelled to over 1 million, and their collective agendas had touched on virtually all of the social and moral issues of the day.

Clubs also played a major role in the lives of middle-class African-American women. Club pioneers Josephine Ruffin and Fannie Barrier Williams had membership in the prestigious NEWC and the Chicago Woman's Club, respectively. Both women came from prestigious families; in addition, Ruffin's husband was a Harvard-trained judge and Williams's spouse was a successful lawyer. The white club members limited their activities, and controversy continually swirled around Ruffin and Williams. Black activists, realizing their limiting and discriminatory positions in the white associations, increasingly founded exclusively black clubs. Ruffin organized Boston's Era Club and put together a National Conference of Colored Women in 1895, and Williams joined the National Association of Colored Women, a collaboration of two earlier federations.

In 1896, Margaret Murray Washington, educator and wife of Tuskeegee's founder Booker T. Washington, and Mary Church Terrell, college-educated and daughter of the first black millionaire in the United States, formed the National Association of Colored Women. In many respects, the black women's clubs were similar to white female associations serving the needs of their communities. They established day nurseries, staffed reading rooms, and directed welfare projects, as well as addressed women's education, employment, and suffrage issues. In a very significant way, however, black women's clubs differed in that their agendas often included issues of specific concern to their race.

Having been denied basic social, civil, and legal rights, these club activists championed the cause of their people. They fought against lynching, and a one-woman crusade led by suffragist, club woman, and educator Ida B. Wells argued for moral purity and sought freedom from white male exploitation. They contended that white society viewed black women as morally loose, thus enticing white male sexual emotions. Following this line of thought, black men could not control their sexual nature and thrust themselves onto unwitting white women. Through example, these innovators intended to change such stereotypes by acting in a manner reflecting the epitome of moral purity and intellectual ability. Eventually, they hoped to beat down prejudice, provide opportunities for women of all races, and elevate the lives of African Americans.

TEMPERANCE

The early nineteenth century had witnessed the emergence of an anti-saloon campaign affiliated with the evangelical notion that drinking alcohol is a sin. Women had organized and participated in moral reform activities, often condemning alcohol and taverns, which they viewed as destructive to the stability of home and family. In the 1870s, a movement in Ohio against the use of alcohol again emerged, associated with female prayer groups—small cadres of women who congregated together usually outside of the church in their homes to worship God. Acquainted with poverty, crime, family abuse, loss of job, and ill repute, female and male evangelists had long struggled against the saloon and fought to close its doors. Their successes were short-lived, however, and soon after the shutting of a saloon, it often was reopened. With the founding of the Women's Christian Temperance Union (WCTU) in 1874, the crusade against alcohol surged full steam ahead.

In the early 1870s, a "Woman's Crusade" barreled through the Midwest. Ohio reformer and Civil War relief worker Annie Wittenmyer quickly climbed on

RESOLUTION IN WASHINGTON COURT HOUSE, OHIO December 25, 1873

The Woman's Christian Temperance Union was founded in 1874 by women who believed that alcohol consumption contributed to problems in families and social harmony. The organization advocated that only through abstaining from alcohol could families be protected. The following is the Resolution in Washington Court House that led to the formation of the organization.

Knowing as you do the fearful effects of intoxicating drinks, we, the women of Washington, after earnest prayer and deliberation, have decided to appeal to you to desist from this ruinous traffic, that our husbands and sons be no longer exposed to this terrible temptation, and that we may no longer see them led into these paths that go down to ruin, and bring both soul and body to destruction.

We appeal to the better instincts of your hearts in the name of desolated homes, blasted hopes, ruined lives, widowed hearts; for the honor of our community; for our prosperity; for our happiness; for our good name as a town; in the name of God, who will judge you, as well as ourselves; for the sake of your souls, which are to be saved or lost, we beg, we implore you to cleanse yourselves from this heinous sin, and place yourselves in the ranks of those who are striving to elevate the ennoble themselves and their follow men: and to this we ask you to pledge yourselves.

Source: Ohio Historical Society, Columbus, Ohio.

the band wagon, and in 1874 she helped to organize the National Woman's Christian Temperance Union. Along with the corresponding secretary, Frances Willard, Wittenmyer traveled on the lecture circuit and tirelessly circulated pamphlets to recruit followers and spread the WCTU's message. Within a few years, an ideological rift emerged between younger members, led by Willard, who embraced a wide range of causes including women's rights, and Wittenmyer, who wanted to focus exclusively on temperance. Eventually, Willard's group gained control, and when she took over the presidency in 1879, the organization rapidly grew in strength. Proselytizing a "do it all" philosophy and possessing expert organizational and strategic skills, Willard brought the WCTU onto the national stage.

Under Willard's tutelage, the WCTU took on issues of a radical flavor. The association not only desired to rid society of alcohol, but now its members also advocated societal reform generally. Championing causes from prostitution to political corruption to women's suffrage, members blamed men for tainting their world and demanded that they change their sinful ways. Willard, like many of her female counterparts, relied on traditional arguments of religion and social welfare to rally support for her concerns. Women, for example, should advocate suffrage, for having the right to vote would help them protect their homes. The National WCTU stood behind all these issues, but members could choose to embrace those most dear to their hearts. This strategy allowed for many different people with many views to join the WCTU, and ignited a large, diverse following.

The WCTU was organized on many levels, including local, state, and federal chapters. Participants held annual conventions with all the trimmings and overtones of politics, with "delegates, banners, flags, and music" permeating. This temperance group clearly gave women a sense of self outside of the home and family, and despite the differences in their priorities, WCTU affiliates proudly displayed their association with badges and white ribbons. Willard managed to mobilize thousands of women, and by 1911 they claimed membership of 245,000, comprising the single largest women's group to date.

More and more, Willard grew restless, and as illness befell her, she spent extended periods of time in England. Although her unorthodox views faced harsh criticism, she managed to maintain her leadership role. At the openly contentious national convention in 1897, Willard continued to hold onto the WCTU's presidency and her uncompromising, comprehensive agenda. But in less than a year she died at the age of fifty-eight of anemia. At her funeral service, followers displayed an outpouring of love and support, with over 2,000 attending. After Willard's death, the WCTU took on a more moderate tone, emphasizing its original message of temperance.

WOMEN PROGRESSIVES

By the late nineteenth century, U.S. society had grown increasingly impersonal. With the rise in urbanization, immigration, and industrialization, the gap between rich and poor had steadily widened. Growth in industry required a large, cheap pool of labor, with southeastern European immigrants responding to the call for an inexpensive labor supply. Now, in addition to economic factors, cultural and racial factors deepened the tensions between labor and management. In

FRANCES ELIZABETH WILLARD
(1839–1898)

Born on September 28, 1839, in Churchville, New York, Frances Willard grew up in Oberlin, Ohio, and in Janesville, Wisconsin Territory. Known as Frank to her friends, she was a sturdy, independent, and strong-willed child of the frontier who graduated from Northwestern Female College in 1859. In 1871, she was named president of Evanston College for Ladies and dean of women at Northwestern University when the latter absorbed Evanston. After leaving the university in 1874, she helped organize the Woman's Christian Temperance Union and in 1879 became its president. She devoted most of her life to the organization of women for the prohibition of alcoholic beverages but was active in other causes as well, especially that of woman suffrage.

In the 1870s, as the prohibition movement gained credence among women, a group of Chicago women invited Willard to become president of their temperance organization. In October 1874, she was elected secretary of the newly organized state temperance society, and in November, at the Cleveland organizing convention, she was chosen corresponding secretary of the National Woman's Christian Temperance Union (WCTU). The latter post led to considerable demand for her services as a lecturer. In 1876, she also became head of the National WCTU's publications committee.

She resigned as president of the Chicago WCTU in 1877 and worked briefly as director of women's meetings for the evangelist Dwight L. Moody. Later in the year she left the National WCTU, in large part because of the resistance of President Annie Wittenmyer to her wish to link the issues of liquor prohibition and woman suffrage. Her attempts to gain women the vote in Illinois failed. At the National WCTU's 1879 convention, Willard succeeded Wittenmyer and remained president of the WCTU for the rest of her life.

Under her leadership, the WCTU quickly became an organization able to mount campaigns of public education and political pressure on many fronts. Willard traveled constantly and spoke frequently—in 1883 she spoke in every state of the Union—and was a regular lecturer at the summer Lake Chautauqua meetings in New York. She then took the movement global. When a convention of delegates from twenty-one nations met in Boston in 1891 to form the World's WCTU, Willard was elected president. In 1888, she joined May Wright Sewall at the International Council of Women meeting in Washington, D.C., and laid the groundwork for a permanent National Council of Women, of which she was first president in 1888–1890. She also helped organize the General Federation of Women's Clubs in 1889.

Willard's attempt to push the WCTU into active politics ultimately failed in part because of her continued efforts to link suffrage with prohibition. Over the years she wrote frequently for periodicals and for WCTU publications. Her autobiography, *Glimpses of Fifty Years*, was published in 1889. In her later years she spent much time in England, where she came under the influence of the Fabian Socialists. After a year of failing health, she died in New York City on February 18, 1898. In 1905, a statue of her became one of Illinois's two submissions to Statuary Hall in the U.S. Capitol.

James G. Lewis

---

the early and mid-nineteenth century, manufacturers had largely relied on native-born workers to fill their employment needs. Undoubtedly, early factory conditions were not ideal, but owners had felt a certain social and moral responsibility toward their employees, many of whom attended the same churches and lived in the same neighborhoods they did. Proprietors now had to deal with people with whom they shared few social or cultural connections and who looked, acted, and spoke differently. Viewing the immigrant as inferior, employers showed little concern for this new breed of worker, who lived in unsanitary, crowded tenements and who toiled for little pay and long hours in dangerous, filthy work environments. In an attempt to overcome these horrific conditions, middle-class women and men sought to alleviate worker exploitation.

Depending on the cultural expectations of an immigrant group, many women, alongside husbands and children, toiled in the factories. Others found alternative ways to meet family needs. Some took care of boarders in crowded one-room apartments; others scavenged the streets for food and other necessities; and yet other female family members participated in the outwork system. This type of job involved piecework, and compensation depended on the speed with which one could accomplish the various manual tasks required to put together an item. Children as young as three years old worked alongside their mothers in tenements with little lighting, ventilation, and sanitation. Survival required contributions from all family members, and even then immigrant factory workers could barely make ends meet. Such devastating and deplorable living and working conditions drew the attention of the Progressives, young journalists, photographers, social scientists, and intellectuals who demanded change to this inhumane situation. A massive social reform campaign emerged, with women, mostly college-educated, at the forefront of the immigrant's plight.

Jane Addams and the Settlement House Movement

Jane Addams, born in 1860 into a prominent Illinois family, was a pioneer in the settlement house movement. In 1881, she graduated from Rockford Female Seminary, a girl's college patterned after the all-female colleges in the East. Much to the surprise of many, she thrived in this intellectual and community-spirited environment, actively participating in and organizing numerous clubs, including the debating team and literary society. Unlike many of her peers Addams never considered marriage, wanting to continue her studies. Unfortunately, within a few weeks after graduation her father died and she fell ill to a childhood illness. Sick and increasingly depressed, she decided to take a European tour to cure herself, but Addams returned to the States even more downhearted and restless. Lacking any direction, she lived with various family members as the spinster aunt and sister. Hoping to gain purpose and her health, in 1887 she again traveled to Europe, and this time Addams discovered what would become her lifelong work. For reasons unexplained she became more and more drawn to the poor, and at the end of her European trip she visited Toynbee Hall, a settlement house in one of London's worst slums. Toynbee, founded and run by young radical male college graduates, catered to poor men, providing job training and shelter. This house of social welfare inspired Addams to establish Hull-House in Chicago, a settlement focusing on the concerns of the working poor, especially women and children.

In 1889, Addams, along with the support of her school friend Ellen Gates Starr, established Hull-House, one of the first and most prominent settlement houses in U.S. history. The idea of a settlement patterned after that in London was not new. About the same time Hull-House opened, Smith College graduates founded the College Settlement, later known as Henry Street Settlement, in New York. Both centers were responding to the growing concern over urban social problems, especially those of the poor, immigrant laboring classes. As the hub of the meat-packing industry, Chicago provided Addams a perfect place to showcase her cause.

Addams had inherited ample funds from her father and so had the resources with which to begin her crusade. In contrast to other social service centers, one of the first priorities of the founders of the Hull-House in 1889 was to locate their settlement in the midst of those who would most need its services instead of in a respectful, safe neighborhood. Carefully choosing a building in one of Chicago's poorest immigrant districts, the activists moved into a rundown mansion and promptly opened its doors to the needy. Hull-House sponsored a wide array of programs, including classes on child rearing and nutrition, and it also provided resources for working mothers such as day nurseries, kindergartens, and youth clubs. Education played an important role in this settlement, and Addams and her coworkers established debating clubs, reading rooms, and art galleries. They also offered university extension classes. Addams and her fellow settlement house workers essentially provided social welfare services to the poorest of the poor, while also encouraging the immigrants to adopt Western ways of language, dress, food, religion, and culture.

Florence Kelley and Women's Activism

Settlement houses also filled a void for their college-educated, middle-class female participants. Like the sorority and leadership built during their college days, settlements provided these women with a place in which they could use their talents and skills, often in decision-making roles. With the rising interest in the poor and the establishment of Hull House, alumnae now had a recognizably important and significant role in the public sphere. Because of the notion of a woman's natural moral righteousness, female reformers had a special mission to improve the lives of women and children and to clean up the ills of society. With the growing interest in the rapidly changing societal landscape created by industry, women could use their natural abilities to aid the plight of the immigrant worker. In many ways, Florence Kelley's life epitomized the settlement experience.

Born in 1859 into an elite Philadelphia Quaker family, Kelley grew up in an atmosphere filled with politics and social activism. Her father had been one of the founders of the antislavery Republican Party, and her aunt Sarah Pugh, who largely raised her, was president of the important Philadelphia Female Anti-Slavery Society and regularly attended women's suf-

FLORENCE KELLEY SPEAKS OUT ON CHILD LABOR AND WOMAN SUFFRAGE
PHILADELPHIA, PA, July 22, 1905

In a speech in Philadelphia on July 22, 1905, Florence Kelley—an advocate of socialism, women's rights, and civil rights—explains the relationship between child labor and the absence of women's suffrage rights.

We have, in this country, two million children under the age of sixteen years who are earning their bread. They vary in age from six and seven years (in the cotton mills of Georgia) and eight, nine and ten years (in the coal-breakers of Pennsylvania), to fourteen, fifteen and sixteen years in more enlightened states.

No other portion of the wage earning class increased so rapidly from decade to decade as the young girls from fourteen to twenty years. Men increase, women increase, youth increase, boys increase in the ranks of the breadwinners; but no contingent so doubles from census period to census period (both by percent and by count of heads), as does the contingent of girls between twelve and twenty years of age. They are in commerce, in offices, in manufacturing.

Tonight while we sleep, several thousand little girls will be working in textile mills, all the night through, in the deafening noise of the spindles and the looms spinning and weaving cotton and wool, silks and ribbons for us to buy.

In Alabama the law provides that a child under sixteen years of age shall not work in a cotton mill at night longer than eight hours, and Alabama does better in this respect than any other southern state. North and South Carolina and Georgia place no restriction upon the work of children at night; and while we sleep little white girls will be working tonight in the mills in those states, working eleven hours at night.

In Georgia there is no restriction whatever! A girl of six or seven years, just tall enough to reach the bobbins, may work eleven hours by day or by night. And they will do so tonight, while we sleep.

Nor is it only in the South that these things occur. Alabama does better than New Jersey. For Alabama limits the children's work at night to eight hours, while New Jersey permits it all night long. Last year New Jersey took a long backward step. A good law was repealed which had required women and [children] to stop work at six in the evening and at noon on Friday. Now, therefore, in New Jersey, boys and girls, after their 14th birthday, enjoy the pitiful privilege of working all night long.

In Pennsylvania, until last May it was lawful for children, 13 years of age, to work twelve hours at night. A little girl, on her thirteenth birthday, could start away from her home at half past five in the afternoon, carrying her pail of midnight luncheon as happier people carry their midday luncheon, and could work in the mill from six at night until six in the morning, without violating any law of the Commonwealth.

If the mothers and the teachers in Georgia could vote, would the Georgia Legislature have refused at every session for the last three years to stop the work in the mills of children under twelve years of age?

Would the New Jersey Legislature have passed that shameful repeal bill enabling girls of fourteen years to work all night, if the mothers in New Jersey were enfranchised? Until the mothers in the great industrial states are enfranchised, we shall none of us be able to free our consciences from participation in this great evil. No one in this room tonight can feel free from such participation. The children make our shoes in the shoe factories; they knit our stockings, our knitted underwear in the knitting factories. They spin and weave our cotton underwear in the cotton mills. Children braid straw for our hats, they spin and weave the silk and velvet wherewith we trim our hats. They stamp buckles and metal ornaments of all kinds, as well as pins and hat-pins. Under the sweating system, tiny children make artificial flowers and neckwear for us to buy. They carry bundles of garments from the factories to the tenements, little beasts of burden, robbed of school life that they may work for us.

We do not wish this. We prefer to have our work done by men and women. But we are almost powerless. Not wholly powerless, however, are citizens who enjoy the right of petition. For myself, I shall use this power in every possible way until the right to the ballot is granted, and then I shall continue to use both.

What can we do to free our consciences? There is one line of action by which we can do much. We can enlist the workingmen on behalf of our enfranchisement just in proportion as we strive with them to free the children. No labor organization in this country ever fails to respond to an appeal for help in the freeing of the children.

For the sake of the children, for the Republic in which these children will vote after we are dead, and for the sake of our cause, we should enlist the workingmen voters, with us, in this task of freeing the children from toil!

Source: PBS. *Great American Speeches: 80 Years of Political Oratory.* Available at www.pbs.org/greatspeeches/timeline/f_kelley_s.html.

frage meetings. Educated at Cornell University, Kelley had hopes of graduate study but was shut out of the University of Pennsylvania. She then went to Zurich where women could receive a Ph.D. There she married, had three children, and became radicalized as a Socialist. She and her husband returned to the States, where she obtained various newspaper jobs but quickly tired of the female-centered pieces assigned to her. After a while, her husband grew frustrated over his failed attempts at practicing medicine, and he started beating her. After a year or so, she fled to Chicago and ended up as a resident of Hull House where she found the companionship and resources to pursue goals outside of domesticity. Like many of her peers, Kelley became involved in fighting worker exploitation.

Kelley wanted more than the traditional role allotted to women, especially married ones, and Hull House and its network of activists provided her with the niche she long desired. After several years working with women and children through settlement activities, in 1893 Illinois governor John Peter Altgeld appointed her chief factory inspector. During her term, she managed to get legislation passed that limited the age, hours, and working conditions of women and children. In 1899, she returned to New York where she served as secretary of the National Consumers' League from 1899 to 1932, the year of her death.

Founded in 1899 in New York, the League sought to bring working- and middle-class women together. League founders Maud Nathan and Josephine Lowell believed that laboring women should be provided a safe place in which to work and that they should be paid a livable wage. Nathan and Lowell asserted that middle-class women had the domestic responsibility to ensure that the goods they purchased were produced in safe, sanitary environments. In this way, the concerns of working- and middle-class women intersected, and under Kelley's leadership the NCL instituted the "white label," indicating that members had inspected these factories and that they found safe, clean labor conditions. The working woman could hope to be employed in decent workplaces and to receive fair wages, and the female consumer could aid her immigrant sister, as well as her family, by buying merchandise and food produced in sanitary and respectable workplaces. As can be seen through Kelley's experiences, settlement social reform activities propelled women into local, state, and federal politics, and were both an acceptable alternative to and compatible with marriage.

College-educated African-American women also established settlement houses. The end of the Civil War freed millions of slaves, most of whom lived in the South and were homeless, jobless, and penniless, and were surrounded by racism and violence. In 1908, wives of professors at the all-black Spelman and Morehouse colleges founded the Atlanta Neighborhood Union. These settlements provided many of the same services as the white centers, but they also encompassed a broader agenda, including race-specific issues. Members argued that racial exclusion and prejudice could not be separated from the economic problems facing African Americans. Until segregation and racial violence were alleviated, African Americans would stand very little chance of rising out of poverty. These female activists viewed lynching as a poignant example of the problems of their people; they flew into action and, along with programs to improve education, health, and employment, energetically campaigned against racism.

Suffrage

The organized suffrage movement can be traced to 1848 with the Seneca Falls Convention. Female abolitionists Elizabeth Cady Stanton and Lucretia Mott had been denied seats at the World Anti-Slavery Convention in London in 1840. At that time the two women, appalled that they could not participate in a conference devoted to human rights, vowed to hold a meeting focusing on women's issues. Because of family responsibilities and distance constraints, it took eight years for the women to put together a convention, but their dedication to this cause never waned. In 1848 in upstate New York, many of these activists were meeting to discuss the role of Quakers in the antislavery campaign and saw this as a perfect opportunity to investigate women's issues. In an atmosphere of reform, the women organized a conference in less than two weeks with over 200 in attendance and with manifold concerns on the agenda, including women's education, employment, legal status, dress reform, and the vote.

By all accounts, the meeting was a success and saw all of their concerns, except the most radical—that of suffrage—unanimously passing. From then on, women held annual women's rights meetings, and by the start of the Civil War, numerous organizations had sprung up throughout the nation. Most were on local or regional levels without formal state or national networks and without written rules, officers, or managers. A tone of spontaneity thus guided the women, with small groups going on speaking engagements, organizing petitions, and lobbying state legislatures. The signing of the Fifteenth Amendment, which granted black men the legal right to suffrage, stirred the women's rights' voting advocates.

In 1869, the women's coalition splintered into two opposing factions. One side, led by Elizabeth Cady Stanton and Susan B. Anthony, organized the National Woman Suffrage Association and advocated universal suffrage, arguing that all, black and white, women and men, should receive the vote. With Lucy Stone at the helm, the other side founded the American Woman Suffrage Association and maintained that it was "the Negro's Hour," that activists should concentrate on securing the vote for black men who had been denied rights for centuries. As the argument went, after freed men were ensured of the right to exercise suffrage, it would then be woman's turn. During the next couple of decades, the women did not make much progress, often fighting one another and lacking their base constituency, which had been grounded in the antislavery crusade. In 1890, after years of struggle, the groups reunited forming the National American Woman Suffrage Association (NAWSA). Suffragists established formal channels for campaign strategy, and the membership and leadership of the NAWSA overlapped with the temperance, club, settlement house, and labor movements. As seen in other crusades, however, women organized along racial lines, denying African-American and foreign-born females meaningful membership in the mainstream groups.

Growth of the Suffrage Movement

By the early twentieth century, suffrage had become a controversial issue and, led by mostly white middle- and upper-class women, had become the central issue of the feminist crusade. Although most organizing women belonged to charity, prohibition, or literary clubs, the issue of women voting had now taken center stage. The exact number of proponents is unclear, but it is evident that suffragists did not encompass a monolithic group, and, depending on temperament, personality, and policy, they drew attention to their cause in a multitude of ways.

As the suffrage campaign grew stronger, so did its critics. Opponents of women's emancipation argued that women and men had inherently different roles and functions in society. Women were the moral caretakers, and they had a special responsibility to care for home and family. It was the men in their families, usually husbands, who should manage affairs outside the domestic realm. Men therefore took care

of politics, and their vote would consider the best interests of the entire household. Some suffragists seized this argument based on "difference" to mold support for their cause.

Increasingly, suffragists themselves differed over why women should receive the vote. All agreed that women possessed a moral superiority and that with their vote society would take on a cleaner, purer tone, which was especially important at a time of grave political and corporate corruption. But was it because of a woman's difference that she deserved suffrage or was it because of her equality to man? In addition, disagreement deepened over the best and most effective strategies to use to achieve women's suffrage. Again a split in the movement occurred; this time the controversy involved ideology and strategy.

Two basic views emerged. On the one hand, proponents argued that it was exactly because of woman's difference that she should directly participate in political matters. Because of her moral righteousness and her concern for those less fortunate, she would act for the best interests of society as a whole, not allowing greed to interfere with her decisions. On the other side, most advocates did not dispute the notion of difference but maintained that women deserved suffrage, as well as other legal and civil rights, because of their equality to men. At the same time, arguments ensued over the best ways to go about working toward female enfranchisement. One faction asserted that modest, traditional tactics, such as petitions, lobbying, and speeches, should be used to garner support for women's suffrage, while others proclaimed that militant approaches such as hunger strikes, arson, and disruption should be utilized. Alice Paul, lawyer and feminist, led the way for a militant struggle.

Paul, inspired by leading British suffragettes and mother-and-daughter team Emmeline and Christabel Pankhurst, insisted on using aggressive confrontation tactics. With Paul's encouragement, militant supporters broke away from the NAWSA and in 1913 founded the Congressional Union. But it was with the establishment of the National Woman's Party (NWP) in 1916 that Paul and her followers appeared on the suffrage stage as a major force.

From its inception, the NWP adopted a militant agitation strategy. The group organized rallies and marches, often with overtones of violence. To draw attention to their plight, NWP members, largely white and from the upper and middle classes, burned effigies of President Woodrow Wilson, chained themselves to the White House fence, and had to be

Five men peer into the window of the headquarters of the National Association Opposed to Woman Suffrage. Many Americans feared that woman suffrage would divide families, disrupt marriages, and undermine society. *(Library of Congress)*

force-fed in jail. These unladylike actions evoked much attention from the press, putting the suffrage campaign into the national limelight. At the same time, Paul had shifted her group's strategy to obtain the vote. Instead of legislating female enfranchisement state by state, Paul and her followers lobbied for a constitutional amendment. They argued that trying to change laws in individual states would take too long and that in the end women would still not have a guaranteed national right to legal enfranchisement. Women had received the vote in some Western states, and Paul had seen the long and bitter fights suffragists had encountered in their struggles to obtain the

vote there. She maintained that a federal amendment would be the only way to ensure female enfranchisement for all women. Carrie Chapman Catt, feminist, president of the NAWSA, and a prominent international suffragist, had a long history of state legislating and led her group in this direction. Both sides tirelessly worked on gaining the vote for women, and in spite of their personal and political squabbles, each played a vital role in female enfranchisement in the United States. After seventy-two years of struggle, on August 26, 1920, with the ratification of Tennessee, women finally received the right to vote with the Nineteenth Amendment.

African-American Women and Suffrage

African-American women also participated in the campaign for women's suffrage. In their numerous social and political groups such as the Alpha Club, established by Ida B. Wells in Chicago, and the National Association of Colored Women, a collaboration of black female activists, African-American women organized fundraisers, circulated petitions, lobbied legislators, and participated in suffrage parades. They regarded female enfranchisement as especially important because in their eyes racism and sexism were intimately intertwined. Ida B. Wells had long insisted that the widespread use of lynching to punish male crimes was associated with male and female, black and white stereotypes of lust and sexuality. Possessing the right to vote would give these female innovators leverage in their struggle against racism, enabling them to bring justice to their unfairly accused brothers, to improve education, to protect themselves against while male abuse, and to secure working rights and opportunities. Similarly, politicians would now have to take heed and consider the needs and concerns of African Americans inasmuch as the black vote could be a critical turning point in deciding the outcome of an election.

From its inception, Paul proclaimed that the NWP welcomed black membership; it even had some prominent black participants such as Mary Church Terrell. To keep the support of their white membership, especially in the South, however, black suffragists were not placed in visible decision-making positions, nor were they welcomed openly to participate in the NWP's activities. An incident in 1917 summarizes the African Americans' position in the white suffrage campaign. The NWP had orchestrated a march down Pennsylvania Avenue in front of the White House to bring attention to the cause of women's suffrage. This was to be a well-publicized and important demonstration. Mary Church Terrell, who had insisted on joining the NWP, was now informed that she could not march arm-in-arm with her sister suffragists as Paul had promised her. On the urging of other members who refused to participate in the protest if Terrell did, Paul thought it best to discourage Terrell from attending. Mary Terrell and other Black suffragists, like their white counterparts, nevertheless played an important role in alleviating the widespread use of lynching, increased opportunities in education, and provided role models for both white and black young women.

BIRTH CONTROL

Until the last quarter of the nineteenth century, custom had largely dictated the use of contraceptives with little interference from the law. The legal system traditionally stayed out of such family affairs, stepping in only under questionable circumstances surrounding the death of a mother or child. Passage of the Comstock Law in 1873 forbidding the sale, manufacture, mailing, importation, and distribution of birth control information or devices changed all that. Now anyone who disseminated birth control literature, advice, or instruments was often arrested and jailed. This shift had little impact on middle-class women, who had personal physicians to take care of their health concerns. Those most affected were the poor, immigrant women, who did not have access to health services, whose culture did not freely discuss contraception, and whose husbands often objected to their wives exercising reproductive autonomy.

Margaret Sanger

Margaret Sanger, anarchist, labor organizer, and settlement house nurse, saw firsthand the devastation of these women's plights. Born in 1879 into a family of eleven, Sanger witnessed her own mother's health problems associated with childbirth and the stress of unrelenting debt to provide for a large family. Educated at a private preparatory school, in spite of her father's objections, Sanger refused to lead the life of a housewife. Similar to other educated women of her day, she tried her hand at teaching but realized that it did not suit either her temperament or her ambitions. After marrying and having three children, she tried to settle into a traditional home life, but she found herself restless. Eventually, she and her husband moved to Manhattan where she found the female companionship and radical causes she had longed for. Working as a home nurse to immigrants, Sanger discovered her calling.

As a healthcare giver to the poor, Sanger witnessed the complications of births, abortions, poor nutrition, and large families. To solve and alleviate these dreary situations, she proposed that women understand their bodies and that an integral part of this care included reproductive knowledge. Sanger went so far as to advocate that women control their own bodies. In order to provide information to those who lacked access to physicians, Sanger researched and published pamphlets outlining the medical aspects of reproduction and contraception. Under the Comstock Law, she was indicted for illegal dissemination of obscene material; to avoid jail, she went to Europe on a self-imposed exile. She returned to the United States a year later, when the government dropped its case against her. According to Sanger, the death of Sadie Sachs, a poor immigrant in a New York tenement, caused her to take even more legal risks, plunging her into an aggressive birth control campaign.

Sachs had experienced several complicated births and had asked her doctor for reproductive information. The physician advised her to have her husband sleep on the roof. Needless to say, Sachs again became pregnant and performed a self-induced abortion, resulting in a slow and painful death. Sanger had counseled Sachs, but she did not have the medical resources to help her prevent pregnancies. Sachs's death stirred such deep emotions in Sanger that she decided to spend her life helping women acquire safe and accurate birth control information. Sanger used this tragedy, whether myth or not, to marshal support for her cause and was more determined than ever to open a clinic where poor women would have access to medical advice and contraceptive materials.

Sanger, with the assistance of her sister, realized her dream with the opening of the Brownsville Clinic in 1916 in Brooklyn. In the ten days before the police closed its doors, over 450 women swarmed to the center seeking professional healthcare. With the arrest and jailing of Sanger and her sister, her cause drew national attention, evoking great sentiment. Although she lost her court case, which pleaded for women's access to reproductive information, the judge ruled that doctors could dispense contraceptive information to women for the prevention of disease. This legal decision paved the way for the ultimate success of the birth control crusade, for until then, only men could receive medical information to prevent venereal disease.

By the end of the second decade of the twentieth century, Sanger had shifted gears and had adopted a "doctors-only" policy, which reinforced the professional position and control of doctors over women's bodies. She divorced her husband in 1922 and married millionaire J. Noah Slee, who provided her the freedom and financial backing to continue her crusade. Sanger broke ties with the radical vanguard, supported eugenics as a rationale for birth control, and utilized her elite social contacts to raise funds for her cause. Even though Sanger's philosophy of reproductive autonomy ceased, she established a prototype for the modern birth control movement. In 1921, she founded the American Birth Control League, which in 1942 became the Planned Parenthood Federation of America, arguably the most vocal and influential force on women's reproduction today. Two years later, she organized the Birth Control Clinical Research Bureau, a teaching and research facility intended to disseminate accurate medical birth control information and to uncover and dispel birth control myths. The center, staffed mostly by female doctors, also created a network of clinics throughout the United States, reaching 300 clinics by 1938.

Mary Ware Dennett

A history of the birth control movement in the United States would not be complete without an examination of Sanger's rival Mary Ware Dennett. Home decorator, suffragist, pacifist, and sex education advocate, Dennett was born in 1872 into a family of Old New England stock. Educated at the local schools and then at the Boston Museum of Fine Arts, Dennett became a prominent artist. Despite her artistic acclaim and recognition, she was unsure of her ability and grew increasingly interested in political affairs such as women's suffrage, socialism, and pacifism. At the same time, Dennett, like many other Progressive reformers, fought against the ills of population explosion. In 1914, with Sanger exiled in Europe, Dennett, along with other birth control advocates, seized her absence as an opportunity to reshape the movement into a more moderate group that rejected militant tactics in favor of legal reform.

Dennett was never able to galvanize a large following comparable to those of her counterparts, but she never lost sight of the need for woman's reproductive autonomy and continued to work on the right of women to control their own bodies. As Sanger grew increasingly conservative, arguing that women should rely on doctors for their reproductive information, Dennett became more and more radical, insisting that sex education and birth control were intimately linked. Until women understood how their bodies functioned sexually, they would not fully comprehend contraception, and to assist women Dennett wrote numerous articles on the pleasures and joys of sex. Her uncompromising stance did not go unnoticed, and in 1928 she was fined $3,000 for circulating her essay. Her conviction drew an outpouring of support, and for awhile she had the recognition that had eluded her. In the 1930s, as women gained access to safer birth control information and as rumors of war swirled, Dennett turned to her earlier cause for peace. Unlike Sanger, Dennett continued to take the bumpier road of radical causes. Even though the two activists remained rivals and never collaborated, they acknowledged their mutual worth and efforts in the birth control campaign. And despite the movement's twists and turns, the early birth control crusade led to the collapse of antilegislation providing access to reproductive information and helping to shape and give rise to the struggle for reproductive autonomy— a struggle that still goes on today.

LABOR ACTIVISM

In contrast to the other movements examined, lower-class working women unquestionably played a major role in labor activism. Labor organizing revolved around the unskilled who often toiled under sweat-shop conditions or around the skilled tradesmen who had organized somewhat successfully in the American Federation of Labor, established in 1886 by Samuel Gompers. Women, usually excluded from all unions, found uneasy allies with the reform-minded middle-class females. Together they strove to improve working conditions and wages, to provide training for increased employment opportunity, and to include women's issues on union agendas.

By the early twentieth century, women's work patterns had changed. In addition to finding employment in jobs directly related to the domestic sphere such as boarding, outwork, service, and sewing, women also filled positions as secretaries, retail clerks, and teachers. Although the type of work a woman performed depended on local opportunities, ethnic attitudes, and family traditions, the single largest area of female employment was in factories. With the rise in urbanization and industrialization, an increased demand for a large, cheap pool of labor emerged, and immigrant women, alongside their male counterparts, gained employment in the unskilled sectors of manufacturing, especially in the textile end. Despite her dominance in this industry, the female worker was often excluded from joining the International Ladies' Garment Workers' Union, the organizing arm of the garment industry.

Women's Exclusion from Unions

Traditionally, union structures were not conducive to female participation. Often labor groups revolved around skills, and women were not welcome to join trade apprenticeships. Similarly, union members held meetings late at night when women had the responsibilities of home and family; moreover, the meetings took place in saloons, which were bastions of male superiority and dominance, and in many cases male unionists showed outright hostility toward female workers. Perhaps the biggest obstacle, however, lay in

the women themselves. Most were young and viewed factory work as temporary until they married. Consequently, they were willing to put up with poor working conditions for a short period if their only other choice was to go to meeting halls late at night in unfamiliar neighborhoods to encounter hostile union members. A couple of unions, however, welcomed women.

The Knights of Labor, founded in 1869, and the Industrial Workers of the World (IWW), established in 1905, were the two notable exceptions. Both groups welcomed blacks and whites, women and men, skilled and unskilled, and the IWW even invited employers to join with the hope of forming a cooperative type of industry. These associations encompassed a wide range of issues but were largely unsuccessful. Agendas were too diffuse, infighting broke out, and unskilled workers did not have much bargaining power over management. By the late 1880s, the Knights had lost what little power they had to the AFL, and the IWW's alliances with radical political groups as well as their support of violent agitation made them too extreme for most workers. In the end, the female worker would find her bargaining chip in the garment industry organizing with other women.

Textile manufacturing, dependent on immigrant labor, was the largest industry in New York, with workers, often entire families, toiling up to eighty hours a week under sweatshop conditions. Whether engaged in outwork at home or laboring on the machines in factories, workers were exposed to polluted, unhealthy work environments. By the second decade of the twentieth century, New York monopolized the women's clothing industry, including the latest trend, the shirtwaist. By 1900, 65,000 women worked in textile manufacturing, with most of them making women's clothing. In fact, they dominated the shirtwaist industry, comprising four-fifths of the 40,000-member workforce, most of whom were immigrants: two-thirds were Russian Jews, one-quarter Italian, and a small portion native-born whites. Only a few hundred black women worked in the industry, for they were virtually excluded from industrial work, except in the busy season or as scabs or in other menial roles. Not surprisingly, throughout the garment trade, men usually held the most skilled and highest paying positions either as supervisors or in the skilled position of cutter. Women and children, in defiance of child labor laws, were at the bottom, were paid by the piece with speed determining wage, and were forced to work up to fifteen hours a day.

To make matters even worse, factory owners

hired subcontractors to handle much of the piece-work, and this middleman received a lump sum for completing the required tasks. The work was performed in the factory on machines rented from the owner, and the profit for the subcontractor depended on the quickness of the workers. In an attempt to increase profits and cut down on overhead expenses, supervisors often physically and verbally abused employees. Known for the harmful tactics that employers used, subcontracting ignited a rallying cry around which women organized.

The Women's Trade Union League

By the early 1900s, 25 percent of the shirtwaist workers participated in subcontracting. All female garment workers were especially subject to layoffs, economic depressions, and wage cuts, but women who toiled under a middleman were even more vulnerable to employment fluctuations. In the 1890s and early 1900s, the workers' condition worsened. Depression and panic caused layoffs and wage cuts, and increasingly employers squeezed labor to make more profits. In 1906, with the founding of Local 25, the Ladies Waistmakers Union, women gained a foothold in union organizing in the textile sector.

Young women under the age of twenty-five dominated the shirtwaist industry. Foreign-born or the daughters of immigrants, these women received hostility from all sides. Working for low pay and long hours in filthy, unsafe conditions, many of them strove to better their situations. Seven women and six men started Local 25, a division of the International Ladies' Garment Workers' Union, an organization for those who worked on women's clothing. The local had few expectations of success. The garment industry had a bleak record when it came to organizing, and three years after its origins Local 25 still only had 100 members and a treasury of less than $5. Opportunity came about as an unexpected result of a strike in 1909.

In 1903, with the founding of the Women's Trade Union League, middle-class reformers and female workers had formed an alliance. The League had a dual purpose: to organize women into the trade union movement and to integrate working-class women's concerns into the women's rights campaign. Because of the male-dominated culture of unions and because of indifference, even hostility, toward female members, the middle-class reformers and their working-class collaborators realized that they had huge obstacles to overcome, not only with management but among themselves as well.

Much to the surprise of many, the 1909 shirtwaist strike grew rapidly. Spontaneously, 200 employees at the Rosen Brothers Shirtwaist Company left their jobs and demanded higher pay. Their success, a 20 percent wage increase and union recognition, encouraged others to do the same. Membership in Local 25 swelled dramatically, with over 1,000 joining in the first few weeks, and workers of other shirtwaist companies began striking. At first, employers did not fear the interruptions, for it was the slow season and there were plenty of unemployed ready to take the place of the striking workers. With the assistance of the well-connected WTUL, however, the strikes became a powerful force with which factory owners had to reckon.

Coalitions between the middle and working classes were hard to come by. Priorities often differed, and antagonisms flared over agendas and leadership. This time, however, a united front emerged. Middle-class reformers could provide many resources such as money, food, and child care, and their mere presence gave credibility to the labor movement, eliciting media attention to the workers' plight. In the early strikes, the activists decided that men should stay behind, having only females on the picket lines. This tactic, they hoped, would limit or even alleviate completely the violence from police as well as from the "thugs" hired by employers. Even with only females picketing and with the presence of New York socialites, violence broke out.

Union leaders, including Clara Lemlich, Local 25, cofounder and Russian immigrant, organized a mass meeting to call for a general strike; over 5,000 attended. After an impassioned speech by Lemlich (an employee of the Leiserson factory) and in defiance of prominent labor leader Samuel Gompers, the workers voted for a general strike. To the great surprise of many, within a few days 20,000 to 30,000 walked off their jobs, virtually crippling their employers. To galvanize even more support, WTUL members launched a citywide campaign recruiting lawyers, patrons, and volunteers to staff picket lines, relief stations, and information centers. The women managed to gain positive attention from many spheres and through marches and rallies extended its support to a broad base, including Socialists, male unionists, and the local elites. The strike quickly spread to Philadelphia, and WTUL activists organized their Chicago and New York branches to help out. Such widespread activism renewed the controversy over black workers. Few had managed to join the unions not only because of their scarce numbers or because owners largely exploited them as scabs, but also because of the racism exhibited by the female employees themselves. It would be decades before any effective measures would change the black worker's struggle.

Within a month, the manufacturer's association made an agreement with officers of Local 25 promising safer work environments, reduction in hours, provisions for free work materials, paid holidays, and the rehiring of strikers. But employers refused to recognize unions and implement closed shops. Workers turned down the contract, maintaining that without the backing of unions enforcement of the agreement would be impossible. By January, public support for the strikers had waned, and it was more and more difficult for those left on the picket lines. Within a month Local 25 signed a contract. Employers granted strikers many of their demands, such as pay increases, better working conditions, and fewer hours, but they still would not accept the union.

Within a couple of years the workers' world was again shattered. Despite laws forbidding the locking of emergency doors, the Triangle Shirtwaist Company continued this dangerous practice. In 1911, amidst the flammable textile work environment, a fire quickly spread throughout the building. Unable to escape, 146 of 400 female workers perished, with many jumping from ninth-story windows to flee the flames of the inferno. As a crowd gathered in the street below, the woes of the worker were reawakened.

Clearly, working women and men still had a long hill to climb, but the activism of these early female organizers provided inroads for all of labor, with at least some improvement in factory conditions. Even though management did not meet all of labor's demands and repeatedly fell back into old habits, the garment worker had proven that she could muster the support needed to galvanize a large and successful strike. This early labor activism showed how much enthusiasm could be garnered and the power of workers, even those unskilled, when united. This event thus evoked a sense of pride in the working man and woman, and instilled fear in the factory boss, for he now had a vision of what was yet to come. And at least for a while, working- and middle-class women formed an alliance, albeit uneasy, for the betterment of their gender. Nonetheless, concerns over protective legislation would hamper the cooperation of these diverse groups of women. Just how much would laws limiting the hours and type of work that a woman was allowed to do benefit her? Or would they exclude women from precious positions in the better paid skilled sectors?

CONCLUSION

By 1920, women had organized on many fronts and had succeeded in achieving many of their goals. They had the right to suffrage, had access to institutions of higher learning, had made inroads to birth control information, and had increasingly created new opportunities in the public sphere in the areas of teaching, social work, labor organizing, and civic affairs. All women benefited, but clearly the white, middle-class woman gained the most. Despite such achievements, there were limits on women's acceptable role, and in many ways the traditional tenets of womanhood and motherhood persisted. Still women had carved out a niche for themselves and had broadened their sphere to include activities in the public realm, paving the path for future generations of organizing women.

Sue Wamsley

BIBLIOGRAPHY

Baer, Judith A. *The Chains of Protection: The Judicial Response to Women's Labor Legislation.* Westport, CT: Greenwood Press, 1978.

Berg, Barbara J. *The Remembered Gate: Origins of American Feminism, The Woman and the City, 1800–1860.* New York: Oxford University Press, 1978.

Blair, Karen J. *The Clubwoman as Feminist: True Womanhood Redefined.* New York: Holmes & Meier, 1980.

Blocker, Jack. *American Temperance Movements: Cycles of Reform.* Boston: Twayne, 1989.

Bordin, Ruth. *Women and Temperance: The Quest for Power and Liberty, 1873–1900.* Philadelphia: Temple University Press, 1981.

Boris, Eileen. *Home to Work: Motherhood and the Politics of Industrial Homework in the United States.* New York: Cambridge University Press, 1994.

Brodie, Janet Farrell. *Contraception and Abortion in Nineteenth-Century America.* Ithaca, NY: Cornell University Press, 1994.

Bryan, Mary L., and Allen F. Davis, eds. *One Hundred Years at Hull House.* Bloomington: Indiana University Press, 1990.

Camhi, Jane Jerome. *Women Against Women: American Anti-Suffragism, 1880–1920.* Brooklyn, NY: Carlson, 1994.

Cantor, Milton, and Bruce Laurie, eds. *Class, Sex, and the Woman Worker.* Westport, CT: Greenwood Press, 1977.

Carson, Mina. *Settlement Folk: The Evolution of Social Ideology in the American Settlement House Movement, 1883–1930.* Chicago: University of Chicago Press, 1990.

Clark, Claudia. *Radium Girls: Women and Industrial Health Reform, 1910–1935.* Chapel Hill: University of North Carolina Press, 1997.

Cross, Barbara M., ed. *The Educated Woman in America.* New York: Teachers College, 1965.

Davis, Allen F. *American Heroine: The Life and Legend of Jane Addams.* New York: Oxford University Press, 1973.

———. *Spearheads for Reform: The Social Settlement and the Progressive Movement, 1890–1914.* New York: Oxford University Press, 1967.

Dubois, Ellen. *Feminism and Suffrage: The Emergence of an Independent Women's Movement, 1848–1869.* Ithaca, NY: Cornell University Press, 1978.

Dye, Nancy Schrom. *As Equals and Sisters: Feminism, the Labor Movement and the Women's Trade Union League of New York.* Columbia: University of Missouri Press, 1980.

Epstein, Barbara Leslie. *The Politics of Domesticity: Women, Evangelism, and Temperance in Nineteenth-Century America.* Middletown, CT: Wesleyan University Press, 1981.

Fitzpatrick, Ellen. *Endless Crusade: Women Social Scientists and Progressive Reform.* New York: Oxford University Press, 1990.

Foner, Philip S. *Women and the American Labor Movement.* New York: Free Press, 1979.

Gabaccia, Donna. *From the Other Side: Women, Gender, and Immigrant Life in the U.S., 1820–1990.* Bloomington: Indiana University Press, 1994.

Gilmore, Glenda Elizabeth. *Gender and Jim Crow: Women and the Politics of White Supremacy in North Carolina, 1896–1920.* Chapel Hill: University of North Carolina Press, 1996.

Ginzberg, Lori D. *Women and the Work of Benevolence: Morality, Politics, and Class in the Nineteenth Century.* New Haven, CT: Yale University Press, 1990.

Gordon, Linda. *Woman's Body, Woman's Right: A Social History of Birth Control in America.* New York: Grossman, 1976.

Gordon, Lynn D. *Gender and Higher Education in the Progressive Era.* New Haven, CT: Yale University Press, 1990.

Green, Elna C. *Southern Strategies: Southern Women Southern Women and the Woman Suffrage Question.* Chapel Hill: University of North Carolina Press, 1997.

Green, Nancy L. *Ready-to-Wear and Ready-to-Work: A Century of Industry in Paris and New York.* Durham, NC: Duke University Press, 1997.

Harris, Alice Kessler. *Out to Work: A History of Wage-Earning Women in America.* New York: Oxford University Press, 1982.

Hendricks, Wanda A. *Gender, Race, and Politics in the Midwest: Black Clubwomen in Illinois.* Bloomington: Indiana University Press, 1998.

Hewitt, Nancy A. *Women's Activism and Social Change: Rochester, New York, 1822–1872.* Ithaca, NY: Cornell University Press, 1984.

Hoffert, Sylvia D. *When Hens Crow: The Women's Rights Movement in Antebellum America.* Bloomington: Indiana University Press, 1995.

Horowitz, Helen Lefkowitz. *Alma Mater: Design and Experience in the Women's Colleges from Their Nineteenth-Century Beginnings to the 1930s.* New York: Knopf, 1984.

Hunter, Tera W. *To Joy My Freedom: Southern Black Women's Lives and Labor after the Civil War.* Cambridge, MA: Harvard University Press, 1997.

Kerber, Linda K. *Women of the Republic: Intellect & Ideology in Revolutionary America.* New York: W.W. Norton, 1986.

Knupfer, Anne Meis. *Toward a Tenderer Humanity and a Nobler Womanhood: African American Women's Clubs in Turn-of-the-Century Chicago.* New York: New York University Press, 1996.

Kraditor, Aileen. *The Ideas of the Woman Suffrage Movement, 1890–1920.* New York: Columbia University Press, 1965.

Lasch-Quinn, Elisabeth. *Black Neighbors: Race and the Limits of Reform in the American Settlement House Movement, 1890–1945.* Chapel Hill: University of North Carolina Press, 1993.

Lehrer, Susan. *Origins of Protective Labor Legislation for Women, 1905–1925.* Albany: State University of New York Press, 1987.

Levine, Louis. *The Women's Garment Workers: A History of the International Ladies Garment Workers Union.* New York: B.W. Huebsch, 1924.

Litwack, Leon. *Been in the Storm So Long: The Aftermath of Slavery.* New York: Knopf, 1979.

Lubove, Roy. *The Professional Altruist: The Emergence of Social Work as a Career, 1880–1930.* Cambridge, MA: Harvard University Press, 1965.

Lunardini, Christine. *From Equal Suffrage to Equal Rights: Alice Paul and the National Woman's Party.* New York: New York University Press, 1986.

Marshall, Susan E. *Splintered Sisterhood: Gender and Class in the Campaign Against Woman Suffrage.* Madison: University of Wisconsin Press, 1997.

Melder, Keith. *Beginnings of Sisterhood: The American Women's Rights Movement 1800–1850.* New York: Schocken Books, 1977.

Milkman, Ruth, ed. *Women, Work, and Protest: A Century of U.S. Labor History.* Boston: Routledge & Kegan Paul, 1985.

Mohr, James C. *Abortion in America: The Origins and Evolution of National Policy, 1800–1900.* New York: Oxford University Press, 1978.

Muncy, Robyn. *Creating a Female Dominion in American Reform, 1890–1935.* New York: Oxford University Press, 1991.

O'Neill, William L. *Feminism in America: A History.* 2d ed. New Brunswick, NJ: Transaction Books, 1989.

Orleck, Annelise. *Common Sense and a Little Fire: Women and Working Class Politics in the United States, 1900–1965.* Chapel Hill: University of North Carolina Press, 1995.

Rothman, Shelia M. *Woman's Proper Place: A History of Changing Ideals and Practices.* New York: Basic Books, 1978.

Sklar, Kathryn Kish. *Catharine Beecher: A Study in American Domesticity.* New Haven, CT: Yale University Press, 1973.

———. *Florence Kelley and the Nation's Work: The Rise of Women's Political Culture, 1830–1900.* New Haven, CT: Yale University Press, 1995.

Solomon, Barbara Miller. *In the Company of Educated Women: A History of Women and Higher Education in America.* New Haven, CT: Yale University Press, 1985.

Tax, Meredith. *The Rising of the Women: Feminist Solidarity and Class Conflict, 1880–1917*. Urbana: University of Illinois Press, 2001.

Tentler, Leslie Woodcock. *Wage-Earning Women: Industrial Work and Family Life in the United States, 1900–1930*. New York: Oxford University Press, 1979.

Terborg-Penn, Rosalyn. *African American Women in the Struggle for the Vote, 1850–1920*. Bloomington: Indiana University Press, 1998.

Wertheimer, Barbara Meyer. *We Were There: The Story of Working Women in America*. New York: Pantheon Books, 1977.

Woody, Thomas A. *A History of Women's Education in the United States*. New York: Science, 1929.

AFRICAN-AMERICAN WOMEN'S MOVEMENT

Frances Ellen Watkins Harper (1825–1911) was the leading "race woman" of her era. Born to free blacks in Baltimore, Harper received a good education, taught school, and wrote poetry, novels, and political tracts. When Maryland passed a law in 1853 that forbade free blacks from crossing its borders, Harper left her teaching job and joined the antislavery circuit. Nicknamed the "Bronze Muse," Harper combined her commanding stage presence with an unmatched command of language to become the leading symbol of black womanhood of her era. After the Emancipation Proclamation, Harper continued her work for racial uplift through temperance, moral reform, and women's rights by joining Elizabeth Cady Stanton and Susan B. Anthony in the formation of the American Equal Rights Association (AERA). But when Stanton and Anthony opposed the Fifteenth Amendment because it failed to give women the vote, Harper left the AERA and joined the American Woman Suffrage Association, which had supported the Reconstruction Amendments, the three post–Civil War additions to the Constitution that abolished slavery, guaranteed black citizenship, and secured black male suffrage. She was present when Anna Julia Cooper and Fannie Barrier Williams challenged white women to protest the rape of black women in the South and was a founding member of the National Association of Colored Women. In 1892, she published her most famous work, *Iola Leroy*, which explored the meaning of race and the responsibility of African-American women to racial equality. Harper's career served as a bridge between African-American women's antislavery work and their post–Reconstruction civil rights movement.

AFRICAN-AMERICAN WOMEN AND WORKERS RIGHTS

This civil rights movement emerged out of the failures and disappointments of Reconstruction. In the years following the Civil War, former slaves and free blacks alike attempted to reunite families and seek economic opportunities that would free them from white control. For a brief period, Reconstruction offered hope as African-American men gained citizenship rights and actively participated in Southern political life. But for most freedmen and women economic opportunities proved more elusive as Black Codes and sharecropping prevented many from owning their own land. Still, former slaves sought to control their own labor, especially that of women as black women's ability to labor for their own families rather than for whites became an important symbol of that independence.

Despite their efforts to labor on behalf of their own families, 70 percent of African-American women in the South worked for a wage. Younger women generally worked as house maids and child nurses, while older women chose occupations that gave them more flexibility. For women in Atlanta, the occupation of choice was that of laundress because they could work outside the homes of whites and control the pace of their work. This desire to control the conditions under which they worked brought laundresses into conflict with their white employers. When those employers attempted to gain more control over the rates they paid or when they encouraged competition from Chinese men, African-American women organized boycotts. Large-scale job actions took place throughout the South in the post–Reconstruction period. For example, in 1866 in Jackson, Mississippi, laundry workers called a citywide strike, while in Atlanta laundresses boycotted their white patrons in 1881. In both instances, women drew on the political skills they had learned as Republican Party workers and as members of labor unions and churches. Their actions resulted in less competition from Chinese laundries and, in some instances, in establishing uniform pay rates. Their actions demonstrated the desire of

FRANCES ELLEN WATKINS HARPER (1825–1911)

Born in Baltimore, Maryland, on September 24, 1825, Frances Watkins was the daughter of free black parents. Born free in a slave city, she was raised by an abolitionist uncle whose school for black children she attended and was well enough educated that by 1845 she published her first volume of poetry, *Forest Leaves*. At age thirteen she went to work as a domestic in a Baltimore household but continued her education on her own. She also taught sewing to support herself.

In 1854, she gave her first antislavery lecture and thereafter continued to give such lectures throughout the Northeast. She also gave recitations of her poems and published her second volume, *Poems on Miscellaneous Subjects* (1854), which soon made her the best-known African-American poet of the era. It addressed the subjects of motherhood, separation, and death and contained the antislavery poem "Bury Me in a Free Land." Its narrative voice reflected the storytelling style of the oral tradition. She also contributed to various periodicals. Her story, "The Two Offers," published in 1859, was said to be the first published by a black American author.

The abolitionist controversy and the consequent increasing stringency of slave laws in the South drew her into the public arena. In August 1854 in New Bedford, Massachusetts, she delivered a public address on "Education and the Elevation of the Colored Race." Her success there led to a two-year lecture tour in Maine for the state Anti-Slavery Society, and from 1856 to 1860 she spoke throughout the East and Midwest. She then married Fenton Harper in 1860. But when he died in 1864, she returned to lecturing on a variety of social causes.

After the Civil War, Harper made several lecture tours of the South speaking on education, temperance, and other topics, and in 1872 she published *Sketches of Southern Life*, a series of poems told in black vernacular. From 1883 to 1890, she was in charge of activities among blacks for the National Woman's Christian Temperance Union. She became a director of the American Association of Education of Colored Youth in 1894, and in 1896 she helped organize the National Association of Colored Women, of which she was elected a vice president in 1897. In her later years, she also took up the cause of women's rights. Her extensive writings—including more volumes of poetry, a travel book, and a novel—no longer have much literary status, but they were important in providing a new image of and for African Americans. She died in Philadelphia, Pennsylvania, on February 22, 1911.

James G. Lewis

African-American women to control their workplace and their ability to draw on past political experience to effect change.

While working-class women organized to gain control of their work, middle-class African-American women looked to education and social welfare institutions to improve not only their status but that of the folk—the poor African Americans. In the years following the Civil War, former abolitionists and ministers looked to the "talented tenth" to lead African Americans. White allies sought out the best men and women of the race to infuse middle-class values into poor communities and to serve as a bridge between blacks and whites. To this end, white religious leaders and former abolitionists sponsored educational institutions, such as Spelman College, to train the talented tenth. Founded in 1881 by the Woman's American Baptist Home Mission Society and run by white missionaries Sophia Packard and Harriet Giles, Spelman trained African-American women to become teachers, nurses, and missionaries. A donation from John D. Rockefeller allowed the seminary to move into its own building; it was named after Rockefeller's first wife, Laura Spelman Rockefeller. Within one year, the seminary grew from eleven students to over 200. In 1901, it awarded its first college degrees, and in the 1920s, it hired its first African-American women faculty members.

CHURCHES AND RELIGION

The movement toward self-help through moral uplift only grew stronger as Reconstruction fell apart and African-American men lost most of the political opportunities they had gained in the 1860s and 1870s. With the failure of Reconstruction, African-American communities turned inward, developing businesses and social institutions that catered to their communities rather than to white patrons. As the institutions most independent of white control, black churches became the leading social, cultural, and political institutions within their communities. African-American women raised funds for these churches and built their social welfare programs. Although African-American women played a key organizational role within black churches, they were often excluded from leadership positions and the ministry. Increasingly, African-American women found this exclusion intolerable as their education provided them with the tools to interpret the Bible and make complex theological arguments. Frustrated by their exclusion, Baptist women such as Virginia Broughton and Mary Cook looked to the Bible for examples of female leadership and developed arguments based on religion for women's leadership. Both organized local women's organizations in their respective states of Tennessee and Kentucky and developed effective statewide women's groups. In 1900, five years after African Americans had formed their own arm of the Baptist Church—the National Baptist Convention—Nannie Helen Burroughs (1879–1961) addressed its national convention. In a speech entitled "How Sisters Are Hindered from Helping," Burroughs claimed that African-American women felt a "righteous discontent" at their marginalized role within the church. That speech, combined with the power women's organizations had gained within state churches, convinced the Baptist Convention to approve a separate women's arm—the Woman's Convention.

Burroughs became the leading force within the Woman's Convention. She served as its secretary until 1948 when she assumed its presidency, a position she held until her death in 1961. Throughout her tenure, she worked to maintain the autonomy of the Woman's Convention. In 1907, Burroughs claimed that the Woman's Convention represented 1.5 million Baptist women. In the years following the founding of the Woman's Convention, its leaders practiced "Social Christianity," a Progressive-era movement that linked individual salvation to improving social conditions. Northern Baptist women worked to mitigate the effects of urbanization on African-American women by developing vocational schools and allying with white Progressives such as Frances Kellor. In 1909, Burroughs founded the National Training School for Women and Girls, which continues to operate today. The goal of these schools was to professionalize domestic service by training African-American women to apply middle-class values to their work. Burroughs and her supporters believed that such training would elevate African-American women's status and provide them with living wages.

The Woman's Convention did not shy away from political issues. In 1914, it joined the National Association for the Advancement of Colored People (NAACP) campaign to eradicate racist stereotypes in textbooks and movies. The Woman's Convention also advocated boycotting newspapers and organizations that mistreated African-American people, and it worked for woman's suffrage.

CALL FOR RIGHTS IN THE CHURCH

Although most African-American women were Protestant, Catholic women also organized institutions for self- and community improvement. In New Orleans, African-American women of the Sisters of the Holy Family founded a convent that educated African-American girls and provided individual African-American women to play an influential role in their community. Faced with continuous poverty and racism both within and outside the Catholic Church, the convent's Mother Superiors were forced to negotiate with church officials and move the convent around the city while continuing to provide social welfare services and educational opportunities to young women. Like their Protestant counterparts, the Sisters of the Holy Family believed that combating vice and infusing middle-class moral (Catholic) values into the poor African-American community that surrounded the convent was essential to uplift and racial advancement.

A strong belief in women's ability to change the course of civilization motivated women's demands for an expanded role within their churches and within the African-American community in general. As African-American men were politically disenfranchised, lynched, and economically marginalized, African-American women argued that they had a responsibility and opportunity to take up the fight that African-American men appeared to be losing. This fight entailed not only fighting for their own rights within the African-American community but also organizing against the violence that terrorized African-American communities. African-American women took leadership roles in the antilynching movement.

ANTILYNCHING

In March of 1892, Thomas Moss and two other men were lynched in Memphis, Tennessee. On the surface, this lynching was like the hundreds of lynchings of African Americans that had occurred in the last two decades of the nineteenth century. But this event would galvanize the political careers of two of the most prominent "race women" of the period—Ida B. Wells (1862–1931) and Mary Church Terrell (1863–1964)—both of whom were friends of Moss and both of whom were outraged by his lynching. The co-owner and editor of Memphis's African-American newspaper, *The Free Speech*, Ida B. Wells responded to Moss's lynching with a blistering editorial that instructed African Americans to leave Memphis. Her words began a large black migration west to Oklahoma. For two months, Wells's attacks on the white leaders of Memphis were relentless. In May, Wells anonymously penned her most famous editorial, which challenged the myth that African-American men raped white women. "Nobody in this country believes that old threadbare lie that Negro men rape white women," Wells wrote, "if Southern men are not careful, they will overreach themselves and public sentiment will have a reaction; a conclusion will then be reached that will be very damaging to the moral reputation of their women." Outraged by the editorial, white newspapers called for its author's removal and a mob burned the offices of the *Free Speech*. Fearing for her life, Wells moved to Chicago and began an antilynching campaign that secured her place as the leading race woman of her era.

Wells's antilynching campaign was the most famous of a long line of civil rights activities that defined her life. Born in Holly Springs, Mississippi, a few months before President Abraham Lincoln issued the Emancipation Proclamation, Wells left college early to support her siblings through a teaching career after her parents died. In 1884, she gained national attention when she sued the Chesapeake, Ohio and Southwestern Railroad for forcing her to move from the first-class car to a "colored" car. When the Tennessee Supreme Court reversed the decision of a lower court's ruling that had decided in Wells's favor, Wells turned to journalism to fight racial oppression. In 1889, she became the co-owner of the *Free Speech*. Two years later she was fired from her teaching job for an editorial that criticized the lack of support for African-American schools. For the next twenty years, Wells used pen and podium to expose the idea that organized political violence was rooted in the nexus between race, sexuality, and gender. She also organized African-American suffrage clubs and community groups in her adopted city of Chicago.

To challenge the myth that the lynching of African-American men was justified by their inherent desire to rape white women, Wells gathered statistics from the *Chicago Tribune* and her own research into hundreds of lynchings. She discovered that less than one-third of those cases involved even an accusation of rape. Wells noted that the deciding factor in lynchings was not rape but rather economic competition. Lynchings, Wells concluded (and historians have since verified her claims), were designed to maintain white

control over the labor of African-American people. Wells published her findings in a series of pamphlets that included *Southern Horrors: Lynch Law in All Its Phases* (1892) and *A Red Record* (1895); *Southern Horrors* was published after African-American women's groups raised $500. When her writings failed to sway Northern opinion, Wells traveled to England in an effort to exert economic pressure on Southern societies dependent on the English cotton market. Wells's campaigns resulted in a decrease in the number of lynchings in the first decade of the twentieth century.

Wells's writing on lynching attacked the popular belief that white women were more moral than African-American women. This idea, Wells argued, encouraged violence against African-American women and excepted white women from moral responsibility for their own sexual choices. Instead, Wells argued that virtuous womanhood was based on behavior, specifically on the willingness to stand up to and testify against racial violence.

THE NATIONAL ASSOCIATION OF COLORED WOMEN

Such attacks on the monopoly that white women claimed on morality were essential to the political organizing of African-American women. One way that African-American women accommodated to sexual violence and charges of sexual immorality was through what one historian has called "the culture of dissemblance"—that is, "a code of silence around intimate matters as a response to discursive and literal attacks on black sexuality." Middle-class African-American women attempted to silence such attacks by practicing the "politics of respectability," a strategy through which African-American women attempted to build coalitions with white women based on their common identification as mothers and Christian women. These strategies had limited success. For example, African-American women formed alliances within the Woman's Christian Temperance Union over a common desire to eliminate drinking. But as African-American women increasingly recognized, such strategies failed to strike at the heart of a racialized discourse that allowed for individual exceptions but still defined blacks as inferior. As Josephine St. Pierre Ruffin, the African-American suffragist who fought against slavery, explained at the founding of the National Association of Colored Women, "year after year, southern women have protested against the admission of colored women into any organization on the ground of the immorality of our women and because our reputations have only been tried by individual work, the charge has never been crushed." The importance of crushing this charge was brought home to Ruffin and other leaders of the black community when whites attacked the reputation of Wells in particular and African-American women in general to silence the antilynching movement.

When Ruffin moved to organize a national response to such charges, she called on the leaders of state and local women's clubs. Although African-American women had organized clubs since the 1790s, the last two decades of the nineteenth century had witnessed an explosion in the number of these clubs. In 1892, Mary Church Terrell, Anna Julia Cooper, and Mary Jane Patterson organized the Colored Woman's League of Washington, D.C. Soon women along the Eastern seaboard as well as in the South and Midwest began forming women's clubs. These clubs subscribed to ideals of racial uplift through self-help and believed that the home in general and mothers in particular held the key to the future of the race. They designed their programs to assist poor blacks through the creation of kindergartens and home visits. Club women believed that the adoption of middle-class ideals of respectability by all segments of the African-American population was essential to racial progress.

As historian Deborah Gray White notes, "for the women who proclaimed the 'woman's era,' the sum of their equation was the superiority of women in matters concerning the moral welfare of black people, and the equality of black men and women in everything else." These ideas were formulated by the organic intellectuals of the African-American women's movement. Perhaps the most famous of these intellectuals was Anna Julia Cooper, whose seminal work, *A Voice from the South* (1892), criticized African-American men for limiting black women's educational opportunities. Like other African-American women intellectuals, Cooper argued that the progress of the race was dependent on the status of women. In one of the most famous expressions of black feminist thought, Cooper wrote, "only the Black Woman can say 'where and when I enter, in the quiet, undisputed dignity of my womanhood, without violence and without suing or special patronage, then and there the whole Negro race enters with me." Like many white reformers, Cooper argued that black women's role as mothers uniquely positioned them to influence society and promoted within them values for a more just and less violent society. She called on white women to use their positions as mothers and teachers to teach anti-racism, and she urged black men to support women's desire for political and religious leadership. One of the first African-American women to obtain a bachelor's, master's, and Ph.D., Cooper was more comfortable with books and ideas than with the day-to-day demands of political organizing.

The formation of a national organization that could enact this vision was left to leaders like Mary Terrell, who would become the first president of the National Association of Colored Women, and Josephine St. Pierre Ruffin, the founder of Boston's New Era Club. Born in Memphis, Tennessee to former slaves who built a successful business, Terrell lived a relatively privileged life. She eventually earned a master's degree from Oberlin College and, like upper-class white women, toured Europe after her graduation. That tour enabled Terrell to master a number of European languages, which later proved useful when she lectured on American racism in Europe. After her tour, Terrell returned home to begin her career as an educator. But Moss's lynching interrupted Terrell's plans. Outraged by her friend's murder, Terrell joined Frederick Douglass in protesting Moss's lynching and sought an audience with President Benjamin Harrison. Denied that audience, Terrell channeled her frustrations into a sixty-year political career that relentlessly attacked racial injustice. To this end, she allied with controversial leader Booker T. Washington. That alliance and her emphasis on pragmatic politics brought her into conflict with Wells; when Terrell actively sought to prevent Wells from taking over the presidency of the NACW in 1907, some began to question Terrell's leadership style. Terrell remained a charismatic speaker and effective organizer who inspired African-American women and formed effective alliances with white women. Despite her alliance with Washington, she did not share his view that it was imprudent to argue for equal political rights. She organized African-American women for woman's suffrage and was a member of the National American Woman Suffrage Association. In 1908, she joined Washington's arch-rival, W.E.B. Du Bois, in forming the NAACP.

DEFENDING BLACK WOMEN

In 1895, Josephine St. Pierre Ruffin (1842–1924) called club women together in defense of black womanhood. A leader among Northeastern club women, Ruffin began her political career before the Civil War when, along with her husband, she recruited black men into the colored regiments of Massachusetts. In 1893, Ruffin edited the *Women's Era*, the first African-American newspaper owned and run by African-American women. Club women met at Ruffin's behest to protest a letter written by James Jack, president of the Missouri Press Association, which accused African-American women of "having no sense of virtue and of being altogether without character." A year after meeting to protest this letter, African-American club women founded the National Association of Colored Women. With the motto, "Lifting as we climb," the NACW sought to provide a national voice to the community work done by African-American women. They established regional networks to coordinate the work of otherwise autonomous clubs. The responsibility of the NACW was to communicate on the national level the messages that club women promoted in their local work. Those messages emphasized the importance of women's work to the creation of the nation and the "uplift of the race." The national organization also hoped to promote issues of concern to African-American women within predominantly white women's organizations. Upon its founding, the NACW had a membership of 200 clubs; by 1916, it had grown to over 1,500 affiliates.

Although the NACW was the largest national organization of African-American women, other more specialized groups also emerged on the national stage. The Association for the Protection of Colored Women helped rural women migrating to Northern cities to find housing, community, and employment. Such organizations often emerged from the experiences of African-American women. For example, the Phillis Wheatley Association, a settlement house for African-American women, was the result of a decade-long project begun by Jane Edna Hunter, who sought to help migrating black women because of her own inability to find decent housing and wages when she migrated to Cleveland in 1905. In 1908, at Howard University, African-American women formed the first black sorority—Alpha Kappa Alpha. In the years that followed, black sororities formed throughout the East to support and provide professional networks to educated African-American women.

UNFULFILLED EXPECTATIONS

African-American women expected that these national organizations would strengthen their position within the women's movements in general. Although some white women formed alliances with African-American women, most white women's clubs were segregated or excluded African-American women altogether. In 1900, in what became known as the "Ruffin incident," the General Federation of Women's Clubs (GFWC) refused to recognize Josephine Ruffin as a delegate from the New Era Club when its members realized that it was a black club. The GFWC subsequently instructed its state federations not to approve applications from black clubs, effectively keeping the GFWC an all-white organization. A similar incident took place in 1913 during the parade for woman's suffrage sponsored by the NAWSA. Bowing to the desires of Southern representatives, the leaders of the NAWSA segregated the parade, refusing to allow Ida B. Wells to march with the Illinois contingent. Wells waited for the parade to begin and joined the Illinois delegates. Individuals like Ruffin and Wells simply refused to leave "white-only" conventions and demonstrations, in essence forcing white women to integrate their organizations. Nonetheless, such humiliations increasingly frustrated efforts by white and black women to ally on common issues such as woman's suffrage.

African-American women not only pressed for inclusion, but they also demanded that whites incorporate issues of violence against African-American people within their political agendas. For example, during the World's Columbian Exposition in 1893, white women invited a carefully selected group of African-American women to address the Exposition in part to protest the exclusion of African Americans from that event. Rather than bowing to white women's desire for inoffensive addresses, Fannie Barrier Williams and Anna Julia Cooper challenged the sexual mythology that defined black women as inherently sexually promiscuous and protested their continued rape in the South. They also called on white women to protest this violence. Similarly, Mary Terrell and other African-American women joined the predominantly white International League for Peace and Freedom to use that organization's resources to combat lynchings. Their activity encouraged peace organizations to incorporate issues of racial justice into their definitions of peace work.

DISUNITY IN THE MOVEMENT

As historians of African-American women have illustrated, African-American women and men were not always united in their quest for racial equality. Personality clashes as well as disagreements over strategy and goals divided the women's movement and sometimes alienated it from lower class women and

African-American men. African-American women's claims that they were the new leaders of the black community offended some African-American men, who felt either betrayed by African-American women's criticisms of their leadership or simply believed that women had overstepped their boundaries through their public demands for equal rights. Some African-American men argued that women's participation in politics was unladylike and threatened the home. More conservative African-American women such as Margaret Murray Washington agreed. They challenged the need for suffrage, arguing instead that African-American women should restrict their work to the home and traditional community-based social welfare work rather than arguing for equal citizenship. To some degree, these debates mirrored those between Booker T. Washington, who emphasized self-help and economic advancement over political goals, and W.E.B. Du Bois, who emphasized higher education and citizenship.

The African-American women's movement's emphasis on respectability and investment in middle-class values alienated them from the folk. Like their white counterparts, middle-class African-American women often defined poverty, as at least in part a problem of the folk culture and values. They looked toward vocational training and the acceptance of middle-class moral standards as the means by which poor African-American peoples could combat economic marginalization.

Improving the status of the folk also included attacks on the religious and cultural expressions of poor blacks. African American middle-class women formed anti-vice societies that attacked not only organized prostitution and drinking but also dance halls and musical expression in which sexuality seemed to be on public display. Teachers such as Mamie Fields, who worked in rural communities, often attacked the values of rural blacks, demanding that her students re-learn domestic habits more in keeping with the middle-class home. Fields also criticized rural churches and ministers as corrupt and inefficient. The Sisters of the Holy Name expelled students who did not adopt their standards of Catholic middle-class womanhood. Middle-class African-American reformers saw the seeds of the race's destruction within the cultural expressions of poor rural and urban communities; as members of the talented tenth they were responsible for instilling respectability within the homes of all African Americans.

Despite these limitations, African-American women developed social welfare institutions and political organizations and shaped feminist ideologies that challenged the racial and sexual violence of post–Reconstruction society. Their work reduced lynchings, built community institutions, improved educational opportunities for women, and shaped a literary culture that nurtured future African-American women. It is no coincidence that the Harlem Renaissance, which spawned a new generation of African-American women intellectuals, followed this work. Like the organic intellectuals who preceded them, the women of the Harlem Renaissance critiqued lynching, examined racial oppression, and offered new explorations of such issues as passing and lesbianism. The works of intellectuals like Anna Julia Cooper and Ida B. Wells are now recognized as founding texts in American feminist thought. Both the NACW and the Woman's Convention remain important organizations within the black community as they continue to provide social welfare institutions and political opportunities for African-American women. These organizations would prove vitally important to and thrust women into the forefront of the modern civil rights movement.

Kathleen Kennedy

BIBLIOGRAPHY

Blackwell-Johnson, Joyce. " 'Now We Got Another Chance to Do Something for 'Em': African American Activists in the Women's International League for Peace and Freedom, 1920s–1950s." *Peace and Change* 23:4 (September 1998).

Boris, Eileen. "The Power of Motherhood: Black and White Activist Women." *Yale Journal of Law and Feminism* 2:1 (1989): 25–49.

Cooper, Anna Julia. *A Voice from the South: By a Black Woman of the South.* 1892. Reprint, New York: Oxford University Press, 1988.

Deggs, Sister Mary Benard. *No Cross, No Crown: Black Nuns in Nineteenth-Century New Orleans.* Eds. Virginia Meacham Gould and Charles E. Nolan. Bloomington: Indiana University Press, 2001.

Giddings, Paula. *When and Where I Enter: The Impact of Black Women on Race and Sex in America.* New York: Bantam, 1984.

Gordon, Linda. "Black and White Women's Visions of Welfare: Women's Welfare Activism, 1890–1945." *Journal of Women's History* 78:2 (September 1991).

Higginbotham, Evelyn Brooks. *Righteous Discontent: The Women's Movement in the Black Baptist Church, 1880–1920.* Cambridge, MA: Harvard University Press, 1993.

Hine, Darlene Clark. "Rape and the Inner Lives of Black Women in the Middle-West: Preliminary Thoughts on the Culture of Dissemblance." *Signs* 14 (Summer 1989).

Jones, Jacqueline. *Labor of Love, Labor of Sorrow: Black Women, Work and the Family from Slavery to the Present.* New York: Basic Books, 1985.

McMurry, Linda. *To Keep the Waters Troubled: The Life of Ida B. Wells.* New York: Oxford University Press, 1998.

Shaw, Stephanie J. "Black Club Women and the Creation of the National Association of Colored Women." *Journal of Women's History* 3:2 (Fall 1991): 1–25.

Wells, Ida B. *Selected Writings of Ida B. Wells-Barnett.* Edited by Trudier Harris. New York: Oxford University Press, 1991.

White, Deborah Gray. *Too Heavy A Load: Black Women in Defense of Themselves, 1894–1994.* New York: W.W. Norton, 1999.

WOMEN AND THE PROGRESSIVE MOVEMENT

Women were intensely involved in the Progressive movements of the early twentieth century, demanding equal rights and social justice for themselves but also advocating a wide variety of other reforms. Progressivism was a complex phenomenon that defies easy characterization because it encompasses so many different groups and goals, but there are several common elements. In general, Progressives opposed political and economic monopolies, worried about social disruptions resulting from rapid industrialization, immigration, and urbanization, and placed great confidence in science and efficient management techniques to solve contemporary public policy issues. Women reformers often worked with male colleagues on important projects, but males usually dominated mixed-sex efforts, so that much female activism arose from independent women's organizations with distinct and sometimes feminist objectives. There were many race, class, and other differences among reformers, however, which made coalitional efforts difficult and fractured the organized women's movement in the 1920s.

WOMEN'S REFORM

Theories about social movements stress several elements, all of which catalyze female reform activity during this period: political opportunity, resource mobilization, and ideological framing. Distrusting established political parties and machines as monopolistic and corrupt, Progressives formed special interest groups and adopted indirect political methods such as lobbying and petitioning that disfranchised women had used for years. The extensive network of clubs and organizations developed by activist women in the late nineteenth century provided a crucial base of experience and resources. Finally, women used various rationales to justify their involvement in the public sphere. Some activists sought social justice through utopian socialism, labor organizing, or expanded social welfare and public health programs. Others challenged the confinement of women to the private, domestic sphere with the discourse of maternalism, or "municipal housekeeping." Arguing that the commercialization of many household functions and contemporary social problems required female involvement in public life, many women became radicalized by their experiences as reformers.

Special interest advocacy during the Progressive Era was widespread, but it was often fragmented, episodic, and hampered by race and class conflict. African-American women activists like Mary Church Terrell, Anna Julia Cooper, and Ida B. Wells-Barnett criticized the exclusionary practices of white women and formed independent organizations, including the National Association of Colored Women (1896). Female activists helped establish the National Association for the Advancement of Colored People in 1909 but were frequently overshadowed by male leaders. As "race women" during a period of harsh segregation and disfranchisement, African-American women reformers sponsored improvement projects to "uplift" their communities and addressed pressing issues relating to female work, poverty, racial oppression, and domestic violence. Chinese-American, Mexican-American, and other racial-ethnic women shared similar concerns, but few native white women understood or appreciated these efforts, and many continued to target women of color in social control and "Americanization" campaigns.

Similar tensions characterized many Progressive reform efforts. Settlement houses, clinics, kindergartens, parks, and other facilities were often intended to help assimilate large populations of recent immigrants and to dampen potential social unrest. Jane Addams and Ellen Gates Starr established the first settlement house, Hull-House, in Chicago in 1889. By 1900, there were nearly 100 similar community centers in operation, providing helpful services to clients (although utilization was selective). In addition, settlement houses gave many educated middle-class women new opportunities for constructive engagement, and some began to professionalize their activities into the new field of social work. During the Progressive period, they built and staffed both private and governmental organizations devoted to social welfare and public health. One of the most important of these was the Children's Bureau, established within the U.S. Department of Labor in 1912 and led by Julia Lathrop, a former resident of Hull House.

SUFFRAGE

Probably the most familiar aspect of Progressive women's activism is the final achievement of woman suffrage. By 1915, years of work resulted in a large, highly mobilized grassroots movement, four million women voters in the Western states, and experienced national leaders like Carrie Chapman Catt and Anna Howard Shaw of the National American Woman Suffrage Association (NAWSA). In addition, energetic younger women like Alice Paul and Lucy Burns of the National Women's Party (NWP) adopted direct action techniques and began confronting politicians with the demand for the federal amendment. Suffragists used many arguments to claim the vote, sometimes arguing that it was necessary to facilitate other reforms, but the demand for equal justice remained primary. This rhetoric seemed hypocritical to many observers, however, because white suffragists did not challenge the concurrent disfranchisement of African Americans in the South, hoping to win the support of Southern politicians for their cause. As a result, African-American activists like Wells-Barnett worked independently through their own suffrage organizations and clubs. The effect of World War I on the final passage of the federal suffrage amendment is debatable. Male politicians praised the NAWSA moderates under Catt's leadership for their patriotic participation but condemned Paul and the radicals, who served time in prison (complete with force feeding) for picketing the White House with signs that referred to "Kaiser [President] Wilson." Nevertheless, the suffrage amendment won ratification in 1920.

WOMEN AND LABOR

Modern suffragists adopted ideas and direct tactics from the labor movement and appealed to working-class constituencies partly because the presence of women in the workforce was a major social issue by the beginning of the twentieth century. Women wage-earners contravened Victorian mores about feminine domesticity, but many middle-class women sought ex-

panded professional opportunities, while working-class families often relied upon female contributions for survival. Women workers were not generally welcome within the male-dominated trade unions, which tried to protect male jobs through gender and racial discrimination and segregation, so women had to organize separately or submit to male control in mixed locals. Reacting to the intransigence of the American Federation of Labor, middle-class reformers and women trade unionists formed a new organization in 1903, the Women's Trade Union League (WTUL). Despite internal class tensions, the League took an active role in many women's labor actions, most notably the great New York City garment workers strike in 1909–1910, the "Uprising of the Twenty Thousand." Disproving popular notions that young women were temporary workers who never organized, thousands of Jewish and Italian women went out on strike, and they received invaluable material and emotional support from the middle- and upper-class women of the WTUL. Although the male leaders of the International Ladies' Garment Workers' Union considered the strike a great victory, some shops refused to settle, including the Triangle Shirtwaist Company, the site of a terrible fire a year later.

The deaths of 146 people in the Triangle Shirtwaist Fire in May 1911 galvanized reformers, especially those who considered protective labor legislation as preferable to labor organization. Activists like Josephine Goldmark and Florence Kelley, who formed the National Consumers League in 1899, vigorously pursued this goal despite judicial resistance. Finally, Goldmark helped her brother-in-law, Louis Brandeis, win a landmark case in *Muller v. Oregon* (1908). They convinced the U.S. Supreme Court that the state had an interest in protecting women workers as the present and future "mothers of the race." Using this precedent, reformers won passage of maximum hours legislation for women in nineteen states between 1909 and 1917, and minimum wage laws in twelve states during this period. This argument was problematic, however, because it defined women as a separate and inferior class of workers, and it generated divisive conflict within the women's movement for many years. Another flawed but highly successful effort resulted in the establishment of "mother's pensions" in forty states between 1911 and 1920. In these programs, the government substituted for absent male breadwinners by providing "deserving" mothers with payments to support their children. Although inadequate funds carried the stigma of charity, and administrators discriminated on racial, moral, or other grounds, these state programs provided the model for federal aid to dependent children as first established in the Social Security Act of 1935.

Labor legislation did not supplant the efforts of women labor organizers like Pauline Newman, Rosa Schneiderman, Elizabeth Gurley Flynn, and others. Many working-class women and quite a few middle-class women were Socialists, usually as firm believers in the democratic process, but those who moved further left toward anarchism or communism found themselves systematically persecuted and their organizations crushed. This trend accelerated during and after World War I, which many scholars mark as the end of the Progressive period. After the war, foreign-born radicals were deported, including Emma Goldman, a famous free love and free speech advocate. Native-born radicals like birth control activist Margaret Sanger fared slightly better but usually by moderating their positions to avoid prosecution.

WOMEN AND SEXUAL MORES

The popularity of the birth control movement reflected a mini sexual revolution that occurred as economic advances and other factors helped modern women establish independent lives. Expectations about love, sex, and marriage shifted to emphasize personal fulfillment and companionate marriage, but these changes were very controversial. Conservatives condemned the decline of Victorian moral values, while Progressives complained that selfish individualism distracted women from reform activism. Efforts to control female sexual behavior were nothing new, and anti-prostitution campaigns were common in many urban areas, but reformers disagreed over whether abolition or regulation was the better approach. Middle-class women who campaigned to eliminate this social problem demonstrated ambivalent Progressive attitudes toward social justice and social control. Claiming sympathy for women forced into prostitution by poverty, they attacked the sexual "double standard" and the largely male interests that controlled the trade. Unfortunately, successful efforts to close bordellos resulted in the eviction of many prostitutes who found themselves in the streets with little protection.

As a social movement, Progressivism also needs to be understood within the international context of early twentieth-century modernism. Great hopes as well as deep concerns about the consequences of rapid economic, political, and social change were widespread at this time. Many countries were experiencing democratization movements, if not revolutions, with women prominently involved in these struggles. Women began to establish transnational organizations in the late nineteenth century with the International Council of Women, the International Woman Suffrage Association, the World's Woman's Christian Temperance Union, the Second Socialist International, and other groups. In the late 1910s, these connections were crucial to the growing peace movement, and many prominent Progressive women, notably Jane Addams, were active pacifists. The movement itself was not really an expression of progressive optimism, however, but rather a reaction to the dark forces of militarism and war. Many moralists and traditionalists were upset by the disruptions of modernism, and they responded with political repression nativism, and moral crusades, including prohibition. The Woman's Christian Temperance Union (WCTU) lost its radical edge after the death of its dynamic leader, Frances Willard, in 1898. In the twentieth century, the WCTU remained a large influential organization, but male leaders dominated the movement through the Anti-Saloon League. With much female support, the prohibitionists mobilized grassroots pressure to pass the federal Prohibition amendment in 1917.

CONCLUSION

Debate over reform goals, strategies, and achievements of women during the Progressive period has often stressed the difficulty of generalizing about this diverse social movement. A major source of Progressive-strength, middle-class white women won concrete legal rights, most notably the vote, helped redefine the nature of political power and influence, and established the organizational basis of the social welfare state. Their elitist assumptions often offended working-class and racial-ethnic reformers, limiting their cooperation and success as a coherent social movement, but the sum of female reform efforts during the Progressive period resulted in major gains for many women and recognition of their new public roles in modern society.

Rebecca J. Mead

BIBLIOGRAPHY

Baker, Paula. "The Domestication of Politics: Women and American Political Society, 1780–1920." *American Historical Review* 89 (June 1984): 620–647.

Blair, Karen J. *The Clubwoman as Feminist: True Womanhood Redefined, 1868–1914.* New York: Holmes & Meier, 1980.

Buhle, Mari Jo. *Women and American Socialism, 1870–1920*. Urbana: University of Illinois Press, 1981.

Cott, Nancy F. *The Grounding of Modern Feminism*. New Haven, CT: Yale University Press, 1987.

DuBois, Ellen Carol. *Harriot Stanton Blatch and the Winning of Woman Suffrage*. New Haven, CT: Yale University Press, 1997.

Evans, Sara M. *Born for Liberty: A History of Women in America*. New York: Free Press Paperbacks, 1997.

Frankel, Noralee, and Nancy S. Dye, eds. *Gender, Class, Race, and Reform in the Progressive Era*. Lexington: University Press of Kentucky, 1991.

Gordon, Linda. "Black and White Visions of Welfare: Women's Welfare Activism, 1890–1945." *Journal of American History* 78 (September 1991): 559–590.

Marilley, Suzanne M. *Woman Suffrage and the Origins of Liberal Feminism in the United States, 1820–1920*. Cambridge, MA: Harvard University Press, 1996.

Muncy, Robyn. *Creating a Female Dominion in American Reform, 1890–1935*. New York: Oxford University Press, 1991.

Orleck, Annelise. *Common Sense and Little Fire: Women and Working-Class Politics in the United States, 1900–1965*. Chapel Hill: University of North Carolina Press, 1995.

Rosen, Ruth. *The Lost Sisterhood: Prostitution in America, 1900–1918*. Baltimore, MD: Johns Hopkins University Press, 1982.

Sklar, Kathryn Kish. *Florence Kelley & the Nation's Work: The Rise of Women's Political Culture, 1830–1900*. New Haven, CT: Yale University Press, 1995.

Skocpol, Theda. *Protecting Soldiers and Mothes: The Political Origins of Social Policy in the United States*. Cambridge, MA: Belknap Press of Harvard University Press, 1992.

Terborg-Penn, Rosalyn. *African American Women in the Struggle for the Vote, 1850–1860*. Bloomington: Indiana University Press, 1998.

Wheeler, Marjorie Spruill, ed. *One Woman, One Vote*. Troutdale, OR: NewSage, 1995.

Women and the Anti-Imperialist Movement

Nineteenth-Century Origins

American women's activism against American imperialism traces back to their involvement in the abolitionist movement. Imperialism is a policy of expansion promulgated by Western nations since the sixteenth century in which European powers and, later, the United States annexed, militarily suppressed, and extracted economic gains from poorer countries around the world. From the late nineteenth century to the early twentieth century, the United States began to expand militarily and economically in the Americas and Southeast Asia. Many women and men who opposed slavery protested the war against Mexico (1846–1848), particularly because of its potential for expanding slave territory. Women drafted and signed petitions as individuals, as church members, and as groups of "ladies" with a particular moral interest in ending slavery. These protests, like later attempts to oppose American imperialism, failed in their immediate goals, but they provided rare opportunities for women to enter national debates over foreign policy.

Anti-imperialism was relatively dormant in American politics during the ensuing decades. Women's devotion to the movement revived in the late nineteenth century, however, through their support for peace and international arbitration. Tellingly, arbitration committees formed within flourishing women's reform organizations like the Woman's Christian Temperance Union (WCTU, founded 1874) and the National American Woman Suffrage Association (NAWSA, founded 1890). Although these national groups formed around issues that appeared to be quite distinct from imperialism, their support for peace activism was consistent with their broader political critiques. Both the temperance movement and the suffrage movement protested violence; they regarded it as a social problem rooted in male aggres-

sion, exacerbated by the abuse of alcohol and by the political and legal oppression of women. Both movements promoted women's increased public participation because women's influence would counteract male tendencies toward violence and militarism. This outlook led them to make peace, arbitration, and anti-imperialism part of their agenda. In international conflicts, women's groups urged that Congress not resort to military intervention and pressed leaders to put aside their desires to acquire new territory to enrich the United States. S. Lillie Devereux Blake, a novelist, suffragist, and reformer, expressed this view at the 1895 NAWSA convention, when she condemned the greed of politicians who would "deluge the world in blood for a strip of land in Venezuela or a gold mine in Africa."

The Anti-Imperialist League

Anti-imperialist sentiments finally coalesced into an independent movement in reaction to the Spanish-American War in 1898. Some women activists continued to call for negotiation instead of violence, as they had in international conflicts earlier in the decade. Partly because the United States explained its involvement in the war as necessary to defend Cuban independence from Spanish brutality, and partly because of popular outrage over the explosion of the U.S. battleship *Maine* in Havana Harbor, by the spring of 1898 there was little vocal opposition to the United States' declaration of war. Even the major peace organizations, such as the Lake Mohonk Conference on International Arbitration, chose to remain silent about U.S. intervention. Indeed, the conflict was soon nicknamed the "splendid little war" because of its brevity, popularity, and success.

As the armed conflict drew to a close, however, it became clear that the United States stood poised to gain an overseas empire as a result of the war. When the McKinley administration publicly announced its intent to annex the Philippines, various new groups formed to counter imperialist policies. The most prominent of these organizations began at an anti-imperialist meeting at Boston's Faneuil Hall on June 15, 1898, some two months before the fight against Spain ended. Women comprised more than half the audience and remained crucial supporters when the Anti-Imperialist League officially formed in November of that year. Josephine Shaw Lowell is typical of former abolitionists who dominated the anti-imperialist movement. Originally supportive of American intervention in Cuba, she thought of the Philippine War as profoundly different: not a noble fight (as the U.S. Civil War had been) but a betrayal of America's principles and of its own revolutionary heritage. In consonance with her convictions, she became an active member of both the New England Anti-Imperialist League and the New York Anti-Imperialist League. She regularly provided the latter's founder, Edward L. Ordway, with advice based on her own lifetime of experience as an activist. Only illness and advanced age prevented her from doing more.

The movement raised various sets of objections to imperialism: constitutional, economic, racial, and historical (that is, it violated American traditions and ideals). Yet the Anti-Imperialist League's (AIL) failure to block ratification of the Treaty of Paris meant that in 1899 the United States gained possession of the Philippines, Puerto Rico, and Guam, and established a military occupation of Cuba. The annexation of Hawaii in the midst of the Spanish-American War added to the new overseas empire. In the face of such developments, the AIL and its local branches across the country pressed for withdrawal of American troops from the Philippines and an end to colonization there. Through rallies, newsletters, and pamphlets, they publicized atrocities committed by the U.S. military during the Philippine Insurrection (1899–1902) that followed occupation—a brutal guerrilla war in which over 4,000 U.S. soldiers and over 220,000 Filipino insurgents and civilians were killed. The AIL's membership of over 30,000 drew from a remarkably broad spectrum, including Democrats and Republicans, labor activists and industrialists, urban reformers and isolationists. In time, the diverse constituency proved to be both a strength and a weakness.

Unsuccessful in obtaining the withdrawal of American troops from the Philippines, the movement faded after President William McKinley's decisive reelection in 1900. The AIL's subsequent goal of Philippine independence met with similar frustrations.

Factions in Chicago and New England broke away to form the Philippine Independence League and the Philippine Information Society, respectively. The organization continued to be active through the 1920s, however, by which time even imperialists had turned away from the direct acquisition of colonies to less direct economic, political, military, and cultural influence in the Pacific and Caribbean.

WOMEN'S CONTRIBUTIONS: MANY KINDS OF ACTIVISM

Although the AIL leadership was dominated by men, women contributed to the movement in crucial ways. First, women remained vital members of the AIL throughout its history; their visible support is evident from newspaper accounts of meetings, which regularly reported on the high percentage of women in attendance. Their presence was both active and vocal, including fundraising work, writing, and speaking on behalf of the movement. Jane Addams, for example, was among the most famous signers and speakers at the important Chicago Liberty Meeting in 1899. Beyond this, they forged key alliances with women's groups, including the WCTU and women's clubs, which helped to distribute pamphlets, tracts, and other anti-imperialist literature through their better established networks and stable memberships. Initially barred from elected positions, women were finally allowed to join the AIL's formal leadership after 1904. At that point, long-time members Jane Addams, Alice Thatcher Post, Josephine Shaw Lowell, and Lucia Ames Mead became vice presidents of the AIL.

Most importantly, women added their own analysis and concerns to the anti-imperialist platform. In contrast with anti-imperialist men, women activists tended to see imperialism, militarism, and women's oppression as inseparable issues that had repercussions beyond anticolonialism. Concerns about imperialism and colonization were, after all, not limited to the AIL but rather were shared by women's groups, including the WCTU, the National Council of Women, and the NAWSA, all of which publicly criticized U.S. occupation of the Philippines. Anti-imperialism enjoyed strong support from peace advocates as well, including prominent women pacifists such as Anna Garlin Spencer and May Wright Sewall. Many women chose to work and lobby against imperialism primarily from within those groups, as opposed to working within the AIL itself; only some, like Jane Addams, were active members in several organizations. Individual expression might also contribute to the cause, as in the case of Katherine Lee Bates, author of "America the Beautiful" (originally written in 1893 and revised in 1904). Several of her poems from this period, including "The Pity of It," condemned American brutality in the Philippines as a violation of the ideal of freedom.

Lucia Ames Mead provides an excellent example of how intertwined anti-imperialism, peace, and women's rights could be for activists. Mead consistently held a "peace-first" policy but saw her work for the pacifist, anti-imperialist, and suffrage movements as all of a piece. She spoke at AIL rallies, often addressing women in particular, and published widely on the subject of the Philippines. Her writings, too (such as her later book, *Swords and Ploughshares*, 1912), criticized imperialism, militarism, and nationalism, sharply denying Admiral Alfred Thayer Mahan's contention that expansion would lead to domestic security and even "moral elevation." Fittingly, she ascended simultaneously to leadership positions in the American Peace Society, the AIL, and the woman suffrage movement.

Women's groups and the peace movement often afforded women much greater opportunities for leadership than did the AIL. Moreover, these other organizations enabled women to carry the torch of anti-imperialism after the AIL had begun to decline. By 1900—when the AIL was attempting to recover from major electoral defeats—the WCTU took a particularly strong moral stand against U.S. military policies in the Philippines. Frances Willard, leader of the WCTU, protested that imperialist policies were the framework within which alcohol and drugs were being manufactured and exported to colonized natives of overseas possessions. She argued that this was both an immoral and ultimately untenable basis for empire.

Moral Criticism

Women, therefore, brought a particular focus of their own to the movement; for them, imperialism represented the excesses of a government that excluded women from political participation and that upheld aggression, competitiveness, and commercialism instead of purer "women's values." In her celebrated address, "Democracy or Militarism," delivered in Chicago on April 30, 1899, Jane Addams traced a recent rash of murders in her neighborhood to the nation's enthusiasm for war. Local violence should come as no surprise, she declared, when even "the little children on the street played at war, day after day, killing Spaniards." Women involved in Progressivism feared

that an imperialist political agenda would edge out domestic reforms, as some believed had happened in Britain because of the Boer War.

Beyond a moral indictment of masculine values, women's anti-imperialism often expressed itself as a pointed critique of American soldiers' immoral conduct. The WCTU and other social purity organizations, in particular, condemned the prostitution, drunkenness, venereal disease, and vice that in their view characterized conditions in and around military canteens in the Philippines. Suffragists denounced the idea of introducing regulated prostitution to the islands as a public health measure. Using such examples, many women's groups reported that the actual effects of American occupation were not "civilizing" as imperialists claimed, but on the contrary, brutalizing and vicious. They wondered whether even American women like themselves could resist the dangers and temptations of the colonial tropics. Lobbying around these types of moral concerns outweighed campaigns against other components of imperialism, such as increased military spending.

To this view, suffragists added a more abstract feminist critique of imperialism. They pointed out an affinity between colonized peoples and themselves, neither of whom could participate directly in the government imposed on them. They also decried the type of gender oppression which the United States would bring to its colonies. It should be no surprise, then, that imperialism came under intense discussion at the 1899 NAWSA convention. Anna Garlin Spencer's address on "Duty to the Women of Our New Possessions" warned against imposing patriarchy and men's "subjection of women" on Hawaiian, Cuban, and Filipino society. Susan B. Anthony agreed, declaring, "I have been overflowing with wrath ever since the proposal was made to engraft our half-barbaric form of government on Hawaii and our other new possessions. I have been studying how to save, not them, but ourselves from the disgrace." These sentiments echoed earlier declarations by the more radical Emma Goldman, who publicly questioned whether the United States could really lead its protectorates to true freedom and democracy when it did not follow such principles at home.

Women, like men, embraced anti-imperialism from a wide range of perspectives, though also with a racist skepticism over imperialism's supposedly civilizing mission. "My most serious objection to making the Philippines American territory is because three-fourths of the population is made up of negroes," wrote Varina Davis, widow of the Confederate president, in an article for *The Arena* (January 1900) supporting Filipino independence. "What [else] are we to do with this mighty negro population, who do not speak our language and come to us in enforced citizenship and full of smoldering discontent?" she asked. Davis was not alone in this rationale. In private letters and reports, peace advocate Hannah Bailey expressed similar views on the Filipino's racial inferiority, though her public comments focused on humanitarian concerns instead. Attitudes within the WCTU and NAWSA could be equally patronizing, assuming a maternal obligation toward colonized peoples.

CRITICISMS FROM CONTEMPORARIES

Although women contributed much to anti-imperialism, both in pragmatic and in intellectual ways, they could also be liabilities to the movement. With the charged rhetoric of gender that ruled contemporary politics, groups like the Grand Army of the Republic disparaged the anti-imperialists as "aunties" and "sissies." Some scholars believe that, over time, women (like Josephine Shaw Lowell) may have turned to increasingly private and less visible forms of support in order to avoid adding to this effeminate image. The phenomenon certainly helps explain why women's participation in the anti-imperialist movement has been overlooked for so long.

Yet men were not the only ones to lead the attack. American women did not align themselves universally with the anti-imperialists. Younger women in particular tended to support expansion and colonization. Even some of the older leaders, including Elizabeth Cady Stanton and Julia Ward Howe, believed imperialism could be part of America's civilizing mission. Enthusiasts of internationalism saw it as a way for the United States to increase its influence in the world. Like the general population, most women were caught up in the nationalist fervor that celebrated the Spanish-American War and that persisted in spite of—or because of—staunch resistance to U.S. rule in the Philippines. If they had not, the movement would have seen more dramatic success.

In the end, however, American women's anti-imperialist activities, rhetoric, and ideology helped to strengthen the whole movement. Despite only limited success in achieving their political goals, women extended the reach of the AIL. They called attention to the moral problems inherent in American expansion and to their interconnectedness with domestic reform issues. In the process, they also broadened the agendas of the temperance, peace, and suffrage organizations to include anti-imperialism, thus making their cause a central part of public debate at the turn of the twentieth century.

Laura R. Prieto

BIBLIOGRAPHY

Alonso, Harriet Hyman. *Peace as a Women's Issue: A History of the U.S. Movement for World Peace and Women's Rights*. New York: Syracuse University Press, 1993.

Beisner, Robert L. *Twelve against Empire: The Anti-Imperialists, 1898–1900*. New York: McGraw-Hill, 1968.

Bresnahan, Roger. *In Time of Hesitation: American Anti-Imperialism and the Philippine-American War*. Quezon City, Philippines: New Day, 1981.

Foner, Philip S., and Richard C. Winchester, eds. *The Anti-Imperialist Reader: A Documentary History of Anti-Imperialism in the United States*. New York: Holmes & Meier, 1984.

Hoganson, Kristin. *Fighting for American Manhood: How Gender Politics Provoked the Spanish-American and Philippine-American Wars*. New Haven, CT: Yale University Press, 1998.

Papachristou, Judith. "American Women and Foreign Policy, 1898–1905: Exploring Gender in Diplomatic History." *Diplomatic History* 14 (Fall 1990): 493–509.

Schirmer, Daniel B. *Republic or Empire: American Resistance to the Philippine War*. Cambridge, MA: Schenkman, 1972.

Tyrrell, Ian. *Woman's World, Woman's Empire: The Women's Christian Temperance Union in International Perspective, 1880–1930*. Chapel Hill: University of North Carolina Press, 1991.

WORKING WOMEN'S MOVEMENT
EARLY TWENTIETH CENTURY

The 1900 American census recorded 5,319,400 women engaged in wage labor, reflecting their broadened employment opportunities in the industrial world. However, women's role in the workforce was ambiguous, and many tensions surrounded the representation of women in the labor movement as a result of prevailing notions of gender. The labor force in which women toiled was gendered; workers, unions, and employers understood skilled craft work as men's work, leaving women largely restricted to semi- and unskilled positions. Such positions increased with the mechanization of trades; technological advances facilitated the division of skilled workers' jobs into multiple lesser-skilled tasks. The newly created semi- and unskilled jobs were more accessible to women than skilled jobs had been, particularly as employers viewed women as a cheaper, more docile labor force, and thus the mechanization of a trade was often accompanied by its feminization.

RACE, GENDER, AND LABOR

The female workforce was further complicated by a racial dynamic with African-American women at the bottom of the labor ladder. In this period, among both blacks and whites most wage-earning women were employed as domestic workers. For black women laundry work was often the only alternative, whereas white women could more readily find employment in clerical work, the garment trades, and department stores, and had greater opportunities to move into the newly mechanized industries.

Labor unions and reform organizations represented a minority of these working women in the early twentieth century. For the majority who were not represented by these social movements, day-to-day resistance ensured women greater control of their working environment, albeit to a limited degree. In the workplace, working women were often isolated from male workers and even from each other. Some

employers encouraged such isolation, but it also often resulted from the work women undertook. For example, domestic service often meant working with only one or two other workers, making it notoriously difficult to unionize; consequently, women who worked in this trade benefited little from union representation or political education. However, women who worked in such circumstances, along with those who worked in other trades that were not yet organized, could still resist their employers' control in a variety of ways. Slowdowns, pilfering, and quitting occurred much more often than strikes and in general involved a lesser risk. By challenging their employers' power to independently dictate the terms of employment, such forms of resistance offered workers at least a modicum of control over their working conditions.

In a much less obvious way, a sense of workplace community also empowered working women. By celebrating birthdays and anniversaries and gossiping about friends and family, women humanized the shop-floor experience, reasserted their independence from employers' control and the monotony of the job, and reaffirmed their relationship to the community in which they lived and worked. Such forms of resistance were chiefly individual in character and thus did not constitute an organized social movement, but they were often the only form of protest working women could engage in.

THE MARGINALIZATION OF WOMEN IN ORGANIZED LABOR

Working women were very much on the periphery of the American labor movement in the early twentieth century. The central labor organization in the United States, the American Federation of Labor (AFL), largely failed to address the needs of working women. Its focus on craft workers and its policy of voluntarism (the AFL saw a limited role for the state within the world of industrial relations) marginalized women workers, recent immigrants, and African Americans. The AFL's failure to address the racial component within the American labor movement meant that African-American working women were even more marginalized by the mainstream labor movement in the early twentieth century than white women.

Underlying AFL policy toward women workers was the fear that women would displace men in the labor force and that the rightful place of women, especially married women, was in the home. As noted above, mechanization was accompanied by an expansion of the female labor force. Craft workers represented in the AFL were concerned that not only would they lose their traditional skilled jobs but that women would dominate the new unskilled labor force. Instead of attempting to organize these women, the AFL, and many of its craft union affiliates, frequently attempted to limit the number of women workers moving into these trades, for example, by denying them access to apprenticeships.

THE AFL AND IWW

The AFL was not the only national labor organization in the early twentieth century. Its most notable rival was the Industrial Workers of the World (IWW, or as they were more commonly known, the Wobblies), first organized in Chicago in 1905. The AFL viewed the IWW as a "dual union" in that it duplicated (and threatened) the AFL's role in the labor movement. The IWW advocated industrial unionism—the organization of factory workers and others involved in mass production. The AFL, on the other hand, sought to organize workers on the basis of craft. The IWW considered the trade union as a vehicle through which the abolition of capitalism could be achieved, a position far removed from the AFL's "pure and simple" craft-oriented unionism that concentrated on improving wages and working conditions but not on abolishing capitalism. Unlike the AFL, the IWW was far more concerned with semi- and unskilled workers, and this helped contribute to the greater role white women played in the organization. However, although the IWW did not oppose the organization of African-American workers, Wobblies only rarely ventured into trades or regions in which blacks constituted a significant proportion of the labor force.

The Lawrence, Massachusetts, textile strike of 1912 demonstrated the Wobblies' commitment to mass organization. The strike began as a spontaneous walkout of the mostly immigrant and female work-

force in response to short pay. IWW activists reacted quickly and began to organize the disparate workers, showing far greater concern for the semi- and unskilled women workers than did the AFL and its affiliate unions. The Wobblies arranged mass pickets to keep strikebreakers out of the mills and inadvertently served to boost morale and to involve large numbers of the community in a productive way. Success came in March, with the strikers' demands largely granted and a huge increase in membership for the IWW, including many women. Indeed, women had played a vocal part in the strike; the most notable female Wobbly, "Rebel Girl" Elizabeth Gurley Flynn, had been elected to the national executive in 1909.

The IWW was male dominated, however, and Flynn stands out, in part because she was exceptional. Many individual Wobblies were less enthusiastic about women's right to work, especially married women, and traditional conceptions of the domestic role for women were revealed in debates within the organization. Moreover, in the months following strikes such as at Lawrence, the Wobblies rarely maintained the gains they had made, thus further weakening their potential power base. Ultimately, the IWW suffered from the interwar Red Scare, and, although it was not officially disbanded, its importance and position in the labor movement diminished after the mid-1920s.

WOMEN'S TRADE UNIONS

Labor unions in trades in which women traditionally constituted a large percentage of the workforce were more inclined to accept the image of a unionized woman worker. This was particularly true as the twentieth century progressed and there was a growth of industrial unions that moved away from the craft focus dominant in the late nineteenth century.

Two of the most important unions for women in the early twentieth century were the Amalgamated Clothing Workers of America (ACWA) and the International Ladies' Garment Workers' Union (ILGWU). Both these organizations presented far greater opportunities for women to be union activists. The ILGWU was founded in 1900 and organized the women's garment trade. The ACWA was founded in 1914 as a breakaway union from the United Garment Workers (UGW), on the grounds that the UGW was too focused on skilled workers and that industrial organization was needed in the men's clothing trade. Both grew rapidly and included the semi- and unskilled female workers who constituted the majority in the clothing trade. The far greater acceptance and concern

Many American women found employment as seamstresses in the early twentieth century. In this gender-divided system of labor, they often worked under the supervision of men. *(Brown Brothers)*

for women workers was reflected in women holding office at both the local and national level, in the women's page that the union journals had for many years, and in the adoption of policy that advocated women's inclusion. For example, in 1916 the ILGWU established a General Educational Committee under Fannia Cohn, who became the first female vice president of a major international union. With support from the union, Cohn worked to promote the necessity of education for workers, especially women workers, and organized extensive educational programs. This set a precedent that many unions adopted as the twentieth century progressed, a precedent that acknowledged the changing role and demands of workers and unions.

African-American women had far fewer employment opportunities available to them and rarely benefited from such labor movements. However, as the twentieth century progressed, mainstream labor organizations offered black women more opportunities for inclusion, particularly in trades and regions in which they dominated. For example, in 1920 black domestic workers made up at least ten locals of the Hotel and Restaurant Employees Union in Southern cities. However, the potential for interracial unions was limited, and racial tensions and discrimination meant that black working women often turned to their own communities and formed cross-class support organizations.

SEGREGATION OF WOMEN'S WORK

Important labor organizations also developed among the growing body of professional women workers, the majority of whom were native-born white Americans. For example, the American Federation of Teachers (AFT) was founded in Chicago in 1916. Teaching was one of the most popular occupations open to educated women, and, faced with attacks from the Chicago Board of Education, teachers turned to unionization as a way of voicing and strengthening their position. However, the ideological position of the union created considerable tension within the AFT. Some members opposed its affiliation to the AFL; they argued that the union should focus on improving their professional skills, not obtaining political power. This indicated the ambiguous relationship between the professions and manual labor, which was also present in the organization of clerical workers.

The early twentieth century witnessed the feminization of clerical work, with the percentage of women clerical workers more than doubling by the 1930s. However, despite the potential for a feminine labor voice this represented, clerical workers did not constitute a significant group within the organized labor movement. In part, this resulted from the different discourses surrounding clerical and nonmanual labor. Clerical workers considered office work to be more prestigious than manual labor, and, with the close association of trade unions with manual occupations, many office workers looked down upon labor unions.

THE WOMEN'S TRADE UNION LEAGUE

On the periphery of the American labor movement was the Women's Trade Union League (WTUL), founded in 1903 by Jane Addams, Mary Anderson, and other trade unionists. The WTUL was the first national organization with a cross-class membership to seriously and solely address the concerns of working women. The majority of the social reformers and settlement house workers at the founding meeting were women, whereas only one of the labor representatives was female, reflecting the masculine nature of the labor movement at the time. In terms of race, the League also conformed to the dominant pattern of the American labor movement, being essentially a white organization. Although the League more readily accepted black women workers than many labor organizations, African-American women played a very limited role in the League, and it was rare for the WTUL to specifically address the grievances of black working women. However, there were occasions when the League organized or supported striking African-American women workers.

The League was organized on a national basis with regional Leagues where they were required, of which New York and Chicago were the largest and most active. Although the intention was to achieve an equal balance between working class and middle-class women, in general the latter dominated. This was particularly so at the national level, with the middle-class activist Margaret Dreier Robins dominating the organization as national president from 1907 to 1922. The program for the League was threefold: organizing women into existing trade unions; educating working women about the importance of labor organization and middle-class women about the conditions and needs of working women; and campaigning for protective labor legislation.

Central to the WTUL's organizing campaign was the recognition that one of the main causes of the low level of female unionization was the male-dominated structure of the labor movement. The AFL and the majority of individual trade unions focused on the interests of skilled white male workers and thus marginalized women workers. The WTUL recognized the exclusionary nature of masculine trade unionism and the cultural disparity between male and female workers; thus, it organized in a different way so as to make unionism more attractive and accessible to women. It arranged meetings in more congenial locations, such as schools or town halls instead of public houses, and at more convenient times, to limit conflict with familial commitments. To further encourage participation, the local Leagues partook in activities that their male counterparts did not, for example, establishing lending libraries, swimming clubs, food cooperatives, socials, and folk dancing lessons. Through such events, a culture of unionism developed among women workers. However, because the WTUL remained on the margins of the labor movement, as the twentieth century progressed many of the most active union women disassociated themselves from the League in favor of full integration into their own unions, thereby accentuating the middle-class presence in the League.

The second component of the League's activities was its educational program. The WTUL was particularly aware of the importance of industrial education for immigrant women. The language difficulties immigrant workers faced were addressed in an original and productive way by turning English lessons into vehicles for trade union education, for example, using an English primer that had lessons entitled "A Trade Without a Union," "A Trade with a Union," and "Joining the Union." In 1913, labor leader Agnes Nestor became president of the Chicago Women's Trade Union League; that same year the League established the Training School for Women Organizers in Chicago, the first residential workers' education program in the United States. It ran until 1926 and involved field work as well as classroom teaching. Other organizations began to see the importance of industrial education, and the League school inspired similar efforts on the part of both unions and women's groups. However, the training programs were expensive to run, and increasingly the League sacrificed organizational campaigns in favor of education, thereby limiting the number of working women who came into contact with the WTUL.

Finally, the League campaigned for improvements in hours, wages, and working conditions. Although this was a major activity of both the male and female labor movements, they tended to differ in approach. Male trade unionists preferred to attain such ameliorations via collective bargaining, whereas women increasingly turned toward protective labor legislation. Collective bargaining relied on an organized workforce; it would not work if only a minority of the workforce was unionized. As repeated attempts failed to organize a majority of the female workforce, the WTUL increasingly turned toward protective legislation. In part, this policy shift was influenced by the involvement of many of its middle-class members in other reform organizations.

Members of the Women's Trade Union League take to the streets to promote union membership, the eight-hour workday, and an end to child labor. *(Brown Brothers)*

AGNES NESTOR (1880–1948)

Agnes Nestor was one of the foremost women labor leaders during the first half of the twentieth century. Not limiting herself to union activities, she also worked vigorously for women's rights, education, and various social causes.

Nestor was born in Grand Rapids, Michigan, on June 24, 1880. In 1897, she began working at the Eisendrath Glove Company in Chicago. In 1898, the women glove makers went on strike. It was during this strike that young Agnes made a name for herself. The strike at Eisendrath was a victory, and out of the event a glovemaker's local union was established.

Nestor's impressive command of the glovemaking business and the lives of the workers won her many admirers. In 1903, she was elected the union's national vice president. She served in this capacity until 1906 when she then became secretary-treasurer, keeping that post until 1913. Her other offices with this union then included president from 1913 to 1915, vice president again from 1915 to 1938, and finally director of Research and Education from 1938 to 1948.

Nestor was also involved with the Chicago Federation of Labor (CFL) both as the president of her local and as a representative to the CFL. In 1919, the CFL began a bold attempt to create a labor party on local, state, and national levels. In that same year, Nestor served as a delegate to the first national convention of what would eventually become the Farmer-Labor Party (FLP). In 1920, as part of the Illinois Labor Party, Nestor was nominated for one of the university trustees positions. She did not gain office, and the FLP as a whole would face utter defeat. In 1928, she again ran

for public office, this time for state representative. Curiously enough, her campaign flyer made no mention of her previous political affiliation with the FLP.

Nestor's other labor activities included serving as president of the Chicago Women's Trade Union League (WTUL) from 1913 to 1948, as well as on the executive board of the national WTUL. She also assisted in organizing workers in industries such as the garment workers and needle trades. She often participated in strikes as a negotiator, speaker, and overall organizer. Nestor was always willing to travel around the country to assist women strikers whenever the need arose.

In terms of social work, Nestor again served on various boards. Such memberships include the Governor's Commission on Unemployment and Relief (1918), the Joint Emergency Relief Fund of Cook County (1931), the Advisory Council on Employment Security (1931), and the Social Security Board (1934).

Nestor lobbied the Illinois legislature to limit the number of hours women, and others, could work each day and week. The first victory was the 1909 Illinois law that created the ten-hour day, although Nestor's goal was to eventually establish an eight-hour day, which came to fruition in 1937. Even so, between 1909 and 1937 Nestor, along with other advocates of the eight-hour day, had to fight strenuously to amend and keep any such laws. Nestor also fought for a minimum wage law, woman suffrage, and legislation addressing maternity health.

Nestor lived in Chicago until her death in 1948. She worked as a labor and social advocate to the very end of her life.

Mitchell Newton-Matza

This panoramic portrait taken in Washington, D.C., on October 28, 1919, shows the attendees of the First International Congress of Working Women, a convention called by the National Women's Trade Union League. Composed of women from all classes, the League focused on industrial education and the rights and conditions of working women. *(Library of Congress)*

OPPOSITION FROM MALE-DOMINATED UNIONS

At its founding, the Women's Trade Union League had represented an unprecedented opportunity for the cross-class feminist organization of working women. However, the failure of the male-dominated mainstream labor movement to respond positively meant that the WTUL soon shifted closer to the women's movement than to the labor movement. The continued presence of middle-class women and the League's emphasis on legislation and education further encouraged both association with the women's movement and alienation from the wider labor movement. Furthermore, by the 1920s, many women unionists chose to work within the mixed-sex labor movement instead of within the WTUL. Although the AFL continued to marginalize women workers, other unions such as the International Ladies' Garment Workers' Union and the Amalgamated Clothing Workers of America began to give women workers a greater role.

An alternative route to trade union organization was amelioration of working women's conditions via reform organizations. The expansion of women's university education in the late nineteenth century resulted in a surplus of educated women with few employment opportunities available to them. These public-spirited women, such as Florence Kelley (head of the National Consumers League from 1899 to 1932), Jane Addams (founder of Hull House settlement house), and Margaret Dreier Robins, carved out a niche for themselves in social improvement work, poor relief, and industrial amelioration.

THE NATIONAL CONSUMERS LEAGUE

The National Consumers League (NCL) was one such group. Founded in 1899 from a number of regional organizations, the NCL was very much part of the broader discourse of social reform that was characteristic of late nineteenth- and early twentieth-century America. The middle-class feminists who led the NCL believed that their "feminine values" provided them with a particular aptitude to empower workers, economically and politically. However, their empowering program was not as direct as those of labor organizations, and the NCL had its greatest impact among middle-class women. It called for ethical consumption and encouraged middle-class female consumers to buy goods from the "white list" or with the "white label," which indicated that the goods were produced under fair conditions. Although these tactics had lim-

ited results in changing working conditions for wage-earning women, they were important in educating more middle- and upper-class women about working conditions and in leading some such women to involve themselves in the Women's Trade Union League.

Closely tied to the NCL was the settlement house movement, another product of the discourse of social reform. Chicago's Hull House and New York's Henry Street Settlement, among others, provided a range of services to the local working-class community, such as nursery care, and nutrition and hygiene education. However, as with the NCL, perhaps their greatest accomplishment was the education of middle-class women as to the living and working conditions of the urban working poor. Like the NCL, settlement house workers were active within the campaign for protective labor legislation, at times working alongside the WTUL. Seemingly beneficial to working women, the campaign for legislation to improve working conditions, hours, and wages encompassed the assumption that women were the weaker sex and in need of such protection. Furthermore, calls for protective legislation often reinforced gender roles that did not recognize women's right to work; these calls were regularly accompanied by claims that it was only financial necessity that "forced" women to engage in wage labor and that their "true" place was the home.

These organizations were predominantly based in the Northeast and Midwest and had their greatest influence on white immigrant communities. In both the South and the black ghettoes of the North and Midwest, in lieu of African-American unions black women often turned to mutual aid groups within the black community. These groups, such as the Federation of Colored Women's Clubs, had a long tradition in African-American culture, stemming from the need for self-reliance in the face of racial discrimination. These groups crossed class boundaries as the common adversity of racism encouraged cross-class black solidarity instead of interracial working-class unity.

The organization and representation of wage-earning women in the early twentieth century took a variety of forms. However, despite considerable progress, women remained marginal within the mainstream labor movement primarily because of the persistence of conventional gender roles that assigned women to the home and family; the opposition of skilled craftsmen to the feminization and de-skilling of their trade; and the male-dominated labor movement's reluctance to seriously consider wage-earning women's grievances and demands. Wage-earning women were also represented by a number of social reform movements that operated in early twentieth-century urban America. Middle class and often feminist, these organizations took on the charge of improving working and living conditions for working women, but in so doing they enforced their own perceptions of women's role in society and the workforce.

Ruth Percy

BIBLIOGRAPHY

Argersinger, Jo Ann E. *Making the Amalgamated: Gender, Ethnicity, and Class in the Baltimore Clothing Industry, 1899–1939*. Baltimore, MD: Johns Hopkins University Press, 1999.

Dubofsky, Melvyn. *We Shall Be All: A History of the Industrial Workers of the World*. Chicago: Quadrangle Books, 1969.

Dye, Nancy Schrom. *As Equals and as Sisters: Feminism, the Labor Movement, and the Women's Trade Union League of New York*. Columbia: University of Missouri Press, 1980.

Foner, Philip S. *Women and the American Labor Movement: From the First Trade Unions to the Present*. New York: Free Press, 1979.

Greene, Julie. *Pure and Simple Politics: The American Federation of Labor and Political Activism, 1881–1917*. Cambridge, UK: Cambridge University Press, 1998.

Jacoby, Robin Miller. *The British and American Women's Trade Union Leagues, 1890–1925*. New York: Carlson, 1994.

Jones, Jacqueline. *Labor of Love, Labor of Sorrow: Black Women, Work and the Family, from Slavery to the Present*. New York: Basic Books, 1985.

Kessler-Harris, Alice. *Out to Work: A History of Wage-Earning Women in the United States*. New York: Oxford University Press, 1982.

Payne, Elizabeth Anne. *Reform, Labor, and Feminism: Margaret Dreier Robins and the Women's Trade Union League*. Urbana: University of Illinois Press, 1988.

Sklar, Kathryn Kish. *Florence Kelley and the Nation's Work: The Rise of Women's Political Culture, 1830–1900*. New Haven, CT: Yale University Press, 1995.

Storrs, Landon R.Y. *Civilizing Capitalism: The National Consumers' League, Women's Activism, and Labor Standards in the New Deal Era*. Chapel Hill: University of North Carolina Press, 2000.

Tax, Meredith. *The Rising of Women: Feminist Solidarity and Class Conflict, 1880–1917*. New York: Monthly Review, 1980.

General Index

A

A. Philip Randolph Institute, **1**:154
AA. *See* Alcoholics Anonymous
AA Grapevine (newsletter), **3**:912
AARP. *See* American Association of
Retired Persons
Abbey, Edward, **4**:1280
Abbott, Grace, **2**:364
Abern, Martin, **2**:573
Abernathy, Ralph David, **1**:197, 200;
3:1088
Abolition movement
as biracial, **1**:27–28, 66, 98
black *vs.* white, **1**:32, 58, 98
distinct from antislavery movement,
1:4, 62, 96
evangelicalism and, **1**:19–20, 23,
31–32, 49–50, 52
founding of, **3**:946–947
and free blacks, **1**:98
gender and, **1**:54–58
governmental censure, **1**:50, 91, 99–101
immediatism, **1**:20–24, 49, 50, 62–63
market revolution and, **1**:18–19
militant, **1**:52, 58–59, 64–67, 93–94
moderate, **1**:63
and nonviolence, **1**:49, 50, 55, 63, 64,
67
North–South reactions to, **1**:96–104
opposition, **1**:98–103
overview of, **1**:4, 47
politics of, **1**:27–29, 53–54, 64
radical, **1**:27–28, 64
reasons for, **1**:47–48, 89, 96–98
religious strains of, **1**:68–69
schism, **1**:25, 27, 51–52, 63, 86
social arena of, **1**:29–32, 89–90
success of, **1**:94, 103
and the temperance movement,
3:866
violence against supporters of, **1**:50,
65, 100, 103

Abolition movement *(continued)*
See also Abolition newspapers;
African Americans; Anti-
slavery movement; Miscege-
nation; Slaveholders; Slaves
Abolition newspapers
Antislavery Bugle, **1**:52
Colored American, **1**:22
Frederick Douglass's Paper, **1**:77, 84
Freedom's Journal, **1**:14–15, 22, 84, 98
Genius of Universal Emancipation,
1:22
Liberator, **1**:21, 22, 49, 60, 89
The North Star, **1**:58, 75, 77, 84
The Rights of All, **1**:84
The Weekly Advocate, **1**:84, 85
Abortion Counseling Service, **2**:404
Abortion legislation
Florynce Rae Kennedy and, **1**:199
Hyde Amendment (1976), **2**:382,
430; **3**:847
Mexico City Policy (1984), **3**:847
Roe v. Wade (1973), **2**:381–382, 426;
3:847
*Webster v. Reproductive Health
Services* (1988), **2**:382; **3**:847
Abortion rights movement
African-American women and,
2:395
impact of *Roe v. Wade*, **2**:381–382
National Organization for Women
and, **2**:398
National Young Women's Day of
Action, **2**:430–431
19th century, **2**:378–380
reframing issues, **2**:380–381
resurgence of, **2**:382–385, 402–404,
426
See also Abortion legislation; Anti-
abortion movement
Abraham, Spencer, **1**:247
Abraham Lincoln Brigade, **1**:162
Abstinence, **1**:82; **3**:852, 931–932

Abstinence from the Flesh of Animals
(Metcalfe, 1827), **3**:1015
Abu-Jamal, Mumia, **1**:218
Abzug, Bella, **4**:1326
ACLU. *See* American Civil Liberties
Union
ACLU, Reno v. (1997), **3**:851
Acosta, Oscar Zeta, **2**:754; **4**:1214, 1217
Act Now to Stop War and End Racism
(ANSWER), **3**:1100–1101,
1106–1111
ACT UP. *See* AIDS Coalition to Unleash
Power
Acuña, Rodolfo, **4**:1214
ADA. *See* Americans with Disabilities Act
Adams, Abigail, **1**:294
Adams, Ansel, **4**:1269
Adams, Circuit City Stores v. (2001),
1:248
Adams, Hannah, **3**:1029
Adamson Act, **2**:515, 537
Adarand Constructors v. Pena (1995),
1:248
Addams, Jane, **3**:1142
activism of, **2**:366
and anti-imperialism, **1**:342
"Democracy or Militarism," **1**:343
Hull-House, **1**:317, 337; **2**:366; **3**:1141
and peace movement, **3**:1044,
1067–1068
and trade unions, **1**:348; **3**:890
Why Women Should Vote (1915),
1:303
*Address to the Slaves in the United States
of America* (Smith, 1842), **1**:27, 64
Adirondack Park, **4**:1286
Adler, Felix, **3**:1007–1011
Adolescent Family Life Program, **3**:852
Adult entertainment. *See* Sex establishments
Advertisements
boycott, **2**:685
union label, **2**:682–683

Advocate of Moral Reform, **1:**264

AFDC. *See* Aid to Families with Dependent Children

Affirmative Action, **1:**213, 215
in higher education, **1:**248–249
opponents of, **1:**217, 218
reversal of, **1:**221
viewpoint diversity, **1:**249

Afghanistan, antiwar movement, **3:**1100, 1104–1105

AFL. *See* American Federation of Labor

AFL-CIO. *See* American Federation of Labor-Congress of Industrial Organizations

Africa
colonization of, **1:**11–13, 83
emigration to, **1:**112–114

African American Women in Defense of Ourselves, **2:**395

African Americans
abolition movement efforts, **1:**98
and Afrocentricism, **1:**149
agriculture and, **1:**70
and anti-communism, **1:**168–169
and antiwar movement, **3:**1087–1088, 1104
blacklisted, **1:**169, 170–171
Civil War and citizenship, **1:**4, 36–38, 41
clubwomen, **1:**116–118, 129, 300
colonization of, **1:**3–4, 11–13, 48, 83
colonization resistance, **1:**14–16, 22, 50, 62, 84
and Communist Party, **2:**572
community building, **1:**80–82
convict leasing, **1:**122–126
culture
Harlem Renaissance, **1:**145–146, 159
1930s, **1:**161–162
education and economic advance, **1:**43–45, 69–70
emigration, **1:**32–34, 70, 83, 86–87, 112–114, 143, 144, 149
establishment of churches, **1:**80–82; **3:**930
establishment of schools, **1:**82
free black press, **1:**84, 85
and fundamentalist religion, **1:**145
in government, **1:**169, 194, 212, 218, 251–253
and labor, **1:**114–116, 145, 152–156
mayors, **1:**251–253
migration, **1:**114, 141–143, 158, 164; **2:**517, 562; **3:**773–776, 884
mutual aid societies, **1:**81–82

African Americans *(continued)*
the "New Negro," **1:**146, 148, 159, 223
petition for freedom (Massachusetts, 1777), **1:**9
political organizations (1860s), **1:**111–112
in the public workers movement, **2:**641
racial uplift, **1:**43–45
and railway worker movement, **2:**539, 540, 541
and religious movements, **3:**953–954
response to civil rights violence, **1:**224–225
restrictions on emancipated, **1:**111
and self-defense, **1:**206, 209–210, 223, 224
settlement houses, **3:**1143
and socialism, **1:**145
socioeconomic differences, **1:**215
southern Black Codes, **1:**111
in Union troops, **1:**4, 39–41, 43
and war, **1:**139–141, 158, 164–165
wildcat strikes, **2:**677–678
women
and abortion rights, **2:**395
and anti-lynching, **1:**130–133; **2:**390
and the anti-rape movement, **2:**446–447
and the birth control movement, **2:**358
clubs, **1:**314, 333, 334
disunity among, **1:**334–335
economic uplift, **2:**387–388, 390
education for, **1:**330, 331
feminism, **2:**391–396, 408–410
in government, **2:**367, 389
and health reform, **2:**389, 395, 405
and the labor movement, **1:**347, 348, 351; **2:**513
racial uplift, **2:**387
rejection of separatism, **2:**443
role in churches and religion, **1:**330–331; **3:**930
and settlement houses, **1:**319, 334
sororities, **1:**334
and suffrage, **1:**300–301, 322; **2:**361
voter registration drives, **2:**361
and white organizations, **1:**334
as womanists, **2:**395, 410
and women's studies movement, **2:**419–420
and worker rights, **1:**329–330

African Americans *(continued)*
See also Black backlash; Black nationalism; Lynching; Race riots; Segregation; Slavery; Slaves

African Benevolent Society, **1:**81

African Blood Brotherhood, **1:**131, 145; **2:**570

African Communities League, **1:**149

African Free Society, **1:**81

African Institution, **1:**13

African Methodist Episcopal Church Magazine, **1:**84

African National Congress, **1:**236

Afrikaner National Party, **1:**235, 236

Afro-American League. *See* National Afro-American League

Afrocentricism, **1:**149

Age Discrimination in Employment Act (1967), **2:**620; **4:**1242

Agee, James, **3:**1124

Ageism, **4:**1230

Agnew, Spiro T., **3:**1130

Agrarian movements
Agrarian Socialist Movement, **3:**796–801
American Agriculture Movement, **3:**835–839
Exodusters Movement, **1:**114; **3:**773–776
Farm Workers Labor Movement, **3:**822–834
Farmers' Alliance Movement, **3:**783–786
Grange Movement, **3:**777–782
Liberty Men, **3:**764–766
Regulators, **3:**761–764
Whiskey Rebellion, **3:**763–764
See also Agricultural workers; Agriculture

Agrarian organizations, **3:**886, 888–889

Agrarian Socialist Movement, **3:**796–801

Agricultural Adjustment Act, **3:**811–812

Agricultural Adjustment Administration, **3:**1123–1124

Agricultural workers
and labor movement, **2:**621–623; **3:**1123
Mexican-American farm laborers, **4:**1216–1217
migrant, **2:**621; **3:**1123–1124, 1125, 1131
See also Agrarian movements; Agrarian organizations; Agriculture

Agricultural Workers Organization, **2:**531
Agriculture
  and animal rights, **4:**1316
  for black economic self-sufficiency, **1:**70
  farm worker boycotts, **2:**683–685
  farmer loans, **3:**1125
  New York tenant farmers, **3:**769
  organic farming, **3:**1017
  sustainable, **4:**1320–1321
  transnational corporations, **4:**1459
  See also Agrarian movements;
      Agrarian organizations;
      Agricultural workers
AHA. *See* American Humane Association
Ahmanson, Howard, **4:**1404
Aid to Families with Dependent
    Children (AFDC), **3:**1128, 1132,
    1134, 1136–1137
AIDS
  and bisexuality, **4:**1369
  early response to, **4:**1373
  and harm reduction movement, **3:**877–878
  and LGBT mobilization, **4:**1348, 1349, 1353
  NIH research, **4:**1354
  outcome of 1987 march for, **3:**854
  and prostitutes, **3:**861
  Religious Right's attack on, **3:**855
AIDS Coalition to Unleash Power (ACT
    UP), **3:**854; **4:**1348, 1373–1378
AIM. *See* American Indian Movement
Air pollution
  Clean Air Act, **4:**1276
  industrialization and, **4:**1260
Air traffic controllers (PATCO strikes), **2:**635–636, 642, 661–664
Aird, George, **2:**715
Akwesasne Mohawk, **2:**745–746
Alabama
  Bloody Sunday, **1:**194
  convict labor and leasing, **1:**125
  King's civil rights efforts, **1:**185–188, 193–194
  Montgomery Bus Boycott, **1:**172, 177–178, 204, 209
  racist violence, **1:**183, 187, 188–190, 193–194, 206
Albany Congress, **2:**739
Albany (Georgia), civil rights in, **1:**185, 206
Albany Plan of Union, **2:**739
Alcatraz, Native American occupation
    of, **2:**725–726

Alcohol and Substance Abuse Treat-
    ment Program, **3:**916
Alcohol recovery movements, **3:**915
  See also Alcoholics Anonymous;
    Temperance movement
Alcoholic Foundation, **3:**911, 912
Alcoholics Anonymous (AA)
  "Big Book" (AA Bible), **3:**911
  founders of, **3:**909–911
  helping others, **3:**913–914
  legacy of, **3:**915–916
  meetings, **3:**914–915
  membership growth, **3:**912
  origins of, **3:**907–908, 910–911
  Oxford Group Movement and, **3:**908–909, 911
  as a social movement, **3:**906–907, 915–916
  Twelve Step work, **3:**907
  Twelve Steps, **3:**906, 907, 912–913
  Twelve Traditions, **3:**906–907, 912
  use of religion in, **3:**916
  See also Alcohol recovery move-
    ments; Temperance movement
*Alcoholics Anonymous: The Story of How
    Many Thousands of Men and Women
    Have Recovered from Alcoholism*
    (1939), **3:**911
Alcott, William A., **3:**1015
Alexander, Will W., **1:**131
Alexander v. Sandoval (2001), **1:**249
Ali, Muhammad, **3:**1088
All S-He Wanted (Jones, 1996), **4:**1381
All Tribe Inc., **2:**725
Allen, Pam, **2:**401
Allen, Richard, **1:**15, 81; **3:**930
Almanac Singers, **2:**688, 689
Almshouses, **4:**1237, 1243
Alpha Kappa Alpha, **1:**334; **2:**389
Alpha Suffrage Club, **1:**300, 322
Alternative religious movements, **3:**953–955
AMA. *See* American Medical Association
Amalgamated Association of Iron,
    Steel, and Tin Workers, **2:**543, 544
Amalgamated Clothing and Textile
    Workers of America, **2:**682
Amalgamated Clothing Workers of
    America, **1:**346; **2:**502, 682, 685
Amana Inspirationist communes, **1:**287
Amana Society, **3:**1001
Ambrose, Myles, **3:**874
America First Committee, **3:**1079
American Academy of Asian Studies, **3:**1031

American Agricultural Strike. *See*
    American Agriculture Movement
American Agriculture Movement, **3:**835–839
American and Foreign Anti-Slavery
    Society, **1:**31, 52, 63; **3:**949
American Anti-Boycott Association, **2:**683
American Anti-Slavery Society, **1:**24–25
  founding of, **1:**89; **3:**946
  goals of, **1:**63
  women in, **3:**949
American Association for Old Age
    Assistance, **4:**1240
American Association of Retired
    Persons (AARP), **4:**1230, 1232, 1241
American Association of University
    Women, **2:**363
American Birth Control League, **2:**355, 357, 358
American Breeding Association, **3:**900
American Buddhism. *See* Buddhism
American Civil Liberties Union (ACLU)
  challenges Communications
    Decency Act, **3:**851
  Ethical Culture and, **3:**1011, 1012
  and gay/lesbian rights, **4:**1339, 1341
  See also Civil Liberties Bureau
American Colonization Society, **1:**3–4, 12–13, 48, 83, 113
  opponents of, **1:**14, 20–22, 50, 62, 84
American Committee on Africa, **1:**236
American Conservative Union, **4:**1393–1394
American Council on Education, Office
    of Women's Affairs, **2:**416
American Council on Human Rights, **2:**389–390
American Dietetic Association, **3:**1018
American Equal Rights Association, **1:**273, 297
American Ethical Union, **3:**1012
American Eugenics Society, **3:**901
American Federation of Labor (AFL), **1:**152, 153, 324
  African-American men and, **2:**512–513
  anti-communism activities, **2:**627
  conservative stance, **2:**510, 559, 593
  critics of, **2:**593
  David Dubinsky and, **2:**605
  drive for southern unions, **2:**626
  Industrial Workers of the World as a
    threat to, **2:**527
  membership growth, **2:**512

American Federation of Labor (AFL)
  (continued)
  merger with Congress of Industrial
    Organizations, 2:614–615, 630,
    631
  in the 1920s, 2:559–560
  racial discrimination, 2:631
  Railway Employees' Department,
    2:538
  successor to Knights of Labor,
    2:508–509
  union label campaigns, 2:681
  Union Label and Service Trades
    Department, 2:681, 682
  and welfare reform, 3:889
  women and, 1:345–346; 2:513
  See also Gompers, Samuel
American Federation of Labor-Con-
    gress of Industrial Organizations
    (AFL-CIO)
  formation of, 2:630, 631
  New Voice, 2:642, 653–655
    organizing, 2:656–658
    politics, 2:659
  racial issues, 2:631–632
  railroad unions and, 2:541
  response to employee offensive,
    2:651–653
  support for PATCO, 2:662–663
  and Vietnam War, 2:643–644
  against war in Iraq, 3:1104
  and WTO, 4:1485
American Federation of State, County
    and Municipal Employees
    (AFSCME), 2:639
American Federation of Teachers (AFT),
    1:348; 2:602, 634, 641
American Female Guardian Society, 1:265
American Female Moral Reform
    Society, 1:264
American Forestry Association, 4:1286,
    1288
American Free Dress League, 1:271
American Geriatrics Society, 4:1241
American Humane Association (AHA),
    4:1312
American Indian. See Native Americans
American Indian Chicago Conference,
    2:726
American Indian Day, 2:701
American Indian Defense Association,
    2:703
American Indian Magazine, 2:701
American Indian Movement (AIM)
  chapters and alliances, 2:708–709
  founders of, 2:707

American Indian Movement (AIM)
  (continued)
  government drive to destroy, 2:711,
    712, 714, 715–723
  trials, 2:714–715
  and Wounded Knee siege (1973),
    2:711–714, 727
  See also Pine Ridge reservation
American Indian Religious Freedom
    Act (1978), 2:728
American Institute of Homeopathy,
    3:990
American League Against War and
    Fascism, 3:1078
American Medical Association (AMA)
  and anti-abortion legislation, 2:379
  Gray Panthers protest, 4:1233
  and homeopathy, 3:993, 994–996
  support of prohibition, 3:866
American Medical Women's Associa-
    tion, 2:367–368
American Methodist Episcopal Church,
    3:930
American Missionary Association, 1:32,
    59, 63, 68
American Negro Labor Congress, 2:572
American Neurological Association,
    3:903
American Peace Society, 1:343; 3:1064
American Physiology Association, 3:1015
American Plan, 2:561
American Protective League, 3:1122
American Railway Union, 2:511, 534,
    535–536, 675
American Rehabilitation Act (1973),
    4:1245
American Revolution, slavery and,
    1:8–10
American Rivers, 4:1283
American Socialist Party, 1:145
American Society for Colonizing the
    Free People of Colour of the United
    States. See American Colonization
    Society
American Society for the Prevention of
    Cruelty to Animals (ASPCA),
    4:1311
American Temperance Society, 1:263
American Union Against Militarism,
    3:1044–1045, 1046, 1068–1070
American Woman Suffrage Association,
    1:266, 273–274, 276
  founding of, 1:297, 320
  relationship with National Woman
    Suffrage Association, 1:297,
    299

The American Woman's Home (Beecher
    and Stowe), 1:286
American Women (report), 2:400
American Women's Voluntary Services,
    2:368
Americans with Disabilities Act (ADA),
    4:1245, 1249
Ames, Jessie Daniel, 1:132, 134; 2:366
Amish, 3:969
Amistad, 1:91
Anarchists
  communes, 3:1024
  deportation of, 2:503
  the Diggers, 3:1022, 1025
  eco-anarchists, 4:1320
  and eight-hour workdays, 2:485
  and European émigrés, 2:499–500
  and global justice movement, 4:1464
  Haymarket Square. See Haymarket
    Square
  intentional communities, 3:1003,
    1005
  Italian, 2:502–503, 580–581
  Jewish influence in the, 2:500–502
Anarcho-syndicalism, 2:503, 524
Anderson, Marian, 1:164
Anderson, Mary, 1:348; 2:362, 369
Andrus, Ethel Percy, 4:1241
Anglo-African Magazine (1859), 1:84
Animal Legal Defense Fund, 4:1315
Animal Liberation (Singer, 1975),
    4:1313–1314
Animal rights, 4:1257, 1281
  and anti-cruelty, 4:1310–1312
  and humane work, 4:1312–1314
  1970s–1990s, 4:1314–1315
  organizations, 4:1310–1312, 1313,
    1314
  overview, 4:1309–1310
  twenty-first century, 4:1315–1316
Animal Welfare Act, 4:1313, 1314–1315
Animal Welfare Institute, 4:1312
Anniston (Alabama), attack on Free-
    dom Riders, 1:183, 205, 209
Anslinger, Harry J., 3:873
ANSWER. See Act Now to Stop War
    and End Racism
Anthony, Aaron, 1:72
Anthony, Susan B., 1:263, 266, 273, 298
  on anti-imperialism, 1:343
  attempt to vote, 1:297, 298
  relationship with Stanton, 1:296–297
  and temperance movement, 1:298;
    3:866
  and woman suffrage, 1:276, 296–299,
    320

Anti-abortion movement
    American Medical Association and,
        2:379
    Catholic Church and, 2:381; 3:847
    legislation and, 2:382, 385
    militant resistance, 2:382, 384; 3:847
    See also Abortion legislation;
        Abortion rights movement
Anti-apartheid movement
    historical background, 1:235–236
    United States and, 1:220, 236–240
Anti-Catholicism
    and the Know-Nothings, 4:1429–1430
    nineteenth century, 4:1428–1429
    and twentieth-century politics,
        4:1430–1431
    vestiges of, 4:1431–1432
    See also Catholics
Anti-colonial movements, 1:14–16, 159,
        167
    See also Anti-imperialist movement;
        Colonialism
Anti-communism, 1:167–170; 2:578
    Taft-Hartley Act and, 2:619,
        626–628
    See also Communist Party; Palmer
        Raids; Red Scare
Anti-cruelty movement, 4:1310–1312
Anti-Drug Abuse Act (1988), 3:876
Anti-drug movement
    Clinton administration, 3:876–877
    constructing a drug panic,
        3:875–876
    early campaigns, 3:873–874
    effects of the, 3:879
    and harm reduction movement,
        3:877–879
    Nixon administration, 3:874
    origins of, 3:872–873
    Reagan administration, 3:875–876
    temperance movement compared
        with, 3:873
    War on Drugs, 3:874, 875–877
    See also Drugs
Anti-gay movement
    and legislation, 4:1353
    and Miami gay rights, 4:1362–1363
    Religious Right, 4:1353, 1365, 1370,
        1371, 1404
    repeal of antidiscrimination laws,
        4:1363–1365
    See also Gays/lesbians
Anti-immigration. *See* Immigration
Anti-Imperialist League, 1:341–342
Anti-imperialist movement, 1:341–344
Anti-Lynching Crusaders, 1:130

Anti-lynching movement
    African-American women and,
        1:130–133; 2:390
    Commission on Interracial Coopera-
        tion and, 1:131–132
    legislation, 1:130, 131, 134
    mobilization, 1:127–129
    NAACP and, 1:129–130, 138, 222
    white women and, 1:132–134; 2:366
    See also Lynching
Anti-nuclear movement
    and activism, 4:1295–1297
    revival and decline, 4:1294
    scientists and, 4:1293–1294
    See also Atomic weapons; Nuclear
        power; Nuclear weapons
Anti-obscenity movement. *See* Obscenity
    and pornography
Anti-poverty movement, 1:200;
        3:1131–1134, 1138
    See also Poverty; Settlement House
        movement
Anti-preparedness movement, 3:1060–1063
Anti-prostitution movement. *See*
    Prostitution reform
Anti-rape movement
    African-American women and,
        2:446–447
    campus activism, 2:450
    emergence of, 2:445
    legislation, 2:406, 448–449
    in the media, 2:450
    and the public agenda, 2:449–450
    rape crisis centers, 2:406, 426, 447, 448
    self-defense, 2:447
    Take Back the Night, 2:406, 447
    women's liberation movement and,
        2:445–446
    See also Rape
Anti-rent movement, 3:768–772
Anti-Saloon League, 3:869
Anti-Semitism, 1:163, 167, 220, 230;
        4:1418, 1420
    See also Jews
Anti-slavery movement
    distinct from abolition movement,
        1:4, 62, 96
    legislation, 1:7–8, 48
    overview of, 1:3–4
    politics of, 1:27–29
    reasons for, 1:5–11
    repatriation, 1:3–4, 11–13, 48
    resistance to colonization, 1:14–16, 84
    See also Abolition movement; African
        Americans; Miscegenation;
        Slaveholders; Slaves

Anti-Stalinism, 2:577
Anti-Strikebreaker Law. *See* Byrnes Act
Anti-sweatshop movement. *See*
    Sweatshops
Anti-Trotskyism, 2:575
Anti-vice movements. *See* Moral reform
    movement
Antimilitarism. *See* Antiwar movement
Antiquities (National Monuments) Act
    (1906), 4:1289
Antislavery Bugle, 1:52
Antitrust laws, 2:618
Antiwar agenda, 3:1109
Antiwar movement
    Afghanistan, 3:1100
    African Americans and, 3:1087–1088,
        1104
    Chicanos and the, 3:1087–1088
    Civil War, 3:1041–1042
    conscientious objectors, 3:1045–1046,
        1048–1050, 1071
    counterculture and, 3:1086–1087
    decline of, 3:1053, 1095–1096
    early America, 3:1039
    Gulf War, 3:1057–1058
    during interwar years, 3:1046
    Iraq, 3:1100–1111
    McCarthy era, 3:1050–1052
    nineteenth century, 3:1040–1041
    overview, 3:1037–1039
    policymakers, 3:1088
    post Vietnam, 3:1056
    pre-World War I, 3:1042–1044
    sedition arrests, 3:1045, 1074–1075
    and September 11, 3:1100–1102
    twenty-first century, 3:1100–1111
    Vietnam War, 3:1053–1054,
        1080–1096; 4:1183–1184, 1230
    women and, 3:1046–1047,
        1067–1068, 1085, 1104–1105
    World War I, 3:1044–1046,
        1064–1072
    World War II, 3:1048, 1077–1079
    See also Pacifism; Peace movement;
        specific war
Antonio, Wards Cove Packing Company v.
    (1989), 1:221
Anything that Moves (magazine), 4:1371
Anzaldua, Gloria, 2:411
Apache, 2:751
Apartheid. *See* Anti-apartheid move-
    ment
Apostolic Faith Missions, 3:951, 981
Appeal to Reason (newspaper), 2:569
*Appeal to the Christian Women of the
    South* (Grimké, 1836), 1:23, 24

Appeal to the Colored Citizens of the World
    (Walker, 1829), **1:**15, 16, 66, 89, 98
Apprenticeships, **2:**459
Appropriate technology movement
    organizations and alliances,
        4:1319–1320
    relationship to other movements,
        4:1320–1321
    Schumacher and, **4:**1317–1318
    Small is Beautiful and, **4:**1318–1319
Appropriate Technology Transfer for
    Rural Areas, **4:**1319
Appuzzo, Virginia, **4:**1346
Aptheker, Herbert, **2:**530
Aptheker v. Secretary of State (1964),
    2:530
Aquash, Anna Mae Pictou, **2:**722
Arab immigrants, discrimination
    against, **3:**1058
Arapaho, **2:**749
Arbeiter Ring, **2:**502
Arctic National Wildlife Refuge
    Athabaskans against drilling, **2:**746
    Bush and the, **4:**1281
Argonauts, **2:**489–490
Arkansas, Little Rock Nine, **1:**180, 224
Armed services. *See* United States
    Military
Arnall, Ellis, **1:**166
Arrears of Pension Act (1879), **4:**1246
Art
    homoerotic, **4:**1353
    and moral reform, **3:**850–851
Artificial insemination, **3:**904
Artists, intentional communities, **3:**1005
Artists United to Win Without War,
    3:1106
Ashbrook, John, **4:**1395
Ashcroft v. Free Speech Coalition (2002),
    3:853
Ashwood, Amy, **1:**148
Asian-American Studies, **4:**1209, 1221
Asian Americans
    Alien Land Laws, **4:**1220
    and American Buddhism, **3:**1029–1030
    attacks on, **2:**653
    feminist movement, **2:**411
    imagined communities, **4:**1221
    music and journals, **4:**1221
    and public programs, **4:**1221–1222
    Red Guards, **4:**1219
    reparations, **4:**1223–1224
    stereotypes, **4:**1220–1221
    and stereotypes, **4:**1222
    white fear of, **3:**884–885, 1030;
        4:1416

Asian Americans *(continued)*
    See also Chinese Americans; Japanese
        Americans
Asian-based religious communities,
    3:1005, 1006
Asian Religions, Dictionary of (Adams,
    1817), **3:**1029
ASPCA. *See* American Society for the
    Prevention of Cruelty to Animals
Assemblies of God, **3:**982
Assembly-line work, **2:**556–557;
    3:884
Association Against the Prohibition
    Amendment, **3:**870
Association for the Protection of
    Colored Women, **1:**334
Association of Collegiate Alumnae, **2:**363
Association of Disabled Miners and
    Widows, **2:**647
Association of Southern Women for the
    Prevention of Lynching, **1:**132–134;
    2:366
Associationalism, **3:**887
Associationism, **3:**972–973
Associationist experiments, **1:**287
Astin, Helen, **2:**415
Atlanta Compromise speech, **1:**136,
    227–228
Atlanta Neighborhood Union, **1:**319
Atomic Energy Act (1946), **4:**1293
Atomic Energy Commission, **4:**1277, 1293
Atomic Scientists, **4:**1293
Atomic weapons
    fallout from, **4:**1275
    See also Anti-nuclear movement;
        Nuclear weapons
Attorney General's Commission on
    Pornography. *See* Meese Commis-
    sion
Attorney General's list of subversive
    organizations, **3:**1126
Auburn System, **1:**122
Audubon Society, **4:**1267
Auld, Hugh, **1:**73
Auld, Thomas, **1:**73, 74
Austin, Alice Constance, **1:**289
Austin, Harriet N., **1:**269
Austin, James T., **1:**50
Auto-Lite strike, **2:**564, 591, 593–595
The Autobiography of a Brown Buffalo
    (Acosta, 1972), **2:**754
Automation (of labor), **2:**629–630, 650
Automotive industry
    concession bargaining, **2:**651–652
    Just-In-Time production, **2:**656
    See also United Automobile Workers

Axelrod, Beverly, **1:**232
Aztlán, **4:**1214–1215
Azusa Street mission, **3:**951, 981

B

Back-to-Africa, **1:**113–114, 148, 149, 159,
    228
Back to the land, **4:**1318
Backlash. *See* Black backlash; White
    backlash
*Backlash: The Undeclared War Against
    American Women* (Faludi, 1991), **2:**433
Bad Heart Bull, John Wesley, **2:**711
Bad Heart Bull, Sarah, **2:**712
Bad-jacketed, **2:**722
Bagley, Sarah, **2:**467, 470
Baher v. Lewin (1993), **4:**1326
Bai, Jane, **1:**254
Bailey, Gamaliel, **1:**28–29, 63
Bailey, Hannah, **1:**344
Bailey, Harriet, **1:**72
Baird, Eisenstadt v. (1972), **2:**358; **3:**847
Baker, Ella Josephine, **1:**180, 181, 182
Baker, Helen, **4:**1230
Bakke, Allen, **1:**215
Bakke decision (1978), **1:**248
Baldwin, Clarence Benham, **1:**166
Baldwin, Robert, **3:**1011
Baldwin, Tammy, **4:**1357
Ballads and Anti-Slavery Poems
    (Whittier), **1:**51
Ballanger, Pat, **2:**707
Ballinger, Richard A., **4:**1290
Bankhead Jones Farm Tenant Act
    (1937), **3:**1125
Banks, Dennis, **2:**707, 708
    at AIM trials, **2:**715
    as a fugitive, **2:**714–715
    Longest Walk, **2:**722
    retirement from AIM, **2:**722
    at Wounded Knee, **2:**712, 714
Banneker, Benjamin, **1:**83
Baptist Convention, **1:**331
Baraka, Amiri, **1:**212
Barnett, Ross, **1:**185
Barry, Marion, **1:**182
Bascom, John, **3:**957
Baseball, segregated teams, **1:**162
Bates, Daisy, **1:**180, 224
Bates, Katherine Lee, **1:**343
Bathhouses, gay, **3:**855
Battle Creek Sanitarium, **1:**282; **3:**1016
Battle of Seattle (WTO protests), **4:**1460,
    1468
    overview, **4:**1482

Battle of Seattle (WTO protests)
  (*continued*)
    participants in, **4:**1486–1488
    protest narrative, **4:**1488–1490
    successes, **4:**1490
    See also World Trade Organization
Bauer, Gary, **4:**1404
Bauman, Robert E., **4:**1393
Baumgardner, Jennifer, **2:**431
Beach, Henry L. (Mike), **4:**1441
*Bean v. Southwestern Waste-Management
  Corporation* (1976), **4:**1300
Beat Generation, **3:**953, 1023, 1031
Beecher, Catherine, **1:**286; **3:**948
Beecher, Henry Ward, **1:**297; **3:**957
Beecher, Lyman, **1:**51; **3:**948
Beecroft, Carol, **4:**1380
*Being a Christian: What it Means and How
  to Begin* (Gladden, 1876), **3:**959
Beissel, Johann Conrad, **3:**998
Belknap, Jeremy, **3:**941
Bell, Buck v. (1927), **3:**902; **4:**1247
*The Bell Curve: Intelligence and Class
  Structure in American Life* (Herrnstein
  and Murray, 1994), **3:**904
Bellamy, Edward, **3:**957, 1120, 1135
Belleville (Illinois), coal miner wildcat
  strikes, **2:**676
Benezet, Anthony, **1:**8
Benjamin, Herbert, **2:**585, 591
Bennett, Anne, **4:**1230
Bentley, Elizabeth, **2:**578; **4:**1412
Benton, Thomas Hart, **2:**489
Berdaches, **4:**1379
Berea College, **1:**59
Berger, Victor, **2:**569; **3:**1074
Bergh, Henry, **4:**1311
Berkeley University. *See* University of
  California at Berkeley
Berkman, Alexander, **2:**501, 503; **3:**1075
Berrigan, Daniel, **3:**1057
Berrigan, Philip, **3:**1057
Bessemer steelmaking, **2:**543; **3:**883
Betha, Rainey, **2:**388–389
Bethune, Mary McLeod, **1:**160, 161;
  2:361, 367
Bevel, Diane Nash. *See* Nash, Diane
Bevel, James, **1:**182, 187
Bi/Trans Action, **4:**1370
BIA. *See* Bureau of Indian Affairs
Biafra, Jello, **3:**850
Bias, Len, **3:**876
Biberman, Herbert, **2:**690
Bible Christian Church, **3:**1015
Big Four railroad brotherhoods, **2:**533,
  536, 537

Big Mama Rag collective, **2:**442
Bikini Kill, **2:**432
Biko, Steve, **1:**236
Bilingual education, **4:**1210
Billings, Richard Mohawk, **2:**715
Billy Graham Evangelistic Association,
  3:951
BiNet USA, **4:**1369
Biometrics, **3:**899
Bioregionalism, **4:**1320
Biracial mixture. *See* Miscegenation
*The Birch-bark Roll of the Woodcraft
  Indians* (Seton, 1900s), **2:**741
Birdsong Incident, **3:**813–814
Birmingham, Alabama
    attack on Freedom Riders, **1:**183, 205,
      209
    King's civil rights efforts, **1:**185–188,
      206; **3:**1127
    racist violence, **1:**187, 188–190, 205
Birney, James G., **1:**25, 53, 64
Birth Control Clinical Research Bureau,
  1:323; **2:**355, 358
Birth Control Federation of America,
  2:358
    See also Planned Parenthood
      Federation of America
Birth control movement
    African Americans and, **2:**358
    legislation, **2:**358; **3:**847
    Margaret Sanger and, **1:**322–323;
      2:354–358, 365
    Mary Ware Dennett, **1:**323–324; **2:**354
    opponents of, **1:**322; **2:**353
    roots of, **2:**353–354
The Birth Control Review, **2:**354
Birth of a Nation (film), **1:**138–139;
  4:1435
Bisexual movement
    AIDS and activism, **4:**1369
    backlash, **4:**1370–1371
    bisexuality explained, **4:**1367–1368
    and the LGBT movement,
      4:1369–1370
    organizing strategy, **4:**1368–1369
    See also Gays/lesbians; Transgender
      activism
Bisexual Network, East Coat, **4:**1369
Bisexual Pride Day, **4:**1369
Bisexual Resource Center, **4:**1369
Bisexual Youth Initiative, **4:**1370
Bishop Hill, **3:**1001
Bisno, Abraham, **2:**485–486
Bissonette, Pedro, **2:**716
Bittelman, Alexander, **2:**570
Black, Algernon D., **3:**1011–1012

Black backlash
    commodity riots, **1:**198, 206–207, 225
    Red Summer, **1:**223
Black Bear Ranch, **3:**1024, 1027
Black Codes, **1:**111
Black Congressional Caucus, **1:**212, 241
Black feminism. *See* African Americans,
  women
Black Hills, federal seizure of, **2:**729
Black-Jewish conflict, **1:**213
Black Kettle, **2:**749, 750
Black Lung Association, **2:**647
Black lung movement, **2:**646–649
Black Muslims. *See* Nation of Islam
Black nationalism, **1:**143–145, 148–149,
    159, 195, 206
    civil rights and, **1:**227–234
    temporary decline of, **1:**228–229
    See also Black Panthers; Nation of
      Islam
Black Panthers, **1:**199–200, 203, 214,
    231–232
    FBI and, **1:**200, 203, 213–215, 233;
      2:715; **3:**1130–1131
    influence on Native Americans,
      2:706–707
    and Weatherman, **4:**1197–1198
Black Power, **1:**198–199, 210
Black Star Line, **1:**144, 145, 149, 150
Black Voices for Peace, **3:**1104
Black Women Organized for Action,
  2:393–394
Black Women's Alliance, **2:**408
Black Women's Health Project, **2:**405
Black Women's Liberation Committee,
  2:392, 408
Black Zionism. *See* Black nationalism
Blacklists
    African Americans on, **1:**169
    film makers on, **2:**690
Blacks. *See* African Americans
Blackwell, Antoinette, **1:**297
Blackwell, Henry Brown, **1:**273, 297, 300
Blades, Joan, **3:**1102
Blake, Lillie Devereux, **1:**276, 341
Blanket injunctions, **2:**618
Blatch, Harriot Stanton, **1:**301; **3:**1044
"Bleeding Kansas," **1:**58
Bloodletting (form of medicine), **1:**280;
  3:990
Bloody Sunday, **1:**194
Bloody Thursday, **2:**564
Bloomer, Amelia, **1:**263, 269
Blyden, Edward Wilmont, **1:**113–114
Board of Indian Commissioners, **2:**750
Boarding schools. *See* Schools

Body image, **2:**432
Boer War (1899–1902), **1:**235
Boggs Act (1951), **3:**874
Bohr, Niels, **4:**1293
Boland, Edward, **4:**1362
Boldt decision, **2:**727
Bolshevik revolution. *See* Russian
    revolution
Bonfield, John, **2:**484
Bonnin, Gertrude, **2:**703
Bonnin, Raymond T., **2:**703
Bonus March, **2:**563, 590
Book of Mormon, **3:**931
Bookchin, Murray, **4:**1320
Booker, Cory, **1:**251, 252
Booth, Heather, **2:**400
Border crossing rights, Canadian
    Indian, **2:**703–704, 736
Boring from within, **2:**527
Bork, Robert, **1:**221
Born again Christians, **3:**951
Borsodi, Ralph, **3:**1005
Bosacker, Steven, **4:**1359
Boston Female Anti-Slavery Society,
    1:263, 264
Boston Police Strike (1919), **2:**559, 639
Boston Tea Party "Mohawks," **2:**739
Boston Women's Health Collective,
    2:404
Boudinot, Elias, **2:**699
Bowers v. Hardwick (1986), **3:**854, 857;
    4:1325, 1352, 1366
Boxing, **1:**162
Boy Scouts of America, **2:**741
Boy Scouts of America v. Dale (2000),
    4:1352
Boycotts
    ban of, **2:**626, 683
    history of, **2:**680
    under judicial attack, **2:**511
    use of, **2:**683–685
Boyd, Norma, **2:**389
Boyd, Wes, **3:**1102
Boyle, Tony, **2:**634
Boynton v. Virginia (1960), **1:**183, 205, 209
Boys Don't Cry (film), **4:**1381
Bra burnings, **2:**401
Bracero program, **3:**829–830
Bradley, James R., **1:**69
Bradley, Mamie Till, **1:**176
Brainerd, Dave, **3:**928
Braintree robbery, **2:**580
Brakemen's Brotherhood and
    Trainmen's Union, **2:**534
Branch Davidians, **3:**954
Brand, Stewart, **4:**1318–1319

Brandeis, Louis, **3:**1010
Brayman, Brandon, **4:**1381
Brazile, Donna, **4:**1346
Bread and Roses, **2:**424
Breakfast cereal, **3:**1016, 1017
Breitman, George, **2:**591
Bresee, Phineas F., **3:**950
Brewer, Duane, **2:**715–716, 717
Breyer, Stephen G., **1:**247
Bridges, Harry, **2:**564, 593, 594
Brigade, Jeanette Rankin, **2:**436
Briggs, Cyril B., **1:**131; **2:**570
Briggs, John, **4:**1364
Briggs Initiative (1978), **3:**852
Bright, Bill, **3:**950
Brisbane, Albert, **1:**287
Britain. *See* Great Britain
British Contagious Disease Act (1864),
    3:859
Brook Farm, **1:**287; **3:**923, 971, 972, 1002
Brookwood Labor College
    curriculum, **2:**599–600
    decline of, **2:**601–602
    denunciation of, **2:**601–602
    faculty and students, **2:**597–599
    founding of, **2:**596–597
    legacy of, **2:**602
Brophy, John, **2:**605–606
Brotherhood, League of Universal,
    3:1041
Brotherhood of Locomotive Engineers,
    2:533, 537
Brotherhood of Locomotive Firemen,
    2:533
Brotherhood of Locomotive Firemen
    and Enginemen, **2:**537, 539
*Brotherhood of Locomotive Firemen and
    Enginemen, Tunstall v.* (1944), **2:**541
Brotherhood of Railroad Brakemen, **2:**533
Brotherhood of Railroad Trainmen,
    2:533, 537, 539
Brotherhood of Railway and Airline
    Clerks, **2:**541
Brotherhood of Sleeping Car Porters
    (BSCP), **1:**145, 152–156, 159; **2:**539,
    540
Broughton, Virginia, **1:**331
Browder, Earl, **2:**575, 577
Brown, Charlotte Emerson, **2:**361
Brown, Clara, **2:**467, 471
Brown, Dee, **2:**707
Brown, H. Rap, **1:**199
Brown, Jerry, **2:**714
Brown, John, **1:**58–60, 66, 94
    Garrison's support for, **3:**1042
    meeting with Frederick Douglass, **1:**77

Brown, Judith, **2:**425, 441
Brown, Oliver, **1:**174
Brown, Rita Mae, **2:**441
Brown, William Wells, **1:**33, 36–38, 41
Brown Berets, **3:**1130; **4:**1215–1216
    COINTELPRO and, **4:**1208–1209
Brown v. Board of Education (1954), **1:**163,
    171, 173–174, 175, 223; **3:**1126
Brownmiller, Susan, **2:**437, 446
Brownsville Clinic, **1:**323; **2:**354
Bruce, Lenny, **3:**850
Brundage, Avery, **1:**163
Bryan, William Jennings, **3:**793
Bryant, Anita, **3:**852; **4:**1362
Bryant, Carolyn, **1:**176
Bryant, Roy, **1:**176–177
Buchanan, Patrick, **3:**1135
Buchanan v. Warley (1917), **1:**138
Buchman, Frank, **3:**908, 911
Buck v. Bell (1927), **3:**902; **4:**1247
Buckley, William, **4:**1389, 1390
Buddhism, **3:**936, 953
    communal societies, **3:**1005
    counterculture movement and, **3:**1031
    famous converts to, **3:**1030–1031
    origin and development of,
        3:1029–1030
    popularization and institutionaliza-
        tion of, **3:**1030–1032
    stagnation of, **3:**1030
Buddhist-Poetics-Humanist Psychology
    community, **3:**1031
Budenz, Louis F., **2:**601
Buff, I.E., **2:**646–647, 648
Buffalo hunts, **2:**750
Bukharin, Nikolai, **2:**575
Bullard, Robert, **4:**1300
Bulletin of the Atomic Scientists, **4:**1293
Bulter, Dino, **2:**719
Bunche, Ralph, **1:**169
Bundy, Ted, **3:**849
Bundy Act, **3:**849
Bunker Hill and Sullivan Mining
    Company (BH&S), **2:**493–494
Bunting, Mary, **2:**415
Bureau of Biological Survey, **4:**1288
Bureau of Indian Affairs (BIA)
    crimes against American Indian
        Movement, **2:**712, 716, 718
    fraudulence of, **2:**711, 737
    Native American infiltration of,
        2:710–711
    role of, **2:**725
Bureau of Legal Advice, **3:**1046
Burger, Warren, **1:**213
Burke Act (1906), **2:**700

Burks, Mary Fair, **1**:178
Burleigh machine drills, **2**:493–494
Burleson, Albert S., **3**:1074
Burlingame Treaty (1868), **2**:475
Burlington & Quincy Railroad strike (1888), **2**:534
Burn, Febb Ensminger, **1**:307
Burn, Harry, **1**:307
Burns, Anthony, **1**:93
Burns, Lucy, **2**:361
Burns and Ward Transfer Company, **4**:1302
Burnside, John, **4**:1335
Burritt, Elihu, **3**:1041
Burroughs, Nannie Helen, **1**:331
Burson Bill (1922), **2**:703
Buses, segregated, **1**:177–178
Bush, George H.W.
    anti-abortion stance, **3**:847
    and 1991 Civil Rights Act, **1**:244
Bush, George W.
    antiwar caricatures, **3**:1103
    and governmental racial diversity, **1**:247
    and Log Cabin Republicans, **4**:1351
    refusal to attend World Conference Against Racism, **1**:255
    War on Terror, **3**:1058
    See also Bush (George W.) administration
Bush (George W.) administration
    environmentalism during the, **4**:1281
    gays appointed during the, **4**:1358
    See also Bush, George W.
Bush v. Gore (2000), **1**:248
Bush v. Vera (1996), **1**:248
Bushnell, Horace, **1**:296; **3**:957
Business, and the conservatives, **4**:1395–1396
Business regulation, **3**:891–892
Business unionism, **2**:512
Butler, Benjamin, **1**:39
Butler, Elizabeth, **2**:699
Butler, Richard G., **4**:1442
Butler v. State of Michigan, **3**:848
Butte Miners' Union, **2**:495
Buy American campaigns, **2**:682–683
Byrd, Harry, **3**:1125
Byrd, James, **1**:134, 242
Byrdcliffe, **3**:1005
Byrnes Act (1936), **2**:619

C

C-R groups. *See* Consciousness raising groups

Cabet, Etienne, **3**:973, 1002–1003
Cable, George Washington, **1**:122
Cable Act (1922), **2**:364
Cable Splicer, **2**:717
Calhoun, Arthur W., **2**:599, 601
Calhoun, John C., **1**:99–100, 101
Calhoun, Patrick, **3**:762
California
    Compassionate Use Act (1996), **3**:876
    Los Angeles. *See* Los Angeles
    McMartin preschool, **3**:853
    migrant workers, **3**:1123, 1131
    miners and mining. *See* Mining
    Proposition 187, **1**:250; **3**:1135–1136
    Proposition 215, **3**:876
    Proposition 229, **4**:1209
    San Francisco. *See* San Francisco
    three-strikes law (1994), **3**:879
    Watts riot (1965), **1**:225
California, Miller v. (1973), **3**:848
California, O'Connor v. (1993), **3**:916
California Civil Liberties Public Education Funds, **4**:1209
California farmers. *See* Farm Workers Labor Movement
California Workingmen's Party, **3**:824
Call, Hal, **4**:1336
Calvin, John, **3**:886–887, 938, 942
Calvinists, **3**:938–939
Cambodia, **3**:1094
Cambridge Cooperative Housekeeping Society, **1**:288–289
Camp, Carter, **2**: 713, 714
Camp, Ellen Moves, **2**:716
Camp meetings, Socialist, **3**:799
Camp Paradise, **3**:1154
Camphill movement, **3**:1005
Campus Antiwar Network, **3**:1104
Campus Crusade for Christ, **3**:950
Campus Life, **3**:950
Canada
    African American emigration to, **1**:32–33
    draft resisters in, **3**:1089, 1097–1098
    Native Indians. *See* Canadian Indians
    Quebec City free trade protests, **4**:1467
Canadian Indians
    Aboriginal rights, **2**:735, 736–737
    border crossing rights, **2**:703–704, 736
The Cancer Journals (Lorde, 1980), **2**:409
Cane Ridge, **3**:929
Cannery and Agricultural Workers' Industrial Union, **2**:621; **3**:827–828

Cannery workers movement, **2**:621–623
Cannon, James P., **2**:571, 574, 575
Cannon, Joseph, **4**:1290
Cape Town, South Africa, **1**:235
Capitalism, Christianity and, **4**:1399
Carey, James, **2**:614
Carey, Ron, **2**:668, 669
Carlin, George, **3**:850
Carlisle Indian School, **2**:701, 752
Carmichael, Stokely, **1**:198, 231; **2**:400, 706
Carnegie, Andrew, **2**:543–544
Carnegie Endowment for International Peace, **3**:1066
Carney, William H., **1**:40
Carson, Rachel, **4**:1273–1274
Carter, Jimmy, **3**:835–837
    and civil rights movement, **1**:214–215
    and gay/lesbian relations, **4**:1345, 1358
Carus, Paul, **3**:1030
Cary, Lott, **1**:14
Cary, Samuel F., **3**:788–789
Casinos, Native American, **2**:729, 737
Castillo, Ana, **2**:410
Catholic Charismatic Movement, **3**:952
Catholic Church, **3**:933
    attack on abortion, **2**:381; **3**:847
    birth control, **3**:847
    See also Catholics
Catholics
    discrimination of, **3**:1117; **4**:1416
    ethnic variations of, **3**:933–934
    Latinos, **3**:933–934
    priests and sexual abuse, **3**:853
    Protestant opposition to, **3**:948
    traditional, **3**:952
    See also Anti-Catholicism; Catholic Church
Catt, Carrie Chapman, **1**:299, 301–308, 321; **2**:361–362
    clash with Alice Paul, **2**:373
    and the peace movement, **3**:1044, 1047
Celestial Seasoning Corporation, **3**:1018
Celo Community, **3**:1006
Censorship
    of art and music, 850–851
    Internet, **3**:851
    of obscenity and pornography. *See* Obscenity and pornography
Central Labor Union (New York), **2**:508
Cereal, **3**:1016, 1017
Ceremony (Silko, 1977), **2**:755
Chamberlain, Neville, **1**:164
Chambers, Whittaker, **2**:578
Chandler, Elizabeth, **1**:54

Chaney, James, **1:**134, 192, 216
Chao, Elaine, **1:**247
Chaplin, Ralph H., **2:**687
Charismatic movement, **3:**951–952
Charismatic Renewal, **3:**982
Charney, George Blake, **2:**576
Chase, Salmon P., **1:**28–29, 63
Chastity, adolescent, **3:**852
Chauncy, Charles, **3:**940
Chavez, Cesar, **2:**683; **3:**830–834, 1131; **4:**1206, 1216
Chavez-Thompson, Linda, **2:**653, 655, 659
Chernobyl, **4:**1257, 1296
Cherokee, **2:**698–699, 748
Cherrystone Club, **4:**1381
Chester Residents Concerned for Quality of Living, **4:**1307
Cheyenne, **2:**749
Chicago, Illinois
    Democratic National Convention (1968), **3:**1092; **4:**1187–1188
    Haymarket Square. *See* Haymarket Square
    Hull-House, **1:**317, 319; **2:**366; **3:**1141
    King's campaign against housing discrimination, **1:**197–198
    race riots 1943, **1:**223
Chicago Defender, **1:**143, 156
Chicago Eight, **3:**1092
Chicago Federation of Labor, **1:**350
Chicago Idea, **2:**499
Chicago Women's Trade Union League, **1:**349, 350
Chicana Service Action Center (1972), **2:**411
Chicano Manifesto (Rendón), **4:**1208, 1212, 1217
Chicano Moratorium Committee, **3:**1088
Chicano movement, **4:**1212–1214
    See also Latinos; Mexican Americans
Chief Fools Crow, **2:**716
Chief Mitchell, **2:**736
Chief Red Cloud, **2:**749, 750, 752
Chief Spotted Tail, **2:**750
Chief Tammany, **2:**740
Child, Lydia Maria, **2:**699
Child care facilities, war time, **2:**369
Child development
    Adler's interest in, **3:**1009
    settlement houses and, **3:**1142–1143
Child Exploitation and Obscenity Section, **3:**849
Child labor
    Felix Adler and, **3:**1009

Child labor *(continued)*
    Florence Kelley on, **1:**318
    industrialization and, **2:**506
    mill work, **3:**1121
    mine workers, **2:**516
Child Obscenity and Pornography Act, **3:**853
Child Online Protection Act (1998), **3:**851
Child pornography, **3:**853–854
Child Pornography Prevention Act (1996), **3:**853
Child Protection and Obscenity Enforcement Act (1988), **3:**853
Child Sexual Abuse and Pornography Act (1986), **3:**853
Child Study Association, **3:**1009
Child welfare
    moral reform and, **3:**864
    sex education and, **3:**582
    Social Security Act and, **2:**366–367
    women and, **2:**364
Children, and sexual abuse panics, **3:**852–853
Children, Prevention of Cruelty to, **4:**1311
Children of God, **3:**1005
Children's Bureau, **1:**338; **2:**364
Children's Institute International, **3:**853
Children's Internet Protection Act (2000), **3:**851
Chin, Vincent, **2:**653
The China Syndrome (film), **4:**1277
Chinese Americans
    discrimination of, **4:**1219–1220
    immigration quotas, **3:**885, 1030; **4:**1424
    union labels and, **2:**680
    See also Asian Americans
Chinese Exclusion Act (1882), **3:**1030; **4:**1219, 1424
Chinese Workers and Staff Association, **2:**659
Chiswick Women's Aid, **2:**406
Chivington, John, **2:**749
Chmielewski, Florian, **4:**1362
Chodorov, Frank, **4:**1388–1389, 1390
Christian anarchism, **1:**64
Christian Anti-Communism Crusade, **4:**1399
Christian Businessman's Committee, **3:**950
Christian Coalition of America, **4:**1403–1404
Christian communal living, **1:**286–287
Christian Defense League, **4:**1442
Christian Economics (journal), **4:**1399

Christian Freedom Foundation, **4:**1399
Christian Herald (newspaper), **1:**84
Christian Identity Movement, **4:**1442
Christian Labor Union, **3:**957
Christian physiologists, **3:**1014–1015
Christian Recorder (newspaper), **1:**84
Christian Right. *See* Religious Right
Christian Science movement, **3:**934
Christian socialism, **3:**957
Christian Voice, **4:**1402
Christianity
    abolition movement and, **1:**19–20, 22, 23, 31–32, 49–50
    antislavery movement and, **1:**3, 5, 6
    blended with socialism, **3:**957
    and capitalism, **4:**1399
    forced upon Native Americans, **2:**696, 697, 698, 701
    repatriation and, **1:**12
    Social, **1:**331
    support of slavery, **1:**7
    and women's rights, **1:**277, 296
    See also specific denomination
Christianity and the Social Crisis (Rauschenbusch, 1907), **3:**959
Chubb, Percival, **3:**1011
Church of God in Christ, **3:**981
Church of Jesus Christ of Latterday Saints. *See* Mormons
Church of Jesus Christ of the Aryan Nations, **4:**1442
Church of the Nazarene, **3:**950
Churches
    African American establishment of, **1:**80–82, 330–331
    and women's rights, **1:**277, 296
Churchill, Ward, **2:**746
Cigar Makers' Association of the Pacific Coast, **2:**680
Cigar Makers International Union, **2:**476–477
Cigar Makers' International Union of America, **2:**680
Cincinnati, racial riots (2001), **1:**242
Cincinnati Contemporary Arts Association, **3:**850
Cinque, Joseph, **1:**92
CIO. *See* Congress of Industrial Organizations
Circuit City Stores v. Adams (2001), **1:**248
Citizen militia groups, **4:**1440, 1443–1446
Citizens' Alliance, **2:**564
Citizens' Equal Rights Association, **1:**114
Citizen's Protective Association, **2:**492

Citizenship
    immigrant. *See* Immigration
    Native Americans and, **2:**701, 702
City Care, **4:**1300
City on the Edge (video), **2:**673
City Repair project, **3:**1156
City University of New York (CUNY),
    1:213
Civil disobedience
    for civil rights, **3:**1052
    as a protest of slavery, **1:**36
    Thoreau and, **3:**1041
Civil Liberties Bureau, **3:**1046, 1068,
    1075
Civil religion, **3:**921, 928
Civil rights
    Asian Americans, **4:**1220
    effect of September 11 on, **1:**250
    Ethical Culture and, **3:**1012
    government enforcement of, **1:**180,
        190, 224
    and self-defense, **1:**206, 209–210, 223,
        224
    U.S. Supreme Court and, **1:**220–221
    war against poverty and, **3:**1126–1127
Civil Rights Act
    1957, **1:**229
    1960, **1:**229
    1964, **1:**229; **2:**620
        Title VI, **1:**249–250
        Title VII, **2:**400
        Title VII, Section 703, **1:**190
    1991, **1:**243–244
Civil Rights Bill (1867), **1:**111
Civil Rights Congress, **1:**171
Civil rights movement
    and black nationalism, **1:**227–234
    Civil War victories, **1:**4, 45
    college students and, **1:**181–182
    constitutional amendments, **1:**111, 112
    Freedom Rides, **1:**182–184, 205, 209
    and Harlem Renaissance, **1:**145–146
    impact of, **1:**109–110
    Jimmy Carter and, **1:**214–215
    legislation, **1:**243–245
    Mexican Americans and, **4:**1213–1214
    militant resistance. *See* Militant
        resistance
    nonviolent direct action. *See* Nonvio-
        lent direct action
    overview of, **1:**107–108
    peace and the, **3:**1052
    presidential action, **1:**246–247
    and racist violence, **1:**170–171, 180, 182
    return of during 1950s, **1:**171–172
    revival in 1980s, **1:**218–220

Civil rights movement *(continued)*
    rolling back, **1:**115–118
    Ronald Reagan and, **1:**216–217, 218
    setbacks during Cold War, **1:**167–169,
        171
    women in the, **2:**400, 423
Civil Service Act (1883), **2:**638
Civil Service Commission, **3:**1074
Civil War
    abolition movement during, **1:**94
    affect on Native Americans, **2:**748–749
    antidiscrimination laws, **1:**41
    blacks fighting for citizenship,
        1:36–38
    blacks in Union troops, **1:**4, 39–41, 43
    civil rights victories, **1:**4, 45
    discrimination of blacks, **1:**41–42
    draft riot, **3:**1042, 1118
    Pacifism and the, **3:**1041–1042
    recruiters, **1:**42
    as a religious event, **3:**947
    and woman suffrage, **1:**297–300, 310
Civilian Conservation Corps, **2:**591
Civilian Public Service camps,
    3:1048–1050
Claim-patent system, **2:**490, 491
Clamshell Alliance, **4:**1277
The Clansman. See Birth of a Nation
Clapp, Moses A., **2:**700
Clark, Jim, **1:**193
Clark, Mark, **1:**203; **3:**1131
Clark-McNary Act (1924), **4:**1291
Clarke, Edward, **1:**312
Clay, Edward W., **1:**50
Clayton Act, **2:**515, 517, 618
Clean Air Act, **4:**1276
Clean Living movements, **1:**282
Clean Water Act, **4:**1276
Cleaver, Eldridge, **1:**231–233
Clement, Victor, **2:**494
Clergy and Laity Concerned About
    Vietnam, **3:**1054
Clerical work, **1:**348
Clinton, Bill
    apology for slavery, **1:**247
    attempted impeachment, **3:**856
    and governmental diversity,
        1:246–247; **4:**1358
    National Dialogue on Race, **1:**255
    and "New Democrats," **4:**1388
    See also Clinton administration
Clinton administration
    assault on welfare, **3:**1136–1139
    conservatism under, **4:**1397
    "Don't Ask, Don't Tell," **4:**1328, 1354
    gays appointed during the, **4:**1358

Clinton administration *(continued)*
    and illegal immigrant legislation,
        3:1136
    labor relations, **2:**655–656
    See also Clinton, Bill
"Close Ranks" editorial (Du Bois), **1:**141
Closed shops, **2:**492, 626
Clothing, women's. *See* Women's
    clothing
Cloud, Henry Roe, **2:**703
Cloward, Richard, **3:**1131
Club movement. *See* Women's clubs
CNVA. *See* Committee for Nonviolent
    Action
Coal mining. *See* Mining
Coalition for Health Sex, **3:**855
Coalition for Labor Union Women,
    2:411–412, 633
Coalition of Black Trade Unionists,
    1:212
Coalition of Labor Union Women, **2:**641
CODEPINK, **3:**1105, 1108
Coeur d'Alenes, Miners' Union of the,
    2:494–495
Coffee, Linda, **2:**381
Coffee trade. *See* Fair Trade Coffee
    campaign
Cohen, Julius, **3:**1010
Cohn, Fannia, **1:**347
Cohousing. *See* Cooperative housing
COINTELPRO, **1:**233; **2:**717, 722
    and Brown Berets, **4:**1208–1209
    and ethnic movements, **4:**1208–1209
    and student movements, **4:**1165, 1192
    and Students for a Democratic
        Society, **4:**1175, 1187, 1188, 1192
Coit, Stanton, **3:**1009
Colburn, Marshal Wayne, **2:**715
Colby, Josephine, **2:**599
Coleman, Norm, **4:**1370
Coler, Jack, **2:**717, 718
Coll, Tom, **2:**718
Collective bargaining, **1:**349; **2:**628–629
College Settlement. *See* Henry Street
    Settlement
Colleges. *See* Universities
Collier, John, **2:**703, 704
Collins, Patricia Hill, **2:**410
Colonial America
    abolition societies, **1:**7
    antislavery movement, **1:**3–11
    apprenticeships, **2:**459
    free labor, **2:**458–459
    immigrant exclusion, **4:**1422–1423
    indentured servants, **2:**459–460
    labor law, **2:**617

Colonial America (continued)
  labor strikes, 2:462
  miscegenation legislation, 1:8
  missionaries, 2:697; 3:961
  Native American movement,
    2:697–699
  organized, 2:462–463
  pacifism in, 3:1039–1040
  petition from slaves, 1:9
  religion, 3:925–928
  repatriation of blacks, 1:3–4, 11–13,
    48
  senior citizens, 4:1236–1237
  slave labor, 2:460–461
  women and, 2:461–462
Colonialism
  apartheid and, 1:235–236
  global, 1:159, 164, 167
  of Philippines, 1:342–343
  See also Anti-colonial movements
Colonization
  black resistance of, 1:14–16, 20–25,
    50, 62, 84
  of blacks, 1:3–4, 11–16, 31, 48, 83
  of Native Americans, 2:695–696
Colorado
  Amendment 2, 4:1366
  Ludlow Massacre, 2: 514
  Mutualistas movement, 4:1227–1228
Colorado Cooperative Colony, 3:983–989
Colored American (newspaper, 1837),
  1:22, 84
Colored Association of Railroad
  Employees, 2:539
Colored Farmers' National Alliance,
  3:784–785
The Colored Patriots of the American
  Revolution (Nell, 1855), 1:38
Colored Trainmen of America, 2:539,
  541
Colored Woman's League (1892), 1:300,
  333
Columbia (Tennessee), racial violence,
  1:223
Columbian Order. See Sons of St.
  Tammany
Columbus, Christopher, 2:695
Columbus Day, protest of, 2:722
Combahee River Collective, 2:393–394,
  410, 443
Coming Nation (socialist newspaper),
  3:1003
Comintern. See Communist Interna-
  tional
Comisión Femenil Mexicana, 2:410–411
Commerford, John, 2:469

Commission on Interracial Coopera-
  tion, 1:131–132
Commissions of the Status of Women,
  2:400
Committee Against Jim Crow in Military
  Service and Training, 1:170
Committee for a Sane Nuclear Policy
  (SANE), 3:1052, 1053
Committee for Nonviolent Action,
  3:1052, 1053, 1083
Committee of Industrial Organizations.
  See Congress of Industrial Organi-
  zations
Committee of One Hundred, 2:703
Committee on Economic Security,
  4:1240
Committee on Maternal Health, 2:356
Committee on Public Information,
  3:1073–1074
Commodification, 3:883
Commodity riots, 1:198, 206–207, 225;
  3:1129
  See also Race riots
Common Threads, 2:554
Commoner, Barry, 4:1275
Commonwealth v. Hunt (1842), 2:617
Commonwealth v. Pullis (1806), 2:617
Communal living
  decline of, 3:1027
  hippies, 3:1023, 1024–1025
  origins of, 1:286–287
  pietist groups, 3:969
  social relations of, 3:1024–1025
  types of, 3:923
  See also Intentional communities;
    Utopian movements; specific
    commune
Communications Decency Act (1996),
  3:851
Communist Control Act (1954), 1:171
Communist International (Comintern),
  2:570–571, 575–576
Communist Labor Party, 2:570
Communist League of America, 2:575
Communist Party
  and African-American labor, 1:145,
    160
  and African-American rights, 1:131,
    159–160, 164; 2:572
  and anticolonialism, 1:159, 164
  and antiracist policies, 1:164
  factionalism, 2:574–575
  fragmentation, 2:575–576
  and global justice movement, 4:1464
  help for the poor, 3:1122–1124
  and immigrant rights, 2:572

Communist Party (continued)
  legacy of, 2:576–578
  and 1930s culture, 1:162
  origins, 2:568–570
  political accomplishments, 2:571–574
  under Stalin, 2:575–576
  and Unemployed Councils, 2:588;
    3:1123
  and unemployment movement,
    2:584–585; 3:1148, 1149–1150
  weakening of, 1:164
  women membership, 2:572
  and women's rights, 2:572–573
  youth membership, 2:573
  See also Anti-communism; Palmer
    Raids; Red Scare
Communist Party (Majority Group). See
  Communist Party Opposition
Communist Party Opposition, 2:575
Community of True Inspiration, 3:1001
Community Service Organization,
  3:831–832
Community United for Sexual Privacy,
  3:855
Company unions, 2:561–562
Compassionate Use Act (1996), 3:876
Complex marriage. See Marriage
Comprehensive Drug Abuse Prevention
  and Control Act (1970), 3:874
Compromise of 1850, 1:29, 87
Comstock, Anthony, 1:277; 2:353;
  3:862–863
Comstock Law (1873), 1:322; 2:353,
  379–380; 3:862
Comstock unions, 2:491–493
Comstockery, 3:863, 864
Concerned Women for America, 4:1402
Concession bargaining, 2:635–636,
  651–652
The Condition, Elevation, Emigration, and
  Destiny of the Colored People of the
  United States, Politically Considered
  (Delany, 1852), 1:31, 32, 36, 38, 67
Conference for Progressive Labor
  Action, 2:589, 601; 3:1150
Conference for Progressive Political
  Action, 2:540, 574
Congress of Industrial Organizations
  (CIO), 3:819–820
  Almanac Singers and, 2:688
  anti-communism and, 2:604, 614
  black membership, 1:164–165
  communist purges, 1:169; 2:627
  condemnation of, 1:163
  founding of, 2:595, 604–606
  ideology, 2:604

Congress of Industrial Organizations (CIO) *(continued)*
    leaders of, **2:**605–606
    leadership and strategy, **2:**610–611
    lift of No Strike Pledge, **2:**624
    merger with American Federation of Labor, **2:**614–615, 630, 631
    Operation Dixie, **2:**611–612, 626
    Political Action Committee, **1:**166; **2:**609–610
    post–World War II, **2:**624–626
    steelmakers and, **2:**545–546
    strikes and politics, **2:**606–609, 611
    support of Roosevelt, **2:**606
    Taft-Hartley Act and, **2:**612–614, 627
    welfare state and, **3:**1124–1125
    and World War II, **2:**609–610
Congress of Racial Equality (CORE), **1:**166
    early years, **1:**208–209
    expansion of, **1:**209
    focus on poverty, **1:**210
    Freedom Highways, **1:**209
    Freedom Rides, **1:**182–184, 205, 209
    Journey of Reconciliation, **1:**203, 208–209
    and nonviolent direct action, **1:**202–203, 205; **3:**1050
    ousted white members, **1:**199, 211
    radicalization and demise, **1:**206, 209–211
    victims of racial violence, **1:**224
Congress of Spanish Speaking People, **2:**622
Congress to Unite Women, **2:**441
Congressional Black Caucus. *See* Black Congressional Caucus
Congressional Dillingham Commission on Immigration, **3:**902
Congressional Union for Woman Suffrage, **1:**300; **2:**361
Conn, Billy, **1:**162
Connecticut, Griswold v. (1965), **2:**355, 358; **3:**847
Connor, Eugene "Bull," **1:**183, 185, 187, 206
Conscientious objectors (COs), **3:**1045–1046, 1048–1050, 1071
Consciousness raising groups, **2:**401, 425, 438–440
Conscription. *See* Drafts
Conservation movement
    federal intervention, **4:**1287–1288
    individuals and organizations, **4:**1285–1287
    opponents, **4:**1289–1290

Conservation movement *(continued)*
    origins of, **4:**1285
    Progressive Era, **4:**1261–1262
    during Taft and Wilson years, **4:**1290–1291
    Theodore Roosevelt and, **4:**1288–1289
Conservationism, **4:**1256
Conservatism, and the American people, **4:**1406–1408
Conservative Christian movements, **3:**950–952
    See also Religious Right
Conservative Mind, from Burke to Eliot (Kirk, 1995), **4:**1388
Conservatives
    ascendancy of, **4:**1395, 1402
    and Clinton, **4:**1397
    discontent with Eisenhower, **4:**1391–1392
    and Ford, **4:**1395
    and Gingrich, **4:**1398–1399
    and Goldwater, **4:**1392–1393
    and Nixon, **4:**1394–1395
    pioneering intellectuals, **4:**1388–1391
    and Reagan, **4:**1396–1397
    and Religious Right alliance, **4:**1399–1404
    and Religious Right friction, **4:**1404–1406
    shared interest with business, **4:**1395–1397
    women as, **4:**1411–1413
Consol Number 9, **2:**646
Constitution. *See* United States Constitution
Constructive engagement, **1:**236, 238
Consultation of Older and Younger Adults for Social Change, **4:**1230
Consumer boycotts. *See* Boycotts
Consumerism, **2:**556–557
Consumers, and the labor movement, **2:**680–685
Consumption campaigns, **2:**680–681
Contraception. *See* Birth control movement
Contract labor, convict. *See* Convict labor and leasing
Contract with America, **3:**1136; **4:**1398–1399
Contracts Clause, **3:**770
Controlled Substance Act, **3:**874
Controlled Substances Analogue Enforcement Act, **3:**876
Convict labor and leasing, **1:**122–126
Conyers, John, **1:**245
Cook, Cara, **2:**599

Cook, Mary, **1:**331
Cooked-food delivery services, **1:**284
Cooley, Harris R., **4:**1238
Coolidge, Calvin, **2:**559, 639
Coolidge, Sherman, **2:**701
Cooper, Anna Julia, **1:**333, 334
Cooper, Peter, **3:**788–789
Cooperative Housekeeping movement
    communes and, **1:**286–288
    reasons for founding, **1:**284
    societies, **1:**288–289
    types of work, **1:**284–286
Cooperative housing, **1:**286; **3:**1006
Cooperatives
    origins of public, **1:**286–288
    worker, **2:**473
Coordinating Committee to End the War in Vietnam, **4:**1186
Corcoran Gallery, **3:**850
CORE. *See* Congress of Racial Equality
Cornish, Samuel, **1:**14, 22, 68, 69, 84, 85, 98
Corporate Campaign Inc., **2:**652
Corporate Consensus, **2:**628
Corporate crimes, **2:**656
Corporations
    and conservatives, **4:**1395–1396
    transnational, **4:**1459
Cost of living allowance (COLA), **2:**628–629
Costigan, Edward, **1:**134
Costigan-Wagner Bill (1934), **1:**134
Coughlin, Charles E., **4:**1240
Council of Energy Resources Tribes, **2:**745
Council on African Affairs, **1:**236
Council on Religion and the Homosexual, **3:**846, 847
Counterculture
    and antiwar, **3:**1086–1087
    "back to the land," **4:**1318
    and Buddhism, **3:**1031
    and class, race, and ethnicity, **3:**1025–1026
    communes, **3:**1024–1025, 1027
    and gender, **3:**1025–1027
    locating the, **3:**1020–1021
    origins and enclaves, **3:**1023
    schools of thought, **3:**1022
    See also Anarchists; Communal living; Hippies
Counterinsurgency warfare, **2:**717
Country Life Commission, **3:**889; **4:**1289
Country Life Movement, **3:**888, 889
Couzins, Phoebe, **1:**276
Covenant against Genocide, **1:**171

Covey, Edward, **1:**73
Coward, Fred, **2:**720
Cowboys and Indians, **2:**741
Cox, James R., **2:**590
Coxey, Jacob, **3:**1120–1121
CPLA. *See* Conference for Progressive
    Labor Action
Craddock, Ida, **3:**862
Craig, Minnie D., **3:**806
Crane, Frederick, **2:**354
Crazy Horse, **2:**751
Crime
    drugs and, **3:**879
    racial divide and, **1:**242
    See also Criminal justice
Criminal justice
    racial divide and, **1:**242
    reform, **1:**122
    See also Crime; Death penalty;
        Prisons
Criminal Sexual Conduct statute, **2:**448
The Crisis, **1:**137, 139
    "Close Ranks" editorial, **1:**141
    and Harlem Renaissance, **1:**146
Crisis of the 1890s, **3:**887
Crispins. *See* Order of the Knights of St.
    Crispin
Croly, Jane, **1:**313; **2:**361
Cromartie, Easley v. (2001), **1:**248
Cronaca Sovversiva (Italian anarchist
    newspaper), **2:**580
Crooks, Lynn, **2:**721
Crop lien system, **3:**783
Cross burnings, **1:**248
"Cross of Gold" speech (Bryan), **3:**793
Crosswaith, Frank, **1:**154
Crow Dog, Leonard, **2:**709, 714
Cruikshank, United States v. (1876), **1:**112
Crummell, Alexander, **1:**34, 69
Cuba, **1:**341; **3:**1060
Cuffee, Paul, **1:**13, 83
Cullen, William, **3:**991
Cult deprogrammers, **3:**953
Cults, **3:**923, 954
Cultural anxieties, **3:**863–864
Cultural feminism, **2:**427
Culture
    archetypal model of American
        Indians, **2:**739–743
    commodification of, **3:**883
    women's movement effect on,
        2:412–413
    See also Popular culture
Culture war, **3:**852
Cumbie, Rev. J.T., **3:**798–801
Currency, saving, **3:**788

"Curse of Ham," **1:**7
Cushing, Ned, **4:**1392
Custer, George Armstrong, **2:**751
Custer Died for Your Sins (Deloria, 1969),
    2:707
Cuthbertson, Polly, **4:**1230
Cutting, Nathaniel, **1:**10–11
Cycles of contention, **2:**483

D

Dahlgren, Mrs., **1:**276
Daily Worker, **2:**573
Dalai Lama, **3:**1032
Dale, Boy Scouts of America v. (2000),
    4:1352
Daley, Richard, **1:**197, 198, 203;
    4:1187–1188
Daly, Jo, **4:**1359
Dams
    Earth First! and, **4:**1280
    Echo Park, **4:**1269–1271
    Hetch Hetchy, **4:**1265–1266
    and river restoration, **4:**1282–1283
Danbury Hatters case, **2:**683
DanceSafe, **3:**879
Daniels, Newell, **2:**475
Darrow, Clarence, **2:**496
Darwin, Charles, **3:**899, 956
Darwinian evolution. *See* Evolution
Daughters of St. Crispin, **2:**476
Daughters of Temperance, **1:**263
Daughters of the American Revolution,
    1:164
Daughters of the Bilitis, **2:**370; **3:**846;
    4:1337–1339
Davenport, Charles B., **3:**900
Davis, Adelle, **3:**1017
Davis, Angela, **1:**214
Davis, Benjamin, **1:**171; **2:**572
Davis, David, **2:**475
Davis, Elizabeth Gould, **2:**443
Davis, Gray, **1:**250; **4:**1359
Davis, Henrietta Vinton, **1:**149
Davis, Madeline, **4:**1345
Davis, Paulina Wright, **1:**296
Davis, Rebecca Harding, **2:**690
Davis, Varina, **1:**343–344
Davis-Bacon Act (1931), **2:**618
Dawes, Henry, **2:**700
Dawes Act. *See* General Allotment Act
Day nurseries, **1:**285
DDT, **4:**1273
De Beauvoir, Simone, **2:**370, 391
De Caux, Len, **2:**597
De Gouges, Olympe, **1:**287

De Leon, Daniel, **2:**525, 527, 528; **3:**796
De Saint Simon, Henri, **1:**287
De Witt, Benjamin Park, **3:**881
Deacons for Defense and Justice, **1:**209,
    224
Dead Kennedys, **3:**850
Dearborn Independent (Ford), **4:**1420
Death penalty, **1:**220
    race and, **1:**244–245
    Racial Justice Act, **1:**244–245
    Reagan administration's support for,
        1:217–218
    See also Criminal justice; Prisons
Debs, Eugene, **1:**145; **2:**535, 569, 618;
    3:796
    and Industrial Workers of the World,
        2:495, 496
    sedition arrest, **3:**1074–1075
Decker, Sara, **3:**859
Declaration of Rights of Indigenous
    Peoples (1992), **2:**726
Declaration of Sentiments, **1:**291, 292
Decolonization, **4:**1207–1208, 1214
DeCora, Angel, **2:**701
Dedwell, John, **3:**867
Defense industry. *See* Wartime indus-
    tries
Defense of Marriage Act, **3:**852;
    4:1326–1327, 1354
Deindustrialization, **1:**217; **2:**635, 650
Deists, **3:**943
Delany, Martin R., **1:**30–34, 38, 67, 68
    on Abraham Lincoln, **1:**37
    agriculture in Africa, **1:**70
    as Civil War recruiter, **1:**42–43
    on danger to blacks, **1:**36
    in Harvard, **1:**69
Dellinger, David, **3:**1049, 1079
Deloria, Vine, Jr., **2:**707, 726
Democratic Leadership Council,
    4:1387–1388
Democratic National Convention
    Chicago (1968), **3:**1092, **4:**1187–1188
    Credentials Committee (1964), **1:**191
    gay fundraisers, **4:**1346
    Mississippi Freedom Democratic
        Party at, **1:**192–193
    openly gay members, **4:**1346–1347
Democratic Party
    African American switch to, **2:**389
    civil rights plank (1948), **1:**170
    divisions over Vietnam, **3:**1088
    gay/lesbians and the, **4:**1344–1346
    New Democrats, **4:**1388
Demonstration clubs, **3:**810
Dempsey, Moore v., **1:**138

Dennett, Mary Ware, **1:**323–324; **2:**354
Dennis, Peggy, **2:**575–576
Department of Labor, **2:**618
    Children's Bureau, **1:**338; **2:**364
    creation of, **2:**557
    Women's Bureau, **2:**362
Dependent Pension Act (1890), **4:**1246
Depugh, Robert, **4:**1440–1441
Des Verney, W.H., **1:**153
DeSersa, Byron, **2:**716
Detroit, Michigan
    hunger marches, **3:**1148–1149
    Treaty of Detroit, **2:**625, 628–629, 636
    wildcat strikes, **2:**678
Detwiller, Henry, **3:**990
Detzer, Dorothy, **3:**1047
DeVos family, **4:**1404
Dew, Thomas Roderick, **1:**99
Dewson, Mary Williams, **2:**367
The Dharma Bums (Keroyac, 1958), **3:**1031
Dharmapala, Anagarika, **3:**1030
Diablo Canyon Power Plant, **4:**1277
The Dial, **3:**1029
The Dialectic of Sex: The Case for Feminist Revolution (Firestone, 1970), **2:**425
Diallo, Amadou, **1:**242
The Diary of a Shirtwaist Striker (Malkiel, 1910), **2:**690
Dibble, C.H., **3:**814–816
Dickinson, Robert, **2:**356
Dickson Mounds, **2:**730
A Dictionary of Asian Religions (Adams, 1817), **3:**1029
Die-in, **3:**1108
Diem regime, **3:**1081
Dies, Martin, **3:**1125
Diet for a Small Planet (Lappé, 1971), **3:**1018
Diggers, **3:**1022, 1025
Diggs, Charles, **1:**212
Dignity Village, **3:**1156
Dilling, Elizabeth, **4:**1411
Dining club, **1:**284
Dinkins, David, **1:**218
Dinosaur National Monument, **4:**1269, 1271
Direct Action to Stop the War, **3:**1101, 1107–1108
Direct actions, **3:**1109
Direct aid, for anti-apartheid movement, **1:**239
Dirksen, Everett, **1:**190
Disabilities, learning and psychiatric, **4:**1249–1251

Disabilities movement
    defining disability, **4:**1245–1246
    and eugenics, **4:**1246–1247
    legislation, **4:**1248–1249
    organizations, **4:**1247
    private and government efforts, **4:**1246
    and public attitudes, **4:**1247
Disarmament, **3:**1057
Dixie Chicks, **3:**1105
Dixon, Joseph, **2:**702
Doar, John, **1:**185
Dobson, James, **3:**850; **4:**1402, 1404–1405
Documentary film, labor reflected in, **2:**691
Dodge, David Low, **3:**1041
Dodge Revolutionary Union Movement, **1:**212; **2:**678
Doherty, Clay, **4:**1347
Dohrn, Bernadine, **4:**1196
Dole, Robert, **1:**250; **3:**837
Dole, Vincent, **3:**877
Domestic violence, **2:**406, 426
Donaghey, George W., **1:**125
Donahue, Thomas, **2:**653
Donnelly, Ignatius, **3:**792
Donnerstein, Edward, **3:**849
"Don't Ask, Don't Tell," **4:**1328, 1354
Dotson, Donald, **2:**651
"Double V" campaign, **1:**166
Douglas, H. Ford, **1:**41, 69
Douglas, Satirra, **1:**44
Douglass, Frederick, **1:**30, 58
    biography, **1:**72–79
    and black economics, **1:**118
    at National Convention of Colored Men, **1:**87
    support of temperance, **3:**866
    and women's rights, **1:**118, 294
Dowie, John Alexander, **3:**1004
Downer, Carol, **2:**405
Downsizing, **2:**656
Drafts
    burning draft cards, **4:**1186–1187
    draft riots, **3:**1042, 1118
    resisters in Canada, **3:**1089, 1097–1098
    Vietnam War, **3:**1089–1090
    World War I, **3:**1045, 1071
Drake, Jennifer, **2:**432
Draper, Alonzo B., **2:**471
Dred Scott decision, **1:**29, 33, 36, 41, 58, 87
    nullification of, **1:**111
Dress reform movement
    abandonment of, **1:**271
    after women's rights, **1:**270–271

Dress reform movement *(continued)*
    reasons for, **1:**268
    and utopian communities, **1:**262, 268–269
    women and, **1:**265–266
    and women's rights, **1:**269–270
Drop City, **3:**1005
Drug Enforcement Administration (1973), **3:**874
Drug law reform, **3:**876
Drug panics
    governmental construction of, **3:**875–876
    See also Anti-drug movement; Drugs
Drugs
    counterculture's use of, **3:**1022
    crime and, **3:**879
    harm reduction movement and, **3:**877–879
    racial discrimination and, **3:**876, 879
    See also Anti-drug movement; Drug panics
Du Bois, W.E.B., **1:**119–120, 129–130
    arrest of, **1:**170–171
    biography, **1:**137
    The Crisis, **1:**136, 137, 139, 146
    and Harlem Renaissance, **1:**145–146
    and NAACP, **1:**136, 141
    and Pan-Africanism, **1:**144–145
    response to black repression, **1:**228
    rivalry with Garvey, **1:**144
    on self-defense, **1:**223
    support of birth control, **2:**358
Dubinsky, David, **2:**548, 605
In Dubious Battle (Steinbeck, 1936), **3:**1123
Dukakis, Michael, **1:**220
Duke, David, **4:**1440
Dull Knife, Guy, **2:**716
Duncan, Donald, **3:**1090
Dunne, Ray, **2:**564
Dunne, Vincent Raymond, **2:**593, 594
Durant, Paul Skyhorse, **2:**715
Durazo, Maria Elena, **2:**671–673
Durham, Jimmie, **2:**713, 722
Duss, John, **3:**1001
Dutch colonialism, **1:**235
Dworkin, Andrea, **3:**849
Dyer, Leonidas, **1:**130
Dyer Bill (1922), **1:**130, 131, 138
Dylan, Bob, **3:**1087

E

Eagle, Jimmy, **2:**716, 718, 719
Earth Day, **4:**1299
Earth First!, **4:**1280

Earth Liberation Front, **4**:1281

Easley v. Cromartie (2001), **1**:248

Eason, James, **1**:149

East Coast Bisexual Network, **4**:1369

East Coast Homophile Organization, **4**:1340

Eastern Religions, **3**:952–953

Eastland, James, **1**:183

Eastman, Charles, **2**:701, 703

Eastman, George, **3**:901

Eastman, Max, **2**:571

Ebenezer, **3**:1001

Ebens, Ronald, **2**:653

ECHO. *See* East Coast Homophile Organization

Echo Park Dam, **4**:1269–1271

Echohawk, John, **2**:727

Echols, Alice, **2**:437

Eckford, Elizabeth, **1**:180

Eco-anarchists, **4**:1320

Eco-saboteurs, **4**:1280

Ecologism, radical, **4**:1320

Ecology, social, **4**:1320

Economic Bill of Rights (1944), **1**:167; **3**:1126

Economic Justice movement, **2**:744

Economic Research and Action Project, **3**:1127; **4**:1175

Economic Security Act (1935), **2**:366

Economics

  abolition movement and, **1**:47–48, 101, 102

  antislavery movement and, **1**:6–7, 18–19

  free *vs.* convict labor, **1**:124, 126

  slavery and, **1**:10

Ecovillages, **3**:1006

Ecumenical Christian Movements, **3**:952

Ecumenical Coalition, **2**:653

Eddy, Mary Baker, **3**:934

Edelstadt, David, **2**:501

Edelman, Marian Wright, **3**:1135

Education

  bilingual, **4**:1210

  for ex-slaves, **1**:43–45, 69–70

  improvement in black, **1**:169

  industrial, **1**:348–349

  labor. *See* Brookwood Labor College

  learning disabilities and, **4**:1249–1251

  medical, **3**:994–996

  Native American Heat of the Earth, **2**:728

  See also Schools; Teachers; Universities; Women's education

Education Amendment, Title IX, **2**:402, 415–416

Education policy, and civil rights, **1**:250

Edwards, Jonathan, **3**:927–928, 940, 941–942

Edwards Dam, **4**:1282–1283

EEOC. *See* Equal Employment Opportunity Commission

E.F. Schumacher Society, **4**:1320

Ehrlich, Paul, **3**:1018; **4**:1276

Eight Hour Associations, **2**:484–485

Eight-hour workday movement, **2**:473–474, 484–485, 520–523, 537

Eight Hours (music, by Jesse Henry Jones), **2**:522

Eighteenth Amendment, **3**:869

Einsiedel, Edna, **3**:849

Eisendrath Glove Company, **1**:350

Eisenhower, Dwight, conservatives' discontent with, **4**:1391–1392

Eisenstadt v. Baird (1972), **2**:358; **3**:847

El Congreso de los Pueblos de Habla Español (1938), **2**:622

El Teatro Campesino, **4**:1217

Elders, Joycelyn, **1**:246; **3**:852

Electronic Frontier Foundation, **3**:851

ELF (Earth Liberation Front), **4**:1281

Eliot, John, **2**:697

Ellen, Jane, **4**:1380

Elliot, John Lovejoy, **3**:1010–1011

Ellis, Havelock, **4**:1246–1247

Ellison, Ralph, **1**:228

Ellsberg, Daniel, **3**:1094–1095

Ely, Richard, **3**:884, 960

Emancipation Proclamation, **1**:35, 39, 94

Emergency Peace Campaign, **3**:1048

Emergency Peace Federation, **3**:1044

Emergency Relief Appropriation Act (1935), **2**:586

Emerson, Ralph Waldo, **3**:936, 943, 1007, 1029

Emigration, African-American, **1**:32–34, 70, 83, 86–87, 112–114, 143, 144, 149

Emissary communities, **3**:1005

Emma Willard School. *See* Troy Female Seminary

Employee representation plans. *See* Company unions

Employee Retirement Income Security Act (1974), **2**:620; **4**:1242

Employees Representation Plan (Pullman's), **1**:153

Employer-sponsored benefits, **2**:562

Employment. *See* Labor

Employment Non-Discrimination Bill, **4**:1381

Employment Nondiscrimination Act, **4**:1326–1327, 1354

Encampment for Citizenship, **3**:1012

End Poverty in California, **4**:1240

Endangered Species Act, **4**:1275–1276

Engel, George, **2**:499, 500

England. *See* Great Britain

Engels, Friedrich, on Knights of Labor, **2**:480

English, as the official language, **1**:249

English, William, **2**:469

English as a Second Language (ESL), **4**:1209–1210

Ensler, Eve, **2**:450

Entertainment

  and moral reform, **3**:850

  whites use of Native Americans for, **2**:732

Environmental dangers, man-made, **4**:1273–1276

Environmental disenfranchisement, poverty and, **4**:1299–1300

Environmental Equity Cluster, **4**:1305

Environmental justice movement, **4**:1281–1282

  first steps, **4**:1304–1307

  ideologies and philosophies, **4**:1299–1300

  overview, **4**:1298–1299

  principles of, **4**:1306

Environmental movement, divisions within, **4**:1320

Environmental policy, and civil rights, **1**:250

Environmental Protection Agency (EPA), **4**:1275

Environmental Equity report, **4**:1304

Environmental racism, **2**:744; **4**:1302–1304

Environmental rights, Native American, **2**:729

Environmentalism

  during conservative ascendancy, **4**:1279–1281

  food choice and, **3**:1018

  growth of, **4**:1270–1271, 1280

  and indigenous peoples, **2**:744–747

  industrialization and, **4**:1260–1261

  literature, **4**:1273–1274

  and nuclear power, **4**:1257, 1276–1277

  origins, **4**:1258

  and population growth, **4**:1276

  post-World War II, **4**:1268–1271

  for wilderness, **4**:1271–1273

  for wildlife, **4**:1267

  women and, **4**:1274

EPA. *See* Environmental Protection Agency

Ephrata Community, **3**:998

Epstein, Abraham, **4**:1240
Equal Employment Opportunity Commission (EEOC), **1**:161; **2**:400
Clinton's appointments to, **1**:246–247
Equal Pay Act (1963), **2**:369
Equal Rights Amendment (ERA), **2**:364–365, 373–376, 402
Equal Rights (journal), **2**:364
Equal Rights Party, **3**:1117
Equality Begins at Home, **4**:1371
Equality (journal), **3**:957
Equality League of Self-Supporting Women, **1**:301
ERA. *See* Equal Rights Amendment
Era Club, **1**:314
Erdman Act (1898), **2**:537
Erdrich, Louise, **2**:754–755
ESL. *See* English as a Second Language
Espionage Act (1917), **3**:1045, 1068, 1074
Ethical Culture
decline of, **3**:1011
founder, **3**:1007
and labor movement, **3**:1009–1010
leaders, **3**:1009
legacy, **3**:1011–1012
new leadership, **3**:1010–1011
philosophy, **3**:1007
Settlement Houses, **3**:1009–1010
and social reform, **3**:1008–1009
Ethnic Studies, **4**:1209
Ethnocentrism, **3**:1121–1122
Ethology, **4**:1313
Ettor, Joseph, **2**:529, 530
EU. *See* European Union
Eugene (Oregon), homeless camp, **3**:1154
Eugenics movement
American Eugenics Society, **3**:901
historical roots, **3**:899–900
ideology, **3**:900–901
Margaret Sanger and, **2**:356–358; **3**:901
opposition to, **3**:902–903
reform, **3**:903
revival of, **3**:903–904
target populations, **3**:901–902; **4**:1246–1247
European Union (EU), **4**:1459, 1467
Evan, Thomas, **3**:1079
Evangelicalism
abolition movement and, **1**:19–20, 31–32, 49–50, 52
labor movement and, **2**:466
politics and, **4**:1402
women and, **3**:948–949
See also Christianity

Evangelism
Oxford Group Movement and, **3**:908–909
televised, **3**:951
Evans, George Henry, **2**:469, 470
Evans, Hiram, **4**:1437
Evans, Romer v. (1996), **3**:854; **4**:1325, 1352, 1366
Everett Massacre, **2**:531
Everglades, **2**:746
Evers, Medgar, **1**:184, 185
Evictions of planters, **3**:814–816
Evolution
Darwinism, **3**:934
teacher arrested for teaching, **3**:950
theories of, **3**:899–900
Ex-Gay Movement, **4**:1371
Exodusters Movement, **1**:114; **3**:773–776
Exotic Dancer's Union, **3**:861
Experimental Negotiating Agreement, **2**:546

F

"The Factory Bell" (poem), **2**:470
"Factory Girl's Reverie" (fiction), **2**:689–690
Factory inspections, **1**:319
Factory work, **1**:315–317, 324–325
Lowell System rules, **2**:465
women in, **2**:505
Fair Employment Practices Committee, **1**:152, 161, 168, 202; **2**:541
Fair Labor Standards Act (1938), **2**:369, 374–375, 522
Fair Trade Coffee campaign
coffee crisis, **4**:1497–1499
competition and sustainability, **4**:1501–1502
ethical consumption and fair trade, **4**:1499–1500
making a fair trade market, **4**:1500–1501
overview, **4**:1497
Fairfax, Francis, **4**:1380
Fall, Albert, **2**:703
Faludi, Susan, **2**:433
Falwell, Jerry, **3**:855, 856; **4**:1400, 1402
Familistere, **1**:287
Family and Medical Leave Act (1993), **2**:655
Family Assistance Plan, **3**:1132–1133
Family planning. *See* Birth control movement
Family Research Council, **4**:1404
Family roles, 1830–1840, **1**:19

Family values
post–World War II, **2**:370
Religious Right and, **3**:852
Fantasia Fair, **4**:1381
Farah Manufacturing Company, **2**:685
Fard, Wallace D., **1**:145, 229; **3**:935–936
The Farm, **3**:1005, 1024–1025
See also Gaskin, Stephen
Farm Animal Reform Movement, **4**:1316
Farm ownership, **3**:822–823
Farm Sanctuary, **4**:1316
Farm Security Administration, **1**:166; **3**:1125
Farm worker boycotts, **2**:683–685
Farm Workers Labor Movement, **3**:822–834
Farmer-Labor Party, **1**:350; **3**:818–821
Farmers' Alliance Movement, **3**:783–786
Farmers' Protective League, **3**:826
Farming, organic, **3**:1017
Farrakhan, Louis, **1**:230, 241, 242–243; **4**:1210
FAS. *See* Federation of American Scientists
Fashion industry
sweatshop labor and, **2**:554
See also Women's clothing
Father Divine, **3**:953–954, 1005
Faubus, Orval, **1**:180
Fauntroy, Walter E., **3**:1104
Fauset, Crystal Bird, **2**:367
FBI. *See* Federal Bureau of Investigation
FCC v. Pacifica Foundation (1978), **3**:850
Federal Administration on Aging, **4**:1242
Federal Bureau of Investigation (FBI)
and American Indian Movement, **2**:711, 712, 714, 715–723
and Black Panthers, **1**:200, 203, 213–214, 233; **2**:715; **3**:1130
COINTELPRO. *See* COINTELPRO
and Industrial Workers of the World, **2**:531
investigation of Martin Luther King Jr., **1**:188
during McCarthy era, **1**:169, 171
and militia groups, **4**:1441
RESMURS investigation, **2**:719–721
surveillance of Vietnam War activists, **3**:1095; **4**:1187–1188
and Wounded Knee siege (1973), **2**:712, 714
Federal Bureau of Narcotics, **3**:873
Federal Coal Mine Health and Safety Act (1969), **2**:646, 649

Federal Emergency Management Agency (FEMA), **2:**717
Federal Emergency Relief Administration (FERA), **3:**1151
Federal Organic Food Production Act (1990), **3:**1019
Federal Society of Journeymen Cordwainers, **2:**464
Federalists, antiwar sentiments of, **3:**1040
Federation of Agricultural Workers Union of America, **2:**622
Federation of American Scientists, **4:**1293
Federation of Atomic Scientists, **4:**1293
Federation of Colored Women's Clubs, **1:**351
Federation of Organized Trades and Labor Unions
  craftworkers and, **2:**507
  eight-hour workday strike, **2:**484, 521
  solidarity with Knights of Labor, **2:**483
Fee, John G., **1:**59
Feinstein, Dianne, **3:**855
Feldman, Sandra, **2:**641
Fellowship of Reconciliation, **1:**166, 202, 208; **3:**1047, 1050, 1079, 1085–1086
FEMA. *See* Federal Emergency Management Agency
The Female Eunuch (Greer, 1970), **2:**403
Female to Male, **4:**1381
Female voting rights. *See* Voting rights
The Feminine Mystique (Friedan, 1963), **2:**398, 400, 422
Femininity, **2:**432–433
Feminism
  African American, **2:**391–396, 408–410
  and the anti-rape movement, **2:**446
  cultural, **2:**427
  culture and, **2:**412–413
  and diversity, **2:**429
  domestic, **3:**948
  dual stance on pornography, **3:**849–850
  gay-straight split, **2:**442
  latina, **2:**410–411
  lesbian, **2:**370, 406–408, 427
  men and, **2:**430
  men as the enemy, **2:**440
  radical, **2:**436–442
  separatism. *See* Separatism
  sex wars, **3:**849–850
  temperance movement and, **3:**866–867
  Third Wave. *See* Third Wave women's movement
  See also Women's liberation movement

Feminist, negative meaning of, **2:**433, 437
Feminist Alliance Against Rape, **2:**448
Feminist Studies (journal), **2:**419
Feminist Women's Health Center, **2:**405
Femme Mirror (magazine), **4:**1380
Fenian movement, **4:**1416
FERA. *See* Federal Emergency Relief Administration
Ferber, New York v. (1982), **3:**853
Ferebee, Dorothy, **2:**389
Ferguson, Plessy v. (1896), **1:**115, 129, 173
Ferringer, Harold Price, **3:**856
Festival of Life, **3:**1092
Fetal rights, **2:**385
  See also Anti-abortion movement
Fetterman, William, **2:**749
Fiction. *See* Literature
Field, James G., **3:**791–792
Fielden, Samuel, **2:**499, 500
Fields, Mamie, **1:**335
Fieldston Plan, **3:**1009
Fifteenth Amendment, **1:**111, 112, 297
Filene, A. Lincoln, **3:**1010
Film
  labor reflected in, **2:**690–691
  movie rating system, **3:**850
Fincke, Helen, **2:**596
Fincke, William, **2:**596
Finkbine, Sherri, **2:**380
Finley, NEA v. (1998), **3:**851
Finney, Charles Grandison, **3:**929–930, 944
Firestone, Shulamith, **2:**401, 425, 427
The First Sex (Gould, 1971), **2:**443
First White House Conference on Children, **2:**364
Fischer, Adolph, **2:**499, 500
Fish-ins, **2:**726–727
Fishbein, Morris, **3:**996
Fishing rights, **2:**726–727, 746
Fiske Award (1951), **3:**993
Fitzhugh, George, **1:**99
Fitzpatrick, John, **2:**544, 574
Five Civilized Tribes, **2:**698–699, 703, 748
Five C's, **3:**908
Flaxer, Abram, **2:**639
Flexner, Abraham, **3:**995–996
Flexner Report, **3:**995–996
Flint (Michigan), automobile worker strikes, **2:**607–608
Florida
  convict labor and leasing, **1:**125
  Everglades, **2:**746
Florida Federation of Colored Women, **2:**361
Florida Paper, **2:**425

Flynn, Elizabeth Gurley, **1:**346; **2:**530
Focus on the Family, **4:**1402, 1404
Fong-Torres, Ben, **4:**1207, 1220
Food, Tobacco, Agricultural and Allied Workers of America, **2:**622–623
Food, Tobacco, Agricultural Workers Union, **3:**1124
Food and Agriculture Act, **3:**835–836
Food and Drug Administration, **3:**872
Food security, **4:**1459
Food Stamp Plan (1939), **3:**1125
Food stamps, **3:**1125, 1128
Foods, genetically modified, **4:**1459
Fools Crow, **2:**716
Football, segregated teams, **1:**162
Ford, Gerald, **4:**1395
Ford, Henry, **4:**1420
Ford, James W., **2:**572
Ford, Patrick, **2:**482
Ford Highland Park plant, **2:**556, 557
Ford Hunger March, **3:**1148–1149
Foreman, Dave, **4:**1280
Forest Management Act (1897), **4:**1288
Forest Reserve Act, **4:**1288
Forest Service, **4:**1291
Forests
  national, **4:**1289
  protection of, **4:**1286–1287
  timber sales, **4:**1288, 1291
Forman, James, **1:**191, 200–201
Forsberg, Randall, **4:**1296
Fort Hood Three, **3:**1090
Fort Wagner, **1:**40
Fort-Whiteman, Lovett, **2:**572
Forten, Charlotte, **1:**44
Forten, James, **1:**13, 14, 22, 84
Fortune, T. Thomas, **1:**114, 128, 222
Foster, Abigail Kelley. *See* Kelley, Abigail
Foster, Jim, **4:**1345
Foster, William Z., **2:**544, 571, 574, 575
Foster Bill, **3:**872
Foucault, Michel, **4:**1329
Fourier, Charles, **1:**287; **3:**972, 1002
Fourierist Associations, **1:**287
Fourierist Phalanxes , **3:**923, 972–973, 1002
Fourteenth Amendment, **1:**111, 112, 297
Framing (in social movement formation), **2:**483
France
  communes, **1:**287
  demise of colonialism, **1:**167
  slave retaliation, **1:**10–11
Frankfurter, Felix, **1:**174
Frankhauser, Roy, **4:**1441

Franklin, Benjamin
    founding of abolition society, **1**:7
    and image of Native Americans,
        2:739
    on limiting growth of slaves, **1**:8
Fraser, Doug, **2**:651–652
Frederick Douglass's Paper (newspaper),
    1:77, 84
Fredonia New York, **3**:778
Free African Union Society, **1**:81
Free-enterprise capitalism, new
    conservatives and, **4**:1391
Free labor, **2**:458–459
Free labor colonies, **1**:59–60
Free market
    effect on abolition movement, **1**:47–48
    See also Market revolution
Free Soil Party, **1**:29, 53–54, 64
Free speech, restricted under Sedition
    Act, **3**:1075
Free Speech Coalition, Ashcroft v. (2002),
    3:853
Free speech fights, **2**:529
Free Speech Movement, **3**:1082,
    4:1178–1182
The Free Speech (newspaper), **1**:332
Free trade
    initiatives, **2**:656
    vs. fair trade, **4**:1455–1456
Free Trade Area of the Americas, **4**:1459
Freedmen's Bureau, **1**:111
Freedom dress, **1**:269
Freedom Highways, **1**:209
Freedom of Access to Clinic Entrances
    Act (1994), **2**:384
Freedom Rides, **1**:182–184, 205, 209
Freedom Schools, **1**:191
Freedom Summer, **1**:190–193;
    3:1127–1128
Freedom's Journal (newspaper), **1**:14–15,
    22, 84, 98
Freemasons, **3**:777–778
Freie Arbeiter Stimme (anarchist newspa-
    per), **2**:500–501
French, Eleanor, **4**:1230
French colonists, and Native Americans
    miscegenation, **2**:696
Frick, Henry Clay, **2**:501, 543
Friedan, Betty, **2**:398
    The Feminine Mystique, **2**:398, 400,
        422
Friedman, Molly, **2**:553
Friends. *See* Quakers
Friends Committee on National
    Legislation, **3**:1079
Friends of the Negro Freedom, **1**:131

Froebel, Friedrich, **1**:285
Frohnmeyer, John, **3**:851
Front Door Lobby, **1**:305
Frontier Hotel and Gambling Hall (Las
    Vegas), **2**:671
Frontiers (journal), **2**:419
Frye, Phyllis, **4**:1381
Fugitive Slave Law (1850), **1**:29, 32, 36,
    58, 65–66, 87, 92
    northern opposition to, **1**:93
Fulbright, J. William, **3**:1088
Full Gospel Business Men's Fellowship,
    3:951
Full Personality Expression, **4**:1380
Fuller, Ida M., **4**:1241
Fulton, Charles W., **4**:1290
Fundamentalist movement, **3**:950–951
Furies Collective, **2**:407–408

G

G8, **4**:1459, 1467
G-O Road case, **2**:722, 728
Gag rules
    abortion, **3**:847
    antislavery, **1**:101
    on government labor unions, **2**:639
Gage, Matilda Joslyn
    family influences on, **1**:272–273
    focus of, **1**:273
    and the *National Citizen and Ballot
        Box*, **1**:274–275
    at Syracuse Convention of 1852,
        1:272
    unity and reformer division, **1**:273–274
    and woman suffrage, **1**:273–277, 296,
        297, 299
Gaines v. Missouri (1938), **1**:162
Gale, William Potter, **4**:1441
Galleani, Luigi, **2**:580, 581
Galton, Francis, **3**:899–900
Games, cowboys and Indians, **2**:741
Gaming, Native American, **2**:729, 737
Gandhi, Mohandas, **1**:166, 202, 204, 208;
    3:1047
Garden Plot, **2**:717
Gardner, Gerald, **3**:955
Garfield, James R., **4**:1289
Garland, Hamlin, **3**:883
Garment industry, **1**:324–325, 338
    activism in, **2**:548–549
    globalization, **2**:554
    labor violations, **2**:554
    sweatshop revival, **2**:554
    union labels, **2**:681
    unions, **1**:346–347; **2**:513

Garment industry *(continued)*
    worker conditions, **2**:550
    See also Sweatshops; Textile industry
Garner, Fred, **3**:1090
Garnet, Henry Highland, **1**:28, 42, 52,
    58, 66–67, 68
Garrison, Althea, **4**:1357
Garrison, William Lloyd, **1**:4, 20–25,
    29–31, 48–51, 89
    bounty on, **1**:99
    free blacks' support for, **1**:86
    and pacifism, **3**:1041
    support of Harpers Ferry raid,
        3:1042
    support of temperance, **3**:866
Garvey, Amy Jacques, **1**:150
Garvey, Marcus
    demise of, **1**:145, 149–150, 159, 228
    later years, **1**:150
    response to black repression, **1**:228
    rivalry with Du Bois, **1**:144
    and Universal Negro Improvement
        Association, **1**:143–144, 148–150,
        159, 228
Garvin, W.L., **3**:783
Gary, Elbert, **2**:544
Gaskin, Stephen, **3**:1005, 1026
    See also The Farm
Gates, Darryl, **1**:216
GATT. *See* General Agreement on
    Tariffs and Trade
Gay Activists Alliance, **4**:1342, 1347
Gay and Lesbian HIV Prevention
    Activists, **3**:855
Gay and Lesbian Task Force, **4**:1346,
    1349, 1350, 1351
Gay and Lesbian Victory Fund, **4**:1351
Gay bathhouses, **3**:855
Gay Leadership Conference, **4**:1349
Gay Liberation Front, **2**:407; **4**:1342,
    1347
Gay Republicans, **4**:1345, 1346, 1351
Gay Rights National Lobby, **4**:1349
Gay sex panics, **3**:855
Gay Vote, **4**:1345, 1346
Gay Women's Alliance, **2**:407
Gays, Parents, Families, and Friends of
    Lesbians and (PFLAG), **4**:1351
Gays/lesbians
    bisexuals in LGBT movement,
        4:1369–1370
    and employment discrimination,
        4:1326, 1339, 1354
    gay liberation movement, **3**:847;
        4:1347
    interest groups, **4**:1349–1351, 1353

Gays/lesbians (continued)
    and marriage, 3:856–857; 4:1326–1327
    in the military, 4:1327–1328, 1333, 1354
    openly gay public officials, 4:1356–1359
    and political parties, 4:1345–1347
    protests, 4:1340, 1347–1348
    and public opinion, 4:1359–1360
    and public policy, 4:1352–1356
    queer culture, 4:1330–1331
    same-sex marriages, 3:856–857; 4:1326–1327, 1354
    sex panics, 3:855
    state and local groups, 4:1351–1352
    voting behavior of, 4:1344–1345
    See also Anti-gay movement; Bisexual movement; Homosexuality; Lesbianism; Sexuality
Gehlke, Charles Elmer, 4:1230
Gender
    abolition movement and, 1:19, 54–58
    counterculture movement and, 3:1025–1027
    missionaries and, 3:962–963
    union labels and, 2:681–682
    Weatherman and, 4:1198–1199
Gender Identity Service, 4:1381
General Agreement on Tariffs and Trade (GATT), 2:656, 682
General Agreement on Trade and Services (GATS), 4:1459
General Allotment Act (Dawes Act) (1887), 2:700, 752; 3:885
General Federation of Women's Clubs, 1:314, 316, 334; 2:361, 703; 3:859–860
General Motors (GM)
    contract with United Automobile Workers, 2:628–629
    1946 strike, 2:626
    Treaty of Detroit, 2:625, 628–629, 636
General Trades' Union, 2:468
Genes, dominant and recessive, 3:900
Genetically modified foods, 4:1459
Genius of Universal Emancipation (newspaper), 1:22
Genoa, 4:1467–1468
Genocide, Covenant against, 1:171
Gentleman's Agreement (1907), 3:1030
George, Henry, 2:487; 3:957, 1003, 1118–1119
Georgia
    civil rights in, 1:185, 206
    sodomy laws, 3:854
Gerber, Henry, 4:1331, 1332

Germ plasma theory, 3:900
German-Americans, discrimination of, 3:1075; 4:1416
German Anarchists, 2:499
German Mennonites, 1:3, 5, 8
German Pietism, 3:969, 1000, 1001
German-Soviet Non-Aggression Pact (1939), 1:160, 164
Germany, Nazi Party, 1:163, 164, 167
Germer, Adolph, 2:605
Germinal choice, 3:904
Geronimo, 2:751
Gerontological Society, 4:1241
Gerry, Elbridge T., 4:1311
Ghana, 1:143
Ghost Dance, 2:752; 3:934
Gibbs, Lois, 4:1275, 1302
Gibson, Gideon, 3:762
Gibson, Kenneth, 1:251
Giger, H.R., 3:850
Gilchrist, Robert, 2:474
Gilded Age
    labor movement, 2:507–512; 3:886
    peace reform, 3:1043
Gildersleeve, Virginia, 2:363
Giles, Harriet, 1:330
Gilman, Caroline Howard, 1:287, 288, 289
Gingrich, Newt, 4:1398–1399
Ginsberg, Allen, 3:1031, 1032
Ginsburg, Ruth Bader, 1:247
Giovannitti, Arturo, 2:529, 530
Girl Power, 2:432
Girlie culture, 2:432–433
Gitlow, Ben, 2:574, 578
Gitlow, Kate, 2:572
Gittings, Barbara, 4:1338, 1339
Giuffrida, Louis O., 2:717
Giuliani, Rudolph, 3:856
Gladden, Washington, 3:957, 958, 959, 960
Glen Canyon Dam, 4:1280
Global financial institutions, 4:1458–1459
    See also specific institution
Global justice movement
    history, 4:1459–1462
    the issues, 4:1458–1459, 1485
    nonviolent vs. violent action, 4:1466–1468
    overview, 4:1455–1457
    participants of, 4:1462–1463
    reform vs. revolution, 4:1468
    and repression, 4:1468
    successes, 4:1468
    tactics, 4:1464–1466, 1468–1469

Globalization
    corporate, 2:635
    missionaries and, 3:961–962
    offshore cannery work, 2:623
    offshore sweatshops, 2:554
    outsourcing, 2:635, 656
    and plant closings, 2:652–653, 656
    racism and, 2:653
    steel industry and, 2:546
    unemployment and, 2:635
    of work, 2:456
Glossolalia, 3:951, 952
GM. See General Motors
GM Fisher Body plant, 2:607–608
Goddard, Dwight, 3:1005
Goddard, Henry, 3:900; 4:1247
Goddess worship, 2:413
Gold rush
    California, 2:489–490
    See also Mining
Goldbert, Art, 4:1179, 1180, 1181
Goldbert, Jackie, 4:1179, 1180
Golden Rule, 1:47
Goldman, Emma, 1:343; 2:354, 501
    deportation of, 2:503; 3:1075
    on prostitution, 3:860
Goldmark, Josephine, 1:338
Goldwater, Barry, 3:874, 1128; 4:1392–1393
Goldwater Girls, 4:1412
Gompers, Samuel, 1:324; 2:509
    and Knights of Labor, 2:510
    on labor violence, 2:507
    support for Haymarket leaders, 2:485
    trade unionism, 3:887–888
    and welfare reform, 3:889
    See also American Federation of Labor
Gonzales, Rodolfo "Corky," 4:1214–1215
Gonzalez, Henry B., 4:1210
Goo-goos, 3:886
Good Neighbor Association, 3:1010
Good roads movement, 1:124–125
Goode, Wilson, 1:216
Gooding, James Henry, 1:39–40
Goodman, Andrew, 1:134, 192, 216
GOONS. See Guardians of the Oglala Nation
Gore, Al, 4:1346
Gore, Bush v. (2000), 1:248
Gore, Tipper, 3:850
Gospel of Wealth, 3:886–887
Gospelgate scandals, 4:1402
Gottlieb, Lou, 3:1005, 1024
Gould, Jay, 2:483

Government workers movement. *See*
    Public workers movement
Graham, Billy, **3**:951
Graham, Sylvester, **1**:281; **3**:1015
Gram, Hans, **1**:281; **3**:990
Grand Eight Hour League, **2**:474
Grange Movement, **3**:777–782
Grant, Madison, **3**:901
Grant, Ulysses S., **1**:78
The Grapes of Wrath (film), **2**:690
The Grapes of Wrath (novel), **3**:1124
Graves, Henry, **4**:1291
Gray, John F., **1**:281
Gray Panthers movement, **4**:1230–1235
    See also Senior citizen relief
Great Ape Project, **4**:1315
Great Awakening, **3**:926–928
    Second, **3**:928, 929, 943–944,
        1040–1041
Great Britain
    abolition movement, **1**:12
    antislavery movement, **1**:6–7
    colonization of Native Americans,
        2:696
    demise of colonialism, **1**:167
    emigration to America, **2**:459
    repatriation of blacks, **1**:11–12
    and South Africa, **1**:235
Great Depression
    communal living during, **3**:1005
    decline of reform activities, **2**:365–366
    novels, **2**:690
    poverty during, **3**:1122–1123
    private charity and government
        relief, **3**:1145–1147
    unemployment during, **2**:562–563,
        588
Great Lakes Indian Fish and Wildlife
    Commission, **2**:729
Great Migration, **1**:141–143; **2**:562; **3**:884
Great Postal Campaign (1835), **1**:51, 91,
    100–101
Great Railroad Strike (1877), **3**:1118
Great Sioux Nation, **2**:749, 750–751
Great Society, **3**:1127–1131
Great Upheaval of 1877, **2**:482, 508
Greater Liberia Bill, **1**:150
Green, Alfred M., **1**:38
Green, Beriah, **1**:64
Green, William, **1**:156; **2**:559, 560
Green Party, gay/lesbians and, **4**:1347
Green technology, **4**:1320
Greenback-Labor Party, **3**:789
Greenbacker Movement, **3**:787–790
Greengrocer Code of Conduct, **2**:654
Greenpeace, **4**:1278–1279

Greer, Germaine, **2**:403
Gregg, Richard, **3**:1047
Gregory, Dick, **3**:1018
Grew, Mary, **1**:56
Griffin, David, **3**:916
Griffin, Marvin, **1**:180
Griffin, Susan, **2**:445
Griffith, D.W., **1**:138–139; **4**:1435
Griffiths, Julia, **1**:77
Griffiths, Martha, **2**:415
Grimké, Angelina, **1**:22, 23, 24, 56, 263;
    3:1042
Grimké, Sarah, **1**:22, 56, 263
Grinde, Donald, **2**:746
Grinnell, George, **4**:1267
Griswold v. Connecticut (1965), **2**:355,
    358; **3**:847
Gritz, James, **4**:1444
Grossup, Peter, **2**:590
Ground Zero Week, **4**:1296
Grrrl, **2**:432
Guardians of the Oglala Nation
    (GOONs), **2**:711–717
Guerilla Girls, **2**:433, 434
Guiliani, Carlo, **4**:1467
Guinier, Lani, **1**:246, 253
Guinn v. United States (1915), **1**:137–138
Gulf War, antiwar movement,
    3:1057–1058
Gun laws, weakening of, **1**:217
Gurus, **3**:953
Guthrie, Woody, **2**:689
Gutierrez, José Angel, **4**:1215
Gwich'in Athabaskans, **2**:746
Gynecology, self-help, **2**:405

H

Haber, Robert Alan, **4**:1173
Hagerty, Thomas J., **2**:526
Hague Peace Conferences, **3**:1043, 1065
Hahnemann, Samuel, **1**:281; **3**:991
Haig, Alexander, **2**:712
Haight-Ashbury, **3**:1023
Haitian Revolution (1791), **1**:10–11
Hall, Tony, **1**:245
"Ham, Curse of ," **1**:7
Ham and Eggs, **4**:1240
Hamer, Fannie Lou Townsend, **1**:191,
    192
Hamilton, Alexander, **3**:763
Hamilton, Alice, **3**:890; **4**:1258–1259, 1260
Hamilton, Robert, **1**:44
Hamilton, Thomas, **1**:59
Hamilton, William, **1**:69
Hammer v. Dagenhart, **3**:1122

Hammond, James Henry, **1**:99
Hammond, John Jays, **2**:494
Hampshire College, **1**:238
Hampton, Fred, **1**:203, 233; **3**:1131
Handsome Lake, **2**:698
Hanley, Edward T., **2**:671
Hanna, Kathleen, **2**:432
Hanover, Joe, **1**:306–307
Hanrahan, Edward V., **1**:203
Hansberry, **2**:391
Happersett, Minor v. (1874), **1**:274
Harbinger (periodical), **3**:972
The Harbor (Poole, 1915), **2**:690
Harding, Warren G., **2**:561
Hardwick, Bowers v. (1986), **3**:854, 857;
    4:1325, 1352, 1366
Hare, Leslie, **2**:709
Hare, Melvin, **2**:709
Hare Krishnas, **3**:953, 1006
Harlem, protests (1935), **1**:162
Harlem Hellfighters, **1**:140–141
Harlem Renaissance, **1**:145–146, 159
Harm Reduction Coalition (1993), **3**:878
Harm reduction movement, **3**:877
Harmony Society (Harmonists/
    Rappites), **1**:287; **3**:1000–1001
Harper, Frances Ellen Watkins, **1**:68,
    329, 330; **2**:361
Harper, William, **1**:99
Harpers Ferry, **1**:60, 94; **3**:1042
Harris, David, **3**:1089
Harrison, Carter, **2**:484, 521
Harrison, Stafford v. (1991), **3**:916
Harrison Narcotic Act (1914), **3**:872–873
Hart-Cellar Act (1965), **3**:1031
Hartford Convention, **3**:1040
Hartman, George W., **3**:1079
Harvan, George, **2**:691
Hasbrouck, Lydia Sayer, **1**:271
Hastie, William, **1**:169
Hatcher, Richard, **1**:212
Hate crimes, **1**:242, 248; **4**:1355
Hate Crimes Statistic Act (1990), **4**:1353
Hate speech, **1**:248
Hate strikes, **2**:677–678
Haven House, **2**:406
Hawley, Nancy, **2**:404
Hawthorne Works, **2**:562
Hay, Harry, **3**:845; **4**:1334–1336
Hayakawa, S.I., **1**:213
Hayden, Casey, **2**:392, 400, 436
Hayden, Tom, **4**:1174, 11745
Hayes, Rutherford B., **1**:78
Hayes, Ted, **3**:1155
Haymarket Square, **2**:485–486, 500; **3**:1118
    defendants, **2**:499

Hays Production Code, **3**:850

Haywood, Harry, **2**:572

Haywood, William D. (Big Bill), **2**:495, 496, 526, 527, 532

Hazard, Rowland, **3**:909

Health, racial divide and, **1**:242

Health Food

    and the countercuisine, **3**:1017–1018

    institutionalizing, **3**:1015–1016

    mainstreaming of, **3**:1018–1019

    roots of, **3**:1014–1015

    See also Health Reform

Health Reform

    African-American women and, **2**:389, 395, 405

    herbalism, **1**:281

    Ladies' Physiological Societies, **1**:282

    overview, **1**:279

    philosophies, **1**:280–281

    women and, **1**:265; **2**:404–406, 427

    See also Health Food; Homeopathy; Hydrotherapy

Healthcare, Gray Panthers and, **4**:1233

Heaven's Gate, **3**:954

Hebrew Union College, **3**:933

Hechler, Ken, **2**:646–647

Heighton, William, **2**:469

Held, Richard G., **2**:715, 719

Helderberg War, **3**:769

Hellfighters, Harlem, **1**:140–141

Hell's Angels, **3**:1025

Helms, J. Lynn, **2**:662

Helms, Jesse, **3**:851, 855; **4**:1353

Helms, Mary, **4**:1364

Hemenway, Augustus, **4**:1267

Henry Street Settlement, **1**:317; **3**:1141

Herbalism, **1**:281

Herberg, Will, **2**:578; **3**:935

Hereditarianism, **3**:900

Hereditary Genius: An Inquiry into Its Laws and Consequences (Galton, 1869), **3**:899

Hering, Constantine, **3**:990

Herndon, Angelo, **2**:572; **3**:1123

Heroic medicine, **1**:280

Hershey, Lewis B., **3**:1089

Hetch Hetchy battle, **4**:1265–1266

Heye Foundation, **2**:730

Heywood, Leslie, **2**:432

Hicklin test, **3**:848

Higginson, Thomas Wentworth, **1**:66

Higher education

    Affirmative Action in, **1**:248–249

    six periods of, **4**:1167–1169

    student movements and, **4**:1165–1167

    See also Universities

Higher Education Act, drug offenses and, **3**:876

Highland Park plant. *See* Ford Highland Park plant

Hill, Anita, **1**:221; **2**:395

Hill, David B., **2**:486

Hill, Herbert, **2**:632

Hill, Joe, **2**:531, 687

Hill-Burton Act (1946), **4**:1243

Hillard, Earl, **1**:253

Hillman, Sidney, **2**:609

Hillquit, Morris, **2**:569

Hillsborough, North Carolina, **3**:761–762

Hinduism, **3**:936, 952–953, 1005

Hine, Lewis, **2**:691; **3**:1121

Hippies

    and the antiwar movement, **3**:1087

    communes, **3**:1023, 1024–1025, 1027

    ideology, **3**:1020–1021

    types of, **3**:1022

History of Woman Suffrage (Anthony, Stanton, and Gage), **1**:276, 290, 291

Hitchcock, Ethan Allen, **4**:1265

Hitchcock, Lone Wolf v. (1903), **2**:726

Hitler-Stalin Non-Aggression Pact (1939), **2**:592

HIV. *See* AIDS

Hobby, Oveta Culp, **2**:368

Hocking, William Ernest, **3**:964

Hodge, Evan, **2**:720–721

Hofstadter, Richard, **3**:783

Holbrook, M.L., **3**:1016

Holder, Stan, **2**:714

Holley, Myron, **1**:25, 53

Holmes, Oliver Wendell, **3**:902, 992, 1075

Holtzman, Elizabeth, **2**:449

Home colony, **3**:1003

Homeless, **3**:1135, 1152–1157

Homeopathic Medical College of Pennsylvania, **3**:990

Homeopathy, **1**:281–282

    AMA and, **3**:993–996

    decline of, **3**:994–995, 996

    impact of Flexner Report, **3**:996

    opponents, **3**:992–993

    origins, **3**:990, 991

    revival of, **3**:996–997

    rise of, **3**:994

Homes for Disable Volunteer Soldiers, **4**:1238

Homestead Steel Strike (1892), **2**:501, 511, 543–544

Homoerotic art, **4**:1353

Homophile Movement, **4**:1334–1339

Homophile Organizations, North American Conference of (NACHO), **4**:1341

Homophiles. *See* Homosexuality

Homosexual League, **4**:1339

Homosexuality

    defining, **4**:1329–1330

    and discrimination, **3**:845–846, 852, 855

    and identity, **4**:1332

    organizations, **4**:1339–1340, 1342

    resurgence, **4**:1339–1342

    Supreme Court legislation and rulings on, **3**:854, 857

    target of moral crusaders, **3**:845–846, 852

    See also Gays/lesbians; Sexuality

Honkala, Cheri, **3**:1138

Hooker, Evelyn, **4**:1339

Hooker, Worthington, **3**:993

hooks, bell, **2**:410, 420

Hoover, Edgar J., **1**:188; **2**:563; **3**:845, 1145

Hope, Lugenia Burns, **3**:1143

Hopi, NativeSun project, **2**:746–747

Hopkins, Harry, **3**:811–812, 1125

Hormel, **2**:652

Horton, Willie, **1**:220

Hose and Heels Club, **4**:1380

Hospital unions, **2**:640–641

Hospital Workers Union 1199, **2**:641

Hotel and Restaurant Employee Union, **1**:347

Hotel and restaurant workers movement, **2**:671–673

Hotel Employees and Restaurant Employees Union (HERE), **2**:671–673

Hough, Franklin, **4**:1286

Hourwich, Nicholas, **2**:570

House of David, **3**:1004

House Un-American Activities Committee (HUAC), **1**:163, 168, 169; **2**:614; **3**:845, 1051

Household income, racial divide and, **1**:242

Households, two *vs.* one parent, **1**:242

Housekeeping Cooperative movement. *See* Cooperative Housekeeping movement

Houser, George, **1**:208

Housewives' League of Detroit, **2**:390

Housework

    pay-for-housework movement, **1**:287

    See also Cooperative Housekeeping movement

Housing
    discrimination, 1:197–198
    funding for, 3:1153
    See also Cooperative housing;
        Intentional communities
Houston, Charles Hamilton, 1:162, 163,
    174; 2:541
How the Other Half Lives (Riis, 1890), 3:1121
How to Play Indian (Seton, 1903), 2:741
Howard, Perry, 1:155
Howe, Florence, 2:416
Howe, Julia Ward, 1:297, 313, 344; 3:1044
Howe, Samuel Gridley, 4:1246
HSUS. *See* Humane Society of the
    United States
Hubbard, Elbert, 3:1005
Hudson Guild Settlement, 3:1010
Huerta, Dolores, 2:411; 3:830–834
Huie, William, 1:177
Hull-House, 1:317, 319, 337; 2:366; 3:1141
Human rights, Eleanor Roosevelt and,
    2:369
Human Rights Campaign, 4:1349, 1351
Human traits, 3:900
Humane Farming Association, 4:1316
Humane Methods of Slaughter Act
    (1958), 4:1313
Humane Society of the United States
    (HSUS), 4:1312, 1314
Humphrey, Hubert, 1:192; 3:1088
Hunger marches, 3:1148–1149
Hunt, Commonwealth v. (1842), 2:617
Hunt, H.L., 4:1399
Hunt, James, 4:1302–1303
Hunter, David, 1:39
Hunter, Jane Edna, 1:334
Huntington, Emily, 1:285
Hunton, Addie W., 1:301
Hunt's Dump, 4:1302–1303
Husband, Herman, 3:761
Hutchenson, William L., 2:559–560
Hutchinson, Dorothy, 3:1079
Hutterites, 3:1004
Hyde Amendment (1976), 2:382, 430; 3:847
Hydropathy. *See* Hydrotherapy
Hydrotherapy, 3:1015
    and dress reform, 1:269
    origin in U.S., 1:282
    Shew's review of, 3:1016
    women and, 1:265, 282

I

"I Am a Union Woman" (song), 2:688
"I Have a Dream" speech, 1:188, 189
Icarians, 3:1002–1003

Idaho miners, 2:493–496
ILGWU. *See* International Ladies'
    Garment Workers' Union
Illegal Immigration Reform and Immi-
    grant Responsibility Act (1996),
    3:1136
Illinois
    Belleville coal miner wildcat strikes,
        2:676
    Chicago. *See* Chicago, Illinois
    Dickson Mounds, 2:730
ILO. *See* International Labor Organization
Immediatism, 1:20–24, 49, 50, 62–63
Immigrant exclusion movement
    early America, 4:1422–1423
    and economics, 4:1426–1427
    and family, 4:1426
    and isolation, 4:1424–1425
    opponents, 4:1424, 1426
    and racial competition, 4:1423–1424
    war and ideology, 4:1425–1426
    See also Immigrants; Immigration
Immigrants
    aid societies, 4:1423
    backlash on illegal, 3:1135–1136
    Communist Party USA and, 2:572
    and community-based labor groups,
        2:659
    growth of, 3:884
    industrial education for female, 1:348–
        349
    as industrial workers, 2:481
    and labor on farms, 3:826–827
    white fear of, 3:863, 884–885
    worker benefits for, 2:673
    See also specific immigrant exclusion
        movement; specific immigrant
        group; specific immigration
Immigrants Protective League, 3:888,
    889, 897
Immigration
    ban of lesbian/gay aliens, 4:1330,
        1354
    and civil rights, 1:250
        after September 11, 1:250,
            253–254
    eugenics movement and, 3:901–902
    Johnson-Reed Act, 2:365
    quota systems, 3:885, 1030; 4:1420, 1424
    and religious diversity, 3:935
    repeal of quota systems, 1:216; 3:1031
    See also Immigrant exclusion
        movement; Immigrants
Immigration Act (1965), 1:216
Immigration and Naturalization Service
    (INS), 3:1136

Immigration Restriction League, 4:1419
Improved Order of Red Men, 2:740
"In Search of Progressivism" (Rodgers),
    3:883
Income. *See* Household income
Indentured servants, 2:459–460, 462–463
Independent Media Center (IndyMedia),
    4:1466
Independent Voters Association,
    3:806–807
Indian Bureau. *See* Bureau of Indian
    Affairs
Indian Child Welfare Act (1978), 2:728
Indian Citizenship Act (1924), 2:703
Indian Civil Rights Act, 2:725
Indian Claims Commission, 2:725
Indian Defense League of America,
    2:703–704
Indian Health Service, 2:711
Indian Manifesto (*Custer Died for Your
    Sins*) (Deloria, 1969), 2:707
Indian New Deal, 2:704
Indian Point, 4:1296
Indian Removal Act (1830), 2:699
Indian Reorganization Act, 2:704, 725
Indian Rights Association, 2:703
Indian Self-Determination and Assis-
    tance Act, 2:729
Indian Self-Determination and Education
    Assistance Act (1975), 2:728
Indians of All Tribes, 2:707
Indians of the Americas: The Long Hope
    (Collier, 1947), 2:704
Indichona Peace Campaign, 3:1095
Indigenous environmental movement,
    2:744–747
Indigenous Peoples, Declaration of
    Rights of (1992), 2:726
Industrial accidents, 2:506
Industrial armies, 3:1120–1121
Industrial Association of San Francisco,
    2:564
Industrial education, 1:348–349
Industrial era (1877–1920)
    American workers, 2:504–506
    cultural perspective of work, 2:505
    poverty, 2:505–506
    See also Factory work
Industrial labor, World War II, 1:164–165
Industrial unions. *See* Labor unions
Industrial Workers of the World (IWW),
    1:324
    Cold War purges, 2:559
    decline of, 2:528–532
    direct action and self-organization,
        2:503, 514

Industrial Workers of the World (IWW)
    (continued)
    and farm laborers, 3:824–825
    founding of, 2:525–526
    free speech fights, 2:529
    ideology, 2:529
    leaders, 2:495
        arrest of, 2:531–532
    legacy of, 2:532
    opponents, 2:527
    preamble, 2:495–496
    sedition arrests, 3:1045
    supporters, 2:513–514, 525–527
    use of song, 2:687
    women and, 1:346
Industrial working class, formation of,
    2:480–483
Industrialization, and pollution,
    4:1260
IndyMedia (Independent Media
    Center), 4:1466
Infant mortality
    concern over, 2:364
    racial divide and, 1:242
Innis, Roy, 1:211
INS. See Immigration and Naturaliza-
    tion Service
Inspirationists, 3:1001
Institute for Sex Research, 3:845
Institutional Church. See Social Gospel
Intentional communities
    cohousing, 1:286; 3:1006
    first American, 3:998
    Harmony Society (Harmonists/
        Rappites), 1:287; 3:1000–1001
    Hutterites, 3:1004
    Inspirationists and Amana, 3:1001
    Mormons. See Mormons
    New Age, 3:1004
    1960s–1970s, 3:1005–1006
    Oneida Community. See Oneida
        Perfectionists
    secular, 3:1002–1003
    Shakers. See Shakers
    tent city, 3:1152–1157
    See also Communal living
Intercollegiate Chinese for Social
    Action, 4:1222
Intercollegiate Society of Individualists,
    4:1389
Intermediate Technology Development
    Group, 4:1317
Internal Revenue Service, surveillance
    of Vietnam War activists, 3:1095
International Association of Machinists,
    2:538

International Brotherhood of Teamsters,
    2:623
International Confederation of Free
    Trade Unions, 2:627
International Council of Women, 1:298
International Executive Board, 2:644
International Federation of University
    Women, 2:363
International Foundation for Gender
    Education (IFGE), 4:1381
International Indian Treaty Council,
    2:713, 722, 726
International Industrial Assembly of
    North America, 2:474
International Labor Defense, 1:131, 160;
    2:571–572
International Labor Organization, 4:1483,
    1484
International Ladies' Garment Workers'
    Union (ILGWU), 1:324, 338, 346
    Cold War purges, 2:553
    David Dubinsky and, 2:605
    disputes within, 2:552
    founding of, 2:549
    General Educational Committee, 1:347
    Jewish Anarchists and, 2:502
    Los Angeles (Local 52), 2:552–553
    New York (Local 25), 2:550–551
    shirtwaist strikes, 2:550–552
    union labels, 2:681, 682
International League for Peace and
    Freedom, 1:334
International Longshoremen's Associa-
    tion, 2:564, 630
International Monetary Fund (IMF),
    4:1458
International Planned Parenthood
    Foundation, 2:355
International Socialist Organization, 3:1101
International Society for Krishna
    Consciousness, 3:953, 1006
International Unemployment Day, 3:1123,
    1148
International Union of Electrical
    Workers, 2:614
International Union of Mine, Mill, and
    Smelter Workers, 2:496
International Woman Suffrage Alliance,
    1:298
International Workers Order, 2:572
Internet
    censorship issues, 3:851
    and child pornography, 3:853–854
    and the global justice movement,
        4:1465–1466
    and grassroots organizations, 2:745

Interracial mixture. See Miscegenation
Interstate Commerce Act (1887), 2:618
Interstate travel, de-segregation, 1:183,
    184, 208, 209
Intervarsity Christian Fellowship, 3:950
Inuit whaling, 2:746
Invisible Man (Ellison, 1952), 1:228
Involuntary sterilization. See Sterilization,
    involuntary
Iraq
    antiwar movement, 3:1100–1111
    February 14–16, 2002 protests,
        3:1106–1107
    war operations in, 3:1058
Irish immigrants
    as anti-abolitionist, 1:102–103
    discrimination of, 4:1415–1416
Irish National Land League, 2:482
Iron Molders' International Union,
    2:471, 473
Iron workers, 2:473
Italian Anarchists, 2:502–503, 580–581
IWW. See Industrial Workers of the World
Izaak Walton League, 4:1267
Izumazaki, James, 4:1207

J

J-curve theory, 1:228
Jack, James, 1:334
Jack Kerouac School of Disembodied
    Poetics, 3:1031–1032
Jackson, Andrew, 1:38, 50, 99–100, 279
Jackson, Aunt Molly, 2:688
Jackson, George, 1:214
Jackson, James Caleb, 1:269, 270; 3:1015
Jackson, Jesse, 1:218, 219, 220, 241; 4:1300
Jackson, Jimmie Lee, 1:193
Jackson, Vic, 2:717
Jails. See Prisons
James, Sharpe, 1:251, 252
Jane, 2:404
Janklow, William, 2:714–715, 718
Japanese American Citizens League,
    4:1220
Japanese Americans, 3:1030
    civil rights, 4:1220
    immigration quotas, 3:885; 4:1424
    reparations, 4:1209
    See also Asian Americans
Japanese Christians, 3:964
Jarrico, Paul, 2:690
Jay Treaty (1794), 2:704, 736
Jefferson, Thomas, 1:3, 10–11; 2:698
Jenkins, Alvin, 3:835–838
Jenkins, Maxine, 2:641

Jennings, Herbert, **3:**903
Jensen, Arthur, **3:**904
Jesus People USA, **3:**1006
Jews
    in the Anarchist movement,
        2:500–502
    and blacks, **1:**213
    Conservative, **3:**933
    in the counterculture movement,
        3:1025–1026
    Orthodox, **3:**933
    Reform, **3:**933, 1007–1009
    women's organizations, **2:**365
    See also Anti-Semitism
Jim Crow laws, **1:**115
Jiménez, Rosie, **2:**430
Johansen, Bruce, **2:**746
John Birch Society, **4:**1394
Johns, Barbara, **1:**174
Johnson, Andrew, **1:**255
Johnson, Charles S., **1:**146
Johnson, Gary, **3:**876
Johnson, Jack, **1:**162
Johnson, James Weldon, **1:**130, 139,
    146
Johnson, Lyndon, **1:**190–193, 194;
    3:1128–1129
Johnson, Miller v. (1995), **1:**248
Johnson-Reed Act (1924), **2:**365; **3:**902;
    4:1420
Johnson's Pastures commune, **3:**1025
Jones, Absalom, **1:**81
Jones, Aphrodite, **4:**1381
Jones, Beverly, **2:**425, 441
Jones, Jesse Henry, **2:**522; **3:**957
Jones, Jim, **3:**954
Jones, Mary Harris (Mother Jones),
    2:510
Jones v. Smid (1993), **3:**916
Jordan, David Starr, **3:**901
Jorgenson, Christine, **4:**1380
Josiah Macy Jr. Foundation, **4:**1241
Joss houses, **3:**1029
Journey of Reconciliation, **1:**203,
    208–209
Journeymen Cordwainers, **2:**617
Judaism. *See* Jews
Jumping Bull, Harry and Cecelia,
    2:717
The Jungle (Sinclair, 1906), **2:**690
Just-in-Time production, **2:**656, 658
"Just Say No" campaign, **3:**875
Justice for Janitors, **2:**653, 658
Justice movements, women and,
    2:365–367
Justiceville, **3:**1155

K

Kagi, John Henry, **1:**66
The Kallikak Family: A Study in the
    Heredity of Feeble-Mindedness
    (Goddard, 1912), **3:**900
Kameny, Franklin, **4:**1326, 1339, 1340
Kane, Ari, **4:**1381
Kanka, Megan, **3:**853
Kansas
    African-American migration to,
        3:773–776
    Pottawatomie Creek massacre, **1:**58, 60
Kansas Fever Exodus, **1:**114
Kansas-Nebraska Act, **1:**29, 58, 93–94
Kant, Immanuel, **3:**1007
Karpman, Benjamin, **3:**848
Kaufman, Paul, **2:**647
Kaweah Cooperative Commonwealth,
    3:1003
Kay, RISE v. (1991), **4:**1305
Keating-Owen Child Labor Bill (1916),
    3:1122
Keep America Out of War campaign
    (1938), **3:**1079
Kefauver, Estes, **3:**848
Kelley, Abigail, **1:**25, 30, 52, 64
Kelley, Florence, **1:**317–319, 338; **2:**364
Kelley, Oliver Hudson, **3:**777–778
Kellogg, James Harvey, **3:**1016, 1017
Kellogg, W.K., **3:**1017
Kellogg-Briand Pact (1928), **3:**1077
Kellor, Frances, **1:**331
Kelly, Clarence, **2:**719–720
Kemp, McCleskey v. (1987), **1:**220, 245
Kendall, Amos, **1:**100
Kennebec River Coalition, **4:**1282
Kennedy, Anthony M., **1:**221, 247; **3:**857;
    4:1326
Kennedy, Florynce, **1:**199, 200; **2:**391
Kennedy, John F.
    as a Catholic, **4:**1431
    and civil rights bill, **1:**188
    and Martin Luther King Jr., **1:**180–181
    and women's rights, **2:**375, 400
Kennedy, Robert
    assassination of, **3:**1055
    and Freedom Rides, **1:**183, 184
Kenngott, Christine, **4:**1347
Kensington Welfare Rights Union,
    3:1138
Kent State, **4:**1191–1192
Kentucky miners, and convict leasing,
    1:124
Kerner, Otto, **1:**198
Kerner Commission, **1:**198

Kerouac, Jack, **3:**1031
Kerr, Clark, **4:**1178, 1179
Kerry, John, **3:**1090
Kershner, Howard E., **4:**1399
Khmer Rouge, **3:**1094
Kilpatrick, Kwame, **1:**252
Kindergarten movement, **1:**285
King, Clennon, **1:**184
King, Martin Luther, Jr., **1:**179
    in Albany, Georgia, **1:**185, 206
    and antiwar movement, **3:**1084–1085
    assassination of, **1:**200, 207, 225;
        3:1055
    in Birmingham, Alabama, **1:**185–188,
        206
    in Chicago, **1:**197–198
    and civil rights for the poor,
        3:1127–1129
    "I Have a Dream" speech, **1:**188, 189
    "Letter from Birmingham Jail,"
        1:186, 187, 229
    and Montgomery Bus Boycott, **1:**172,
        177–178, 204, 209
    and nonviolent direct action, **1:**178,
        179, 206
    Poor People's Campaign, **2:**641;
        3:1153; **4:**1299
    popularity of, **1:**188
    and Selma to Montgomery march,
        1:194
    and Southern Christian Leadership
        Conference, **1:**179, 180, 185,
        204; **3:**1127
King, Mary, **2:**392, 400, 436
King, Matthew, **2:**716
King, Rodney, **1:**242
Kingsley, Bathsheba, **3:**928
Kingston, Maxine Hong, **4:**1220
Kinsey, Alfred, **3:**845
Kinsey reports, **2:**370, **3:**845
Kirk, Russell, **4:**1388
Kirkland, Lane, **2:**651, 653
Kirkland, Moses, **3:**762
Kirkpatrick, Jean, **3:**915
Kitchen gardens, **1:**285
Kitchens, public, **1:**286
Kitson, Frank, **2:**717
KKK. *See* Ku Klux Klan
Klonsky, Mike, **4:**1196
Knights of Labor, **1:**265, 324
    and anti-Chinese violence, **2:**508
    biracial approach, **2:**513
    decline of, **2:**485–487, 508–510
    denounce David B. Hill, **2:**486
    diversified membership, **2:**507–508
    founder, **2:**481–482

Knights of Labor (continued)
    and Irish Americans, 2:482–483
    legacy of the, 2:487–488, 512
    membership growth, 2:483–484, 508
    and railway unions, 2:534
    as a secret society, 2:482
    as a social movement, 2:480
    and temperance, 3:866
Knights of St. Crispin. See Order of the
    Knights of St. Crispin
Know-Nothings, 3:1117; 4:1429–1430
Knox, Henry, 2:698
Knox, James, 1:125
Koernke, Mark, 4:1442
Kolbe, Jim, 4:1346
Kollias, Karen, 2:448
Korean War, 1:170–171; 2:628
Koresh, David, 3:954
Koreshan Unity community, 3:1004
Kozachenko, Kathy, 4:1357
Kramer, Larry, 4:1373
Ku Klux Klan (KKK)
    1920s, 4:1435–1437
    1960–1968, 1:206, 224
    desegregation and, 1:223
    against Freedom Schools, 1:191
    growth of, 1:170; 3:1122
    and militia groups, 4:1440
    post 1954, 4:1437–1438
    and the Reconstruction revolution,
        4:1433–1435
    revival of, 4:1420–1421
    women in, 4:1436–1437
Kuhn, Margaret E., 4:1230, 1231
Kunstler, William, 2:715, 719

                    L

La Confederación de Uniones de
    Campesinos y Obreros Mexicanos,
    2:622
La Follette, Robert M., 2:540, 574, 600,
    3:895
La Marcha de la Reconquista, 4:1207
La Sociedad Protección Mutua de
    Trabajadores Unidos, 4:1227–1228
Labadist Community, 3:998
Label campaigns. See Union labels
Labor
    anti-strike legislation, 2:611
    assembly-line work, 2:556–557; 3:884
    automation of, 2:629–630, 650
    ban on racial discrimination, 1:190
    convict labor and leasing, 1:122–126
    culture, 2:687–691
    employer-sponsored benefits, 2:562

Labor (continued)
    factory work, 1:315–317, 324–325
    free, 2:458–459
    globalization of, 2:456
    law, 2:617–620
    manufacturing jobs, 2:556
    Open Shop employers, 2:561
    racial discrimination, 1:116, 243–244
    replacement workers, 2:661
    right-to-work laws, 1:168–169; 2:612
    scientific management, 2:556
    standards through ILO, 4:1483–1484
    women in war industries, 2:368–369
    See also Labor movement; Labor
        strikes; Labor unions; Unem-
        ployment
The Labor Herald (periodical), 2:571
Labor Leadership Assembly for Peace,
    2:644
Labor-Management Reporting and
    Disclosure Act (1959), 2:619–620
Labor movement
    antebellum period, 2:464–471
    challenges to, 2:653–656
    colonial America, 2:462–463
    decline of, 2:624
    effects of Red Scare on, 2:559
    Felix Adler and, 3:1009–1010
    Gilded Age, 2:507–512; 3:886
    and global justice movement,
        4:1462–1463
    1950s, 2:629–630
    1960s, 2:633–634
    1970s, 2:634–636
    post–World War II, 2:624–626
    and Progressive Era, 2:514–517;
        3:890–891
    Southern, 1:166
    and the Vietnam War, 2:643–645
    and the war in Iraq, 3:1104
    World War I, 2:517–518
    See also Labor; Labor strikes; Labor
        unions; Unemployment
Labor strikes
    after lift of No Strike Pledge,
        2:624–626
    after New Deal legislation, 2:564–565
    after World War II, 2:624–626
    agricultural, 2:621; 3:1131
    antebellum period, 2:468–469, 471
    Auto-Lite, 2:564, 591, 593–595
    automobile, 2:607–608
    by black women, 1:329
    Boston Police, 2:559, 639
    casino and hotel workers, 2:671
    colonial America, 2:462

Labor strikes (continued)
    to defeat concessions, 2:652
    for eight-hour workdays, 2:484–485,
        521
    General Motors, 2:626
    glovemaker, 1:350
    government intervention of, 2:676,
        677, 678; 3:1118
    Great Upheaval, 2:482
    hate strikes, 2:677–678
    Homestead Steel, 2:501, 511, 543–544
    as illegal conspiracies, 2:617
    by immigrants, 1:346
    under judicial attack, 2:511
    Little Steel, 2:546
    maritime workers,' 2:564–565, 593–595
    miner, 2:494
    Minneapolis Teamsters, 2:564, 593–595
    National Strike of 1877, 2:478, 506–507
    1919, 2:558–599
    1934, 2:563–565, 593–595
    1990s-2000s, 2:658–659
    PATCO (air traffic controllers),
        2:635–636, 642, 661–664
    Paterson, New Jersey, 2:514, 530
    post–WWI, 2:517–518
    postal workers,' 2:634
    public sector, 2:641
    Pullman Company, 2:511, 535–536,
        618, 676
    railway. See Railway strikes
    replacement workers, 2:661, 663–666
    shirtwaist, 1:325, 338; 2:513, 549,
        550–552
    Southern Pecan, 2:621
    stopped with violence, 2:558–559
    strikebreakers, 2:676
    Taft-Hartley Act and, 2:626–628
    for the ten-hour workday, 2:468–469
    textile, 1:346; 2:514, 529–530, 565
    wildcat, 1:165; 2:478, 633–634, 674–679
    Willys-Overland, 2:558–559
    by women, 1:346, 350; 2:411, 469,
        549, 550–552
Labor unions
    anti-union campaigns, 1:217; 2:544–545,
        564, 612, 639, 642, 690
    biracial, 2:512–513
    black, 1:212
    black participation in, 1:114
    community-based, 2:659
    concession bargaining, 2:635–636,
        651–652
    decline of, 2:650
    deindustrialization and, 1:217
    drive for southern, 2:611–612, 626

Labor unions (continued)
employer offensive, **2:**650–651
and employer resistance, **2:**485
foremen and, **2:**627
government, **2:**639
government attack on, **2:**636
as illegal conspiracies, **2:**617
injunctions against, **2:**612, 618, 626–627
labels. See Union labels
membership decline, **2:**636
mergers, **2:**653, 658
outlaw, **2:**676
public sector, **2:**634, 639–642
union busting, **2:**651
women marginalized in, **1:**345–346
World War I, **2:**557
See also Company unions; specific union
The Ladder (newsletter), **2:**370; **4:**1337
Ladies' Home Journal, **2:**402
Ladies' Physiological Societies, **1:**282
Ladies Waistmakers Union, **1:**325
LaDuke, Winona, **2:**745
Ladysmith mining case, **2:**729
LaHaye, Beverly, **4:**1402
Lakota, Black Hills land rights, **2:**729
Lambda Legal Defense and Education Fund, **4:**1349, 1351
Lancaster, Roy, **1:**153
Land loss, *Mutualista* response to, **4:**1226–1227
Land tax, **3:**798
Landrum-Griffin Act. *See* Labor-Management Reporting and Disclosure Act
Lane, Franklin, **2:**702; **4:**1290
Lange, Dorothea, **1:**162
Lanham Act (1942), **2:**369
Lappé, Francis, **3:**1018
Largen, Mary Ann, **2:**446
Las Vegas, casino strikes, **2:**671
Lasser, David, **2:**585, 591
Lathrop, Julia Clifford, **2:**364
Latin American mission fields, **3:**964
Latina feminism, **2:**410–411
Latino mutual aid societies, **4:**1226–1228
Latinos
and the antiwar movement, **3:**1087–1088
Catholic, **3:**933–934
and poverty, **3:**1135–1136
See also Chicano movement
Latterday Saints. See Mormons
Lau v. Nichols (1974), **4:**1209
Laughlin, Harry, **3:**902; **4:**1247
Lavender Hill Mob, **4:**1375

Lavender menace, **2:**406–407, 441
Lavender Vote thesis, **4:**1344
Law of Ancestral Heredity, **3:**899
Lawlor, Loewe v. (1908), **2:**683
Lawrence and Garner v. Texas (2003), **3:**857; **4:**1325, 1352
Lawrence (Massachusetts), textile strike (1912), **1:**346; **2:**514, 529–530
Lawson, James, **1:**182
Laymen's Inquiry (to missionaries), **3:**962, 964
Lea, Luke, **2:**699
League for Industrial Democracy, **2:**585; **3:**1123; **4:**1173
League of Revolutionary Black Workers, **1:**212; **2:**633
League of United Latin American Citizens, **4:**1214
League of Universal Brotherhood, **3:**1041
League of Women Voters, **2:**361–362, 374
Lean production, **2:**656
Learning disabilities, **4:**1249–1251
Leavitt, Joshua, **1:**52, 63
Lee, Ann, **1:**287; **3:**931–932, 970
See also Shakers
Lee, Barbara, **3:**1111
Lee, Bill Lann, **1:**247
Lee, Day Kellogg, **2:**689
Lee, Jarena, **3:**930
Legal Aid Society, **3:**1009
Lemlich, Clara, **1:**325; **2:**550
Leopold, Aldo, **4:**1272–1273, 1291
Lesbian Avengers, **4:**1348
Lesbian feminism, **2:**370, 406–408, 427
Lesbian Feminist Liberation, **4:**1348
Lesbian Health Fund, **2:**405
Lesbian Resource Center, **2:**407
Lesbian separatism, **2:**436, 442
Lesbianism
chosen, **2:**442
counterculture of the gay rights movement, **4:**1347–1348
fear of, **2:**441
illegal in certain states, **2:**370
See also Gays/lesbians; Homosexuality
Lester, Peter, **1:**70
"Letter from Birmingham Jail" (King, Jr.), **1:**186, 187, 229
Lewin, Baher v. (1993), **4:**1326
Lewis, John, **1:**182, 183; **2:**545, 546, 560, 604, 609, 610, 676–677
Leyden, John, **2:**662
The Liberal Thinker (newspaper), **1:**277

Liberation (magazine), **2:**436
Liberator (newspaper), **1:**21, 22, 49, 60, 89; **3:**946
Liberia, **1:**4, 13, 14, 31, 113, 149, 150
Libertarian Party, **4:**1347, 1388
Liberty Bonds, World War I, **2:**702–703
Liberty City race riot, **1:**216
Liberty (journal), **2:**496
Liberty Men, **3:**764–766
Liberty Party, **1:**28–29, 53–54, 64
Libraries
Children's Internet Protection Act (2000), **3:**851
removal of Du Bois' books, **1:**171
Liebman, Marvin, **4:**1389, 1393
Life expectancy, racial divide and, **1:**242
Life in the Iron Mills (Davis, 1861), **2:**690
Lifestyles of Health and Sustainability Market, **3:**1018–1019
Lincoln, Abraham, **1:**35, 37, 39, 94; **3:**865
Lind, Betty Ann, **4:**1381
Lindbergh, Charles, **3:**1079
Lingg, Louis, **2:**499, 500
Literary societies, African-American, **1:**82
Literature
environmental, **4:**1273–1274
feminist, **2:**412
labor portrayed in, **2:**689–690
Mexican migrant worker, **3:**1123–1124
Native American, **2:**754–755
utopian, **3:**1119
wartime, **3:**1046, 1077
Little, Frank, **2:**531
Little, Jim, **2:**716
Little Crow, **2:**748
Little Rock Nine, **1:**180, 224
Little Sisters of the Poor, **4:**1238
Little Steel, **2:**546
Liuzzo, Viola, **1:**194
Living Wage Act, **2:**657
Living wage movement
campaign locations, **4:**1476–1479
coalitions, **4:**1474–1475
community organizations, **4:**1473–1474
effects of campaigns and ordinances, **4:**1479–1480
labor organizations, **4:**1471–1473
overview, **4:**1471
religious organizations, **4:**1473
successes, **4:**1475–1476
Llano Colony, **3:**1003
Llano del Rio, **1:**289
Lloyd, Edward, **1:**72–73
Lloyd-La Follette Act (1912), **2:**639
Loan, Nguyen Loc, **3:**1092
Local 25, **1:**325–326

Lockhart Commission, **3**:849
Locofocos, **3**:1117
Loewe, Dietrich, **2**:683
Loewe v. Lawlor (1908), **2**:683
Log Cabin Republicans, **4**:1345, 1346, 1351
Logan, Adella Hunt, **1**:300
London, Julia, **2**:406
Lone Wolf v. Hitchcock (1903), **2**:726
Long, Huey, **4**:1240
Longest Walk, **2**:722
Longshoremen's strike, **2**:564–565, 593, 594
"Look for the Union Label," **2**:682–683
Looking Backward (Bellamy, 1888), **3**:957, 1120, 1135
Lorde, Audre, **2**:409, 410
Lore, Ludwig, **2**:575
Lorenz, Konrad, **4**:1313
Los Angeles, California
    City on the Edge (video), **2**:673
    HERE Local 11, **2**:671–673
    police brutality, **1**:216, 242
    tent city, **3**:1155–1156
Loud Hawk, Kenny, **2**:715
Louis, Joe, **1**:162
Louisiana, African-American migration from, **3**:775–776
Louisville & Nashville R.R. Co., Steele v. (1944), **2**:541
Love, Alfred H., **3**:1044
Love Canal, **4**:1275, 1301–1302
Lovejoy, Elijah P., **1**:4, 50, 65
Lovestone, Jay, **2**:571, 574, 575, 578
Lowell, Frances Cabot, **2**:465
Lowell, Josephine, **1**:319, 342
Lowell Female Labor Reform Association, **1**:265; **2**:470
Lowell System, **2**:465
Lower Snake River, **4**:1269
LSD, **3**:1022
Lucas, Donald, **4**:1336
Luce, Henry, **1**:167
Lundy, Benjamin, **1**:22
Luther, Seth, **2**:466, 469–470
Lykes Corporation, **2**:635
Lynching, **1**:115–116, 127, 136
    Barry Winchell, **4**:1328
    black response to, **1**:222
    Emmet Till, **1**:134, 176–177, 223
    James Byrd, **1**:134, 242
    John Wesley Bad Heart Bull, **2**:711
    of Mormons, **3**:931
    Raymond Yellow Thunder, **2**:709
    See also Anti-lynching movement

Lyng v. Northwest Indian Cemetery Protective Association (1988), **2**:722, 728
Lynn, Merissa Sherrill, **4**:1381
Lynn shoemakers' strike (1860), **2**:471
Lyon, Mary, **3**:948, 962
Lyon, Phyllis, **2**:370; **4**:1337
Lysistrata Project, **3**:1105

M

Mackay Radio and Telegraph, NLRB v. (1938), **2**:661
MacKinnon, Catharine, **3**:849
Maclure, William, **3**:979
Macune, Charles, **3**:791
Macune, William, **3**:784
Macy Foundation, **4**:1241
MADD. *See* Mothers Against Drunk Driving
Madrigal v. Quilligan (1975), **2**:405
Magdalen Societies, **1**:264; **3**:859
Mahan, Alfred Thayer, **1**:343
Mahoney, William, **3**:818–819
Mail campaigns. *See* Postal campaigns
Main Law crusades, **1**:263
Maines, Natalie, **3**:1105–1106
Malcolm X, **1**:196, 206, 229, 230–231
Male-identified woman, **2**:441
Malkiel, Theresa Server, **2**:690
Malloy, Terry, **2**:690
Maltovich, Leonard, **4**:1327
Mamselle, Sorority, **4**:1380
"Man and His Years" (conference), **4**:1242
Mandela, Nelson, **1**:239
Manhattan Project, **4**:1293
Manhattan Twelve, **4**:1395
Mankiller, Wilma, **2**:726
Mann Act (1910), **3**:860
Manpower, **2**:656
Manufacturing jobs, **2**:556
    effect of automation on, **2**:629–630, 650
Manypenny, George, **2**:699
Mapplethorpe, Robert, **3**:850
Marable, Manning, **1**:253
March, Artemis, **2**:441
March Against Fear, **1**:198
March on Washington, **1**:188–190
Marijuana
    decriminalization of, **3**:875
    drug reform and, **3**:876
    laws banning, **3**:873–874
    medicinal use of, **3**:876
Marijuana Policy Project, **3**:876
Marijuana Tax Act (1937), **3**:873

Maritime workers' strike, **2**:564–565, 593–595
Market revolution, **2**:464
    effect on antislavery movement, **1**:18–19, 96–97
    See also Free market
Marriage
    Defense of Marriage Act, **3**:852; **4**:1326–1327, 1354
    group (complex), **3**:972, 1001
    same-sex, **3**:856–857; **4**:1326–1327, 1354
Married Women's Property Act (1860), **1**:298
Marsh, George Perkins, **4**:1285–1286
Marshall, Robert, **4**:1267–1268
Marshall, Thurgood, **1**:162, 174, 194, 221
Martha Washingtonians, **3**:866
Martin, Del, **2**:370; **4**:1337
Martin v. Wilkes (1990), **1**:221
Martinez, Elizabeth, **3**:1104
Martinez, Mel, **1**:247
Martinez, Santa Clara v. (1978), **2**:728
Masaoka, Mike, **4**:1206, 1220
Mason, Charles H., **3**:981
Massachusetts
    antislavery movement, **1**:51
    Boston Police Strike (1919), **2**:559, 639
    Lawrence textile strike (1912), **1**:346; **2**:514, 529–530
    Regulators, **3**:762–763
    same-sex marriages, **4**:1327
    slaves' petition for freedom (1777), **1**:9
Massachusetts Anti-Slavery Society, **1**:74
Massachusetts Fifty-fourth Regiment, **1**:40
Massachusetts Peace Society, **3**:1041
Massachusetts School for Idiotic Children and Youth, **4**:1246
The Masses (journal), **3**:1074
Materia Medica Pura (Hahnemann, 1811), **3**:991
Maternal mortality, racial divide and, **1**:242
Maternity and Infancy Act. *See* Sheppard-Towner Maternity and Infancy Protection Act
Mathews, Robert, **4**:1443
Mathias, Charles, **2**:449
Mathiasen, Geneva, **4**:1242
Mattachine Foundation, **4**:1334–1336
Mattachine Review (newsletter), **4**:1336
Mattachine Society, **3**:846; **4**:1336, 1339
Maurer, James, **2**:596

May-Johnson bill, **4:**1293
Mayo, George Elton, **2:**561
Mayo, Mary, **3:**781
Mays, Robert L., **2:**539
Mazey, Emil, **2:**644
McCaffrey, Barry, **3:**876
McCain, John, **4:**1346
McCarran Internal Security Act (1950), **1:**171
McCarran Walker Act (1952), **3:**845
McCarthy, Eugene, **3:**1054–1055, 1086
McCarthy, Joseph, **1:**168; **3:**845
McCarthyism
    Ethical Culture and, **3:**1012
    the peace movement and, **3:**1050–1051
    rise of, **3:**845–846
    See also Anti-communism; Palmer
        Raids; Red Scare
McCleskey v. Kemp (1987), **1:**220, 245
McCormick Reaper Works, **2:**500, 521
McCoy, Isaac, **2:**699
McCulloh, Henry, **3:**761–762
McDonald, David J., **2:**606
McDonald, Lawrence, **4:**1362
McGee, William, **1:**171
McGillivray, Alexander, **2:**698
McGovern, George, **3:**1056; **4:**1345
McIntire, Carl, **4:**1399
McKenzie, Fayette, **2:**701
McKim, J. Miller, **1:**56
McKinney, Cynthia, **1:**253
McKinney, Ernest Rice, **2:**591
McKissick, Floyd B., **1:**210
McLean, Alice Throckmorton, **2:**368
McMartin, Buckey, **3:**853
McMartin, Virginia, **3:**853
McMartin preschool, **3:**853
McPadden, Myles, **2:**483
McPherson, Aimee Semple, **3:**981–982
McVeigh, Timothy, **4:**1446
Meacham, Joseph, **3:**970
Mead, Lucia Ames, **1:**342, 343
The Meaning of July Fourth for the Negro
    (Douglass, 1852), **1:**76
Means, Russell, **2:**708, 709, 727;
    4:1206–1207
    at AIM trials, **2:**714
    barred from Pine Ridge, **2:**711
    electoral challenge to Wilson, **2:**716
    expelled from IITC, **2:**722
    government drive to destroy, **2:**714
    shot on Pine Ridge, **2:**716
    and Yellow Thunder Camp, **2:**722
Meany, George, **2:**613, 614, 630, 643
Mechanics' Union of Trade Associa-
    tions, **2:**464

Media
    and American Indian Movement,
        2:711, 718
    and Earth First!, **4:**1281
    and the global justice movement,
        4:1465–1466
    and Gulf War, **3:**1057
    homosexuals in the, **4:**1339
    and Oglala shootout, **2:**718
    portrayal of Asian Americans, **4:**1220
    and United Farm Workers boycott,
        2:684
    and Vietnam War protests, **4:**1187
    and the War on Drugs, **3:**874, 876
    and wildcat strikes, **2:**678
    See also Advertisements
Medical education, Flexner Report and,
    3:994–996
Medicare/Medicaid, **3:**1128; **4:**1242
Medicine
    doctors and birth control, **2:**355–356
    1830s–1840s culture and, **1:**279–280
    eighteenth century, **3:**990
    elitism and licensure, **1:**280
    geriatrics, **4:**1241
    heroic, **1:**280; **3:**990
    See also American Medical Associa-
        tion; Homeopathy; Medical
        education
Meek, Marvin, **3:**838
Meese Commission, **3:**848–849
Megan's laws, **3:**853
Mellis, David M., **1:**297
Memorial Day Massacre, **2:**546
Memphis sanitation strike, **2:**641
Men and Religion Forward Movement,
    3:935
Mendel, Gregor, **3:**900
Mennonites. *See* German Mennonites
Menominee reservation, **2:**727
Menominee Warrior Society, **2:**727
Mercer, Charles Fenton, **1:**13
Meredith, James, **1:**184–185, 198
Meriam Report, **2:**703
The Messenger, **1:**145, 154
Metcalfe, William, **3:**1014–1015
Methadone maintenance therapy,
    3:877–879
Methodists, **3:**929, 947
Métis, **2:**696
Metz, Christian, **3:**1001
Mexican-American Anti-Defamation
    Committee, **4:**1215
Mexican-American Movement, **4:**1214
Mexican American National Issues
    Conference, **2:**410

Mexican-American War, **3:**1040, 1041
Mexican-American Women's National
    Association, **2:**411
Mexican Americans
    activist groups, **3:**1130
    Brown Berets, **3:**1130; **4:**1208–1209,
        1215–1216
    farm laborers, **4:**1216–1217
    feminist movement, **2:**410–411
    stereotypes, **4:**1215–1216
    women in the labor movement,
        2:621–623
    and World War II, **4:**1212–1213
    See also Chicano movement; Latinos
Mexican workers, agricultural, **2:**621;
    3:1123, 1131; **4:**1213
Mexico, Treaty of Guadeloupe Hidalgo
    (1848), **4:**1212
Mexico City Policy (1984), **3:**847
Miami, Florida
    gay rights laws, **4:**1362–1363
    Liberty City race riot, **1:**216
Michigan
    automobile worker strikes, **2:**607–608
    Detroit. *See* Detroit, Michigan
Michigan Women's Task Force on Rape,
    2:448–449
Migration, African-American. *See*
    African Americans
Milam, J.W., **1:**176–177
Militant resistance
    anti-abortion groups, **2:**382, 384;
        3:847
    Black Panthers, **1:**199–200, 203, 214
    Black Power, **1:**198–199
    CORE and, **1:**210–211
    environmental, **4:**1280–1281
    and global justice movement,
        4:1463–1464
    Malcolm X and, **1:**196
    of miners, **2:**494–495
    National Woman's Party, **1:**320–321
    of nonwhite groups, **4:**1207
    transition to during civil rights era,
        1:194–195
    violence against black, **1:**214
    See also Nonviolent direct action
Military. *See* United States Military
Military veterans. *See* Veterans
Militia movement
    citizen militia groups, **4:**1443–1446
    overview, **4:**1439
    paramilitary white-wing groups,
        4:1440–1443
    public opinion and, **4:**1449–1451
    2003 and beyond, **4:**1451–1452

Milk, Harvey, **4:**1356
Millennialism, **3:**943, 969–970
Miller, David, **3:**1089
Miller, Elizabeth Smith, **1:**269
Miller, Herman, **3:**904
Miller, William, **3:**931
Miller v. California (1973), **3:**848
Miller v. Johnson (1995), **1:**248
Millet, Kate, **2:**407
Million Man March, **1:**242–243; **2:**396
Mills, Samuel, **1:**13
Milwaukee Leader (newspaper), **3:**1074
Mime Troupe, San Francisco, **3:**1022
Mine Owners' Protective Association,
    2:494
Miners, free *vs.* convict, **1:**124
Miners for Democracy, **2:**634
Miners' League, **2:**492
Miners' Union of the Coeur d'Alenes,
    2:494–495
Mineta, Norman, **1:**247
Minimum Drinking Age Law (1984),
    3:870
Mining
    black lung movement, 646–649
    child labor, **2:**516
    claim-patent system, **2:**490, 491
    Comstock unions, **2:**491–493
    dangers of, **2:**494
    Idaho, **2:**493–496
    laws, **2:**489, 490–491
    miner strikes, **2:**494
    miner wage reduction, **2:**491–492,
        493
    "people's" mines, **2:**489–490
    privatization, **2:**489, 491–492, 494
    union camps, **2:**492
    wildcat strikes, **2:**648–649, 676–677
    women in, **2:**490
Mining Law (1872), **2:**490
Minneapolis Teamster's strike, **2:**564,
    593–595
Minnesota
    opposition to the Nonpartisan
        League, **3:**804–805
    White Earth reservation, **2:**700–701
Minnesota Farmer-Labor Party. *See*
    Farmer-Labor Party
Minor, Virginia, **1:**297
Minor v. Happersett (1874), **1:**274
Minutemen, **4:**1440–1441
Miscegenation, fear of, **1:**8, 50, 101
Miss America Pageant, **2:**401, 425
Missionaries
    colonial America, **2:**697, 698, 750;
        3:926, 961

Missionaries *(continued)*
    decline of Protestant American, **3:**965
    evaluating western, **3:**964–965
    gender and, **3:**962–963
    globalization and, **3:**961–962
    overseas, **3:**963, 964
    youth and, **3:**963–964
Missionary Review of the Word (journal),
    3:963
Mississippi
    African-American migration from,
        3:775–776
    civil rights at University, **1:**184–185
    Freedom Riders imprisoned,
        1:183–184
    Freedom Summer, **1:**190–193;
        3:1127–1128
    racist violence, **1:**191–192, 209
    voting rights, **1:**191
Mississippi Freedom Democratic Party,
    1:181, 191, 192–193
Missouri, Gaines v. (1938), **1:**162
Missouri Compromise (1850), **1:**58, 94
Mitchell, George, **2:**707
Mitchell, H.L., **3:**1123
Mitchell, John, **3:**874
Mitchell, O. M., **1:**43
Mitchell, Wisconsin v. (1993), **1:**248
Mitchell v. MNR (2001) (Canada), **2:**736
Miyamoto, Nobuko Joanne, **4:**1220
MNR, Mitchell v. (2001) (Canada), **2:**736
Mobilization Committee to End the War
    in Vietnam, **3:**1092
Model Christian Neighborhood
    (Stowes), **1:**287–288
Mohawk (Richard Billings), **2:**715
Mojave Desert, **4:**1296
Molly Clubs, **4:**1379–1380
Mondragón, Celedonio, **4:**1227
The Monkey Wrench Gang (Abbey, 1975),
    4:1280
Monroe, Sarah, **2:**469
Montezuma, Carlos, **2:**701
Montgomery (Alabama), attack on
    Freedom Riders, **1:**183, 205, 209
Montgomery Bus Boycott, **1:**152, 172,
    177–178, 204, 209
Montgomery Improvement Association,
    1:178
Montgomery Race Conference of 1900,
    1:129
Moody, Dwight L., **3:**966
Mooney, Tom, **2:**676
Moore, Ely, **2:**469
Moore, Fred H., **2:**580, 581
Moore, Richard B., **2:**570

Moore v. Dempsey, **1:**138
Moor's Charity School, **2:**697
Moraga, Cherrie, **2:**411
Moral Majority, **4:**1402
Moral panics, **3:**844
Moral reform movement
    and child welfare, **3:**864
    due to cultural anxieties, **3:**863–864
    overview, **3:**843–844
    women and, **1:**264–265, 343; **3:**949
    See also Anti-abortion movement;
        Anti-drug movement; Obscen-
        ity and pornography; Prostitu-
        tion reform; Religious Right;
        Temperance movement
Moral suasion, **1:**4, 20, 35, 63, 67, 97
    failure of, **1:**103–104
Moral uplift, **1:**67–68
Moreno, Luisa, **2:**621, 622
Morgan, Arthur, **3:**1005
Morgan, Robin, **2:**400, 407, 440
Morgan v. Virginia, **1:**203, 208
Morlan, Robert, **3:**802–803
Mormons
    communal living, **3:**1004
    and dress reform, **1:**269
    founder, **3:**931
    lynching of, **3:**931
    and utopianism, **1:**262; **3:**923
Morning Star Ranch, **3:**1005, 1024
Morris, Glen, **2:**722
Morrison, Toni, **1:**247
Morrison, United States v. (2002), **2:**450
Moscow Treaty (2002), **4:**1296
Moses, Robert, **1:**191, 192
Moskowitz, Henry, **3:**1010
Moss, Thomas, **1:**331–332
Most, Johann, **2:**499
Mother Earth (magazine), **2:**501; **3:**1074
Mother Jones. *See* Jones, Mary Harris
    (Mother Jones)
Mothers Against Drunk Driving
    (MADD), **3:**870
Mother's Milk Project, **2:**745
Mother's pension, **1:**338
Mother's Society to Study Child
    Nature, **3:**1009
Motion Picture Association of America,
    3:850
Mott, James, **1:**56
Mott, John R., **3:**962, 966
Mott, Lucretia Coffin, **1:**55, 56, 92, 263,
    266
    and abolition movement, **1:**290
    and woman suffrage, **1:**290, 319
Moultrie, Mary, **2:**641

Mount Holyoke Female Seminary, 3:948, 962
Mousseau, Johnny, 2:716
MOVE, 1:216
MoveOn.org, 3:1102–1103, 1111
Movies. *See* Film
Moyer, Charles, 2:495, 496, 527
Mrs. Warren's Profession (play), 3:863
Ms. (magazine), 2:403, 404, 426
Muckraking, 3:1121
Mugwumps, 3:886
Muhammad, Elijah, 1:195–196, 229–230; 3:935–936
Muhammad, Wallace, 4:1210
Muhammad Speaks (newspaper), 1:229
Muir, John, 4:1256, 1263–1265
    See also Sierra Club
Mujeres Activas en Letras y Cambio Social, 2:411
Muller v. Oregon (1908), 1:338; 2:521
Multiuniversity, 4:1168
Munaker, Sue, 2:425
Munger, Theodore, 3:957
Municipal housekeeping movement, 1:286
Municipal reform, 3:1143–1144
Murray, Anna, 1:74
Murray, Judith S., 1:287
Murray, Pauli, 2:391–392
Murray, Philip, 2:606, 612–614
Music
    antiwar movement and, 3:1087
    Asian-American, 4:1221
    feminist, 2:412–413
    labor reflected in, 2:687–689
    and moral reform, 3:850
    and war on Iraq, 3:1105
    warning stickers on albums, 3:850
Muslim Mosque Inc., 1:230
Muslims, and Islam, 3:935
Muste, A.J., 1:166
    at Brookwood Labor College, 2:597–602
    on 1934 labor strikes, 2:594
    and unemployment movement, 2:586, 589, 591
    war relief services, 3:1079
Musteites, 3:1147–1148, 1150
Mutual aid, railroad brotherhoods and, 2:534
Mutual aid societies
    African American, 1:81–82
    for alcoholics, 3:906, 908
    Latino, 4:1226–1228
Mutualista movement, 4:1226–1228
Muzzey, David, 3:1011

MX missile program, 4:1296
My Bondage and My Freedom (Douglass), 1:77
Myers, Isaac, 2:475
Mygatt, Tracy, 3:1046
Mystical hippies, 3:1022, 1026

N

NAACP. *See* National Association for the Advancement of Colored People
Nader, Ralph, 3:1138
NAFTA (North American Free Trade Agreement), 2:656; 3:1136
Narcotic Control Act (1956), 3:874
Naropa Institute (University), 3:1031, 1032
Narrative of Sojourner Truth (Truth, 1850), 1:55, 57
Narrative of the Life of Frederick Douglass (Douglass, 1845), 1:58, 74, 75
Nash, Diane, 1:182, 183, 193
Nashoba commune, 1:287
Nashville, Tennessee, student sit-ins, 1:182
Nathan, Maud, 1:319
Nation, Carry, 3:867, 868
Nation of Islam, 1:145, 172, 195–196, 229–231, 241; 3:936
National Abortion and Reproductive Rights Action League, 2:382, 383
National Afro-American League, 1:114, 128, 129
National Alliance of Black Feminists, 2:393
National American Indian Movement, 2:723
National American Woman Suffrage Association, 1:291, 299, 300, 305, 320, 334; 2:360
National Asian Women's Health Organization, 2:405
National Association for Office Workers, 2:412
National Association for the Advancement of Colored People (NAACP), 1:119, 129–130
    and anti-lynching movement, 1:129–130, 138, 222
    and *Birth of a Nation* (film), 1:138–139
    and *Brown v. Board of Education*, 1:173–174
    Ethical Culture and, 3:1011
    founding of, 1:136; 3:1121
    and future of civil rights, 1:241

National Association for the Advancement of Colored People (NAACP) *(continued)*
    legal successes, 1:137–138, 162
    and nonviolent direct action, 1:206
    and Scottsboro case, 1:160
    Silent Parade (1917), 1:141
    support of blacklist purges, 1:171
    support of Truman administration, 1:170
    and University of Mississippi desegregation, 1:184–185
National Association for the Repeal of Abortion Laws, 2:402–403
National Association of Colored Women, 1:314, 332–333, 334; 2:361, 387
National Association of Colored Women's Clubs, 1:116–118, 129, 300
National Association of Letter Carriers, 2:638
National Association of Manufacturers, 2:513; 3:891
National Baptist Convention, 1:331
National Birth Control League, 2:354
National Black Feminist Organization, 2:408, 410
National Black Women's Health Project, 2:395
National Center for the Prevention and Control of Rape, 2:449
National Child Labor Committee, 3:1009
National Christian Action Coalition, 4:1402
National Citizen and Ballot Box (newspaper), 1:274–275
National Civic Federation, 2:513; 3:891
National Civil Liberties Bureau, 3:1046, 1068, 1075
National Civil Rights Association, 1:129
National Coalition Against Domestic Violence, 2:406
National Coalition Against Sexual Abuse, 2:406
National Coalition Against Sexual Assault, 2:448
National Coalition for Research on Women's Education and Development, 2:415
National Commission on Marijuana and Drug Abuse, 3:875
National Committee for Organizing Iron and Steel Workers, 2:544–545
National Committee on the Cause and Cure of War, 3:1046, 1047

National Conference of Colored Women, 1:314
National Conference of Social Work, 3:897
National Consumers League (NCL), 1:319, 338, 351–352; 3:889
union labels, 2:681
National Consumers Union, 3:888
National Convention of Colored Men, 1:87
National Conventions of Colored Citizens, 1:75
National conventions of free blacks, 1:84, 85, 86–87, 98, 112
National Conversation Association, 4:1290
National Conversation on Race, 1:247
National Council for Prevention of War, 3:1078
National Council for Research on Women, 2:419
National Council for the Protection of the Foreign Born, 2:572
National Council of American Indians, 2:703
National Council of Catholic Women, 2:365
National Council of Jewish Women, 2:365
National Council of Negro Women, 2:388–389
National Council of Senior Citizens, 4:1230, 1232
National Council of Women, 1:316
National Council on Aging, 4:1242
National debt, 3:763–764
National Defense Mediation Board, 2:609, 677
National Dialogue on Race, 1:255
National Dress Reform Association, 1:265–266, 270–271
National Drug Trade Conference, 3:872
National Economy Act (Section 213) (1932), 2:365
National Education Association, 2:641
National Endowment for the Arts, 3:850, 851; 4:1353
National Equal Rights Council, 1:128
National Equal Rights League, 1:87, 112, 131
National Federation of Afro-American Women, 2:361
National Female Anti-Slavery Convention, 1:263
National Gay and Lesbian Task Force, 4:1346, 1349, 1350, 1351, 1371

National Gay Leadership Conference, 4:1349
National health system, 3:1136
National Indian Welfare Committee, 2:703
National Indian Youth Council, 2:706, 726
National Industrial Conference, 3:897
National Industrial Recovery Act, 2:545, 563–564, 565, 604, 619
National Institutes for Health, HIV/ AIDs research, 4:1354
National Labor and Reform Party, 2:475
National Labor Relations Act. See Wagner Act
National Labor Relations Board, 2:565, 619, 651
National Labor Union, 1:265; 2:474–475
National League of American Penwomen, 2:362
National League of Colored Women, 2:361
National Mobilization Committee to End the War, 2:437
National Monuments Act (1906), 4:1289
National Negro Business League, 1:119
National Negro Congress, 1:160
National Negro Conventions, 1:52, 86
National Negro Labor Council, 1:171
National Organization for the Reform of Marijuana Laws, 3:876
National Organization for Women (NOW)
and abortion rights, 2:398
Betty Friedan and, 2:398
and the Equal Rights Amendment, 2:402
goals of, 2:400
and lesbian rights, 2:407
Rape Task Force, 2:446
statement of purpose, 2:399
National Origins Quota System, 3:885
National Peace Action Coalition, 3:1096
National Progressive Republican League, 3:895
National Prohibition Enforcement Act (1919), 3:869
National Prohibition Party, 3:867
National Recovery administration, 2:563–564, 604
National Reform Association, 2:470
National Reformers, 3:771
National Relations Act, 1:168–169
National Resources Planning Board, 3:1125
National Retired Teachers Association, 4:1241

National Right to Life Committee, 3:847
National Stonewall Democrats, 4:1346–1347
National Strike of 1877, 2:478
National Student and Youth Peace Coalition, 3:1104
National Student Association, 4:1173, 1189–1190
National Trades' Union, 2:468
National Training School for Women and Girls, 1:331
National Transgender Advocacy Coalition, 4:1381
National Unemployed League, 2:586–587
National Unemployed Leagues, 2:589
National Union for Social Justice, 4:1240
National Urban League, 1:139; 3:1143; 4:1301
National War Labor Board. See War Labor Board
National Welfare Rights Organization, 3:1131–1134
National Woman Suffrage Association, 1:266; 2:360–361
and American Woman Suffrage Association, 1:297, 299
founding of, 1:272, 291, 297, 320
National Woman's Party, 1:300, 301, 305, 320–322; 2:361
merge with Women's Joint Congressional Committee, 2:364
National Woman's Rights Convention, 1:295, 296
National Women's Party, 2:373–374
National Women's Political Caucus, 2:402
National Women's Studies Association, 2:418–420
National Young Women's Day of Action, 2:430
National Youth Administration, 2:367, 389
Native American Graves Protection and Repatriation Act (1990), 2:730
Native American reservations
abolishment of, 2:700–701
development of, 2:699, 725, 749
economic development, 2:729, 737–738
Menominee, 2:727
Northern Cheyenne, 2:729, 745
Pine Ridge, 2:711, 712, 716–719
residents' lack of voice on, 2:725
resistance to, 2:750–751
White Earth, 2:700–701, 746

Native American Rights Fund, **2:**727
Native American Women's Health
    Education Resource Center, **2:**405
Native Americans
    AIM. *See* American Indian Movement
    Alcatraz occupation, **2:**725–726
    Americanization of, **2:**700
    Black Panthers' influence on, **2:**706–707
    boarding schools, **2:**701, 751, 752
    border-crossing rights, **2:**703–704, 736
    Christian 'civilization' of, **2:**696, 697,
        698, 701, 732
    and citizenship, **2:**701, 702, 703
    Civil War and, **2:**748–749
    colonial boarding schools for, **2:**701,
        732
    environmental concerns of, **2:**729,
        744–747
    expropriation and annihilation,
        2:750
    federal recognition of tribes, **2:**737
    forced concessions of, **2:**748–749
    gaming and casinos, **2:**729, 737
    Ghost Dance, **2:**752; **3:**934
    identity and literature, **2:**754–755
    Indian New Deal, **2:**704
    land allotment, **2:**751–752; **3:**885
    land claims, **2:**728, 729
    militarism and repression of, **2:**749–750
    1920s reform efforts, **2:**703–704
    Pan-Indianism movement,
        2:732–734
    powwows, **2:**732–734
    preservation of language, **2:**735
    Red Power, **2:**707, 726
    religious revitalization, **3:**930
    religious rights, **2:**728, 729
    relocation of, **2:**699
    reservations. *See* Native American
        reservations
    resistance to colonization, **2:**695–696,
        698, 750–751
    Sand Creek Massacre, **2:**749
    treaty rights, **2:**725–728, 730
    tribal rights, **2:**725–730, 736
    tribal self-determination, **2:**727–730,
        735–738
    U.S. policy toward land, **2:**698–699,
        700–701, 704
    white archetypal model of, **2:**739–743
    white entertainment from, **2:**732
    as the white man's mascot, **2:**741–743
    women
        as first laborers, **2:**461
        involuntary sterilization of, **2:**711
        during World War I, **2:**702

Native Americans *(continued)*
    in World War I, **2:**702–703, 732–733
    Wounded Knee massacre (1890),
        2:752–753
    Wounded Knee siege (1973), **2:**711–
        715, 727
Native Son (Wright), **1:**162
NativeSun project, **2:**746–747
Nativism
    1860s–1880s, **4:**1415–1417
    late 1800s–World War I, **4:**1417–1419
    1920s, **4:**1419–1421
    organizations, **4:**1416, 1418–1419,
        1420
    overview, **4:**1414–1415
*Natural Diet for Folks Who Eat: Cookin'
    with Mother Nature* (Gregory, 1973),
    3:1018
The Nature Conservancy, **4:**1282
Navajo, NativeSun project, **2:**746–747
Naval Act (1925), **2:**367
Nazi Party, **1:**163, 164, 167
NEA v. Finley (1998), **3:**851
Neebe, Oscar, **2:**499
Needle exchange programs, **3:**878
Negro American Political League, **1:**131
Negro Factories Corporation, **1:**149
The Negro Liberator, **2:**572
Negro World (newspaper), **1:**144, 148–149
Negro Zionism. *See* Black nationalism
Neighborhood Guild, **3:**1009
Nell, William Cooper, **1:**30, 38, 68, 69
Neo-Lamarckism, **3:**900
Neolin, **2:**696, 697
Neopaganism, **3:**955
Neotechnic revolution, **3:**883
Nestor, Agnes, **1:**349, 350
Neumann, Henry, **3:**1011
Nevada
    atomic testing and fallout, **4:**1275
    legal prostitution, **3:**861
    mining conflicts, **2:**490, 491–493
New Age movement, **3:**923, 936, 954
    intentional communities, **3:**1004–1005
New Alchemy Institute, **4:**1320
New Conservatives, **4:**1388
New Deal
    African Americans and, **2:**389
    anti-sweatshop movement,
        4:1493–1494
    civil rights and, **1:**160–164, 166–167
    failure of, **3:**1151
    labor relations and legislation,
        2:563–565
    opponents of, **3:**1125
    and public labor unions, **2:**639–641

New Deal *(continued)*
    and railway legislation, **2:**540
    social welfare, **2:**366; **3:**1122–1124
    work relief programs, **2:**586, 591–592
    See also Indian New Deal; Roosevelt,
        Franklin D.; Welfare programs;
        Works Progress Administration
New Democrats, **4:**1388
New England, antislavery legislation,
    1:7–8
New England Anti-Slavery Society,
    1:24, 49
New England Association of Farmers,
    Mechanics and Other Working
    Men, **2:**468
New England Emigrant Aid Society,
    1:58
New England Labor Reform League,
    1:265
New England Non-Resistance Society,
    1:51; **3:**1041
New England Woman's Club, **1:**313–314
New England Women's Club of Boston,
    1:271
New England Workingmen's Associa-
    tion, **2:**470
New Harmony, **1:**262, 268, **3:**923, 975–980,
    1002
New industrialism, **3:**883
New interventionism, **3:**887–889
New Jersey
    Newark's black mayors, **1:**251–252
    Paterson textile strikes, **2:**514, 530
    same-sex marriages, **4:**1327
New Left, **2:**400, 401, 423; **3:**1020
New Left National Conference for a
    New Politics, **2:**400–401
New Lights, **3:**940–941
New Negro, **1:**146, 148, 159, 223
New Religion. *See* Social Gospel
New Right. *See* Religious Right
New Social Movement, **4:**1307
New Theology, **3:**957
New York
    Adirondack Park, **4:**1286
    anti-rent movement, **3:**768–772
    City University of New York
        (CUNY), **1:**213
    community-controlled school
        districts, **1:**213
    draft riots (1863), **3:**1042
    first women's rights convention at
        Seneca Falls, **1:**290–294, 319
    fiscal crisis (1975), **3:**1131–1134
    gay public health issues, **3:**855
    police brutality, **1:**242

New York (continued)
    slum riots (1857), 3:1117
    Stonewall riots (1969), 3:847;
        4:1341–1342, 1380–1381
    Times Square clean up, 3:856
New York African Free School, 1:69
New York Anti-Slavery Society, 1:49–50
New York College Settlement, 3:1141
New York Federation of Labor, 3:891
New York Female Benevolent Society,
    1:264
New York Female Moral Reform
    Society, 1:264
New York Olive Plant (newspaper), 1:263
New York Peace Society, 3:1041
New York Radical Feminists, 2:401, 406,
    424, 445–446
New York Radical Women, 2:401, 424,
    436, 437
New York State Woman Suffrage
    Association, 1:272, 276–277
New York Tailoresses' Society, 2:469
New York v. Ferber (1982), 3:853
New York Women Against Rape, 2:446
New York World, 1:125
New Yorkers for Abortion Law Repeal,
    2:402
Newark, black mayors, 1:251–252
Newell, Frederick, 4:1288–1289
Newell, William Wells, 2:741
Newman, Pauline, 2:552
Newton, Huey P., 1:199–200, 231
Niagara Movement, 1:119, 129, 136
Nice, United States v. (1916), 2:702
Nichiren Shoshu, 3:953
Nicholas II (Russian czar), 3:1043
Nichols, Jack, 4:1339
Nichols, Lau v. (1974), 4:1209
Nichols, Mary Gove, 1:282
Nichols, Terry, 4:1446
Niebuhr, Reinhold, 1:178
Nine to Five, 2:412
Nineteenth Amendment, 1:300, 305–307
Nisga'a, 2:737
Nishimura Ekiu v. United States (1891),
    4:1424
Nitz, Michael, 2:653
Nixon, E.D., 1:152, 172, 177–178
Nixon, Richard, 3:1130
    and anti-civil rights, 1:213–214
    anti-drug campaign, 3:874
    conservatism of, 4:1394–1395
    and Martin Luther King Jr., 1:180
    and Trail of Broken Treaties, 2:709–711
Nixon administration, and Native
    American treaty rights, 2:727–728

NLRB v. Mackay Radio and Telegraph
    (1938), 2:661
"No promo homo," 3:855
No Rest for the Weary: Children in the
    Coal Mines (Spargo), 2:516
No Strike Pledge, 2:624, 625, 674
Noble, Elaine, 4:1357
Noble, Robert, 4:1240
Non-Aggression Pact (1939), 1:160, 164
Non-Partisan Council on Public Affairs,
    2:389
Non-Resistance Society, New England,
    3:1041
Non-Violent Action to Abolish Nuclear
    Weapons, 3:1052
Nongovernmental organizations, and
    global justice movement, 4:1462
Nonpartisan Leader (newspaper), 3:803
Nonpartisan League, 3:802–807
    opposition to, 3:804–805
Nonviolent direct action
    CORE and, 1:166, 202–203, 205,
        208–209
    Freedom Rides, 1:182–184, 205, 209
    global justice movement and,
        4:1466–1467
    limitations and demise of, 1:197–198,
        206–207
    Martin Luther King Jr. and, 1:178,
        179, 204
    Montgomery Bus Boycott, 1:178, 204,
        209
    roots and early activism, 1:202–204
    sit-ins, 1:181–182, 185, 204
    skeptics of, 1:204, 206
    success of, 1:207
    See also Militant resistance
Nonwhite ethnic movements
    backlash, 4:1209–1210
    decline of, 4:1208–1209
    militant resistance, 4:1207
    tension between, 4:1208
Nordin, D. Sven, 3:780–782
Norquist, Grover, 4:1397
Norris-LaGuardia Anti-Junction Act
    (1932), 2:563, 618–619, 683
North American Conference of Ho-
    mophile Organizations (NACHO),
    4:1341
North American Free Trade Agreement
    (NAFTA), 2:656; 3:1136; 4:1459
North Carolina
    Hillsborough, 3:761–762
    Hunts Dump, 4:1302
    racial redistricting, 1:248
    Regulators, 3:761

North Carolina (continued)
    student sit-ins, 1:181, 204; 3:1127
    textile industry strikes, 2:565, 594
North Dakota, poverty in, 3:802–803
The North Star (newspaper, 1847), 1:58,
    75, 77, 84
Northern Cheyenne reservation, 2:745
Northern states
    acceptance of abolition, 1:103–104
    African American migration to,
        1:142–143, 158, 164; 2:517;
        3:884
    anti-abolition, 1:101–103
    growth of KKK, 1:170
    race riots, 1:222–223
Northrop, Solomon, 1:93
Northwest Indian Cemetery Protective
    Association, Lyng v. (1988), 2:722, 728
Northwest Ordinance (1787), 2:698
Not in Our Name, 3:1100–1101, 1106
Novak, Michael, 4:1208
NOW. See National Organization for
    women
Noyes, John Humphrey, 1:64; 3:932,
    972, 1001
    and dress reform, 1:262, 268–269
    founder of communes, 1:287
    See also Oneida Perfectionists
Nuclear Freeze campaign, 3:1057
Nuclear power, 4:1257, 1276–1277
    See also Anti-nuclear movement;
        Nuclear weapons
Nuclear weapons
    opponents of, 3:1057
    and terrorism, 4:1297
    See also Anti-nuclear movement;
        Nuclear power
Nullification, 1:99–100
Nurses, visiting, 3:1008–1009
Nursing homes. See Senior citizen relief
The NWSA Journal, 2:420
Nye, James, 2:492
Nyswander, Maria, 3:877

                    O

Oberlin College, 1:312; 3:930, 947
O'Brian, Robert, 2:722
Obscenity and pornography
    child pornography, 3:853–854
    Comstock Law (1873), 1:322; 2:353,
        379–380; 3:862
    feminist sex wars, 3:849–859
    Internet, 3:851
    legislation, 3:848, 849, 851
    Meese Commission, 3:848–849

Obscenity and pornography *(continued)*
prosecutions and charges against,
3:848, 850
Obscenity Enforcement Unit, **3:**849
Occupational Safety and Health Act
(1970), **2:**620
O'Clock, George, **2:**716
O'Connor, Charles, **2:**475
O'Connor, Sandra Day, **1:**248; **4:**1326
O'Connor v. California (1993), **3:**916
Office of Drug Abuse Law Enforcement,
3:874
Office of Economic Opportunity, **3:**1128
Office of Environmental Equity, **4:**1305
Office of National Drug Control Policy,
3:876
Office of National Narcotics Intelli-
gence, **3:**874
Offshore jobs. *See* Globalization
Oglala, FBI counterinsurgency at,
2:717–718
Oglala Sioux Civil Rights Organization,
2:711
Ohio
Kent State, **3:**1093; **4:**1191–1192
Resolution in Washington Court
House, **1:**315
statement from African-American
students, **1:**63
Toledo Auto-Lite strike, **2:**564, 591,
593–595
Oil exploration, Athabaskans against,
2:746
Oklahoma, **2:**703; **3:**797–798
Oklahoma City bombing, **4:**1446–1449
Olazábal, Francisco, **3:**981
Old Age, Survivors, and Disability
Insurance (OASDI). *See* Social
Security
Old age homes. *See* Senior citizen relief
Old Lights, **3:**940–941
"Old" Poor Laws, **4:**1236
Older Americans Act, **4:**1242
Older Women's League, **2:**405
Olesen, One Inc. v. (1958), **3:**846
Oliphant v. Suquamish (1978), **2:**728
Olson, Floyd, **2:**564
Olson, Floyd B., **3:**819–820
Olympics (1936), **1:**163
Omaha Platform of the People's Party,
3:886
"On Civil Disobedience" (Thoreau),
3:1041
On the Waterfront (film), **2:**690
ONE (magazine), **3:**846; **4:**1336
One Inc. v. Olesen (1958), **3:**846

One Institute of Homophile Studies,
4:1336
One Package of Japanese Pessaries, U.S. v.,
2:355, 358; **3:**847
Oneida Perfectionists, **1:**287
complex marriage, **3:**1001, 1002
and dress reform, **1:**268–269
ideology, **3:**932, 972
inventions of, **1:**262; **3:**933
and utopianism, **1:**262
Open Court Publishing Company, **3:**1030
Operation Breadbasket, **1:**219
Operation Dewy Cannon III, **3:**1094
Operation Dixie, **2:**611–612, 626
Operation Intercept, **3:**874
Operation PUSH (People United to
Save Humanity), **1:**219
Operation Rescue, **2:**384; **3:**847
Opium laws, **3:**872
Oppenheimer, J. Robert, **4:**1293
Opportunity (journal), **1:**145
The Order, **4:**1443
Order of Patrons of Husbandry. *See*
Grange Movement
Order of Railway Conductors, **2:**533, 537
Order of the Knights of St. Crispin,
2:475–476
Ordway, Edward L., **1:**342
Oregon
anti-gay discrimination laws,
4:1365–1366
Eugene's homeless camp, **3:**1154
Oregon, Muller v. (1908), **1:**338; **2:**521
Oregon Citizens Alliance, **4:**1365–1366
Organic farming, **3:**1017
Organic Food Production Act (1990),
3:1019
Organization of Afro-American Unity,
1:196, 230
Organizational revolution, **2:**487
Organon of Homeopathic Medicine
(Hahnemann, 1810), **3:**991
The Origins of the Species (1859), **3:**899
Osage Indians, **2:**703
Osawatomie Brown (play), **1:**60
Osborn, Frederick, **3:**903
OSHA Act. *See* Occupational Safety and
Health Act
O'Sullivan, Elizabethann, **2:**448
Our Bodies, Our Selves (1969), **2:**404, 426
*Our Country: Its Possible Future and Its
Present Crisis* (Strong, 1885), **3:**959
Our Home on the Hillside, **3:**1015
Outlaw strikes. *See* Wildcat strikes
Outreach Institute of Gender Studies,
4:1381

Outsourcing. *See* Globalization
Overton, William, **1:**307
Ovington, Mary White, **1:**136
Owen, Chandler, **1:**131, 145
Owen, John, **1:**287
Owen, Robert, **3:**970, 975–980, 1002
See also New Harmony
Owenite communes, **1:**287
Oxford Group Movement, **3:**908–909, 911
Oxford Pledge, **3:**1047

P

Pacifica Foundation, FCC v. (1978), **3:**850
Pacifism
Civil War and, **3:**1041–1042
early America, **3:**1039–1041
pre–World War I, **3:**1042–1044
religion and, **3:**1039–1041
World War II, **3:**1048
See also Antiwar movement; Peace
movement
Packard, Sophia, **1:**330
Pagans, and global justice movement,
4:1464
"Pageant of the Paterson Strike," **2:**691
Paige, Rod, **1:**247
Paine, Thomas, **3:**943
Painter, Sweatt v. (1950), **1:**174
Palestine, **1:**167
Palmer, A. Mitchell, **2:**559; **3:**1076
Palmer, Phoebe, **3:**933
Palmer Raids
and Industrial Workers of the World,
2:532
See also Anti-communism; Red Scare
Pan-African Congresses, **1:**137, 144
Pan-Africanism. *See* Black nationalism
Pan-Indian movement, **2:**701, 732–734
Panic of 1873, **2:**477, 506
Panics, social construction of. *See* Drug
panics; Sex panics
"Paramilitary Operations in Indian
Country," **2:**715
Paramilitary white-wing groups,
4:1440–1443
Parents, Families, and Friends of
Lesbians and Gays (PFLAG), **4:**1351
Parents' Music Resource Center, **3:**850
Parham, Charles, **3:**951, 981
Park, Maud Wood, **1:**305; **2:**364
Parker, Arthur C., **2:**701, 703
Parker, John, **3:**878
Parker, Mack Charles, **1:**224
Parks, Rosa, **1:**172, 177
Parnell, Charles, **2:**482

Parsons, Albert, **2:**499, 500, 521
Part-time employment, **2:**656
Partial Birth Abortion Ban, **2:**385; **3:**847
Partial Test Ban treaty (1963), **3:**1053
PATCO. *See* Professional Air Traffic Controller Organization
Paterson Silk Strike (1913), **2:**691
Patman Bill, **2:**590
Patrician strain, **3:**886
Patriot Act. *See* USA Patriot Act
Patriot Movement, **4:**1442
Patterson, William, **2:**572
Patterson v. McClean Credit Union (1989), **1:**221
Paul, Alice, **1:**300–304, 320–322; **2:**361
    clash with Carrie Chapman Catt, **2:**373
    and Equal Rights Amendment, **2:**364, 373
Pay-for-housework movement, **1:**287
PBCs, **4:**1302–1303
Peabody, Elizabeth, **1:**285
Peace Action (news bulletin), **3:**1078
Peace Conferences, Hague, **3:**1043, 1065
Peace movement
    civil rights and the, **3:**1052
    Civil War, **3:**1041–1042
    Gilded Age, **3:**1043
    Gulf War, **3:**1057–1058
    international, **3:**1064–1067
    McCarthy era, **3:**1050–1052
    nineteenth-century, **3:**1040–1041
    opposition to nuclear weapons, **3:**1057
    post Vietnam, **3:**1056
    societies, **3:**1041, 1046
    students and, **3:**1047
    Vietnam War, **3:**1053–1056
    waning of, **3:**1050
    women and the, **3:**1046–1047, 1067–1068, 1085
    World War I, **3:**1044–1046
    World War II, **3:**1077–1079
    See also Antiwar movement; Pacifism; specific war
Peace Movement Now, **3:**1079
Peace reform. *See* Peace movement
Peace Research and Education Project, **4:**1185
Peace Society, American, **1:**343; **3:**1064
Peace Union, Universal, **3:**1044
Peale, Norman Vincent, **4:**1399
Pearson, Karl, **3:**899
Pedophiles, **3:**852–853
Peirce, Melusina Fay, **1:**288–289
Peltier, Leonard, **2:**719–722
Pena, Adarand Constructors v. (1995), **1:**248

Penitentiary models, **1:**122–123
Penn, William, **3:**926
Pennington, J.W.C., **1:**69
Pennsylvania Anti-Slavery Society, **1:**56
Penrod, Immanuel, **2:**490–491
Pension plans, **4:**1238–1239, 1246
Pentagon Papers, **3:**1094–1095
Pentecostalism, **3:**951–952, 981–982
People for Community Recovery, **4:**1307
People for the Ethical Treatment of Animals (PETA), **4:**1281, 1314
People's Coalition for Peace and Justice, **3:**1096
People's Council of American for Peace and Democracy, **3:**1045
People's Front, **2:**577
People's Global Action Against Free Trade and the WTO, **4:**1461
People's Now Committee, **3:**1079
People's Party, **3:**792–793
People's Political Party, **1:**150
People's Temple, **3:**954
Pepper, Claude, **1:**166; **4:**1243
Pepper, John, **2:**574
Perce, Nez, **2:**751
"The Perfect 36," **1:**305
Perkins, Francis, **2:**366; **4:**1240
Permanent Court of Arbitration, **3:**1043
Persian Gulf War. *See* Gulf War
Personal Responsibility and Work Opportunity Reconciliation Act, **3:**1136–1139
Personnel management, **2:**561
Pesotta, Rose, **2:**553
PETA. *See* People for the Ethical Treatment of Animals
Peterson, Esther, **2:**375
Petitions, abolitionist, **1:**101
Pettibone, George A., **2:**527
Pew, J. Howard, **4:**1399
Phelps, John, **1:**39
Phelps Dodge, **2:**652
Philadelphia Female Anti-Slavery Society, **1:**56, 263
Philadelphia Journeymen Cordwainers, **2:**617
Philippine Independence League, **1:**342
Philippine Information Society, **1:**342
Philippine Insurrection, **1:**342–343
Philippine War, **1:**342
Phillips, Howard, **4:**1402
Phillips, Wendell, **1:**50; **2:**474, 699
Phillis Wheatley Association, **1:**334
Phillis Wheatley Settlement, **3:**1143
Photography
    child labor, **3:**1121

Photography *(continued)*
    environmentalism and, **4:**1269, 1271
    labor reflected in, **2:**691
Phrenology, **1:**265
Physicians. *See* Medicine
Physicians for Miners Health and Safety Committee, **2:**646
Physiologists
    Christian, **3:**1014–1015
    Ladies' Physiological Societies, **1:**282
Piercy, Marge, **2:**400, 436
Pierson, Arthur T., **3:**963, 966
Pietism, **3:**969, 1000, 1001
Pillsbury, Parker, **1:**291, 297
Pinchot, Gifford, **4:**1257, 1262, 1288–1290
Pine Ridge reservation, **2:**711, 712
    FBI counterinsurgency on, **2:**716–717
    Wilson's sell out of, **2:**718–719
    See also Wounded Knee siege
Pioneers of Liberty, **2:**500
Pitt, Helen, **1:**78
Pittsburgh, Pennsylvania, effects of industrialization on, **4:**1261
Pittston Coal Company, **2:**652
Piven, Frances Fox, **3:**1131, 1132
The Pivot of Civilization (Sanger, 1922), **2:**357
Planned Parenthood Federation of America, **1:**323; **2:**355
Plant closings, **2:**635, 650, 652–653
Plant relocation, **2:**650, 656
Platt Amendment, **3:**1060
Playboy (magazine), **2:**370
Playground movement, **1:**286
Playing with Fire (report), **4:**1304
Plessy v. Ferguson (1896), **1:**115, 129, 173
Plockhoy, Peter Cornelius, **3:**998
Plockhoy's Commonwealth, **3:**998
Plumb, Glenn E., **2:**539
Plumb Plan, **2:**539
Poetry
    feminist, **2:**412
    labor reflected in, **2:**687
Pogany, John. *See* Pepper, John
Point Defiance program, **3:**878
Poli, Robert, **2:**662
Police brutality
    Birmingham, **1:**187, 206
    Chicago (1968), **3:**1092; **4:**1187–1188
    Cincinnati, **1:**242
    Columbia, Tennessee, **1:**223
    death of George Jackson, **1:**214
    free trade protests, **4:**1467–1468
    Kent State, **3:** 1093; **4:**1191–1192
    Los Angeles Police Department, **1:**216, 242

Police brutality *(continued)*
  against MOVE, **1:**216
  New York, **1:**242
  1960s, **1:**225
  Selma to Montgomery march, **1:**194, 206
  Sharpeville incident, **1:**236
  of shirtwaist strikers, **2:**551
  state terrorism against blacks, **1:**216
  on unemployed council protests, **2:**590
Politico women, **2:**437
Politzer, Anita, **3:**1012
Polk, James K., **1:**53
Polk, Leonidas Lafayette, **3:**791
Poll tax, **1:**229
Pollution
  air. *See* Air pollution
  water. *See* Water pollution
Pontiac, **2:**697
Pontiac's Rebellion, **2:**696
Poole, Elijah. *See* Muhammad, Elijah
Poole, Ernest, **2:**690
Poor, Little Sisters of the, **4:**1238
Poor farms, **4:**1237
Poor Laws, for the aged, **4:**1236
Poor people. *See* Poverty
Poor People's Campaign, **1:**200; **2:**641; **3:**1153; **4:**1299
Poor Relief Act (1601), **4:**1236
Popular culture
  and antiwar movement, **3:**1087
  and moral reform, **3:**850–851
  and war on Iraq, **3:**1105–1106
  See also Culture; specific form of culture
Population Bomb (Ehrlich, 1968), **3:**1018; **4:**1276
Population growth, **4:**1276
Population policy, **3:**903
Population Registration Act (South Africa, 1950), **1:**236
Populist Movement, **3:**791–795
Populist Party, **1:**114–115; **2:**512
Populists, **3:**1119
Pornography. *See* Obscenity and pornography
Pornography Victims Compensation Act, **3:**849
Port Huron Statement, **4:**1174, 1176
Posse Comitatus, **4:**1441–1442
Posse Comitatus Act (1878), **3:**876
Post, Alice Thatcher, **1:**342
Postal campaigns
  abolitionist, **1:**51, 91, 100–101
  and Comstock Law, **2:**353, 354; **3:**846, 862
  sedition-based, **3:**1074

Postal workers
  strikes, **2:**634, 678–679
  unions, **2:**638
Postal Workers' Strike (1970), **2:**634
Pottawatomie Creek massacre, **1:**58, 60
Potter, Julian, **4:**1346
Poverty
  and the aged, **4:**1236–1237
  Asian Americans, **4:**1221–1222
  black, **1:**200, 206, 210, 217, 242
  call for legislation against, **1:**200
  child, **3:**1135
  civil rights and, **3:**1126–1127
  environmental disenfranchisement and, **4:**1299–1300
  hippies and voluntary, **3:**1026
  hispanic, **1:**242
  during industrialization, **2:**505–506
  Native American, **2:**737
  post–World War I, **3:**1122
  pre-civil war, **3:**1117
  racial divide and, **1:**242
  routinization of, **3:**1135
  rural, **3:**783, 1119–1120
  war on, **3:**1128–1129
  See also Homeless; Unemployment; Unemployment movement; Welfare programs
Powderly, Terence, **2:**482, 485
Powell, Adam Clayton, **1:**160
Powell, Colin, **1:**221, 247
Powell, Lewis, **1:**220
Powwows, **2:**732–734
Poyntz, Juliet Stuart, **2:**570, 578
Prabhupada, Swami Srila, **3:**953
Pratt, Larry, **4:**1444
Pratt, Richard Henry, **2:**701
Preparedness Day parade, **3:**1061–1062
Presbyterians, view of slavery, **3:**947–948
Preservationists, **4:**1256, 1286–1287
Presidential Commission on the Status of Women, **2:**400
President's Commission on Obscenity and Pornography (1970), **3:**849
Pressman, Lee, **3:**1123
Prevention of Cruelty to Children, **4:**1311
Prevention Point, **3:**878
Prince, Virginia, **4:**1380
Prisons
  AA's Twelve Steps practices in, **3:**916
  anti-drug movement and, **3:**879
  convict labor and leasing, **1:**122–126
  Freedom Riders in, **1:**183–184
  mistreatment of African-American, **1:**171
  organizations and societies, **1:**123

Prisons *(continued)*
  penitentiary models, **1:**122–123
  race relations and, **1:**123
  racially biased, **1:**215, 220
  See also Crime; Criminal justice; Death penalty
Pritchett, Laurie, **1:**185
Pro-choice movement. *See* Abortion rights movement
Pro-life movement. *See* Anti-abortion movement
The Problem of Indian Administration (1928) (report), **2:**703
Producerism, **2:**490
Professional Air Traffic Controller Organization (PATCO), **2:**635–636, 642, 661–664
Progress and Poverty (George, 1879), **3:**1118–1119
Progressive Era
  anti-sweatshop movement, **4:**1491–1492
  conservation movement, **4:**1261–1262
  great transformation of the, **3:**883–884
  labor legislation, **2:**514–517
  labor reforms, **2:**557
  peace movement, **3:**1044–1045
  religion, **3:**933–935
  social reforms, **2:**569–570
  urban growth, **3:**884
Progressive movement
  business regulation, **3:**891–892
  constructing reform agendas, **3:**893–894
  cultural conflicts, **3:**892–893
  decline, **3:**896–897
  early reform, **3:**886–887
  historical debate over, **3:**881–883
  matured reform, **3:**887
  municipal reform movements, **3:**894
  national arena, **3:**895–896
  political directions, **3:**892
  states and reform, **3:**894–895
  tax reform, **3:**891
  the welfare state, **3:**889–890
  women and, **1:**315–317, 337–339
Progressive movement, new interventionism, **3:**887–889
The Progressive Movement: A Non-Partisan, Comprehensive Discussion of Current Tendencies in American Politics (De Witt), **3:**881
Progressive Party, **1:**170; **3:**896

Prohibition Enforcement Act (1919), **3**:869
Prohibition movement. *See* Temperance movement
Prohibition Party (1869), **3**:867
Proposition 187, **1**:250; **3**:1135–1136
Proposition 215, **3**:876
Proposition 229, **4**:1209
Prosperity, linked to capitalism, **3**:1122
Prostitution reform
    anti-imperialism and, **1**:343
    closing of bordellos, **1**:339; **3**:860
    early nineteenth century, **1**:264
    early twentieth century, **3**:859–860
    origins of, **2**:859
PROTECT Act (2003), **3**:854
Protest-records.com, **3**:1105
Protest songs, **2**:688
Protestants
    and growth of sects, **3**:928–929, 934
    missions, **3**:962, 963
    opposition to Catholicism, **3**:948
Provisional Committee Toward a Democratic Peace, **3**:1079
Public hangings. *See* Lynching
Public housekeeping cooperatives. *See* Cooperative Housekeeping movement
Public kitchen movement, **1**:286
Public lands
    government purchase of, **4**:1291
    planned management of, **4**:1287–1288
Public Workers Administration, **2**:591
Public workers movement
    African Americans in the, **2**:641
    labor unions, **2**:634, 639–642
    nineteenth century, **2**:638
    women in the, **2**:641–642
Puget Sound Cooperative Colony, **3**:1003
Pugh, Sarah, **1**:56
Pulitzer, Joseph, **1**:125
Pullis, Commonwealth v. (1806), **2**:617
Pullman, George, **1**:152–153
Pullman Palace Car Company, **1**:152–156; **2**:536
    strikes, **2**:511, 535–536, 618, 676
Pullman Porters and Maids Protective Association, **1**:153
Puppets, in the global justice movement, **4**:1464
Purchase, Dave, **3**:878
Pure Food and Drug Act (1906), **3**:872
Puritans
    antislavery movement, **1**:6
    communal living, **1**:286–287
    origins of, **3**:925–926, 938

Purnell, Benjamin, **3**:1004
Purnell, Mary, **3**:1004

Q

Quakers
    antislavery movement, **1**:3–8, 48
    ideology, **3**:926
Quality of Work Life, **2**:652
Quebec City, free trade protests, **4**:1467
Queer culture, **4**:1330–1331
Queer Nation, **3**:854, **4**:1348
Quilligan, Madrigal v. (1975), **2**:405
Quimby, Phineas P., **3**:934
Quota Acts (1921, 1924), **3**:1030; **4**:1420

R

Rabinowitch, Eugene, **4**:1293
Race and socialism, **3**:800
Race card, **1**:214
Race relations, study on, **1**:169
Race riots
    after King's assassination, **1**:200
    after World War I, **1**:222–223
    Alabama, **1**:187
    Chicago (1943), **1**:223
    Cincinnati (2001), **1**:242
    Freedom Ride, **1**:183–184, 205, 209
    Los Angeles (1992), **1**:242
    1917, **1**:139, 141; **2**:517
    1919, **2**:518
    1940s, **1**:165, 170, 223
    1960s, **1**:225
    1980, **1**:216
    Red Summer, **1**:158, 223
    Tulsa (1921), **1**:223
    See also Commodity riots
Racial discrimination
    ban of, **1**:190
    drug use and, **3**:876, 879
    workplace, **1**:243–244
    World War I, **1**:139–141
Racial diversity, in government, **1**:246–247
Racial divide, 1990s, **1**:241–242
Racial Justice Act, **1**:244–245
Racial profiling, **1**:242; **3**:1110
Racial redistricting, **1**:248
Racial riots. *See* Race riots
Racial segregation. *See* Segregation
Racial stereotyping, **1**:241–242
Racism
    environmental, **2**:744; **4**:1302–1304
    eugenics and, **3**:901, 904
    rise of, **3**:1121–1122

Racism *(continued)*
    World War I, **3**:1121–1122
    world wide, **1**:167–168
Radical ecologism, **4**:1320
Radical feminism, **2**:436–442
Radicallesbians, **2**:407, 441
Railroad Labor Board, **2**:539, 676
Railroad Retirement Act (1937), **2**:540
Railroad workers movement
    and eight-hour workday, **2**:537
    industrial unionism *vs.* craft unionism, **2**:536
    and political action, **2**:539–540
    racial inequality within, **2**:539, 540, 541
    strikes. *See* Railway strikes
    unions, **2**:533–535, 538–539, 541
    during Word War I, **2**:537
    during World War II, **2**:540–541
Railway Employees' Department, **2**:538
Railway Labor Act (1926), **2**:540, 618
Railway Labor Act (1934), **1**:156; **2**:540
Railway legislation, **2**:540, 541
Railway Men's International Benevolent Industrial Association, **2**:539
Railway strikes
    Burlington & Quincy Railroad strike (1888), **2**:534
    Great Upheaval (1877), **2**:482, 508; **3**:1118
    legal injunctions against, **2**:511, 618
    National Strike (1877), **2**:478, 506–507
    1946, **2**:541
    Pullman, **2**:511, 535–536, 676, 618
    Shopmen's Strike (1922), **2**:539–540
    Wabash, **2**:483
    World War I, **2**:675–677
    See also Railroad workers movement
Rainbow Coalition, **1**:218, 219
Rainbow Warrior (ship), **4**:1278
Rand, Ayn, **4**:1412
Randall, Ollie, **4**:1242
Randolph, A. Philip, **1**:131, 145, 152–154, 159
    and nonviolent direct action, **1**:202
    threat of a national march, **1**:160, 164, 170, 188
Randolph, P.B., **1**:87
Rankin, Jeannette, **3**:1077
Rape
    lynching and, **1**:332
    See also Anti-rape movement
Rape crisis centers. *See* Anti-rape movement
Rape Victims Privacy Act, **2**:449
Rapp, George, **1**:287; **3**:1000–1001

Rasmussen, Donald L., **2:**646–647
Rastafarian faith, African Americans
    and, **1:**145; **3:**953
Rational Recovery, **3:**915
Rauschenbusch, Walter, **3:**959–960
R.A.V. v. St. Paul (1992), **1:**248
Raza Unida Party, **2:**402
Re-Thinking Missions (Rockefeller, 1932),
    3:962
Reagan, Nancy, War on Drugs, **3:**875
Reagan, Ronald,
    anti-abortion stance, **3:**847
    as California governor, **4:**1394
    and civil rights, **1:**216–217, 218
    and conservatives, **4:**1396–1397
    elimination of welfare programs,
        1:217; **3:**1134–1135
    firing of air traffic controllers, **2:**636,
        642, 662
    pro-business, **2:**635–636, 642
    War on Drugs, **3:**875
Reagan administration
    environmentalism during the,
        4:1279–1281
    evangelical support for, **4:**1402
Real Life Experience, **4:**1381
Reason, Charles, **1:**69
Reba Place, **3:**1006
Reclaim the Streets, **4:**1464
Reclamation Act (1902), **4:**1288–1289
Recollections of a Housekeeper (Gilman),
    1:287, 288
Reconstruction Act, **1:**111
Reconstruction Finance Corporation,
    2:563; **3:**1145
Red Cloud, **2:**749, 750, 752
Red Cross, during World War I, **2:**702
Red diaper babies, **2:**578
Red Guards, **4:**1219
Red Power, **2:**707, 726
Red Progressives, **2:**701
Red River War, **2:**750
Red Scare, **1:**158
    deportation of Anarchists, **2:**503
    effects on labor movement, **2:**559
    and Haymarket Square, **2:**485
    rise of, **3:**845–846, 1076
    Sacco and Vanzetti arrests, **2:**580–582
    targets of the, **3:**1046; **4:**1326
    See also Anti-communism; Palmer
        Raids
Red Summer, **1:**158, 223
Redner, Russell, **2:**715
Redstockings, **2:**403, 438, 439
Reducing Americans' Vulnerability to
    Ecstasy (RAVE) Act (2001), **3:**876

Reed, Ralph, **4:**1404
Reed, Simon, **2:**493
Reefer Madness (film), **3:**873
Reese, United States v. (1876), **1:**112
Regina v. Butler (Canada, 1992), **3:**849
Regulators
    Massachusetts, **3:**762–763
    North Carolina, **3:**761–762
    South Carolina, **3:**762
Rehabilitation Act (1973), **4:**1248
Rehnquist, William, **1:**213, 221, 247
Reisman, Judith, **3:**849
Religion
    and the Farmer-Labor Party,
        3:818–819
    the Great Awakening, **3:**926–928
    and pacifism, **3:**1040
    and peace reform, **3:**1040–1041
    reasons for revivals, **3:**926
    and the STFU, **3:**812–813
    and utopian communities, **1:**262
    See also specific religion
Religious communes, **1:**287
Religious conference, **3:**921
Religious freedom, **3:**921
Religious Right
    alliance with conservatives,
        4:1399–1404
    attack on AIDs, **3:**855
    attack on the poor, **3:**1134–1135
    betrayed by conservatives,
        4:1404–1406
    Focus on the Family, **4:**1402, 1404
    ideology, **3:**952
    leaders, **3:**852
    and LGBT backlash. *See* Anti-gay
        movement
    Moral Majority, **4:**1402
    origins, **3:**952
    rise of, **3:**852
Religious Roundtable, **4:**1402
Remond, Charles Lenox, **1:**86
Rendón, Armando, **4:**1208, 1212, 1217
Reno, Shaw v. (1993), **1:**248
Reno v. ACLU (1997), **3:**851
Renters' unions, **3:**799
Replacement workers, **2:**661
Report on the Forests of North America
    (1884), **4:**1286
*Repository of Religion and Literature of
    Science and Art* (newspaper,
    1858–1864), **1:**84
Reproductive Health Services, Webster v.
    (1988), **2:**382; **3:**847
Republican Party
    conservatives and, **4:**1388–1391

Republican Party (*continued*)
    gay/lesbians and the, **4:**1345, 1346, 1351
Reservations. *See* Native American
    reservations
Residents Involved with Saving the
    Environment, **4:**1305
The Resistance, **3:**1089
RESMURS, **2:**719
Resurrection City, **1:**200
Retirement communities. *See* Senior
    citizen relief
Reuther, Roy, **2:**602
Reuther, Victor, **2:**644
Reuther, Walter, **2:**611, 614, 624–626, 630,
    644
Reverse racism, **1:**215
*Review of the Debate in the Virginia
    Legislature* (Dew, 1832), **1:**99
The Revolution (women's rights maga-
    zine), **1:**291, 297
Revolutionary Communist Party, **3:**1100
Revolutionary War-era, pacifism, **3:**1040
Revolutionary Youth Movement, **4:**1189
Reynolds, William Bradford, **1:**218
Rice, Condoleezza, **1:**247
Rich, Adrienne, **2:**408, 442
Richards, Amy, **2:**431
Richards, Ellen Swallow, **1:**286
Rickard, Clinton, **2:**703–704
Ricketson, Shradrach, **3:**1015
Ridge, John, **2:**699
Right to Life Amendment (1974), **2:**382
Right-to-work laws, **1:**168–169; **2:**612
The Rights of All (newspaper), **1:**84
Riis, Jacob, **2:**691; **3:**1121
Riots
    Chicago (1968), **3:**1092; **4:**1187–1188
    commodity. *See* Commodity riots
    draft (1863), **3:**1042, 1118
    Hillsborough, North Carolina (1770),
        3:761–762
    poverty-based, **3:**1117
    race. *See* Race riots
    slum (1857), **3:**1117
    Stonewall (1969), **3:**847; **4:**1341–1342,
        1380–1381
Ripley, George, **1:**287; **3:**971, 972, 1002
    See also Brook Farm
RISE v. Kay (1991), **4:**1305
The Rising Son (Brown), **1:**33, 37–38, 41
Ritschl, Albrecht, **3:**956
River restoration, **4:**1282–1283
Rivera, Diego, **2:**578
The Road to Serfdom (von Hayek, 1944),
    4:1388
Road to Survival (Vogt, 1948), **4:**1276

Roberts, Albert H., **1:**306
Robertson, Pat, **4:**1403–1404
Robeson, Paul, **1:**162, 168, 170
Robideau, Rob, **2:**719, 720
Robins, Margaret Dreier, **1:**348
Robinson, C.H., **3:**988
Robinson, Jo Ann, **1:**178
Robinson, William D., **2:**533
Rochdale Equitable Pioneers, **1:**288
Rochester Resolutions, **1:**274
Rock, John, **1:**42
Rockefeller, John D., **1:**330; **3:**901, 911, 962
Rockefeller, Mary, **2:**682
Rockefeller, Nelson, **3:**874
Rocky Mountain Institute, **4:**1320
Rodale, J.I., **3:**1017
Rodgers, Daniel T., **3:**883
Rodgers, Ward, **3:**813–814
Roe v. Wade (1973), **2:**381–382, 426; **3:**847
Rogers, Don, **3:**876
Rogers, Edith Nourse, **2:**368
Rogers, Ray, **2:**652
Roman Nose, **2:**749
Romer v. Evans (1996), **3:**854; **4:**1325, 1352, 1366
Room, Robin, **3:**906
Roosevelt, Eleanor, **1:**164; **2:**367–368, 369
and union label campaigns, **2:**682
Roosevelt, Franklin D., **1:**160–161, 166, 167, 202; **2:**366
See also New Deal
Roosevelt, Theodore, **2:**514, **3:**895–896; **4:**1290
and environmentalism, **4:**1263–1264, 1288
Rose Valley, **3:**1005
Roselle, Mike, **4:**1280
Ross, Loretta, **2:**447
Rotblat, Joseph, **4:**1296
Roth, Samuel, **3:**848
Roth v. United States (1957), **3:**848
Rothbard, Murray, **4:**1388
Roycrofters, **3:**1005
Rubber workers, **2:**606
Rubin, Gayle, **3:**855
Ruby Ridge, **4:**1444
Rudd, Mark, **4:**1198
Ruffin, Josephine, **1:**314, 332–334
Ruffin incident, **1:**334
Rural Electrification Administration, **3:**1124
Rural poverty. *See* Poverty
Rural utopian movements. *See* Utopian movements
Rush, Benjamin, **1:**280; **3:**865, 907

Rusher, William E., **4:**1391–1392
Ruskin Colony, **3:**1003
Russell, Howard Hyde, **3:**869
Russell Sage Foundation, **4:**1261
Russian revolution, **2:**570
Russwurm, John B., **1:**14, 22, 84, 98
Rustin, Bayard, **1:**204, 208, 209
Ruthenberg, Charles, **2:**574
Ryan White CARE Act (1990), **4:**1353

S

Sabbathday Lake, **3:**999
Sacajawea dollar coin, **2:**740
Sacco, Nicola, **2:**503, 580–582
Sacco-Vanzetti Defense Committee, **2:**581
Sachs, Sadie, **1:**323; **2:**354
Sagan, Carl, **4:**1296
Sage: A Scholarly Journal on Black Women, **2:**419–420
Sager, Manuela Solis, **2:**621
Salazar, Rubin, **3:**1088
Salinas, California, **3:**829
Salt of the Earth (film), **2:**690–691
Salter, William Mackintire, **3:**1009
Sam, Alfred, **1:**143
Same-sex marriages, **3:**856–857; **4:**1326–1327, 1354
The San. *See* Battle Creek Sanitarium
San Carlos de Monterey (1770), **3:**927
San Francisco, California
attack on gays, **4:**1340–1341
gays in, **3:**846, 847, 855
general strike (1934), **2:**564–565, 593–595
same-sex marriages, **4:**1327
San Francisco, Haight-Ashbury, **3:**1023
San Francisco Mime Troupe, **3:**1022
San Francisco Oracle (newspaper), **3:**1023
San Francisco Renaissance (1950s-1960s), **3:**1031
San Francisco State University, **4:**1207
San Francisco Zen Center, **3:**1031
Sanchez, David, **4:**1216
Sanctions, South Africa, **1:**238
Sand Creek Massacre, **2:**749
Sandler, Bernice, **2:**416
Sandoval, Alexander v. (2001), **1:**249
Sandoval, Martha, **1:**249
SANE. *See* Committee for a Sane Nuclear Policy
Sanger, Margaret, **1:**322–323; **2:**354–358, 365
The Pivot of Civilization (1922), **2:**357

Sanger, Margaret *(continued)*
Comstock's opposition to, **3:**862–863
and eugenics movement, **2:**356–358; **3:**901
Sanitation strike (1968), **2:**641
Santa Clara v. Martinez (1978), **2:**728
Saposs, David J., **2:**598–599
Sargent, Charles S., **4:**1286
Sarria, José, **4:**1341, 1356
Satana, **2:**749
Save our Children Campaign, **3:**852; **4:**1362
Save Our Moral Ethics, **4:**1364
Save Our State, **3:**1135
SAVER Act (1997), **4:**1243
Savings are Vital to Everyone's Retirement Act. *See* SAVER act
Savio, Mario, **4:**1179, 1180
Scalia, Antonin, **1:**221, 247; **3:**857; **4:**1325
Schenck v. United States (1919), **3:**1075
Schlafly, Phyllis, **2:**376; **4:**1401
Schmeling, Max, **1:**162
Schmidtz, Darold, **2:**711
Schneiderman, Rose (Rachel), **2:**549
School of Living, **3:**1005
Schools
African-American establishment of, **1:**82
boarding schools for Native Americans, **2:**701, 732, 752
Children's Internet Protection Act (2000), **3:**851
elimination of segregation in, **1:**171, 173–174, 175, 184–185
Ethical Culture, **3:**1009
kindergarten movement, **1:**285
Little Rock desegregation, **1:**180, 224
religious student organizations, **3:**950
and Section 504, **4:**1248–1249
sex education, **3:**852
University of Mississippi desegregation, **1:**184–185
See also Education; Teachers
Schropp, Jill, **4:**1345
Schumacher, E.F., **4:**1257, 1317–1318
Schumacher Society, **4:**1320
Schurz, Carl, **4:**1286
Schwar, Michael, **2:**499
Schwarz, Fred C., **4:**1399
Schwerner, Michael, **1:**134, 192, 216
Scientific management, **2:**556, 561
Scopes, John, **3:**950
Scott, Emmett, **1:**139–140
Scottsboro case, **1:**160; **2:**572
Scudder, Vida, **3:**1141

Seabrook Nuclear Power Plant, **4:**1277
Seale, Bobby, **1:**231, 232; **3:**1131
Seamen's Act, **2:**515
Seattle, Washington
  General Strike (1919), **2:**558
  WTO protests. *See* Battle of Seattle
Seattle Gay Liberation Front, **2:**407
Seattle Housing and Resource Effort
  (SHARE), **3:**1155–1156
Second Great Awakening, **1:**97; **3:**928,
  929, 943–944
  antimilitarism, **3:**1040–1041
The Second Sex (de Beauvoir, 1953),
  2:370, 391
Secret Army Organization, **4:**1440
Secret Six, **1:**49, 60
Secret societies, Knights of Labor, **2:**482
Secretary of State, Apteker v. (1964),
  2:530
Sectarian utopian societies, **3:**923
Sectarians, **3:**990, 991–993
Section 503, **4:**1248–1249
Sects. *See* Cults
Secular Organizations for Sobriety, **3:**915
Sedition Act (1918), **3:**1068, 1074–1075;
  4:1423
Sedition arrests, World War I, **3:**1045,
  1074–1075
Seeger, Pete, **2:**688
Segregation, **1:**115, 158–159
  apartheid, **1:**220, 235–236
  black endorsement of, **1:**118–119
  on buses, **1:**177–178
  challenges to "separate but equal,"
  1:162
  city ordinances (1910s), **1:**138
  elimination of school, **1:**171–175,
  184–185
  German Jews, **1:**163
  government outlawing, **1:**190
  interstate travel, **1:**183, 184, 208, 209
  Mexican Americans, **4:**1213
  nonviolent resistance to. *See* Nonviolent direct action
  sports teams, **1:**162
  women's clubs, **1:**334
  of World War I Native Americans,
  2:702
  See also Race riots
Seigenthaler, John, **1:**183
Selective Service Act, **3:**1045, 1048
Self-Culture Halls Association, **3:**1009
Self-defense, women's, **2:**447
Self-evaluation, **1:**67, 68
Self-help gynecology, **2:**405
Self-Realization Fellowship, **3:**952–953

Self-reliant philosophies, **3:**942–943
Seligman, E.R.A., **3:**1009
Sells, Cato, **2:**702
Selma (Alabama), civil rights protests,
  1:193–194, 206
Sen, Rinku, **1:**255
Seneca Falls, New York, first women's
  rights convention, **1:**290–294, 319
Seneca Falls Resolution (1848), **1:**293
Senior citizen relief
  advocacy organizations, **4:**1241–1242
  colonial America, **4:**1236–1237
  emergence of, **4:**1240–1241
  government social support, **4:**1239–
  1240, 1242–1243
  nineteenth-century, **4:**1237–1238
  nursing homes, **4:**1243
  old age homes, **4:**1238
  pension plans, **4:**1238–1239
  philanthropy, **4:**1241
  post-Civil War, **4:**1238–1239
  private charity, **4:**1237–1238
  retirement communities, **4:**1243
  See also Gray Panthers movement
Separatism
  African-American rejection of, **2:**443
  feminist, **2:**436–438, 440
  lesbian, **2:**436, 442
  personal, **2:**440–441
September 11
  antiwar movement and, **3:**1100–1102
  effect on civil rights, **1:**250, 253–254,
  255
  Ground Zero Week, **4:**1296
  Jerry Falwell's accusations about,
  3:856
  War on Terror, **3:**1058
Serra, Junípero, **3:**926, 927
Serrano, Andres, **3:**850
Service Employees International Union,
  2:653, 658
Service sector
  growth in, **2:**650–651
  lack of unionization, **2:**456
Servicemembers Legal Defense Net-
  work, **4:**1328
Services of Colored Americans (Nell,
  1851), **1:**38
Seton, Ernest Thompson, **2:**741
Settlement house movement, **3:**1121,
  1141–1144
Settlement Houses, **1:**317–319, 334,
  337–338; **2:**366; **3:**1141
  Ethical Culture, **3:**1009–1010
Seventh-day Adventists, **1:**271
  founder of, **3:**931

Seventh-day Adventists *(continued)*
  and health food movement,
  3:1015–1016, 1017
Severance, Caroline, **1:**313
Sewall, May Wright, **1:**342
Sex education
  for children, **3:**852
  for sex workers, **3:**861, 878
Sex establishments
  Comstock and, **3:**862
  gay clubs, **3:**855
  in NYC Times Square, **3:**856
Sex in Education (Clarke, 1873), **1:**312
Sex panics
  gay, **3:**855
  sexual abuse, **3:**852–853
Sex wars, feminist, **3:**849–850
Sex workers movement, **3:**861, 878
Sexual Dialogue, **2:**407
Sexual discrimination, legislation, **2:**400
Sexual Exploitation of Children Act
  (1977), **3:**853
Sexual mores, **1:**339
Sexual revolution, counterculture and
  the, **3:**1026
Sexuality, **2:**432
  African-American women, **2:**394–395
  Kinsey reports, **2:**370; **3:**845
  post World War II, **2:**370
  and World War II, **4:**1333–1334
Seymour, William J., **3:**951, 981
Shachtman, Max, **2:**573
Shadd, Abraham D., **1:**22, 69
Shakers
  and communes, **1:**287; **3:**970
  decline of, **3:**999
  founder of, **3:**931, 998
  ideology, **3:**998–999
  inventions of, **1:**287; **3:**922
  and utopianism, **1:**262; **3:**922
Shaku, Soyen, **3:**1030
Shambhala Meditation Centers, **3:**1032
Shanker, Albert, **1:**213
Share Croppers Union, **3:**1123
Share Our Wealth, **4:**1240
SHARE. *See* Seattle Housing and
  Resource Effort
Sharpeville incident (1960), **1:**236
Shaw, Anna Howard, **1:**302
Shaw, George Bernard, **3:**863, 1118
Shaw v. Reno (1993), **1:**248
Shays, Daniel, **3:**763
Shays' Rebellion, **3:**762–763
Sheet and Tube Company, Youngstown,
  2:635
Sheldon, Walter, **3:**1009

Sheppard-Towner Maternity and
    Infancy Protection Act (1921), **2:**364
Sheridan, Philip, **2:**750
Sherman, Charles O., **2:**527
Sherman, William T., **1:**39
Sherman Anti-Trust Act, **2:**515, 618;
    3:1119
Shew, Joel, **1:**282; **3:**1015, 1016
Shiloh, **3:**1005
Shirtwaist industry, **1:**325–326
    strikes, **1:**325, 338, **2:**513, 549, 550–552
    Triangle Shirtwaist Company Fire,
        2:552
Shoemaker, Samuel, **3:**909
Shoemakers' strike, **2:**471
Shopmen's Strike, **2:**539–540
Shumsky, Ellen, **2:**441
Shuttlesworth, Fred, **1:**185, 187
The Sibyl: A Review of the Tastes, Errors &
    Fashions of Society (Hasbrouck),
    1:271
Sickles, Daniel E., **1:**39
Sidgewick, Rose, **2:**363
Siegel, Mo, **3:**1018
Sierra Club, **4:**1265, 1301
    and Hetch Hetchy battle, **4:**1265–1266
Sierra Leone, **1:**3, 11, 83
Signs: Journal for Women in Culture and
    Society, **2:**419
Silent Parade (1917), **1:**141
Silent Sentinels, **1:**305
Silent Spring (Carson, 1962),
    4:1273–1274
Silko, Leslie Marmon, **2:**755
Silverman, Mervyn, **3:**855
Simmons, William J., **4:**1420–1421
Simone, Nina, **2:**393
Sinclair, Upton, **2:**690
Singer, Peter, **4:**1313–1314
Single-tax, **3:**1003, 1118–1119
Sioux, **2:**748–749, 750–751
Sisters of the Holy Family, **1:**331, 335
Sit-ins, **1:**181–182, 185, 204; **3:**1127
    by CORE, **1:**166
Sitting Bull, **2:**751, 752
Sixteenth Street Baptist Church, **1:**185,
    187, 188
Skidmore, Thomas, **2:**469
Skyhorse (Paul Durant), **2:**715
Slaughter Act, Humane Methods of
    (1958), **4:**1313
Slaughter-House Cases (1873) decision,
    1:112
Slave communities, religious revival in,
    3:930
Slave labor, **2:**460–461

"Slave Power," **1:**27, 29, 66
Slave Trade Act of 1819, **1:**13
Slaveholders
    reaction to abolition movement,
        1:98–100
    rights of, **1:**29
Slavery
    Bill Clinton's apology for, **1:**247
    impact on religion, **3:**947–948
    origins of, **2:**460–461
    reparations for, **1:**201, 245, 249, 255
    white, **3:**860
    See also Abolition movement; African
        Americans; Anti-slavery
        movement; Miscegenation;
        Slaveholders; Slaves
Slaves
    fugitive, **1:**91, 93
    petition for freedom (Massachusetts,
        1777), **1:**9
    repatriation of, **1:**3–4, 11–13, 48
    retaliation, **1:**5–6, 10, 89, 91–92, 94,
        99
    self-emancipation, **1:**94
    white and black, **2:**460, 461
    whites fear of retaliation, **1:**8, 10–11,
        98
    whites helping, **1:**28
    See also Abolition movement; African
        Americans; Anti-slavery
        movement; Miscegenation;
        Slaveholders; Slavery
Sleeping car porters. *See* Brotherhood of
    Sleeping Car Porters
Sloan, Thomas, **2:**703
Small, Albion W., **3:**960
Small is Beautiful: A Study of Economics
    As If People Mattered (Schumacher,
    1318), **4:**1318
Smalls, Robert, **1:**40
Smid, Jones v. (1993), **3:**916
Smiley, Glen, **1:**204
Smith, Barbara, **2:**392, 443
Smith, Gerrit, **1:**27, 49, 60, 64
Smith, Helen, **4:**1230
Smith, James McCune, **1:**69
Smith, Joseph, Jr., **3:**931
Smith, Margaret Chase, **2:**369
Smith, Martin Cruz, **2:**755
Smith, Paul Chaat, **2:**722
Smith, Robert H., **3:**909, 910
Smith, Ruby Doris, **2:**400, 436
Smith, T.O., **3:**988
Smith, Tucker P., **2:**602
Smith Act, **1:**171
Smith-Connally Act, **2:**609–610

Smith v. Allwright (1944), **1:**166
Smithsonian Institute
    repatriation of Native American
        statues, **2:**730
    sweatshop exhibit, **2:**554
The Smoking Gun Memo, **4:**1370
Social Christianity, **1:**331
Social Darwinism, **3:**886, 899, 956
Social ecology, **4:**1320
Social Gospel, **3:**887
    ideology, **3:**934–935
    leaders, **3:**957–958
    legacy of, **3:**960
    missions, **3:**963
    roots, **3:**956–957
    Socialism and New Theology, **3:**957
Social Palace at Guise, France, **1:**287
Social panics. *See* Drug panics; Sex
    panics
Social sciences, rise of, **3:**887
Social Security, founding of,
    4:1240–1241
Social Security Act, **2:**366
Social Security Board, **2:**366
Socialism
    and African-American labor, **1:**145
    Christian, **3:**957
    southwestern, **3:**796
    See also Agrarian Socialist Movement
Socialist camp meetings, **3:**799
Socialist efforts for the unemployed,
    3:1150
Socialist intentional communities, **1:**287,
    289; **3:**1003
Socialist Labor Party (SLP), **2:**526–527
Socialist Organization, International,
    3:1101
Socialist Party of America. *See* Socialist
    Party
Socialist Party (SP), **1:**159; **2:**569–570
    Eugene Debs and, **2:**535
    and global justice movement, **4:**1464
    and Industrial Workers of the World,
        2:526–527
    sedition arrests, **3:**1045, 1074–1075
    supporters, **2:**513
    and temperance, **3:**866
    and unemployment movement,
        2:585, 589–590; **3:**1123,
        1149–1150
Socialist voting, peak of, **3:**799–800
Societies for the prevention of cruelty to
    animals (SPCAs), **4:**1311
Society for Human Abortions, **2:**380
Society for Human Rights, **4:**1331, 1332
Society for Individual Rights, **4:**1341

Society for Promoting the Abolition of Slavery, **1:**7
Society for the Mutual Protection of United Workers, **4:**1227–1228
Society for the Second Self (Tri-Ess), **4:**1380
Society for the Suppression of Vice, **3:**862
Society of American Foresters, **4:**1289
Society of American Indians, **2:**701
Society of Friends. *See* Quakers
Sodomy laws, **3:**854, 857; **4:**1325–1327, 1352, 1362
"Solidarity Forever," **2:**687–688
Solomon, Hannah Greenebaum, **2:**365
Songs, labor reflected in, **2:**687–689
Sons of Liberty, **2:**739–740, **4:**1443
Sons of St. Tammany, **2:**740
Sons of Temperance, **1:**263
Sons of Temperance Convention, **3:**866
Sororities, black, **1:**334
Sorosis Club of New York City, **1:**271, 313
Soul on Ice (Cleaver, 1968), **1:**232, 233
The Souls of Black Folk (Du Bois, 1903), **1:**137
Souter, David H., **1:**247
South Africa, apartheid. *See* Anti-apartheid movement
South Carolina, Regulators, **3:**762
South Dakota, Wounded Knee siege (1973), **2:**711–715, 727
Southern Association of College Women, **2:**363
Southern Baptist Convention, **3:**947
Southern Christian Leadership Conference, **1:**179, 180, 185, 200, 204; **3:**1127
Southern Community Labor Conference for Environmental Justice, **4:**1304
Southern Democrats, **1:**166
Southern Exodusters Movement, **3:**773–776
Southern Horrors: Lynch Law in All Its Phases (Wells-Barnett, 1892), **1:**128, 222, 332
Southern Negro Youth Congress, **1:**161–162
Southern Organizing Committee, **2:**611–612
Southern Pecan Shelling Company, **2:**621
Southern Regional Council, **1:**166
Southern states
    Black Codes, **1:**111
    black outmigration, **1:**158

Southern states *(continued)*
    black representation, **1:**112
    challenges to "separate but equal," **1:**162
    convict labor and leasing, **1:**123, 124–125
    and Fourteenth Amendment, **1:**111
    grandfather clauses, **1:**137–138
    labor unions, **2:**611–612, 626
    pro-slavery, **1:**98–101
    racial violence, **1:**180, 182–184, 198
    resistance to *Brown v. Board of Education* ruling, **1:**174
    sharecropper mobilization, **3:**1123
    sit-ins, **1:**181–182, 204
Southern Tenant Farmers Union, **3:**811–817, 1123
Southwestern Waste-Management Corporation, Bean v. (1976), **4:**1300
Spain, colonization of Native Americans, **2:**695–696
Spanish-American War, **1:**341; **3:**1060
Spargo, John, **2:**516
Sparkman, John, **1:**170
SPCAs (societies for the prevention of cruelty to animals), **4:**1311
Speaking in tongues, **3:**951, 981
Spear, Allan, **4:**1357
Special Field Order No. 15, **1:**255
Spelman College, **1:**330
Spencer, Anna Garlin, **1:**342, 343; **3:**1010
Spencer, Campbell, **4:**1347
Spencer, Herbert, **3:**956
Spencer, Peter, **1:**22
Spencer, Sara, **1:**276
Spengler, Mark, **4:**1347
Spiegelberg, Frederick, **3:**1031
Spies, August, **2:**499, 500, 521
Spira, Henry, **4:**1314, 1316
Spooner, Lysander, **3:**864
Sports teams
    segregated, **1:**162
    use of Native American mascots, **2:**741–743
Spotted Tail, **2:**750
Spring Mobilization, **3:**1088, 1089
Springsteen, Bruce, **2:**689
Spurgeon, Caroline, **2:**363
Squatters, **3:**1154
St. John, Vincent, **2:**528
St. Paul, R.A.V. v. (1992), **1:**248
Stable Family Amendment, **4:**1362
Stafford v. Harrison (1991), **3:**916
Stalin, Josef, **2:**571, 575
    and Trotskyist anti-Stalinism, **2:**577
Stallion Gate (Smith, 1986), **2:**755

Stanford University, **4:**1209
Stanton, Elizabeth Cady, **1:**56, 92, 263, 266, 273, 291
    and abolition movement, **1:**290, 291
    and dress reform, **1:**269, 270
    and peace reform, **3:**1044
    relationship with Anthony, **1:**296
    and temperance movement, **3:**866–867
    view of imperialism, **1:**344
    and woman suffrage, **1:**290, 296–297, 299, 319–320
Stanton, Henry B., **1:**25
Starr, Ellen Gates, **1:**317, 337
Starr, Mark, **2:**599
State, County and Municipal Workers of America, **2:**639
State of Michigan, Butler v., **3:**848
States' rights, **1:**99–100
    lynching and, **1:**131
    Reagan and, **1:**216
Statue of Liberty, irony of, **1:**276
Stearns, Charles B., **1:**66
Steel Chain of Ideas, **3:**886
Steel Workers Organizing Committee, **2:**546, 606
Steele v. Louisville & Nashville R.R. Co. (1944), **2:**541
Steelmaking, Bessemer, **2:**543; **3:**883
Steelworker movement
    early organization, **2:**543
    effect of globalization, **2:**546
    Homestead Steel Strike (1892), **2:**501, 511, 543–544
    independent organizations, **2:**545
    revival, **2:**545–546
    strikes, **2:**544–545, 546
    union busting, **2:**544–545
Steinbeck, John, **2:**690; **3:**1123, 1124
Steinem, Gloria, **2:**404, 426
Stephens, Uriah, **2:**481–482
Sterilization, involuntary, **2:**405, 711
    eugenics movement and, **3:**901–902, 903; **4:**1247
Sterilization legislation, **2:**405
Steunenberg, Frank, **2:**526
Stevens, John Paul, **1:**247
Steward, Ira, **2:**473–474, 520
Steward, Maria W., **1:**54–55
Stewart, Alvan, **1:**53
Stewart, Maria W., **1:**68
Stewart, Potter, **3:**848
Stieglitz, Alfred, **3:**1121
Still, John N., **1:**70
Still, William, **1:**30
Stock market crashes, Panic of 1873, **2:**477, 506

Stone, Chester, **2:**716
Stone, Jesse, **2:**716
Stone, Lucy, **1:**273, 296, 297, 299, 320
Stonewall Democrats, **4:**1346–1347
Stonewall riots (1969), **3:**847; **4:**1341–1342, 1380–1381
Stono Rebellion, **1:**6
Stowe, Harriet Beecher, **1:**93; **3:**947
　and cooperative housekeeping, **1:**286
　Model Christian Neighborhood, **1:**287–288
Strasser, Adolph, **2:**476
Strategic Offensive Reductions (Moscow Treaty) (2002), **4:**1296
Strikes. *See* Labor strikes
Strong, Josiah, **3:**959, 1043
Student activism. *See* Student movements
Student Mobilization Committee to End the War in Vietnam, **3:**1086
Student movements
　effectiveness, **4:**1169–1172
　emergence of, **4:**1164
　and global justice movement, **4:**1463
　history of, **4:**1163–1172
　1930s, **3:**1047
　1960s–1970s, **1:**212–213; **3:**1053
　overview of, **4:**1164–1166
　patterns in higher education and, **4:**1165–1167
　political orientation of, **4:**1163
　twenty-first century, **3:**1104
　See also specific movement; specific tactic; specific war or cause
Student Nonviolent Coordinating Committee, **1:**181, 182, 185
　abandonment of nonviolent direct action, **1:**206
　draft resistance, **3:**1054
　and Freedom Rides, **1:**209
　Freedom Summer, **1:**191
　nonviolent direct action, **1:**204
　ousted white members, **1:**199
　position of women in, **2:**400, 423, 436
　Selma to Montgomery march, **1:**194, 206
　victims of racial violence, **1:**224
Student Peace Union, **3:**1086
Student Union for Peace Action, **3:**1098
Student Volunteer Movement, **3:**963
Students for a Democratic Society, **1:**203; **2:**401, 423–424, 436; **3:**1053–1054, 1083
　agenda, **4:**1173–1175
　decline, **4:**1175–1177, 1196
　emergence, **4:**1173

Students for a Democratic Society *(continued)*
　influences on, **4:**1174
　Port Huron Statement, **4:**1174, 1176
　praxis, **4:**1175
　radicalization of, **4:**1188–1190
　and Vietnam War activism, **4:**1185–1187
Students for Sensible Drug Policy, **3:**876
Students Transforming and Resisting Corporations, **3:**1104
Studio movies. *See* Film
Stuntz Killsright, Joe, **2:**718
Sturges, Jock, **3:**853
Subversive Activities Control Act (1950), **2:**530
Subversive Activities Control Board, **1:**171
Suffrage. *See* Voting rights; Woman suffrage movement
Sullivan, Leon, **1:**238
Sullivan, Louis, **4:**1381
Sullivan Principles, **1:**238
Sumner, William Graham, **3:**956
Supplemental income, by women, **3:**809–810
Supplemental Security Income (SSI), **4:**1242
Supreme Council of the United Orders of Railway Employees, **2:**534
Supreme Court. *See* United States Supreme Court
Suquamish, Oliphant v. (1978), **2:**728
Suzuki, Daisetz Teitaro, **3:**936, 1030
Suzuki, Shunryu, **3:**936, 1031
Swanendael, **3:**998
Sweatshop exhibit (Smithsonian), **2:**554
Sweatshop work, compared with prostitution, **3:**860
Sweatshops
　anti-sweatshop movement, **4:**1491–1496
　revival of, **2:**554, 659
　See also Garment industry
Sweatshops, United Students Against, **3:**1104
Sweatt v. Painter (1950), **1:**174
Sweeney, John, **2:**642, 653, 659
Swift, Wesley, **4:**1442
Swinton, John, **2:**507
Switchmen's Mutual Aid Association, **2:**533
Switchmen's Union of North America, **2:**533
Sylvis, William, **2:**471, 473

Sympathy strikes
　ban of, **2:**626
　under judicial attack, **2:**511
　use of, **2:**677
Syndicalism, **2:**524
Syndicalist Industrial Workers of the World. *See* Industrial Workers of the World
Syracuse Women's Rights Convention, **1:**272
Szilard, Leo, **4:**1293

T

Taft, Robert A., **4:**1391
Taft, William Howard, **2:**557; **3:**895; **4:**1290
Taft-Hartley Act (1947), **1:**168–169; **2:**612–614, 619, 626–628
Take Back the Night, **2:**406, 447
Talbert, Martin, **1:**125
Talbert, Mary B., **1:**130
Tammany, **2:**740
Tammany Society, **2:**740
TANF. *See* Temporary Assistance to Needy Families
Tang, Eric, **1:**254
Tapestry, **4:**1381
Tappan, Arthur, **1:**49
Tappan, Lewis, **1:**24–25, 29, 31–32, 49, 52, 63
　attack on home of, **1:**103
Tarr, Curtis, **3:**1089
Taxes
　cuts, **3:**1134–1135
　equity, **3:**895
　reform, **3:**891
　single-tax, **3:**1003, 1118–1119
　slave importation, **1:**5–6, 8
　state government, **3:**895
　whisky, **3:**763–764
Taylor, Emily, **2:**416
Taylor, Frederick Winslow, **2:**556
Taylor, Glen, **1:**170
Taylor, Graham, **3:**890
Taylor, Hoote, **1:**125
Taylor, Myron, **2:**546
Taylor, Nathaniel William, **3:**947
Taylor, Susie King, **1:**44
Teach-ins, **3:**1053, 1083; **4:**1186
Teachers
　National Retired Teachers Association, **4:**1241
　pension plans, **4:**1238–1239
　unionization of, **1:**348
　women in labor unions, **2:**641
　See also Education; Schools

Teague, Colin, **1:**14
Team Act, **2:**655
Teamsters
  membership decline, **2:**665
  strike against UPS, **2:**659, 665–669
  strikes, **2:**564, 593–595
  United Automobile Workers alliance,
    2:630
Teamsters for a Democratic Union,
  2:652, 668
TeamX, **2:**554–555
Tecumseh, **3:**930
Teed, Cyrus, **3:**1004
Televangelism, **3:**951
Television
  advertisements. *See* Advertisements
  evangelism on, **3:**951
Temperance movement, **1:**68
  abolition movement associated with,
    3:866
  anti-drug movement compared with,
    3:873
  common themes of, **3:**843
  end of prohibition, **3:**870
  and passage of Prohibition, **3:**869–870
  twentieth century, **3:**870
  women and, **1:**262–263, 298, 314–315,
    316; **3:**866–867
  See also Alcoholics Anonymous;
    Temperance societies
Temperance societies
  African American, **1:**82
  first U.S., **3:**865
  women's, **1:**298; **3:**867–869
  See also Temperance movement
Temporary Assistance to Needy
  Families (TANF), **3:**1136, 1137
Ten-hour workday, proponents of,
  2:468–469, 470, 638
Tenayucca, Emma, **2:**621
Tenement House Building Company,
  3:1009
Tennessee
  Columbia racial violence, **1:**223
  Memphis sanitation strike (1968), **2:**641
  miners and convict leasing, **1:**124
  ratification of Nineteenth Amend-
    ment, **1:**305–307
  student sit-ins, **1:**182
Tenskwatawa, **3:**930
Tent city movements, **3:**1152–1157
Terrell, Mary Church, **1:**129, 300, 301,
  314, 322; **2:**361
  and anti-lynching movement,
    1:331–333
  and racial uplift, **2:**388

Terrorism
  and nuclear weapons, **4:**1297
  September 11. *See* September 11
Tet Offensive, **3:**1091
Texas, **3:**798
  African American migration from,
    3:775–776
  Farmers' Alliance, **3:**783–784
  sodomy laws, **3:**857; **4:**1325–1326,
    1352
  Two Rivers, **4:**1213
Texas, Lawrence and Garner v. (2003),
  3:857; **4:**1325, 1352
Texas Alliance, **3:**783–785
Textile industry, **1:**265, 324
  Carolina strikes (1934), **2:**565, 594
  Lawrence, Massachusetts strike
    (1912), **1:**346; **2:**514, 529–530
  Paterson, New Jersey strikes (1912),
    2:514, 530
  See also Garment industry
Thatcher, Ebby, **3:**909
Thayer, Eli, **1:**59–60
Theatre
  El Teatro Campesino, **4:**1217
  guerrilla, **4:**1280
  labor reflected in, **2:**691
  Lysistrata Project, **3:**1105
A Theology for the Social Gospel
  (Rauschenbusch, 1917), **3:**960
Theosophy, **3:**1004–1005
Thernstrom, Abigail, **1:**241
Thernstrom, Stephan, **1:**241
Third International. *See* Communist
  International
Third Wave Foundation, **2:**430
Third Wave women's movement
  diversity, **2:**429–430
  fighting backlash, **2:**433–434
  girlie culture, **2:**432–433
  growing up and, **2:**431–432
  issues of the, **2:**432
  men and feminism, **2:**430
  as a movement?, **2:**434
  organization and activism, **2:**430–431
  popular culture of, **2:**434
Third World Liberation Front, **1:**213;
  4:1207
Third World Women's Alliance, **2:**392,
  393–394, 408
Thirteenth Amendment, **1:**94, 111
Thomas, Clarence, **1:**217, 221, 247;
  2:395; **4:**1210
Thomas, M. Carey, **1:**313
Thomas, Nevil, **1:**131
Thomas, Norman, **3:**1079, 1122

Thomas, Robert K., **2:**706, 707
Thomas, Timothy, **1:**242
Thomas, William S., **1:**22
Thompson, George, **1:**103
Thompson, William, **2:**581
Thomson, Samuel, **1:**281; **3:**991–992,
  1015
Thomsonian Botanics, **1:**281
Thoreau, Henry David, **3:**943, 1029,
  1041; **4:**1259
Thornton, William, **1:**12
Thoughts on African Colonization
  (Garrison, 1832), **1:**20, 48, 62, 86
Three Mile Island, **4:**1257, 1277
Three-strikes law (1994), **3:**879
Thurmond, Strom, **1:**170, 213
Tibetan Buddhism, **3:**953, 1031–1032
Tiegan, Henry, **3:**818–819
Tijerina, Reies, **4:**1214
Till, Emmet, **1:**134, 171, 176–177, 223
Tillman, Benjamin, **3:**958
Tillman, William, **1:**40
Tillotson, Mary, **1:**271
Tinbergen, Niko, **4:**1313
Tingley, Katherine, **3:**1005
Tippet, Tom, **2:**599
To Secure These Rights (1947), **1:**169
Tobias, Andrew, **4:**1346
Todd, John, **4:**1320
Toledo, Ohio
  Auto-Lite strike, **2:**564, 591,
    593–595
  Willys-Overland strike, **2:**558–559
Tolstoy, Leo, **3:**1044
Tolstoy Farm, **3:**1005
Tonkin Gulf Resolution, **3:**1081
Torrey, Charles, **1:**25, 56
Totten, Ashley, **1:**153
Toure, Nkenge, **2:**447
Tourgee, Albion, **1:**129
"Toward a Female Liberation Move-
  ment" (article), **2:**425
Townley, Arthur C., **3:**802–803
Townsend, Francis E., **4:**1240
Townsend plan, **4:**1240
Toynbee Hall, **3:**1141
Tracks (Erdrich, 1989), **2:**754–755
Trade deficit with Britain, **3:**763
Trade Related Aspects of Intellectual
  Property, **4:**1459
Trade Union Committee for Organizing
  Negro Workers, **1:**154
Trade Union Educational League, **2:**571,
  574
The Trades' Union. *See* National Trades'
  Union

Trading with the Enemy Act (1917), **3:**1074
Trail of Broken Treaties, **2:**709–711, 727
Trail of Tears, **2:**699
Train, George Francis, **1:**297
Training School for Women Organizers, **1:**349
Trall, Russell, **1:**282
Trammell, Jeffrey, **4:**1346
Trans Activism, **4:**1381–1382
Transcendentalists, **3:**943, 1002, 1029; **4:**1255
Transformationist perspective, **1:**253
Transgender activism, **4:**1379–1382
Transgender Advocacy Coalition, **4:**1381
Transnational corporations, **4:**1459
Transportation Act (1920), **2:**539
Transvestia (magazine), **4:**1380
Traps for the Young (Comstock, 1883), **3:**862
Trautmann, William E., **2:**527, 530
Treatment Action Group, **4:**1348
Treaty of Detroit, **2:**625, 628–629, 636
Treaty of 1868
    and Alcatraz occupation, **2:**725–726
    U.S. violation of, **2:**714
    Wounded Knee siege and, **2:**727
Treaty of Ghent (1812), **2:**704
Treaty of Guadeloupe Hidalgo (1848), **4:**1212
Treaty of Paris, **1:**342
Treaty rights
    Canadian aboriginal, **2:**736–737
    Native American, **2:**725–728, 730
Trembath, John, **2:**491
Trenton Six, **1:**171
Tresca, Carlo, **2:**530, 580
Triangle Shirtwaist Company, **1:**326, 338; **2:**552
Tribally Controlled Community College Assistance Act (1978), **2:**728
Trochmann, John, **4:**1445
Trotsky, Leon, **2:**571
Trotskyism, **2:**575, 577
Trotter, James Monroe, **1:**43
Trout Unlimited, **4:**1283
Troy Female Seminary, **1:**311–312
Trudell, John, **2:**708, 722
Truman, Harry, **1:**167, 168, 170; **2:**611
Trumka, Richard, **2:**652, 653
Trungpa, Chogyam, **3:**1031, 1032
Truth, Sojourner, **1:**55, 56–57
Tryon, William, **3:**761–762
Tubman, Harriet, **1:**43, 56; **2:**361
Tucker, Benjamin, **2:**496

Tulsa, race riots 1921, **1:**223
Tunstall v. Brotherhood of Locomotive Firemen and Enginemen (1944), **2:**541
Turnaround Tuesday, **1:**194
Turner, Banks, **1:**307
Turner, Elizabeth, **2:**689
Turner, Henry McNeal, **1:**39, 112–113, 128
Turner, Nat, **1:**59, 89, 99
Tuskegee Institute, **1:**118–119
Twelve Steps. *See* Alcoholics Anonymous
Twelve Traditions. *See* Alcoholics Anonymous
Twelve Years a Slave (Northrop, 1853), **1:**93
Twenty-Eight Hour Law (1873), **4:**1311
Twenty-first Amendment, **3:**870
Twenty-sixth Amendment, **3:**870
Twin Oaks, **3:**1006, 1024
Two Live Crew, **3:**850
Two Rivers, Texas, **4:**1213

U

UAW. *See* United Automobile Workers
Unborn Victims of Violence Act (1999), **2:**385
Uncle Tom's Cabin (Stowe, 1852), **1:**93; **3:**947
Underground Railroad, **1:**28, 43, 56, 93
Underwood, John C., **1:**60
Underwood Simmons tariff, **3:**891
Unemployed Councils
    emergence of, **2:**588–590
    protests, **2:**590–591
Unemployed Councils of the United States, **2:**584–585
Unemployed Leagues, **2:**586–587, 589, 591; **3:**1150
Unemployment
    black, **1:**242
    downsizing, **2:**656
    globalization and, **2:**635
    Great Depression, **2:**562–563, 588; **3:**1145
    1920s, **2:**557
    1970s, **2:**634
    1980s rise in, **2:**650–651
    1990s-2000s, **2:**656
    See also Homeless; Poverty; Unemployment movement; Welfare programs
Unemployment Council of Detroit, **3:**1148–1149
Unemployment Day, International, **3:**1123, 1148
Unemployment movement, **3:**1120–1121, 1147–1150

Unemployment movement (*continued*)
    A.J. Muste and, **2:**586, 589, 591
    collective self-help, **2:**588
    Communist Party and, **2:**584–585, **3:**1122–1124, 1148–1150
    decline of, **2:**592
    protests, **2:**590–591
    Socialist Party and, **2:**585, 589–590; **3:**1123, 1149–1150
    unification of groups, **2:**591–592
    See also Poverty; Tent city movements; Unemployment; Welfare programs
Unification Church, **3:**1006
Uniform Narcotic Drug Act (1932), **3:**873
Union busting, **2:**651
Union camps, mining, **2:**492
Union Films, **2:**691
Union labels
    Buy American campaigns, **2:**682–683
    gender and, **2:**681–682
    white men's,' **2:**680–681
Union League, **1:**112
Union of Concerned Scientists, **4:**1277
Union of Needletrades, Industrial and Textile Employees (UNITE), **2:**548–549, 554
Union of Russian Workers, **2:**502
Union-produced goods, **2:**680
Union Summer, **2:**656–658
Unions. *See* Labor unions
Unitarians, **3:**943
UNITE. *See* Union of Needletrades, Industrial and Textile Employees
United Automobile Workers (UAW), **1:**212; **2:**586, 607–608
    concession bargaining, **2:**635, 636, 651–652
    conditions for strike bylaw, **2:**628
    contract with General Motors, **2:**628–629
    General Motors strike (1946), **2:**626
    membership decline, **2:**636, 650
    No Strike Pledge, **2:**625
    racial issues, **2:**631, 632
    Teamsters alliance, **2:**630
    and Vietnam War, **2:**644
    wildcat strikes, **2:**634
    women in, **2:**632
United Brotherhood of Carpenters, **2:**559
United Cannery, Agricultural, Packing, and Allied Workers of America, **2:**622
United Church of Christ Commission for Racial Justice, **4:**1302, 1304
United Council of Working-Class Women, **2:**572

United Electrical Workers (UE), 2:614, 632

United Farm Workers, 2:683–685; 3:1131; 4:1216

United Federation of Teachers, 1:213; 2:641

United Food and Commercial Workers, 2:652

United for Peace and Justice, 3:1102

United Front, 4:1179

United Garment Workers, 1:346; 2:681

United Hatters, 2:683

United Mine Workers (UMW), 2:560, 628–629, 647–649
  concession strikes, 2:652
  strikebreakers, 2:676

United National Caucus, 2:634

United Nations
  Atomic Energy Commission, 4:1293–1294
  Commission on Human Rights, 2:369
  Convention on the Political Rights of Women, 2:370
  Covenant against Genocide, 1:171
  lack of Native American members, 2:735
  meeting of Indigenous Peoples, 2:726
  sanctions against South Africa, 1:238
  Working Group on Indigenous Populations, 2:713, 726

United Order of Enoch, 3:1004

United Parcel Service, strike against, 2:659, 665–669

United Poultry Concerns, 4:1316

United Public Workers of America, 2:640

United Railway Workers of America, 2:676

United Rubber Workers' Union, 2:606

United Service Organizations, 2:368

United Society of Believers in Christ's Second Appearance. *See* Shakers

United States
  and anti-apartheid movement, 1:220, 236–240
  factionalism over slavery, 1:11, 53, 58, 100, 103
  restriction of civil rights, 1:115–118
  See also Northern states; Southern states

United States, Guinn v. (1915), 1:137–138

United States, Nishimura Ekiu v. (1891), 4:1424

United States, Roth v. (1957), 3:848

United States, Schenck v. (1919), 3:1075

United States Constitution
  civil rights amendments to, 1:111, 112
  Eighteenth Amendment, 3:869
  Fifteenth Amendment, 1:111, 112, 297
  Fourteenth Amendment, 1:111, 112, 297
  Nineteenth Amendment, 1:300, 305
  slavery and, 1:53, 64
  Thirteenth Amendment, 1:111
  Twenty-first Amendment, 3:870
  Twenty-sixth Amendment, 3:870

United States Department of Labor, Children's Bureau, 1:338

United States Military
  executive order to integrate, 1:170
  first formally integrated troops, 1:162
  gays/lesbians in, 4:1327–1328, 1333, 1354
  racial discrimination during WWI, 1:139–140, 158; 2:702
  racial discrimination during WWII, 4:1213
  women in, 2:367–368, 416

United States Railroad Administration, 2:537, 539

United States Steel Corporation (1901), 2:544, 546

United States Supreme Court
  abortion legislation, 2:382; 3:847–848
  Brown v. Board of Education, 1:174, 175
  child pornography legislation, 3:853
  color-blind jurisprudence, 1:241, 243, 247–248
  and death penalty, 1:220
  gay/lesbian legislation, 3:854, 857; 4:1325–1326, 1352, 1364, 1366
  immigrant legislation, 4:1424
  legislation during war years, 3:1075–1076
  1930s, 1:162–163
  obscenity legislation, 3:848, 851
  rape legislation, 2:449
  ruling on Montgomery bus segregation, 1:178
  weakening support for civil rights, 1:220–221

United States v. Cruikshank (1876), 1:112

United States v. Morrison (2002), 2:450

United States v. Nice (1916), 2:702

United States v. Reese (1876), 1:112

United Steelworkers of America, 2:546, 650, 652

United Students Against Sweatshops, 3:1104

United Tailoresses Society of New York, 1:265

United Transportation Union, 2:541

Universal Declaration of Human Rights, 2:369

Universal Negro Improvement Association (UNIA), 1:143–145
  decline, 1:149–150, 159
  founding, 1:148–149, 159, 228

Universal Peace Union, 3:1044

Universal suffrage, 1:297

Universalists, 3:943

Universities
  Affirmative Action, 1:248–249
  African-American, 1:330
  and anti-apartheid movement, 1:238–239, 240
  and the anti-rape movement, 2:450
  desegregation of, 1:174
  and disability support services, 4:1249–1251
  religious student organizations, 3:950
  tribal colleges, 2:728
  unionization of graduate students, 2:658
  YAF clubs, 4:1390
  See also Higher education; Women's education; specific university

University of California at Berkeley, 4:1178, 1186, 1207

University of Michigan
  Affirmative Action, 1:248–249
  teach-in, 4:1186

University of Mississippi, civil rights in, 1:184–185

University Settlement, 3:1009

Uprising of 20,000, 2:550–552

UPS. *See* United Parcel Service

Uranium mining, 4:1278

Urban Environment Conference, 4:1300–1301

Urban growth, Progressive Era, 3:884

Urban League. *See* National Urban League

U.S. Division of Forestry, 4:1286

U.S. Geological Survey, 4:1288

U.S. Labor Against the War, 3:1104

U.S. Naval Home (1811), 4:1238

U.S. Treasury Department, farmers' subsidy, 3:785

U.S. v. One Package of Japanese Pessaries, 2:355, 358; 3:847

U.S. v. Washington (1974), 2:727

USA Patriot Act, **1:**253–254
USX Corporation, **2:**546, 652
Ute, **2:**751
Utley, Freda, **4:**1412
Utopian literature, **3:**1119
Utopian movements
    and dress reform, **1:**262, 268–269
    1840s communities, **3:**970–973
    German Pietism, **3:**969
    millennialism and reform, **3:**969–970
    reasons for, **3:**922–923
    women and, **1:**262
    See also Communal living

V

V-Day Campaign, **2:**450
Vagina Monologues (play), **2:**450
Valdez, Luis, **4:**1216–1217
Van Buren, Martin, **1:**54
Van Renssalaer, Stephen, IV, **3:**769
Van Renssalaer, William, **3:**770
Vanzetti, Bartolomeo, **2:**503, 580–582
Varhayt (anarchist newspaper), **2:**500
Varick, James, **1:**82
Vector Magazine, **4:**1341
Vegetarianism, **3:**1005, 1015, 1016, 1018
Vendanta Society, **3:**936, 1005
Ventura, Jesse, **3:**876
Vera, Bush v. (1996), **1:**248
Vermont
    antislavery legislation, **1:**7
    same-sex marriages, **4:**1327, 1354
Vesey, Denmark, **1:**98
Veterans
    disabled, **4:**1247
    and ethnic identity movements,
        4:1206–1207
    old age homes, **4:**1238
    pension plans, **4:**1238, 1246
    Vietnam Veterans Against the War,
        2:644–645; **3:**1090, 1094
Vice, Society for the Suppression of,
    3:862
Vice Versa (newsletter), **4:**1333
Vices Are Not Crimes (Spooner, 1875),
    3:864
Vietnam, Black Power and, **1:**198–199
Vietnam Day Committee, **4:**1186
Vietnam Veterans Against the War,
    2:644–645; **3:**1090, 1094
Vietnam War
    antiwar movement, **3:**1080–1096;
        4:1183–1184, 1230
    the draft, **3:**1089–1090
    GI's and Veterans, **3:**1090

Vietnam War *(continued)*
    labor movement, **2:**643–645
    Moratorium, **3:**1092–1094
    peace movement, **3:**1053–1056
    student protests, **3:**1053–1056,
        1082–1083, 1086
    war on poverty and, **3:**1128–1130
    women-led protests, **2:**401, 436;
        3:1085
    women's liberation movement and
        the, **2:**423
Vietnam War campus activism
    Chicago riots (1968), **3:**1092;
        4:1187–1188
    decline of, **4:**1192–1193
    Kent State, **4:**1191–1192
    movement formation, **4:**1185–1187
    opponents, **4:**1187, 1192–1193
    origins, **4:**1183–1184
    peak of, **4:**1191
    radicalization of, **4:**1188–1190
    slow beginnings, **4:**1184–1185
Viewpoint diversity, Affirmative
    Action, **1:**249
Vigilance Committees, **1:**93
Villard, Fanny Garrison, **3:**1044
Villard, Oswald Garrison, **1:**136
Vinson, Fred, **1:**174
Violence
    labor, **2:**507
    against women, **2:**406
Violence Against Women Act, **2:**450
Virginia
    against emancipation, **1:**99
    Harpers Ferry, **1:**60, 94; **3:**1042
    involuntary sterilization programs,
        3:902
    miscegenation legislation (1691), **1:**8
Virginia, Boynton v. (1960), **1:**183
Virginia, Morgan v., **1:**203, 208
Visiting and Teaching Guild for
    Crippled Children, **3:**1009
Visiting nurses, **3:**1008–1009
Vivekananda, Swami, **3:**936
Vocationalism, **3:**1010
Vogt, William, **4:**1276
Voice from the South, A (Cooper, 1892),
    1:333
Voice of Industry, **2:**470
Volstead Act (1919), **3:**869
Voluntarism, **3:**887
Voluntary motherhood, **2:**353
Volunteers in Service to America,
    3:1132
Von Harnack, Adolph, **3:**956
Von Hayek, Friedrich, **4:**1388

Voter registration drives, African-
    American women, **2:**361
Voting, abolishment of white primary,
    1:166
Voting behavior, gay/lesbian,
    4:1344–1345
Voting rights
    curtailment of black, **1:**227, 300
    legislation, **1:**229
    Mississippi, **1:**191–192
    universal suffrage, **1:**297, 300–301,
        320
    women's. *See* Woman suffrage
        movement
Voting Rights Act
    1965, **1:**191, 194, 195, 229
    1982 amendments, **1:**248
Voyage en Icarie (Cabet, 1839), **3:**973,
    1002
Vygotsky, Lev, **4:**1245

W

Wage slavery, **2:**503
Wagner, Robert, **1:**134
Wagner Act, **2:**565, 605, 619, 661
Wald, Lillian, **3:**1141
Walker, Alice, **2:**394, 395, 410
Walker, David, **1:**15–16, 66, 89, 98
Walker, Rebecca, **2:**430
Walker, Seth, **1:**307
Wallace, George, **1:**187
Wallace, Henry A., **1:**167, 170
Walsh-Healey Public Contracts Act
    (1936), **2:**522
War Labor Board, **2:**557–558, 609,
    674–675
War of 1812, **3:**1040
War of the Roses, **1:**306
War on Drugs. *See* Anti-drug movement
War on Poverty, **3:**1128–1129
War on Terror, **3:**1058
War Resisters League, **3:**1079
Ward, Lester, **3:**957
Ward Valley, **4:**1296
Wards Cove Packing Company v. Antonio
    (1989), **1:**221
Waring, George, **4:**1260
Waring, Mary, **2:**388
Warley, Buchanan v. (1917), **1:**138
Warren, Earl, **1:**174
Warren County, North Carolina,
    4:1302–1303
Warrior, Clyde, **2:**707
Wartime industries
    African American's and, **2:**517, 541

Wartime industries (continued)
    discrimination, 1:161, 164, 202
    labor unions during, 2:557
    women in, 2:368–369, 517
Wartime literature, 3:1046, 1077
Washington
    Everett Massacre, 2:531
    Seattle General Strike (1919), 2:558
    Spokane's free speech fights, 2:529
Washington, Booker T., 1:118–119
    Atlanta Compromise speech, 1:136,
        227–228
    on convict leasing, 1:123
    on lynching, 1:129
    response to black repression,
        1:227–228
Washington, Harold, 1:218
Washington, Madison, 1:92
Washington, Margaret Murray, 1:117,
    314
Washington, U.S. v. (1974), 2:727
Washingtonian movement, 3:908
Water-cure. See Hydrotherapy
Water-Cure Journal, 1:269, 282
Water pollution
    Clean Water Act, 4:1276
    industrialization and, 4:1261
Water rights
    Colorado Cooperative Colony,
        3:988–989
    Native American, 2:729, 736
    and privatization, 4:1459
Waterways Commission, 4:1289
Watson, Paul, 4:1278–1279
Watson, Tom, 3:793–795
Watts, Alan, 3:1031
Watts riot (1965), 1:225
We Charge Genocide (CRC study), 1:171
"We Shall Not Be Moved" (song), 2:688
"We Shall Not Be Overcome" (song),
    2:688
Weatherford, Willis D., 1:131
Weatherman Underground Organiza-
    tion, 4:1189, 1196–1200
Weaver, James B., 3:791–792
Webster, Delia, 1:59
Webster, Milton P., 1:152, 153
Webster, William, 2:721
Webster v. Reproductive Health Services
    (1988), 2:382; 3:847
Weddington, Sarah, 2:381
Wednesday Club, 4:1261
The Weekly Advocate (newspaper, 1837–
    1842), 1:84, 85
Weeks Act (1911), 4:1291
Weinberg, Jack, 4:1178–1179, 1180

Weinstein, Naomi, 2:400
Weismann, August, 3:900
Welch, James, 2:754
Weld, Theodore, 1:25; 3:946–947
Weld, William, 4:1351
Welfare capitalism, 2:561–562
Welfare programs
    advocates of, 3:1131–1134, 1138
    beginnings of, 3:889–890
    CIO and, 3:1124–1126
    effect on women, 3:582
    for the elderly, 4:1239, 1240, 1242
    opposition to, 3:1125–1126, 1129,
        1132–1136
    reduction of, 1:217; 3:1134–1139
    war on poverty, 3:1128
    See also Poverty; Unemployment;
        Unemployment movement
Welfare queens, 3:1133
Welfare rights movement, 3:1131–1134,
    1138
Welfare Rights Organization, National,
    3:1131–1133
Welfare Rights Union, Kensington,
    3:1138
Wells-Barnett, Ida Bell, 1:117, 127–128,
    222, 300, 301, 322
    and anti-lynching movement,
        1:331–332
    and General Federation of Women's
        Clubs, 2:361
    and NAWSA parade, 1:334
Wesley, John, 3:933
Wesleyans, ideology, 3:933
West Coast Lesbian Conference, 2:407
West Virginia, black lung movement,
    2:646–649
Western Association of Collegiate
    Alumnae, 2:363
Western Electric's Hawthorne Works,
    2:561
Western Federation of Miners, 2:493,
    495–496, 526
Western Health Reform Institute, 3:1016
Western Shoshone, 2:746
Weston, S. Burns, 3:1009
Westside Group, 2:401, 424
Weyrich, Paul, 4:1402, 1406
Wheeler-Howard Act. See Indian
    Reorganization Act
Wheelock, Eleazar, 2:697
Whipper, William, 1:68, 69
Whiskey Rebellion, 3:763–764
White, E. Edwin, 4:1240
White, Ellen Gould, 1:271, 282;
    3:1015–1016

White, F. Clifton, 4:1391–1392
White, Garland H., 1:43
White, Jacob C., 1:68
White, Sue Shelton, 1:305
White, Walter, 1:130, 170
White backlash
    on Birmingham marchers, 1:187
    black response to, 1:224–225
    on black voter registration cam-
        paigns, 1:191–192, 209
    on Chicago marchers, 1:198
    during Cold War, 1:171
    on Freedom Riders, 1:183–184, 205,
        209
    on March Against Fear, 1:198
    on Marion marchers, 1:193
    on MOVE, 1:216
    1960–1968, 1:206, 224
    post–World War I, 1:222–223
    post–World War II, 1:223–224
    on railway workers, 2:539
    and reverse racism, 1:215
    right-wing, 1:213–214
    on school desegregation, 1:180,
        185–185
    and state terrorism, 1:216
    on student sit-ins, 1:182
    war industry, 1:165
    See also Police brutality
White Citizens Councils, 1:180, 223;
    3:1126–1127
White Earth Land Recovery Project,
    2:746
White Earth reservation, 2:700–701
White ethnics, 4:1208
White House Conference on Aging,
    4:1232, 1242–1243
White Overalls, 4:1463
White Rose Mission and Industrial
    Association, 3:1143
White Slave Traffic Act. See Mann Act
White supremacy
    1960–1968, 1:206, 224
    world wide, 1:167
Whitefield, George, 3:927, 928, 939
Whitehead, Ralph Radcliffe, 3:1005
Whitman, Walt, 3:1029
Whittier, John Greenleaf, 1:51
Whole Earth Catalog (Brand),
    4:1318–1319
The Whole Woman (Greer, 1999), 2:403
Wiccans, and global justice movement,
    4:1464
Wicker, Randy, 4:1339
Wildcat strikes, 1:165; 2:478, 633, 634
    motivation for, 2:674–675

Wildcat strikes (continued)
  1960s–1970s, 2:678–679
  racially motivated, 2:677–678
  railroad and coal, 2:675–677
  trends of, 2:675
  World War I, 2:675–677
  World War II, 2:677–678
Wilderness ethic, 4:1271–1273
Wilderness movement, 4:1271–1272
Wilderness Society, 4:1268
Wildlife, 4:1267
Wiley, George, 3:1131
Wilkes, Martin v. (1990), 1:221
Wilkins, Roy, 1:178
Willard, Emma Hart, 1:311–312
Willard, Frances Elizabeth, 1:297, 315,
    316, 343
  and temperance movement, 3:867, 869
Williams, Fannie Barrier, 1:314, 334
Williams, Robert F., 1:224
Williams, Ron, 2:717, 718
Willys-Overland strike, 2:558–559
Wilson, Charles, 2:533
Wilson, Dick, 2:711, 712, 715, 716, 718
Wilson, Joseph T., 1:44, 45
Wilson, Mary Jane, 2:707
Wilson, Michael, 2:690
Wilson, Pete, 1:250; 4:1351
Wilson, William G., 3:909–910
Wilson, William Junius, 1:215
Wilson, Woodrow, 2:515; 3:1060–1061;
    4:1290
Wilson administration, Progressive
    legislation, 3:896
Winchell, Barry, 4:1328
Winston, Henry, 1:171
Winter in the Blood (Welch, 1974), 2:754
Winthrop, John, 3:926, 939
Wisconsin v. Mitchell (1993), 1:248
Wise, Isaac Mayer, 3:933
Witherspoon, Frances, 3:1046
Wittenmyer, Annie, 1:314–315
Wobblies. See Industrial Workers of the
    World
Wolfe, Bertram, 2:571, 578
Wollstonecraft, Mary, 1:287
Woman, Church and State (Gage, 1893),
    1:277, 296
Woman-identified woman, 2:441–442
Woman in the Wilderness, 3:998
The Woman Rebel (magazine), 2:354
Woman Suffrage and Politics (Catt, 1923),
    1:307–308
Woman suffrage movement, 1:266
  African-American, 1:300–301, 322;
    2:361

Woman suffrage movement (continued)
  anti-suffragists, 1:296–297, 306, 320
  campaign paraphernalia, 1:299–300
  child labor and absence of, 1:318
  Civil War and, 1:297–300, 310
  first women's rights convention,
    1:290–294, 319
  growth of, 1:301–305, 320–321
  leaders of, 1:290, 338
  National Woman's Rights conven-
    tion, 1:295, 296
  organizations, 2:360–361
  protests, 1:302–304, 320–321
  victory and aftermath, 2:361–363
  See also Voting rights; specific leader
Womanist, 2:395, 410
Woman's American Baptist Home
    Mission Society, 1:330
The Woman's Bible (Stanton, 1895), 1:296
Woman's Building (Los Angeles,
    California), 2:413
Woman's Christian Temperance Union,
    1:276, 297, 314–315; 3:949
  and anti-cruelty movement, 4:1311
  and anti-imperialist movement,
    1:343
  and peace reform, 3:1044
  and temperance movement, 3:867–869
Woman's Convention, 1:331
Woman's National Liberal Union, 1:277,
    299
Woman's National Loyal League, 1:264,
    291, 297
Woman's Peace Party, 3:1044, 1046
Woman's State Temperance Society of
    New York, 1:263, 298; 3:866
Woman's Work for Women, 3:962
Women
  and antiwar movement, 3:1104–1105
  and colonial labor, 2:461–462
  and the conservative movement,
    4:1411–1413
  domesticity of, 1:19
  early common law restrictions,
    1:294, 296
  and evangelicalism, 3:948–949
  in the labor movement, 2:632–633
  in military, 2:367–368, 416
  and the peace movement,
    3:1046–1047
  politico, 2:437
  professionalization of domestic
    tasks, 1:284
  in the public workers movement,
    2:641–642
  role in environmentalism, 4:1274

Women (continued)
  role in missionaries, 3:962–963
  and sexual mores, 1:339
  violence against, 2:406
  in war industries, 2:368–369, 517
  and World War I, 3:1044
  and World War II, 2:368–369
Women Accepted for Voluntary
    Emergency Services (WAVES),
    2:368
Women against Violence against
    Women in Los Angeles, 2:406
Women for Sobriety, 3:915
Women Hurt in Systems of Prostitution
    Engaged in Revolt (WHISPER),
    3:861
Women in the Air Force, 2:368
Women in the Nonpartisan League,
    3:805–806
Women of All Red Nations, 2:726
Women Strike for Peace, 3:1052
Women's, and Men's, Dialogues at
    Creating Change, 4:1370
Women's Armed Services Integration
    Act, 2:368
Women's Army Corps, 2:368
Women's Auxiliary Army Corps, 2:368
Women's Bureau, 2:362, 632
Women's charitable organizations,
    1:287
Women's clothing, 1:269
  See also Dress reform movement
Women's clubs
  black, 1:314, 333, 334
  clubwomen, 1:116–118, 129, 300
  demonstration, 3:810
  organizations, 2:361
  segregated, 1:334
  white, 1:313–314, 334
Women's Cooperative Housekeeping
    movement. See Cooperative
    Housekeeping movement
Women's education
  African-American, 1:330, 331
  all-female colleges, 1:312–313
  industrial education, 1:348–349
  Oberlin College, 1:312
  opponents of, 1:312
  Spelman College, 1:330
  Troy Female Seminary, 1:311–312
  university organizations, 2:363
  and women's studies movement,
    2:415–416
Women's Equal Pay Act (1945), 2:369
Women's Equity Action League, 2:400
Women's Era (newspaper), 1:334

Women's Home Demonstration Movement, 3:808–810
Women's International League for Peace and Freedom, 3:1046–1047, 1051, 1085
Women's International Terrorist Conspiracy from Hell (WITCH), 2:437
Women's Joint Congressional Committee, 2:363, 364
Women's liberation movement, 2:437–442
    anti-rape movement and, 2:445–446
    counterculture movement and, 3:1026–1027
    divisions, 2:426–427
    goals, 2:426
    historical context, 2:422–423
    ideologies and tactics, 2:424
    institutions, 2:426
    intellectual foundations, 2:425–426
    organizations, 2:401, 408, 424
    origins, 2:423–424
    outcomes, 2:427
    See also Feminism
Women's Organization for National Prohibition Reform, 3:870
Women's Peace Party, 2:366
Women's Peace Union, 3:1046, 1047
Women's Political Council, 1:178
Women's Political Union, 1:301
Women's Radical Action Project, 2:401
Women's rights
    Communist Party USA and, 2:572–573
    Felix Adler and, 3:1010
    nonresistance and, 3:1041
Women's Rights Convention
    Frederick Douglass at 1848, 1:75
    Sojourner Truth's speech at 1851, 1:57
Women's rights movement, 1:266
    the church and, 1:277, 296
    dress reform and, 1:269–270
    first convention of, 1:290–294
    Frederick Douglass and, 1:118, 294
    transnational organizations, 1:339
    William Garrison and, 1:21, 30
Women's shelters, 2:406
Women's studies movement
    associations, 2:418–419
    emergence of, 2:415–417
    journals and publications, 2:419–420
Women's Trade Association, 3:889
Women's Trade Union League, 1:325, 338, 348–349; 3:888
    African-American women and, 1:348
    opposition from men and shift to women's movement, 1:351
    Rose Schneiderman and, 2:549

Women's Work Department, 1:132
Woodcock, Leonard, 2:644
Woodhull, Victoria, 1:297
Woodman, Olivia, 3:782
Woodson, Lewis, 1:67
Worcester, Samuel A., 2:699
Word War I
    and railroad workers movement, 2:537
Work, Hubert, 2:703
Work Hours Act (1962), 2:620
Workers Alliance of America, 2:585–587, 591–592
Workers Committee on Unemployment, 2:585
Workers cooperatives, 2:473
Workers Education Local 189, 2:602
Workers' Liberty Defense Union, 2:530
Workers Party of America. See Communist Party
Working class
    industrial, formation of, 2:480–483
    and Vietnam War, 2:644–645
Working Men's parties, 2:468
Working Woman (periodical), 2:572
Workingman's School, 3:1009
Workingmen's Party, 3:789
Workmen's Circle, 2:502
Workplace contractualism, 2:628
Works Progress Administration (WPA), 2:586, 591–592; 3:1124
    Federal Theatre, 1:161
    opposition to, 3:1125–1126
    See also New Deal
World Anti-Slavery Convention (1840), 1:290, 319
World Bank, 4:1458
World Conference Against Racism, 1:255
World Economic Fund, 4:1459
World Trade Organization (WTO)
    AFL-CIO opposition to, 2:659
    Clinton's support for, 2:656
    founding and purpose, 4:1458–1459, 1482–1483
    objections to, 4:1483–1486
    protests, 4:1460–1462
    See also Battle of Seattle
World War I
    African Americans and, 1:139–141, 158, 164
    anti-preparedness movement, 3:1060–1063
    antiwar movement, 3:1044–1046, 1064–1072
    civil liberties, 3:1073–1076

World War I (continued)
    conscientious objectors, 3:1045–1046, 1071
    labor movement, 2:517–518
    labor strikes after, 2:518
    Liberty Bonds, 2:702–703
    Native Americans and, 2:702–703
    pacifism before, 3:1042–1044
    and Pan-Indianism movement, 2:732–733
    peace movement, 3:1044–1045
    poverty after, 3:1122
    racism and ethnocentrism, 3:1121–1122
    sedition arrests, 3:1045, 1074–1075
    veterans' Bonus March, 2:563, 590
    white backlash after, 1:222–223
    wildcat strikes, 2:675–677
World War II
    African Americans and, 1:164–165
    antiwar movement, 3:1077–1079
    Congress of Industrial Organizations and, 2:609–610
    conscientious objectors, 3:1048–1050
    job discrimination, 2:677
    labor movement after, 2:624–626
    Mexican Americans and, 4:1212–1213
    nonwhite veterans, 4:1206–1027
    pacifism, 3:1048
    and Pan-Indianism movement, 2:732–733
    railroad workers movement during, 2:540–541
    white backlash during and after, 1:223–224
    wildcat strikes, 2:677–678
    women and, 2:368–369
World Wide Web. See Internet
World's Columbian Exposition (1893), 1:334
World's Parliament of Religions (1893), 3:921, 1030
World's Temperance Convention (1853), 3:866
Wounded Knee Legal Defense/Offense Committee, 2:714
Wounded Knee massacre (1890), 2:752–753
Wounded Knee siege (1973), 2:711–715, 727
    See also Pine Ridge reservation
Wovoka, 3:934
WPA. See Works Progress Administration
Wright, Elizur, Jr., 1:25
Wright, Fielding, 1:170

Wright, Frances, **1:**287; **3:**970
Wright, Hamilton, **3:**872
Wright, Henry B., **3:**908
Wright, Lucy, **3:**970
Wright, Moses, **1:**176–177
Wright, Richard, **1:**162
WTO. *See* World Trade Organization
Wurf, Jerry, **2:**641
Wurtzel, Elizabeth, **2:**432
WWW. *See* Internet
Wye River plantation, **1:**72

X

Xicanisma. See Latina feminism

Y

Yablonski, Joseph, **2:**634
Yanovsky, Saul, **2:**501
Yellow Thunder, Raymond, **2:**709, 727

Yellow Thunder Camp, **2:**722, 729
Yippies, **3:**1087, 1092
YMCA. *See* Young Men's Christian Association
Yoga, **3:**936
Yogananda, Paramahansa, **3:**952
Young, Andrew, **1:**191
Young, Brigham, **3:**931
Young, Coleman, **1:**169
Young, William F., **2:**470
Young Americans for Freedom, **4:**1389
Young Bear, Severt, **2:**716
Young Communist League, **1:**164; **2:**573
Young Lords, **3:**1130–1131
Young Men's Christian Association (YMCA), **3:**963, 966–968
Young Pioneer (magazine), **2:**573
Young Pioneers of America, **2:**573
Young Republican National Federation, **4:**1391–1392
Young Women's Christian Association (YWCA), **2:**365; **3:**966–968

Young Worker (periodical), **2:**573
Young Workers League. *See* Young Communist League
Youngstown Sheet and Tube Company, **2:**635, 653
Youth for Christ, **3:**950
Youth International Party, **3:**1087
Yucca Mountain, **2:**746
YWCA. *See* Young Women's Christian Association

Z

Zapatistas, **4:**1460
Zen Buddhism, **3:**936, 953, 1030, 1031
Zen Center, San Francisco, **3:**1031
Zero Population Growth, **4:**1276
Zia, Helen, **4:**1220
Zinoviev, Gregory, **2:**571
Zion City, **3:**1004
Zoar Society, **3:**1001

BIOGRAPHICAL INDEX

A

Abbey, Edward, **4:**1280
Abbott, Grace, **2:**364
Abern, Martin, **2:**573
Abernathy, Ralph David, **1:**197, 200; **3:**1088
Abraham, Spencer, **1:**247
Abu-Jamal, Mumia, **1:**218
Abzug, Bella, **4:**1326
Acosta, Oscar Zeta, **2:**754; **4:**1214, 1217
Acuña, Rodolfo, **4:**1214
Adams, Abigail, **1:**294
Adams, Ansel, **4:**1269
Adams, Hannah, **3:**1029
Addams, Jane, **3:**1142
    activism of, **2:**366
    and anti-imperialism, **1:**342
    "Democracy or Militarism," **1:**343
    Hull House, **1:**317, 337; **2:**366; **3:**1141
    and peace movement, **3:**1044, 1067–1068
    and trade unions, **1:**348; **3:**890
    Why Women Should Vote (1915), **1:**303
Adler, Felix, **3:**1007–1011
Agee, James, **3:**1124
Agnew, Spiro T., **3:**1130
Ahmanson, Howard, **4:**1404
Aird, George, **2:**715
Alcott, William A., **3:**1015
Alexander, Will W., **1:**131
Ali, Muhammad, **3:**1088
Allen, Pam, **2:**401
Allen, Richard, **1:**15, 81; **3:**930
Ambrose, Myles, **3:**874
Ames, Jessie Daniel, **1:**132, 134; **2:**366
Anderson, Marian, **1:**164
Anderson, Mary, **1:**348; **2:**362, 369
Andrus, Ethel Percy, **4:**1241
Anslinger, Harry J., **3:**873
Anthony, Aaron, **1:**72
Anthony, Susan B., **1:**263, 266, 273, 298
    on anti-imperialism, **1:**343

Anthony, Susan B. *(continued)*
    attempt to vote, **1:**297, 298
    relationship with Stanton, **1:**296–297
    and temperance movement, **1:**298; **3:**866
    and woman suffrage, **1:**276, 296–299, 320
Anzaldua, Gloria, **2:**411
Appuzzo, Virginia, **4:**1346
Aptheker, Herbert, **2:**530
Aquash, Anna Mae Pictou, **2:**722
Arnall, Ellis, **1:**166
Ashbrook, John, **4:**1395
Ashwood, Amy, **1:**148
Astin, Helen, **2:**415
Auld, Hugh, **1:**73
Auld, Thomas, **1:**73, 74
Austin, Alice Constance, **1:**289
Austin, Harriet N., **1:**269
Austin, James T., **1:**50
Axelrod, Beverly, **1:**232

B

Bad Heart Bull, John Wesley, **2:**711
Bad Heart Bull, Sarah, **2:**712
Bagley, Sarah, **2:**467, 470
Bai, Jane, **1:**254
Bailey, Gamaliel, **1:**28–29, 63
Bailey, Hannah, **1:**344
Bailey, Harriet, **1:**72
Baker, Ella Josephine, **1:**180, 181, 182
Baker, Helen, **4:**1230
Bakke, Allen, **1:**215
Baldwin, Clarence Benham, **1:**166
Baldwin, Robert, **3:**1011
Baldwin, Tammy, **4:**1357
Ballanger, Pat, **2:**707
Ballinger, Richard A., **4:**1290
Banks, Dennis, **2:**707, 708
    at AIM trials, **2:**715
    as a fugitive, **2:**714–715

Banks, Dennis *(continued)*
    Longest Walk, **2:**722
    retirement from AIM, **2:**722
    at Wounded Knee, **2:**712, 714
Banneker, Benjamin, **1:**83
Baraka, Amiri, **1:**212
Barnett, Ross, **1:**185
Barry, Marion, **1:**182
Bascom, John, **3:**957
Bates, Daisy, **1:**180, 224
Bates, Katherine Lee, **1:**343
Bauer, Gary, **4:**1404
Bauman, Robert E., **4:**1393
Baumgardner, Jennifer, **2:**431
Beach, Henry L. (Mike), **4:**1441
Beecher, Catherine, **1:**286; **3:**948
Beecher, Henry Ward, **1:**297; **3:**957
Beecher, Lyman, **1:**51; **3:**948
Beecroft, Carol, **4:**1380
Beissel, Johann Conrad, **3:**998
Belknap, Jeremy, **3:**941
Bellamy, Edward, **3:**957, 1120, 1135
Benezet, Anthony, **1:**8
Benjamin, Herbert, **2:**585, 591
Bennett, Anne, **4:**1230
Bentley, Elizabeth, **2:**578; **4:**1412
Benton, Thomas Hart, **2:**489
Berger, Victor, **2:**569; **3:**1074
Bergh, Henry, **4:**1311
Berkman, Alexander, **2:**501, 503; **3:**1075
Berrigan, Daniel, **3:**1057
Berrigan, Philip, **3:**1057
Betha, Rainey, **2:**388–389
Bethune, Mary McLeod, **1:**160, 161; **2:**361, 367
Bevel, Diane Nash. *See* Nash, Diane
Bevel, James, **1:**182, 187
Biafra, Jello, **3:**850
Bias, Len, **3:**876
Biberman, Herbert, **2:**690
Biko, Steve, **1:**236
Birney, James G., **1:**25, 53, 64

Bisno, Abraham, **2**:485–486
Bissonette, Pedro, **2**:716
Bittelman, Alexander, **2**:570
Black, Algernon D., **3**:1011–1012
Blackwell, Antoinette, **1**:297
Blackwell, Henry Brown, **1**:273, 297, 300
Blades, Joan, **3**:1102
Blake, Lillie Devereux, **1**:276, 341
Blatch, Harriot Stanton, **1**:301; **3**:1044
Bloomer, Amelia, **1**:263, 269
Blyden, Edward Wilmont, **1**:113–114
Bohr, Niels, **4**:1293
Boland, Edward, **4**:1362
Bonfield, John, **2**:484
Bonnin, Gertrude, **2**:703
Bonnin, Raymond T., **2**:703
Bookchin, Murray, **4**:1320
Booker, Cory, **1**:251, 252
Booth, Heather, **2**:400
Bork, Robert, **1**:221
Borsodi, Ralph, **3**:1005
Bosacker, Steven, **4**:1359
Boudinot, Elias, **2**:699
Boyd, Norma, **2**:389
Boyd, Wes, **3**:1102
Boyle, Tony, **2**:634
Bradley, James R., **1**:69
Bradley, Mamie Till, **1**:176
Brainerd, Dave, **3**:928
Brand, Stewart, **4**:1318–1319
Brandeis, Louis, **3**:1010
Brayman, Brandon, **4**:1381
Brazile, Donna, **4**:1346
Breitman, George, **2**:591
Bresee, Phineas F., **3**:950
Brewer, Duane, **2**:715–716, 717
Breyer, Stephen G., **1**:247
Bridges, Harry, **2**:564, 593, 594
Brigade, Jeanette Rankin, **2**:436
Briggs, Cyril B., **1**:131; **2**:570
Briggs, John, **4**:1364
Bright, Bill, **3**:950
Brisbane, Albert, **1**:287
Brophy, John, **2**:605–606
Broughton, Virginia, **1**:331
Browder, Earl, **2**:575, 577
Brown, Charlotte Emerson, **2**:361
Brown, Clara, **2**:467, 471
Brown, Dee, **2**:707
Brown, H. Rap, **1**:199
Brown, Jerry, **2**:714
Brown, John, **1**:58–60, 66, 94
　　Garrison's support for, **3**:1042
　　meeting with Frederick Douglass, **1**:77
Brown, Judith, **2**:425, 441
Brown, Oliver, **1**:174

Brown, Rita Mae, **2**:441
Brown, William Wells, **1**:33, 36–38, 41
Brownmiller, Susan, **2**:437, 446
Bruce, Lenny, **3**:850
Brundage, Avery, **1**:163
Bryan, William Jennings, **3**:793
Bryant, Anita, **3**:852; **4**:1362
Bryant, Carolyn, **1**:176
Bryant, Roy, **1**:176–177
Buchanan, Patrick, **3**:1135
Buchman, Frank, **3**:908, 911
Buckley, William, **4**:1389, 1390
Budenz, Louis F., **2**:601
Buff, I.E., **2**:646–647, 648
Bukharin, Nikolai, **2**:575
Bullard, Robert, **4**:1300
Bulter, Dino, **2**:719
Bunche, Ralph, **1**:169
Bundy, Ted, **3**:849
Bunting, Mary, **2**:415
Burger, Warren, **1**:213
Burks, Mary Fair, **1**:178
Burleson, Albert S., **3**:1074
Burn, Febb Ensminger, **1**:307
Burn, Harry, **1**:307
Burns, Anthony, **1**:93
Burns, Lucy, **2**:361
Burnside, John, **4**:1335
Burritt, Elihu, **3**:1041
Burroughs, Nannie Helen, **1**:331
Bush, George H.W.
　　and 1991 Civil Rights Act, **1**:244
　　anti-abortion stance, **3**:847
Bush, George W.
　　antiwar caricatures, **3**:1103
　　and governmental racial diversity, **1**:247
　　and Log Cabin Republicans, **4**:1351
　　refusal to attend World Conference Against Racism, **1**:255
　　War on Terror, **3**:1058
Bushnell, Horace, **1**:296; **3**:957
Butler, Benjamin, **1**:39
Butler, Elizabeth, **2**:699
Butler, Richard G., **4**:1442
Byrd, Harry, **3**:1125
Byrd, James, **1**:134, 242

C

Cabet, Etienne, **3**:973, 1002–1003
Calhoun, Arthur W., **2**:599, 601
Calhoun, John C., **1**:99–100, 101
Calhoun, Patrick, **3**:762
Call, Hal, **4**:1336
Calvin, John, **3**:886–887, 938, 942

Camp, Carter, **2**: 713, 714
Camp, Ellen Moves, **2**:716
Cannon, James P., **2**:571, 574, 575
Cannon, Joseph, **4**:1290
Carey, James, **2**:614
Carey, Ron, **2**:668, 669
Carlin, George, **3**:850
Carmichael, Stokely, **1**:198, 231; **2**:400, 706
Carnegie, Andrew, **2**:543–544
Carney, William H., **1**:40
Carson, Rachel, **4**:1273–1274
Carter, Jimmy, **3**:835–837
　　and civil rights movement, **1**:214–215
　　and gay/lesbian relations, **4**:1345, 1358
Carus, Paul, **3**:1030
Cary, Lott, **1**:14
Cary, Samuel F., **3**:788–789
Castillo, Ana, **2**:410
Catt, Carrie Chapman, **1**:299, 301–308, 321; **2**:361–362
　　clash with Alice Paul, **2**:373
　　and the peace movement, **3**:1044, 1047
Chamberlain, Neville, **1**:164
Chambers, Whittaker, **2**:578
Chandler, Elizabeth, **1**:54
Chaney, James, **1**:134, 192, 216
Chao, Elaine, **1**:247
Chaplin, Ralph H., **2**:687
Charney, George Blake, **2**:576
Chase, Salmon P., **1**:28–29, 63
Chauncy, Charles, **3**:940
Chavez, Cesar, **2**:683; **3**:830–834, 1131; **4**:1206, 1216
Chavez-Thompson, Linda, **2**:653, 655, 659
Chief Fools Crow, **2**:716
Chief Mitchell, **2**:736
Chief Red Cloud, **2**:749, 750, 752
Chief Spotted Tail, **2**:750
Chief Tammany, **2**:740
Child, Lydia Maria, **2**:699
Chin, Vincent, **2**:653
Chivington, John, **2**:749
Chmielewski, Florian, **4**:1362
Chodorov, Frank, **4**:1388–1389, 1390
Chubb, Percival, **3**:1011
Churchill, Ward, **2**:746
Cinque, Joseph, **1**:92
Clapp, Moses A., **2**:700
Clark, Jim, **1**:193
Clark, Mark, **1**:203; **3**:1131
Clarke, Edward, **1**:312
Clay, Edward W., **1**:50
Cleaver, Eldridge, **1**:231–233
Clement, Victor, **2**:494

Clinton, Bill
  apology for slavery, **1:**247
  attempted impeachment, **3:**856
  and governmental diversity, **1:**246–247; **4:**1358
  National Dialogue on Race, **1:**255
  and "New Democrats," **4:**1388
Cloud, Henry Roe, **2:**703
Cloward, Richard, **3:**1131
Coffee, Linda, **2:**381
Cohen, Julius, **3:**1010
Cohn, Fannia, **1:**347
Coit, Stanton, **3:**1009
Colburn, Marshal Wayne, **2:**715
Colby, Josephine, **2:**599
Coleman, Norm, **4:**1370
Coler, Jack, **2:**717, 718
Coll, Tom, **2:**718
Collier, John, **2:**703, 704
Collins, Patricia Hill, **2:**410
Commerford, John, **2:**469
Commoner, Barry, **4:**1275
Comstock, Anthony, **1:**277; **2:**353; **3:**862–863
Conn, Billy, **1:**162
Connor, Eugene "Bull," **1:**183, 185, 187, 206
Conyers, John, **1:**245
Cook, Cara, **2:**599
Cook, Mary, **1:**331
Cooley, Harris R., **4:**1238
Coolidge, Calvin, **2:**559, 639
Coolidge, Sherman, **2:**701
Cooper, Anna Julia, **1:**333, 334
Cooper, Peter, **3:**788–789
Cornish, Samuel, **1:**14, 22, 68, 69, 84, 85, 98
Costigan, Edward, **1:**134
Coughlin, Charles E., **4:**1240
Couzins, Phoebe, **1:**276
Covey, Edward, **1:**73
Coward, Fred, **2:**720
Cox, James R., **2:**590
Coxey, Jacob, **3:**1120–1121
Craddock, Ida, **3:**862
Craig, Minnie D., **3:**806
Crane, Frederick, **2:**354
Crazy Horse, **2:**751
Croly, Jane, **1:**313; **2:**361
Crooks, Lynn, **2:**721
Crosswaith, Frank, **1:**154
Crow Dog, Leonard, **2:**709, 714
Crummell, Alexander, **1:**34, 69
Cuffee, Paul, **1:**13, 83
Cullen, William, **3:**991
Cumbie, Rev. J.T., **3:**798–801
Cushing, Ned, **4:**1392

Custer, George Armstrong, **2:**751
Cuthbertson, Polly, **4:**1230
Cutting, Nathaniel, **1:**10–11

D

Dahlgren, Mrs., **1:**276
Dalai Lama, **3:**1032
Daley, Richard, **1:**197, 198, 203; **4:**1187–1188
Daly, Jo, **4:**1359
Daniels, Newell, **2:**475
Darrow, Clarence, **2:**496
Darwin, Charles, **3:**899, 956
Davenport, Charles B., **3:**900
Davis, Adelle, **3:**1017
Davis, Angela, **1:**214
Davis, Benjamin, **1:**171; **2:**572
Davis, David, **2:**475
Davis, Elizabeth Gould, **2:**443
Davis, Gray, **1:**250; **4:**1359
Davis, Henrietta Vinton, **1:**149
Davis, Madeline, **4:**1345
Davis, Paulina Wright, **1:**296
Davis, Rebecca Harding, **2:**690
Davis, Varina, **1:**343–344
Dawes, Henry, **2:**700
De Beauvoir, Simone, **2:**370, 391
De Caux, Len, **2:**597
De Gouges, Olympe, **1:**287
De Leon, Daniel, **2:**525, 527, 528; **3:**796
De Saint Simon, Henri, **1:**287
De Witt, Benjamin Park, **3:**881
Debs, Eugene, **1:**145; **2:**535, 569, 618; **3:**796
  and Industrial Workers of the World, **2:**495, 496
  sedition arrest, **3:**1074–1075
Decker, Sara, **3:**859
DeCora, Angel, **2:**701
Dedwell, John, **3:**867
Delany, Martin R., **1:**30–34, 38, 67, 68
  on Abraham Lincoln, **1:**37
  agriculture in Africa, **1:**70
  as Civil War recruiter, **1:**42–43
  on danger to blacks, **1:**36
  in Harvard, **1:**69
Dellinger, David, **3:**1049, 1079
Deloria, Vine, Jr., **2:**707, 726
Dennett, Mary Ware, **1:**323–324; **2:**354
Dennis, Peggy, **2:**575–576
Depugh, Robert, **4:**1440–1441
Des Verney, W.H., **1:**153
DeSersa, Byron, **2:**716
Detwiller, Henry, **3:**990
Detzer, Dorothy, **3:**1047
DeVos family, **4:**1404

Dew, Thomas Roderick, **1:**99
Dewson, Mary Williams, **2:**367
Dharmapala, Anagarika, **3:**1030
Diallo, Amadou, **1:**242
Dibble, C.H., **3:**814–816
Dickinson, Robert, **2:**356
Dies, Martin, **3:**1125
Diggs, Charles, **1:**212
Dilling, Elizabeth, **4:**1411
Dinkins, David, **1:**218
Dirksen, Everett, **1:**190
Dixon, Joseph, **2:**702
Doar, John, **1:**185
Dobson, James, **3:**850; **4:**1402, 1404–1405
Dodge, David Low, **3:**1041
Doherty, Clay, **4:**1347
Dohrn, Bernadine, **4:**1196
Dole, Robert, **1:**250; **3:**837
Dole, Vincent, **3:**877
Donaghey, George W., **1:**125
Donahue, Thomas, **2:**653
Donnelly, Ignatius, **3:**792
Donnerstein, Edward, **3:**849
Dotson, Donald, **2:**651
Douglas, H. Ford, **1:**41, 69
Douglas, Satirra, **1:**44
Douglass, Frederick, **1:**30, 58
  biography, **1:**72–79
  and black economics, **1:**118
  at National Convention of Colored Men, **1:**87
  support of temperance, **3:**866
  and women's rights, **1:**118, 294
Dowie, John Alexander, **3:**1004
Downer, Carol, **2:**405
Drake, Jennifer, **2:**432
Draper, Alonzo B., **2:**471
Du Bois, W.E.B., **1:**119–120, 129–130
  arrest of, **1:**170–171
  biography, **1:**137
  The Crisis, **1:**136, 137, 139, 146
  and Harlem Renaissance, **1:**145–146
  and NAACP, **1:**136, 141
  and Pan-Africanism, **1:**144–145
  response to black repression, **1:**228
  rivalry with Garvey, **1:**144
  on self-defense, **1:**223
  support of birth control, **2:**358
Dubinsky, David, **2:**548, 605
Dukakis, Michael, **1:**220
Duke, David, **4:**1440
Dull Knife, Guy, **2:**716
Duncan, Donald, **3:**1090
Dunne, Ray, **2:**564
Dunne, Vincent Raymond, **2:**593, 594
Durant, Paul Skyhorse, **2:**715

Durazo, Maria Elena, **2:**671–673
Durham, Jimmie, **2:**713, 722
Duss, John, **3:**1001
Dworkin, Andrea, **3:**849
Dyer, Leonidas, **1:**130
Dylan, Bob, **3:**1087

E

Eagle, Jimmy, **2:**716, 718, 719
Eason, James, **1:**149
Eastland, James, **1:**183
Eastman, Charles, **2:**701, 703
Eastman, George, **3:**901
Eastman, Max, **2:**571
Ebens, Ronald, **2:**653
Echohawk, John, **2:**727
Echols, Alice, **2:**437
Eckford, Elizabeth, **1:**180
Eddy, Mary Baker, **3:**934
Edelstadt, David, **2:**501
Edelman, Marian Wright, **3:**1135
Edwards, Jonathan, **3:**927–928, 940, 941–942
Ehrlich, Paul, **3:**1018; **4:**1276
Einsiedel, Edna, **3:**849
Eisenhower, Dwight, **4:**1391–1392
Eliot, John, **2:**697
Ellen, Jane, **4:**1380
Elliot, John Lovejoy, **3:**1010–1011
Ellis, Havelock, **4:**1246–1247
Ellison, Ralph, **1:**228
Ellsberg, Daniel, **3:**1094–1095
Ely, Richard, **3:**884, 960
Emerson, Ralph Waldo, **3:**936, 943, 1007, 1029
Engel, George, **2:**499, 500
Engels, Friedrich, **2:**480
English, William, **2:**469
Ensler, Eve, **2:**450
Epstein, Abraham, **4:**1240
Erdrich, Louise, **2:**754–755
Ettor, Joseph, **2:**529, 530
Evan, Thomas, **3:**1079
Evans, George Henry, **2:**469, 470
Evans, Hiram, **4:**1437
Evers, Medgar, **1:**184, 185

F

Fairfax, Francis, **4:**1380
Fall, Albert, **2:**703
Faludi, Susan, **2:**433
Falwell, Jerry, **3:**855, 856; **4:**1400, 1402
    post–World War II, **2:**370
    Religious Right and, **3:**852
Fard, Wallace D., **1:**145, 229; **3:**935–936

Farrakhan, Louis, **1:**230, 241, 242–243; **4:**1210
Father Divine, **3:**953–954, 1005
Faubus, Orval, **1:**180
Fauntroy, Walter E., **3:**1104
Fauset, Crystal Bird, **2:**367
Fee, John G., **1:**59
Feinstein, Dianne, **3:**855
Feldman, Sandra, **2:**641
Ferebee, Dorothy, **2:**389
Ferringer, Harold Price, **3:**856
Fetterman, William, **2:**749
Field, James G., **3:**791–792
Fielden, Samuel, **2:**499, 500
Fields, Mamie, **1:**335
Filene, A. Lincoln, **3:**1010
Fincke, Helen, **2:**596
Fincke, William, **2:**596
Finkbine, Sherri, **2:**380
Finney, Charles Grandison, **3:**929–930, 944
Firestone, Shulamith, **2:**401, 425, 427
Fischer, Adolph, **2:**499, 500
Fishbein, Morris, **3:**996
Fitzhugh, George, **1:**99
Fitzpatrick, John, **2:**544, 574
Flaxer, Abram, **2:**639
Flexner, Abraham, **3:**995–996
Flynn, Elizabeth Gurley, **1:**346; **2:**530
Ford, Gerald, **4:**1395
Ford, Henry, **4:**1420
Ford, James W., **2:**572
Ford, Patrick, **2:**482
Foreman, Dave, **4:**1280
Forman, James, **1:**191, 200–201
Forsberg, Randall, **4:**1296
Forten, Charlotte, **1:**44
Forten, James, **1:**13, 14, 22, 84
Fortune, T. Thomas, **1:**114, 128, 222
Foster, Abigail Kelley. *See* Kelley, Abigail
Foster, Jim, **4:**1345
Foster, William Z., **2:**544, 571, 574, 575
Foucault, Michel, **4:**1329
Fourier, Charles, **1:**287; **3:**972, 1002
Frankfurter, Felix, **1:**174
Frankhauser, Roy, **4:**1441
Franklin, Benjamin
    founding of abolition society, **1:**7
    and image of Native Americans, **2:**739
    on limiting growth of slaves, **1:**8
Fraser, Doug, **2:**651–652
French, Eleanor, **4:**1230
Frick, Henry Clay, **2:**501, 543
Friedan, Betty, **2:**398
    The Feminine Mystique, **2:**398, 400, 422
Friedman, Molly, **2:**553
Froebel, Friedrich, **1:**285

Frohnmeyer, John, **3:**851
Frye, Phyllis, **4:**1381
Fulbright, J. William, **3:**1088
Fuller, Ida M., **4:**1241
Fulton, Charles W., **4:**1290

G

Gage, Matilda Joslyn
    family influences on, **1:**272–273
    focus of, **1:**273
    and the National Citizen and Ballot Box, **1:**274–275
    at Syracuse Convention of 1852, **1:**272
    unity and reformer division, **1:**273–274
    and woman suffrage, **1:**273–277, 296, 297, 299
Gale, William Potter, **4:**1441
Galleani, Luigi, **2:**580, 581
Galton, Francis, **3:**899–900
Gandhi, Mohandas, **1:**166, 202, 204, 208; **3:**1047
Gardner, Gerald, **3:**955
Garfield, James R., **4:**1289
Garland, Hamlin, **3:**883
Garner, Fred, **3:**1090
Garnet, Henry Highland, **1:**28, 42, 52, 58, 66–67, 68
Garrison, Althea, **4:**1357
Garrison, William Lloyd, **1:**4, 20–25, 29–31, 48–51, 89
    bounty on, **1:**99
    free blacks' support for, **1:**86
    and pacifism, **3:**1041
    support of Harpers Ferry raid, **3:**1042
    support of temperance, **3:**866
Garvey, Amy Jacques, **1:**150
Garvey, Marcus
    demise of, **1:**145, 149–150, 159, 228
    later years, **1:**150
    response to black repression, **1:**228
    rivalry with Du Bois, **1:**144
    and Universal Negro Improvement Association, **1:**143–144, 148–150, 159, 228
Garvin, W.L., **3:**783
Gary, Elbert, **2:**544
Gaskin, Stephen, **3:**1005, 1026
Gates, Darryl, **1:**216
Gehlke, Charles Elmer, **4:**1230
George, Henry, **2:**487; **3:**957, 1003, 1118–1119
Gerber, Henry, **4:**1331, 1332
Germer, Adolph, **2:**605
Gerry, Elbridge T., **4:**1311
Gibbs, Lois, **4:**1275, 1302
Gibson, Gideon, **3:**762

Gibson, Kenneth, **1:**251
Giger, H.R., **3:**850
Gilchrist, Robert, **2:**474
Gildersleeve, Virginia, **2:**363
Giles, Harriet, **1:**330
Gilman, Caroline Howard, **1:**287, 288, 289
Gingrich, Newt, **4:**1398–1399
Ginsberg, Allen, **3:**1031, 1032
Ginsburg, Ruth Bader, **1:**247
Giovannitti, Arturo, **2:**529, 530
Gitlow, Ben, **2:**574, 578
Gitlow, Kate, **2:**572
Gittings, Barbara, **4:**1338, 1339
Giuffrida, Louis O., **2:**717
Giuliani, Rudolph, **3:**856
Gladden, Washington, **3:**957, 958, 959, 960
Goddard, Dwight, **3:**1005
Goddard, Henry, **3:**900; **4:**1247
Goldbert, Art, **4:**1179, 1180, 1181
Goldbert, Jackie, **4:**1179, 1180
Goldman, Emma, **1:**343; **2:**354, 501
    deportation of, **2:**503; **3:**1075
    on prostitution, **3:**860
Goldmark, Josephine, **1:**338
Goldwater, Barry, **3:**874, 1128;
    4:1392–1393
Gompers, Samuel, **1:**324; **2:**509
    and Knights of Labor, **2:**510
    on labor violence, **2:**507
    support for Haymarket leaders, **2:**485
    trade unionism, **3:**887–888
    and welfare reform, **3:**889
Gonzales, Rodolfo "Corky," **4:**1214–1215
Gonzalez, Henry B., **4:**1210
Goode, Wilson, **1:**216
Gooding, James Henry, **1:**39–40
Goodman, Andrew, **1:**134, 192, 216
Gore, Al, **4:**1346
Gore, Tipper, **3:**850
Gottlieb, Lou, **3:**1005, 1024
Gould, Jay, **2:**483
Graham, Billy, **3:**951
Graham, Sylvester, **1:**281; **3:**1015
Gram, Hans, **1:**281; **3:**990
Grant, Madison, **3:**901
Grant, Ulysses S., **1:**78
Graves, Henry, **4:**1291
Gray, John F., **1:**281
Green, Alfred M., **1:**38
Green, Beriah, **1:**64
Green, William, **1:**156; **2:**559, 560
Greer, Germaine, **2:**403
Gregg, Richard, **3:**1047
Gregory, Dick, **3:**1018
Grew, Mary, **1:**56
Griffin, David, **3:**916

Griffin, Marvin, **1:**180
Griffin, Susan, **2:**445
Griffith, D.W., **1:**138–139; **4:**1435
Griffiths, Julia, **1:**77
Griffiths, Martha, **2:**415
Grimké, Angelina, **1:**22, 23, 24, 56, 263;
    3:1042
Grimké, Sarah, **1:**22, 56, 263
Grinde, Donald, **2:**746
Grinnell, George, **4:**1267
Gritz, James, **4:**1444
Grossup, Peter, **2:**590
Guiliani, Carlo, **4:**1467
Guinier, Lani, **1:**246, 253
Guthrie, Woody, **2:**689
Gutierrez, José Angel, **4:**1215

H

Haber, Robert Alan, **4:**1173
Hagerty, Thomas J., **2:**526
Hahnemann, Samuel, **1:**281; **3:**991
Haig, Alexander, **2:**712
Hall, Tony, **1:**245
Hamer, Fannie Lou Townsend, **1:**191, 192
Hamilton, Alexander, **3:**763
Hamilton, Alice, **3:**890; **4:**1258–1259, 1260
Hamilton, Robert, **1:**44
Hamilton, Thomas, **1:**59
Hamilton, William, **1:**69
Hammond, James Henry, **1:**99
Hammond, John Jays, **2:**494
Hampton, Fred, **1:**203, 233; **3:**1131
Hanley, Edward T., **2:**671
Hanna, Kathleen, **2:**432
Hanover, Joe, **1:**306–307
Harding, Warren G., **2:**561
Hare, Leslie, **2:**709
Hare, Melvin, **2:**709
Harper, Frances Ellen Watkins, **1:**68, 329,
    330; **2:**361
Harper, William, **1:**99
Harris, David, **3:**1089
Harrison, Carter, **2:**484, 521
Hartman, George W., **3:**1079
Harvan, George, **2:**691
Hasbrouck, Lydia Sayer, **1:**271
Hastie, William, **1:**169
Hatcher, Richard, **1:**212
Hawley, Nancy, **2:**404
Hay, Harry, **3:**845; **4:**1334–1336
Hayakawa, S.I., **1:**213
Hayden, Casey, **2:**392, 400, 436
Hayden, Tom, **4:**1174, 11745
Hayes, Rutherford B., **1:**78
Hayes, Ted, **3:**1155

Haywood, Harry, **2:**572
Haywood, William D. (Big Bill), **2:**495,
    496, 526, 527, 532
Hazard, Rowland, **3:**909
Hechler, Ken, **2:**646–647
Heighton, William, **2:**469
Held, Richard G., **2:**715, 719
Helms, J. Lynn, **2:**662
Helms, Jesse, **3:**851, 855; **4:**1353
Helms, Mary, **4:**1364
Hemenway, Augustus, **4:**1267
Herberg, Will, **2:**578; **3:**935
Hering, Constantine, **3:**990
Herndon, Angelo, **2:**572; **3:**1123
Hershey, Lewis B., **3:**1089
Heywood, Leslie, **2:**432
Higginson, Thomas Wentworth, **1:**66
Hill, Anita, **1:**221; **2:**395
Hill, David B., **2:**486
Hill, Herbert, **2:**632
Hill, Joe, **2:**531, 687
Hillard, Earl, **1:**253
Hillman, Sidney, **2:**609
Hillquit, Morris, **2:**569
Hine, Lewis, **2:**691; **3:**1121
Hitchcock, Ethan Allen, **4:**1265
Hobby, Oveta Culp, **2:**368
Hocking, William Ernest, **3:**964
Hodge, Evan, **2:**720–721
Hofstadter, Richard, **3:**783
Holbrook, M.L., **3:**1016
Holder, Stan, **2:**714
Holley, Myron, **1:**25, 53
Holmes, Oliver Wendell, **3:**902, 992, 1075
Holtzman, Elizabeth, **2:**449
Honkala, Cheri, **3:**1138
Hooker, Evelyn, **4:**1339
Hooker, Worthington, **3:**993
hooks, bell, **2:**410, 420
Hoover, Edgar J., **1:**188; **2:**563; **3:**845, 1145
Hope, Lugenia Burns, **3:**1143
Hopkins, Harry, **3:**811–812, 1125
Horton, Willie, **1:**220
Hough, Franklin, **4:**1286
Hourwich, Nicholas, **2:**570
Houser, George, **1:**208
Houston, Charles Hamilton, **1:**162, 163,
    174; **2:**541
Howard, Perry, **1:**155
Howe, Florence, **2:**416
Howe, Julia Ward, **1:**297, 313, 344; **3:**1044
Howe, Samuel Gridley, **4:**1246
Hubbard, Elbert, **3:**1005
Huerta, Dolores, **2:**411; **3:**830–834
Huie, William, **1:**177
Humphrey, Hubert, **1:**192; **3:**1088

Hunt, H.L., **4:**1399
Hunt, James, **4:**1302–1303
Hunter, David, **1:**39
Hunter, Jane Edna, **1:**334
Huntington, Emily, **1:**285
Hunton, Addie W., **1:**301
Husband, Herman, **3:**761
Hutchenson, William L., **2:**559–560
Hutchinson, Dorothy, **3:**1079

I

Innis, Roy, **1:**211
Izumazaki, James, **4:**1207

J

Jack, James, **1:**334
Jackson, Andrew, **1:**38, 50, 99–100, 279
Jackson, Aunt Molly, **2:**688
Jackson, George, **1:**214
Jackson, James Caleb, **1:**269, 270; **3:**1015
Jackson, Jesse, **1:**218, 219, 220, 241; **4:**1300
Jackson, Jimmie Lee, **1:**193
Jackson, Vic, **2:**717
James, Sharpe, **1:**251, 252
Janklow, William, **2:**714–715, 718
Jarrico, Paul, **2:**690
Jefferson, Thomas, **1:**3, 10–11; **2:**698
Jenkins, Alvin, **3:**835–838
Jenkins, Maxine, **2:**641
Jennings, Herbert, **3:**903
Jensen, Arthur, **3:**904
Jiménez, Rosie, **2:**430
Johansen, Bruce, **2:**746
Johns, Barbara, **1:**174
Johnson, Andrew, **1:**255
Johnson, Charles S., **1:**146
Johnson, Gary, **3:**876
Johnson, Jack, **1:**162
Johnson, James Weldon, **1:**130, 139, 146
Johnson, Lyndon, **1:**190–193, 194; **3:**1128–1129
Jones, Absalom, **1:**81
Jones, Aphrodite, **4:**1381
Jones, Beverly, **2:**425, 441
Jones, Jesse Henry, **2:**522; **3:**957
Jones, Jim, **3:**954
Jones, Mary Harris (Mother Jones), **2:**510
Jordan, David Starr, **3:**901
Jorgenson, Christine, **4:**1380

K

Kagi, John Henry, **1:**66
Kameny, Franklin, **4:**1326, 1339, 1340

Kane, Ari, **4:**1381
Kanka, Megan, **3:**853
Kant, Immanuel, **3:**1007
Karpman, Benjamin, **3:**848
Kaufman, Paul, **2:**647
Kefauver, Estes, **3:**848
Kelley, Abigail, **1:**25, 30, 52, 64
Kelley, Florence, **1:**317–319, 338; **2:**364
Kelley, Oliver Hudson, **3:**777–778
Kellogg, James Harvey, **3:**1016, 1017
Kellogg, W.K., **3:**1017
Kellor, Frances, **1:**331
Kelly, Clarence, **2:**719–720
Kendall, Amos, **1:**100
Kennedy, Anthony M., **1:**221, 247; **3:**857; **4:**1326
Kennedy, Florynce, **1:**199, 200; **2:**391
Kennedy, John F.
　　as a Catholic, **4:**1431
　　and civil rights bill, **1:**188
　　and Martin Luther King Jr., **1:**180–181
　　and women's rights, **2:**375, 400
Kennedy, Robert
　　assassination of, **3:**1055
　　and Freedom Rides, **1:**183, 184
Kenngott, Christine, **4:**1347
Kerner, Otto, **1:**198
Kerouac, Jack, **3:**1031
Kerr, Clark, **4:**1178, 1179
Kerry, John, **3:**1090
Kershner, Howard E., **4:**1399
Kilpatrick, Kwame, **1:**252
King, Clennon, **1:**184
King, Martin Luther, Jr., **1:**179
　　in Albany, Georgia, **1:**185, 206
　　and antiwar movement, **3:**1084–1085
　　assassination of, **1:**200, 207, 225; **3:**1055
　　in Birmingham, Alabama, **1:**185–188, 206
　　in Chicago, **1:**197–198
　　and civil rights for the poor, **3:**1127–1129
　　"I Have a Dream" speech, **1:**188, 189
　　"Letter from Birmingham Jail," **1:**186, 187, 229
　　and Montgomery Bus Boycott, **1:**172, 177–178, 204, 209
　　and nonviolent direct action, **1:**178, 179, 206
　　Poor People's Campaign, **2:**641; **3:**1153; **4:**1299
　　popularity of, **1:**188
　　and Selma to Montgomery march, **1:**194

King, Martin Luther, Jr., *(continued)*
　　and Southern Christian Leadership Conference, **1:**179, 180, 185, 204; **3:**1127
King, Mary, **2:**392, 400, 436
King, Matthew, **2:**716
King, Rodney, **1:**242
Kingsley, Bathsheba, **3:**928
Kingston, Maxine Hong, **4:**1220
Kinsey, Alfred, **3:**845
Kirk, Russell, **4:**1388
Kirkland, Lane, **2:**651, 653
Kirkland, Moses, **3:**762
Kirkpatrick, Jean, **3:**915
Kitson, Frank, **2:**717
Klonsky, Mike, **4:**1196
Knox, Henry, **2:**698
Knox, James, **1:**125
Koernke, Mark, **4:**1442
Kolbe, Jim, **4:**1346
Kollias, Karen, **2:**448
Koresh, David, **3:**954
Kozachenko, Kathy, **4:**1357
Kramer, Larry, **4:**1373
Kuhn, Margaret E., **4:**1230, 1231
Kunstler, William, **2:**715, 719

L

LaDuke, Winona, **2:**745
LaHaye, Beverly, **4:**1402
Lancaster, Roy, **1:**153
Lane, Franklin, **2:**702; **4:**1290
Lange, Dorothea, **1:**162
Lappé, Francis, **3:**1018
Largen, Mary Ann, **2:**446
Lasser, David, **2:**585, 591
Lathrop, Julia Clifford, **2:**364
Laughlin, Harry, **3:**902; **4:**1247
Lawson, James, **1:**182
Lea, Luke, **2:**699
Leavitt, Joshua, **1:**52, 63
Lee, Ann, **1:**287; **3:**931–932, 970
Lee, Barbara, **3:**1111
Lee, Bill Lann, **1:**247
Lee, Day Kellogg, **2:**689
Lee, Jarena, **3:**930
Lemlich, Clara, **1:**325; **2:**550
Leopold, Aldo, **4:**1272–1273, 1291
Lester, Peter, **1:**70
Lewis, John, **1:**182, 183; **2:**545, 546, 560, 604, 609, 610, 676–677
Leyden, John, **2:**662
Liebman, Marvin, **4:**1389, 1393
Lincoln, Abraham, **1:**35, 37, 39, 94; **3:**865
Lind, Betty Ann, **4:**1381

Lindbergh, Charles, **3:**1079
Lingg, Louis, **2:**499, 500
Little, Frank, **2:**531
Little, Jim, **2:**716
Little Crow, **2:**748
Liuzzo, Viola, **1:**194
Lloyd, Edward, **1:**72–73
Loan, Nguyen Loc, **3:**1092
Loewe, Dietrich, **2:**683
Logan, Adella Hunt, **1:**300
London, Julia, **2:**406
Long, Huey, **4:**1240
Lorde, Audre, **2:**409, 410
Lore, Ludwig, **2:**575
Lorenz, Konrad, **4:**1313
Loud Hawk, Kenny, **2:**715
Louis, Joe, **1:**162
Love, Alfred H., **3:**1044
Lovejoy, Elijah P., **1:**4, 50, 65
Lovestone, Jay, **2:**571, 574, 575, 578
Lowell, Frances Cabot, **2:**465
Lowell, Josephine, **1:**319, 342
Lucas, Donald, **4:**1336
Luce, Henry, **1:**167
Lundy, Benjamin, **1:**22
Luther, Seth, **2:**466, 469–470
Lynn, Merissa Sherrill, **4:**1381
Lyon, Mary, **3:**948, 962
Lyon, Phyllis, **2:**370; **4:**1337

M

MacKinnon, Catharine, **3:**849
Maclure, William, **3:**979
Macune, Charles, **3:**791
Macune, William, **3:**784
Mahan, Alfred Thayer, **1:**343
Mahoney, William, **3:**818–819
Maines, Natalie, **3:**1105–1106
Malcolm X, **1:**196, 206, 229, 230–231
Malkiel, Theresa Server, **2:**690
Malloy, Terry, **2:**690
Maltovich, Leonard, **4:**1327
Mandela, Nelson, **1:**239
Mankiller, Wilma, **2:**726
Manypenny, George, **2:**699
Mapplethorpe, Robert, **3:**850
Marable, Manning, **1:**253
March, Artemis, **2:**441
Marsh, George Perkins, **4:**1285–1286
Marshall, Robert, **4:**1267–1268
Marshall, Thurgood, **1:**162, 174, 194, 221
Martin, Del, **2:**370; **4:**1337
Martinez, Elizabeth, **3:**1104
Martinez, Mel, **1:**247
Masaoka, Mike, **4:**1206, 1220

Mason, Charles H., **3:**981
Mathews, Robert, **4:**1443
Mathias, Charles, **2:**449
Mathiasen, Geneva, **4:**1242
Maurer, James, **2:**596
Mayo, George Elton, **2:**561
Mayo, Mary, **3:**781
Mays, Robert L., **2:**539
Mazey, Emil, **2:**644
McCaffrey, Barry, **3:**876
McCain, John, **4:**1346
McCarthy, Eugene, **3:**1054–1055, 1086
McCarthy, Joseph, **1:**168; **3:**845
McCoy, Isaac, **2:**699
McCulloh, Henry, **3:**761–762
McDonald, David J., **2:**606
McDonald, Lawrence, **4:**1362
McGee, William, **1:**171
McGillivray, Alexander, **2:**698
McGovern, George, **3:**1056; **4:**1345
McIntire, Carl, **4:**1399
McKenzie, Fayette, **2:**701
McKim, J. Miller, **1:**56
McKinney, Cynthia, **1:**253
McKinney, Ernest Rice, **2:**591
McKissick, Floyd B., **1:**210
McLean, Alice Throckmorton, **2:**368
McMartin, Buckey, **3:**853
McMartin, Virginia, **3:**853
McPadden, Myles, **2:**483
McPherson, Aimee Semple, **3:**981–982
McVeigh, Timothy, **4:**1446
Meacham, Joseph, **3:**970
Mead, Lucia Ames, **1:**342, 343
Means, Russell, **2:**708, 709, 727;
      4:1206–1207
   at AIM trials, **2:**714
   barred from Pine Ridge, **2:**711
   electoral challenge to Wilson, **2:**716
   expelled from IITC, **2:**722
   government drive to destroy, **2:**714
   shot on Pine Ridge, **2:**716
   and Yellow Thunder Camp, **2:**722
Meany, George, **2:**613, 614, 630, 643
Meek, Marvin, **3:**838
Mellis, David M., **1:**297
Mendel, Gregor, **3:**900
Mercer, Charles Fenton, **1:**13
Meredith, James, **1:**184–185, 198
Metcalfe, William, **3:**1014–1015
Metz, Christian, **3:**1001
Milam, J.W., **1:**176–177
Milk, Harvey, **4:**1356
Miller, David, **3:**1089
Miller, Elizabeth Smith, **1:**269
Miller, Herman, **3:**904

Miller, William, **3:**931
Millet, Kate, **2:**407
Mills, Samuel, **1:**13
Mineta, Norman, **1:**247
Minor, Virginia, **1:**297
Mitchell, George, **2:**707
Mitchell, H.L., **3:**1123
Mitchell, John, **3:**874
Mitchell, O.M., **1:**43
Miyamoto, Nobuko Joanne, **4:**1220
Mondragón, Celedonio, **4:**1227
Monroe, Sarah, **2:**469
Montezuma, Carlos, **2:**701
Moody, Dwight L., **3:**966
Mooney, Tom, **2:**676
Moore, Ely, **2:**469
Moore, Fred H., **2:**580, 581
Moore, Richard B., **2:**570
Moraga, Cherrie, **2:**411
Moreno, Luisa, **2:**621, 622
Morgan, Arthur, **3:**1005
Morgan, Robin, **2:**400, 407, 440
Morlan, Robert, **3:**802–803
Morris, Glen, **2:**722
Morrison, Toni, **1:**247
Moses, Robert, **1:**191, 192
Moskowitz, Henry, **3:**1010
Moss, Thomas, **1:**331–332
Most, Johann, **2:**499
Mother Jones. *See* Jones, Mary Harris
   (Mother Jones)
Mott, James, **1:**56
Mott, John R., **3:**962, 966
Mott, Lucretia Coffin, **1:**55, 56, 92, 263, 266
   and abolition movement, **1:**290
   and woman suffrage, **1:**290, 319
Moultrie, Mary, **2:**641
Mousseau, Johnny, **2:**716
Moyer, Charles, **2:**495, 496, 527
Muhammad, Elijah, **1:**195–196, 229–230;
      3:935–936
Muhammad, Wallace, **4:**1210
Muir, John, **4:**1256, 1263–1265
Munaker, Sue, **2:**425
Munger, Theodore, **3:**957
Murray, Anna, **1:**74
Murray, Judith S., **1:**287
Murray, Pauli, **2:**391–392
Murray, Philip, **2:**606, 612–614
Muste, A.J., **1:**166
   at Brookwood Labor College,
      2:597–602
   on 1934 labor strikes, **2:**594
   and unemployment movement, **2:**586,
      589, 591
   war relief services, **3:**1079

Muzzey, David, **3:**1011
Myers, Isaac, **2:**475
Mygatt, Tracy, **3:**1046

N

Nader, Ralph, **3:**1138
Nash, Diane, **1:**182, 183, 193
Nathan, Maud, **1:**319
Nation, Carry, **3:**867, 868
Neebe, Oscar, **2:**499
Nell, William Cooper, **1:**30, 38, 68, 69
Nestor, Agnes, **1:**349, 350
Neumann, Henry, **3:**1011
Newell, Frederick, **4:**1288–1289
Newell, William Wells, **2:**741
Newman, Pauline, **2:**552
Newton, Huey P., **1:**199–200, 231
Nicholas II (Russian czar), **3:**1043
Nichols, Jack, **4:**1339
Nichols, Mary Gove, **1:**282
Nichols, Terry, **4:**1446
Niebuhr, Reinhold, **1:**178
Nitz, Michael, **2:**653
Nixon, E.D., **1:**152, 172, 177–178
Nixon, Richard, **3:**1130
    and anti-civil rights, **1:**213–214
    anti-drug campaign, **3:**874
    conservatism of, **4:**1394–1395
    and Martin Luther King Jr., **1:**180
    and Trail of Broken Treaties, **2:**709–711
Noble, Elaine, **4:**1357
Noble, Robert, **4:**1240
Nordin, D. Sven, **3:**780–782
Norquist, Grover, **4:**1397
Novak, Michael, **4:**1208
Noyes, John Humphrey, **1:**64; **3:**932, 972, 1001
    and dress reform, **1:**262, 268–269
    founder of communes, **1:**287
    See also Oneida Perfectionists
Nye, James, **2:**492
Nyswander, Maria, **3:**877

O

O'Brian, Robert, **2:**722
O'Clock, George, **2:**716
O'Connor, Charles, **2:**475
O'Connor, Sandra Day, **1:**248; **4:**1326
Olazabál, Francisco, **3:**981
Olson, Floyd, **2:**564; **3:**819–820
Oppenheimer, J. Robert, **4:**1293
Ordway, Edward L., **1:**342
Osborn, Frederick, **3:**903
O'Sullivan, Elizabethann, **2:**448

Overton, William, **1:**307
Ovington, Mary White, **1:**136
Owen, Chandler, **1:**131, 145
Owen, John, **1:**287
Owen, Robert, **3:**970, 975–980, 1002

P

Packard, Sophia, **1:**330
Paige, Rod, **1:**247
Paine, Thomas, **3:**943
Palmer, A. Mitchell, **2:**559; **3:**1076
Palmer, Phoebe, **3:**933
Parham, Charles, **3:**951, 981
Park, Maud Wood, **1:**305; **2:**364
Parker, Arthur C., **2:**701, 703
Parker, John, **3:**878
Parker, Mack Charles, **1:**224
Parks, Rosa, **1:**172, 177
Parnell, Charles, **2:**482
Parsons, Albert, **2:**499, 500, 521
Patterson, William, **2:**572
Paul, Alice, **1:**300–304, 320–322; **2:**361
    clash with Carrie Chapman Catt, **2:**373
    and Equal Rights Amendment, **2:**364, 373
Peabody, Elizabeth, **1:**285
Peale, Norman Vincent, **4:**1399
Pearson, Karl, **3:**899
Peirce, Melusina Fay, **1:**288–289
Peltier, Leonard, **2:**719–722
Penn, William, **3:**926
Pennington, J.W.C., **1:**69
Penrod, Immanuel, **2:**490–491
Pepper, Claude, **1:**166; **4:**1243
Pepper, John, **2:**574
Perce, Nez, **2:**751
Perkins, Francis, **2:**366; **4:**1240
Pesotta, Rose, **2:**553
Peterson, Esther, **2:**375
Pettibone, George A., **2:**527
Pew, J. Howard, **4:**1399
Phelps, John, **1:**39
Phillips, Howard, **4:**1402
Phillips, Wendell, **1:**50; **2:**474, 699
Piercy, Marge, **2:**400, 436
Pierson, Arthur T., **3:**963, 966
Pinchot, Gifford, **4:**1257, 1262, 1288–1290
Pitt, Helen, **1:**78
Piven, Frances Fox, **3:**1131, 1132
Plockhoy, Peter Cornelius, **3:**998
Pogany, John. *See* Pepper, John
Poli, Robert, **2:**662
Politzer, Anita, **3:**1012

Polk, James K., **1:**53
Polk, Leonidas Lafayette, **3:**791
Poole, Elijah. *See* Muhammad, Elijah
Poole, Ernest, **2:**690
Post, Alice Thatcher, **1:**342
Potter, Julian, **4:**1346
Powderly, Terence, **2:**482, 485
Powell, Adam Clayton, **1:**160
Powell, Colin, **1:**221, 247
Powell, Lewis, **1:**220
Poyntz, Juliet Stuart, **2:**570, 578
Prabhupada, Swami Srila, **3:**953
Pratt, Larry, **4:**1444
Pratt, Richard Henry, **2:**701
Pressman, Lee, **3:**1123
Prince, Virginia, **4:**1380
Pritchett, Laurie, **1:**185
Pugh, Sarah, **1:**56
Pulitzer, Joseph, **1:**125
Pullman, George, **1:**152–153
Purchase, Dave, **3:**878
Purnell, Benjamin, **3:**1004
Purnell, Mary, **3:**1004

Q

Quimby, Phineas P., **3:**934

R

Rabinowitch, Eugene, **4:**1293
Rand, Ayn, **4:**1412
Randall, Ollie, **4:**1242
Randolph, A. Philip, **1:**131, 145, 152–154, 159
    and nonviolent direct action, **1:**202
    threat of a national march, **1:**160, 164, 170, 188
Randolph, P.B., **1:**87
Rankin, Jeannette, **3:**1077
Rapp, George, **1:**287; **3:**1000–1001
Rasmussen, Donald L., **2:**646–647
Rauschenbusch, Walter, **3:**959–960
Reagan, Nancy, **3:**875
Reagan, Ronald,
    anti-abortion stance, **3:**847
    as California governor, **4:**1394
    and civil rights, **1:**216–217, 218
    and conservatives, **4:**1396–1397
    elimination of welfare programs, **1:**217; **3:**1134–1135
    firing of air traffic controllers, **2:**636, 642, 662
    pro-business, **2:**635–636, 642
    War on Drugs, **3:**875
Reason, Charles, **1:**69

Redner, Russell, **2:**715
Reed, Ralph, **4:**1404
Reed, Simon, **2:**493
Rehnquist, William, **1:**213, 221, 247
Reisman, Judith, **3:**849
Remond, Charles Lenox, **1:**86
Rendón, Armando, **4:**1208, 1212, 1217
Reuther, Roy, **2:**602
Reuther, Victor, **2:**644
Reuther, Walter, **2:**611, 614, 624–626, 630, 644
Reynolds, William Bradford, **1:**218
Rice, Condoleezza, **1:**247
Rich, Adrienne, **2:**408, 442
Richards, Amy, **2:**431
Richards, Ellen Swallow, **1:**286
Rickard, Clinton, **2:**703–704
Ricketson, Shradrach, **3:**1015
Ridge, John, **2:**699
Riis, Jacob, **2:**691; **3:**1121
Ripley, George, **1:**287; **3:**971, 972, 1002
Ritschl, Albrecht, **3:**956
Roberts, Albert H., **1:**306
Robertson, Pat, **4:**1403–1404
Robeson, Paul, **1:**162, 168, 170
Robideau, Rob, **2:**719, 720
Robins, Margaret Dreier, **1:**348
Robinson, C.H., **3:**988
Robinson, Jo Ann, **1:**178
Robinson, William D., **2:**533
Rock, John, **1:**42
Rockefeller, John D., **1:**330; **3:**901, 911, 962
Rockefeller, Mary, **2:**682
Rockefeller, Nelson, **3:**874
Rodale, J.I., **3:**1017
Rodgers, Daniel T., **3:**883
Rodgers, Ward, **3:**813–814
Rogers, Don, **3:**876
Rogers, Edith Nourse, **2:**368
Rogers, Ray, **2:**652
Room, Robin, **3:**906
Roosevelt, Eleanor, **1:**164; **2:**367–368, 369
    and union label campaigns, **2:**682
Roosevelt, Franklin D., **1:**160–161, 166, 167, 202; **2:**366
Roosevelt, Theodore, **2:**514; **3:**895–896; **4:**1290
    and environmentalism, **4:**1263–1264, 1288
Roselle, Mike, **4:**1280
Ross, Loretta, **2:**447
Rotblat, Joseph, **4:**1296
Roth, Samuel, **3:**848
Rothbard, Murray, **4:**1388
Rubin, Gayle, **3:**855
Rudd, Mark, **4:**1198

Ruffin, Josephine, **1:**314, 332–334
Rush, Benjamin, **1:**280; **3:**865, 907
Rusher, William E., **4:**1391–1392
Russell, Howard Hyde, **3:**869
Russwurm, John B., **1:**14, 22, 84, 98
Rustin, Bayard, **1:**204, 208, 209
Ruthenberg, Charles, **2:**574

S

Sacco, Nicola, **2:**503, 580–582
Sachs, Sadie, **1:**323; **2:**354
Sagan, Carl, **4:**1296
Sager, Manuela Solis, **2:**621
Salazar, Rubin, **3:**1088
Salter, William Mackintire, **3:**1009
Sam, Alfred, **1:**143
Sanchez, David, **4:**1216
Sandler, Bernice, **2:**416
Sandoval, Martha, **1:**249
Sanger, Margaret, **1:**322–323; **2:**354–358, 365
    The Pivot of Civilization (1922), **2:**357
    Comstock's opposition to, **3:**862–863
    and eugenics movement, **2:**356–358; **3:**901
Saposs, David J., **2:**598–599
Sargent, Charles S., **4:**1286
Sarria, José, **4:**1341, 1356
Savio, Mario, **4:**1179, 1180
Scalia, Antonin, **1:**221, 247; **3:**857; **4:**1325
Schlafly, Phyllis, **2:**376; **4:**1401
Schmeling, Max, **1:**162
Schmidtz, Darold, **2:**711
Schneiderman, Rose (Rachel), **2:**549
Schropp, Jill, **4:**1345
Schumacher, E.F., **4:**1257, 1317–1318
Schurz, Carl, **4:**1286
Schwar, Michael, **2:**499
Schwarz, Fred C., **4:**1399
Schwerner, Michael, **1:**134, 192, 216
Scopes, John, **3:**950
Scott, Emmett, **1:**139–140
Scudder, Vida, **3:**1141
Seale, Bobby, **1:**231, 232; **3:**1131
Seeger, Pete, **2:**688
Seigenthaler, John, **1:**183
Seligman, E.R.A., **3:**1009
Sells, Cato, **2:**702
Sen, Rinku, **1:**255
Serra, Junípero, **3:**926, 927
Serrano, Andres, **3:**850
Seton, Ernest Thompson, **2:**741
Severance, Caroline, **1:**313
Sewall, May Wright, **1:**342
Seymour, William J., **3:**951, 981

Shachtman, Max, **2:**573
Shadd, Abraham D., **1:**22, 69
Shaku, Soyen, **3:**1030
Shanker, Albert, **1:**213
Shaw, Anna Howard, **1:**302
Shaw, George Bernard, **3:**863, 1118
Shays, Daniel, **3:**763
Sheldon, Walter, **3:**1009
Sheridan, Philip, **2:**750
Sherman, Charles O., **2:**527
Sherman, William T., **1:**39
Shew, Joel, **1:**282; **3:**1015, 1016
Shoemaker, Samuel, **3:**909
Shumsky, Ellen, **2:**441
Shuttlesworth, Fred, **1:**185, 187
Sickles, Daniel E., **1:**39
Sidgewick, Rose, **2:**363
Siegel, Mo, **3:**1018
Silko, Leslie Marmon, **2:**755
Silverman, Mervyn, **3:**855
Simmons, William J., **4:**1420–1421
Simone, Nina, **2:**393
Sinclair, Upton, **2:**690
Singer, Peter, **4:**1313–1314
Sitting Bull, **2:**751, 752
Skidmore, Thomas, **2:**469
Skyhorse (Paul Durant), **2:**715
Sloan, Thomas, **2:**703
Small, Albion W., **3:**960
Smalls, Robert, **1:**40
Smiley, Glen, **1:**204
Smith, Barbara, **2:**392, 443
Smith, Gerrit, **1:**27, 49, 60, 64
Smith, Helen, **4:**1230
Smith, James McCune, **1:**69
Smith, Joseph, Jr., **3:**931
Smith, Margaret Chase, **2:**369
Smith, Martin Cruz, **2:**755
Smith, Paul Chaat, **2:**722
Smith, Robert H., **3:**909, 910
Smith, Ruby Doris, **2:**400, 436
Smith, T.O., **3:**988
Smith, Tucker P., **2:**602
Solomon, Hannah Greenebaum, **2:**365
Souter, David H., **1:**247
Spargo, John, **2:**516
Sparkman, John, **1:**170
Spear, Allan, **4:**1357
Spencer, Anna Garlin, **1:**342, 343; **3:**1010
Spencer, Campbell, **4:**1347
Spencer, Herbert, **3:**956
Spencer, Peter, **1:**22
Spencer, Sara, **1:**276
Spengler, Mark, **4:**1347
Spiegelberg, Frederick, **3:**1031
Spies, August, **2:**499, 500, 521

Spira, Henry, 4:1314, 1316
Spooner, Lysander, 3:864
Spotted Tail, 2:750
Springsteen, Bruce, 2:689
Spurgeon, Caroline, 2:363
Stalin, Josef, 2:571, 575
    and Trotskyist anti-Stalinism, 2:577
Stanton, Elizabeth Cady, 1:56, 92, 263, 266, 273, 291
    and abolition movement, 1:290, 291
    and dress reform, 1:269, 270
    and peace reform, 3:1044
    relationship with Anthony, 1:296
    and temperance movement, 3:866–867
    view of imperialism, 1:344
    and woman suffrage, 1:290, 296–297, 299, 319–320
Stanton, Henry B., 1:25
Starr, Ellen Gates, 1:317, 337
Starr, Mark, 2:599
Stearns, Charles B., 1:66
Steinbeck, John, 2:690; 3:1123, 1124
Steinem, Gloria, 2:404, 426
Stephens, Uriah, 2:481–482
Steunenberg, Frank, 2:526
Stevens, John Paul, 1:247
Steward, Ira, 2:473–474, 520
Steward, Maria W., 1:54–55
Stewart, Alvan, 1:53
Stewart, Maria W., 1:68
Stewart, Potter, 3:848
Stieglitz, Alfred, 3:1121
Still, John N., 1:70
Still, William, 1:30
Stone, Chester, 2:716
Stone, Jesse, 2:716
Stone, Lucy, 1:273, 296, 297, 299, 320
Stowe, Harriet Beecher, 1:93; 3:947
    and cooperative housekeeping, 1:286
    Model Christian Neighborhood, 1:287–288
Strasser, Adolph, 2:476
Strong, Josiah, 3:959, 1043
Stuntz Killsright, Joe, 2:718
Sturges, Jock, 3:853
Sullivan, Leon, 1:238
Sullivan, Louis, 4:1381
Sumner, William Graham, 3:956
Suzuki, Daisetz Teitaro, 3:936, 1030
Suzuki, Shunryu, 3:936, 1031
Sweeney, John, 2:642, 653, 659
Swift, Wesley, 4:1442
Swinton, John, 2:507
Sylvis, William, 2:471, 473
Szilard, Leo, 4:1293

T

Taft, Robert A., 4:1391
Taft, William Howard, 2:557; 3:895; 4:1290
Talbert, Martin, 1:125
Talbert, Mary B., 1:130
Tang, Eric, 1:254
Tappan, Arthur, 1:49
Tappan, Lewis, 1:24–25, 29, 31–32, 49, 52, 63
    attack on home of, 1:103
Tarr, Curtis, 3:1089
Taylor, Emily, 2:416
Taylor, Frederick Winslow, 2:556
Taylor, Glen, 1:170
Taylor, Graham, 3:890
Taylor, Hoote, 1:125
Taylor, Myron, 2:546
Taylor, Nathaniel William, 3:947
Taylor, Susie King, 1:44
Teague, Colin, 1:14
Teed, Cyrus, 3:1004
Tenayucca, Emma, 2:621
Terrell, Mary Church, 1:129, 300, 301, 314, 322; 2:361
    and anti-lynching movement, 1:331–333
    and racial uplift, 2:388
Thatcher, Ebby, 3:909
Thayer, Eli, 1:59–60
Thernstrom, Abigail, 1:241
Thernstrom, Stephan, 1:241
Thomas, Clarence, 1:217, 221, 247; 2:395; 4:1210
Thomas, M. Carey, 1:313
Thomas, Nevil, 1:131
Thomas, Norman, 3:1079, 1122
Thomas, Robert K., 2:706, 707
Thomas, Timothy, 1:242
Thomas, William S., 1:22
Thompson, George, 1:103
Thompson, William, 2:581
Thomson, Samuel, 1:281; 3:991–992, 1015
Thoreau, Henry David, 3:943, 1029, 1041; 4:1259
Thornton, William, 1:12
Thurmond, Strom, 1:170, 213
Tiegan, Henry, 3:818–819
Tijerina, Reies, 4:1214
Till, Emmet, 1:134, 171, 176–177, 223
Tillman, Benjamin, 3:958
Tillman, William, 1:40
Tillotson, Mary, 1:271
Tinbergen, Niko, 4:1313
Tingley, Katherine, 3:1005

Tippet, Tom, 2:599
Tobias, Andrew, 4:1346
Todd, John, 4:1320
Tolstoy, Leo, 3:1044
Torrey, Charles, 1:25, 56
Totten, Ashley, 1:153
Toure, Nkenge, 2:447
Tourgee, Albion, 1:129
Townley, Arthur C., 3:802–803
Townsend, Francis E., 4:1240
Train, George Francis, 1:297
Trall, Russell, 1:282
Trammell, Jeffrey, 4:1346
Trautmann, William E., 2:527, 530
Trembath, John, 2:491
Tresca, Carlo, 2:530, 580
Trochmann, John, 4:1445
Trotsky, Leon, 2:571
Trotter, James Monroe, 1:43
Trudell, John, 2:708, 722
Truman, Harry, 1:167, 168, 170; 2:611
Trumka, Richard, 2:652, 653
Trungpa, Chogyam, 3:1031, 1032
Truth, Sojourner, 1:55, 56–57
Tryon, William, 3:761–762
Tubman, Harriet, 1:43, 56; 2:361
Tucker, Benjamin, 2:496
Turner, Banks, 1:307
Turner, Elizabeth, 2:689
Turner, Henry McNeal, 1:39, 112–113, 128
Turner, Nat, 1:59, 89, 99

U

Underwood, John C., 1:60
Utley, Freda, 4:1412

V

Valdez, Luis, 4:1216–1217
Van Buren, Martin, 1:54
Van Renssalaer, Stephen, IV, 3:769
Van Renssalaer, William, 3:770
Vanzetti, Bartolomeo, 2:503, 580–582
Varick, James, 1:82
Ventura, Jesse, 3:876
Vesey, Denmark, 1:98
Villard, Fanny Garrison, 3:1044
Villard, Oswald Garrison, 1:136
Vinson, Fred, 1:174
Vivekananda, Swami, 3:936
Vogt, William, 4:1276
Von Harnack, Adolph, 3:956
Von Hayek, Friedrich, 4:1388
Vygotsky, Lev, 4:1245

W

Wagner, Robert, 1:134
Wald, Lillian, 3:1141
Walker, Alice, 2:394, 395, 410
Walker, David, 1:15–16, 66, 89, 98
Walker, Rebecca, 2:430
Walker, Seth, 1:307
Wallace, George, 1:187
Wallace, Henry A., 1:167, 170
Ward, Lester, 3:957
Waring, George, 4:1260
Waring, Mary, 2:388
Warren, Earl, 1:174
Warrior, Clyde, 2:707
Washington, Booker T., 1:118–119
    Atlanta Compromise speech, 1:136,
        227–228
    on convict leasing, 1:123
    on lynching, 1:129
    response to black repression,
        1:227–228
Washington, Harold, 1:218
Washington, Madison, 1:92
Washington, Margaret Murray, 1:117, 314
Watson, Paul, 4:1278–1279
Watson, Tom, 3:793–795
Watts, Alan, 3:1031
Weatherford, Willis D., 1:131
Weaver, James B., 3:791–792
Webster, Delia, 1:59
Webster, Milton P., 1:152, 153
Webster, William, 2:721
Weddington, Sarah, 2:381
Weinberg, Jack, 4:1178–1179, 1180
Weinstein, Naomi, 2:400
Weismann, August, 3:900
Welch, James, 2:754
Weld, Theodore, 1:25; 3:946–947
Weld, William, 4:1351
Wells-Barnett, Ida Bell, 1:117, 127–128,
    222, 300, 301, 322

Wells-Barnett, Ida Bell (continued)
    and anti-lynching movement, 1:331–332
    and General Federation of Women's
        Clubs, 2:361
    and NAWSA parade, 1:334
Wesley, John, 3:933
Weston, S. Burns, 3:1009
Weyrich, Paul, 4:1402, 1406
Wheelock, Eleazar, 2:697
Whipper, William, 1:68, 69
White, E. Edwin, 4:1240
White, Ellen Gould, 1:271, 282; 3:1015–1016
White, F. Clifton, 4:1391–1392
White, Garland H., 1:43
White, Jacob C., 1:68
White, Sue Shelton, 1:305
White, Walter, 1:130, 170
Whitefield, George, 3:927, 928, 939
Whitehead, Ralph Radcliffe, 3:1005
Whitman, Walt, 3:1029
Whittier, John Greenleaf, 1:51
Wicker, Randy, 4:1339
Wienstein, Naomi, 2:400
Wiley, George, 3:1131
Wilkins, Roy, 1:178
Willard, Emma Hart, 1:311–312
Willard, Frances Elizabeth, 1:297, 315,
    316, 343
    and temperance movement, 3:867, 869
Williams, Fannie Barrier, 1:314, 334
Williams, Robert F., 1:224
Williams, Ron, 2:717, 718
Wilson, Charles, 2:533
Wilson, Dick, 2:711, 712, 715, 716, 718
Wilson, Joseph T., 1:44, 45
Wilson, Mary Jane, 2:707
Wilson, Michael, 2:690
Wilson, Pete, 1:250; 4:1351
Wilson, William G., 3:909–910
Wilson, William Junius, 1:215
Wilson, Woodrow, 2:515; 3:1060–1061;
    4:1290

Winchell, Barry, 4:1328
Winston, Henry, 1:171
Winthrop, John, 3:926, 939
Wise, Isaac Mayer, 3:933
Witherspoon, Frances, 3:1046
Wittenmyer, Annie, 1:314–315
Wolfe, Bertram, 2:571, 578
Wollstonecraft, Mary, 1:287
Woodcock, Leonard, 2:644
Woodhull, Victoria, 1:297
Woodman, Olivia, 3:782
Woodson, Lewis, 1:67
Worcester, Samuel A., 2:699
Work, Hubert, 2:703
Wright, Elizur, Jr., 1:25
Wright, Fielding, 1:170
Wright, Frances, 1:287; 3:970
Wright, Hamilton, 3:872
Wright, Henry B., 3:908
Wright, Lucy, 3:970
Wright, Moses, 1:176–177
Wright, Richard, 1:162
Wurf, Jerry, 2:641
Wurtzel, Elizabeth, 2:432

Y

Yablonski, Joseph, 2:634
Yanovsky, Saul, 2:501
Yellow Thunder, Raymond, 2:709,
    727
Yogananda, Paramahansa, 3:952
Young, Andrew, 1:191
Young, Brigham, 3:931
Young, Coleman, 1:169
Young, William F., 2:470
Young Bear, Severt, 2:716

Z

Zia, Helen, 4:1220
Zinoviev, Gregory, 2:571